Encyclopedia of Crash Dump Analysis Patterns
Third Edition

Detecting Abnormal Software Structure and Behavior in Computer Memory

Dmitry Vostokov
Software Diagnostics Institute

OpenTask

Published by OpenTask, Republic of Ireland

Copyright © 2020 by Dmitry Vostokov

Copyright © 2020 by Software Diagnostics Institute

OpenTask books are available through booksellers and distributors worldwide. For further information or comments, send requests to press@opentask.com.

Product and company names mentioned in this book may be trademarks of their owners.

A CIP catalog record for this book is available from the British Library.

ISBN-13: 978-1-912636-30-3 (eBook)

ISBN-13: 978-1-912636-28-0 (Volume 1, A - J)

ISBN-13: 978-1-912636-29-7 (Volume 2, L - Z)

Version 3.04 (December 2021)

Summary of Contents

Detailed Table of Contents

Preface to the Third Edition

Three and a half years passed since the publication of the second edition, and after the release of volumes 10 – 13 of Memory Dump Analysis Anthology containing new memory analysis patterns, we decided to publish the updated edition. It now includes more than 30 new patterns and pattern variants, more than 30 new comments, and 3 new pattern subcatalogs. We also added 8 structural memory analysis patterns that were excluded from the previous editions. All links and references were checked and corrected if necessary. The bibliography was updated to reflect new book editions. We also improved illustrations and debugger output snippets by adding extra visual highlighting.

Preface to the Second Edition

Two years passed since the publication of the previous edition, and after the release of volumes 8b, 9a, and 9b of Memory Dump Analysis Anthology containing new memory analysis patterns including Linux variants, we decided to publish the updated edition. It now includes more than 50 new patterns and pattern variants, including 5 analysis patterns from the forthcoming volume 10 at the time of this writing, and more than 70 new comments. WinDbg output and code sections were reformatted for easier screen and paperback reading. Some typos were corrected, and punctuation was improved.

In addition to contact details provided in the preface to the first edition, we suggest the following Facebook page and group:

http://www.facebook.com/DumpAnalysis

http://www.facebook.com/groups/dumpanalysis

Preface to the First Edition

We originally planned this book in 2009. At that time, there were less than 100 memory dump analysis patterns. Since then, Software Diagnostics Institute has already added many more patterns. All of them (326 patterns in total) are scattered among 3,300 pages of Memory Dump Analysis Anthology volumes (1 – 7, 8a), and a few can be found only in Software Diagnostics Library. So we decided to reprint all these patterns and their examples in one book for easy reference. During editing, we also corrected various mistakes, added additional comments and cross-references. Most of the patterns are for Windows platforms and WinDbg with a few examples for Mac OS X and GDB. However, this pattern language is easily extendable, and we plan to add more non-Windows examples (including Linux) in the future editions.

If you encounter any error, please send me a personal message using this contact e-mail:

dmitry.vostokov@dumpanalysis.org

Alternatively, via Twitter @ DumpAnalysis

Acknowledgements

Special thanks to Igor Dzyubenko, who suggested corrections and improvements for second and third editions, João Roque and Malcolm McCaffery, who provided encouraging support just after the first edition release, users of Software Diagnostics Library who contributed to comment sections, and customers of Software Diagnostics Services training courses and reference materials who provided financial assistance to continue this project.

About the Author

Dmitry Vostokov is an internationally recognized expert, speaker, educator, scientist, and author. He is the founder of pattern-oriented software diagnostics, forensics and prognostics discipline and Software Diagnostics Institute (DA+TA: DumpAnalysis.org + TraceAnalysis.org). Vostokov has also authored more than 50 books on software diagnostics, anomaly detection and analysis, software and memory forensics, root cause analysis and problem solving, memory dump analysis, debugging, software trace and log analysis, reverse engineering and malware analysis. He has more than 25 years of experience in software architecture, design, development and maintenance in a variety of industries including leadership, technical and people management roles. Dmitry also founded Syndromatix, Anolog.io, BriteTrace, DiaThings, Logtellect, OpenTask Iterative and Incremental Publishing (OpenTask.com), Software Diagnostics Technology and Services (former Memory Dump Analysis Services) PatternDiagnostics.com and Software Prognostics. In his spare time, he presents various topics on Debugging.TV and explores Software Narratology, its further development as Narratology of Things and Diagnostics of Things (DoT), and Software Pathology. His current areas of interest are theoretical software diagnostics and its mathematical and computer science foundations, application of artificial intelligence, machine learning and data mining to diagnostics and anomaly detection, software diagnostics engineering and diagnostics-driven development, diagnostics workflow and interaction. Recent interest areas also include security, functional programming, and applications of category theory to software development and big data.

Abridged Dump

Sometimes we get memory dumps that are difficult to analyze in full because some if not most of the information was omitted while saving them. These are usually small memory dumps (contrasted with kernel and complete) and user process minidumps. We can easily recognize that when we open a dump file:

```
User Mini Dump File: Only registers, stack and portions of memory are available
```

```
Mini Kernel Dump File: Only registers and stack trace are available
```

The same also applies to user dumps where thread times information is omitted (it is not possible to use **!runaway** WinDbg command) or to a dump saved with various options of **.dump** command (including privacy-aware[1]) instead of **/ma** or deprecated **/f** option. On the contrary, manually erased data[2] in crash dumps looks more like an example of another pattern called **Lateral Damage** (page 678).

The similar cases of abridged dumps are discussed in **Wrong Dump**[3] and **Missing Space**[4] antipatterns.

Anyway, we should not dismiss such dump files and should try to analyze them. For example, some approaches (including using image binaries) are listed in kernel minidump analysis series[5]. We can even see portions of the raw stack data when looking for **Execution Residue** (page 395):

```
0: kd> !thread
GetPointerFromAddress: unable to read from 81d315b0
THREAD 82f49020  Cid 0004.0034  Teb: 00000000 Win32Thread: 00000000 RUNNING on processor 0
IRP List:
    Unable to read nt!_IRP @ 8391e008
Not impersonating
GetUlongFromAddress: unable to read from 81d0ad90
Owning Process            82f00ab0       Image:        System
Attached Process          N/A            Image:        N/A
ffdf0000: Unable to get shared data
Wait Start TickCount      4000214
Context Switch Count      21886
ReadMemory error: Cannot get nt!KeMaximumIncrement value.
UserTime                  00:00:00.000
KernelTime                00:00:00.000
Win32 Start Address nt!ExpWorkerThread (0x81c78ea3)
Stack Init 85be0000 Current 85bdf7c0 Base 85be0000 Limit 85bdd000 Call 0
```

[1] WinDbg is Privacy-Aware, Memory Dump Analysis Anthology, Volume 1, page 600
[2] Data Hiding in Crash Dumps, Memory Dump Analysis Anthology, Volume 2, page 397
[3] Wrong Dump, Memory Dump Analysis Anthology, Volume 1, page 496
[4] Missing Space, Memory Dump Analysis Anthology, Volume 3, page 138
[5] Minidump Analysis, Memory Dump Analysis Anthology, Volume 1, page 43

```
Priority 14 BasePriority 12 PriorityDecrement 0 IoPriority 2 PagePriority 5
[...]


0: kd> dps 85bdd000 85be0000
85bdd000  ????????
85bdd004  ????????
85bdd008  ????????
85bdd00c  ????????
85bdd010  ????????
85bdd014  ????????
85bdd018  ????????
85bdd01c  ????????
[...]
85bdf8c4  ????????
85bdf8c8  ????????
85bdf8cc  ????????
85bdf8d0  0000000a
85bdf8d4  a112883e
85bdf8d8  0000001b
85bdf8dc  00000000
85bdf8e0  81c28750 nt!KeSetEvent+0x4d
85bdf8e4  85bdf8e8
85bdf8e8  85bdf970
85bdf8ec  81c28750 nt!KeSetEvent+0x4d
85bdf8f0  badb0d00
85bdf8f4  00000000
85bdf8f8  00000000
85bdf8fc  81cf4820 nt!KiInitialPCR+0x120
85bdf900  00000000
85bdf904  85bdf938
85bdf908  81cf4820 nt!KiInitialPCR+0x120
85bdf90c  00000000
85bdf910  81d32300 nt!IopTimerLock
85bdf914  00000000
85bdf918  81fa0000 nt!_NULL_IMPORT_DESCRIPTOR <PERF> (nt+0x3a0000)
85bdf91c  85bd0023
85bdf920  00000023
85bdf924  00000000
85bdf928  81d323c0 nt!KiDispatcherLock
85bdf92c  a1128828
85bdf930  85bdf9b4
85bdf934  85bdfdb0
85bdf938  00000030
85bdf93c  84ca6f40
85bdf940  84ca6f38
85bdf944  00000001
85bdf948  85bdf970
85bdf94c  00000000
85bdf950  81c28750 nt!KeSetEvent+0x4d
85bdf954  00000008
85bdf958  00010246
85bdf95c  00000000
85bdf960  84ca68a0
[...]
85bdfd2c  82f49020
85bdfd30  835ca4d0
```

```
85bdfd34   a6684538
85bdfd38   81cfde7c   nt!ExWorkerQueue+0x3c
85bdfd3c   00000001
85bdfd40   00000000
85bdfd44   85bdfd7c
85bdfd48   81c78fa0   nt!ExpWorkerThread+0xfd
85bdfd4c   835ca4d0
85bdfd50   00000000
85bdfd54   82f49020
85bdfd58   00000000
85bdfd5c   00000000
85bdfd60   0069000b
85bdfd64   00000000
85bdfd68   00000001
85bdfd6c   00000000
85bdfd70   835ca4d0
85bdfd74   81da9542   nt!PnpDeviceEventWorker
85bdfd78   00000000
85bdfd7c   85bdfdc0
85bdfd80   81e254e0   nt!PspSystemThreadStartup+0x9d
85bdfd84   835ca4d0
85bdfd88   85bd4680
85bdfd8c   00000000
85bdfd90   00000000
85bdfd94   00000000
85bdfd98   00000002
85bdfd9c   00000000
85bdfda0   00000000
85bdfda4   00000001
85bdfda8   85bdfd88
85bdfdac   85bdfdbc
85bdfdb0   ffffffff
85bdfdb4   81c8aad5   nt!_except_handler4
85bdfdb8   81c9ddb8   nt!`string'+0x4
85bdfdbc   00000000
85bdfdc0   00000000
85bdfdc4   81c9159e   nt!KiThreadStartup+0x16
85bdfdc8   81c78ea3   nt!ExpWorkerThread
85bdfdcc   00000001
85bdfdd0   00000000
85bdfdd4   00000000
85bdfdd8   002e0069
85bdfddc   006c0064
85bdfde0   004c006c
85bdfde4   00000000
85bdfde8   000007f0
85bdfdec   00010000
85bdfdf0   0000027f
85bdfdf4   00000000
85bdfdf8   00000000
85bdfdfc   00000000
85bdfe00   00000000
85bdfe04   00000000
85bdfe08   00001f80
85bdfe0c   0000ffff
85bdfe10   00000000
```

```
85bdfe14  00000000
85bdfe18  00000000
[...]
85bdffec  00000000
85bdfff0  00000000
85bdfff4  00000000
85bdfff8  00000000
85bdfffc  00000000
85be0000  ????????
```

User minidumps are similar here:

```
0:001> k
ChildEBP RetAddr
099bfe14 7c90daaa ntdll!KiFastSystemCallRet
099bfe18 77e765e3 ntdll!NtReplyWaitReceivePortEx+0xc
099bff80 77e76caf rpcrt4!LRPC_ADDRESS::ReceiveLotsaCalls+0x12a
099bff88 77e76ad1 rpcrt4!RecvLotsaCallsWrapper+0xd
099bffa8 77e76c97 rpcrt4!BaseCachedThreadRoutine+0x79
099bffb4 7c80b729 rpcrt4!ThreadStartRoutine+0x1a
099bffec 00000000 kernel32!BaseThreadStart+0x37
```

```
0:001> dd 099bfe14
099bfe14  099bfe24 7c90daaa 77e765e3 00000224
099bfe24  099bff74 00000000 2db87ae8 099bff48
099bfe34  fbf58e18 00000040 fd629338 b279dbbc
099bfe44  fd5928b8 fbf58ebc b279dbbc e0c1e002
099bfe54  00000000 00000006 00000001 00000000
099bfe64  e637d218 00000000 00000006 00000006
099bfe74  00000006 e1f79698 e39b8b60 00000000
099bfe84  fbe33c40 00000001 e5ce12f8 b279db9c
```

```
0:001> dd 099bfe14-20
099bfdf4  ???????? ???????? ???????? ????????
099bfe04  ???????? ???????? ???????? ????????
099bfe14  099bfe24 7c90daaa 77e765e3 00000224
099bfe24  099bff74 00000000 2db87ae8 099bff48
099bfe34  fbf58e18 00000040 fd629338 b279dbbc
099bfe44  fd5928b8 fbf58ebc b279dbbc e0c1e002
099bfe54  00000000 00000006 00000001 00000000
099bfe64  e637d218 00000000 00000006 00000006
```

As a warning here it is possible to conclude that minidumps can also reveal the private information especially when ASCII or Unicode buffers are seen in the raw stack data.

We named this pattern by analogy with an abridged book.

Accidental Lock

When a system is unresponsive or sluggish, we usually check _ERESOURCE locks in the kernel or complete memory dumps to see **Deadlock** (page 213) or **High Contention** (page 537) patterns. However, there is some chance that reported locks are purely accidental and appear in a crash dump because they just happened at that time. We need to look at *Contention Count*, *Ticks* and *KernelTime* in both blocking and blocked threads to recognize an **Accidental Lock**. Also, WinDbg may not distinguish between prolonged and accidental locks when we use **!analyze -v -hang** command, and merely reports some lock chain it finds among equal alternatives.

Here is an example. The system was reported hung, and kernel memory dump was saved. WinDbg analysis command reports one thread blocking 3 other threads and the driver on top of the blocking thread stack is *AVDriver.sys*. The algorithm WinDbg uses to point to specific image name is described in minidump analysis article[6] and in our case it chooses *AVDriver* module:

```
BLOCKED_THREAD:   8089d8c0

BLOCKING_THREAD:  8aab4700

LOCK_ADDRESS:  8859a570 -- (!locks 8859a570)

Resource @ 0x8859a570    Exclusively owned
    Contention Count = 3
    NumberOfExclusiveWaiters = 3
     Threads: 8aab4700-01<*>
    Threads Waiting On Exclusive Access:
          885d0020        88a7c020        8aafc7d8

1 total locks, 1 locks currently held

BUGCHECK_STR:  LOCK_HELD

FAULTING_THREAD:  8aab4700

STACK_TEXT:
f592f698 80832f7a nt!KiSwapContext+0x26
f592f6c4 80828705 nt!KiSwapThread+0x284
f592f70c f720a394 nt!KeDelayExecutionThread+0x2ab
WARNING: Stack unwind information not available. Following frames may be wrong.
f592f734 f720ae35 AVDriver+0x1394
f592f750 f720b208 AVDriver+0x1e35
f592f794 f721945a AVDriver+0x2208
f592f7cc 8081dcdf AVDriver+0x1045a
f592f7e0 f5b9f76a nt!IofCallDriver+0x45
f592f7f0 f5b9c621 Driver!FS_Dispatch+0xa4
```

---

[6] Minidump Analysis, Memory Dump Analysis Anthology, Volume 1, page 43

```
f592f7fc 8081dcdf Driver!Kernel_dispatch+0x53
f592f810 f5eb2856 nt!IofCallDriver+0x45
f592f874 8081dcdf AVFilter!QueryFullName+0x5c10
f592f888 f5e9eae3 nt!IofCallDriver+0x45
f592f8b8 f5e9eca4 DrvFilter!PassThrough+0x115
f592f8d4 8081dcdf DrvFilter!Create+0xda
f592f8e8 808f8275 nt!IofCallDriver+0x45
f592f9d0 808f86bc nt!IopParseDevice+0xa35
f592fa08 80936689 nt!IopParseFile+0x46
f592fa88 80932e04 nt!ObpLookupObjectName+0x11f
f592fadc 808ea231 nt!ObOpenObjectByName+0xea
f592fb58 808eb4cb nt!IopCreateFile+0x447
f592fbb4 f57c8efd nt!IoCreateFile+0xa3
f592fc24 f57c9f29 srv!SrvIoCreateFile+0x36d
f592fcf0 f57ca5e4 srv!SrvNtCreateFile+0x5cc
f592fd78 f57adbc6 srv!SrvSmbNtCreateAndX+0x15c
f592fd84 f57c3451 srv!SrvProcessSmb+0xb7
f592fdac 80948bd0 srv!WorkerThread+0x138
f592fddc 8088d4e2 nt!PspSystemThreadStartup+0x2e
00000000 00000000 nt!KiThreadStartup+0x16


STACK_COMMAND:  .thread 0xffffffff8aab4700 ; kb


FOLLOWUP_IP:
AVDriver+1394
f720a394 eb85            jmp     AVDriver+0x131b (f720a31b)


MODULE_NAME: AVDriver


IMAGE_NAME:  AVDriver.sys
```

Motivated by this "discovery" we want to see all locks:

```
0: kd> !locks
**** DUMP OF ALL RESOURCE OBJECTS ****
KD: Scanning for held locks...


Resource @ 0x895a62d8    Shared 1 owning threads
     Threads: 89570520-01<*>


Resource @ 0x897ceba8    Shared 1 owning threads
     Threads: 89584020-01<*>


Resource @ 0x8958e020    Shared 1 owning threads
     Threads: 89555020-01<*>


Resource @ 0x89590608    Shared 1 owning threads
     Threads: 89666020-01<*>


Resource @ 0x89efc398    Shared 1 owning threads
     Threads: 89e277c0-01<*>
```

```
Resource @ 0x88d70820    Shared 1 owning threads
     Threads: 88e43948-01<*>


Resource @ 0x89f2fb00    Shared 1 owning threads
     Threads: 89674688-01<*>


Resource @ 0x89c80370    Shared 1 owning threads
     Threads: 888496b8-01<*>


Resource @ 0x89bfdf08    Shared 1 owning threads
     Threads: 88b62910-01<*>


Resource @ 0x888b5488    Shared 1 owning threads
     Threads: 88536730-01<*>


Resource @ 0x89f2e348    Shared 1 owning threads
     Threads: 89295930-01<*>


Resource @ 0x891a0838    Shared 1 owning threads
     Threads: 88949020-01<*>


Resource @ 0x8825bf08    Shared 1 owning threads
     Threads: 882b9a08-01<*>


Resource @ 0x881a6510    Shared 1 owning threads
     Threads: 88a88338-01<*>


Resource @ 0x885c5890    Shared 1 owning threads
     Threads: 881ab020-01<*>


Resource @ 0x886633a8    Shared 1 owning threads
     Threads: 89b5f8b0-01<*>


Resource @ 0x88216390    Shared 1 owning threads
     Threads: 88820020-01<*>


Resource @ 0x88524490    Shared 1 owning threads
     Threads: 88073020-01<*>


Resource @ 0x88f6a020    Shared 1 owning threads
     Threads: 88e547b0-01<*>


Resource @ 0x88cf2020    Shared 1 owning threads
     Threads: 89af32d8-01<*>


Resource @ 0x889cea80    Shared 1 owning threads
     Threads: 88d18b40-01<*>


Resource @ 0x88486298    Shared 1 owning threads
     Threads: 88af7db0-01<*>
```

```
Resource @ 0x88b22270     Exclusively owned
    Contention Count = 4
    NumberOfExclusiveWaiters = 4
     Threads: 8aad07d8-01<*>
    Threads Waiting On Exclusive Access:
              8ad78020        887abdb0        88eb39a8        8aa1f668


Resource @ 0x88748c20     Exclusively owned
    Contention Count = 2
    NumberOfExclusiveWaiters = 2
     Threads: 8873c8d8-01<*>
    Threads Waiting On Exclusive Access:
              88477478        88db6020


Resource @ 0x8859a570     Exclusively owned
    Contention Count = 3
    NumberOfExclusiveWaiters = 3
     Threads: 8aab4700-01<*>
    Threads Waiting On Exclusive Access:
              885d0020        88a7c020        8aafc7d8


KD: Scanning for held locks...
18911 total locks, 25 locks currently held
```

We can ignore shared locks and then concentrate on the last 3 exclusively owned resources. It looks suspicious that Contention Count has the same number as the number of threads waiting for exclusive access (*NumberOfExclusiveWaiters*). This means that these resources had never been used before. If we dump locks verbosely, we see that blocked threads had been waiting no more than 2 seconds, for example, for resource 0x8859a570:

```
0: kd> !thread 885d0020; !thread 88a7c020; !thread 8aafc7d8
THREAD 885d0020  Cid 0004.1c34  Teb: 00000000 Win32Thread: 00000000 WAIT: (Unknown) KernelMode Non-
Alertable
    89908d50  SynchronizationEvent
    885d0098  NotificationTimer
Not impersonating
DeviceMap                 e10022c8
Owning Process            8ad80648 Image:         System
Wait Start TickCount      7689055  Ticks: 127 (0:00:00:01.984)
Context Switch Count      248
UserTime                  00:00:00.000
KernelTime                00:00:00.000
Start Address srv!WorkerThread (0xf57c3394)
Stack Init b4136000 Current b4135b74 Base b4136000 Limit b4133000 Call 0
Priority 9 BasePriority 9 PriorityDecrement 0
ChildEBP RetAddr
b4135b8c 80832f7a nt!KiSwapContext+0x26
b4135bb8 8082925c nt!KiSwapThread+0x284
b4135c00 8087c1ad nt!KeWaitForSingleObject+0x346
b4135c3c 8087c3a1 nt!ExpWaitForResource+0xd5
b4135c5c f57c9e95 nt!ExAcquireResourceExclusiveLite+0x8d
b4135cf0 f57ca5e4 srv!SrvNtCreateFile+0x510
b4135d78 f57adbc6 srv!SrvSmbNtCreateAndX+0x15c
```

```
b4135d84 f57c3451 srv!SrvProcessSmb+0xb7
b4135dac 80948bd0 srv!WorkerThread+0x138
b4135ddc 8088d4e2 nt!PspSystemThreadStartup+0x2e
00000000 00000000 nt!KiThreadStartup+0x16


THREAD 88a7c020  Cid 0004.3448  Teb: 00000000 Win32Thread: 00000000 WAIT: (Unknown) KernelMode Non-
Alertable
    89908d50  SynchronizationEvent
    88a7c098  NotificationTimer
Not impersonating
DeviceMap                     e10022c8
Owning Process                8ad80648  Image:          System
Wait Start TickCount          7689112    Ticks: 70 (0:00:00:01.093)
Context Switch Count          210
UserTime                      00:00:00.000
KernelTime                    00:00:00.000
Start Address srv!WorkerThread (0xf57c3394)
Stack Init b55dd000 Current b55dcb74 Base b55dd000 Limit b55da000 Call 0
Priority 9 BasePriority 9 PriorityDecrement 0
ChildEBP RetAddr
b55dcb8c 80832f7a nt!KiSwapContext+0x26
b55dcbb8 8082925c nt!KiSwapThread+0x284
b55dcc00 8087c1ad nt!KeWaitForSingleObject+0x346
b55dcc3c 8087c3a1 nt!ExpWaitForResource+0xd5
b55dcc5c f57c9e95 nt!ExAcquireResourceExclusiveLite+0x8d
b55dccf0 f57ca5e4 srv!SrvNtCreateFile+0x510
b55dcd78 f57adbc6 srv!SrvSmbNtCreateAndX+0x15c
b55dcd84 f57c3451 srv!SrvProcessSmb+0xb7
b55dcdac 80948bd0 srv!WorkerThread+0x138
b55dcddc 8088d4e2 nt!PspSystemThreadStartup+0x2e
00000000 00000000 nt!KiThreadStartup+0x16


THREAD 8aafc7d8  Cid 0004.058c  Teb: 00000000 Win32Thread: 00000000 WAIT: (Unknown) KernelMode Non-
Alertable
    89908d50  SynchronizationEvent
    8aafc850  NotificationTimer
Not impersonating
DeviceMap                     e10022c8
Owning Process                8ad80648  Image:          System
Wait Start TickCount          7689171    Ticks: 11 (0:00:00:00.171)
Context Switch Count          310
UserTime                      00:00:00.000
KernelTime                    00:00:00.000
Start Address srv!WorkerThread (0xf57c3394)
Stack Init f592c000 Current f592bb18 Base f592c000 Limit f5929000 Call 0
Priority 9 BasePriority 9 PriorityDecrement 0
ChildEBP RetAddr
f592bb30 80832f7a nt!KiSwapContext+0x26
f592bb5c 8082925c nt!KiSwapThread+0x284
f592bba4 8087c1ad nt!KeWaitForSingleObject+0x346
f592bbe0 8087c3a1 nt!ExpWaitForResource+0xd5
f592bc00 f57c8267 nt!ExAcquireResourceExclusiveLite+0x8d
f592bc18 f57ff0ed srv!UnlinkRfcbFromLfcb+0x33
f592bc34 f57ff2ea srv!SrvCompleteRfcbClose+0x1df
f592bc54 f57b5e8f srv!CloseRfcbInternal+0xb6
f592bc78 f57ce8a9 srv!SrvCloseRfcbsOnSessionOrPid+0x74
```

```
f592bc94 f57e2b22 srv!SrvCloseSession+0xb0
f592bcb8 f57aeb12 srv!SrvCloseSessionsOnConnection+0xa9
f592bcd4 f57c79ed srv!SrvCloseConnection+0x143
f592bd04 f5808c50 srv!SrvCloseConnectionsFromClient+0x17f
f592bdac 80948bd0 srv!WorkerThread+0x138
f592bddc 8088d4e2 nt!PspSystemThreadStartup+0x2e
00000000 00000000 nt!KiThreadStartup+0x16
```

Blocking threads themselves are not blocked and active: the number of ticks passed since their last wait or preemption is 0. This could be a sign of CPU spike pattern. However, their accumulated KernelTime is less than a second:

```
0: kd> !thread 8aad07d8
THREAD 8aad07d8  Cid 0004.0580  Teb: 00000000 Win32Thread: 00000000 WAIT: (Unknown) KernelMode Non-
Alertable
    8aad0850  NotificationTimer
IRP List:
    8927ade0: (0006,0220) Flags: 00000884  Mdl: 00000000
Impersonation token:  eafdc030 (Level Impersonation)
DeviceMap               e5d69340
Owning Process          8ad80648       Image:          System
Wait Start TickCount    7689182        Ticks: 0
Context Switch Count    915582
UserTime                00:00:00.000
KernelTime              00:00:00.125
Start Address srv!WorkerThread (0xf57c3394)
Stack Init f59d8000 Current f59d7680 Base f59d8000 Limit f59d5000 Call 0
Priority 9 BasePriority 9 PriorityDecrement 0


0: kd> !thread 8873c8d8
THREAD 8873c8d8  Cid 0004.2898  Teb: 00000000 Win32Thread: 00000000 WAIT: (Unknown) KernelMode Non-
Alertable
    8873c950  NotificationTimer
IRP List:
    882a8de0: (0006,0220) Flags: 00000884  Mdl: 00000000
Impersonation token:  eafdc030 (Level Impersonation)
DeviceMap               e5d69340
Owning Process          8ad80648       Image:          System
Wait Start TickCount    7689182        Ticks: 0
Context Switch Count    917832
UserTime                00:00:00.000
KernelTime              00:00:00.031
Start Address srv!WorkerThread (0xf57c3394)
Stack Init ac320000 Current ac31f680 Base ac320000 Limit ac31d000 Call 0
Priority 9 BasePriority 9 PriorityDecrement 0
```

```
0: kd> !thread 8aab4700
THREAD 8aab4700  Cid 0004.0588  Teb: 00000000 Win32Thread: 00000000 WAIT: (Unknown) KernelMode Non-
Alertable
    8aab4778  NotificationTimer
IRP List:
    88453008: (0006,0220) Flags: 00000884  Mdl: 00000000
Impersonation token:  e9a82728 (Level Impersonation)
DeviceMap                eb45f108
Owning Process           8ad80648      Image:          System
Wait Start TickCount     7689182       Ticks: 0
Context Switch Count     1028220
UserTime                 00:00:00.000
KernelTime               00:00:00.765
Start Address srv!WorkerThread (0xf57c3394)
Stack Init f5930000 Current f592f680 Base f5930000 Limit f592d000 Call 0
Priority 9 BasePriority 9 PriorityDecrement 0
```

Based on this observation we could say that locks were accidental and when the problem happened again, the new dump did not show them.

Activation Context

This is a new pattern about activation contexts[7]. Here we have **Software Exceptions** (page 977) STATUS_SXS_*, for example:

```
STATUS_SXS_EARLY_DEACTIVATION 0xC015000F
STATUS_SXS_INVALID_DEACTIVATION 0xC0150010


0:000> !analyze -v

[...]


EXCEPTION_RECORD: ffffffff -- (.exr 0xffffffffffffffff)
ExceptionAddress: 77a54441 (ntdll!RtlDeactivateActivationContext+0x00000154)
ExceptionCode: c015000f
ExceptionFlags: 00000000
NumberParameters: 3
Parameter[0]: 00000000
Parameter[1]: 0056cbe8
Parameter[2]: 0056cc18


EXCEPTION_CODE: (NTSTATUS) 0xc015000f - The activation context being deactivated is not the most recently
activated one.


CONTEXT: 003df6c8 -- (.cxr 0x3df6c8)
eax=003df9bc ebx=13050002 ecx=00000000 edx=00000000 esi=0056cbe8 edi=0056cc18
eip=77a54441 esp=003df9b0 ebp=003dfa0c iopl=0 nv up ei pl nz na pe nc
cs=0023 ss=002b ds=002b es=002b fs=0053 gs=002b efl=00000206
ntdll!RtlDeactivateActivationContext+0x154:
77a54441 8b36 mov esi,dword ptr [esi] ds:002b:0056cbe8=0056cbb8
Resetting default scope


STACK_TEXT:
003dfa0c 755aa138 005507d0 13050002 003dfa7c ntdll!RtlDeactivateActivationContext+0x154
003dfa1c 002b1235 00000000 13050002 3a92c68c kernel32!DeactivateActCtx+0x31
003dfa7c 002b13b5 00000001 01f01e98 01f01ec8 TestActCtx!wmain+0x225
003dfac4 75593677 7efde000 003dfb10 77a09f02 TestActCtx!__tmainCRTStartup+0xfa
003dfad0 77a09f02 7efde000 7e35c89d 00000000 kernel32!BaseThreadInitThunk+0xe
003dfb10 77a09ed5 002b140c 7efde000 ffffffff ntdll!__RtlUserThreadStart+0x70
003dfb28 00000000 002b140c 7efde000 00000000 ntdll!_RtlUserThreadStart+0x1b
```

---

[7] https://docs.microsoft.com/en-gb/windows/win32/sbscs/activation-contexts

The ReactOS code for *RtlDeactivateActivationContext*[8] function suggests the following line of inquiry:

```
0:000> dt _TEB
TestActCtx!_TEB
+0x000 NtTib : _NT_TIB
+0x01c EnvironmentPointer : Ptr32 Void
+0x020 ClientId : _CLIENT_ID
+0x028 ActiveRpcHandle : Ptr32 Void
+0x02c ThreadLocalStoragePointer : Ptr32 Void
+0x030 ProcessEnvironmentBlock : Ptr32 _PEB
+0x034 LastErrorValue : Uint4B
+0x038 CountOfOwnedCriticalSections : Uint4B
+0x03c CsrClientThread : Ptr32 Void
+0x040 Win32ThreadInfo : Ptr32 Void
+0x044 User32Reserved : [26] Uint4B
+0x0ac UserReserved : [5] Uint4B
+0x0c0 WOW32Reserved : Ptr32 Void
+0x0c4 CurrentLocale : Uint4B
+0x0c8 FpSoftwareStatusRegister : Uint4B
+0x0cc SystemReserved1 : [54] Ptr32 Void
+0x1a4 ExceptionCode : Int4B
+0x1a8 ActivationContextStack : ACTIVATION CONTEXT STACK
+0x1bc SpareBytes1 : [24] UChar
+0x1d4 GdiTebBatch : _GDI_TEB_BATCH
+0x6b4 RealClientId : _CLIENT_ID
+0x6bc GdiCachedProcessHandle : Ptr32 Void
+0x6c0 GdiClientPID : Uint4B
+0x6c4 GdiClientTID : Uint4B
+0x6c8 GdiThreadLocalInfo : Ptr32 Void
+0x6cc Win32ClientInfo : [62] Uint4B
+0x7c4 glDispatchTable : [233] Ptr32 Void
+0xb68 glReserved1 : [29] Uint4B
+0xbdc glReserved2 : Ptr32 Void
+0xbe0 glSectionInfo : Ptr32 Void
+0xbe4 glSection : Ptr32 Void
+0xbe8 glTable : Ptr32 Void
+0xbec glCurrentRC : Ptr32 Void
+0xbf0 glContext : Ptr32 Void
+0xbf4 LastStatusValue : Uint4B
+0xbf8 StaticUnicodeString : _UNICODE_STRING
+0xc00 StaticUnicodeBuffer : [261] Wchar
+0xe0c DeallocationStack : Ptr32 Void
+0xe10 TlsSlots : [64] Ptr32 Void
+0xf10 TlsLinks : _LIST_ENTRY
+0xf18 Vdm : Ptr32 Void
+0xf1c ReservedForNtRpc : Ptr32 Void
+0xf20 DbgSsReserved : [2] Ptr32 Void
+0xf28 HardErrorMode : Uint4B
+0xf2c Instrumentation : [16] Ptr32 Void
+0xf6c WinSockData : Ptr32 Void
```

---

[8] https://doxygen.reactos.org/de/d9c/sdk_2lib_2rtl_2actctx_8c.html#a52533b501a01935d624ca160b7dd7dc7

```
+0xf70 GdiBatchCount : Uint4B
+0xf74 InDbgPrint : UChar
+0xf75 FreeStackOnTermination : UChar
+0xf76 HasFiberData : UChar
+0xf77 IdealProcessor : UChar
+0xf78 Spare3 : Uint4B
+0xf7c ReservedForPerf : Ptr32 Void
+0xf80 ReservedForOle : Ptr32 Void
+0xf84 WaitingOnLoaderLock : Uint4B
+0xf88 Wx86Thread : _Wx86ThreadState
[...]


0:000> dt _ACTIVATION_CONTEXT_STACK
TestActCtx!_ACTIVATION_CONTEXT_STACK
+0x000 Flags : Uint4B
+0x004 NextCookieSequenceNumber : Uint4B
+0x008 ActiveFrame : Ptr32 _RTL_ACTIVATION_CONTEXT_STACK_FRAME
+0x00c FrameListCache : _LIST_ENTRY


0:000> dt _RTL_ACTIVATION_CONTEXT_STACK_FRAME
ntdll!_RTL_ACTIVATION_CONTEXT_STACK_FRAME
+0x000 Previous : Ptr32 _RTL_ACTIVATION_CONTEXT_STACK_FRAME
+0x004 ActivationContext : Ptr32 _ACTIVATION_CONTEXT
+0x008 Flags : Uint4B


0:000> dd 0056cc18 14
0056cc18 0056cbe8 0056ca6c 00000028 13050003


0:000> dd 0056cbe8
0056cbe8 0056cbb8 0056c934 00000028 13050002
0056cbf8 00000000 00000000 00000000 00000000
0056cc08 00000000 00000000 00000000 00000000
0056cc18 0056cbe8 0056ca6c 00000028 13050003
0056cc28 00000000 00000000 00000000 00000000
0056cc38 00000000 00000000 00000000 00000000
0056cc48 00000000 00000000 0000000c 00000000
0056cc58 00000000 00000000 00000000 00000000


0:000> dd 0056cbb8
0056cbb8 00000000 0056c7fc 00000028 13050001
0056cbc8 00000000 00000000 00000000 00000000
0056cbd8 00000000 00000000 00000000 00000000
0056cbe8 0056cbb8 0056c934 00000028 13050002
0056cbf8 00000000 00000000 00000000 00000000
0056cc08 00000000 00000000 00000000 00000000
0056cc18 0056cbe8 0056ca6c 00000028 13050003
0056cc28 00000000 00000000 00000000 00000000
```

We see that a different cookie was found on top of the thread activation stack and the code raised the runtime exception.

Active Space

When we have **Active Thread** (page 74):

```
0:001> kL
# Child-SP RetAddr Call Site
00 (Inline Function) --------`-------- Windows_Web!JsonParser::ParseString+0x96
01 0000007f`56efdb00 00007fff`700198c5 Windows_Web!JsonParser::ParseValue+0x3b7
02 0000007f`56efdb80 00007fff`70018ab3 Windows_Web!JsonParser::ParseArray+0xf5
03 0000007f`56efdbd0 00007fff`70018f72 Windows_Web!JsonParser::ParseValue+0x663
04 0000007f`56efdc50 00007fff`700186fb Windows_Web!JsonParser::ParseObject+0x422
05 0000007f`56efdda0 00007fff`700198c5 Windows_Web!JsonParser::ParseValue+0x2ab
06 0000007f`56efde20 00007fff`70018ab3 Windows_Web!JsonParser::ParseArray+0xf5
07 0000007f`56efde70 00007fff`70018f72 Windows_Web!JsonParser::ParseValue+0x663
08 0000007f`56efdef0 00007fff`700186fb Windows_Web!JsonParser::ParseObject+0x422
09 0000007f`56efe040 00007fff`70018f72 Windows_Web!JsonParser::ParseValue+0x2ab
0a 0000007f`56efe0c0 00007fff`700186fb Windows_Web!JsonParser::ParseObject+0x422
0b 0000007f`56efe210 00007fff`70011a69 Windows_Web!JsonParser::ParseValue+0x2ab
0c 0000007f`56efe290 00007fff`700119d2 Windows_Web!JsonValueImpl::ParseInternal+0x75
0d 0000007f`56efe2d0 00007fff`700118e8 Windows_Web!JsonValueImpl::InitializeFromString+0x16
0e 0000007f`56efe300 00007fff`70011876 Windows_Web!JsonValueFactory::TryParseInternal+0x50
0f 0000007f`56efe330 00007fff`3a6fe48e Windows_Web!JsonValueFactory::TryParse+0x36
10 0000007f`56efe360 00007fff`3a78f95c eModel!JsonUtils::GetJsonObject+0x82
[...]
```

which is also **Spiking Thread** (page 992):

```
0:001> !runaway f
User Mode Time
Thread Time
1:1a2c 0 days 0:03:37.562
8:52a8 0 days 0:00:36.890
[...]

Kernel Mode Time
Thread Time
8:52a8 0 days 0:00:10.625
1:1a2c 0 days 0:00:18.078
[...]
```

we can look at the relative proportion of User Mode / Kernel Mode times to infer **Active Space**. This can be further confirmed if we have **Step Dumps** (page 1070), for example, in our case we had an earlier memory dump with the same **Active Thread** and **Constant Subtrace** (page 153, with **Variable Subtraces**, page 1175, in the same **Active Space**):

```
0:001> kL
# Child-SP RetAddr Call Site
00 0000007f`56efd8d0 00007fff`a1109453 ntdll!RtlpHpLfhSlotAllocate+0x126
01 0000007f`56efd9c0 00007fff`a110a8db ntdll!RtlpAllocateHeapInternal+0x313
02 0000007f`56efdaa0 00007fff`9ea09960 ntdll!RtlpHpAllocWithExceptionProtection+0x3b
03 0000007f`56efdb70 00007fff`7001ba1b msvcrt!malloc+0x70
04 0000007f`56efdba0 00007fff`700187ca Windows_Web!operator new+0x23
05 (Inline Function) ---`--- Windows_Web!StringBuilder::EnsureBufferSpace+0x18
06 (Inline Function) ---`--- Windows_Web!JsonParser::ParseString+0x59
07 0000007f`56efdbd0 00007fff`70018f72 Windows_Web!JsonParser::ParseValue+0x37a
08 0000007f`56efdc50 00007fff`700186fb Windows_Web!JsonParser::ParseObject+0x422
09 0000007f`56efdda0 00007fff`700198c5 Windows_Web!JsonParser::ParseValue+0x2ab
0a 0000007f`56efde20 00007fff`70018ab3 Windows_Web!JsonParser::ParseArray+0xf5
0b 0000007f`56efde70 00007fff`70018f72 Windows_Web!JsonParser::ParseValue+0x663
0c 0000007f`56efdef0 00007fff`700186fb Windows_Web!JsonParser::ParseObject+0x422
0d 0000007f`56efe040 00007fff`70018f72 Windows_Web!JsonParser::ParseValue+0x2ab
0e 0000007f`56efe0c0 00007fff`700186fb Windows_Web!JsonParser::ParseObject+0x422
0f 0000007f`56efe210 00007fff`70011a69 Windows_Web!JsonParser::ParseValue+0x2ab
10 0000007f`56efe290 00007fff`700119d2 Windows_Web!JsonValueImpl::ParseInternal+0x75
11 0000007f`56efe2d0 00007fff`700118e8 Windows_Web!JsonValueImpl::InitializeFromString+0x16
12 0000007f`56efe300 00007fff`70011876 Windows_Web!JsonValueFactory::TryParseInternal+0x50
13 0000007f`56efe330 00007fff`3a6fe48e Windows_Web!JsonValueFactory::TryParse+0x36
14 0000007f`56efe360 00007fff`3a78f95c eModel!JsonUtils::GetJsonObject+0x82
[...]
```

Even in the absence of **Active Threads** in process memory dumps it is useful to look at time spent in kernel and user modes to see any anomalies, especially when threads are blocked in **System Calls** (page 1084). Then the high value of kernel mode time should suggest inspecting kernel **Activity Space** (for example, via a kernel dump). If we have an indication of high values of user mode time in a kernel memory dump, we may need to obtain process memory **Step Dumps**.

Active Thread

Linux

Here we publish a Linux variant of **Active Thread** pattern that was previously introduced for Mac OS X (page 72) and Windows (page 74). Basically, it is a thread that is not waiting, sleeping, or suspended (most threads are). However, from a memory dump, it is not possible to find out whether it was **Spiking Thread** (page 989) at the dump generation time (unless we have a set of memory snapshots and in each one we have the same or similar backtrace) and we do not have any **Paratext** (page 869) with CPU consumption stats for threads. For example, in one core dump we have this thread:

```
(gdb) info threads
Id Target Id Frame
6 Thread 0x7f560d467700 (LWP 3483) 0x00000000004324a9 in clone ()
5 Thread 0x7f560c465700 (LWP 3485) 0x000000000042fe31 in nanosleep ()
4 Thread 0x7f560bc64700 (LWP 3486) 0x000000000042fe31 in nanosleep ()
3 Thread 0x7f560b463700 (LWP 3487) 0x000000000042fe31 in nanosleep ()
2 Thread 0x18b9860 (LWP 3482) 0x000000000042fe31 in nanosleep ()
1 Thread 0x7f560cc66700 (LWP 3484) 0x000000000042fe31 in nanosleep ()
```

Thread #6 is not waiting so we inspect its back trace:

```
(gdb) thread 6
[Switching to thread 6 (Thread 0x7f560d467700 (LWP 3483))]
#0 0x00000000004324a9 in clone ()

(gdb) bt
#0 0x00000000004324a9 in clone ()
#1 0x0000000000401560 in ?? () at pthread_create.c:217
#2 0x00007f560d467700 in ?? ()
#3 0x0000000000000000 in ?? ()

(gdb) x/i 0x4324a9
=> 0x4324a9 : test %rax,%rax
```

Perhaps the core dump was saved at the thread creation time.

Mac OS X

This pattern was introduced in *Accelerated Mac OS X Core Dump Analysis*[9] training. Basically, it is a thread that is not waiting or suspended (most threads are). However, from a memory dump it is not possible to find out whether it was **Spiking Thread** (page 989) at the dump generation time (unless we have a set of memory snapshots and in each one we have the same or similar backtrace) and we do not have any **Paratext** (page 866) with CPU consumption stats for threads. For example, in one core dump we have these threads:

```
(gdb) info threads
12 0x98c450ee in __workq_kernreturn ()
11 0x98c4280e in semaphore_wait_trap ()
10 0x98c448e2 in __psynch_cvwait ()
9 0x00110171 in std::_Rb_tree<int, std::pair<int const, _iCapture*>, std::_Select1st<std::pair<int const,
_iCapture*> >, std::less<int>, std::allocator<std::pair<int const, _iCapture*> > >::find ()
8 0x98c428e6 in mach_wait_until ()
7 0x98c448e2 in __psynch_cvwait ()
6 0x98c427d2 in mach_msg_trap ()
5 0x98c427d2 in mach_msg_trap ()
4 0x98c428e6 in mach_wait_until ()
3 0x98c427d2 in mach_msg_trap ()
2 0x98c459ae in kevent ()
*  1 0x014bcee0 in cgGLGetLatestProfile ()
```

Threads #9 and #1 are not waiting so we inspect their back traces:

```
(gdb) bt
#0  0x014bcee0 in cgGLGetLatestProfile ()
#1  0x99060dd5 in exit ()
#2  0x001ef859 in os_exit ()
#3  0x001dc873 in luaD_precall ()
#4  0x001e7d9e in luaV_execute ()
#5  0x001dc18b in luaD_rawrunprotected ()
#6  0x001dced4 in lua_resume ()
#7  0x0058a526 in ticLuaManager::executeProgram ()
#8  0x005a09af in ticLuaScript::_execute ()
#9  0x003a6480 in darcScript::execute ()
#10 0x003af4d8 in darcTimeline::execute ()
#11 0x0034a2ba in darcSequenceur::executeAll ()
#12 0x0036904b in darcEventManager::ExecuteEventHandler ()
#13 0x003a37d2 in darcScene::process ()
#14 0x0034a2ba in darcSequenceur::executeAll ()
#15 0x0036904b in darcEventManager::ExecuteEventHandler ()
#16 0x00343ec0 in darcContext::process ()
#17 0x00347339 in darcContext::main ()
#18 0x003cf73d in darcPlayerImpl::renderOneFrame ()
#19 0x003cf078 in darcPlayerImpl::render ()
#20 0x000b1f6f in Run ()
```

---

[9] http://www.patterndiagnostics.com/accelerated-macosx-core-dump-analysis-book

```
#21 0x000b1fe9 in tiMain ()
#22 0x000c73ee in main ()


(gdb) thread 9
[Switching to thread 9 (core thread 8)]
0x00110171 in std::_Rb_tree<int, std::pair<int const, _iCapture*>, std::_Select1st<std::pair<int const,
_iCapture*> >, std::less<int>, std::allocator<std::pair<int const, _iCapture*> > >::find ()


(gdb) bt
#0  0x00110171 in std::_Rb_tree<int, std::pair<int const, _iCapture*>, std::_Select1st<std::pair<int
const, _iCapture*> >, std::less<int>, std::allocator<std::pair<int const, _iCapture*> > >::find ()
#1  0x0010f936 in ticVideoManager::isPaused ()
#2  0x00201801 in ticMLT_VideoCapture::Execute ()
#3  0x0020aa0b in ticModuleGraph::runOnce ()
#4  0x002632be in TrackingApp::ProcessTracking ()
#5  0x005b2f5d in ticMLTTracking::processInternal ()
#6  0x005b322d in ticMLTTracking::processThread ()
#7  0x005b36f3 in trackingThread ()
#8  0x004eaf1e in ticThread::threadFunc ()
#9  0x99023557 in _pthread_start ()
#10 0x9900dcee in thread_start ()
```

Windows equivalent would be a process memory dump which does not have any information saved for **!runaway** WinDbg command.

Windows

We already introduced **Active Thread** (page 72) pattern variant for Mac OS X. Here we provide an example for Windows. Unless we have **Evental Dumps** (page 351), **Active Threads** in Windows are usually threads from **Busy System** (page 110) or **Spiking Threads** (page 992), and, therefore, represent an abnormal behavior since most threads are waiting or calling some API. For **Evental Dumps** they may be just normal threads:

```
0:000> r
rax=0000000000000006 rbx=0000000000000003 rcx=0000000000000018
rdx=0000000000000000 rsi=000000000028c601 rdi=0000000002bee25e
rip=000007feff1a5a09 rsp=000000000028c380 rbp=0000000000000000
r8=0000000000000000 r9=00000000001653a0 r10=000000000000000e
r11=000000000000000a r12=0000000000000006 r13=000000000028ca38
r14=0000000002bec888 r15=0000000000173630
iopl=0 nv up ei pl nz ac po nc
cs=0033 ss=002b ds=002b es=002b fs=0053 gs=002b efl=00000216
usp10!otlChainingLookup::apply+0x2f9:
000007fe`ff1a5a09 498d0c06 lea rcx,[r14+rax]


0:000> k
# Child-SP RetAddr Call Site
00 00000000`0028c380 000007fe`ff19f4f2 usp10!otlChainingLookup::apply+0x2f9
01 00000000`0028c4b0 000007fe`ff19e777 usp10!ApplyLookup+0x592
02 00000000`0028c5a0 000007fe`ff19a634 usp10!ApplyFeatures+0x777
03 00000000`0028c860 000007fe`ff181800 usp10!SubstituteOtlGlyphs+0x224
04 00000000`0028c910 000007fe`ff174cc0 usp10!GenericEngineGetGlyphs+0x1000
05 00000000`0028ccb0 000007fe`ff1389c5 usp10!ShlShape+0x7a0
06 00000000`0028ced0 000007fe`ff147363 usp10!ScriptShape+0x205
07 00000000`0028cf70 000007fe`ff148ac9 usp10!RenderItemNoFallback+0x433
08 00000000`0028d030 000007fe`ff148d86 usp10!RenderItemWithFallback+0x129
09 00000000`0028d080 000007fe`ff14a5f7 usp10!RenderItem+0x36
0a 00000000`0028d0d0 000007fe`ff13b2c9 usp10!ScriptStringAnalyzeGlyphs+0x277
0b 00000000`0028d170 000007fe`fdd616bf usp10!ScriptStringAnalyse+0x399
0c 00000000`0028d1f0 000007fe`fdd614cc lpk!LpkCharsetDraw+0x4eb
0d 00000000`0028d3b0 00000000`774e85c5 lpk!LpkDrawTextEx+0x68
0e 00000000`0028d420 00000000`774e865c user32!DT_DrawStr+0xa6
0f 00000000`0028d4c0 00000000`774e826c user32!DT_DrawJustifiedLine+0xa6
10 00000000`0028d530 00000000`774e6cc8 user32!DrawTextExWorker+0x442
11 00000000`0028d640 000007fe`fbd840d1 user32!DrawTextW+0x57
12 00000000`0028d6b0 000007fe`fbd83e49 comctl32!CLVView::_ComputeLabelSizeWorker+0x1d1
13 00000000`0028da40 000007fe`fbd8cc48 comctl32!CLVView::v_RecomputeLabelSize+0x1f9
14 00000000`0028dd70 000007fe`fbda9d24 comctl32!CLVListView::v_DrawItem+0x284
15 00000000`0028e110 000007fe`fbd9773b comctl32!CLVDrawItemManager::DrawItem+0x4c0
16 00000000`0028e170 000007fe`fbd95f8e comctl32!CLVDrawManager::_PaintItems+0x3df
17 00000000`0028e3b0 000007fe`fbd95e87 comctl32!CLVDrawManager::_PaintWorkArea+0xda
18 00000000`0028e430 000007fe`fbd95cff comctl32!CLVDrawManager::_OnPaintWorkAreas+0x147
19 00000000`0028e4c0 000007fe`fbd06f1b comctl32!CLVDrawManager::_OnPaint+0x14b
1a 00000000`0028e570 000007fe`fbd06011 comctl32!CListView::WndProc+0xebf
1b 00000000`0028e770 00000000`774e9bd1 comctl32!CListView::s_WndProc+0x6cd
1c 00000000`0028e7d0 00000000`774e3bfc user32!UserCallWinProcCheckWow+0x1ad
1d 00000000`0028e890 00000000`774e3b78 user32!CallWindowProcAorW+0xdc
1e 00000000`0028e8e0 000007fe`fbca6215 user32!CallWindowProcW+0x18
1f 00000000`0028e920 000007fe`fbca69a0 comctl32!CallOriginalWndProc+0x1d
20 00000000`0028e960 000007fe`fbca6768 comctl32!CallNextSubclassProc+0x8c
```

```
21 00000000`0028e9e0 000007fe`fde1096a comctl32!DefSubclassProc+0x7c
22 00000000`0028ea30 000007fe`fdde9df4 shell32!DefSubclassProc+0x56
23 00000000`0028ea60 000007fe`fbca69a0 shell32!CListViewHost::s_ListViewSubclassWndProc+0x267
24 00000000`0028eb40 000007fe`fbca6877 comctl32!CallNextSubclassProc+0x8c
25 00000000`0028ebc0 00000000`774e9bd1 comctl32!MasterSubclassProc+0xe7
26 00000000`0028ec60 00000000`774e72cb user32!UserCallWinProcCheckWow+0x1ad
27 00000000`0028ed20 00000000`774e6829 user32!DispatchClientMessage+0xc3
28 00000000`0028ed80 00000000`776211f5 user32!_fnDWORD+0x2d
29 00000000`0028ede0 00000000`774e6e5a ntdll!KiUserCallbackDispatcherContinue
2a 00000000`0028ee68 00000000`774e6e6c user32!NtUserDispatchMessage+0xa
2b 00000000`0028ee70 00000000`774e67c2 user32!DispatchMessageWorker+0x55b
2c 00000000`0028eef0 000007fe`fbcc34a4 user32!IsDialogMessageW+0x153
2d 00000000`0028ef80 000007fe`fbcc583f comctl32!Prop_IsDialogMessage+0x1f0
2e 00000000`0028eff0 000007fe`fbcc5c05 comctl32!_RealPropertySheet+0x31b
2f 00000000`0028f0c0 000007fe`ff214e68 comctl32!_PropertySheet+0x55
30 00000000`0028f100 000007fe`ff214bb1 comdlg32!Print_InvokePropertySheets+0x2c6
31 00000000`0028f660 000007fe`ff21499c comdlg32!PrintDlgExX+0x2be
32 00000000`0028f6c0 00000000`ffec250f comdlg32!PrintDlgExW+0x38
33 00000000`0028f730 00000000`ffec242b notepad!GetPrinterDCviaDialog+0xab
34 00000000`0028f7f0 00000000`ffec23e8 notepad!PrintIt+0x46
35 00000000`0028fb70 00000000`ffec14eb notepad!NPCommand+0xdb
36 00000000`0028fca0 00000000`774e9bd1 notepad!NPWndProc+0x540
37 00000000`0028fce0 00000000`774e98da user32!UserCallWinProcCheckWow+0x1ad
38 00000000`0028fda0 00000000`ffec10bc user32!DispatchMessageWorker+0x3b5
39 00000000`0028fe20 00000000`ffec133c notepad!WinMain+0x16f
3a 00000000`0028fea0 00000000`773c59ed notepad!DisplayNonGenuineDlgWorker+0x2da
3b 00000000`0028ff60 00000000`775fc541 kernel32!BaseThreadInitThunk+0xd
3c 00000000`0028ff90 00000000`00000000 ntdll!RtlUserThreadStart+0x1d
```

We see the thread is active, in the middle of the function. For comparison, the next two threads are waiting and calling API respectively:

```
0:000> ~1k
# Child-SP          RetAddr           Call Site
00 00000000`02edf748 00000000`775eb037 ntdll!NtWaitForMultipleObjects+0xa
01 00000000`02edf750 00000000`773c59ed ntdll!TppWaiterpThread+0x14d
02 00000000`02edf9f0 00000000`775fc541 kernel32!BaseThreadInitThunk+0xd
03 00000000`02edfa20 00000000`00000000 ntdll!RtlUserThreadStart+0x1d


0:000> ~2k
# Child-SP          RetAddr           Call Site
00 00000000`0344e048 000007fe`fd3f403e ntdll!NtUnmapViewOfSection+0xa
01 00000000`0344e050 00000000`774e2edf KERNELBASE!FreeLibrary+0xa4
02 00000000`0344e080 000007fe`fdddaab3 user32!PrivateExtractIconsW+0x34b
03 00000000`0344e5a0 000007fe`fdddac28 shell32!SHPrivateExtractIcons+0x50a
04 00000000`0344e870 000007fe`fdde34b4 shell32!SHDefExtractIconW+0x254
05 00000000`0344eb60 000007fe`fdde3435 shell32!CExtractIcon::_ExtractW+0xcd
06 00000000`0344ebe0 000007fe`fdf0d529 shell32!CExtractIconBase::Extract+0x21
07 00000000`0344ec20 000007fe`fdf0d2da shell32!IExtractIcon_Extract+0x43
08 00000000`0344ec60 000007fe`fdddfff0 shell32!_GetILIndexGivenPXIcon+0x22e
09 00000000`0344f100 000007fe`fdde27a4 shell32!_GetILIndexFromItem+0x87
0a 00000000`0344f1a0 000007fe`fddb6506 shell32!SHGetIconIndexFromPIDL+0x66
0b 00000000`0344f1d0 000007fe`fdedb186 shell32!MapIDListToIconILIndex+0x52
0c 00000000`0344f250 000007fe`fdddc54c shell32!CLoadSystemIconTask::InternalResumeRT+0x110
0d 00000000`0344f2e0 000007fe`fde0efcb shell32!CRunnableTask::Run+0xda
```

```
0e 00000000`0344f310 000007fe`fde12b56 shell32!CShellTask::TT_Run+0x124
0f 00000000`0344f340 000007fe`fde12cb2 shell32!CShellTaskThread::ThreadProc+0x1d2
10 00000000`0344f3e0 000007fe`ff2b3843 shell32!CShellTaskThread::s_ThreadProc+0x22
11 00000000`0344f410 00000000`775f15db shlwapi!ExecuteWorkItemThreadProc+0xf
12 00000000`0344f440 00000000`775f0c56 ntdll!RtlpTpWorkCallback+0x16b
13 00000000`0344f520 00000000`773c59ed ntdll!TppWorkerThread+0x5ff
14 00000000`0344f820 00000000`775fc541 kernel32!BaseThreadInitThunk+0xd
15 00000000`0344f850 00000000`00000000 ntdll!RtlUserThreadStart+0x1d


0:000> ub ntdll!NtUnmapViewOfSection+0xa
ntdll!NtAccessCheckAndAuditAlarm:
00000000`77621540 4c8bd1           mov      r10,rcx
00000000`77621543 b826000000       mov      eax,26h
00000000`77621548 0f05             syscall
00000000`7762154a c3               ret
00000000`7762154b 0f1f440000       nop      dword ptr [rax+rax]
ntdll!NtUnmapViewOfSection:
00000000`77621550 4c8bd1           mov      r10,rcx
00000000`77621553 b827000000       mov      eax,27h
00000000`77621558 0f05             syscall
```

Our **Active Thread** is not **Spiking Thread** since CPU consumption is minimal:

```
0:000> !runaway f
User Mode Time
Thread       Time
0:1ca4       0 days 0:00:00.171
11:1fb0       0 days 0:00:00.000
10:f98        0 days 0:00:00.000
9:eb8        0 days 0:00:00.000
8:1b80       0 days 0:00:00.000
7:139c       0 days 0:00:00.000
6:1d9c       0 days 0:00:00.000
5:1b44       0 days 0:00:00.000
4:1edc       0 days 0:00:00.000
3:830        0 days 0:00:00.000
2:1638       0 days 0:00:00.000
1:1ab0       0 days 0:00:00.000
Kernel Mode Time
Thread       Time
0:1ca4       0 days 0:00:00.421
11:1fb0       0 days 0:00:00.000
10:f98        0 days 0:00:00.000
9:eb8        0 days 0:00:00.000
8:1b80       0 days 0:00:00.000
7:139c       0 days 0:00:00.000
6:1d9c       0 days 0:00:00.000
5:1b44       0 days 0:00:00.000
4:1edc       0 days 0:00:00.000
3:830        0 days 0:00:00.000
2:1638       0 days 0:00:00.000
1:1ab0       0 days 0:00:00.000
Elapsed Time
Thread       Time
11:1fb0       24692 days 13:29:46.335
```

```
0:1ca4    0 days 0:02:39.671
1:1ab0    0 days 0:01:48.239
2:1638    0 days 0:01:18.837
4:1edc    0 days 0:01:18.697
3:830     0 days 0:01:18.697
5:1b44    0 days 0:01:18.497
6:1d9c    0 days 0:01:18.387
7:139c    0 days 0:01:15.957
8:1b80    0 days 0:01:14.397
9:eb8     0 days 0:01:01.485
10:f98     0 days 0:00:39.849
```

However, the huge *Elapsed Time* for the thread #11 (most likely the value is uninitialized) and its stack trace suggest that the dump was saved on *Create Thread* debugging event by a debugger:

```
0:000> ~11k
# Child-SP          RetAddr           Call Site
00 00000000`0666fb08 00000000`00000000 ntdll!RtlUserThreadStart
```

Activity Resonance

This pattern is observed when two products from different vendors compete in some functional domain such malware detection. In the example below *ApplicationA* and *AVDriverA* modules belong to *Vendor A,* and *AV-B* module belongs to *Vendor B*. Both threads are **Spiking Threads** (page 989) blocking all other activity in the system:

```
0: kd> !running

System Processors: (0000000000000003)
Idle Processors: (0000000000000000) (0000000000000000) (0000000000000000) (0000000000000000)


Prcbs           Current         Next
0    fffff80001845e80  fffffa8004350060                        ................
1    fffff880009c4180  fffffa80028e7060                        ................


0: kd> !thread fffffa8004350060 1f
THREAD fffffa8004350060  Cid 14424.14b34  Teb: 000000007efdb000 Win32Thread: fffff900c1d32c30 RUNNING on
processor 0
Not impersonating
DeviceMap               fffff8a00148fe80
Owning Process          fffffa8003d6cb30     Image:         ApplicationA.exe
Attached Process        N/A             Image:      N/A
Wait Start TickCount    10568630        Ticks: 0
Context Switch Count    345                  LargeStack
UserTime                00:02:21.360
KernelTime              01:09:32.130
Win32 Start Address ApplicationA!mainCRTStartup (0x0000000000404c1b)
Stack Init fffff88006c71db0 Current fffff88006c71670
Base fffff88006c72000 Limit fffff88006c6a000 Call 0
Priority 9 BasePriority 8 UnusualBoost 0 ForegroundBoost 0 IoPriority 2 PagePriority 5
Child-SP          RetAddr           Call Site
fffff880`06c70ec0 fffff880`0197d53c AVDriverA+0x15d69
fffff880`06c70f10 fffff880`01988556 AVDriverA+0x1453c
fffff880`06c70fd0 fffff880`019886a8 AVDriverA+0x1f556
fffff880`06c71000 fffff800`0198ebfd AVDriverA+0x1f6a8
fffff880`06c71060 fffff800`019bf4f2 nt! ?? ::NNGAKEGL::`string'+0x2a6fd
fffff880`06c711e0 fffff800`019c3385 nt!PspCreateThread+0x246
fffff880`06c71460 fffff800`016d28d3 nt!NtCreateThreadEx+0x25d
fffff880`06c71bb0 00000000`76e61d9a nt!KiSystemServiceCopyEnd+0x13 (TrapFrame @ fffff880`06c71c20)
00000000`0008e178 00000000`74990411 ntdll!ZwCreateThreadEx+0xa
00000000`0008e180 00000000`7497cf87 wow64!whNtCreateThreadEx+0x815
00000000`0008e350 00000000`748c2776 wow64!Wow64SystemServiceEx+0xd7
00000000`0008ec10 00000000`7497d07e wow64cpu!TurboDispatchJumpAddressEnd+0x2d
00000000`0008ecd0 00000000`7497c549 wow64!RunCpuSimulation+0xa
00000000`0008ed20 00000000`76e54956 wow64!Wow64LdrpInitialize+0x429
00000000`0008f270 00000000`76e51a17 ntdll!LdrpInitializeProcess+0x17e4
00000000`0008f760 00000000`76e3c32e ntdll! ?? ::FNODOBFM::`string'+0x29220
00000000`0008f7d0 00000000`00000000 ntdll!LdrInitializeThunk+0xe
```

```
0: kd> !thread ffffffa80028e7060 1f
THREAD ffffffa80028e7060  Cid 0dc4.0e5c  Teb: 000000007efa4000 Win32Thread: 0000000000000000 RUNNING on
processor 1
Not impersonating
DeviceMap               fffff8a000008b30
Owning Process          ffffffa8002817060        Image:          AV-B.exe
Attached Process        N/A             Image:          N/A
Wait Start TickCount    10568617        Ticks: 13 (0:00:00:00.203)
Context Switch Count    1763138
UserTime                00:04:26.765
KernelTime              03:09:31.140
Win32 Start Address AV-B (0x00000000004289f2)
Stack Init fffff88003b88db0 Current fffff88003b88900
Base fffff88003b89000 Limit fffff88003b83000 Call 0
Priority 15 BasePriority 15 UnusualBoost 0 ForegroundBoost 0 IoPriority 2 PagePriority 5
Child-SP          RetAddr           Call Site
fffff880`03b88660 fffff800`019919a9 nt!ObReferenceObjectSafe+0xf
fffff880`03b88690 fffff800`01991201 nt!PsGetNextProcess+0x81
fffff880`03b886e0 fffff800`019dcef6 nt!ExpGetProcessInformation+0x774
fffff880`03b88830 fffff800`019dd949 nt!ExpQuerySystemInformation+0xfb4
fffff880`03b88be0 fffff800`016d28d3 nt!NtQuerySystemInformation+0x4d
fffff880`03b88c20 00000000`76e6167a nt!KiSystemServiceCopyEnd+0x13 (TrapFrame @ fffff880`03b88c20)
00000000`0118e708 00000000`74987da7 ntdll!NtQuerySystemInformation+0xa
00000000`0118e710 00000000`74988636 wow64!whNT32QuerySystemProcessInformationEx+0x93
00000000`0118e760 00000000`7498a0e9 wow64!whNtQuerySystemInformation_SpecialQueryCase+0x466
00000000`0118e800 00000000`7497cf87 wow64!whNtQuerySystemInformation+0xf1
00000000`0118e840 00000000`748c2776 wow64!Wow64SystemServiceEx+0xd7
00000000`0118f100 00000000`7497d07e wow64cpu!TurboDispatchJumpAddressEnd+0x2d
00000000`0118f1c0 00000000`7497c549 wow64!RunCpuSimulation+0xa
00000000`0118f210 00000000`76e8e707 wow64!Wow64LdrpInitialize+0x429
00000000`0118f760 00000000`76e3c32e ntdll! ?? ::FNODOBFM::`string'+0x29364
00000000`0118f7d0 00000000`00000000 ntdll!LdrInitializeThunk+0xe
```

Affine Thread

Setting a thread affinity mask to a specific processor or core makes that thread running in a single processor environment from that thread point of view. It is always scheduled to run on that processor. This potentially creates a problem found in real single processor environments if the processor runs another higher priority thread (**Thread Starvation** pattern, page 1119) or loops at dispatch level IRQL (**Dispatch Level Spin** pattern, page 261).

Here is one example. A dual core laptop was hanging, and kernel memory dump revealed the following **Wait Chain** pattern (page 1206):

```
Resource @ nt!PopPolicyLock (0x80563080)      Exclusively owned
    Contention Count = 32
    NumberOfExclusiveWaiters = 9
     Threads: 8b3b08b8-01<*>
     Threads Waiting On Exclusive Access:
             872935f0       8744cb30       87535da8       8755a6b0
             8588dba8       8a446c10       85891c50       87250020
             8a6e7da8
```

The thread 8b3b08b8 blocked other 9 threads and had the following stack trace:

```
0: kd> !thread 8b3b08b8 1f
THREAD 8b3b08b8  Cid 0004.002c  Teb: 00000000 Win32Thread: 00000000 READY
Not impersonating
DeviceMap                 e1009248
Owning Process            8b3b2830       Image:         System
Wait Start TickCount      44419          Ticks: 8744 (0:00:02:16.625)
Context Switch Count      4579
UserTime                  00:00:00.000
KernelTime                00:00:01.109
Start Address nt!ExpWorkerThread (0x8053867e)
Stack Init bad00000 Current bacffcb0 Base bad00000 Limit bacfd000 Call 0
Priority 15 BasePriority 12 PriorityDecrement 3 DecrementCount 16
ChildEBP RetAddr
bacffcc8 804fd2c9 nt!KiUnlockDispatcherDatabase+0x9e
bacffcdc 8052a16f nt!KeSetSystemAffinityThread+0x5b
bacffd04 805caf03 nt!PopCompositeBatteryUpdateThrottleLimit+0x2d
bacffd24 805ca767 nt!PopCompositeBatteryDeviceHandler+0x1c5
bacffd3c 80529d3b nt!PopPolicyWorkerMain+0x25
bacffd7c 8053876d nt!PopPolicyWorkerThread+0xbf
bacffdac 805cff64 nt!ExpWorkerThread+0xef
bacffddc 805460de nt!PspSystemThreadStartup+0x34
00000000 00000000 nt!KiThreadStartup+0x16
```

Note this function and its first parameter (shown in smaller font for visual clarity):

```
0: kd> !thread 8b3b08b8
...
bacffcdc 8052a16f 00000002 8a5b8cd8 00000030 nt!KeSetSystemAffinityThread+0x5b
...
```

The first parameter is KAFFINITY mask, and 0x2 is 0y10 (binary) which is the second core. This thread had been already set to run on that core only:

```
0: kd> dt _KTHREAD 8b3b08b8
nt!_KTHREAD
   +0x000 Header          : _DISPATCHER_HEADER
...
   +0x124 Affinity        : 2
...
```

Let's look at our second core:

```
0: kd> ~1s

1: kd> kL 100
ChildEBP RetAddr
a8f00618 acd21947 hal!KeAcquireInStackQueuedSpinLock+0x43
a8f00618 acd21947 tcpip!IndicateData+0x98
a8f00684 acd173e5 tcpip!IndicateData+0x98
a8f0070c acd14ef5 tcpip!TCPRcv+0xbb0
a8f0076c acd14b19 tcpip!DeliverToUser+0x18e
a8f007e8 acd14836 tcpip!DeliverToUserEx+0x95e
a8f008a0 acd13928 tcpip!IPRcvPacket+0x6cb
a8f008e0 acd13853 tcpip!ARPRcvIndicationNew+0x149
a8f0091c ba56be45 tcpip!ARPRcvPacket+0x68
a8f00970 b635801d NDIS!ethFilterDprIndicateReceivePacket+0x307
a8f00984 b63581b4 psched!PsFlushReceiveQueue+0x15
a8f009a8 b63585f9 psched!PsEnqueueReceivePacket+0xda
a8f009c0 ba56c8ed psched!ClReceiveComplete+0x13
a8f009d8 b7defdb5 NDIS!EthFilterDprIndicateReceiveComplete+0x7c
a8f00a08 b7df0f78 driverA+0x17db5
a8f00a64 ba55ec2c driverA+0x18f78
a8f00a88 b6b0962c NDIS!ndisMSendCompleteX+0x8d
a8f00a9c b6b0a36d driverB+0x62c
a8f00ab8 ba55e88f driverB+0x136d
a8f00ae0 b7de003c NDIS!NdisReturnPackets+0xe9
a8f00af0 ba55e88f driverA+0x803c
a8f00b18 b6358061 NDIS!NdisReturnPackets+0xe9
a8f00b30 ba55e88f psched!MpReturnPacket+0x3b
a8f00b58 acc877cc NDIS!NdisReturnPackets+0xe9
87749da0 00000000 afd!AfdReturnBuffer+0xe1

1: kd> r
eax=a8f005f8 ebx=a8f00624 ecx=8a9862ed edx=a8f00b94 esi=874e2ed0 edi=8a9862d0
eip=806e6a33 esp=a8f005ec ebp=a8f00618 iopl=0 nv up ei pl nz na po nc
cs=0008  ss=0010  ds=0023  es=0023  fs=0030  gs=0000  efl=00000202
hal!KeAcquireInStackQueuedSpinLock+0x43:
806e6a33 74ee je hal!KeAcquireInStackQueuedSpinLock+0x33 (806e6a23) [br=0]
```

```
1: kd> !running

System Processors 3 (affinity mask)
  Idle Processors 1

     Prcb      Current   Next
  1  bab38120  8a0c8ae8  8b3a7318  ...........
```

We see the thread 8a0c8ae8 had been spinning on the second core for more than 2 minutes:

```
1: kd> !thread 8a0c8ae8 1f
THREAD 8a0c8ae8  Cid 0660.0124  Teb: 7ffd7000 Win32Thread: e338c498 RUNNING on processor 1
IRP List:
    8a960008: (0006,01b4) Flags: 00000900  Mdl: 87535908
Not impersonating
DeviceMap                  e2f155b8
Owning Process             87373020     Image:        APPLICATION.EXE
Wait Start TickCount       43918        Ticks: 9245 (0:00:02:24.453)
Context Switch Count       690                  LargeStack
UserTime                   00:00:00.000
KernelTime                 00:02:24.453
...
```

Its kernel time looks consistent with the starved thread waiting time:

```
0: kd> !thread 8b3b08b8 1f
THREAD 8b3b08b8  Cid 0004.002c  Teb: 00000000 Win32Thread: 00000000 READY
Not impersonating
DeviceMap                  e1009248
Owning Process             8b3b2830     Image:        System
Wait Start TickCount       44419        Ticks: 8744 (0:00:02:16.625)
...
```

For comparison, the spinning thread has affinity mask 0y11 (0x3) which means that it could be scheduled to run on both cores:

```
0: kd> dt _KTHREAD 8a0c8ae8
nt!_KTHREAD
   +0x000 Header           : _DISPATCHER_HEADER
...
   +0x124 Affinity         : 3
...
```

Aggregate Snapshot

This pattern is any memory dump or software trace file that is combined from **Memory Snapshots** (page 744). Typical examples include:

- A minidump file where only specific memory ranges are included
- A software trace file combined from structured memory snapshots

Aggregated Frames

For completeness, we add **Aggregated Frames** analysis pattern implemented as "aggregated stack trace" in various software performance profiling tools. Such tools periodically record CPU **Stack Trace Collection** (page 1042). Other tools profile memory allocations and their stack traces. By aggregation we mean summing up occurrences of modules and functions from all collected stack traces similar to this table:

```
ModuleA         88%
    +0x234          42%
    +0x123           8%
    !foo            38%
        +0xd            30%
        +0x56            2%
    !bar             6%
        +0x18            6%
ModuleB         12%
    !export         12%
        +0x2380          1%
        +0x1224          6%
        +0x3812          5%
```

Related to memory dump analysis we can either use **Stack Trace Collection** (page 1053) to detect **Ubiquitous Component** in user (page 1138) and kernel (page 1135) spaces, or database **Stack Traces** (page 1026), for example, used in detection of process heap (page 732), handle (page 464), and reference (page 922) **Memory Leaks**.

We do not include "stack" in the name of this pattern because frames are not sorted by the execution direction compared to **Unified Stack Trace** (page 1150) analysis pattern where we have some notion of aggregation depicted as multiplicities.

We can also name it as *Frame Usage Signature* similar to **Stack Trace Signature** (page 1067).

Anchor Region

In order to start the analysis of a structured **Memory Snapshot** (page 744), a debugger engine needs **Anchor Region** that describes memory layout and where to start unfolding of analysis. For example, it can be a list of modules (another forthcoming structural pattern). We can observe the importance of such regions when we try to open corrupt or severely **Truncated Dumps** (page 1130):

```
[...]
KdDebuggerDataBlock is not present or unreadable.
[...]
Unable to read PsLoadedModuleList
[...]
```

For certain types of memory snapshots (like software traces) an anchor region coincides with its structure description (message trace format for structured snapshots) and a trace file header (if any) for **Aggregate Snapshots** (page 83).

Annotated Disassembly

JIT .NET Code

When disassembling JIT code, it is good to see annotated function calls with full type and token information:

```
0:000> !CLRStack
OS Thread Id: 0xbf8 (0)
ESP       EIP
001fef90 003200a4 ClassMain.DoWork()
001fef94 00320082 ClassMain.Main(System.String[])
001ff1b0 79e7c74b [GCFrame: 001ff1b0]


0:000> !U 00320082
Normal JIT generated code
ClassMain.Main(System.String[])
Begin 00320070, size 13
00320070 b960300d00   mov ecx,0D3060h (MT: ClassMain)
00320075 e8a21fdaff   call 000c201c (JitHelp: CORINFO_HELP_NEWSFAST)
0032007a 8bc8         mov ecx,eax
0032007c ff159c300d00 call dword ptr ds:[0D309Ch] (ClassMain.DoWork(), mdToken: 06000002)
>>> 00320082 c3        ret
```

However, this does not work when we disable the output of raw bytes:

```
0:000> !U 00320082
Normal JIT generated code
ClassMain.Main(System.String[])
Begin 00320070, size 13
00320070 mov  ecx,0D3060h
00320075 call 000c201c
0032007a mov  ecx,eax
0032007c call dword ptr ds:[0D309Ch]
>>> 00320082 ret
```

Here we can still double check JIT-ed function calls manually:

```
0:000> dd 0D309Ch l1
000d309c 00320098


0:000> !IP2MD 00320098
MethodDesc:   000d3048
Method Name: ClassMain.DoWork()
Class:        000d1180
MethodTable:  000d3060
mdToken:      06000002
Module:       000d2c3c
IsJitted:     yes
m_CodeOrIL:   00320098
```

Blocked DPC

In this pattern, we have blocked per-processor Deferred Procedure Call[10] queues because of threads running on processors with IRQL > DISPATCH_LEVEL. For example, on the processor 11 (0x0b):

```
11: kd> !dpcs
CPU Type KDPC Function
3: Normal : 0x8accacec 0xf710567a DriverA

5: Normal : 0x89f449e4 0xf595b83a DriverB

7: Normal : 0x8a63664c 0xf59e3f04 USBPORT!USBPORT_IsrDpc

11: Normal : 0x8acb2cec 0xf710567a DriverA
11: Normal : 0x8b5e955c 0xf73484e6 ACPI!ACPIInterruptServiceRoutineDPC


11: kd> !thread
THREAD 89806428  Cid 0934.0944  Teb: 7ffdb000 Win32Thread: bc17dda0 RUNNING on processor b
Not impersonating
DeviceMap              e1002258
Owning Process         89972290      Image:        ApplicationA.exe
Attached Process       N/A           Image:        N/A
Wait Start TickCount   2863772       Ticks: 368905 (0:01:36:04.140)
Context Switch Count   145085                 LargeStack
UserTime               00:00:00.015
KernelTime             01:36:04.203
Win32 Start Address MSVCR90!_threadstartex (0x7854345e)
Start Address kernel32!BaseThreadStartThunk (0x77e617ec)
Stack Init f3f63000 Current f3f62c4c Base f3f63000 Limit f3f5f000 Call 0
Priority 10 BasePriority 10 PriorityDecrement 0
ChildEBP RetAddr  Args to Child
f777d3b0 f3f62d28 00000010 00000000 00000000 hal!KeAcquireInStackQueuedSpinLockRaiseToSynch+0x36
WARNING: Frame IP not in any known module. Following frames may be wrong.
f777d3b4 00000000 00000000 00000000 00000000 0xf3f62d28
```

---

[10] http://en.wikipedia.org/wiki/Deferred_Procedure_Call

Blocked Queue

LPC/ALPC

We provide an example of an ALPC port here. If we see an LPC/ALPC wait chain (page 1214) endpoint or just have a message address (and optionally a port address), we can check the port queue length. For example, in a frozen system we have this WinDbg output:

```
THREAD fffffa8009db7160  Cid 03b0.2ec0  Teb: 000007fffffd5000 Win32Thread: 0000000000000000 WAIT:
(WrLpcReply) UserMode Non-Alertable
     fffffa8009db7520  Semaphore Limit 0x1
Waiting for reply to ALPC Message fffff8a00dbc6650 : queued at port fffffa800577ee60 : owned by process
fffffa80056ddb30
Not impersonating
DeviceMap                   fffff8a000008b30
Owning Process              fffffa8005691b30      Image:        ServiceA.exe
Attached Process            N/A          Image:         N/A
Wait Start TickCount        39742808     Ticks: 3469954 (0:15:02:11.629)
Context Switch Count        9
UserTime                    00:00:00.000
KernelTime                  00:00:00.000
Win32 Start Address 0x0000000076cd8e70
Stack Init fffff8800bf60db0 Current fffff8800bf60620
Base fffff8800bf61000 Limit fffff8800bf5b000 Call 0
Priority 10 BasePriority 9 UnusualBoost 0 ForegroundBoost 0 IoPriority 2 PagePriority 5
Kernel stack not resident.
Child-SP RetAddr Call Site
fffff880`0bf60660 fffff800`016de992 nt!KiSwapContext+0x7a
fffff880`0bf607a0 fffff800`016e0cff nt!KiCommitThreadWait+0x1d2
fffff880`0bf60830 fffff800`016f5d1f nt!KeWaitForSingleObject+0x19f
fffff880`0bf608d0 fffff800`019ddac6 nt!AlpcpSignalAndWait+0x8f
fffff880`0bf60980 fffff800`019dba50 nt!AlpcpReceiveSynchronousReply+0x46
fffff880`0bf609e0 fffff800`019d8fcb nt!AlpcpProcessSynchronousRequest+0x33d
fffff880`0bf60b00 fffff800`016d6993 nt!NtAlpcSendWaitReceivePort+0x1ab
fffff880`0bf60bb0 00000000`76d105aa nt!KiSystemServiceCopyEnd+0x13 (TrapFrame @ fffff880`0bf60c20)
00000000`01efe638 000007fe`fec0aa76 ntdll!ZwAlpcSendWaitReceivePort+0xa
00000000`01efe640 000007fe`fecacb64 RPCRT4!LRPC_CCALL::SendReceive+0x156
00000000`01efe700 000007fe`fecacd55 RPCRT4!NdrpClientCall3+0x244
00000000`01efe9c0 000007fe`fcbf18a1 RPCRT4!NdrClientCall3+0xf2
[...]
```

```
0: kd> !alpc /m fffff8a00dbc6650
 Message @ fffff8a00dbc6650
    MessageID               : 0x0720 (1824)
    CallbackID              : 0x257C575 (39306613)
    SequenceNumber          : 0x00000002 (2)
    Type                    : LPC_REQUEST
    DataLength              : 0x0044 (68)
    TotalLength             : 0x006C (108)
    Canceled                : No
    Release                 : No
    ReplyWaitReply          : No
    Continuation            : Yes
    OwnerPort               : fffffa8006a4bb10 [ALPC_CLIENT_COMMUNICATION_PORT]
    WaitingThread           : fffffa8009db7160
    QueueType               : ALPC_MSGQUEUE_PENDING
    QueuePort               : fffffa800577ee60 [ALPC_CONNECTION_PORT]
    QueuePortOwnerProcess   : fffffa80056ddb30 (ServiceB.exe)
    ServerThread            : fffffa8007ead4d0
    QuotaCharged            : No
    CancelQueuePort         : 0000000000000000
    CancelSequencePort      : 0000000000000000
    CancelSequenceNumber    : 0x00000000 (0)
    ClientContext           : 0000000002a60f40
    ServerContext           : 0000000000000000
    PortContext             : 000000000227a370
    CancelPortContext       : 0000000000000000
    SecurityData            : 0000000000000000
    View                    : 0000000000000000

0: kd> !alpc /p fffffa800577ee60
 Port @ fffffa800577ee60
    Type                      : ALPC_CONNECTION_PORT
    CommunicationInfo         : fffff8a0022435d0
      ConnectionPort          : fffffa800577ee60
      ClientCommunicationPort : 0000000000000000
      ServerCommunicationPort : 0000000000000000
    OwnerProcess              : fffffa80056ddb30 (ServiceB.exe)
    SequenceNo                : 0x0000481A (18458)
    CompletionPort            : fffffa8005728e80
    CompletionList            : 0000000000000000
    MessageZone               : 0000000000000000
    ConnectionPending         : No
    ConnectionRefused         : No
    Disconnected              : No
    Closed                    : No
    FlushOnClose              : Yes
    ReturnExtendedInfo        : No
    Waitable                  : No
    Security                  : Static
    Wow64CompletionList       : No
Main queue is empty.


Large message queue is empty.


Pending queue has 698 message(s)
```

```
fffff8a002355aa0 00000404 0000000000001344:0000000000001358 0000000000000000 fffffa8004c0cb60 LPC_REQUEST
fffff8a00a52f030 00000644 0000000000001078:00000000000024c0 0000000000000000 fffffa80072f1b60 LPC_REQUEST
fffff8a00abb5030 000007a8 000000000000103c:000000000000050c 0000000000000000 fffffa800725b580 LPC_REQUEST
fffff8a00239cab0 000000b8 0000000000000480:00000000000015f8 0000000000000000 fffffa80077f0b60 LPC_REQUEST
fffff8a00ac81a90 00000a18 00000000000028ac:0000000000001e54 0000000000000000 fffffa8007fba060 LPC_CANCELED
fffff8a005879140 00000f80 0000000000001260:0000000000000730 fffffa8006432060 fffffa8006b18060 LPC_REQUEST
fffff8a013720d00 00000c6c 0000000000003764:00000000000032a8 0000000000000000 fffffa8006b00a60 LPC_CANCELED
fffff8a00ac82660 00000810 0000000000003af4:0000000000002a98 0000000000000000 fffffa80068c0b60 LPC_CANCELED
fffff8a00bdeca50 00000ec8 000000000000233c:00000000000013f8 0000000000000000 fffffa80079455b0 LPC_CANCELED
fffff8a00b662830 000005cc 00000000000005e4:0000000000000e0c fffffa800791a7a0 fffffa8007376580 LPC_REQUEST
fffff8a003d57150 00000f08 0000000000002678:0000000000003e0c 0000000000000000 fffffa8007e4a870 LPC_CANCELED
fffff8a00cd08830 00000750 0000000000003408:000000000000003adc 0000000000000000 fffffa8008631b60 LPC_CANCELED
fffff8a01855b2f0 000004f4 0000000000002c74:0000000000002d00 0000000000000000 fffffa800746b890 LPC_CANCELED
fffff8a00da0d0b0 00000db0 0000000000001a34:0000000000002d80 0000000000000000 fffffa800aff4b60 LPC_CANCELED
fffff8a00eddb030 0000059c 0000000000003f34:0000000000003c8c 0000000000000000 fffffa8008f96060 LPC_CANCELED
fffff8a017a14d00 00000920 0000000000003850:0000000000002588 0000000000000000 fffffa8009f66060 LPC_CANCELED
fffff8a01792d030 000007f8 0000000000003844:00000000000028d0 0000000000000000 fffffa800ad56260 LPC_CANCELED
fffff8a00f8d6ae0 00000f30 000000000000239c:0000000000001694 0000000000000000 fffffa8008b86060 LPC_CANCELED
fffff8a01395ab80 00000cdc 0000000000003630:00000000000018f8 0000000000000000 fffffa8005bc0770 LPC_CANCELED
fffff8a0166ff800 00000984 00000000000005e4:00000000000025f4 fffffa8009718910 fffffa8008cbfb60 LPC_REQUEST
fffff8a012b9f5a0 00000ac8 0000000000002d34:0000000000001b24 0000000000000000 fffffa8009cd8410 LPC_CANCELED
fffff8a014313830 00000afc 00000000000005e4:00000000000023bc fffffa80073f0230 fffffa80054d7060 LPC_REQUEST
fffff8a00a34a6b0 00000ca8 0000000000002534:0000000000002dd0 0000000000000000 fffffa80064c3980 LPC_CANCELED
[...]
fffff8a00ad8f610 00000e64 0000000000003714:00000000000030b8 0000000000000000 fffffa800aeea9f0 LPC_REQUEST
fffff8a015720710 00001594 0000000000003638:00000000000029b8 0000000000000000 fffffa800b5359a0 LPC_REQUEST
fffff8a009bac560 00001508 0000000000003994:0000000000001aac 0000000000000000 fffffa800b5359a0 LPC_REQUEST
fffff8a00b6e78f0 00001574 0000000000002938:0000000000001998 0000000000000000 fffffa800aeea9f0 LPC_REQUEST
fffff8a00b5716b0 00001570 0000000000002938:0000000000001698 0000000000000000 fffffa800a3b8620 LPC_REQUEST
fffff8a018531d00 00000db8 00000000000016d8:00000000000031c4 0000000000000000 fffffa800b5359a0 LPC_REQUEST
fffff8a01112f410 000014b0 0000000000001b6c:0000000000001618 0000000000000000 fffffa800a3b8620 LPC_CANCELED


Canceled queue is empty.
```

Comments

Q. Does this mean that no thread in *ServiceB.exe* can accept the ALPC request?

A. We think so because we have not yet seen the opposite: there would be no need to save a memory dump file if ALPC works.

Blocked Thread

Hardware

This is a specialization of **Blocked Thread** pattern where a thread is waiting for hardware I/O response. For example, a frozen system initialization thread is waiting for a response from one of ACPI general register ports:

```
kd> kL 100
ChildEBP RetAddr
f7a010bc f74c5a57 hal!READ_PORT_UCHAR+0x7
f7a010c8 f74c5ba4 ACPI!DefReadAcpiRegister+0xa1
f7a010d8 f74b4d78 ACPI!ACPIReadGpeStatusRegister+0x10
f7a010e4 f74b6334 ACPI!ACPIGpeIsEvent+0x14
f7a01100 8054157d ACPI!ACPIInterruptServiceRoutine+0x16
f7a01100 806d687d nt!KiInterruptDispatch+0x3d
f7a01194 804f9487 hal!HalEnableSystemInterrupt+0x79
f7a011d8 8056aac4 nt!KeConnectInterrupt+0x95
f7a011fc f74c987c nt!IoConnectInterrupt+0xf2
f7a0123c f74d13f0 ACPI!OSInterruptVector+0x76
f7a01250 f74b5781 ACPI!ACPIInitialize+0x154
f7a01284 f74cf824 ACPI!ACPIInitStartACPI+0x71
f7a012b0 f74b1e12 ACPI!ACPIRootIrpStartDevice+0xc0
f7a012e0 804ee129 ACPI!ACPIDispatchIrp+0x15a
f7a012f0 8058803b nt!IopfCallDriver+0x31
f7a0131c 805880b9 nt!IopSynchronousCall+0xb7
f7a01360 804f515c nt!IopStartDevice+0x4d
f7a0137c 80587769 nt!PipProcessStartPhase1+0x4e
f7a015d4 804f5823 nt!PipProcessDevNodeTree+0x1db
f7a01618 804f5ab3 nt!PipDeviceActionWorker+0xa3
f7a01630 8068afc6 nt!PipRequestDeviceAction+0x107
f7a01694 80687e48 nt!IopInitializeBootDrivers+0x376
f7a0183c 806862dd nt!IoInitSystem+0x712
f7a01dac 805c61e0 nt!Phase1Initialization+0x9b5
f7a01ddc 80541e02 nt!PspSystemThreadStartup+0x34
00000000 00000000 nt!KiThreadStartup+0x16

kd> r
eax=00000000 ebx=00000000 ecx=00000002 edx=0000100c esi=00000000 edi=867d8008
eip=806d664b esp=f7a010c0 ebp=f7a010c8 iopl=1     nv up ei pl zr na pe nc
cs=0008  ss=0010  ds=0023  es=0023  fs=0030  gs=0000         efl=00001246
hal!READ_PORT_UCHAR+0x7:
806d664b c20400          ret     4
```

```
kd> ub eip
hal!KdRestore+0x9:
806d663f cc              int     3
806d6640 cc              int     3
806d6641 cc              int     3
806d6642 cc              int     3
806d6643 cc              int     3
hal!READ_PORT_UCHAR:
806d6644 33c0            xor     eax,eax
806d6646 8b542404        mov     edx,dword ptr [esp+4]
806d664a ec              in      al,dx


kd> version
[...]
System Uptime: 0 days 0:03:42.140
[...]


kd> !thread
THREAD 867c63e8  Cid 0004.0008  Teb: 00000000 Win32Thread: 00000000 RUNNING on processor 0
IRP List:
    867df008: (0006,0190) Flags: 00000000  Mdl: 00000000
Not impersonating
DeviceMap                e1005460
Owning Process           0        Image:          <Unknown>
Attached Process         867c6660     Image:         System
Wait Start TickCount     39           Ticks: 1839 (0:00:00:18.416)
Context Switch Count     4
UserTime                 00:00:00.000
KernelTime               00:00:00.911
Start Address nt!Phase1Initialization (0x80685928)
Stack Init f7a02000 Current f7a014a4 Base f7a02000 Limit f79ff000 Call 0
Priority 31 BasePriority 8 PriorityDecrement 0 DecrementCount 0
[...]
```

Software

We often say that particular thread is blocked and/or it blocks other threads. At the same time, we know that almost all threads are "blocked" to some degree except those currently running on processors. They are either preempted and in the ready lists, voluntarily yielded their execution, or they are waiting for some synchronization object. Therefore the notion of **Blocked Thread** is highly context and problem dependent and usually we notice them when comparing current thread stack traces with their expected normal stack traces. Here reference guides (Appendix A) are indispensable especially those created for troubleshooting concrete products.

To show the diversity of "blocked" threads, we can propose the following thread classification:

Running threads

Their EIP (RIP) points to some function different from *KiSwapContext*:

```
3: kd> !running

System Processors f (affinity mask)
  Idle Processors 0

     Prcb        Current   Next
  0  ffdff120    a30a9350            ...............
  1  f7727120    a3186448            ...............
  2  f772f120    a59a1b40            ...............
  3  f7737120    a3085888            ...............

3: kd> !thread a59a1b40
THREAD a59a1b40  Cid 0004.00b8  Teb: 00000000 Win32Thread: 00000000 RUNNING on processor 2
Not impersonating
DeviceMap                  e10028b0
Owning Process             a59aa648      Image:        System
Wait Start TickCount       1450446       Ticks: 1 (0:00:00:00.015)
Context Switch Count       308765
UserTime                   00:00:00.000
KernelTime                 00:00:01.250
Start Address nt!ExpWorkerThread (0x80880356)
Stack Init f7055000 Current f7054cec Base f7055000 Limit f7052000 Call 0
Priority 12 BasePriority 12 PriorityDecrement 0
ChildEBP RetAddr
f7054bc4 8093c55c nt!ObfReferenceObject+0x1c
f7054ca0 8093d2ae nt!ObpQueryNameString+0x2ba
f7054cbc 808f7d0f nt!ObQueryNameString+0x18
f7054d80 80880441 nt!IopErrorLogThread+0x197
f7054dac 80949b7c nt!ExpWorkerThread+0xeb
f7054ddc 8088e062 nt!PspSystemThreadStartup+0x2e
00000000 00000000 nt!KiThreadStartup+0x16

3: kd> .thread a59a1b40
Implicit thread is now a59a1b40
```

```
3: kd> r
Last set context:
eax=00000028 ebx=e1000228 ecx=e1002b30 edx=e1000234 esi=e1002b18 edi=0000001a
eip=8086c73e esp=f7054bc4 ebp=f7054ca0 iopl=0 nv up ei pl nz na po nc
cs=0008 ss=0010 ds=0023 es=0023 fs=0030 gs=0000 efl=00000202
nt!ObfReferenceObject+0x1c:
8086c73e 40                   inc      eax
```

These threads can also be identified by RUNNING attribute in the output of **!process 0 3f** command applied for complete and kernel memory dumps.

Ready threads

These threads can be seen in the output of **!ready** command or identified by READY attribute in the output of **!process 0 3f** command:

```
3: kd> !ready
Processor 0: No threads in READY state
Processor 1: Ready Threads at priority 11
    THREAD a3790790  Cid 0234.1108  Teb: 7ffab000 Win32Thread: 00000000 READY
    THREAD a32799a8  Cid 0234.061c  Teb: 7ff83000 Win32Thread: 00000000 READY
    THREAD a3961798  Cid 0c04.0c68  Teb: 7ffab000 Win32Thread: bc204ea8 READY
Processor 1: Ready Threads at priority 10
    THREAD a32bedb0  Cid 1fc8.1a30  Teb: 7ffad000 Win32Thread: bc804468 READY
Processor 1: Ready Threads at priority 9
    THREAD a52dcd48  Cid 0004.04d4  Teb: 00000000 Win32Thread: 00000000 READY
Processor 2: Ready Threads at priority 11
    THREAD a37fedb0  Cid 0c04.11f8  Teb: 7ff8e000 Win32Thread: 00000000 READY
Processor 3: Ready Threads at priority 11
    THREAD a5683db0  Cid 0234.0274  Teb: 7ffd6000 Win32Thread: 00000000 READY
    THREAD a3151b48  Cid 0234.2088  Teb: 7ff88000 Win32Thread: 00000000 READY
    THREAD a5099d80  Cid 0ecc.0d60  Teb: 7ffd4000 Win32Thread: 00000000 READY
    THREAD a3039498  Cid 0c04.275c  Teb: 7ff7d000 Win32Thread: 00000000 READY
```

If we look at these threads we see that they were either scheduled to run because of a signaled object they were waiting for:

```
3: kd> !thread a3039498
THREAD a3039498  Cid 0c04.275c  Teb: 7ff7d000 Win32Thread: 00000000 READY
IRP List:
    a2feb008: (0006,0094) Flags: 00000870  Mdl: 00000000
Not impersonating
DeviceMap                 e10028b0
Owning Process            a399a770      Image:         svchost.exe
Wait Start TickCount      1450447       Ticks: 0
Context Switch Count      1069
UserTime                  00:00:00.000
KernelTime                00:00:00.000
Win32 Start Address 0x001e4f22
LPC Server thread working on message Id 1e4f22
Start Address KERNEL32!BaseThreadStartThunk (0x77e617ec)
Stack Init f171b000 Current f171ac60 Base f171b000 Limit f1718000 Call 0
Priority 11 BasePriority 10 PriorityDecrement 0
```

```
ChildEBP RetAddr  Args to Child
f171ac78 80833465 a3039498 a3039540 e7561930 nt!KiSwapContext+0x26
f171aca4 80829a62 00000000 00000000 00000000 nt!KiSwapThread+0x2e5
f171acec 80938d0c a301cad8 00000006 f171ad01 nt!KeWaitForSingleObject+0x346
f171ad50 8088978c 00000c99 00000000 00000000 nt!NtWaitForSingleObject+0x9a
f171ad50 7c8285ec 00000c99 00000000 00000000 nt!KiFastCallEntry+0xfc
03d9efa8 00000000 00000000 00000000 00000000 ntdll!KiFastSystemCallRet

3: kd> !object a301cad8
Object: a301cad8  Type: (a59a0720) Event
    ObjectHeader: a301cac0 (old version)
    HandleCount: 1  PointerCount: 3
```

or they were boosted in priority:

```
3: kd> !thread a3790790
THREAD a3790790  Cid 0234.1108  Teb: 7ffab000 Win32Thread: 00000000 READY
IRP List:
    a2f8b7f8: (0006,0094) Flags: 00000900  Mdl: 00000000
Not impersonating
DeviceMap                e10028b0
Owning Process           a554bcc8     Image:          lsass.exe
Wait Start TickCount     1450447      Ticks: 0
Context Switch Count     384
UserTime                 00:00:00.000
KernelTime               00:00:00.000
Win32 Start Address RPCRT4!ThreadStartRoutine (0x77c7b0f5)
Start Address KERNEL32!BaseThreadStartThunk (0x77e617ec)
Stack Init f3ac1000 Current f3ac0ce8 Base f3ac1000 Limit f3abe000 Call 0
Priority 11 BasePriority 10 PriorityDecrement 0
ChildEBP RetAddr  Args to Child
f3ac0d00 80831266 a3790790 a50f1870 a3186448 nt!KiSwapContext+0x26
f3ac0d20 8082833a 00000000 a50f1870 8098b56c nt!KiExitDispatcher+0xf8
f3ac0d3c 8098b5b9 a50f1870 00000000 00f5f8d0 nt!KeSetEventBoostPriority+0x156
f3ac0d58 8088978c a50f1870 00f5f8d4 7c8285ec nt!NtSetEventBoostPriority+0x4d
f3ac0d58 7c8285ec a50f1870 00f5f8d4 7c8285ec nt!KiFastCallEntry+0xfc
00f5f8d4 00000000 00000000 00000000 00000000 ntdll!KiFastSystemCallRet

3: kd> !object a50f1870
Object: a50f1870  Type: (a59a0720) Event
    ObjectHeader: a50f1858 (old version)
    HandleCount: 1  PointerCount: 15
```

or were interrupted and queued to be run again:

```
3: kd> !thread a5683db0
THREAD a5683db0 Cid 0234.0274 Teb: 7ffd6000 Win32Thread: 00000000 READY
IRP List:
  a324d498: (0006,0094) Flags: 00000900 Mdl: 00000000
  a2f97a20: (0006,0094) Flags: 00000900 Mdl: 00000000
  a50c3e70: (0006,0190) Flags: 00000000 Mdl: a50a22d0
  a5167750: (0006,0094) Flags: 00000800 Mdl: 00000000
Not impersonating
DeviceMap e10028b0
Owning Process a554bcc8 Image: lsass.exe
Wait Start TickCount 1450447 Ticks: 0
Context Switch Count 9619
UserTime 00:00:00.156
KernelTime 00:00:00.234
Win32 Start Address RPCRT4!ThreadStartRoutine (0x77c7b0f5)
Start Address KERNEL32!BaseThreadStartThunk (0x77e617ec)
Stack Init f59f3000 Current f59f2d00 Base f59f3000 Limit f59f0000 Call 0
Priority 11 BasePriority 10 PriorityDecrement 0
ChildEBP RetAddr
f59f2d18 80a5c1ae nt!KiDispatchInterrupt+0xb1
f59f2d48 80a5c577 hal!HalpDispatchSoftwareInterrupt+0x5e
f59f2d54 80a59902 hal!HalEndSystemInterrupt+0x67
f59f2d54 77c6928d hal!HalpIpiHandler+0xd2 (TrapFrame @ f59f2d64)
00c5f908 00000000 RPCRT4!OSF_SCALL::GetBuffer+0x37

3: kd> .thread a5683db0
Implicit thread is now a5683db0

3: kd> r
Last set context:
eax=00000000 ebx=00000000 ecx=00000000 edx=00000000 esi=00000000 edi=00000000
eip=8088dba1 esp=f59f2d0c ebp=f59f2d2c iopl=0         nv up di pl nz na po nc
cs=0008 ss=0010 ds=0000 es=0000 fs=0000 gs=0000             efl=00000000
nt!KiDispatchInterrupt+0xb1:
8088dba1 b902000000      mov     ecx,2

3: kd> ub
nt!KiDispatchInterrupt+0x8f:
8088db7f mov     dword ptr [ebx+124h],esi
8088db85 mov     byte ptr [esi+4Ch],2
8088db89 mov     byte ptr [edi+5Ah],1Fh
8088db8d mov     ecx,edi
8088db8f lea     edx,[ebx+120h]
8088db95 call    nt!KiQueueReadyThread (80833490)
8088db9a mov     cl,1
8088db9c call    nt!SwapContext (8088dbd0)

3: kd> u
nt!KiDispatchInterrupt+0xb1:
8088dba1 mov     ecx,2
8088dba6 call    dword ptr [nt!_imp_KfLowerIrql (80801108)]
8088dbac mov     ebp,dword ptr [esp]
8088dbaf mov     edi,dword ptr [esp+4]
8088dbb3 mov     esi,dword ptr [esp+8]
```

```
8088dbb7 add esp,0Ch
8088dbba pop ebx
8088dbbb ret
```

We can get user space thread stack by using **.trap** WinDbg command, but we need to switch to the corresponding process context first:

```
3: kd> .process /r /p a554bcc8
Implicit process is now a554bcc8
Loading User Symbols

3: kd> kL
  *** Stack trace for last set context - .thread/.cxr resets it
ChildEBP RetAddr
00c5f908 77c7ed60 RPCRT4!OSF_SCALL::GetBuffer+0x37
00c5f924 77c7ed14 RPCRT4!I_RpcGetBufferWithObject+0x7f
00c5f934 77c7f464 RPCRT4!I_RpcGetBuffer+0xf
00c5f944 77ce3470 RPCRT4!NdrGetBuffer+0x2e
00c5fd44 77ce35c4 RPCRT4!NdrStubCall2+0x35c
00c5fd60 77c7ff7a RPCRT4!NdrServerCall2+0x19
00c5fd94 77c8042d RPCRT4!DispatchToStubInCNoAvrf+0x38
00c5fde8 77c80353 RPCRT4!RPC_INTERFACE::DispatchToStubWorker+0x11f
00c5fe0c 77c68e0d RPCRT4!RPC_INTERFACE::DispatchToStub+0xa3
00c5fe40 77c68cb3 RPCRT4!OSF_SCALL::DispatchHelper+0x149
00c5fe54 77c68c2b RPCRT4!OSF_SCALL::DispatchRPCCall+0x10d
00c5fe84 77c68b5e RPCRT4!OSF_SCALL::ProcessReceivedPDU+0x57f
00c5fea4 77c6e8db RPCRT4!OSF_SCALL::BeginRpcCall+0x194
00c5ff04 77c6e7b4 RPCRT4!OSF_SCONNECTION::ProcessReceiveComplete+0x435
00c5ff18 77c7b799 RPCRT4!ProcessConnectionServerReceivedEvent+0x21
00c5ff84 77c7b9b5 RPCRT4!LOADABLE_TRANSPORT::ProcessIOEvents+0x1b8
00c5ff8c 77c8872d RPCRT4!ProcessIOEventsWrapper+0xd
00c5ffac 77c7b110 RPCRT4!BaseCachedThreadRoutine+0x9d
00c5ffb8 77e64829 RPCRT4!ThreadStartRoutine+0x1b
00c5ffec 00000000 kernel32!BaseThreadStart+0x34
```

Waiting threads (wait originated from user space)

```
THREAD a34369d0  Cid 1fc8.1e88  Teb: 7ffae000 Win32Thread: bc6d5818 WAIT: (Unknown) UserMode Non-
Alertable
    a34d9940  SynchronizationEvent
    a3436a48  NotificationTimer
Not impersonating
DeviceMap              e12256a0
Owning Process        a3340a10      Image:          IEXPLORE.EXE
Wait Start TickCount  1450409       Ticks: 38 (0:00:00.593)
Context Switch Count  7091                     LargeStack
UserTime              00:00:01.015
KernelTime            00:00:02.250
Win32 Start Address mshtml!CExecFT::StaticThreadProc (0x7fab1061)
Start Address kernel32!BaseThreadStartThunk (0x77e617ec)
Stack Init f252b000 Current f252ac60 Base f252b000 Limit f2528000 Call 0
Priority 11 BasePriority 10 PriorityDecrement 0
ChildEBP RetAddr
f252ac78 80833465 nt!KiSwapContext+0x26
f252aca4 80829a62 nt!KiSwapThread+0x2e5
```

```
f252acec 80938d0c nt!KeWaitForSingleObject+0x346
f252ad50 8088978c nt!NtWaitForSingleObject+0x9a
f252ad50 7c8285ec nt!KiFastCallEntry+0xfc (TrapFrame @ f252ad64)
030dff08 7c827d0b ntdll!KiFastSystemCallRet
030dff0c 77e61d1e ntdll!NtWaitForSingleObject+0xc
030dff7c 77e61c8d kernel32!WaitForSingleObjectEx+0xac
030dff90 7fab08a3 kernel32!WaitForSingleObject+0x12
030dffa8 7fab109c mshtml!CDwnTaskExec::ThreadExec+0xae
030dffb0 7fab106e mshtml!CExecFT::ThreadProc+0x28
030dffb8 77e64829 mshtml!CExecFT::StaticThreadProc+0xd
030dffec 00000000 kernel32!BaseThreadStart+0x34
```

If we had taken user dump of iexplore.exe we would have seen the following stack trace there:

```
030dff08 7c827d0b ntdll!KiFastSystemCallRet
030dff0c 77e61d1e ntdll!NtWaitForSingleObject+0xc
030dff7c 77e61c8d kernel32!WaitForSingleObjectEx+0xac
030dff90 7fab08a3 kernel32!WaitForSingleObject+0x12
030dffa8 7fab109c mshtml!CDwnTaskExec::ThreadExec+0xae
030dffb0 7fab106e mshtml!CExecFT::ThreadProc+0x28
030dffb8 77e64829 mshtml!CExecFT::StaticThreadProc+0xd
030dffec 00000000 kernel32!BaseThreadStart+0x34
```

Another example:

```
THREAD a31f2438  Cid 1fc8.181c  Teb: 7ffaa000 Win32Thread: 00000000 WAIT: (Unknown) UserMode Non-
Alertable
    a30f8c20  NotificationEvent
    a5146720  NotificationEvent
    a376fbb0  NotificationEvent
Not impersonating
DeviceMap               e12256a0
Owning Process          a3340a10        Image:          IEXPLORE.EXE
Wait Start TickCount    1419690         Ticks: 30757 (0:00:08:00.578)
Context Switch Count    2
UserTime                00:00:00.000
KernelTime              00:00:00.000
Win32 Start Address USERENV!NotificationThread (0x76929dd9)
Start Address kernel32!BaseThreadStartThunk (0x77e617ec)
Stack Init f5538000 Current f5537900 Base f5538000 Limit f5535000 Call 0
Priority 10 BasePriority 10 PriorityDecrement 0
Kernel stack not resident.
ChildEBP RetAddr
f5537918 80833465 nt!KiSwapContext+0x26
f5537944 80829499 nt!KiSwapThread+0x2e5
f5537978 80938f68 nt!KeWaitForMultipleObjects+0x3d7
f5537bf4 809390ca nt!ObpWaitForMultipleObjects+0x202
f5537d48 8088978c nt!NtWaitForMultipleObjects+0xc8
f5537d48 7c8285ec nt!KiFastCallEntry+0xfc (TrapFrame @ f5537d64)
0851fec0 7c827cfb ntdll!KiFastSystemCallRet
0851fec4 77e6202c ntdll!NtWaitForMultipleObjects+0xc
0851ff6c 77e62fbe kernel32!WaitForMultipleObjectsEx+0x11a
0851ff88 76929e35 kernel32!WaitForMultipleObjects+0x18
0851ffb8 77e64829 USERENV!NotificationThread+0x5f
0851ffec 00000000 kernel32!BaseThreadStart+0x34
```

Waiting threads (wait originated from kernel space)

Examples include explicit wait as a result from calling potentially blocking API:

```
THREAD a33a9740  Cid 1980.1960  Teb: 7ffde000 Win32Thread: bc283ea8 WAIT: (Unknown) UserMode Non-
Alertable
    a35e3168  SynchronizationEvent
Not impersonating
DeviceMap                    e689f298
Owning Process               a342d3a0      Image:         explorer.exe
Wait Start TickCount         1369801       Ticks: 80646 (0:00:21:00.093)
Context Switch Count         1667                     LargeStack
UserTime                     00:00:00.015
KernelTime                   00:00:00.093
Win32 Start Address Explorer!ModuleEntry (0x010148a4)
Start Address kernel32!BaseProcessStartThunk (0x77e617f8)
Stack Init f258b000 Current f258ac50 Base f258b000 Limit f2585000 Call 0
Priority 13 BasePriority 10 PriorityDecrement 1
Kernel stack not resident.
ChildEBP RetAddr
f258ac68 80833465 nt!KiSwapContext+0x26
f258ac94 80829a62 nt!KiSwapThread+0x2e5
f258acdc bf89abd3 nt!KeWaitForSingleObject+0x346
f258ad38 bf89da43 win32k!xxxSleepThread+0x1be
f258ad4c bf89e401 win32k!xxxRealWaitMessageEx+0x12
f258ad5c 8088978c win32k!NtUserWaitMessage+0x14
f258ad5c 7c8285ec nt!KiFastCallEntry+0xfc (TrapFrame @ f258ad64)
0007feec 7739bf53 ntdll!KiFastSystemCallRet
0007ff08 7c8fadbd USER32!NtUserWaitMessage+0xc
0007ff14 0100fff1 SHELL32!SHDesktopMessageLoop+0x24
0007ff5c 0101490c Explorer!ExplorerWinMain+0x2c4
0007ffc0 77e6f23b Explorer!ModuleEntry+0x6d
0007fff0 00000000 kernel32!BaseProcessStart+0x23
```

and implicit wait when a thread yields execution to another thread voluntarily via explicit context swap:

```
THREAD a3072b68  Cid 1fc8.1d94  Teb: 7ffaf000 Win32Thread: bc1e3c20 WAIT: (Unknown) UserMode Non-
Alertable
    a37004d8  QueueObject
    a3072be0  NotificationTimer
IRP List:
    a322be00: (0006,01fc) Flags: 00000000  Mdl: a30b8e30
    a30bcc38: (0006,01fc) Flags: 00000000  Mdl: a35bf530
Not impersonating
DeviceMap                    e12256a0
Owning Process               a3340a10      Image:         IEXPLORE.EXE
Wait Start TickCount         1447963       Ticks: 2484 (0:00:00:38.812)
Context Switch Count         3972                     LargeStack
UserTime                     00:00:00.140
KernelTime                   00:00:00.250
Win32 Start Address ntdll!RtlpWorkerThread (0x7c839efb)
Start Address kernel32!BaseThreadStartThunk (0x77e617ec)
Stack Init f1cc3000 Current f1cc2c38 Base f1cc3000 Limit f1cbf000 Call 0
Priority 10 BasePriority 10 PriorityDecrement 0
ChildEBP RetAddr
```

```
f1cc2c50 80833465 nt!KiSwapContext+0x26
f1cc2c7c 8082b60f nt!KiSwapThread+0x2e5
f1cc2cc4 808ed620 nt!KeRemoveQueue+0x417
f1cc2d48 8088978c nt!NtRemoveIoCompletion+0xdc
f1cc2d48 7c8285ec nt!KiFastCallEntry+0xfc (TrapFrame @ f1cc2d64)
06ceff70 7c8277db ntdll!KiFastSystemCallRet
06ceff74 7c839f38 ntdll!ZwRemoveIoCompletion+0xc
06ceffb8 77e64829 ntdll!RtlpWorkerThread+0x3d
06ceffec 00000000 kernel32!BaseThreadStart+0x34


THREAD a3612020  Cid 1980.1a48  Teb: 7ffd9000 Win32Thread: 00000000 WAIT: (Unknown) UserMode Alertable
    a3612098  NotificationTimer
Not impersonating
DeviceMap                 e689f298
Owning Process            a342d3a0       Image:         explorer.exe
Wait Start TickCount      1346718        Ticks: 103729 (0:00:27:00.765)
Context Switch Count      4
UserTime                  00:00:00.000
KernelTime                00:00:00.000
Win32 Start Address ntdll!RtlpTimerThread (0x7c83d3dd)
Start Address kernel32!BaseThreadStartThunk (0x77e617ec)
Stack Init f2453000 Current f2452c80 Base f2453000 Limit f2450000 Call 0
Priority 10 BasePriority 10 PriorityDecrement 0
Kernel stack not resident.
ChildEBP RetAddr
f2452c98 80833465 nt!KiSwapContext+0x26
f2452cc4 80828f0b nt!KiSwapThread+0x2e5
f2452d0c 80994812 nt!KeDelayExecutionThread+0x2ab
f2452d54 8088978c nt!NtDelayExecution+0x84
f2452d54 7c8285ec nt!KiFastCallEntry+0xfc (TrapFrame @ f2452d64)
0149ff9c 7c826f4b ntdll!KiFastSystemCallRet
0149ffa0 7c83d424 ntdll!NtDelayExecution+0xc
0149ffb8 77e64829 ntdll!RtlpTimerThread+0x47
0149ffec 00000000 kernel32!BaseThreadStart+0x34
```

Explicit waits in the kernel can be originated from GUI threads and their message loops, for example, **Main Thread** (page 694). Blocked GUI thread, **Message Box** pattern (page 743) can be seen as an example of a genuine **Blocked Thread.** Some "blocked" threads are just really **Passive Threads** (page 879).

Comments

An example of a blocked thread that is trying to load a library and blocked in the kernel:

```
ntdll!KiFastSystemCallRet
ntdll!NtQueryAttributesFile+0xc)
ntdll!RtlDoesFileExists_UstrEx+0x6b
ntdll!RtlDoesFileExists_UEx+0x27
ntdll!RtlDosSearchPath_U+0x14f
ntdll!LdrpResolveDllName+0x12d
ntdll!LdrpMapDll+0x140
ntdll!LdrpLoadDll+0x1e9
ntdll!LdrLoadDll+0x230
kernel32!LoadLibraryExW+0x18e
kernel32!LoadLibraryExA+0x1f
[…]
WINMM!DrvSendMessage+0x18
MSACM32!IDriverMessageId+0x81
MSACM32!acmFormatSuggest+0x28b
mmdriver!DriverProc+0x8e52
[…]
mmdriver!wodMessage+0x76
WINMM!waveOutOpen+0x2a2
[...]
```

Another example of the blocked thread on a uniprocessor VM:

```
kd> !running

System Processors: (00000001)
Idle Processors: (00000000)

Prcbs Current Next
0 82944d20 85a575c0 ..........

kd> !thread
THREAD 85a575c0 Cid 0004.00e0 Teb: 00000000 Win32Thread: 00000000 RUNNING on processor 0
Not impersonating
DeviceMap 8a209d68
Owning Process 8523e660 Image: System
Attached Process N/A Image: N/A
Wait Start TickCount 4392621 Ticks: 0
Context Switch Count 414195
UserTime 00:00:00.000
KernelTime 17:59:14.739
Win32 Start Address DriverA (0x8900ab4e)
Stack Init 8d1c0fd0 Current 8d1c0950 Base 8d1c1000 Limit 8d1be000 Call 0
Priority 16 BasePriority 8 UnusualBoost 0 ForegroundBoost 0 IoPriority 2 PagePriority 5
ChildEBP RetAddr Args to Child
8d1c0c48 82c34117 ffd090f0 85a32008 85a5a000 nt!READ_REGISTER_ULONG+0x6 (FPO: [1,0,0])
8d1c0c68 82c347a1 8d1c0c84 82c38b53 8d1c0c7c hal!HalpHpetQueryCount+0x4b (FPO: [Non-Fpo])
8d1c0c70 82c38b53 8d1c0c7c 00da7a64 00000000 hal!HalpHpetQueryPerformanceCounter+0x1d (FPO: [Non-Fpo])
8d1c0c84 89007e52 8d1c0cbc 85a5a0d0 85a5a000 hal!KeQueryPerformanceCounter+0x3d (FPO: [Non-Fpo])
```

```
WARNING: Stack unwind information not available. Following frames may be wrong.
8d1c0ce4 89007938 85a5a000 00000000 85a5a000 DriverA+0x7e52
8d1c0cf8 8900ae9a 85a5a000 00000000 00000000 DriverA+0x7938
8d1c0d50 82a23056 85a32008 a9492f18 00000000 DriverA+0xae9a
8d1c0d90 828cb1a9 8900ab4e 85a5a000 00000000 nt!PspSystemThreadStartup+0x9e
00000000 00000000 00000000 00000000 00000000 nt!KiThreadStartup+0x19


kd> !ready
Processor 0: Ready Threads at priority 15
THREAD 861a2590 Cid 0460.0464 Teb: 7ffdf000 Win32Thread: fe9dbb18 ????
THREAD 853cac98 Cid 0460.0670 Teb: 7ffd6000 Win32Thread: 00000000 ????
THREAD 852fda88 Cid 0004.0084 Teb: 00000000 Win32Thread: 00000000 ????
THREAD 8534ad48 Cid 0004.0090 Teb: 00000000 Win32Thread: 00000000 ????
THREAD 852f1d48 Cid 0004.0080 Teb: 00000000 Win32Thread: 00000000 ????
THREAD 852fd4f0 Cid 0004.0088 Teb: 00000000 Win32Thread: 00000000 ????
THREAD 85340020 Cid 0004.008c Teb: 00000000 Win32Thread: 00000000 ????
THREAD 852e67c8 Cid 0004.0078 Teb: 00000000 Win32Thread: 00000000 ????
THREAD 85de77a8 Cid 01e4.026c Teb: 7ffda000 Win32Thread: ffb2c008 ????
THREAD 85da7d48 Cid 01e4.0234 Teb: 7ffdf000 Win32Thread: ffad0d38 ????
THREAD 85a7c678 Cid 0004.00f0 Teb: 00000000 Win32Thread: 00000000 ????
[...]
```

Timeout

This is a special variant of **Blocked Thread** pattern where we have a timeout value: a thread is temporarily blocked. For example, this **Main Thread** (page 694) is blocked while waiting for the beep sound to finish after a minute:

```
0:000> kvL
ChildEBP RetAddr Args to Child
0291f354 7c90d21a 7c8023f1 00000001 0291f388 ntdll!KiFastSystemCallRet
0291f358 7c8023f1 00000001 0291f388 7c90d27e ntdll!NtDelayExecution+0xc
0291f3b0 7c837beb 0000ea60 00000001 00000004 kernel32!SleepEx+0x61
0291f404 004952a2 00000370 0000ea60 004d6ae2 kernel32!Beep+0x1b3
0291f410 004d6ae2 00000370 0000ea60 004d6ed4 Application!DoBeep+0x16
[...]
0291ffec 00000000 0045aad0 00e470a0 00000000 kernel32!BaseThreadStart+0x37


0:000> ? ea60/0n1000
Evaluate expression: 60 = 0000003c
```

Blocking File

This pattern often happens (but not limited to) in roaming profile scenarios In addition to **Blocked Thread** (page 93), endpoint threads of **Wait Chain** patterns (page 1209), and **Blocking Module** (page 107). For example, an application was reported hanging, and in a complete memory dump we could see a thread in **Stack Trace Collection** (page 1052):

```
THREAD fffffa8005eca060 Cid 14b0.1fec Teb: 000000007ef84000 Win32Thread: fffff900c26c2c30 WAIT:
(Executive) KernelMode Non-Alertable
fffffa80048e6758 NotificationEvent
IRP List:
fffffa8005a6c160: (0006,03e8) Flags: 00060000 Mdl: 00000000
Not impersonating
DeviceMap fffff8a0055b6620
Owning Process fffffa80063dd970 Image: Application.exe
Attached Process N/A Image: N/A
Wait Start TickCount 171988390 Ticks: 26963639 (4:21:01:46.859)
Context Switch Count 226 LargeStack
UserTime 00:00:00.015
KernelTime 00:00:00.015
Win32 Start Address 0x000000006d851f62
Stack Init fffff880075a9db0 Current fffff880075a9770
Base fffff880075aa000 Limit fffff880075a4000 Call 0
Priority 10 BasePriority 8 UnusualBoost 0 ForegroundBoost 2 IoPriority 2 PagePriority 5
Child-SP RetAddr Call Site
fffff880`075a97b0 fffff800`0167f752 nt!KiSwapContext+0x7a
fffff880`075a98f0 fffff800`016818af nt!KiCommitThreadWait+0x1d2
fffff880`075a9980 fffff800`019b612a nt!KeWaitForSingleObject+0x19f
fffff880`075a9a20 fffff800`0198feaa nt! ?? ::NNGAKEGL::`string'+0x1d61a
fffff880`075a9a60 fffff800`018ed0e3 nt!IopSynchronousServiceTail+0x35a
fffff880`075a9ad0 fffff800`01677853 nt!NtLockFile+0x514
fffff880`075a9bb0 00000000`77840cea nt!KiSystemServiceCopyEnd+0x13 (TrapFrame @ fffff880`075a9c20)
00000000`0798e488 00000000`7543293b ntdll!ZwLockFile+0xa
00000000`0798e490 00000000`7541cf87 wow64!whNtLockFile+0x7f
00000000`0798e510 00000000`7536276d wow64!Wow64SystemServiceEx+0xd7
00000000`0798edd0 00000000`7541d07e wow64cpu!TurboDispatchJumpAddressEnd+0x24
00000000`0798ee90 00000000`7541c549 wow64!RunCpuSimulation+0xa
00000000`0798eee0 00000000`7786d177 wow64!Wow64LdrpInitialize+0x429
00000000`0798f430 00000000`7782308e ntdll! ?? ::FNODOBFM::`string'+0x2bfe4
00000000`0798f4a0 00000000`00000000 ntdll!LdrInitializeThunk+0xe
```

We immediately spot the anomaly of a lock file attempt and look at its IRP:

```
0: kd> !irp fffffa8005a6c160
Irp is active with 7 stacks 7 is current (= 0xfffffa8005a6c3e0)
No Mdl: No System Buffer: Thread fffffa8005eca060: Irp stack trace.
cmd flg cl Device File Completion-Context
[ 0, 0] 0 2 00000000 00000000 00000000-00000000

Args: 00000000 00000000 00000000 fffffffffc000020c
[ 0, 0] 0 0 00000000 00000000 00000000-00000000
```

```
Args: 00000000 00000000 00000000 00000000
[ 0, 0] 0 0 00000000 00000000 00000000-00000000

Args: 00000000 00000000 00000000 00000000
[ 0, 0] 0 0 00000000 00000000 00000000-00000000

Args: 00000000 00000000 00000000 00000000
[ 0, 0] 0 0 00000000 00000000 00000000-00000000

Args: 00000000 00000000 00000000 00000000
[ 11, 0] 0 2 fffffa8004da0620 00000000 fffff8800177d9cc-fffffa800710e580
\FileSystem\mrxsmb mup!MupiUncProviderCompletion
Args: 00000000 00000000 00000000 00000000
>[ 11, 1] 0 0 fffffa8004066400 fffffa80048e66c0 00000000-00000000
\FileSystem\Mup
Args: fffffa8004a98120 00000001 00000000 00000000
```

From that IRP we see a file name:

```
0: kd> !fileobj fffffa80048e66c0

[...]\AppData\Roaming\Vendor\Product\Recent\index.dat

LockOperation Set Device Object: 0xfffffa8004066400 \FileSystem\Mup
Vpb is NULL
Access: Read SharedRead SharedWrite SharedDelete

Flags: 0x40002
Synchronous IO
Handle Created

File Object is currently busy and has 0 waiters.

FsContext: 0xfffff8a00e8d9010 FsContext2: 0xfffff8a012e4d688
CurrentByteOffset: 0
Cache Data:
Section Object Pointers: fffffa8006086928
Shared Cache Map: 00000000
File object extension is at fffffa8005c8cbe0:
```

Alternatively we get a 32-bit stack trace from **Virtualized Process** (page 1185):

```
0: kd> .process /r /p fffffa80063dd970
Implicit process is now fffffa80`063dd970
Loading User Symbols

0: kd> .thread /w fffffa8005eca060
Implicit thread is now fffffa80`05eca060
The context is partially valid. Only x86 user-mode context is available.
x86 context set
```

```
0: kd:x86> .reload
Loading Kernel Symbols
Loading User Symbols
Loading unloaded module list
Loading Wow64 Symbols


0: kd:x86> kv
*** Stack trace for last set context - .thread/.cxr resets it
ChildEBP RetAddr Args to Child
07ac8510 774f033f 00000390 00000000 00000000 ntdll_779d0000!ZwLockFile+0x12
07ac8590 774f00d3 061b2b68 ada9964d c0000016 kernel32!BaseDllOpenIniFileOnDisk+0x246
07ac85d0 774efae9 061b2b68 00001000 6d352f20 kernel32!BaseDllReadWriteIniFileOnDisk+0x2d
07ac85e8 775001bf 00000001 00000000 061b2b68 kernel32!BaseDllReadWriteIniFile+0xed
07ac861c 6d928401 07aca71c 00000000 00001000 kernel32!GetPrivateProfileStringW+0x35
WARNING: Stack unwind information not available. Following frames may be wrong.
07ac8640 6d9282f5 07aca71c 00000000 00000000 DLL+0x618401
[...]
07acfb14 774e3677 06757d20 07acfb60 77a09d72 DLL+0x541f6d
07acfb20 77a09d72 06757d20 eca51e43 00000000 kernel32!BaseThreadInitThunk+0xe
07acfb60 77a09d45 6d851f62 06757d20 ffffffff ntdll_779d0000!__RtlUserThreadStart+0x70
07acfb78 00000000 6d851f62 06757d20 00000000 ntdll_779d0000!_RtlUserThreadStart+0x1b
```

We get the same file name from a file handle:

```
0: kd> !handle 00000390
processor number 0, process fffffa80063dd970
PROCESS fffffa80063dd970
SessionId: 5 Cid: 14b0 Peb: 7efdf000 ParentCid: 1fac
DirBase: 48293000 ObjectTable: fffff8a010515f90 HandleCount: 342.
Image: Application.exe

Handle table at fffff8a0083e9000 with 444 Entries in use
0390: Object: fffffa80048e66c0 GrantedAccess: 00120089 Entry: fffff8a00866fe40
Object: fffffa80048e66c0 Type: (fffffa8003cf0b40) File
ObjectHeader: fffffa80048e6690 (new version)
HandleCount: 1 PointerCount: 3
Directory Object: 00000000 Name: [...]\AppData\Roaming\Vendor\Product\Recent\index.dat {Mup}
```

Also, we have c0000016 error code on raw stack and examine it too:

```
0: kd> !error c0000016
Error code: (NTSTATUS) 0xc0000016 (3221225494) - {Still Busy} The specified I/O request packet (IRP)
cannot be disposed of because the I/O operation is not complete.
```

Blocking Module

We would like to add this pattern in addition to **Blocked Thread** (page 93) and endpoint threads of **Wait Chain** (page 1209) patterns to account for modules calling waiting or delaying functions, for example:

```
0:017> kL
ChildEBP RetAddr
02c34100 7c90df5a ntdll!KiFastSystemCallRet
02c34104 7c8025db ntdll!ZwWaitForSingleObject+0xc
02c34168 7c802542 kernel32!WaitForSingleObjectEx+0xa8
02c3417c 009f0ed9 kernel32!WaitForSingleObject+0x12
02c34a08 00bc2c9a ModuleA!DLLCanUnloadNow+0x6db39
02c3526c 00bc2fa4 ModuleA!DLLCanUnloadNow+0x23f8fa
02c35ae0 00f6413c ModuleA!DLLCanUnloadNow+0x23fc04
02c363e8 00c761ab ModuleA!DLLCanUnloadNow+0x5e0d9c
02c36c74 00c74daa ModuleA!DLLCanUnloadNow+0x2f2e0b
02c374e4 3d1a9eb4 ModuleA!DLLCanUnloadNow+0x2f1a0a
02c3753c 3d0ed032 mshtml!CView::SetObjectRectsHelper+0x98
02c37578 3cf7e43b mshtml!CView::EndDeferSetObjectRects+0x75
02c375bc 3cf2542d mshtml!CView::EnsureView+0x39f
02c375d8 3cf4072c mshtml!CElement::EnsureRecalcNotify+0x17c
02c37614 3cf406ce mshtml!CElement::get_clientHeight_Logical+0x54
02c37628 3d0822a1 mshtml!CElement::get_clientHeight+0x27
02c37648 3cf8ad53 mshtml!G_LONG+0x7b
02c376bc 3cf96e21 mshtml!CBase::ContextInvokeEx+0x5d1
02c3770c 3cfa2baf mshtml!CElement::ContextInvokeEx+0x9d
02c37738 3cf8a751 mshtml!CElement::VersionedInvokeEx+0x2d
[...]
```

Comments

!stacks command may show the possible candidates too.

Broken Link

Sometimes we have a broken linked list for some reason, either from memory corruption, **Lateral Damage** (page 678) or **Truncated Dump** (page 1130). For example, an active process list enumeration stopped after showing some processes (**!for_each_thread** and **!vm** also do not work):

```
0: kd> !process 0 3f

[...]

TYPE mismatch for process object at fffffa80041da5c0

0: kd> !validatelist nt!PsActiveProcessHead
Blink at address fffffa80041da748 does not point back to previous at fffffa8005bc8cb8
```

Here we can either try to repair or navigate links manually or use other means such as dumping pool allocations for process structures with *Proc* pool tag:

```
0: kd> !poolfind Proc

Searching NonPaged pool (fffffa80032fc000 : fffffffe000000000) for Tag: Proc

*fffffa80033879a0 size:   510 previous size:    a0  (Allocated) Proc (Protected)
*fffffa80033ffad0 size:   530 previous size:   280  (Allocated) Proc (Protected)
*fffffa80041a2af0 size:   510 previous size:    90  (Allocated) Proc (Protected)
*fffffa800439c5c0 size:   530 previous size:    80  (Allocated) Proc (Protected)
[...]
*fffffa8007475ad0 size:   530 previous size:    30  (Allocated) Proc (Protected)
*fffffa80074e8490 size:   530 previous size:   100  (Allocated) Proc (Protected)
*fffffa80075ee0b0 size:   530 previous size:    b0  (Free)      Pro.
*fffffa800761d000 size:   530 previous size:     0  (Free)      Pro.
*fffffa8007645ad0 size:   530 previous size:    b0  (Allocated) Proc (Protected)


0: kd> dc fffffa8007645ad0
fffffa80`07645ad0  0253000b e36f7250 07644030 fffffa80  ..S.Pro.0.d.....
fffffa80`07645ae0  00001000 00000528 00000068 fffff800  ....(...h.......
fffffa80`07645af0  01a1a940 fffff800 00080090 00490024  @...........$.I.
fffffa80`07645b00  000000c4 00000000 00000008 00000000  ................
fffffa80`07645b10  00000000 00000000 00080007 00300033  ............3.0.
fffffa80`07645b20  01a1a940 fffff800 013cfeae fffff8a0  @.........<.....
fffffa80`07645b30  00580003 00000000 05ba19a0 fffffa80  ..X.............
fffffa80`07645b40  05ba19a0 fffffa80 07645b48 fffffa80  ........H[d.....
```

```
0: kd> !process fffffa80`07645b30 3f
PROCESS fffffa8007645b30
SessionId: 0  Cid: 14c4    Peb: 7fffffd4000  ParentCid: 02c4
DirBase: 7233e000  ObjectTable: fffff8a0014d4220  HandleCount: 399.
Image: AppA.exe
VadRoot fffffa80072bc5b0 Vads 239 Clone 0 Private 24675. Modified 23838. Locked 0.
DeviceMap fffff8a0000088f0
Token                             fffff8a000f28060
ElapsedTime                       00:00:53.066
UserTime                          00:00:00.000
KernelTime                        00:00:00.000
QuotaPoolUsage[PagedPool]         0
QuotaPoolUsage[NonPagedPool]      0
Working Set Sizes (now,min,max)   (11960, 50, 345) (47840KB, 200KB, 1380KB)
PeakWorkingSetSize                74346
VirtualSize                       331 Mb
PeakVirtualSize                   478 Mb
PageFaultCount                    92214
MemoryPriority                    BACKGROUND
BasePriority                      8
CommitCharge                      25905

[...]
```

Busy System

If there are no CPU-bound threads in a system, then most of the time processors are looping in the so-called idle thread where they are halted waiting for an interrupt to occur (HLT instruction). When an interrupt occurs, they process a DPC list and then do thread scheduling if necessary as evident from the stack trace and its functions disassembly below. If we have a memory dump, one of running threads would be the one that called *KeBugCheck(Ex)* function.

```
3: kd> !running

System Processors f (affinity mask)
  Idle Processors d


    Prcb      Current   Next
  1  f7737120  8a3da020              . . . . . . . . . . . . . . .


3: kd> !thread 8a3da020 1f
THREAD 8a3da020  Cid 0ebc.0dec  Teb: 7ffdf000 Win32Thread: bc002328 RUNNING on processor 1
Not impersonating
DeviceMap             e3e3e080
Owning Process        8a0aea88       Image:        SystemDump.exe
Wait Start TickCount  17154          Ticks: 0
Context Switch Count  568                     LargeStack
UserTime              00:00:00.046
KernelTime            00:00:00.375
Win32 Start Address 0x0040fe92
Start Address 0x77e6b5c7
Stack Init f4266000 Current f4265c08 Base f4266000 Limit f4261000 Call 0
Priority 11 BasePriority 10 PriorityDecrement 0
ChildEBP RetAddr
f4265bec f79c9743 nt!KeBugCheckEx+0x1b
WARNING: Stack unwind information not available. Following frames may be wrong.
f4265c38 8081dce5 SystemDump+0x743
f4265c4c 808f4797 nt!IofCallDriver+0x45
f4265c60 808f5515 nt!IopSynchronousServiceTail+0x10b
f4265d00 808ee0e4 nt!IopXxxControlFile+0x5db
f4265d34 80888c6c nt!NtDeviceIoControlFile+0x2a
f4265d34 7c82ed54 nt!KiFastCallEntry+0xfc


3: kd> !ready
Processor 0: No threads in READY state
Processor 1: No threads in READY state
Processor 2: No threads in READY state
Processor 3: No threads in READY state


3: kd> ~2s
```

```
2: kd> !thread -1 1f
THREAD f7742090  Cid 0000.0000  Teb: 00000000 Win32Thread: 00000000 RUNNING on processor 2
Not impersonating
Owning Process            8089db40       Image:          Idle
Wait Start TickCount      0              Ticks: 17154 (0:00:04:28.031)
Context Switch Count      193155
UserTime                  00:00:00.000
KernelTime                00:03:23.328
Stack Init f78b7000 Current f78b6d4c Base f78b7000 Limit f78b4000 Call 0
Priority 0 BasePriority 0 PriorityDecrement 0
ChildEBP RetAddr
f78b6d50 8088d262 intelppm!AcpiC1Idle+0x12
f78b6d54 00000000 nt!KiIdleLoop+0xa


2: kd> .asm no_code_bytes
Assembly options: no_code_bytes


2: kd> uf intelppm!AcpiC1Idle
intelppm!AcpiC1Idle:
f6e73c90 push    ecx
f6e73c91 push    0
f6e73c93 call    intelppm!KeQueryPerformanceCounter (f6e740c6)
f6e73c98 mov     ecx,dword ptr [esp]
f6e73c9b mov     dword ptr [ecx],eax
f6e73c9d mov     dword ptr [ecx+4],edx
f6e73ca0 sti
f6e73ca1 hlt
f6e73ca2 push    0
f6e73ca4 call    intelppm!KeQueryPerformanceCounter (f6e740c6)
f6e73ca9 pop     ecx
f6e73caa mov     dword ptr [ecx+8],eax
f6e73cad mov     dword ptr [ecx+0Ch],edx
f6e73cb0 xor     eax,eax
f6e73cb2 ret


2: kd> uf nt!KiIdleLoop
nt!KiIdleLoop:
8088d258 jmp     nt!KiIdleLoop+0xa (8088d262)


nt!KiIdleLoop+0x2:
8088d25a lea     ecx,[ebx+0EC0h]
8088d260 call    dword ptr [ecx]


nt!KiIdleLoop+0xa:
8088d262 pause
8088d264 sti
8088d265 nop
8088d266 nop
8088d267 cli
8088d268 mov     eax,dword ptr [ebx+0A4Ch]
8088d26e or      eax,dword ptr [ebx+0A88h]
8088d274 or      eax,dword ptr [ebx+0C10h]
8088d27a je      nt!KiIdleLoop+0x37 (8088d28f)
```

```
nt!KiIdleLoop+0x24:
8088d27c mov     cl,2
8088d27e call    dword ptr [nt!_imp_HalClearSoftwareInterrupt (808010a8)]
8088d284 lea     ecx,[ebx+120h]
8088d28a call    nt!KiRetireDpcList (80831be8)


nt!KiIdleLoop+0x37:
8088d28f cmp     dword ptr [ebx+128h],0
8088d296 je      nt!KiIdleLoop+0xca (8088d322)


nt!KiIdleLoop+0x44:
8088d29c mov     ecx,1Bh
8088d2a1 call    dword ptr [nt!_imp_KfRaiseIrql (80801100)]
8088d2a7 sti
8088d2a8 mov     edi,dword ptr [ebx+124h]
8088d2ae mov     byte ptr [edi+5Dh],1
8088d2b2 lock bts dword ptr [ebx+0A7Ch],0
8088d2bb jae     nt!KiIdleLoop+0x70 (8088d2c8)


nt!KiIdleLoop+0x65:
8088d2bd lea     ecx,[ebx+0A7Ch]
8088d2c3 call    nt!KefAcquireSpinLockAtDpcLevel (80887fd0)


nt!KiIdleLoop+0x70:
8088d2c8 mov     esi,dword ptr [ebx+128h]
8088d2ce cmp     esi,edi
8088d2d0 je      nt!KiIdleLoop+0xb3 (8088d30b)


nt!KiIdleLoop+0x7a:
8088d2d2 and     dword ptr [ebx+128h],0
8088d2d9 mov     dword ptr [ebx+124h],esi
8088d2df mov     byte ptr [esi+4Ch],2
8088d2e3 and     byte ptr [ebx+0AA3h],0
8088d2ea and     dword ptr [ebx+0A7Ch],0


nt!KiIdleLoop+0x99:
8088d2f1 mov     ecx,1
8088d2f6 call    nt!SwapContext (8088d040)
8088d2fb mov     ecx,2
8088d300 call    dword ptr [nt!_imp_KfLowerIrql (80801104)]
8088d306 jmp     nt!KiIdleLoop+0xa (8088d262)


nt!KiIdleLoop+0xb3:
8088d30b and     dword ptr [ebx+128h],0
8088d312 and     dword ptr [ebx+0A7Ch],0
8088d319 and     byte ptr [edi+5Dh],0
8088d31d jmp     nt!KiIdleLoop+0xa (8088d262)


nt!KiIdleLoop+0xca:
8088d322 cmp     byte ptr [ebx+0AA3h],0
8088d329 je      nt!KiIdleLoop+0x2 (8088d25a)
```

```
nt!KiIdleLoop+0xd7:
8088d32f sti
8088d330 lea      ecx,[ebx+120h]
8088d336 call     nt!KiIdleSchedule (808343e6)
8088d33b test     eax,eax
8088d33d mov      esi,eax
8088d33f mov      edi,dword ptr [ebx+12Ch]
8088d345 jne      nt!KiIdleLoop+0x99 (8088d2f1)


nt!KiIdleLoop+0xef:
8088d347 jmp      nt!KiIdleLoop+0xa (8088d262)
```

In some memory dumps taken when systems or sessions were hanging or very slow for some time we might see **Busy System** pattern where all processors execute non-idle threads, and there are threads in ready queues waiting to be scheduled:

```
3: kd> !running

System Processors f (affinity mask)
  Idle Processors 0


    Prcb       Current   Next
 0  ffdff120   88cef850            ...............
 1  f7727120   8940b7a0            ...............
 2  f772f120   8776f020            ...............
 3  f7737120   87b25360            ...............


3: kd> !ready
Processor 0: Ready Threads at priority 8
    THREAD 88161668  Cid 3d58.43a0  Teb: 7ffdf000 Win32Thread: bc1eba48 READY
    THREAD 882d0020  Cid 1004.0520  Teb: 7ffdf000 Win32Thread: bc230838 READY
    THREAD 88716b40  Cid 2034.241c  Teb: 7ffdd000 Win32Thread: bc11b388 READY
    THREAD 88bf7978  Cid 2444.2564  Teb: 7ffde000 Win32Thread: bc1ccc18 READY
    THREAD 876f7a28  Cid 2308.4bfc  Teb: 7ffdd000 Win32Thread: bc1f7b98 READY
Processor 0: Ready Threads at priority 0
    THREAD 8a3925a8  Cid 0004.0008  Teb: 00000000 Win32Thread: 00000000 READY
Processor 1: Ready Threads at priority 9
    THREAD 87e69db0  Cid 067c.3930  Teb: 7ffdb000 Win32Thread: bc180990 READY
Processor 1: Ready Threads at priority 8
    THREAD 88398c70  Cid 27cc.15b4  Teb: 7ffde000 Win32Thread: bc159ea8 READY
Processor 2: Ready Threads at priority 8
    THREAD 8873cdb0  Cid 4c24.4384  Teb: 7ffdd000 Win32Thread: bc1c9838 READY
    THREAD 89f331e0  Cid 453c.4c68  Teb: 7ffdf000 Win32Thread: bc21dbd0 READY
    THREAD 889a03f0  Cid 339c.2fcc  Teb: 7ffdf000 Win32Thread: bc1cdbe8 READY
    THREAD 87aacdb0  Cid 3b80.4ed0  Teb: 7ffde000 Win32Thread: bc1c5d10 READY
Processor 3: No threads in READY state
```

Here is another example from a busy 8-processor system where only one processor was idle at the time of the bugcheck:

```
5: kd> !ready
Processor 0: No threads in READY state
Processor 1: No threads in READY state
Processor 2: No threads in READY state
Processor 3: No threads in READY state
Processor 4: No threads in READY state
Processor 5: No threads in READY state
Processor 6: No threads in READY state
Processor 7: No threads in READY state


5: kd> !running

System Processors ff (affinity mask)
  Idle Processors 1


    Prcb      Current    Next
  1 f7727120  8713a5a0              ...............
  2 f772f120  86214750              ...............
  3 f7737120  86f87020              ...............
  4 f773f120  86ffe700              ...............
  5 f7747120  86803a90              ...............
  6 f774f120  86043db0              ...............
  7 f7757120  86bcbdb0              ...............


5: kd> !thread 8713a5a0 1f
THREAD 8713a5a0  Cid 4ef4.4f04  Teb: 7ffdd000 Win32Thread: bc423920 RUNNING on processor 1
Not impersonating
DeviceMap                 e44e9a40
Owning Process            864d1d88       Image:         SomeExe.exe
Wait Start TickCount      1415535        Ticks: 0
Context Switch Count      7621092                    LargeStack
UserTime                  00:06:59.218
KernelTime                00:19:26.359
Win32 Start Address BROWSEUI!BrowserProtectedThreadProc (0x75ec1c3f)
Start Address kernel32!BaseThreadStartThunk (0x77e617ec)
Stack Init b68b8a70 Current b68b8c28 Base b68b9000 Limit b68b1000 Call b68b8a7c
Priority 13 BasePriority 13 PriorityDecrement 0
ChildEBP RetAddr
00c1f4fc 773dc4e4 USER32!DispatchHookA+0x35
00c1f528 7739c9c6 USER32!fnHkINLPCWPRETSTRUCTA+0x60
00c1f550 7c828536 USER32!__fnDWORD+0x24
00c1f550 808308f4 ntdll!KiUserCallbackDispatcher+0x2e
b68b8a94 8091d6d1 nt!KiCallUserMode+0x4
b68b8aec bf8a26d3 nt!KeUserModeCallback+0x8f
b68b8b70 bf89dd4d win32k!SfnDWORD+0xb4
b68b8be8 bf89d79d win32k!xxxHkCallHook+0x22c
b68b8c90 bf89da19 win32k!xxxCallHook2+0x245
b68b8cac bf8a137a win32k!xxxCallHook+0x26
b68b8cec bf85af67 win32k!xxxSendMessageTimeout+0x1e3
b68b8d10 bf8c182c win32k!xxxWrapSendMessage+0x1b
b68b8d40 8088978c win32k!NtUserMessageCall+0x9d
```

```
b68b8d40 7c8285ec nt!KiFastCallEntry+0xfc
00c1f550 7c828536 ntdll!KiFastSystemCallRet
00c1f57c 7739d1ec ntdll!KiUserCallbackDispatcher+0x2e
00c1f5b8 7738cee9 USER32!NtUserMessageCall+0xc
00c1f5d8 01438f73 USER32!SendMessageA+0x7f


5: kd> !thread 86214750
THREAD 86214750  Cid 0b94.1238  Teb: 7ffdb000 Win32Thread: bc2f5ea8 RUNNING on processor 2
Not impersonating
DeviceMap                 e3482310
Owning Process            85790020      Image:          SomeExe.exe
Wait Start TickCount      1415535       Ticks: 0
Context Switch Count      1745682                   LargeStack
UserTime                  00:01:20.031
KernelTime                00:04:03.484
Win32 Start Address 0x75ec1c3f
Start Address kernel32!BaseThreadStartThunk (0x77e617ec)
Stack Init b4861000 Current b4860558 Base b4861000 Limit b4856000 Call 0
Priority 13 BasePriority 13 PriorityDecrement 0
ChildEBP RetAddr
b4860bd8 bf8da699 nt!PsGetThreadProcess
b4860bf4 bf89d6e6 win32k!IsRestricted+0x2f
b4860c90 bf89da19 win32k!xxxCallHook2+0x12d
b4860cac bf8a137a win32k!xxxCallHook+0x26
b4860cec bf85af67 win32k!xxxSendMessageTimeout+0x1e3
b4860d10 bf8c182c win32k!xxxWrapSendMessage+0x1b
b4860d40 8088978c win32k!NtUserMessageCall+0x9d
b4860d40 7c8285ec nt!KiFastCallEntry+0xfc
00c1f5fc 00000000 ntdll!KiFastSystemCallRet


5: kd> !thread 86f87020 1f
THREAD 86f87020  Cid 0238.0ae8  Teb: 7ffa5000 Win32Thread: 00000000 RUNNING on processor 3
IRP List:
    86869200: (0006,0094) Flags: 00000900  Mdl: 00000000
    85b2a7f0: (0006,0094) Flags: 00000900  Mdl: 00000000
    86f80a20: (0006,0094) Flags: 00000800  Mdl: 00000000
    85e6af68: (0006,0094) Flags: 00000900  Mdl: 00000000
    892a6c78: (0006,0094) Flags: 00000900  Mdl: 00000000
    85d06070: (0006,0094) Flags: 00000900  Mdl: 00000000
    85da35e0: (0006,0094) Flags: 00000900  Mdl: 00000000
    87216340: (0006,0094) Flags: 00000900  Mdl: 00000000
Not impersonating
DeviceMap                 e1003940
Owning Process            8850e020      Image:          lsass.exe
Wait Start TickCount      1415535       Ticks: 0
Context Switch Count      39608
UserTime                  00:00:01.625
KernelTime                00:00:05.437
Win32 Start Address RPCRT4!ThreadStartRoutine (0x77c7b0f5)
Start Address kernel32!BaseThreadStartThunk (0x77e617ec)
Stack Init f4925000 Current f4924c38 Base f4925000 Limit f4922000 Call 0
Priority 10 BasePriority 9 PriorityDecrement 0
ChildEBP RetAddr
f4924640 80972e8e nt!SePrivilegeCheck+0x24
f4924678 80944aa0 nt!SeSinglePrivilegeCheck+0x3a
f4924770 8088978c nt!NtOpenProcess+0x13a
```

```
f4924770 8082eff5 nt!KiFastCallEntry+0xfc
f49247f8 f6037bee nt!ZwOpenProcess+0x11
WARNING: Stack unwind information not available. Following frames may be wrong.
f4924830 f6002996 SomeDrv+0x48bee


5: kd> !thread 86ffe700 1f
THREAD 86ffe700  Cid 1ba4.1ba8  Teb: 7ffdf000 Win32Thread: bc23cea8 RUNNING on processor 4
Not impersonating
DeviceMap                 e44e9a40
Owning Process            87005708        Image:          WINWORD.EXE
Wait Start TickCount      1415535         Ticks: 0
Context Switch Count      1547251                 LargeStack
UserTime                  00:01:00.750
KernelTime                00:00:45.265
Win32 Start Address WINWORD (0x300019b0)
Start Address kernel32!BaseProcessStartThunk (0x77e617f8)
Stack Init f3465000 Current f3464c48 Base f3465000 Limit f345e000 Call 0
Priority 8 BasePriority 8 PriorityDecrement 0
ChildEBP RetAddr
f3464d64 7c8285eb nt!KiFastCallEntry+0x91
f3464d68 badb0d00 ntdll!KiFastSystemCall+0x3


5: kd> !thread 86803a90 1f
THREAD 86803a90  Cid 3c20.29f8  Teb: 7ffdf000 Win32Thread: bc295480 RUNNING on processor 5
Not impersonating
DeviceMap                 e518c6b8
Owning Process            857d5500        Image:          SystemDump.exe
Wait Start TickCount      1415535         Ticks: 0
Context Switch Count      310                     LargeStack
UserTime                  00:00:00.015
KernelTime                00:00:00.046
*** ERROR: Module load completed but symbols could not be loaded for SystemDump.exe
Win32 Start Address SystemDump_400000 (0x0040fe92)
Start Address kernel32!BaseProcessStartThunk (0x77e617f8)
Stack Init b38a4000 Current b38a3c08 Base b38a4000 Limit b389f000 Call 0
Priority 11 BasePriority 8 PriorityDecrement 2
ChildEBP RetAddr  Args to Child
b38a3bf0 f79e3743 000000e2 cccccccc 866962b0 nt!KeBugCheckEx+0x1b
WARNING: Stack unwind information not available. Following frames may be wrong.
b38a3c3c 8081df65 SystemDump+0x743
b38a3c50 808f5437 nt!IofCallDriver+0x45
b38a3c64 808f61bf nt!IopSynchronousServiceTail+0x10b
b38a3d00 808eed08 nt!IopXxxControlFile+0x5e5
b38a3d34 8088978c nt!NtDeviceIoControlFile+0x2a
b38a3d34 7c8285ec nt!KiFastCallEntry+0xfc
0012efc4 7c826fcb ntdll!KiFastSystemCallRet
0012efc8 77e416f5 ntdll!NtDeviceIoControlFile+0xc
0012f02c 00402208 kernel32!DeviceIoControl+0x137
0012f884 00404f8e SystemDump_400000+0x2208
```

```
5: kd> !thread 86043db0 1f
THREAD 86043db0  Cid 0610.55dc  Teb: 7ffa1000 Win32Thread: 00000000 RUNNING on processor 6
IRP List:
    86dc99a0: (0006,0094) Flags: 00000a00  Mdl: 00000000
Impersonation token:  e7b30030 (Level Impersonation)
DeviceMap            e4e470a8
Owning Process       891374a8    Image:          SomeSvc.exe
Wait Start TickCount 1415215     Ticks: 320 (0:00:00:05.000)
Context Switch Count 11728
UserTime             00:00:02.546
KernelTime           00:02:57.765
Win32 Start Address 0x0082b983
LPC Server thread working on message Id 82b983
Start Address kernel32!BaseThreadStartThunk (0x77e617ec)
Stack Init b49c1000 Current b49c0a7c Base b49c1000 Limit b49be000 Call 0
Priority 8 BasePriority 8 PriorityDecrement 0
ChildEBP RetAddr
b49c0b80 8087c9c0 hal!KeReleaseQueuedSpinLock+0x2d
b49c0ba0 8087ca95 nt!ExReleaseResourceLite+0xac
b49c0ba4 f6faa5ae nt!ExReleaseResourceAndLeaveCriticalRegion+0x5
b49c0bb8 f6faad05 termdd!_IcaCallStack+0x60
b49c0bdc f6fa6bda termdd!IcaCallDriver+0x71
b49c0c34 f6fa86dc termdd!IcaWriteChannel+0xd8
b49c0c50 f6fa8cc6 termdd!IcaWrite+0x40
b49c0c68 8081df65 termdd!IcaDispatch+0xd0
b49c0c7c 808f5437 nt!IofCallDriver+0x45
b49c0c90 808f3157 nt!IopSynchronousServiceTail+0x10b
b49c0d38 8088978c nt!NtWriteFile+0x663
b49c0d38 7c8285ec nt!KiFastCallEntry+0xfc
0254d814 7c827d3b ntdll!KiFastSystemCallRet
0254d818 77e5b012 ntdll!NtWriteFile+0xc
0254d878 004389f2 kernel32!WriteFile+0xa9


5: kd> !thread 86bcbdb0 1f
THREAD 86bcbdb0  Cid 34ac.1b04  Teb: 7ffdd000 Win32Thread: bc3d9a48 RUNNING on processor 7
IRP List:
    8581d900: (0006,01fc) Flags: 00000884  Mdl: 00000000
Not impersonating
DeviceMap            e153fc48
Owning Process       872fb708    Image:          SomeExe.exe
Wait Start TickCount 1415535     Ticks: 0
Context Switch Count 7655285                 LargeStack
UserTime             00:10:09.343
KernelTime           00:30:21.296
Win32 Start Address 0x75ec1c3f
Start Address 0x77e617ec
Stack Init b86cb000 Current b86ca58c Base b86cb000 Limit b86c2000 Call 0
Priority 13 BasePriority 13 PriorityDecrement 0
ChildEBP RetAddr
b86ca974 f724ffc2 fltmgr!FltpPerformPostCallbacks+0x260
b86ca988 f72504f1 fltmgr!FltpProcessIoCompletion+0x10
b86ca998 f7250b83 fltmgr!FltpPassThroughCompletion+0x89
b86ca9c8 f725e5de fltmgr!FltpLegacyProcessingAfterPreCallbacksCompleted+0x269
b86caa04 8081df65 fltmgr!FltpCreate+0x26a
b86caa18 f75fa8c7 nt!IofCallDriver+0x45
b86caa40 f75faa5a SomeFlt!PassThrough+0xbb
```

```
b86caa5c 8081df65 SomeFlt!Create+0xda
b86caa70 808f8f71 nt!IofCallDriver+0x45
b86cab58 80937942 nt!IopParseDevice+0xa35
b86cabd8 80933a76 nt!ObpLookupObjectName+0x5b0
b86cac2c 808eae25 nt!ObOpenObjectByName+0xea
b86caca8 808ec0bf nt!IopCreateFile+0x447
b86cad04 808efc4f nt!IoCreateFile+0xa3
b86cad44 8088978c nt!NtOpenFile+0x27
b86cad44 7c8285ec nt!KiFastCallEntry+0xfc
```

Running threads have good chance to be **Spiking Threads** (page 992).

C

C++ Exception

Linux

This is a Linux variant of **C++ Exception** pattern previously described for Mac OS X (page 120) and Windows (page 121) platforms:

```
(gdb) bt
#0 0x00007f0a1d0e5165 in *__GI_raise ()
at ../nptl/sysdeps/unix/sysv/linux/raise.c:64
#1 0x00007f0a1d0e83e0 in *__GI_abort () at abort.c:92
#2 0x00007f0a1db5789d in __gnu_cxx::__verbose_terminate_handler() ()
from /usr/lib/x86_64-linux-gnu/libstdc++.so.6
#3 0x00007f0a1db55996 in ?? () from /usr/lib/x86_64-linux-gnu/libstdc++.so.6
#4 0x00007f0a1db559c3 in std::terminate() ()
from /usr/lib/x86_64-linux-gnu/libstdc++.so.6
#5 0x00007f0a1db55bee in __cxa_throw ()
from /usr/lib/x86_64-linux-gnu/libstdc++.so.6
#6 0x0000000000400dcf in procB() ()
#7 0x0000000000400e26 in procA() ()
#8 0x0000000000400e88 in procNH() ()
#9 0x0000000000400ea8 in bar_one() ()
#10 0x0000000000400eb3 in foo_one() ()
#11 0x0000000000400ec6 in thread_one(void*) ()
#12 0x00007f0a1d444b50 in start_thread ()
#13 0x00007f0a1d18e95d in clone ()
at ../sysdeps/unix/sysv/linux/x86_64/clone.S:112
#14 0x0000000000000000 in ?? ()
```

Mac OS X

This is a Mac OS X / GDB counterpart to **C++ Exception** pattern:

```
(gdb) bt
#0 0x00007fff88bd582a in __kill ()
#1 0x00007fff8c184a9c in abort ()
#2 0x00007fff852f57bc in abort_message ()
#3 0x00007fff852f2fcf in default_terminate ()
#4 0x00007fff852f3001 in safe_handler_caller ()
#5 0x00007fff852f305c in std::terminate ()
#6 0x00007fff852f4152 in __cxa_throw ()
#7 0x000000010e402be8 in bar ()
#8 0x000000010e402c99 in foo ()
#9 0x000000010e402cbb in main (argc=1, argv=0x7fff6e001b18)
```

The modeling application source code:

```cpp
class Exception
{
        int code;
        std::string description;
public:
        Exception(int _code, std::string _desc) : code(_code), description(_desc) {}
};

void bar()
{
        throw new Exception(5, "Access Denied");
}

void foo()
{
        bar();
}

int main(int argc, const char * argv[])
{
        foo();
        return 0;
}
```

Windows

This is a very simple pattern, and it is similar to **Managed Code Exception** (page 697) and can be manifested by the same *RaiseException* function call on top of the stack (bold). It is called by Visual C runtime (I consider Microsoft C/C++ implementation here, msvcrt.dll, bold italic). The typical example of it might be checking the validity of a C++ stream operator data format (bold underlined):

```
STACK_TEXT:
09d6f264 78007108 KERNEL32!RaiseException+0x56
09d6f2a4 677f2a88 msvcrt!_CxxThrowException+0x34
09d6f2bc 6759afff DLL!MyInputStream::operator>>+0x34
```

Also, some Visual C++ STL implementations check for out of bounds or invalid parameters and call unhandled exception filter directly, for example:

```
STACK_TEXT:
0012d2e8 7c90e9ab ntdll!KiFastSystemCallRet
0012d2ec 7c8094e2 ntdll!ZwWaitForMultipleObjects+0xc
0012d388 7c80a075 kernel32!WaitForMultipleObjectsEx+0x12c
0012d3a4 6945763c kernel32!WaitForMultipleObjects+0x18
0012dd38 694582b1 faultrep!StartDWException+0x5df
0012edac 7c8633b1 faultrep!ReportFault+0x533
0012f44c 004409b3 kernel32!UnhandledExceptionFilter+0x587
0012f784 00440a1b Application!_invoke_watson+0xc4
0012f79c 00406f4f Application!_invalid_parameter_noinfo+0xc
0012f7a0 0040566b Application!std::vector<std::basic_string<char, std::char_traits<char>,
std::allocator<char> >, std::allocator<std::basic_string<char, std::char_traits<char>,
std::allocator<char> > > >::operator[]+0x12
```

The latter example also shows how an unhandled exception filter in an application itself calls a postmortem debugger specified by *AeDebug* registry key (see also the article[11] for the detailed explanation).

Comments

There is also **!cppexr** WinDBg extension command to format C++ exception record contents.

---

[11] Who Calls the Postmortem Debugger? Memory Dump Analysis Anthology, Volume 1, page 113

Caller-n-Callee

We noticed this pattern when analyzing the output of **!DumpStack** WinDbg SOS extension command:

```
0:011> !DumpStack
OS Thread Id: 0xac (11)
[...]
ChildEBP RetAddr  Caller, Callee
[...]
0b73f65c 77c416dc ntdll!RtlAllocateHeap+0x17c, calling ntdll!RtlpLowFragHeapAllocFromContext
0b73f688 77c486cd ntdll!RtlAllocateHeap+0x193, calling ntdll!memset
0b73f6b0 7653a467 kernel32!TlsSetValue+0x4c, calling ntdll!RtlAllocateHeap
0b73f6cc 77a01c48 urlmon!CUrlMkTls::TLSAllocData+0x3f, calling kernel32!TlsSetValue
0b73f6dc 77a0198d urlmon!CUrlMkTls::CUrlMkTls+0x29, calling urlmon!CUrlMkTls::TLSAllocData
0b73f6e8 77a01be5 urlmon!TlsDllMain+0x100, calling urlmon!EnsureFeatureCache
0b73f6f4 6d016a21 mshtml!DllMain+0x10, calling kernel32!GetCurrentThreadId
0b73f704 6d016b6c mshtml!_CRT_INIT+0x281, calling mshtml!DllMain
0b73f71c 7239133e msimtf!_CRT_INIT+0x281, calling msimtf!DllMain
0b73f728 72391375 msimtf!_CRT_INIT+0x3e7, calling msimtf!_SEH_epilog4
0b73f764 6d016ad0 mshtml!_DllMainStartup+0x56, calling mshtml!_DllMainCRTStartup
0b73f778 72391375 msimtf!_CRT_INIT+0x3e7, calling msimtf!_SEH_epilog4
0b73f77c 77c4a604 ntdll!LdrpCallInitRoutine+0x14
0b73f7a4 77c1ab6c ntdll!LdrpInitializeThread+0x1e9, calling ntdll!RtlLeaveCriticalSection
0b73f7ac 77c1a9ea ntdll!LdrpInitializeThread+0x1cd, calling ntdll!_SEH_epilog4
0b73f800 77c1ab15 ntdll!LdrpInitializeThread+0x11f, calling ntdll!RtlActivateActivationContextUnsafeFast
0b73f804 77c1ab53 ntdll!LdrpInitializeThread+0x167, calling
ntdll!RtlDeactivateActivationContextUnsafeFast
0b73f838 77c1a9ea ntdll!LdrpInitializeThread+0x1cd, calling ntdll!_SEH_epilog4
0b73f83c 77c405a0 ntdll!NtTestAlert+0xc
0b73f840 77c1a968 ntdll!_LdrpInitialize+0x29c, calling ntdll!_SEH_epilog4
0b73f8a0 77c3f3d0 ntdll!NtContinue+0xc
0b73f8a4 77c1a98a ntdll!LdrInitializeThunk+0x1a, calling ntdll!NtContinue
0b73fb30 6afd59f6 clr!Thread::intermediateThreadProc+0x39, calling clr!_alloca_probe_16
0b73fb44 76573833 kernel32!BaseThreadInitThunk+0xe
0b73fb50 77c1a9bd ntdll!_RtlUserThreadStart+0x23
```

Obviously the command collected "call-type" **Execution Residue** (page 395) from the raw stack. The "calling" part was not found in the nearby region:

```
0:011> dps 0b73f7a4-20 0b73f7a4+20
0b73f784 72390000 msimtf!_imp__RegOpenKeyW <PERF> (msimtf+0x0)
0b73f788 00000002
0b73f78c 00000000
0b73f790 00000001
0b73f794 0b73f80c
0b73f798 0b73f80c
0b73f79c 00000001
0b73f7a0 05636578
0b73f7a4 0b73f83c
0b73f7a8 77c1ab6c ntdll!LdrpInitializeThread+0x1e9
0b73f7ac 77ca5340 ntdll!LdrpLoaderLock
0b73f7b0 77c1a9ea ntdll!LdrpInitializeThread+0x1cd
0b73f7b4 0b7321f2
```

```
0b73f7b8 7ff4e000
0b73f7bc 7ffdf000
0b73f7c0 77ca51f4 ntdll!LdrpProcessInitialized
0b73f7c4 00000000
```

We tried to disassemble backward the addresses and found the callees:

```
0:011> ub 77c1ab6c
ntdll!LdrpInitializeThread+0x16b:
77c1ab57 90 nop
77c1ab58 90 nop
77c1ab59 90 nop
77c1ab5a 90 nop
77c1ab5b 90 nop
77c1ab5c ff054452ca77 inc dword ptr [ntdll!LdrpActiveThreadCount (77ca5244)]
77c1ab62 684053ca77 push offset ntdll!LdrpLoaderLock (77ca5340)
77c1ab67 e8bd820000 call ntdll!RtlLeaveCriticalSection (77c22e29)


0:011> ub 77a01be5
urlmon!TlsDllMain+0x2f:
77a01bce 8d4510 lea eax,[ebp+10h]
77a01bd1 50 push eax
77a01bd2 8d4d0c lea ecx,[ebp+0Ch]
77a01bd5 e88efdffff call urlmon!CUrlMkTls::CUrlMkTls (77a01968)
77a01bda 397d10 cmp dword ptr [ebp+10h],edi
77a01bdd 7c09 jl urlmon!TlsDllMain+0x103 (77a01be8)
77a01bdf 56 push esi
77a01be0 e887fcffff call urlmon!EnsureFeatureCache (77a0186c)
```

In the past, we were frequently referencing this pattern especially when discussing **Coincidental Symbolic Information** (page 148) but didn't name it.

We can also run **!DumpStack** command against every thread (including non-managed) to get the summary of the call-type execution residue:

```
0:011> ~4s
eax=76573821 ebx=00000002 ecx=00000000 edx=74d01909 esi=00000000 edi=00000000
eip=77c40f34 esp=0478f8a0 ebp=0478f93c iopl=0 nv up ei pl zr na pe nc
cs=001b ss=0023 ds=0023 es=0023 fs=003b gs=0000 efl=00000246
ntdll!KiFastSystemCallRet:
77c40f34 c3 ret


0:004> k
ChildEBP RetAddr
0478f89c 77c40690 ntdll!KiFastSystemCallRet
0478f8a0 76577e09 ntdll!ZwWaitForMultipleObjects+0xc
0478f93c 7674c4af kernel32!WaitForMultipleObjectsEx+0x11d
0478f990 76748b7b user32!RealMsgWaitForMultipleObjectsEx+0x13c
0478f9ac 74d01965 user32!MsgWaitForMultipleObjects+0x1f
0478f9f8 76573833 GdiPlus!BackgroundThreadProc+0x59
0478fa04 77c1a9bd kernel32!BaseThreadInitThunk+0xe
0478fa44 00000000 ntdll!_RtlUserThreadStart+0x23
```

```
0:004> !DumpStack
OS Thread Id: 0x950 (4)
Current frame: ntdll!KiFastSystemCallRet
ChildEBP RetAddr Caller, Callee
0478f89c 77c40690 ntdll!ZwWaitForMultipleObjects+0xc
0478f8a0 76577e09 kernel32!WaitForMultipleObjectsEx+0x11d, calling ntdll!NtWaitForMultipleObjects
0478f914 76751a91 user32!UserCallWinProcCheckWow+0x5c, calling
ntdll!RtlActivateActivationContextUnsafeFast
0478f918 76751b41 user32!UserCallWinProcCheckWow+0x16a, calling
ntdll!RtlDeactivateActivationContextUnsafeFast
0478f93c 7674c4af user32!RealMsgWaitForMultipleObjectsEx+0x13c, calling kernel32!WaitForMultipleObjectsEx
0478f968 76752a65 user32!DispatchMessageWorker+0x396, calling user32!_SEH_epilog4
0478f980 76743c64 user32!PeekMessageA+0x129, calling user32!_PeekMessage
0478f990 76748b7b user32!MsgWaitForMultipleObjects+0x1f, calling user32!MsgWaitForMultipleObjectsEx
0478f9ac 74d01965 GdiPlus!BackgroundThreadProc+0x59, calling user32!MsgWaitForMultipleObjects
0478f9f8 76573833 kernel32!BaseThreadInitThunk+0xe
0478fa04 77c1a9bd ntdll!_RtlUserThreadStart+0x23
```

Changed Environment

Sometimes the change of operating system version or installing an intrusive product reveals hidden bugs in software that was working perfectly before that.

What happens after installing the new software? If we look at the process dump, we see many DLLs loaded at their specific virtual addresses. Here is the output from **lm** WinDbg command after attaching to *iexplore.exe* process running on Windows XP SP2 workstation:

```
0:000> lm
start    end      module name
00400000 00419000 iexplore
01c80000 01d08000 shdoclc
01d10000 01fd5000 xpsp2res
022b0000 022cd000 xpsp3res
02680000 02946000 msi
031f0000 031fd000 LvHook
03520000 03578000 PortableDeviceApi
037e0000 037f7000 odbcint
0ffd0000 0fff8000 rsaenh
20000000 20012000 browselc
30000000 302ee000 Flash9b
325c0000 325d2000 msohev
4d4f0000 4d548000 WINHTTP
5ad70000 5ada8000 UxTheme
5b860000 5b8b4000 NETAPI32
5d090000 5d12a000 comctl32_5d090000
5e310000 5e31c000 pngfilt
63000000 63014000 SynTPFcs
662b0000 66308000 hnetcfg
66880000 6688c000 ImgUtil
6bdd0000 6be06000 dxtrans
6be10000 6be6a000 dxtmsft
6d430000 6d43a000 ddrawex
71a50000 71a8f000 mswsock
71a90000 71a98000 wshtcpip
71aa0000 71aa8000 WS2HELP
71ab0000 71ac7000 WS2_32
71ad0000 71ad9000 wsock32
71b20000 71b32000 MPR
71bf0000 71c03000 SAMLIB
71c10000 71c1e000 ntlanman
71c80000 71c87000 NETRAP
71c90000 71cd0000 NETUI1
71cd0000 71ce7000 NETUI0
71d40000 71d5c000 actxprxy
722b0000 722b5000 sensapi
72d10000 72d18000 msacm32
72d20000 72d29000 wdmaud
73300000 73367000 vbscript
73760000 737a9000 DDRAW
73bc0000 73bc6000 DCIMAN32
73dd0000 73ece000 MFC42
```

```
74320000 7435d000 ODBC32
746c0000 746e7000 msls31
746f0000 7471a000 msimtf
74720000 7476b000 MSCTF
754d0000 75550000 CRYPTUI
75970000 75a67000 MSGINA
75c50000 75cbe000 jscript
75cf0000 75d81000 mlang
75e90000 75f40000 SXS
75f60000 75f67000 drprov
75f70000 75f79000 davclnt
75f80000 7607d000 BROWSEUI
76200000 76271000 mshtmled
76360000 76370000 WINSTA
76390000 763ad000 IMM32
763b0000 763f9000 comdlg32
76600000 7661d000 CSCDLL
767f0000 76817000 schannel
769c0000 76a73000 USERENV
76b20000 76b31000 ATL
76b40000 76b6d000 WINMM
76bf0000 76bfb000 PSAPI
76c30000 76c5e000 WINTRUST
76c90000 76cb8000 IMAGEHLP
76d60000 76d79000 iphlpapi
76e80000 76e8e000 rtutils
76e90000 76ea2000 rasman
76eb0000 76edf000 TAPI32
76ee0000 76f1c000 RASAPI32
76f20000 76f47000 DNSAPI
76f60000 76f8c000 WLDAP32
76fc0000 76fc6000 rasadhlp
76fd0000 7704f000 CLBCATQ
77050000 77115000 COMRes
77120000 771ac000 OLEAUT32
771b0000 77256000 WININET
773d0000 774d3000 comctl32
774e0000 7761d000 ole32
77920000 77a13000 SETUPAPI
77a20000 77a74000 cscui
77a80000 77b14000 CRYPT32
77b20000 77b32000 MSASN1
77b40000 77b62000 appHelp
77bd0000 77bd7000 midimap
77be0000 77bf5000 MSACM32_77be0000
77c00000 77c08000 VERSION
77c10000 77c68000 msvcrt
77c70000 77c93000 msv1_0
77d40000 77dd0000 USER32
77dd0000 77e6b000 ADVAPI32
77e70000 77f01000 RPCRT4
77f10000 77f57000 GDI32
77f60000 77fd6000 SHLWAPI
77fe0000 77ff1000 Secur32
7c800000 7c8f4000 kernel32
7c900000 7c9b0000 ntdll
```

```
7c9c0000 7d1d5000 SHELL32
7dc30000 7df20000 mshtml
7e1e0000 7e280000 urlmon
7e290000 7e3ff000 SHDOCVW
```

Installing or upgrading software can change the distribution of loaded DLLs and their addresses. This also happens when we install some monitoring software which usually injects their DLLs into every process. As a result, some DLLs might be relocated, or even the new ones appear loaded. And this might influence 3rd-party program behavior therefore exposing its hidden bugs being dormant when executing the process in the old environment. I call this pattern **Changed Environment**.

Let's look at some hypothetical example. Suppose our program has the following code fragment

```
if (*p)
{
// do something useful
}
```

Suppose the pointer p is invalid, dangling, its value has been overwritten, and this happened because of some bug. Being invalid that pointer can point to a valid memory location nevertheless and the value it points to most likely is non-zero. Therefore, the body of the "if" statement will be executed. Suppose it always happens when we run the program and every time we execute it the value of the pointer happens to be the same.

Here is the picture illustrating the point:

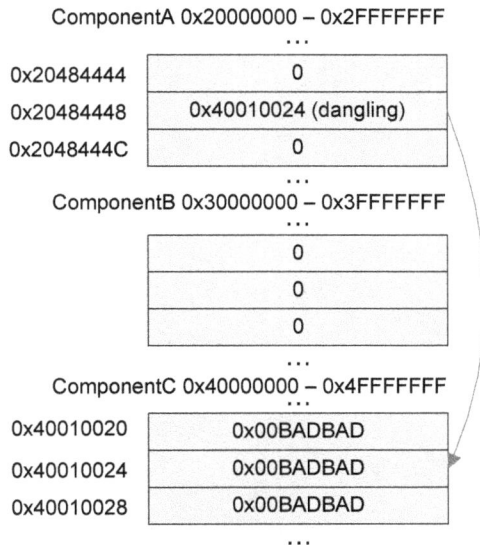

The pointer value 0x40010024 due to some reason always points to the value 0x00BADBAD. Although in the correct program the pointer itself should have had a completely different value and pointed to 0x1, for example, we see that dereferencing its current invalid value does not crash the process.

After installing the new software, *NewComponent* DLL is loaded at the address range previously occupied by *ComponentC*:

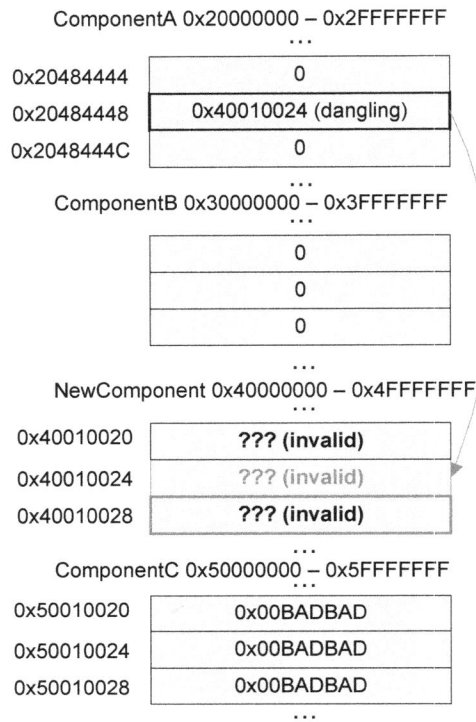

ComponentA 0x20000000 – 0x2FFFFFFF

...

0x20484444	0
0x20484448	0x40010024 (dangling)
0x2048444C	0

...

ComponentB 0x30000000 – 0x3FFFFFFF

...

0
0
0

...

NewComponent 0x40000000 – 0x4FFFFFFF

...

0x40010020	**??? (invalid)**
0x40010024	??? (invalid)
0x40010028	**??? (invalid)**

...

ComponentC 0x50000000 – 0x5FFFFFFF

...

0x50010020	0x00BADBAD
0x50010024	0x00BADBAD
0x50010028	0x00BADBAD

...

Now the address 0x40010024 happens to be completely invalid, and we have an access violation and the crash dump.

Comments

Sometimes changes in physical memory size may also affect process behavior. Other examples include an application running under a user mode debugger which effects a different type of runtime heap used.

Clone Dump

With the possibility of process cloning (reflection) starting from Windows 7 it is possible to get memory snapshots (**Clone Dump**) from a process clone (similar to *fork* API in Unix). The procdump[12] tool has **-r** switch for that purpose. We checked this with x64 Windows 7 *notepad.exe*. We got two memory dumps: one is a clone with this stack trace:

```
Loading Dump File [C:\DebuggingTV\Procdump\notepad.exe_151117_000755.dbgcfg.dmp]
User Mini Dump File with Full Memory: Only application data is available


Comment: '
*** procdump -ma -r Notepad.exe
*** Manual dump'


0:000> ~*k

. 0 Id: 25ec.147c Suspend: 1 Teb: 000007ff`fffdb000 Unfrozen
# Child-SP RetAddr Call Site
00 00000000`02c8fd38 00000000`7733aae7 ntdll!NtSuspendThread+0xa
01 00000000`02c8fd40 00000000`77165a4d ntdll!RtlpProcessReflectionStartup+0x2e7
02 00000000`02c8fe30 00000000`7729b831 kernel32!BaseThreadInitThunk+0xd
03 00000000`02c8fe60 00000000`00000000 ntdll!RtlUserThreadStart+0x1d
```

The process memory has all address space of the original process including module list and heap structure:

```
0:000> lmn
start end module name
00000000`77050000 00000000`7714a000   user32    user32.dll
00000000`77150000 00000000`77270000   kernel32  kernel32.dll
00000000`77270000 00000000`77419000   ntdll     ntdll.dll
00000000`ff030000 00000000`ff065000   notepad   notepad.exe
000007fe`f57d0000 000007fe`f5841000   winspool  winspool.drv
000007fe`fb730000 000007fe`fb786000   uxtheme   uxtheme.dll
000007fe`fb910000 000007fe`fbb04000   comctl32  comctl32.dll
000007fe`fbf00000 000007fe`fbf0c000   version   version.dll
000007fe`fceb0000 000007fe`fcebf000   CRYPTBASE CRYPTBASE.dll
000007fe`fd310000 000007fe`fd37c000   KERNELBASE KERNELBASE.dll
000007fe`fd3d0000 000007fe`fd499000   usp10     usp10.dll
000007fe`fd4a0000 000007fe`fd511000   shlwapi   shlwapi.dll
000007fe`fd520000 000007fe`fd64d000   rpcrt4    rpcrt4.dll
000007fe`fd650000 000007fe`fd66f000   sechost   sechost.dll
000007fe`fd680000 000007fe`fd6ae000   imm32     imm32.dll
000007fe`fd6b0000 000007fe`fd78b000   advapi32  advapi32.dll
000007fe`fd810000 000007fe`fd8a7000   comdlg32  comdlg32.dll
000007fe`fdd60000 000007fe`fddff000   msvcrt    msvcrt.dll
000007fe`fdfe0000 000007fe`fed69000   shell32   shell32.dll
000007fe`fed70000 000007fe`fedd7000   gdi32     gdi32.dll
```

---

[12] https://docs.microsoft.com/en-gb/sysinternals/downloads/procdump

```
000007fe`ff0b0000 000007fe`ff1b9000   msctf    msctf.dll
000007fe`ff1c0000 000007fe`ff1ce000   lpk      lpk.dll
000007fe`ff1d0000 000007fe`ff2a7000   oleaut32 oleaut32.dll
000007fe`ff2b0000 000007fe`ff349000   clbcatq  clbcatq.dll
000007fe`ff350000 000007fe`ff553000   ole32    ole32.dll


0:000> !address -summary


Mapping file section regions...
Mapping module regions...
Mapping PEB regions...
Mapping TEB and stack regions...
Mapping heap regions...
Mapping page heap regions...
Mapping other regions...
Mapping stack trace database regions...
Mapping activation context regions...


--- Usage Summary --------------- RgnCount ----------- Total Size -------- %ofBusy %ofTotal
Free                             48       7ff`faa06000 (   8.000 TB)               100.00%
Image                            129      0`01e79000 (  30.473 MB)      35.47%     0.00%
<unknown>                        21       0`01d10000 (  29.063 MB)      33.83%     0.00%
Other                            9        0`016be000 (  22.742 MB)      26.47%     0.00%
Heap                             26       0`00320000 (   3.125 MB)       3.64%     0.00%
Stack                            3        0`00080000 ( 512.000 kB)       0.58%     0.00%
TEB                              1        0`00002000 (   8.000 kB)       0.01%     0.00%
PEB                              1        0`00001000 (   4.000 kB)       0.00%     0.00%

--- Type Summary (for busy) ------ RgnCount ----------- Total Size -------- %ofBusy %ofTotal
MEM_IMAGE                        130      0`01e7a000 (  30.477 MB)      35.47%     0.00%
MEM_PRIVATE                      47       0`01449000 (  20.285 MB)      23.61%     0.00%
MEM_MAPPED                       11       0`00c97000 (  12.590 MB)      14.65%     0.00%

--- State Summary --------------- RgnCount ----------- Total Size -------- %ofBusy %ofTotal
MEM_FREE                         50       7ff`fc096000 (   8.000 TB)               100.00%
MEM_COMMIT                       176      0`02c10000 (  44.063 MB)      51.29%     0.00%
MEM_RESERVE                      12       0`0134a000 (  19.289 MB)      22.45%     0.00%

--- Protect Summary (for commit) - RgnCount ----------- Total Size -------- %ofBusy %ofTotal
PAGE_READONLY                    83       0`01b46000 (  27.273 MB)      31.75%     0.00%
PAGE_EXECUTE_READ                25       0`00f6d000 (  15.426 MB)      17.95%     0.00%
PAGE_WRITECOPY                   48       0`00126000 (   1.148 MB)       1.34%     0.00%
PAGE_READWRITE                   18       0`00032000 ( 200.000 kB)       0.23%     0.00%
PAGE_READWRITE|PAGE_GUARD        2        0`00005000 (  20.000 kB)       0.02%     0.00%

--- Largest Region by Usage ----------- Base Address -------- Region Size ----------
Free                                    0`ff065000     7fd`f676b000 (   7.992 TB)
Image                                   7fe`fe4cb000   0`0089e000 (   8.617 MB)
<unknown>                               0`7f0e0000     0`00f00000 (  15.000 MB)
Other                                   0`00610000     0`01590000 (  21.563 MB)
Heap                                    0`003b8000     0`000c8000 ( 800.000 kB)
Stack                                   0`02c10000     0`0006c000 ( 432.000 kB)
TEB                                     7ff`fffdb000   0`00002000 (   8.000 kB)
PEB                                     7ff`fffdf000   0`00001000 (   4.000 kB)
```

```
0:000> !heap -s

***************************************************
NT HEAP STATS BELOW
***************************************************
LFH Key                  : 0x000000381021167d
Termination on corruption : ENABLED
Heap    Flags   Reserv  Commit Virt   Free  List  UCR  Virt  Lock  Fast
(k)     (k)     (k)     (k) length     blocks cont. heap
-----------------------------------------------------------------------------
0000000000280000 00000002   1024    412   1024    14    4    1    0     0  LFH
0000000000250000 00001002   1088    256   1088     5    2    2    0     0  LFH
0000000001cc0000 00001002     64      8     64     3    1    1    0     0
0000000001e60000 00001002    512    120    512    49    3    1    0     0
0000000001dc0000 00001002    512      8    512     2    1    1    0     0
-----------------------------------------------------------------------------
```

The other dump saved is a minidump from which we can get thread information for **Execution Residue** (page 395, raw stack data) and reconstruct stack traces in **Clone Dump**:

```
Loading Dump File [C:\DebuggingTV\Procdump\notepad.exe_151117_000755.dmp]
Comment: '
*** procdump -ma -r Notepad.exe
*** Manual dump'
User Mini Dump File: Only registers, stack and portions of memory are available

0:000> ~
.  0  Id: 87c.27f4 Suspend: 0 Teb: 000007ff`fffdd000 Unfrozen


0:000> k
# Child-SP RetAddr Call Site
00 00000000`0016fac8 00000000`77069e9e 0x77069e6a
01 00000000`0016fad0 00000000`00000000 0x77069e9e


0:000> r
rax=0000000000000000 rbx=000000000016fb40 rcx=0000000000280000
rdx=0000000000000000 rsi=0000000000000001 rdi=0000000000000000
rip=0000000077069e6a rsp=000000000016fac8 rbp=00000000ff030000
r8=000000000016f8e8 r9=00000000000a0cdc r10=0000000000000000
r11=0000000000000000 r12=0000000000000000 r13=0000000000000000
r14=0000000000000000 r15=0000000000000000
iopl=0         nv up ei pl zr na po nc
cs=0033 ss=002b ds=002b es=002b fs=0053 gs=002b efl=00000246
00000000`77069e6a c3              ret
```

Now we can see the original stack trace in **Clone Dump**:

```
0:000> k =000000000016fac8 ff
# Child-SP RetAddr Call Site
00 00000000`0016fac8 00000000`77069e9e ntdll!NtSuspendThread+0xa
01 00000000`0016fad0 00000000`ff031064 user32!GetMessageW+0x34
02 00000000`0016fb00 00000000`ff03133c notepad!WinMain+0x182
03 00000000`0016fb80 00000000`77165a4d notepad!DisplayNonGenuineDlgWorker+0x2da
```

```
04 00000000`0016fc40 00000000`7729b831 kernel32!BaseThreadInitThunk+0xd
05 00000000`0016fc70 00000000`00000000 ntdll!RtlUserThreadStart+0x1d
```

Since we know TEB address from the minidump we can get stack region boundaries in **Clone Dump**:

```
0:000> dt _NT_TIB 000007fffffdd000
ntdll!_NT_TIB
   +0x000 ExceptionList    : (null)
   +0x008 StackBase        : 0x00000000`00170000 Void
   +0x010 StackLimit       : 0x00000000`0015b000 Void
   +0x018 SubSystemTib     : (null)
   +0x020 FiberData        : 0x00000000`00001e00 Void
   +0x020 Version          : 0x1e00
   +0x028 ArbitraryUserPointer : (null)
   +0x030 Self             : 0x000007ff`fffdd000 _NT_TIB
```

Now we can check **Execution Residue** (for example, for signs of **Hidden Exceptions**, page 506):

```
0:000> dpS 0x00000000`0015b000 0x00000000`00170000
[...]
```

Cloud Environment

This pattern is specific to cloud platforms. It covers both development (emulator, if it exists) and real (staging and deployment) environments and is best diagnosed by looking at specific infrastructure modules:

```
0:016> lm m Wa*
start end module name
00000000`00b00000 00000000`00b0c000  WaWorkerHost
00000000`74fb0000 00000000`74fbd000  WaRuntimeProxy

0:016> lm m *Azure*
start end module name
00000000`57cd0000 00000000`57d26000  Microsoft_WindowsAzure_StorageClient
00000000`58820000 00000000`5886c000  Microsoft_WindowsAzure_Diagnostics
00000000`5c750000 00000000`5c764000  Microsoft_WindowsAzure_ServiceRuntime
```

Development platform can be distinguished by looking at versions of system modules such as *ntdll*:

```
0:016> lmv m ntdll
start                 end              module name
00000000`76de0000 00000000`76f5f000  ntdll
Loaded symbol image file:       ntdll.dll
Image path:                     D:\Windows\System32\ntdll.dll
Image name:                     ntdll.dll
Timestamp:                      Fri May 13 21:45:21 2011 (4DCD9861)
CheckSum:                       00188814
ImageSize:                      0017F000
File version:                   6.0.6002.18446
Product version:                6.0.6002.18446
File flags:                     0 (Mask 3F)
File OS:                        40004 NT Win32
File type:                      2.0 Dll
File date:                      00000000.00000000
Translations:                   0409.04b0
CompanyName:                    Microsoft Corporation
ProductName:                    Microsoft® Windows® Operating System
InternalName:                   ntdll.dll
OriginalFilename:               ntdll.dll
ProductVersion:                 6.0.6002.18446
FileVersion:                    6.0.6002.18446 (rd_os_v1.110513-1321)
FileDescription:                NT Layer DLL
LegalCopyright:                 © Microsoft Corporation. All rights reserved.
```

```
0:016> lmv m ntdll
start                 end                  module name
00000000`775a0000 00000000`7774b000 ntdll
Loaded symbol image file:       ntdll.dll
Image path:                     C:\Windows\System32\ntdll.dll
Image name:                     ntdll.dll
Timestamp:                      Tue Jul 14 02:32:27 2009 (4A5BE02B)
CheckSum:                       001B1CB5
ImageSize:                      001AB000
File version:                   6.1.7600.16385
Product version:                6.1.7600.16385
File flags:                     0 (Mask 3F)
File OS:                        40004 NT Win32
File type:                      2.0 Dll
File date:                      00000000.00000000
Translations:                   0409.04b0
CompanyName:                    Microsoft Corporation
ProductName:                    Microsoft® Windows® Operating System
InternalName:                   ntdll.dll
OriginalFilename:               ntdll.dll
ProductVersion:                 6.1.7600.16385
FileVersion:                    6.1.7600.16385 (win7_rtm.090713-1255)
FileDescription:                NT Layer DLL
LegalCopyright:                 © Microsoft Corporation. All rights reserved.
```

CLR Thread

In cases where we do not see **Managed Code Exceptions** (page 697) or **Managed Stack Traces** (page 704) by default, we need to identify **CLR Threads** in order to try various SOS commands and start digging into a managed realm. These threads are easily distinguished by *mscorwks* module on their stack traces (do not forget to list full stack traces[13]):

```
0:000> ~*kL 100


.  0  Id: 658.4ec Suspend: 1 Teb: 7ffdf000 Unfrozen
ChildEBP RetAddr
0007fc98 7c827d19 ntdll!KiFastSystemCallRet
0007fc9c 77e6202c ntdll!NtWaitForMultipleObjects+0xc
0007fd44 7739bbd1 kernel32!WaitForMultipleObjectsEx+0x11a
0007fda0 6c296601 user32!RealMsgWaitForMultipleObjectsEx+0x141
0007fdc0 6c29684b duser!CoreSC::Wait+0x3a
0007fdf4 6c29693d duser!CoreSC::xwProcessNL+0xab
0007fe14 773b0c02 duser!MphProcessMessage+0x2e
0007fe5c 7c828556 user32!__ClientGetMessageMPH+0x30
0007fe84 7739c811 ntdll!KiUserCallbackDispatcher+0x2e
0007fea4 7f072fd6 user32!NtUserGetMessage+0xc
0007fec0 010080ef mfc42u!CWinThread::PumpMessage+0x16
0007fef0 7f072dda mmc!CAMCApp::PumpMessage+0x37
0007ff08 7f044d5b mfc42u!CWinThread::Run+0x4a
0007ff1c 01034e19 mfc42u!AfxWinMain+0x7b
0007ffc0 77e6f23b mmc!wWinMainCRTStartup+0x19d
0007fff0 00000000 kernel32!BaseProcessStart+0x23


   1  Id: 658.82c Suspend: 1 Teb: 7ffde000 Unfrozen
ChildEBP RetAddr
003afea0 7c827d19 ntdll!KiFastSystemCallRet
003afea4 7c80e5bb ntdll!NtWaitForMultipleObjects+0xc
003aff48 7c80e4a2 ntdll!EtwpWaitForMultipleObjectsEx+0xf7
003affb8 77e6482f ntdll!EtwpEventPump+0x27f
003affec 00000000 kernel32!BaseThreadStart+0x34


   2  Id: 658.648 Suspend: 1 Teb: 7ffdd000 Unfrozen
ChildEBP RetAddr
00f3fe18 7c827859 ntdll!KiFastSystemCallRet
00f3fe1c 77c885ac ntdll!NtReplyWaitReceivePortEx+0xc
00f3ff84 77c88792 rpcrt4!LRPC_ADDRESS::ReceiveLotsaCalls+0x198
00f3ff8c 77c8872d rpcrt4!RecvLotsaCallsWrapper+0xd
00f3ffac 77c7b110 rpcrt4!BaseCachedThreadRoutine+0x9d
00f3ffb8 77e6482f rpcrt4!ThreadStartRoutine+0x1b
00f3ffec 00000000 kernel32!BaseThreadStart+0x34
```

---

[13] Common Mistakes, Memory Dump Analysis Anthology, Volume 2, page 39

```
3  Id: 658.640 Suspend: 1 Teb: 7ffdb000 Unfrozen
ChildEBP RetAddr
0156fdb4 7c827d19 ntdll!KiFastSystemCallRet
0156fdb8 77e6202c ntdll!NtWaitForMultipleObjects+0xc
0156fe60 7739bbd1 kernel32!WaitForMultipleObjectsEx+0x11a
0156febc 6c296601 user32!RealMsgWaitForMultipleObjectsEx+0x141
0156fedc 6c29684b duser!CoreSC::Wait+0x3a
0156ff10 6c28f9e6 duser!CoreSC::xwProcessNL+0xab
0156ff30 6c28bce1 duser!GetMessageExA+0x44
0156ff84 77bcb530 duser!ResourceManager::SharedThreadProc+0xb6
0156ffb8 77e6482f msvcrt!_endthreadex+0xa3
0156ffec 00000000 kernel32!BaseThreadStart+0x34


   4  Id: 658.e74 Suspend: 1 Teb: 7ffda000 Unfrozen
ChildEBP RetAddr
01d1fe30 7c827d19 ntdll!KiFastSystemCallRet
01d1fe34 77e6202c ntdll!NtWaitForMultipleObjects+0xc
01d1fedc 77e62fbe kernel32!WaitForMultipleObjectsEx+0x11a
01d1fef8 79f02541 kernel32!WaitForMultipleObjects+0x18
01d1ff58 79f0249e mscorwks!DebuggerRCThread::MainLoop+0xe9
01d1ff88 79f023c5 mscorwks!DebuggerRCThread::ThreadProc+0xe5
01d1ffb8 77e6482f mscorwks!DebuggerRCThread::ThreadProcStatic+0x9c
01d1ffec 00000000 kernel32!BaseThreadStart+0x34


   5  Id: 658.4d4 Suspend: 1 Teb: 7ffd8000 Unfrozen
ChildEBP RetAddr
03dffcc4 7c827d19 ntdll!KiFastSystemCallRet
03dffcc8 77e6202c ntdll!NtWaitForMultipleObjects+0xc
03dffd70 77e62fbe kernel32!WaitForMultipleObjectsEx+0x11a
03dffd8c 79f92bcb kernel32!WaitForMultipleObjects+0x18
03dffdac 79f97028 mscorwks!WKS::WaitForFinalizerEvent+0x77
03dffdc0 79e9845f mscorwks!WKS::GCHeap::FinalizerThreadWorker+0x49
03dffdd4 79e983fb mscorwks!Thread::DoADCallBack+0x32a
03dffe68 79e98321 mscorwks!Thread::ShouldChangeAbortToUnload+0xe3
03dffea4 79eef6cc mscorwks!Thread::ShouldChangeAbortToUnload+0x30a
03dffecc 79eef6dd mscorwks!ManagedThreadBase_NoADTransition+0x32
03dffedc 79f3c63c mscorwks!ManagedThreadBase::FinalizerBase+0xd
03dfff14 79f92015 mscorwks!WKS::GCHeap::FinalizerThreadStart+0xbb
03dfffb8 77e6482f mscorwks!Thread::intermediateThreadProc+0x49
03dfffec 00000000 kernel32!BaseThreadStart+0x34


   6  Id: 658.f54 Suspend: 1 Teb: 7ffd6000 Unfrozen
ChildEBP RetAddr
040afec4 7c826f69 ntdll!KiFastSystemCallRet
040afec8 77e41ed5 ntdll!NtDelayExecution+0xc
040aff30 79fd8a41 kernel32!SleepEx+0x68
040affac 79fd88ef mscorwks!ThreadpoolMgr::TimerThreadFire+0x6d
040affb8 77e6482f mscorwks!ThreadpoolMgr::TimerThreadStart+0x57
040affec 00000000 kernel32!BaseThreadStart+0x34
```

```
  7  Id: 658.988 Suspend: 1 Teb: 7ffd5000 Unfrozen
ChildEBP RetAddr
0410fc2c 7c827d29 ntdll!KiFastSystemCallRet
0410fc30 77e61d1e ntdll!ZwWaitForSingleObject+0xc
0410fca0 79e8c5f9 kernel32!WaitForSingleObjectEx+0xac
0410fce4 79e8c52f mscorwks!PEImage::LoadImage+0x1af
0410fd34 79e8c54e mscorwks!CLREvent::WaitEx+0x117
0410fd48 79ee3f35 mscorwks!CLREvent::Wait+0x17
0410fe14 79f92015 mscorwks!AppDomain::ADUnloadThreadStart+0x308
0410ffb8 77e6482f mscorwks!Thread::intermediateThreadProc+0x49
0410ffec 00000000 kernel32!BaseThreadStart+0x34


  8  Id: 658.e0 Suspend: 1 Teb: 7ff4f000 Unfrozen
ChildEBP RetAddr
0422fcec 7c827d19 ntdll!KiFastSystemCallRet
0422fcf0 7c83c7be ntdll!NtWaitForMultipleObjects+0xc
0422ffb8 77e6482f ntdll!RtlpWaitThread+0x161
0422ffec 00000000 kernel32!BaseThreadStart+0x34


  9  Id: 658.db4 Suspend: 1 Teb: 7ff4e000 Unfrozen
ChildEBP RetAddr
0447fec0 7c827d19 ntdll!KiFastSystemCallRet
0447fec4 77e6202c ntdll!NtWaitForMultipleObjects+0xc
0447ff6c 77e62fbe kernel32!WaitForMultipleObjectsEx+0x11a
0447ff88 76929e35 kernel32!WaitForMultipleObjects+0x18
0447ffb8 77e6482f userenv!NotificationThread+0x5f
0447ffec 00000000 kernel32!BaseThreadStart+0x34


 10  Id: 658.e7c Suspend: 1 Teb: 7ff4c000 Unfrozen
ChildEBP RetAddr
0550ff7c 7c8277f9 ntdll!KiFastSystemCallRet
0550ff80 71b25914 ntdll!NtRemoveIoCompletion+0xc
0550ffb8 77e6482f mswsock!SockAsyncThread+0x69
0550ffec 00000000 kernel32!BaseThreadStart+0x34


[...]
```

Comments

Silverlight applications use *coreclr*.

In CLR 4.0 the module has changed to just *clr*:

```
0:000> lmv m clr
start             end                 module name
000007fe`eadc0000 000007fe`eb725000   clr        (pdb symbols)
    Loaded symbol image file: clr.dll
    Image path: C:\Windows\Microsoft.NET\Framework64\
v4.0.30319\clr.dll
    Image name: clr.dll
    Timestamp:        Thu Mar 18 12:39:07 2010 (4BA21EEB)
    CheckSum:         00959DBD
    ImageSize:        00965000
    File version:     4.0.30319.1
    Product version:  4.0.30319.1
    File flags:       8 (Mask 3F) Private
    File OS:          4 Unknown Win32
    File type:        2.0 Dll
    File date:        00000000.00000000
    Translations:     0409.04b0
    CompanyName:      Microsoft Corporation
    ProductName:      Microsoft® .NET Framework
    InternalName:     clr.dll
    OriginalFilename: clr.dll
    ProductVersion:   4.0.30319.1
    FileVersion:      4.0.30319.1 (RTMRel.030319-0100)
    PrivateBuild:     DDBLD431
    FileDescription:  Microsoft .NET Runtime Common Language Runtime - WorkStation
    LegalCopyright:   © Microsoft Corporation. All rights reserved.
    Comments:         Flavor=Retail

0:000> ~16kc
Call Site
ntdll!NtWaitForSingleObject
KERNELBASE!WaitForSingleObjectEx
clr!CLREvent::WaitEx
clr!CLREvent::WaitEx
clr!CLREvent::WaitEx
clr!Thread::WaitSuspendEventsHelper
clr!Thread::WaitSuspendEvents
clr! ?? ::FNODOBFM::`string'
clr!Thread::RareDisablePreemptiveGC
clr!GCHolderBase<1,0,0,1>::EnterInternal
clr!AddTimerCallbackEx
clr!ThreadpoolMgr::AsyncTimerCallbackCompletion
clr!UnManagedPerAppDomainTPCount::DispatchWorkItem
clr!ThreadpoolMgr::NewWorkerThreadStart
clr!ThreadpoolMgr::WorkerThreadStart
clr!Thread::intermediateThreadProc
kernel32!BaseThreadInitThunk
ntdll!RtlUserThreadStart
```

Coincidental Error Code

Address space-wide search for errors and status codes[14] may show **Coincidental Error Codes**:

```
0:000> !heap -x -v c0000005
Search VM for address range c0000005 - c0000005 : 028690b8 (c0000005), [...]


0:000> dd 028690b8 l1
028690b8 c0000005
```

In such cases we need to check whether the addresses belong to volatile regions such as stack because it is possible to have such values as legitimate code and image data:

```
0:000> !address 028690b8
Usage:                 Image
Allocation Base:       02700000
Base Address:          02869000
End Address:           02874000
Region Size:           0000b000
Type:                  01000000 MEM_IMAGE
State:                 00001000 MEM_COMMIT
Protect:               00000002 PAGE_READONLY
More info: lmv m ModuleA
More info: !lmi ModuleA
More info: ln 0x28690b8


0:000> u 028690b8
ModuleA!ComputeB:
028690b8 050000c000 add eax,0C00000h
[...]
```

Another example (x64):

```
0:000> !heap -x -v c0000005
Search VM for address range 00000000c0000005 - 00000000c0000005 : 7feff63ab60 (c0000005),


0:000> !address 7feff63ab60
Usage: Image
Allocation Base: 000007fe`ff460000
Base Address:      000007fe`ff635000
End Address:     000007fe`ff63c000
Region Size:     00000000`00007000
Type:           01000000 MEM_IMAGE
State:          00001000 MEM_COMMIT
Protect:        00000004 PAGE_READWRITE
More info: lmv m ole32
```

---

[14] WinDbg Shortcuts, Memory Dump Analysis Anthology, Volume 7, page 29

```
More info: !lmi ole32
More info: ln 0x7feff63ab60
```

```
0:000> dp 7feff63ab60
000007fe`ff63ab60 00000000`c0000005 c0000194`00000001
000007fe`ff63ab70 00000001`00000000 00000000`c00000aa
000007fe`ff63ab80 80000002`00000001 00000001`00000000
000007fe`ff63ab90 00000000`c0000096 c000001d`00000001
000007fe`ff63aba0 00000001`00000000 00000000`80000003
000007fe`ff63abb0 c00000fd`00000001 00000001`00000000
000007fe`ff63abc0 00000000`c0000235 c0000006`00000001
000007fe`ff63abd0 00000001`00000000 00000000`c0000420
```

In the latter case, the data structure suggests a table of errors:

```
0:000> ln 7feff63ab60
(000007fe`ff63ab60) ole32!gReportedExceptions
```

Coincidental Frames

For certain stack traces, we should always be aware of coincidental frames similar to **Coincidental Symbolic Information** pattern (page 148) for raw stack data. Such frames can lead to a wrong analysis conclusion. Consider this stack trace fragment from a kernel memory dump:

```
0: kd> kL 100
ChildEBP RetAddr
9c5b6550 8082d9a4 nt!KeBugCheckEx+0x1b
9c5b6914 8088befa nt!KiDispatchException+0x3a2
9c5b697c 8088beae nt!CommonDispatchException+0x4a
9c5b699c 80a6056d nt!KiExceptionExit+0x186
9c5b69a0 80893ae2 hal!KeReleaseQueuedSpinLock+0x2d
9c5b6a08 b20c3de5 nt!MiFreePoolPages+0x7dc
WARNING: Stack unwind information not available. Following frames may be wrong.
9c5b6a48 b20c4107 DriverA+0x17de5
[...]
```

The frame with *MiFreePoolPages* symbol might suggest some sort of a pool corruption. We can even double check return addresses and see the valid common-sense assembly language code:

```
0: kd> ub 8088beae
nt!KiExceptionExit+0x167:
8088be8f 33c9            xor     ecx,ecx
8088be91 e81a000000      call    nt!CommonDispatchException (8088beb0)
8088be96 33d2            xor     edx,edx
8088be98 b901000000      mov     ecx,1
8088be9d e80e000000      call    nt!CommonDispatchException (8088beb0)
8088bea2 33d2            xor     edx,edx
8088bea4 b902000000      mov     ecx,2
8088bea9 e802000000      call    nt!CommonDispatchException (8088beb0)


0: kd> ub 80a6056d
hal!KeReleaseQueuedSpinLock+0x1b:
80a6055b 7511            jne     hal!KeReleaseQueuedSpinLock+0x2e (80a6056e)
80a6055d 50              push    eax
80a6055e f00fb119        lock cmpxchg dword ptr [ecx],ebx
80a60562 58              pop     eax
80a60563 7512            jne     hal!KeReleaseQueuedSpinLock+0x37 (80a60577)
80a60565 5b              pop     ebx
80a60566 8aca            mov     cl,dl
80a60568 e8871e0000      call    hal!KfLowerIrql (80a623f4)


0: kd> ub 80893ae2
nt!MiFreePoolPages+0x7c3:
80893ac9 761c            jbe     nt!MiFreePoolPages+0x7e1 (80893ae7)
80893acb ff75f8          push    dword ptr [ebp-8]
80893ace ff7508          push    dword ptr [ebp+8]
80893ad1 e87ea1fcff      call    nt!MiFreeNonPagedPool (8085dc54)
80893ad6 8a55ff          mov     dl,byte ptr [ebp-1]
80893ad9 6a0f            push    0Fh
```

```
80893adb 59                    pop      ecx
80893adc ff1524118080          call     dword ptr [nt!_imp_KeReleaseQueuedSpinLock (80801124)]


0: kd> ub b20c3de5
DriverA+0x17dcf:
b20c3dcf 51                    push     ecx
b20c3dd0 ff5010                call     dword ptr [eax+10h]
b20c3dd3 eb10                  jmp      DriverA+0x17de5 (b20c3de5)
b20c3dd5 8b5508                mov      edx,dword ptr [ebp+8]
b20c3dd8 52                    push     edx
b20c3dd9 8d86a0000000          lea      eax,[esi+0A0h]
b20c3ddf 50                    push     eax
b20c3de0 e8ebf1ffff            call     DriverA+0x16fd0 (b20c2fd0)
```

However, if we try to reconstruct the stack trace manually[15] we would naturally skip these three frames (shown in underlined bold):

```
9c5b6550 8082d9a4 nt!KeBugCheckEx+0x1b
9c5b6914 8088befa nt!KiDispatchException+0x3a2
9c5b697c 8088beae nt!CommonDispatchException+0x4a
9c5b699c 80a6056d nt!KiExceptionExit+0x186
9c5b69a0 80893ae2 hal!KeReleaseQueuedSpinLock+0x2d
9c5b6a08 b20c3de5 nt!MiFreePoolPages+0x7dc
9c5b6a48 b20c4107 DeriverA+0x17de5
[...]


0: kd> !thread
THREAD 8f277020  Cid 081c.7298  Teb: 7ff11000 Win32Thread: 00000000 RUNNING on processor 0
IRP List:
    8e234b60: (0006,0094) Flags: 00000000  Mdl: 00000000
Not impersonating
DeviceMap               e1002880
Owning Process          8fc78b80        Image:          ProcessA.exe
Attached Process        N/A             Image:          N/A
Wait Start TickCount    49046879        Ticks: 0
Context Switch Count    10
UserTime                00:00:00.000
KernelTime              00:00:00.000
Win32 Start Address DllA!ThreadA (0x7654dc90)
Start Address kernel32!BaseThreadStartThunk (0x77e617dc)
Stack Init 9c5b7000 Current 9c5b6c50 Base 9c5b7000 Limit 9c5b4000 Call 0
Priority 10 BasePriority 10 PriorityDecrement 0
ChildEBP RetAddr  Args to Child
[...]


0: kd> dds 9c5b4000 9c5b7000
9c5b4000  00000000
9c5b4004  00000000
9c5b4008  00000000
```

---

[15] Manual Stack Trace Reconstruction, Memory Dump Analysis Anthology, Volume 1, page 157

```
[...]
9c5b6290   ffdff13c
9c5b6294   9c5b6550
9c5b6298   80827e01 nt!KeBugCheckEx+0x1b
9c5b629c   00000008
9c5b62a0   00000286
[...]
9c5b654c   00000000
9c5b6550   9c5b6914
9c5b6554   8082d9a4 nt!KiDispatchException+0x3a2
9c5b6558   0000008e
9c5b655c   c0000005
[...]
9c5b6910   ffffffff
9c5b6914   9c5b6984
9c5b6918   8088befa nt!CommonDispatchException+0x4a
9c5b691c   9c5b6930
9c5b6920   00000000
[...]
9c5b6980   8088beae nt!KiExceptionExit+0x186
9c5b6984   9c5b6a08
9c5b6988   b20c3032 DriverA+0x17032
9c5b698c   badb0d00
9c5b6990   00000006
9c5b6994   8dc11cec
9c5b6998   808b6900 nt!KiTimerTableLock+0x3c0
9c5b699c   9c5b69d4
9c5b69a0   80a6056d hal!KeReleaseQueuedSpinLock+0x2d
9c5b69a4   80893ae2 nt!MiFreePoolPages+0x7dc
9c5b69a8   808b0b40 nt!NonPagedPoolDescriptor
9c5b69ac   03151fd0
9c5b69b0   00000000
9c5b69b4   00000000
[...]
9c5b6a04   8f47123b
9c5b6a08   9c5b6a48
9c5b6a0c   b20c3de5 DriverA+0x17de5
9c5b6a10   8e3640a0
9c5b6a14   8f4710d0
[...]
9c5b6a44   00000000
9c5b6a48   9c5b6a80
9c5b6a4c   b20c4107 DriverA+0x18107
9c5b6a50   8f4710d0
9c5b6a54   9c5b6a6c
[...]
```

If we try to find a pointer to the exception record we get this crash address:

```
0: kd> .exr 9c5b6930
ExceptionAddress: b20c3032 (DriverA+0x00017032)
   ExceptionCode: c0000005 (Access violation)
  ExceptionFlags: 00000000
NumberParameters: 2
   Parameter[0]: 00000000
   Parameter[1]: 00000157
Attempt to read from address 00000157
```

If we disassemble it we see **Inline Function Optimization** pattern (page 578) for string or memory copy, perhaps *wcscpy* function:

```
0: kd> u b20c3032
DriverA+0x17032:
b20c3032 f3a5          rep movs dword ptr es:[edi],dword ptr [esi]
b20c3034 8bcb          mov     ecx,ebx
b20c3036 83e103        and     ecx,3
b20c3039 f3a4          rep movs byte ptr es:[edi],byte ptr [esi]
b20c303b 8b750c        mov     esi,dword ptr [ebp+0Ch]
b20c303e 0fb7ca        movzx   ecx,dx
b20c3041 894e14        mov     dword ptr [esi+14h],ecx
b20c3044 8b700c        mov     esi,dword ptr [eax+0Ch]
```

So the problem happened in *DriverA* code, not in functions *MiFreePoolPages* or *KeReleaseQueuedSpinLock*.

Comments

This often happens when we have some "boundary" such as in **Exception Stack Trace** pattern (page 386).

Coincidental Symbolic Information

Linux

This is a Linux variant of **Coincidental Symbolic Information** pattern previously described for Mac OS X (page 146) and Windows (page 148) platforms. The idea is the same: to disassemble the address to see if the preceding instruction is a call. If it is indeed then most likely the symbolic address is a return address from past **Execution Residue** (page 389):

```
(gdb) x/i 0x4005e6
0x4005e6 <_Z6work_3v+9>: pop     %rbp


(gdb) disassemble 0x4005e6
Dump of assembler code for function _Z6work_3v:
0x00000000004005dd <+0>: push    %rbp
0x00000000004005de <+1>: mov     %rsp,%rbp
0x00000000004005e1 <+4>: callq   0x4005d2 <_Z6work_4v>
0x00000000004005e6 <+9>: pop     %rbp
0x00000000004005e7 <+10>: retq
End of assembler dump.


(gdb) x/4i 0x49c740-4
0x49c73c: add     %al,(%rax)
0x49c73e: add     %al,(%rax)
0x49c740 <default_attr>: add     %al,(%rax)
0x49c742 <default_attr+2>: add     %al,(%rax)
```

Mac OS X

This is a Mac OS X / GDB counterpart to **Coincidental Symbolic Information** pattern previously described for Windows platforms. The idea is the same: to disassemble the address to see if the preceding instruction is a call. If it is indeed then most likely the symbolic address is a return address from past **Execution Residue** (page 389):

```
(gdb) x $rsp
0x7fff6a162a38: 0x8fab9a9c


(gdb) x/1000a 0x7fff6a162000
[...]
0x7fff6a162960: 0x7fff6a162980 0x7fff6a167922
0x7fff6a162970: 0x0 0x0
0x7fff6a162980: 0x7fff6a162a50 0x7fff8a31e716 <dyld_stub_binder_+13>
0x7fff6a162990: 0x1 0x7fff6a162b00
0x7fff6a1629a0: 0x7fff6a162b10 0x7fff6a162bc0
0x7fff6a1629b0: 0x8 0x0
[...]
0x7fff6a162a00: 0x0 0x0
0x7fff6a162a10: 0x0 0x0
0x7fff6a162a20: 0x0 0x0
0x7fff6a162a30: 0x7fff6a162a60 0x7fff8fab9a9c <abort+177>
0x7fff6a162a40: 0x0 0x0
0x7fff6a162a50: 0x7fffffffffdf 0x0
[...]
0x7fff6a163040: 0x35000 0x0
0x7fff6a163050: 0x35000 0x500000007
0x7fff6a163060: 0x7 0x747865745f5f
0x7fff6a163070: 0x0 0x545845545f5f
0x7fff6a163080: 0x0 0x7fff5fc01000 <__dyld_stub_binding_helper>
0x7fff6a163090: 0x22c9d 0xc00001000
0x7fff6a1630a0: 0x0 0x80000400
[...]


(gdb) disass 0x7fff8a31e716
Dump of assembler code for function dyld_stub_binder_:
0x00007fff8a31e709 <dyld_stub_binder_+0>: mov 0x8(%rbp),%rdi
0x00007fff8a31e70d <dyld_stub_binder_+4>: mov 0x10(%rbp),%rsi
0x00007fff8a31e711 <dyld_stub_binder_+8>: callq 0x7fff8a31e86d <_Z21_dyld_fast_stub_entryPv1>
0x00007fff8a31e716 <dyld_stub_binder_+13>: mov %rax,%r11
0x00007fff8a31e719 <dyld_stub_binder_+16>: movdqa 0x40(%rsp),%xmm0
0x00007fff8a31e71f <dyld_stub_binder_+22>: movdqa 0x50(%rsp),%xmm1
0x00007fff8a31e725 <dyld_stub_binder_+28>: movdqa 0x60(%rsp),%xmm2
0x00007fff8a31e72b <dyld_stub_binder_+34>: movdqa 0x70(%rsp),%xmm3
0x00007fff8a31e731 <dyld_stub_binder_+40>: movdqa 0x80(%rsp),%xmm4
0x00007fff8a31e73a <dyld_stub_binder_+49>: movdqa 0x90(%rsp),%xmm5
0x00007fff8a31e743 <dyld_stub_binder_+58>: movdqa 0xa0(%rsp),%xmm6
0x00007fff8a31e74c <dyld_stub_binder_+67>: movdqa 0xb0(%rsp),%xmm7
0x00007fff8a31e755 <dyld_stub_binder_+76>: mov (%rsp),%rdi
0x00007fff8a31e759 <dyld_stub_binder_+80>: mov 0x8(%rsp),%rsi
0x00007fff8a31e75e <dyld_stub_binder_+85>: mov 0x10(%rsp),%rdx
0x00007fff8a31e763 <dyld_stub_binder_+90>: mov 0x18(%rsp),%rcx
0x00007fff8a31e768 <dyld_stub_binder_+95>: mov 0x20(%rsp),%r8
0x00007fff8a31e76d <dyld_stub_binder_+100>: mov 0x28(%rsp),%r9
```

```
0x00007fff8a31e772 <dyld_stub_binder_+105>: mov 0x30(%rsp),%rax
0x00007fff8a31e777 <dyld_stub_binder_+110>: add $0xc0,%rsp
0x00007fff8a31e77e <dyld_stub_binder_+117>: pop %rbp
0x00007fff8a31e77f <dyld_stub_binder_+118>: add $0x10,%rsp
0x00007fff8a31e783 <dyld_stub_binder_+122>: jmpq *%r11


(gdb) x/2i 0x7fff8fab9a9c
0x7fff8fab9a9c <abort+177>: mov $0x2710,%edi
0x7fff8fab9aa1 <abort+182>: callq 0x7fff8fab9c43 <usleep$nocancel>


(gdb) disass 0x7fff8fab9a9c-5 0x7fff8fab9a9c
Dump of assembler code from 0x7fff8fab9a97 to 0x7fff8fab9a9c:
0x00007fff8fab9a97 <abort+172>: callq 0x7fff8fb1f54a <dyld_stub_kill>
End of assembler dump.


(gdb) disass 0x7fff5fc01000
Dump of assembler code for function __dyld_stub_binding_helper:
0x00007fff5fc01000 <__dyld_stub_binding_helper+0>: add %al,(%rax)
0x00007fff5fc01002 <__dyld_stub_binding_helper+2>: add %al,(%rax)
0x00007fff5fc01004 <__dyld_stub_binding_helper+4>: add %al,(%rax)
0x00007fff5fc01006 <__dyld_stub_binding_helper+6>: add %al,(%rax)
End of assembler dump.


(gdb) x/10 0x7fff5fc01000-0x10
0x7fff5fc00ff0: 0x00000000 0x00000000 0x00000000 0x00000000
0x7fff5fc01000 <__dyld_stub_binding_helper>: 0x00000000 0x00000000 0x00000000 0x00000000
0x7fff5fc01010 <__dyld_offset_to_dyld_all_image_infos>: 0x00000000 0x00000000
```

Windows

Raw stack dumps can be useful for finding any suspicious modules that might have caused the problem. For example, it is common for some programs to install hooks to monitor GUI changes, intercept window messages to provide value added services on top of the existing applications. These hooks are implemented as DLLs. Another use would be to examine raw stack data for printer drivers that caused problems before. The fact that these modules had been loaded does not mean that they were used. If we find references to their code, it means that they might have been used.

However, when looking at raw stack dump with symbol information, we should be aware of **Coincidental Symbolic Information** pattern. Here is the first example. Loading the crash dump and displaying the problem thread stack shows the following reference:

```
...
...
...
00b1ed00   0063006f
00b1ed04   006d0075
00b1ed08   006e0065
00b1ed0c   00200074
00b1ed10   006f004c
00b1ed14   00640061
00b1ed18   00720065
00b1ed1c   005b0020
00b1ed20   00500055
00b1ed24   003a0044
00b1ed28   00430050 Application!Array::operator=+0x2f035
00b1ed2c   0035004c
00b1ed30   005d0063
00b1ed34   00630000
00b1ed38   0000005d
...
...
...
```

Applying symbols gives us a more meaningful name:

```
...
...
...
00b1ed00   0063006f
00b1ed04   006d0075
00b1ed08   006e0065
00b1ed0c   00200074
00b1ed10   006f004c
00b1ed14   00640061
00b1ed18   00720065
00b1ed1c   005b0020
00b1ed20   00500055
00b1ed24   003a0044
00b1ed28   00430050 Application!Print::DocumentLoad+0x5f
```

```
00b1ed2c  0035004c
00b1ed30  005d0063
00b1ed34  00630000
...
...
...
```

However, this is the pure coincidence. The data pattern 00NN00NN clearly belongs to a Unicode string:

```
0:020> du 00b1ed00
00b1ed00  "ocument Loader [UPD:PCL5c]"
```

It just happens that 00430050 value can be interpreted as an address that falls within *Application* module address range and its code section:

```
0:020> lm
start     end        module name
00400000 0044d000   Application
```

In the second example, the crash dump is from some 3rd-party application called *AppSql* for which we do not have PDB files. Also, we know that *myhook.dll* is installed as a system-wide hook, and it had some problems in the past. It is loaded into any address space but is not necessarily used. We want to see if there are traces of it on the problem thread stack. Dumping stack contents shows us the only one reference:

```
...
...
...
00118cb0  37302f38
00118cb4  00000000
00118cb8  10008e00 myhook!notify_me+0x22c
00118cbc  01400000
00118cc0  00118abc
00118cc4  06a129f0
00118cc8  00118d04
00118ccc  02bc57d0
00118cd0  04ba5d74
00118cd4  00118d30
00118cd8  0000001c
00118cdc  00000010
00118ce0  075922bc
00118ce4  04a732e0
00118ce8  075922bc
00118cec  04a732e0
00118cf0  0066a831 AppSql+0x26a831
00118cf4  04a732d0
00118cf8  02c43190
00118cfc  00000001
00118d00  0000001c
00118d04  00118d14
00118d08  0049e180 AppSql+0x9e180
00118d0c  02c43190
00118d10  0000001c
```

```
00118d14   00118d34
…
…
…


0:020> lm
start     end        module name
00400000 00ba8000   AppSql
...
...
...
10000000 100e0000   myhook
```

The address 10008e00 looks very "round" and it might be the set of bit flags, and also, if we disassemble the code at this address backward, we do not see the usual *call* instruction that saved that address on the stack:

```
0:000> ub 10008e00
myhook!notify_me+0x211
10008de5 81c180000000    add     ecx,80h
10008deb 899578ffffff    mov     dword ptr [ebp-88h],edx
10008df1 89458c          mov     dword ptr [ebp-74h],eax
10008df4 894d98          mov     dword ptr [ebp-68h],ecx
10008df7 6a01            push    1
10008df9 8d45ec          lea     eax,[ebp-14h]
10008dfc 50              push    eax
10008dfd ff75e0          push    dword ptr [ebp-20h]
```

In contrast, the other two addresses are return addresses saved on the stack:

```
0:000> ub 0066a831
AppSql+0x26a81e:
0066a81e 8bfb            mov     edi,ebx
0066a820 f3a5            rep movs dword ptr es:[edi],dword ptr [esi]
0066a822 8bca            mov     ecx,edx
0066a824 83e103          and     ecx,3
0066a827 f3a4            rep movs byte ptr es:[edi],byte ptr [esi]
0066a829 8b00            mov     eax,dword ptr [eax]
0066a82b 50              push    eax
0066a82c e8affeffff      call    AppSql+0x26a6e0 (0066a6e0)


0:000> ub 0049e180
AppSql+0x9e16f:
0049e16f cc              int     3
0049e170 55              push    ebp
0049e171 8bec            mov     ebp,esp
0049e173 8b4510          mov     eax,dword ptr [ebp+10h]
0049e176 8b4d0c          mov     ecx,dword ptr [ebp+0Ch]
0049e179 50              push    eax
0049e17a 51              push    ecx
0049e17b e840c61c00      call    AppSql+0x26a7c0 (0066a7c0)
```

Therefore, the appearance of *myhook!notify_me+0x22c* could be a coincidence unless it was a pointer to a function. However, if it was the function pointer address then it wouldn't have pointed to the middle of the function call sequence that pushes arguments:

```
0:000> ub 10008e00
myhook!notify_me+0x211
10008de5 81c180000000    add     ecx,80h
10008deb 899578ffffff    mov     dword ptr [ebp-88h],edx
10008df1 89458c          mov     dword ptr [ebp-74h],eax
10008df4 894d98          mov     dword ptr [ebp-68h],ecx
10008df7 6a01            push    1
10008df9 8d45ec          lea     eax,[ebp-14h]
10008dfc 50              push    eax
10008dfd ff75e0          push    dword ptr [ebp-20h]


0:000> u 10008e00
myhook!notify_me+0x22c
10008e00 e82ff1ffff      call    myhook!copy_data (10007f34)
10008e05 8b8578ffffff    mov     eax,dword ptr [ebp-88h]
10008e0b 3945ac          cmp     dword ptr [ebp-54h],eax
10008e0e 731f            jae     myhook!notify_me+0x25b (10008e2f)
10008e10 8b4598          mov     eax,dword ptr [ebp-68h]
10008e13 0fbf00          movsx   eax,word ptr [eax]
10008e16 8945a8          mov     dword ptr [ebp-58h],eax
10008e19 8b45e0          mov     eax,dword ptr [ebp-20h]
```

Also, because we have a source code and private symbols, we know that if it was a function pointer, then it would have been *myhook!notify_me* address and not *notify_me+0x22c* address.

All this evidence supports the hypothesis that *myhook* occurrence on the problem stack is just the coincidence and should be ignored.

To add, the most coincidental symbolic information we have found so far in one crash dump is an accidental correspondence between exported *_DebuggerHookData* and the location of the postmortem debugger NTSD:

```
002dd434 003a0043
002dd438 0057005c
002dd43c 004e0049 LegacyApp!_DebuggerHookData+0xc4a5
002dd440 004f0044 LegacyApp!_DebuggerHookData+0x1c4a0
002dd444 00530057
002dd448 0073005c
002dd44c 00730079
002dd450 00650074
002dd454 0033006d
002dd458 005c0032
002dd45c 0074006e
002dd460 00640073
002dd464 0065002e


0:000> du 002dd434
002dd434 "C:\WINDOWS\system32\ntsd.exe"
```

Comments

Due to possible **Disassembly Ambiguity** (page 256) we should try to specify the different number of instructions to disassembly, for example, **ub** L1, **ub** L2.

Constant Subtrace

Variable Subtrace (page 1175) analysis pattern was introduced for inter-correlational (**Inter-Correlation**[16]) analysis of CPU spikes across memory snapshots with just one thread involved. In contrast, we found **Constant Subtrace** pattern useful in **Wait Chain** (page 1199) analysis involving several threads in just one memory snapshot (intra-correlational analysis, **Intra-Correlation**[17]). Here a constant subtrace groups stack traces from **Stack Trace Collection** (page 1052) with a bifurcation stack trace frame (similar to **Bifurcation Point** trace analysis pattern[18]) providing some wait chain relationship hint. Such traces may be initially found by the preceding wait chain analysis or by technology-specific subtraces such as ALPC/RPC server thread frames (as seen in an example stack from COM interface invocation, **Technology-Specific Subtrace**, page 1103). Here is a minimal stack trace diagram (similar to minimal trace graphs introduced in *Accelerated Windows Software Trace Analysis* training[19]) illustrating the pattern (it also shows **Spiking Thread** pattern in user space as seen from a complete memory dump, page 992):

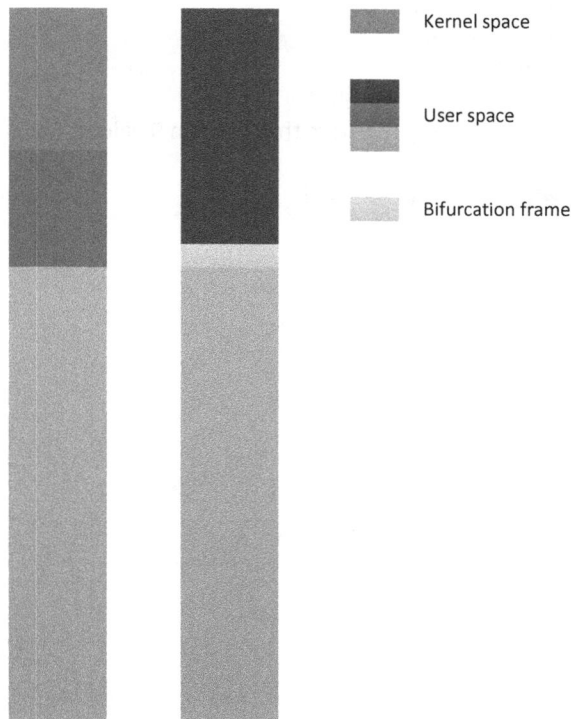

- Kernel space
- User space
- Bifurcation frame

---

[16] Memory Dump Analysis Anthology, Volume 4, page 350

[17] Ibid., Volume 3, page 347

[18] Ibid., Volume 4, page 343

[19] http://www.patterndiagnostics.com/Training/Accelerated-Software-Trace-Analysis-Part1-Public.pdf

Context Pointer

The collection of register values can be interpreted as **Context Pointer** to various memory locations:

```
0:000> !for_each_register -c:.if (${@#RegisterValue} > 0xFFFF) {.printf "${@#RegisterName}: %p -> %p\n",
${@#RegisterValue}, poi(${@#RegisterValue})}
rdx: 000000e4c0afe888 -> 00000000000000b4
rsp: 000000e4c0afe488 -> 00007ffecc888037
r9: 00000000ffffffff -> Memory access error at ')'
r11: 000000e4c0afdc30 -> 0000000000000090
r12: 00000000ffffffff -> Memory access error at ')'
r13: 000000e4c0afe888 -> 00000000000000b4
rip: 00007ffecf6bcbc4 -> 00841f0fc32ecdc3
edx: 00000000c0afe888 -> Memory access error at ')'
esp: 00000000c0afe488 -> Memory access error at ')'
r9d: 00000000ffffffff -> Memory access error at ')'
r11d: 00000000c0afdc30 -> Memory access error at ')'
r12d: 00000000ffffffff -> Memory access error at ')'
r13d: 00000000c0afe888 -> Memory access error at ')'
eip: 00000000cf6bcbc4 -> Memory access error at ')'
```

We filter pointer values to avoid printing many registers that contain 0 values.

Individual pointers can also be **Pointer Cones** (page 895).

Corrupt Dump

This is quite a frequent pattern and usually becomes the consequence of **Truncated Dump** pattern (page 1130). When we open such crash dumps, we usually notice immediate errors in WinDbg output. We can distinguish between two classes of corrupt memory dumps: totally corrupt and partially corrupt. Total corruption is less frequent, results from invalid file header and manifests itself in an error message box with the following Win32 error:

```
Loading Dump File [C:\Documents and Settings\All Users\Application Data\Microsoft\Dr
Watson\user_corrupted.dmp]
ERROR: Directory not present in dump (RVA 0x20202020)
Could not open dump file [C:\Documents and Settings\All Users\Application Data\Microsoft\Dr
Watson\user_corrupted.dmp], Win32 error 1392
    "The file or directory is corrupted and unreadable."
```

Partially corrupt files can be loaded, but some critical information is missing, for example, the list of loaded modules and context for all or some processors. We can see lots of messages in WinDbg output like:

```
GetContextState failed, 0x80070026
Unable to get current machine context, Win32 error 0n38
```

or

```
GetContextState failed, 0x80004005
```

or

```
GetContextState failed, 0xD0000147
```

which mean:

```
?: kd> !error 0x80070026
Error code: (HRESULT) 0x80070026 (2147942438) - Reached the end of the file.

?: kd> !error 0x80004005
Error code: (HRESULT) 0x80004005 (2147500037) - Unspecified error

?: kd> !error 0xD0000147
Error code: (NTSTATUS) 0xd0000147 (3489661255) - {No Paging File Specified}  No paging file was specified
in the system configuration.
```

However, in many such cases we can still see system information and bugcheck parameters:

```
***********************************
THIS DUMP FILE IS PARTIALLY CORRUPT.
KdDebuggerDataBlock is not present or unreadable.
***********************************
Unable to read PsLoadedModuleList
KdDebuggerData.KernBase < SystemRangeStart
Windows Server 2003 Kernel Version 3790 MP (4 procs) Free x86 compatible
Product: Server, suite: TerminalServer
Kernel base = 0x00000000 PsLoadedModuleList = 0x808af9c8
```

```
Debug session time: Wed Nov 21 20:29:31.373 2007 (GMT+0)
System Uptime: 0 days 0:45:02.312
Unable to read PsLoadedModuleList
KdDebuggerData.KernBase < SystemRangeStart
Loading Kernel Symbols
Unable to read PsLoadedModuleList
GetContextState failed, 0x80070026
GetContextState failed, 0x80070026
CS descriptor lookup failed
GetContextState failed, 0x80070026
GetContextState failed, 0x80070026
GetContextState failed, 0x80070026
GetContextState failed, 0x80070026
Unable to get program counter
GetContextState failed, 0x80070026
Unable to get current machine context, Win32 error 0n38
GetContextState failed, 0x80070026
GetContextState failed, 0x80070026

Use !analyze -v to get detailed debugging information.

BugCheck 20, {0, ffff, 0, 1}

***** Debugger could not find nt in module list, module list might be corrupt, error 0x80070057.

GetContextState failed, 0x80070026
Unable to read selector for PCR for processor 0
GetContextState failed, 0x80070026
Unable to read selector for PCR for processor 0
GetContextState failed, 0x80070026
Unable to read selector for PCR for processor 0
GetContextState failed, 0x80070026
GetContextState failed, 0x80070026
Unable to get current machine context, Win32 error 0n38
GetContextState failed, 0x80070026
Unable to get current machine context, Win32 error 0n38
GetContextState failed, 0x80070026
```

Looking at bugcheck number and parameters, we can form some signature and check in our crash database. We can also request a kernel minidump corresponding to debug session time.

Comments

The main point is that if you have a corrupt dump, you may still identify the problem. Also, system administrators and support engineers can identify corrupt dumps earlier and request the new ones.

Corrupt Structure

Typical signals of **Corrupt Structure** include:

- **Regular Data** (page 925) such as ASCII and UNICODE fragments over substructures and pointer areas
- Large values where you expect small and vice versa
- User space address values where we expect kernel space and vice versa
- Malformed and partially zeroed _LIST_ENTRY data (see exercise C3[20] for linked list navigation)
- Memory read errors for pointer dereferences or inaccessible memory indicators (**??**)
- Memory read error at the end of the linked list while traversing structures

```
0: kd> dt _ERESOURCE ffffd0002299f830
ntdll!_ERESOURCE
+0x000 SystemResourcesList : _LIST_ENTRY [ 0xffffc000`07b64800 - 0xffffe000`02a79970 ]
+0x010 OwnerTable       : 0xffffe000`02a79940 _OWNER_ENTRY
+0x018 ActiveCount      : 0n0
+0x01a Flag             : 0
+0x01a ReservedLowFlags : 0 ''
+0x01b WaiterPriority   : 0 ''
+0x020 SharedWaiters    : 0x00000000`00000001 _KSEMAPHORE
+0x028 ExclusiveWaiters : 0xffffe000`02a79a58 _KEVENT
+0x030 OwnerEntry       : _OWNER_ENTRY
+0x040 ActiveEntries    : 0
+0x044 ContentionCount  : 0
+0x048 NumberOfSharedWaiters : 0x7b64800
+0x04c NumberOfExclusiveWaiters : 0xffffc000
+0x050 Reserved2        : (null)
+0x058 Address          : 0xffffd000`2299f870 Void
+0x058 CreatorBackTraceIndex : 0xffffd000`2299f870
+0x060 SpinLock         : 1


0: kd> dt _ERESOURCE ffffd0002299d830
ntdll!_ERESOURCE
+0x000 SystemResourcesList : _LIST_ENTRY [ 0x000001e0`00000280 - 0x00000000`00000004 ]
+0x010 OwnerTable       : 0x00000000`0000003c _OWNER_ENTRY
+0x018 ActiveCount      : 0n0
+0x01a Flag             : 0
+0x01a ReservedLowFlags : 0 "
+0x01b WaiterPriority   : 0 "
+0x020 SharedWaiters    : 0x0000003c`000001e0 _KSEMAPHORE
+0x028 ExclusiveWaiters : (null)
+0x030 OwnerEntry       : _OWNER_ENTRY
+0x040 ActiveEntries    : 0
+0x044 ContentionCount  : 0x7f
+0x048 NumberOfSharedWaiters : 0x7f
+0x04c NumberOfExclusiveWaiters : 0x7f
```

---

[20] Advanced Windows Memory Dump Analysis with Data Structures, Third Edition, http://www.patterndiagnostics.com/advanced-windows-memory-dump-analysis-book

```
+0x050 Reserved2          : 0x00000001`00000001 Void
+0x058 Address            : 0x00000000`00000005 Void
+0x058 CreatorBackTraceIndex : 5
+0x060 SpinLock           : 0
```

However, we need to be sure that we supplied the correct pointer to **dt** WinDbg command. One of the signs that the pointer was incorrect is memory read errors or all zeroes:

```
0: kd> dt _ERESOURCE ffffd000229af830
ntdll!_ERESOURCE
+0x000 SystemResourcesList : _LIST_ENTRY [ 0x00000000`00000000 - 0x00000000`00000000 ]
+0x010 OwnerTable : (null)
+0x018 ActiveCount : 0n0
+0x01a Flag : 0
+0x01a ReservedLowFlags : 0 ''
+0x01b WaiterPriority : 0 ''
+0x020 SharedWaiters : (null)
+0x028 ExclusiveWaiters : (null)
+0x030 OwnerEntry : _OWNER_ENTRY
+0x040 ActiveEntries : 0
+0x044 ContentionCount : 0
+0x048 NumberOfSharedWaiters : 0
+0x04c NumberOfExclusiveWaiters : 0
+0x050 Reserved2 : (null)
+0x058 Address : (null)
+0x058 CreatorBackTraceIndex : 0
+0x060 SpinLock : 0


0: kd> dt _ERESOURCE ffffd00022faf830
ntdll!_ERESOURCE
+0x000 SystemResourcesList : _LIST_ENTRY
+0x010 OwnerTable       : ????
+0x018 ActiveCount      : ??
+0x01a Flag             : ??
+0x01a ReservedLowFlags : ??
+0x01b WaiterPriority   : ??
+0x020 SharedWaiters    : ????
+0x028 ExclusiveWaiters : ????
+0x030 OwnerEntry       : _OWNER_ENTRY
+0x040 ActiveEntries    : ??
+0x044 ContentionCount  : ??
+0x048 NumberOfSharedWaiters : ??
+0x04c NumberOfExclusiveWaiters : ??
+0x050 Reserved2        : ????
+0x058 Address          : ????
+0x058 CreatorBackTraceIndex : ??
+0x060 SpinLock         : ??
Memory read error ffffd00022faf890
```

Coupled Machines

Sometimes we have threads that wait for a response from another machine (for example, via RPC). For most of the time, **Coupled Processes** pattern (page 162) covers that if we assume that processes in that pattern are not restricted to the same machine. However, sometimes we have threads that provide hints for dependency on another machine through their data, and that could also involve additional threads from different processes to accomplish the task. Here we need another pattern that we call **Coupled Machines**. For example, the following thread on a computer SERVER_A is trying to set the current working directory that resides on a computer SERVER_B:

```
kd> kv 100
ChildEBP RetAddr  Args to Child
b881c8d4 804e1bf2 89cd9c80 89cd9c10 804e1c3e nt!KiSwapContext+0x2f
b881c8e0 804e1c3e 00000000 89e35b08 89e35b34 nt!KiSwapThread+0x8a
b881c908 f783092e 00000000 00000000 00000006 nt!KeWaitForSingleObject+0x1c2
b881c930 f7830a3b 89e35b08 00000000 f78356d8 Mup!PktPostSystemWork+0x3d
b881c94c f7836712 b881c9b0 b881c9b0 b881c9b8 Mup!PktGetReferral+0xce
b881c980 f783644f b881c9b0 b881c9b8 00000000 Mup!PktCreateDomainEntry+0x224
b881c9d0 f7836018 0000000b 00000000 b881c9f0 Mup!DfsFsctrlIsThisADfsPath+0x2bb
b881ca14 f7835829 89a2e130 899ba350 b881caac Mup!CreateRedirectedFile+0x2cd
b881ca70 804e13eb 89f46ee8 89a2e130 89a2e130 Mup!MupCreate+0x1cb
b881ca80 805794b6 89f46ed0 89df3c44 b881cc18 nt!IopfCallDriver+0x31
b881cb60 8056d03b 89f46ee8 00000000 89df3ba0 nt!IopParseDevice+0xa12
b881cbd8 805701e7 00000000 b881cc18 00000042 nt!ObpLookupObjectName+0x53c
b881cc2c 80579b12 00000000 00000000 00003801 nt!ObOpenObjectByName+0xea
b881cca8 80579be1 00cff67c 00100020 00cff620 nt!IopCreateFile+0x407
b881cd04 80579d18 00cff67c 00100020 00cff620 nt!IoCreateFile+0x8e
b881cd44 804dd99f 00cff67c 00100020 00cff620 nt!NtOpenFile+0x27
b881cd44 7c90e514 00cff67c 00100020 00cff620 nt!KiFastCallEntry+0xfc
00cff5f0 7c90d5aa 00cff67c 00100020 ntdll!KiFastSystemCallRet
00cff5f4 7c91e8dd 00cff67c 00100020 00cff620 ntdll!ZwOpenFile+0xc
00cff69c 7c831e58 00cff6a8 00460044 0078894a ntdll!RtlSetCurrentDirectory_U+0x169
00cff6b0 7731889e 0078894a 00000000 00000001 kernel32!SetCurrentDirectoryW+0x2b
00cffb84 7730ffbb 00788450 00788b38 00cffbe0 schedsvc!CSchedWorker::RunNTJob+0x221
00cffe34 7730c03a 01ea9108 8ed032d4 00787df8 schedsvc!CSchedWorker::RunJobs+0x304
00cffe74 77310e4d 7c80a749 00000000 00000000 schedsvc!CSchedWorker::RunNextJobs+0x129
00cfff28 77310efc 7730b592 00000000 000ba4bc schedsvc!CSchedWorker::MainServiceLoop+0x6d9
00cfff2c 7730b592 00000000 000ba4bc 0009a2bc schedsvc!SchedMain+0xb
00cfff5c 7730b69f 00000001 000ba4b8 00cfffa0 schedsvc!SchedStart+0x266
00cfff6c 010011cc 00000001 000ba4b8 00000000 schedsvc!SchedServiceMain+0x33
00cfffa0 77df354b 00000001 000ba4b8 0007e898 svchost!ServiceStarter+0x9e
00cfffb4 7c80b729 000ba4b0 00000000 0007e898 ADVAPI32!ScSvcctrlThreadA+0x12
00cfffec 00000000 77df3539 000ba4b0 00000000 kernel32!BaseThreadStart+0x37

kd> du /c 90 0078894a
0078894a  "\\SERVER_B\Share_X$\Folder_Q"
```

Coupled Modules

Often we identify a pattern that points to a particular module such as a driver or DLL other modules could use functional services from and, therefore, the latter modules can be implicated in abnormal software behavior. For example, detected **Insufficient Memory** in kernel paged pool (page 599) pointed to a driver that owns a pool tag DRV:

```
1: kd> !poolused 4
Sorting by Paged Pool Consumed

Tag  Allocs  Frees   Diff  Used
DRV  1466496 1422361 44135 188917256 UNKNOWN pooltag 'DRV ', please update pooltag.txt
File 6334830 6284036 50794 6735720 File objects
Thre 53721 45152 8569 4346432 Thread objects , Binary: nt!ps
[...]
```

This module is known to be **Directing Module** (page 255) to other drivers (from the stack trace perspective), but we also know that other (directed) modules use its services that require memory allocation.

Comments
___

We can also see if 2 modules are coupled statically by examining their import tables (**!dh**).

Coupled Processes

Semantics

In addition to **Strong** (page 162) and **Weak** (page 164) process coupling patterns, we also have another variant that we call **Semantic** coupling. Some processes (not necessarily from the same vendor) cooperate to provide certain functionality. The cooperation might not involve trackable and visible inter-process communication such as (A)LPC/RPC or pipes but involve events, shared memory, and other possible mechanisms not explicitly visible when we look at memory dumps. In many cases, after finding problems in one or several processes from a semantic group, we also look at the remaining processes from that group to see if there are some anomalies there as well. The one example I encounter often can be generalized as follows: we have an ALPC wait chain *ProcessA -> ProcessB <-> ProcessC* (not necessarily **Deadlock**, page 217) but the crucial piece of functionality is also implemented in *ProcessD*. Sometimes *ProcessD* is healthy, and the problem resides in *ProcessC* or *ProcessB*, and sometimes, when we look at *ProcessD* we find evidence of an earlier problem pattern there so the focus of recommendations shifts to one of the *ProcessD* modules.

Strong

Sometimes we have a problem that some functionality is not available, or it is unresponsive when we request it. Then we can suppose that the process implementing that functionality has crashed or hangs. If we know the relationship between processes, we can request several user dumps at once or a complete memory dump to analyze the dependency between processes by looking at their stack traces. This is an example of the system level crash dump analysis pattern that we call **Coupled Processes.**

Process relationship can be implemented via different interprocess communication mechanisms (IPC), for example, Remote Procedure Call (RPC) via LPC (Local Procedure Call) which can be easily identified in **Stack Traces** (page 1033).

Our favorite example here is when some application tries to print and hangs. Printing API is exported from *WINSPOOL.DLL*, and it forwards via RPC most requests to Windows Print Spooler service. Therefore, it is logical to take two dumps, one from that application, and one from *spoolsv.exe*. A similar example is from Citrix terminal services environments related to printer autocreation when there are dependencies between Citrix Printing Service *CpSvc.exe* and *spoolsv.exe*. Therefore if new user connections hang and restarting both printing services resolves the issue then we might need to analyze memory dumps from both services together to confirm this **Procedure Call Chain**[21] and find the problem 3rd-party printing component or driver.

Back to our favorite example. In the hang application we have the following thread:

```
  18  Id: 2130.6320 Suspend: 1 Teb: 7ffa8000 Unfrozen
ChildEBP RetAddr
01eae170 7c821c94 ntdll!KiFastSystemCallRet
01eae174 77c72700 ntdll!NtRequestWaitReplyPort+0xc
01eae1c8 77c713ba rpcrt4!LRPC_CCALL::SendReceive+0x230
01eae1d4 77c72c7f rpcrt4!I_RpcSendReceive+0x24
01eae1e8 77ce219b rpcrt4!NdrSendReceive+0x2b
01eae5d0 7307c9ef rpcrt4!NdrClientCall2+0x22e
01eae5e8 73082d8d winspool!RpcAddPrinter+0x1c
01eaea70 0040d81a winspool!AddPrinterW+0x102
01eaef58 0040ee7c App!AddNewPrinter+0x816
...
...
...
```

Notice *winspool* and *rpcrt4* modules. The application is calling spooler service using RPC to add a new printer and waiting for a reply back. Looking at spooler service dump shows several threads displaying message boxes and waiting for user input:

---

[21] https://www.dumpanalysis.org/blog/index.php/2020/09/18/crash-dump-analysis-patterns-part-272/

```
 20   Id: 790.5950 Suspend: 1 Teb: 7ffa2000 Unfrozen
ChildEBP RetAddr  Args to Child
03deea70 7739d02f 77392bf3 00000000 00000000 ntdll!KiFastSystemCallRet
03deeaa8 7738f122 03dd0058 00000000 00000001 user32!NtUserWaitMessage+0xc
03deead0 773a1722 77380000 00123690 00000000 user32!InternalDialogBox+0xd0
03deed90 773a1004 03deeeec 03dae378 03dae160 user32!SoftModalMessageBox+0x94b
03deeee0 773b1a28 03deeeec 00000028 00000000 user32!MessageBoxWorker+0x2ba
03deef38 773b19c4 00000000 03defb9c 03def39c user32!MessageBoxTimeoutW+0x7a
03deef58 773b19a0 00000000 03defb9c 03def39c user32!MessageBoxExW+0x1b
03deef74 021f265b 00000000 03defb9c 03def39c user32!MessageBoxW+0x45
WARNING: Stack unwind information not available. Following frames may be wrong.
03deef88 00000000 03dae160 03deffec 03dae16a PrinterDriver!UninstallerInstall+0x2cb
```

Dumping the 3rd parameter of *MessageBoxW* using WinDbg **du** command shows the message:

> "Installation of the software for your printer is now complete. Restart your computer to make the new settings active."

Another example is when one process starts another and then waiting for it to finish:

```
0 Id: 2a34.24d0 Suspend: 1 Teb: 7ffde000 Unfrozen
ChildEBP RetAddr
0007ec8c 7c822124 ntdll!KiFastSystemCallRet
0007ec90 77e6bad8 ntdll!NtWaitForSingleObject+0xc
0007ed00 77e6ba42 kernel32!WaitForSingleObjectEx+0xac
0007ed14 01002f4c kernel32!WaitForSingleObject+0x12
0007f79c 01003137 userinit!ExecApplication+0x2d3
0007f7dc 0100366b userinit!ExecProcesses+0x1bb
0007fe68 010041fd userinit!StartTheShell+0x132
0007ff1c 010056f1 userinit!WinMain+0x263
0007ffc0 77e523e5 userinit!WinMainCRTStartup+0x186
```

Comments

Good diagrams explaining basic printing architecture[22].
Print driver isolation in W2K8 R2/W7[23].

---

[22] http://blogs.technet.com/b/askperf/archive/2007/06/19/basic-printing-architecture.aspx
[23] http://blogs.technet.com/b/askperf/archive/2009/10/08/windows-7-windows-server-2008-r2-print-driver-isolation.aspx

Weak

Previously introduced **Strong** version of **Coupled Processes** (page 162) pattern involves an active request (or an action) and an active wait for a response (or the action status):

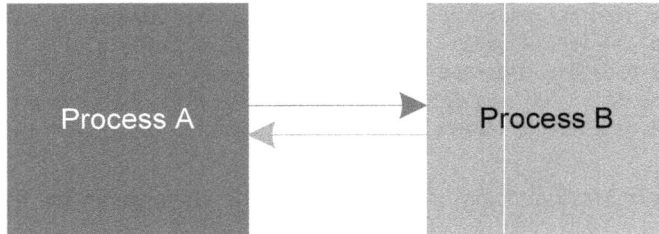

It is illustrated on this simple UML sequence diagram (process timeline represent collective request-response threads):

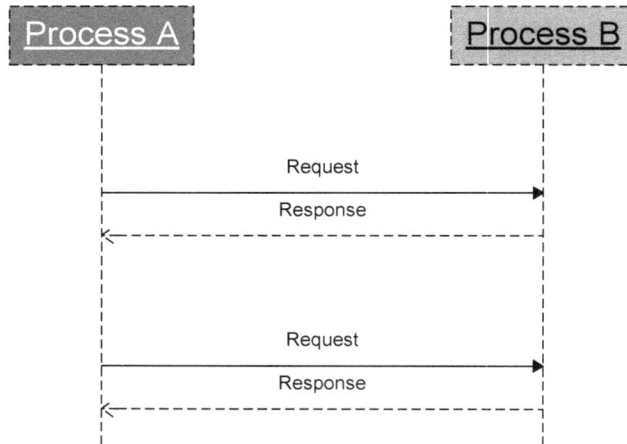

However, there is so-called **Weak** coupling when a process subscribes for notifications. Such threads, for the most time, are **Passive Threads** (page 879), and processes are not blocked:

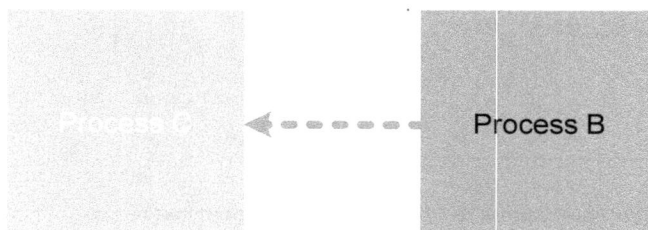

The coupling manifests itself when notifier threads start spiking CPU (**Spiking Thread**, page 992) and bring their share of CPU consumption to the notified threads:

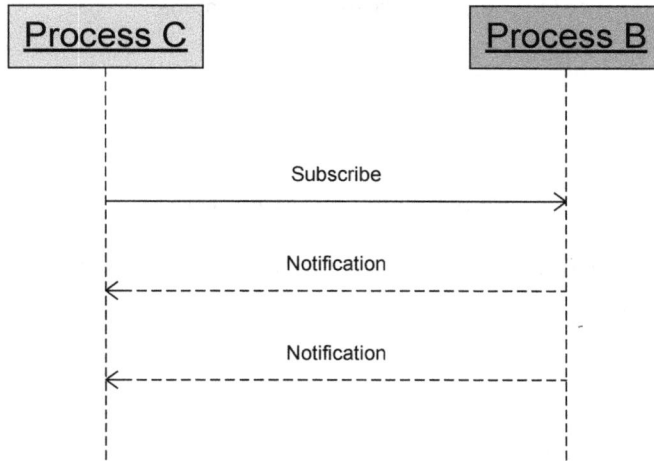

Here is an example of such threads:

```
   5  Id: 61018.dbec Suspend: 1 Teb: 7ffae000 Unfrozen
ChildEBP RetAddr
01e3fa68 7c82787b ntdll!KiFastSystemCallRet
01e3fa6c 77c80a6e ntdll!NtRequestWaitReplyPort+0xc
01e3fab8 77c7fcf0 rpcrt4!LRPC_CCALL::SendReceive+0x230
01e3fac4 77c80673 rpcrt4!I_RpcSendReceive+0x24
01e3fad8 77ce315a rpcrt4!NdrSendReceive+0x2b
01e3fec0 771f4fbd rpcrt4!NdrClientCall2+0x22e
01e3fed8 771f4f60 winsta!RpcWinStationWaitSystemEvent+0x1c
01e3ff20 6582116c winsta!WinStationWaitSystemEvent+0x51
[...]
01e3ffec 00000000 kernel32!BaseThreadStart+0x34
```

In cases of synchronous notifications, if a notified thread is blocked we have an instance of a reversed strong coupling.

Crash Signature

This is one of the most common patterns. It consists of a set of attributes derivable from saved execution context for exceptions, faults, and traps. For example, on x64 Windows, it is usually RIP and RSP addresses. For x86, it is usually EIP, ESP, and EBP. It can also include the application module name.

```
0:009> !analyze -v

[...]

FAILURE_BUCKET_ID: SOFTWARE_NX_FAULT_c0000005_ApplicationA.exe!Unknown

BUCKET_ID: APPLICATION_FAULT_SOFTWARE_NX_FAULT_STACK_CORRUPTION_BAD_IP_ApplicationA+2d560

[...]

0:009> kL
ChildEBP RetAddr
0354f270 75bc0962 ntdll!NtWaitForMultipleObjects+0x15
0354f30c 7651162d KERNELBASE!WaitForMultipleObjectsEx+0x100
0354f354 76511921 kernel32!WaitForMultipleObjectsExImplementation+0xe0
0354f370 76539b0d kernel32!WaitForMultipleObjects+0x18
0354f3dc 76539baa kernel32!WerpReportFaultInternal+0x186
0354f3f0 765398d8 kernel32!WerpReportFault+0x70
0354f400 76539855 kernel32!BasepReportFault+0x20
0354f48c 77750727 kernel32!UnhandledExceptionFilter+0x1af
0354f494 77750604 ntdll!__RtlUserThreadStart+0x62
0354f4a8 777504a9 ntdll!_EH4_CallFilterFunc+0x12
0354f4d0 777387b9 ntdll!_except_handler4+0x8e
0354f4f4 7773878b ntdll!ExecuteHandler2+0x26
0354f5a4 776f010f ntdll!ExecuteHandler+0x24
0354f5a4 0354f958 ntdll!KiUserExceptionDispatcher+0xf
WARNING: Frame IP not in any known module. Following frames may be wrong.
0354f908 02ff0340 0x354f958
00000000 00000000 0x2ff0340


0:009> kv
ChildEBP RetAddr Args to Child
[...]
0354f5a4 0354f958 0154f5bc 0354f60c 0354f5bc ntdll!KiUserExceptionDispatcher+0xf (CONTEXT @ 0354f60c)
WARNING: Frame IP not in any known module. Following frames may be wrong.
0354f908 02ff0340 00000000 00000000 00000000 0x354f958
00000000 00000000 00000000 00000000 00000000 0x2ff0340


0:009> .cxr 0354f60c
eax=80010105 ebx=0354f924 ecx=00000003 edx=0000ffff esi=00d7dce0 edi=00d7e0c8
eip=0354f958 esp=0354f8f4 ebp=0354f908 iopl=0         nv up ei pl zr na pe nc
cs=0023 ss=002b ds=002b es=002b fs=0053 gs=002b             efl=00010246
0354f958 64f9            stc
```

```
0:009> !address 0354f958
TEB 7efdd000 in range 7efdb000 7efde000
TEB 7efda000 in range 7efd8000 7efdb000
TEB 7efd7000 in range 7efd5000 7efd8000
TEB 7efaf000 in range 7efad000 7efb0000
TEB 7efac000 in range 7efaa000 7efad000
TEB 7efa9000 in range 7efa7000 7efaa000
TEB 7efa6000 in range 7efa4000 7efa7000
TEB 7efa3000 in range 7efa1000 7efa4000
TEB 7ef9f000 in range 7ef9d000 7efa0000
TEB 7ef9c000 in range 7ef9a000 7ef9d000
TEB 7ef99000 in range 7ef97000 7ef9a000
ProcessParametrs        007714b0 in range 00770000 00870000
Environment             007707f0 in range 00770000 00870000
03450000 : 0354d000 - 00003000
Type                    00020000 MEM_PRIVATE
Protect                 00000004 PAGE_READWRITE
State                   00001000 MEM_COMMIT
Usage                   RegionUsageStack
Pid.Tid                 1ea0.12dc


0:009> !address 02ff0340
TEB 7efdd000 in range 7efdb000 7efde000
TEB 7efda000 in range 7efd8000 7efdb000
TEB 7efd7000 in range 7efd5000 7efd8000
TEB 7efaf000 in range 7efad000 7efb0000
TEB 7efac000 in range 7efaa000 7efad000
TEB 7efa9000 in range 7efa7000 7efaa000
TEB 7efa6000 in range 7efa4000 7efa7000
TEB 7efa3000 in range 7efa1000 7efa4000
TEB 7ef9f000 in range 7ef9d000 7efa0000
TEB 7ef9c000 in range 7ef9a000 7ef9d000
TEB 7ef99000 in range 7ef97000 7ef9a000
ProcessParametrs        007714b0 in range 00770000 00870000
Environment             007707f0 in range 00770000 00870000
02fc0000 : 02fc0000 - 00043000
Type                    00020000 MEM_PRIVATE
Protect                 00000004 PAGE_READWRITE
State                   00001000 MEM_COMMIT
Usage                   RegionUsageHeap
Handle                  00d70000
```

Stack Trace (page 1033) may or may not be included here, and it might be **Incorrect Stack Trace** (page 563), heuristic[24] and not fully discernible automatically (requires raw stack semantic analysis) like in the example above. In some cases, we may have **Invalid Exception Information** (page 638) though, for example, in the case of **Laterally Damaged** (page 678) memory dumps or **Truncated Dump** (page 1130) files.

---

[24] Heuristic Stack Trace, Memory Dump Analysis Anthology, Volume 2, page 43

Crash Signature Invariant

Sometimes there are crashes in multiplatform products where only some portion of **Crash Signature** (page 166) is similar, for example:

```
x86: cmp dword ptr [eax], 1
x64: cmp dword ptr [r10]. 1
```

One crash dump had the following condensed stack trace:

```
0: kd> kc
DriverA
win32k!DrvSetMonitorPowerState
win32k!xxxSysCommand
win32k!xxxRealDefWindowProc
win32k!NtUserfnNCDESTROY
win32k!NtUserMessageCall
nt!KiSystemServiceCopyEnd
```

With the following faulting instruction:

```
DriverA+0x1234:
cmp      dword ptr [r11],1 ds:002b:00000000`00000000=????????
```

A search for DriverA led to this x86 crash analyzed some time ago:

```
0: kd> kc
DriverA
nt!IopfCallDriver
win32k!GreDeviceIoControl
win32k!DrvSetMonitorPowerState
win32k!xxxSysCommand
win32k!xxxRealDefWindowProc
win32k!xxxWrapRealDefWindowProc
win32k!NtUserfnNCDESTROY
win32k!NtUserMessageCall
nt!KiSystemServicePostCall

0: kd> r
DtiverA+0x1423:
cmp      dword ptr [ecx],1    ds:0023:00000000=????????
```

We see common function names on both stack traces, and overall flow is the same (only 3 functions are omitted in x64 trace); we see the same NULL pointer dereference for the same comparison instruction with the same comparison operand, #1.

Crashed Process

Sometimes we can see signs of **Crashed Processes** in the kernel and complete memory dumps. By "crashes" [25] we mean the sudden disappearance of processes from Task Manager, for example. In memory dumps, we can still see such processes as **Zombie Processes** (page 1278). **Special Processes** (page 980) found in the process list may help to select the possible candidate among many **Zombie Processes**. If a process is supposed to be launched only once (as a service) but found several times as **Zombie Process** and also as a normal process later in the process list (for example, as **Last Object**, page 675), then this may point to possible past crashes (or silent terminations). We also have a similar trace analysis pattern: **Singleton Event**[26]. The following example illustrates both signs:

```
0: kd> !process 0 0

[...]

PROCESS fffffa80088a5640
SessionId: 0 Cid: 2184 Peb: 7fffffd7000 ParentCid: 0888
DirBase: 381b8000 ObjectTable: 00000000 HandleCount: 0.
Image: WerFault.exe

PROCESS fffffa8007254b30
SessionId: 0 Cid: 20ac Peb: 7fffffdf000 ParentCid: 02cc
DirBase: b3306000 ObjectTable: 00000000 HandleCount: 0.
Image: ServiceA.exe

[...]

PROCESS fffffa8007fe2b30
SessionId: 0 Cid: 2a1c Peb: 7fffffdf000 ParentCid: 02cc
DirBase: 11b649000 ObjectTable: fffff8a014939530 HandleCount: 112.
Image: ServiceA.exe
```

---

[25] Crashes and Hangs Differentiated, Memory Dump Analysis Anthology, Volume 1, page 36
[26] Singleton Event, Memory Dump Analysis Anthology, Volume 8a, page 108

Critical Region

We first introduced **Critical Region** pattern in *Accelerated Mac OS X Core Dump Analysis*[27] training but didn't submit the pattern itself to the catalog at that time.

A critical region is usually a region of code protected by synchronization objects such as critical sections and mutexes. However, **Critical Region** analysis pattern is about identifying code regions "sandwiched" between contending function calls (which may or may not involve synchronization objects and corresponding synchronization calls such as identified in **Contention** patterns, page 1288), and then identifying any possibly shared data referenced by such code regions:

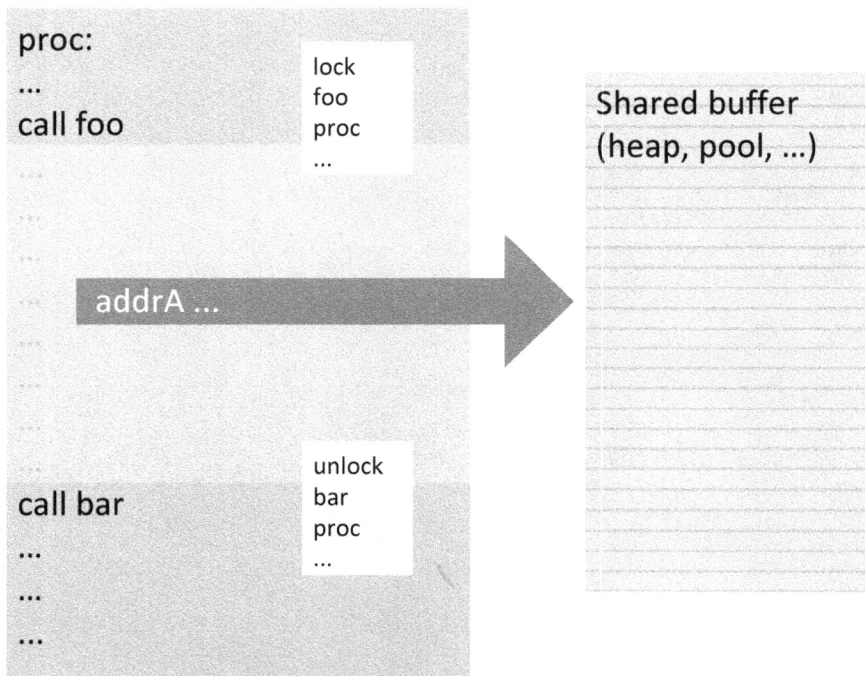

---

[27] http://www.patterndiagnostics.com/accelerated-macosx-core-dump-analysis-book

```
(gdb) thread apply all bt

Thread 6 (Thread 0x7f2665377700 (LWP 17000)):
#0  0x00000000004151a1 in _int_malloc ()
#1  0x0000000000416cf8 in malloc ()
#2  0x00000000004005a4 in proc ()
#3  0x0000000000400604 in bar_two ()
#4  0x0000000000400614 in foo_two ()
#5  0x000000000040062c in thread_two ()
#6  0x00000000004016c0 in start_thread (arg=<optimized out>)
at pthread_create.c:304
#7  0x0000000000432589 in clone ()
#8  0x0000000000000000 in ?? ()

Thread 5 (Thread 0x7f2664b76700 (LWP 17001)):
#0  __lll_unlock_wake_private ()
at ../nptl/sysdeps/unix/sysv/linux/x86_64/lowlevellock.S:343
#1  0x000000000041886d in _L_unlock_9670 ()
#2  0x0000000000416d22 in malloc ()
#3  0x00000000004005a4 in proc ()
#4  0x0000000000400641 in bar_three ()
#5  0x0000000000400651 in foo_three ()
#6  0x0000000000400669 in thread_three ()
#7  0x00000000004016c0 in start_thread (arg=<optimized out>)
at pthread_create.c:304
#8  0x0000000000432589 in clone ()
#9  0x0000000000000000 in ?? ()

Thread 4 (Thread 0x7f2665b78700 (LWP 16999)):
#0  __lll_lock_wait_private ()
at ../nptl/sysdeps/unix/sysv/linux/x86_64/lowlevellock.S:97
#1  0x0000000000418836 in _L_lock_9558 ()
#2  0x0000000000416c1c in free ()
#3  0x0000000000400586 in proc ()
#4  0x00000000004005c7 in bar_one ()
#5  0x00000000004005d7 in foo_one ()
#6  0x00000000004005ef in thread_one ()
#7  0x00000000004016c0 in start_thread (arg=<optimized out>)
at pthread_create.c:304
#8  0x0000000000432589 in clone ()
#9  0x0000000000000000 in ?? ()

Thread 3 (Thread 0x1ab1860 (LWP 16998)):
#0  0x000000000042fed1 in nanosleep ()
#1  0x000000000042fda0 in sleep ()
#2  0x000000000040078a in main ()

Thread 2 (Thread 0x7f2663b74700 (LWP 17003)):
#0  __lll_lock_wait_private ()
at ../nptl/sysdeps/unix/sysv/linux/x86_64/lowlevellock.S:97
#1  0x0000000000418836 in _L_lock_9558 ()
#2  0x0000000000416c1c in free ()
#3  0x0000000000400586 in proc ()
#4  0x00000000004006bb in bar_five ()
#5  0x00000000004006cb in foo_five ()
```

```
#6  0x00000000004006e3 in thread_five ()
#7  0x00000000004016c0 in start_thread (arg=<optimized out>)
at pthread_create.c:304
#8  0x0000000000432589 in clone ()
#9  0x0000000000000000 in ?? ()


Thread 1 (Thread 0x7f2664375700 (LWP 17002)):
#0  0x000000000043ef65 in raise ()
#1  0x0000000000409fc0 in abort ()
#2  0x000000000040bf5b in __libc_message ()
#3  0x0000000000412042 in malloc_printerr ()
#4  0x0000000000416c27 in free ()
#5  0x0000000000400586 in proc ()
#6  0x000000000040067e in bar_four ()
#7  0x000000000040068e in foo_four ()
#8  0x00000000004006a6 in thread_four ()
#9  0x00000000004016c0 in start_thread (arg=<optimized out>)
at pthread_create.c:304
#10 0x0000000000432589 in clone ()
#11 0x0000000000000000 in ?? ()
```

From threads #4 and #5 we can identify one such a region with a shared buffer 0x6b8fc0 which may further point to heap entries.

```
(gdb) disassemble proc
Dump of assembler code for function proc:
0x00000000004004f0 <+0>:  push   %rbp
0x00000000004004f1 <+1>:  mov    %rsp,%rbp
0x00000000004004f4 <+4>:  push   %rbx
0x00000000004004f5 <+5>:  sub    $0x18,%rsp
0x00000000004004f9 <+9>:  callq  0x40ac70 <rand>
0x00000000004004fe <+14>: mov    %eax,%ecx
0x0000000000400500 <+16>: mov    $0x68db8bad,%edx
0x0000000000400505 <+21>: mov    %ecx,%eax
0x0000000000400507 <+23>: imul   %edx
0x0000000000400509 <+25>: sar    $0xc,%edx
0x000000000040050c <+28>: mov    %ecx,%eax
0x000000000040050e <+30>: sar    $0x1f,%eax
0x0000000000400511 <+33>: mov    %edx,%ebx
0x0000000000400513 <+35>: sub    %eax,%ebx
0x0000000000400515 <+37>: mov    %ebx,%eax
0x0000000000400517 <+39>: mov    %eax,-0x14(%rbp)
0x000000000040051a <+42>: mov    -0x14(%rbp),%eax
0x000000000040051d <+45>: imul   $0x2710,%eax,%eax
0x0000000000400523 <+51>: mov    %ecx,%edx
0x0000000000400525 <+53>: sub    %eax,%edx
0x0000000000400527 <+55>: mov    %edx,%eax
0x0000000000400529 <+57>: mov    %eax,-0x14(%rbp)
0x000000000040052c <+60>: callq  0x40ac70 <rand>
0x0000000000400531 <+65>: mov    %eax,%ecx
0x0000000000400533 <+67>: mov    $0x68db8bad,%edx
0x0000000000400538 <+72>: mov    %ecx,%eax
0x000000000040053a <+74>: imul   %edx
0x000000000040053c <+76>: sar    $0xc,%edx
0x000000000040053f <+79>: mov    %ecx,%eax
```

```
0x0000000000400541 <+81>:  sar    $0x1f,%eax
0x0000000000400544 <+84>:  mov    %edx,%ebx
0x0000000000400546 <+86>:  sub    %eax,%ebx
0x0000000000400548 <+88>:  mov    %ebx,%eax
0x000000000040054a <+90>:  mov    %eax,-0x18(%rbp)
0x000000000040054d <+93>:  mov    -0x18(%rbp),%eax
0x0000000000400550 <+96>:  imul   $0x2710,%eax,%eax
0x0000000000400556 <+102>: mov    %ecx,%edx
0x0000000000400558 <+104>: sub    %eax,%edx
0x000000000040055a <+106>: mov    %edx,%eax
0x000000000040055c <+108>: mov    %eax,-0x18(%rbp)
0x000000000040055f <+111>: mov    -0x14(%rbp),%eax
0x0000000000400562 <+114>: cltq
0x0000000000400564 <+116>: mov    0x6b8fc0(,%rax,8),%rax
0x000000000040056c <+124>: test   %rax,%rax
0x000000000040056f <+127>: je     0x400597 <proc+167>
0x0000000000400571 <+129>: mov    -0x14(%rbp),%eax
0x0000000000400574 <+132>: cltq
0x0000000000400576 <+134>: mov    0x6b8fc0(,%rax,8),%rax
0x000000000040057e <+142>: mov    %rax,%rdi
0x0000000000400581 <+145>: callq  0x416bc0 <free>
0x0000000000400586 <+150>: mov    -0x14(%rbp),%eax
0x0000000000400589 <+153>: cltq
0x000000000040058b <+155>: movq   $0x0,0x6b8fc0(,%rax,8)
0x0000000000400597 <+167>: mov    -0x18(%rbp),%eax
0x000000000040059a <+170>: cltq
0x000000000040059c <+172>: mov    %rax,%rdi
0x000000000040059f <+175>: callq  0x416c90 <malloc>
0x00000000004005a4 <+180>: mov    %rax,%rdx
0x00000000004005a7 <+183>: mov    -0x14(%rbp),%eax
0x00000000004005aa <+186>: cltq
0x00000000004005ac <+188>: mov    %rdx,0x6b8fc0(,%rax,8)
0x00000000004005b4 <+196>: jmpq   0x4004f9 <proc+9>
End of assembler dump.
```

Critical Section Corruption

Dynamic Memory Corruption patterns in user (page 330) and kernel (page 315) spaces are specializations of one big parent pattern called **Corrupt Structure** (page 157) because crashes happen there due to corrupt or overwritten heap or pool control structures (for the latter see **Double Free** pattern, page 281). Critical sections are linked together through statically pre-allocated or heap-allocated helper structure (shown in bold italic) although themselves they can be stored anywhere from static and stack area to process heap:

```
0:001> dt -r1 ntdll!_RTL_CRITICAL_SECTION 77795240
   +0x000 DebugInfo       : 0x00175d28 _RTL_CRITICAL_SECTION_DEBUG
      +0x000 Type                 : 0
      +0x002 CreatorBackTraceIndex : 0
      +0x004 CriticalSection  : 0x77795240 _RTL_CRITICAL_SECTION
      +0x008 ProcessLocksList : _LIST_ENTRY [ 0x173a08 - 0x173298 ]
      +0x010 EntryCount           : 0
      +0x014 ContentionCount  : 0
      +0x018 Spare                : [2] 0
   +0x004 LockCount        : -1
   +0x008 RecursionCount   : 0
   +0x00c OwningThread     : (null)
   +0x010 LockSemaphore    : (null)
   +0x014 SpinCount        : 0

0:001> !address 77795240
   77670000 : 77792000 - 00005000
                   Type       01000000 MEM_IMAGE
                   Protect    00000004 PAGE_READWRITE
                   State      00001000 MEM_COMMIT
                 Usage      RegionUsageImage
                   FullPath C:\WINDOWS\system32\ole32.dll

0:001> !address 0x00175d28
   00140000 : 00173000 - 0000d000
                   Type       00020000 MEM_PRIVATE
                   Protect    00000004 PAGE_READWRITE
                   State      00001000 MEM_COMMIT
                 Usage      RegionUsageHeap
                   Handle     00140000
```

```
0:000> !locks

CritSec ntdll!LdrpLoaderLock+0 at 7c8877a0
WaiterWoken        No
LockCount          0
RecursionCount     1
OwningThread       1184
EntryCount         0
ContentionCount    b04707
*** Locked

0:000> dt -r1 _RTL_CRITICAL_SECTION 7c8877a0
   +0x000 DebugInfo          : 0x7c8877c0 _RTL_CRITICAL_SECTION_DEBUG
      +0x000 Type               : 0
      +0x002 CreatorBackTraceIndex : 0
      +0x004 CriticalSection    : 0x7c8877a0 _RTL_CRITICAL_SECTION
      +0x008 ProcessLocksList : _LIST_ENTRY [ 0x7c887be8 - 0x7c887bc8 ]
      +0x010 EntryCount         : 0
      +0x014 ContentionCount  : 0xb04707
      +0x018 Spare              : [2] 0
   +0x004 LockCount          : -2
   +0x008 RecursionCount     : 1
   +0x00c OwningThread       : 0x00001184
   +0x010 LockSemaphore      : 0x0000013c
   +0x014 SpinCount          : 0

0:000> !address 7c8877a0
   7c800000 : 7c887000 - 00003000
                  Type        01000000 MEM_IMAGE
                  Protect     00000004 PAGE_READWRITE
                  State       00001000 MEM_COMMIT
                  Usage       RegionUsageImage
                  FullPath C:\WINDOWS\system32\ntdll.dll

0:000> !address 0x7c8877c0
   7c800000 : 7c887000 - 00003000
                  Type        01000000 MEM_IMAGE
                  Protect     00000004 PAGE_READWRITE
                  State       00001000 MEM_COMMIT
                  Usage       RegionUsageImage
                  FullPath C:\WINDOWS\system32\ntdll.dll
```

Consider the case when CRITICAL_SECTION structure is defined on a stack, and there was **Local Buffer Overflow** (page 688) overwriting *DebugInfo* pointer. Then we have an example of **Wild Pointer** pattern (page 1271) and traversing the list of critical sections from this point will diverge into completely unrelated memory area or stop there. Consider another example of heap corruption or race condition overwriting *ProcessLocksList* or *CriticalSection* pointer. Then we have another instance of **Wild Pointer** pattern illustrated below:

```
0:000> !locks

CritSec ntdll!LdrpLoaderLock+0 at 7c8877a0
WaiterWoken        No
LockCount          0
RecursionCount     1
OwningThread       1184
EntryCount         0
ContentionCount    b04707
*** Locked

CritSec +1018de08 at 1018de08
WaiterWoken        Yes
LockCount          -49153
RecursionCount     5046347
OwningThread       460050
EntryCount         0
ContentionCount    0
*** Locked

CritSec +1018ddd8 at 1018ddd8
WaiterWoken        Yes
LockCount          -1
RecursionCount     0
OwningThread       0
*** Locked

CritSec +1018de28 at 1018de28
WaiterWoken        Yes
LockCount          -1
RecursionCount     0
OwningThread       0
*** Locked

CritSec +1018de08 at 1018de08
WaiterWoken        Yes
LockCount          -49153
RecursionCount     5046347
OwningThread       460050
EntryCount         0
ContentionCount    0
*** Locked

CritSec +1018de28 at 1018de28
WaiterWoken        Yes
LockCount          -1
RecursionCount     0
OwningThread       0
*** Locked
```

```
CritSec +1018ddd8 at 1018ddd8
WaiterWoken          Yes
LockCount            -1
RecursionCount       0
OwningThread         0
*** Locked
```

```
Scanned 841 critical sections
```

We see the signs of corruption at 1018de08 address which is interpreted as pointing to a locked critical section. To see where the corruption started we need to look at the list of all critical sections either locked or not locked:

```
0:000> !locks -v

CritSec ntdll!RtlCriticalSectionLock+0 at 7c887780
LockCount            NOT LOCKED
RecursionCount       0
OwningThread         0
EntryCount           0
ContentionCount      28

CritSec ntdll!LdrpLoaderLock+0 at 7c8877a0
WaiterWoken          No
LockCount            0
RecursionCount       1
OwningThread         1184
EntryCount           0
ContentionCount      b04707
*** Locked

CritSec ntdll!FastPebLock+0 at 7c887740
LockCount            NOT LOCKED
RecursionCount       0
OwningThread         0
EntryCount           0
ContentionCount      42c9

CritSec ntdll!RtlpCalloutEntryLock+0 at 7c888ea0
LockCount            NOT LOCKED
RecursionCount       0
OwningThread         0
EntryCount           0
ContentionCount      0

CritSec ntdll!PMCritSect+0 at 7c8883c0
LockCount            NOT LOCKED
RecursionCount       0
OwningThread         0
EntryCount           0
ContentionCount      0

CritSec ntdll!UMLogCritSect+0 at 7c888400
LockCount            NOT LOCKED
RecursionCount       0
OwningThread         0
```

```
EntryCount          0
ContentionCount     0

CritSec ntdll!RtlpProcessHeapsListLock+0 at 7c887960
LockCount           NOT LOCKED
RecursionCount      0
OwningThread        0
EntryCount          0
ContentionCount     0

CritSec +80608 at 00080608
LockCount           NOT LOCKED
RecursionCount      0
OwningThread        0
EntryCount          0
ContentionCount     22


...


CritSec cabinet!_adbgmsg+13c at 74fb4658
LockCount           NOT LOCKED
RecursionCount      0
OwningThread        0
EntryCount          0
ContentionCount     0

CritSec +c6c17c at 00c6c17c
LockCount           NOT LOCKED
RecursionCount      0
OwningThread        0
EntryCount          0
ContentionCount     0

CritSec +c6c0e4 at 00c6c0e4
LockCount           NOT LOCKED
RecursionCount      0
OwningThread        0
EntryCount          0
ContentionCount     0

CritSec at 1018de08 does not point back to the debug info at 00136a40
Perhaps the memory that held the critical section has been reused without calling DeleteCriticalSection()
?

CritSec +1018de08 at 1018de08
WaiterWoken         Yes
LockCount           -49153
RecursionCount      5046347
OwningThread        460050
EntryCount          0
ContentionCount     0
*** Locked

CritSec at 1018ddd8 does not point back to the debug info at 00136a68
Perhaps the memory that held the critical section has been reused without calling DeleteCriticalSection()
?
```

```
CritSec +1018ddd8 at 1018ddd8
WaiterWoken        Yes
LockCount          -1
RecursionCount     0
OwningThread       0
*** Locked
```

...

We see that the problem appears when the heap-allocated critical section at 00c6c0e4 address is linked to an inconsistent critical section at the 0x1018de08 address where its memory data contains UNICODE string fragment:

```
0:000> !address 00c6c0e4
   00c60000 : 00c60000 - 00010000
                  Type      00020000 MEM_PRIVATE
                  Protect   00000004 PAGE_READWRITE
                  State     00001000 MEM_COMMIT
                  Usage     RegionUsageHeap
                  Handle    00c60000

0:000> dt -r1 _RTL_CRITICAL_SECTION 00c6c0e4
   +0x000 DebugInfo        : 0x00161140 _RTL_CRITICAL_SECTION_DEBUG
      +0x000 Type              : 0
      +0x002 CreatorBackTraceIndex : 0
      +0x004 CriticalSection   : 0x00c6c0e4 _RTL_CRITICAL_SECTION
      +0x008 ProcessLocksList  : _LIST_ENTRY [ 0x136a48 - 0x119f58 ]
      +0x010 EntryCount        : 0
      +0x014 ContentionCount   : 0
      +0x018 Spare             : [2] 0
   +0x004 LockCount        : -1
   +0x008 RecursionCount   : 0
   +0x00c OwningThread     : (null)
   +0x010 LockSemaphore    : (null)
   +0x014 SpinCount        : 0

0:000> dt -r _RTL_CRITICAL_SECTION_DEBUG 0x00136a48-0x008
   +0x000 Type             : 0
   +0x002 CreatorBackTraceIndex : 0
   +0x004 CriticalSection  : 0x1018de08 _RTL_CRITICAL_SECTION
      +0x000 DebugInfo         : 0x000d001b _RTL_CRITICAL_SECTION_DEBUG
         +0x000 Type              : 0
         +0x002 CreatorBackTraceIndex : 0
         +0x004 CriticalSection   : (null)
         +0x008 ProcessLocksList  : _LIST_ENTRY [ 0x0 - 0x0 ]
         +0x010 EntryCount        : 0
         +0x014 ContentionCount   : 0x37e3c700
         +0x018 Spare             : [2] 0x8000025
      +0x004 LockCount         : 196609
      +0x008 RecursionCount    : 5046347
      +0x00c OwningThread      : 0x00460050
      +0x010 LockSemaphore     : 0x00310033
      +0x014 SpinCount         : 0x520044
   +0x008 ProcessLocksList : _LIST_ENTRY [ 0x136a70 - 0x161148 ]
      +0x000 Flink             : 0x00136a70 _LIST_ENTRY [ 0x136a98 - 0x136a48 ]
         +0x000 Flink              : 0x00136a98 _LIST_ENTRY [ 0x136ae8 - 0x136a70 ]
```

```
        +0x004 Blink              : 0x00136a48 _LIST_ENTRY [ 0x136a70 - 0x161148 ]
      +0x004 Blink              : 0x00161148 _LIST_ENTRY [ 0x136a48 - 0x119f58 ]
        +0x000 Flink            : 0x00136a48 _LIST_ENTRY [ 0x136a70 - 0x161148 ]
        +0x004 Blink            : 0x00119f58 _LIST_ENTRY [ 0x161148 - 0x16cc3c0 ]
   +0x010 EntryCount       : 0
   +0x014 ContentionCount  : 0
   +0x018 Spare            : [2] 0x2e760000

0:000> !address 0x1018de08
   10120000 : 10120000 - 00100000
                    Type     00020000 MEM_PRIVATE
                    Protect  00000004 PAGE_READWRITE
                    State    00001000 MEM_COMMIT
                    Usage    RegionUsageIsVAD
```

The address points miraculously to some DLL:

```
0:000> du 1018de08
1018de08  "....componentA.dll"
```

We might suggest that componentA.dll played some role there.

There are other messages from verbose version of **!locks** WinDbg command pointing to critical section problems:

```
CritSec componentB!Section+0 at 74004008
LockCount          NOT LOCKED
RecursionCount     0
OwningThread       0
EntryCount         0
ContentionCount    0


The CritSec componentC!Info+c at 72455074 has been RE-INITIALIZED.
The critical section points to DebugInfo at 00107cc8 instead of 000f4788

CritSec componentC!Info+c at 72455074
LockCount          NOT LOCKED
RecursionCount     0
OwningThread       0
EntryCount         0
ContentionCount    0

CritSec componentD!foo+8ec0 at 0101add0
LockCount          NOT LOCKED
RecursionCount     0
OwningThread       0
EntryCount         0
ContentionCount    0
```

Critical Stack Trace

This pattern addresses abnormal behavior such as the page fault processing or any other critical system activity that is waiting for too long. Such activity is either finishes quickly or leads to normal bugcheck processing code. For example, this thread is stuck in the page fault processing for 32 minutes while loading a resource:

```
THREAD fffffa80f0603c00  Cid 376.3d6  Teb: 000007fffffd6000 Win32Thread: fffff900c09e0640 WAIT:
(Executive) KernelMode Non-Alertable
[...]
Wait Start TickCount        6281298        Ticks: 123391 (0:00:32:04.102)
[...]
Child-SP          RetAddr           Call Site
fffff880`3fc99030 fffff800`01882bd2 nt!KiSwapContext+0x7a
fffff880`3fc99170 fffff800`01893f8f nt!KiCommitThreadWait+0x1d2
fffff880`3fc99200 fffff880`016283ff nt!KeWaitForSingleObject+0x19f
fffff880`3fc992a0 fffff880`01620fc6 Ntfs!NtfsNonCachedIo+0x23f
fffff880`3fc99470 fffff880`01622a68 Ntfs!NtfsCommonRead+0x7a6
fffff880`3fc99610 fffff880`00fb4bcf Ntfs!NtfsFsdRead+0x1b8
fffff880`3fc99820 fffff880`00fb36df fltmgr!FltpLegacyProcessingAfterPreCallbacksCompleted+0x24f
fffff880`3fc998b0 fffff800`018b44f5 fltmgr!FltpDispatch+0xcf
fffff880`3fc999a0 fffff800`018b3fc9 nt!IoPageRead+0x255
fffff880`3fc99a30 fffff800`0189a85a nt!MiIssueHardFault+0x255
fffff880`3fc99ac0 fffff800`0188b2ee nt!MmAccessFault+0x146a
fffff880`3fc99c20 00000000`779da643 nt!KiPageFault+0x16e (TrapFrame @ fffff880`3fd99c20)
00000000`039ff4f0 00000000`779d8b1e ntdll!LdrpGetRcConfig+0xcd
00000000`039ff580 00000000`779da222 ntdll!LdrIsResItemExist+0x1e
00000000`039ff5c0 00000000`779f82c4 ntdll!LdrpSearchResourceSection_U+0xa4
00000000`039ff6e0 000007fe`fe0075c1 ntdll!LdrFindResource_U+0x44
00000000`039ff720 000007fe`fb217777 KERNELBASE!FindResourceExW+0x85
[...]
```

The **Top Module** (page 1127) and **Blocking Module** (page 107) is NTFS, so we might want to look for other similar stack traces from **Stack Trace Collection** (page 1052).

Custom Exception Handler

Kernel Space

This is a kernel space counterpart to **Custom Exception Handler** pattern in user space (page 184). In the following stack trace below we see that *DriverA* code intercepted an access violation exception resulted from dereferencing **NULL Pointer** (page 838) and generated a custom bugcheck:

```
kd> !analyze -v

[...]


EXCEPTION_RECORD: fffff8801c757158 -- (.exr 0xfffff8801c757158)
ExceptionAddress: fffff88003977de1 (DriverA!foo+0x0000000000000381)
ExceptionCode: c0000005 (Access violation)
ExceptionFlags: 00000000
NumberParameters: 2
Parameter[0]: 0000000000000000
Parameter[1]: 0000000000000070
Attempt to read from address 0000000000000070


TRAP_FRAME: fffff8801c757200 -- (.trap 0xfffff8801c757200)
NOTE: The trap frame does not contain all registers.
Some register values may be zeroed or incorrect.
rax=0000000000000000 rbx=0000000000000000 rcx=fffff8a00da3f3c0
rdx=0000000000000000 rsi=0000000000000000 rdi=0000000000000000
rip=fffff88003977de1 rsp=fffff8801c757390 rbp=fffffa8009a853f0
r8=0000000000000000 r9=0000000000000000 r10=006800740020006e
r11=fffff8a00da3f3c6 r12=0000000000000000 r13=0000000000000000
r14=0000000000000000 r15=0000000000000000
iopl=0 nv up ei pl zr na po nc
DriverA!foo+0x381:
fffff880`03977de1 0fb74070 movzx eax,word ptr [rax+70h] ds:0703:0070=????
Resetting default scope


[...]


kd> kL 100
Child-SP RetAddr Call Site
fffff880`1c7560f8 fffff880`039498f7 nt!KeBugCheckEx
fffff880`1c756100 fffff880`039352a0 DriverA!MyBugCheckEx+0x93
fffff880`1c756140 fffff800`016f1d1c DriverA!MyExceptionFilter+0x1d0
fffff880`1c756210 fffff800`016e940d nt!_C_specific_handler+0x8c
fffff880`1c756280 fffff800`016f0a90 nt!RtlpExecuteHandlerForException+0xd
fffff880`1c7562b0 fffff800`016fd9ef nt!RtlDispatchException+0x410
fffff880`1c756990 fffff800`016c2d82 nt!KiDispatchException+0x16f
fffff880`1c757020 fffff800`016c18fa nt!KiExceptionDispatch+0xc2
fffff880`1c757200 fffff880`03977de1 nt!KiPageFault+0x23a
fffff880`1c757390 fffff880`03977754 DriverA!foo+0x381
fffff880`1c757430 fffff880`0396f006 DriverA!bar+0x74
[...]
fffff880`1c7579b0 fffff800`019a6e0a DriverA!QueryInformation+0x30b
```

```
fffff880`1c757a70 fffff800`016c2993 nt!NtQueryInformationFile+0x535
fffff880`1c757bb0 00000000`76e5fe6a nt!KiSystemServiceCopyEnd+0x13
00000000`0a08dfe8 00000000`00000000 0x76e5fe6a


kd> !exchain
24 stack frames, scanning for handlers...
Frame 0x05: nt!RtlpExecuteHandlerForException+0xd (fffff800`016e940d)
ehandler nt!RtlpExceptionHandler (fffff800`016e93d0)
Frame 0x07: nt!KiDispatchException+0x16f (fffff800`016fd9ef)
ehandler nt!_GSHandlerCheck_SEH (fffff800`0169aec0)
Frame 0x0b: DriverA!bar+0x74 (fffff880`03977754)
ehandler DriverA!__GSHandlerCheck (fffff880`039a12fc)
[...]
Frame 0x14: DriverA!QueryInformation+0x30b (fffff880`039303ab)
ehandler DriverA!_C_specific_handler (fffff880`039a1864)
Frame 0x15: nt!NtQueryInformationFile+0x535 (fffff800`019a6e0a)
ehandler nt!_C_specific_handler (fffff800`016f1c90)
Frame 0x16: nt!KiSystemServiceCopyEnd+0x13 (fffff800`016c2993)
ehandler nt!KiSystemServiceHandler (fffff800`016c2580)
Frame 0x17: error getting module for 0000000076e5fe6a
```

User Space

As discussed in **Early Crash Dump** pattern (page 335) saving crash dumps on first-chance exceptions helps to diagnose components that might have caused corruption and later crashes, hangs or CPU spikes by ignoring abnormal exceptions like access violation. In such cases, we need to know whether an application installs its own **Custom Exception Handler** or several of them. If it uses only default handlers provided by runtime or windows subsystem then most likely a first-chance access violation exception will result in a last-chance exception and a postmortem dump. To check a chain of exception handlers, we can use WinDbg **!exchain** extension command. For example:

```
0:000> !exchain
0017f9d8: TestDefaultDebugger!AfxWinMain+3f5 (00420aa9)
0017fa60: TestDefaultDebugger!AfxWinMain+34c (00420a00)
0017fb20: user32!_except_handler4+0 (770780eb)
0017fcc0: user32!_except_handler4+0 (770780eb)
0017fd24: user32!_except_handler4+0 (770780eb)
0017fe40: TestDefaultDebugger!AfxWinMain+16e (00420822)
0017feec: TestDefaultDebugger!AfxWinMain+797 (00420e4b)
0017ff90: TestDefaultDebugger!_except_handler4+0 (00410e00)
0017ffdc: ntdll!_except_handler4+0 (77961c78)
```

We see that *TestDefaultDebugger* does not have its own exception handlers except ones provided by MFC and C/C++ runtime libraries which were linked statically. Here is another example. It was reported that a 3rd-party application was hanging and spiking CPU (**Spiking Thread** pattern, page 992), so a user dump was saved using command line *userdump.exe*:

```
0:000> vertarget
Windows Server 2003 Version 3790 (Service Pack 2) MP (4 procs) Free x86 compatible
Product: Server, suite: TerminalServer
kernel32.dll version: 5.2.3790.4062 (srv03_sp2_gdr.070417-0203)
Debug session time: Thu Nov 22 12:45:59.000 2007 (GMT+0)
System Uptime: 0 days 10:43:07.667
Process Uptime: 0 days 4:51:32.000
Kernel time: 0 days 0:08:04.000
User time: 0 days 0:23:09.000


0:000> !runaway 3
User Mode Time
Thread       Time
0:1c1c       0 days 0:08:04.218
1:2e04       0 days 0:00:00.015
Kernel Mode Time
Thread       Time
0:1c1c       0 days 0:23:09.156
1:2e04       0 days 0:00:00.031
```

```
0:000> kL
ChildEBP RetAddr
0012fb80 7739bf53 ntdll!KiFastSystemCallRet
0012fbb4 05ca73b0 user32!NtUserWaitMessage+0xc
WARNING: Stack unwind information not available. Following frames may be wrong.
0012fd20 05c8be3f 3rdPartyDLL+0x573b0
0012fd50 05c9e9ea 3rdPartyDLL+0x3be3f
0012fd68 7739b6e3 3rdPartyDLL+0x4e9ea
0012fd94 7739b874 user32!InternalCallWinProc+0x28
0012fe0c 7739c8b8 user32!UserCallWinProcCheckWow+0x151
0012fe68 7739c9c6 user32!DispatchClientMessage+0xd9
0012fe90 7c828536 user32!__fnDWORD+0x24
0012febc 7739d1ec ntdll!KiUserCallbackDispatcher+0x2e
0012fef8 7738cee9 user32!NtUserMessageCall+0xc
0012ff18 0050aea9 user32!SendMessageA+0x7f
0012ff70 00452ae4 3rdPartyApp+0x10aea9
0012ffac 00511941 3rdPartyApp+0x52ae4
0012ffc0 77e6f23b 3rdPartyApp+0x111941
0012fff0 00000000 kernel32!BaseProcessStart+0x23
```

Exception chain listed **Custom Exception Handler**s:

```
0:000> !exchain
0012fb8c: 3rdPartyDLL+57acb (05ca7acb)
0012fd28: 3rdPartyDLL+3be57 (05c8be57)
0012fd34: 3rdPartyDLL+3be68 (05c8be68)
0012fdfc: user32!_except_handler3+0 (773aaf18)
  CRT scope  0, func:    user32!UserCallWinProcCheckWow+156 (773ba9ad)
0012fe58: user32!_except_handler3+0 (773aaf18)
0012fea0: ntdll!KiUserCallbackExceptionHandler+0 (7c8284e8)
0012ff3c: 3rdPartyApp+53310 (00453310)
0012ff48: 3rdPartyApp+5334b (0045334b)
0012ff9c: 3rdPartyApp+52d06 (00452d06)
0012ffb4: 3rdPartyApp+38d4 (004038d4)
0012ffe0: kernel32!_except_handler3+0 (77e61a60)
  CRT scope  0, filter: kernel32!BaseProcessStart+29 (77e76a10)
             func:    kernel32!BaseProcessStart+3a (77e81469)
```

The customer then enabled MS Exception Monitor and selected only "Access violation exception code" (c0000005) to avoid **False Positive Dumps** (page 419). During application execution various 1st-chance exception crash dumps were saved pointing to numerous access violations including function calls into unloaded modules, for example:

```
0:000> kL 100
ChildEBP RetAddr
WARNING: Frame IP not in any known module. Following frames may be wrong.
0012f910 7739b6e3 <Unloaded_Another3rdParty.dll>+0x4ce58
0012f93c 7739b874 user32!InternalCallWinProc+0x28
0012f9b4 7739c8b8 user32!UserCallWinProcCheckWow+0x151
0012fa10 7739c9c6 user32!DispatchClientMessage+0xd9
0012fa38 7c828536 user32!__fnDWORD+0x24
0012fa64 7739d1ec ntdll!KiUserCallbackDispatcher+0x2e
0012faa0 7738cee9 user32!NtUserMessageCall+0xc
0012fac0 0a0f2e01 user32!SendMessageA+0x7f
0012fae4 0a0f2ac7 3rdPartyDLL+0x52e01
0012fb60 7c81a352 3rdPartyDLL+0x52ac7
0012fb80 7c839dee ntdll!LdrpCallInitRoutine+0x14
0012fc94 77e6b1bb ntdll!LdrUnloadDll+0x41a
0012fca8 0050c9c1 kernel32!FreeLibrary+0x41
0012fdf4 004374af 3rdPartyApp+0x10c9c1
0012fe24 0044a076 3rdPartyApp+0x374af
0012fe3c 7739b6e3 3rdPartyApp+0x4a076
0012fe68 7739b874 user32!InternalCallWinProc+0x28
0012fee0 7739ba92 user32!UserCallWinProcCheckWow+0x151
0012ff48 773a16e5 user32!DispatchMessageWorker+0x327
0012ff58 00452aa0 user32!DispatchMessageA+0xf
0012ffac 00511941 3rdPartyApp+0x52aa0
0012ffc0 77e6f23b 3rdPartyApp+0x111941
0012fff0 00000000 kernel32!BaseProcessStart+0x23
```

D

Data Alignment

Page Boundary

Most of the time, this pattern manifests itself on Intel platforms from performance perspective and via GP faults for some instructions that require natural boundary for their qword operands. There are no exceptions generally if we move a dword value from or to an odd memory location address when the whole operand fits into one page. However, we need to take the possibility of the page boundary spans into account when checking memory addresses for their validity. Consider this exception:

```
0: kd> .trap 0xfffffffffa38df520
ErrCode = 00000002
eax=b6d9220f ebx=b6ab4ffb ecx=00000304 edx=eaf2fdea esi=b6d9214c edi=b6ab8189
eip=bfa10e6e esp=a38df594 ebp=a38df5ac iopl=0 nv up ei ng nz ac po cy
cs=0008  ss=0010  ds=0023  es=0023  fs=0030  gs=0000  efl=00010293
driver+0x2ae6e:
bfa10e6e 895304  mov     dword ptr [ebx+4],edx ds:0023:b6ab4fff=????????
```

The address seems to be valid:

```
0: kd> !pte b6ab4fff
              VA b6ab4fff
PDE at   C0300B68        PTE at C02DAAD0
contains 7F0DD863     contains 426B0863
pfn 7f0dd —DA—KWEV    pfn 426b0 —DA—KWEV
```

But a careful examination of the instruction reveals that it writes 32-bit value, so we need to inspect the next byte too because it is on another page:

```
0: kd> !pte b6ab4fff+1
              VA b6ab5000
PDE at   C0300B68        PTE at C02DAAD4
contains 7F0DD863     contains 00000080
pfn 7f0dd —DA—KWEV                            not valid
                      DemandZero
                      Protect: 4 - ReadWrite
```

Although the page is demand zero and this should have been satisfied by creating a new page filled with zeroes, the point here is that the page could have been completely invalid or paged out in the case of IRQL >= 2.

Data Contents Locality

This is a comparative pattern that helps not only in identifying the class of the problem but increases our confidence and degree of belief in the specific hypothesis. Suppose we have a database of notes on previous problems. If we see the same or similar data accessed in the new memory dump, we may suppose that the issue is similar. If **Data Contents Locality** is complemented by **Code Path Locality**[28] (similar partial stack traces and code **Execution Residues**, page 395) it even greater boosts our confidence in suggesting specific troubleshooting steps, recommending fixes and service packs or routing the problem to the next support or development service supply chain (like escalating the issue).

Suppose we got a new kernel memory dump with IRQL_NOT_LESS_OR_EQUAL (A) bugcheck pointing to our module, and we notice the write access to a structure in the nonpaged pool having specific pool tag:

```
3: kd> .trap 9ee8d9b0
ErrCode = 00000002
eax=85407650 ebx=858f6650 ecx=ffffffff edx=85407648 esi=858f65a8 edi=858f6620
eip=8083df4c esp=9ee8da24 ebp=9ee8da64 iopl=0 nv up ei pl zr na pe nc
cs=0008  ss=0010  ds=0023  es=0023  fs=0030  gs=0000 efl=00010246
nt!KeWaitForSingleObject+0x24f:
8083df4c 8919    mov     dword ptr [ecx],ebx  ds:0023:ffffffff=????????

STACK_TEXT:
9ee8d9b0 8083df4c badb0d00 85407648 00000000 nt!KiTrap0E+0x2a7
9ee8da64 80853f3f 85407648 0000001d 00000000 nt!KeWaitForSingleObject+0x24f
9ee8da7c 8081d45f 865b18d8 854076b0 f4b9e53b nt!KiAcquireFastMutex+0x13
9ee8da88 f4b9e53b 00000004 86940110 85407638 nt!ExAcquireFastMutex+0x20
9ee8daa8 f4b9ed98 85407638 00000000 86940110 driver!Query+0x143
...

3: kd> !pool 85407648
Pool page 85407648 region is Nonpaged pool
  85407000 size:    80 previous size:     0  (Allocated)  Mdl
  85407080 size:    30 previous size:    80  (Allocated)  Even (Protected)
  854070b0 size:    28 previous size:    30  (Allocated)  Ntfn
  854070d8 size:    28 previous size:    28  (Allocated)  NtFs
  85407100 size:    28 previous size:    28  (Allocated)  Ntfn
...
  85407570 size:    28 previous size:    70  (Allocated)  Ntfn
  85407598 size:    98 previous size:    28  (Allocated)  File (Protected)
 *85407630 size:    b0 previous size:    98  (Free )      *DrvA
```

Dumping the memory address passed to *KeWaitForSingleObject* function shows simple but a peculiar pattern:

```
3: kd> dd 85407648
85407648  ffffffff ffffffff ffffffff ffffffff
85407658  ffffffff ffffffff ffffffff ffffffff
85407668  ffffffff ffffffff ffffffff ffffffff
85407678  ffffffff ffffffff ffffffff ffffffff
85407688  ffffffff ffffffff ffffffff ffffffff
85407698  ffffffff ffffffff ffffffff ffffffff
854076a8  ffffffff ffffffff ffffffff ffffffff
854076b8  ffffffff ffffffff ffffffff ffffffff
```

We find several similar cases in our database but with different overall call stacks, except the topmost wait call. Then we notice that in previous cases there were mutants associated with their thread structure, and we have the same now:

```
0: kd> !thread
THREAD 858f65a8 Cid 474c.4530 Teb: 7ffdf000 Win32Thread: bc012410 RUNNING on processor 0
...

3: kd> dt /r _KTHREAD 858f65a8 MutantListHead
nt!_KTHREAD
   +0x010 MutantListHead : _LIST_ENTRY [ 0x86773040 - 0x86773040 ]

3: kd> !pool 86773040
Pool page 86773040 region is Nonpaged pool
*86773000 size:   50 previous size:    0  (Allocated) *Muta (Protected)
  Pooltag Muta : Mutant objects
...
```

This narrows the issue to only a few previous cases. In one previous case, *WaitBlockList* associated with a thread structure had 0xffffffff in its pointers. Our block shows the same pattern:

```
0: kd> dt -r _KTHREAD 858f65a8 WaitBlockList
nt!_KTHREAD
   +0x054 WaitBlockList : 0x858f6650 _KWAIT_BLOCK

0: kd> dt _KWAIT_BLOCK 0x858f6650
nt!_KWAIT_BLOCK
   +0x000 WaitListEntry    : _LIST_ENTRY [ 0x85407650 - 0xffffffff ]
   +0x008 Thread           : 0x858f65a8 _KTHREAD
   +0x00c Object           : 0x85407648
   +0x010 NextWaitBlock    : 0x858f6650 _KWAIT_BLOCK
   +0x014 WaitKey          : 0
   +0x016 WaitType         : 0x1 "
   +0x017 SpareByte        : 0 "
```

We have probably narrowed down the issue to a specific case. Although this does not work always and mostly based on intuition, there are spectacular cases where it really helps in troubleshooting. Here is another example where the contents of EDI register from exception context provided specific recommendation hints. When looking at the crash point, we see an instance of **Wild Code** pattern (page 1268):

```
0:000> kv
ChildEBP RetAddr  Args to Child
WARNING: Frame IP not in any known module. Following frames may be wrong.
49ab5bba 00000000 00000000 00000000 00000000 0x60f1011a

0:000> r
eax=38084ff0 ebx=52303340 ecx=963f1416 edx=0000063d esi=baaff395 edi=678c5804
eip=60f1011a esp=5a9d0f48 ebp=49ab5bba iopl=0   nv up ei pl nz na pe nc
cs=001b  ss=0023  ds=0023  es=0023  fs=003b  gs=0000  efl=00210206
60f1011a cd01            int     1

0:000> u
60f1011a cd01            int     1
60f1011c cc              int     3
60f1011d 8d              ???
60f1011e c0eb02          shr     bl,2
60f10121 0f840f31cd01    je      62be3236
60f10127 8d              ???
60f10128 c0cc0f          ror     ah,0Fh
60f1012b 0bce            or      ecx,esi
```

Looking at raw stack data, we notice the presence of a specific component that is known to patch the process import table. Applying techniques outlined in **Hooked Functions** pattern (page 548) we notice two different 3rd-party components that patched two different modules (*kernel32* and *user32*):

```
0:000> !chkimg -lo 50 -d !kernel32 -v
Searching for module with expression: !kernel32
Will apply relocation fixups to file used for comparison
Will ignore NOP/LOCK errors
Will ignore patched instructions
Image specific ignores will be applied
Comparison image path: c:\mss\kernel32.dll\4626487F102000\kernel32.dll
No range specified

Scanning section:     .text
Size: 564709
Range to scan: 77e41000-77ecade5
    77e41ae5-77e41ae9  5 bytes - kernel32!LoadLibraryExW
 [ 6a 34 68 48 7b:e9 16 e5 f4 07 ]
    77e44a8a-77e44a8e  5 bytes - kernel32!WaitNamedPipeW (+0x2fa5)
 [ 8b ff 55 8b ec:e9 71 b5 f9 07 ]
    77e5106a-77e5106e  5 bytes - kernel32!CreateProcessInternalW (+0xc5e0)
...
Total bytes compared: 564709(100%)
Number of errors: 49
49 errors : !kernel32 (77e41ae5-77e9aa16)
```

```
0:000> u 77e41ae5
kernel32!LoadLibraryExW:
77e41ae5 jmp       7fd90000
77e41aea out       77h,al
77e41aec call      kernel32!_SEH_prolog (77e6b779)
77e41af1 xor       edi,edi
77e41af3 mov       dword ptr [ebp-28h],edi
77e41af6 mov       dword ptr [ebp-2Ch],edi
77e41af9 mov       dword ptr [ebp-20h],edi
77e41afc cmp       dword ptr [ebp+8],edi

0:000> u 7fd90000
*** ERROR: Symbol file could not be found.  Defaulted to export symbols for ComponentA.dll -
7fd90000 jmp       ComponentA!DllUnregisterServer+0x2700 (678c4280)
7fd90005 push      34h
7fd90007 push      offset kernel32!`string'+0xc (77e67b48)
7fd9000c jmp       kernel32!LoadLibraryExW+0x7 (77e41aec)
7fd90011 add       byte ptr [eax],al
7fd90013 add       byte ptr [eax],al
7fd90015 add       byte ptr [eax],al
7fd90017 add       byte ptr [eax],al

0:000> !chkimg -lo 50 -d !user32 -v
Searching for module with expression: !user32
Will apply relocation fixups to file used for comparison
Will ignore NOP/LOCK errors
Will ignore patched instructions
Image specific ignores will be applied
Comparison image path: c:\mss\user32.dll\45E7BFD692000\user32.dll
No range specified

Scanning section:    .text
Size: 396943
Range to scan: 77381000-773e1e8f
   77383f38-77383f3c  5 bytes - user32!EnumDisplayDevicesW
 [ 8b ff 55 8b ec:e9 c3 c0 82 08 ]
   77384406-7738440a  5 bytes - user32!EnumDisplaySettingsExW (+0x4ce)
 [ 8b ff 55 8b ec:e9 f5 bb 7e 08 ]
   773844d9-773844dd  5 bytes - user32!EnumDisplaySettingsW (+0xd3)
 [ 8b ff 55 8b ec:e9 22 bb 80 08 ]
   7738619b-7738619f  5 bytes - user32!EnumDisplayDevicesA (+0x1cc2)
 [ 8b ff 55 8b ec:e9 60 9e 83 08 ]
   7738e985-7738e989  5 bytes - user32!CreateWindowExA (+0x87ea)
 [ 8b ff 55 8b ec:e9 76 16 8c 08 ]
...
Total bytes compared: 396943(100%)
Number of errors: 119
119 errors : !user32 (77383f38-773c960c)
```

```
0:000> u 77383f38
user32!EnumDisplayDevicesW:
77383f38 e9c3c08208     jmp     7fbb0000
77383f3d 81ec58030000   sub     esp,358h
77383f43 a1ac243e77     mov     eax,dword ptr [user32!__security_cookie (773e24ac)]
77383f48 8b5508         mov     edx,dword ptr [ebp+8]
77383f4b 83a5acfcffff00 and     dword ptr [ebp-354h],0
77383f52 53             push    ebx
77383f53 56             push    esi
77383f54 8b7510         mov     esi,dword ptr [ebp+10h]

0:000> u 7fbb0000
*** ERROR: Symbol file could not be found.  Defaulted to export symbols for ComponentB.dll -
7fbb0000 e91b43d5e5     jmp     ComponentB+0x4320 (65904320)
7fbb0005 8bff           mov     edi,edi
7fbb0007 55             push    ebp
7fbb0008 8bec           mov     ebp,esp
7fbb000a e92e3f7df7     jmp     user32!EnumDisplayDevicesW+0x5 (77383f3d)
7fbb000f 0000           add     byte ptr [eax],al
7fbb0011 0000           add     byte ptr [eax],al
7fbb0013 0000           add     byte ptr [eax],al
```

Which one should we try to eliminate first to test our assumption that they somehow resulted in application faults? Looking at register context again we see that one specific register (EDI) has a value that lies in *ComponentA* address range:

```
0:000> r
eax=38084ff0 ebx=52303340 ecx=963f1416 edx=0000063d esi=baaff395 edi=678c5804
eip=60f1011a esp=5a9d0f48 ebp=49ab5bba iopl=0  nv up ei pl nz na pe nc
cs=001b  ss=0023  ds=0023  es=0023  fs=003b  gs=0000 efl=00210206
60f1011a cd01           int     1

0:000> lm
start    end      module name
00400000 01901000  Application
...
678c0000 6791d000  ComponentA    ComponentA.DLL
...
```

Comments

The second example is about Locality[29] but the first is about Similarity. The former example here will be moved to a new pattern with the possible name **Data Contents Similarity**.

---

[29] https://en.wikipedia.org/wiki/Locality_of_reference

Data Correlation

CPU Times

This is a variant of **Data Correlation** (function parameters, page 195) analysis pattern where we look at correlations across memory structures. Simple arithmetical ratios may link such structures and correlate corresponding behavioral processes. Here we look at a recent instance of *calc.exe* consuming much CPU. Upon the discovery of that process, we were curious and saved its full process memory dump via Task Manager. In the dump we discovered 4 **Spiking Threads** (page 992):

```
0:000> !runaway f
User Mode Time
Thread       Time
13:1b68      0 days 1:51:39.906
10:23a8      0 days 1:51:37.796
11:1b98      0 days 0:00:09.890
14:88c       0 days 0:00:09.828
1:2eb4       0 days 0:00:00.390
18:2a44      0 days 0:00:00.015
19:28f0      0 days 0:00:00.000
17:22c0      0 days 0:00:00.000
16:232c      0 days 0:00:00.000
15:2008      0 days 0:00:00.000
12:2880      0 days 0:00:00.000
9:2f38       0 days 0:00:00.000
8:1a98       0 days 0:00:00.000
7:1dcc       0 days 0:00:00.000
6:c58        0 days 0:00:00.000
5:1550       0 days 0:00:00.000
4:2938       0 days 0:00:00.000
3:2b64       0 days 0:00:00.000
2:2f90       0 days 0:00:00.000
0:dc4        0 days 0:00:00.000
[...]
```

We see that #10/#13 approximately equals 1 and #11/#14 too, or #10/#11 approximately equals #13/#14 in user mode CPU consumption. If we look at kernel times, we see the same ratios:

```
[...]
Kernel Mode Time
Thread Time
10:23a8      0 days 0:10:36.718
13:1b68      0 days 0:10:32.968
14:88c       0 days 0:00:23.859
11:1b98      0 days 0:00:23.812
1:2eb4       0 days 0:00:00.218
2:2f90       0 days 0:00:00.015
0:dc4        0 days 0:00:00.015
19:28f0      0 days 0:00:00.000
18:2a44      0 days 0:00:00.000
17:22c0      0 days 0:00:00.000
```

```
16:232c          0 days 0:00:00.000
15:2008          0 days 0:00:00.000
12:2880          0 days 0:00:00.000
9:2f38           0 days 0:00:00.000
8:1a98           0 days 0:00:00.000
7:1dcc           0 days 0:00:00.000
6:c58            0 days 0:00:00.000
5:1550           0 days 0:00:00.000
4:2938           0 days 0:00:00.000
3:2b64           0 days 0:00:00.000
[...]
```

Elapsed times are also correlated, and we see that correlated threads were created in pairs {#10, #11} and {#13, #14}:

```
[...]
Elapsed Time
Thread Time
0:dc4            0 days 18:20:55.778
1:2eb4           0 days 18:20:55.731
2:2f90           0 days 18:20:55.725
3:2b64           0 days 18:20:55.721
4:2938           0 days 18:20:55.715
5:1550           0 days 18:20:55.582
6:c58            0 days 18:20:55.522
7:1dcc           0 days 18:20:55.522
8:1a98           0 days 18:20:55.522
9:2f38           0 days 18:20:55.522
10:23a8          0 days 16:12:52.330
11:1b98          0 days 16:12:52.329
12:2880          0 days 16:12:52.195
13:1b68          0 days 16:11:44.822
14:88c           0 days 16:11:44.821
15:2008          0 days 16:11:44.693
16:232c          0 days 2:09:35.021
17:22c0          0 days 2:05:13.038
18:2a44          0 days 0:23:38.000
19:28f0          0 days 0:00:24.261
```

This suggests that the threads are related. We call such analysis pattern variant **Data Correlation (CPU times)**. It may also help in finding weak **Coupled Processes** (page 164).

Function Parameters

This is a general pattern where values found in different parts of a memory dump correlate between each other according to some rules, for example, in some proportion. Here we show a variant for function parameters.

A process user memory dump had **C++ Exception** (page 119) inside:

```
0:000> kL
*** Stack trace for last set context - .thread/.cxr resets it
ChildEBP RetAddr
0012e950 78158e89 kernel32!RaiseException+0x53
0012e988 7830770c msvcr80!_CxxThrowException+0x46
0012e99c 783095bc mfc80u!AfxThrowMemoryException+0x19
0012e9b4 02afa8ca mfc80u!operator new+0x27
0012e9c8 02b0992f ModuleA!std::_Allocate<...>+0x1a
0012e9e0 02b09e7c ModuleA!std::vector<double,std::allocator<double>
>::vector<double,std::allocator<double> >+0x3f
[...]
```

We suspected an out-of-memory condition and looked for function parameters:

```
0:000> kv 5
ChildEBP RetAddr Args to Child
0012e950 78158e89 e06d7363 00000001 00000003 kernel32!RaiseException+0x53
0012e988 7830770c 0012e998 783b0110 783c8d68 msvcr80!_CxxThrowException+0x46
0012e99c 783095bc 0000a7c0 0012ea40 000014f8 mfc80u!AfxThrowMemoryException+0x19
0012e9b4 02afa8ca 0000a7c0 089321b0 089321f0 mfc80u!operator new+0x27 (FPO: [Uses EBP] [1,0,0])
0012e9c8 02b0992f 000014f8 00000000 00000008 ModuleA!std::_Allocate<...>+0x1a (FPO: [2,3,0])
```

Because of **Frame Pointer Omission** (page 438) we originally thought that stack arguments would be invalid. However, knowing the function prototype and semantics of operator *new*[30] and *std::vector double* element type we immediately see the correlation between 0xa7c0 and 0x14f8 which are proportional to *sizeof(double) == 8*:

```
0:000> ? 0000a7c0/000014f8
Evaluate expression: 8 = 00000000`00000008
```

---

[30] https://docs.microsoft.com/en-us/cpp/cpp/new-and-delete-operators

We, therefore, conclude without looking at the disassembly that memory allocation size was 42944 bytes:

```
0:000> .formats 0000a7c0
Evaluate expression:
Hex:      00000000`0000a7c0
Decimal: 42944
Octal:    0000000000000000123700
Binary:   00000000 00000000 00000000 00000000 00000000 00000000 10100111 11000000
Chars:    ........
Time:     Thu Jan 01 11:55:44 1970
Float:    low 6.01774e-041 high 0
Double:   2.12172e-319
```

Deadlock

.NET Finalizer

In one .NET process memory dump we noticed **Managed Stack Trace** (page 704) pointing that the thread was waiting for .NET Finalizer to finish its work:

```
0:000> !CLRStack
OS Thread Id: 0x60b0 (0)
ESP       EIP
00a585d8 773dca2c [HelperMethodFrame: 00a585d8] System.GC.WaitForPendingFinalizers()
00a58628 10105bbb ComponentA.FreeMemory()
```

The unmanaged stack trace involved Windows forms and COM object modal loops:

```
0:000> k
ChildEBP RetAddr
00a58034 7644112f ntdll!NtWaitForMultipleObjects+0xc
00a581c0 75ecd433 KERNELBASE!WaitForMultipleObjectsEx+0xcc
00a58224 7655fab4 user32!MsgWaitForMultipleObjectsEx+0x163
00a5825c 7656097c combase!CCliModalLoop::BlockFn+0x111
00a58314 765591fa combase!ClassicSTAThreadWaitForHandles+0x9e
00a58344 6e59103d combase!CoWaitForMultipleHandles+0x84
00a58364 6e590f9e mscorwks!NT5WaitRoutine+0x51
00a583d0 6e590f02 mscorwks!MsgWaitHelper+0xa5
00a583f0 6e6665e8 mscorwks!Thread::DoAppropriateAptStateWait+0x28
00a58474 6e66667d mscorwks!Thread::DoAppropriateWaitWorker+0x13c
00a584c4 6e666801 mscorwks!Thread::DoAppropriateWait+0x40
00a58520 6e5056b8 mscorwks!CLREvent::WaitEx+0xf7
00a58534 6e59eea3 mscorwks!CLREvent::Wait+0x17
00a58584 6e59ec19 mscorwks!WKS::GCHeap::FinalizerThreadWait+0xfb
00a58620 10105bbb mscorwks!GCInterface::RunFinalizers+0x99
00a58684 6cd8683b 0x10105bbb
00a586a0 6c4f5a52 System_Windows_Forms_ni+0xa5683b
00a586e4 6cd8e8f4 System_Windows_Forms_ni+0x1c5a52
00a586f8 6c529a00 System_Windows_Forms_ni+0xa5e8f4
00a58700 6c529981 System_Windows_Forms_ni+0x1f9a00
00a58714 6c52985a System_Windows_Forms_ni+0x1f9981
00a58778 75ec8e71 System_Windows_Forms_ni+0x1f985a
00a587a4 75ec90d1 user32!_InternalCallWinProc+0x2b
00a58838 75ec932c user32!UserCallWinProcCheckWow+0x18e
00a58898 75ec9529 user32!DispatchClientMessage+0xdc
00a588d8 773e07d6 user32!__fnDWORD+0x49
00a588ec 01293a30 ntdll!KiUserCallbackDispatcher+0x36
00a58998 75ecb0f8 0x1293a30
00a589e8 75ec8e71 user32!DefWindowProcW+0x118
00a58a14 75ec90d1 user32!_InternalCallWinProc+0x2b
00a58aa8 75ecddd5 user32!UserCallWinProcCheckWow+0x18e
00a58ae4 6c52a033 user32!CallWindowProcW+0x8d
00a58b3c 6c5331a9 System_Windows_Forms_ni+0x1fa033
00a58b84 6c529b1e System_Windows_Forms_ni+0x2031a9
00a58bdc 6c53310a System_Windows_Forms_ni+0x1f9b1e
00a58be8 6c5330c0 System_Windows_Forms_ni+0x20310a
```

```
00a58bf0 6c532d80 System_Windows_Forms_ni+0x2030c0
00a58c04 6c529a00 System_Windows_Forms_ni+0x202d80
00a58c0c 6c529981 System_Windows_Forms_ni+0x1f9a00
00a58c20 6c52985a System_Windows_Forms_ni+0x1f9981
00a58c84 75ec8e71 System_Windows_Forms_ni+0x1f985a
00a58cb0 75ec90d1 user32!_InternalCallWinProc+0x2b
00a58d44 75ec932c user32!UserCallWinProcCheckWow+0x18e
00a58da4 75ec9529 user32!DispatchClientMessage+0xdc
00a58de4 773e07d6 user32!__fnDWORD+0x49
00a58df8 011efaa0 ntdll!KiUserCallbackDispatcher+0x36
00a58e48 75eca989 0x11efaa0
00a58e7c 765603c3 user32!PeekMessageW+0x135
00a58ed0 76560436 combase!CCliModalLoop::MyPeekMessage+0x31
00a58f10 76560630 combase!CCliModalLoop::PeekRPCAndDDEMessage+0x31
00a58f3c 76560506 combase!CCliModalLoop::FindMessage+0x2b
00a58fa0 765605fb combase!CCliModalLoop::HandleWakeForMsg+0x44
00a58fc4 7656097c combase!CCliModalLoop::BlockFn+0x19d
00a5907c 765591fa combase!ClassicSTAThreadWaitForHandles+0x9e
00a590ac 6e59103d combase!CoWaitForMultipleHandles+0x84
00a590cc 6e590f9e mscorwks!NT5WaitRoutine+0x51
00a59138 6e590f02 mscorwks!MsgWaitHelper+0xa5
00a59158 6e6665e8 mscorwks!Thread::DoAppropriateAptStateWait+0x28
00a591dc 6e66667d mscorwks!Thread::DoAppropriateWaitWorker+0x13c
00a5922c 6e666801 mscorwks!Thread::DoAppropriateWait+0x40
00a59288 6e5056b8 mscorwks!CLREvent::WaitEx+0xf7
00a5929c 6e59eea3 mscorwks!CLREvent::Wait+0x17
00a592ec 6e59ec19 mscorwks!WKS::GCHeap::FinalizerThreadWait+0xfb
00a59388 10105bbb mscorwks!GCInterface::RunFinalizers+0x99
00a593ec 6cd8683b 0x10105bbb
00a59408 6ca863bd System_Windows_Forms_ni+0xa5683b
00a59438 6cd90b7e System_Windows_Forms_ni+0x7563bd
00a59480 6c539eee System_Windows_Forms_ni+0xa60b7e
00a5951c 6c539bf7 System_Windows_Forms_ni+0x209eee
00a59574 6c539a41 System_Windows_Forms_ni+0x209bf7
00a595a4 6ca4fc97 System_Windows_Forms_ni+0x209a41
00a595bc 6ca84598 System_Windows_Forms_ni+0x71fc97
00a59648 6ca847af System_Windows_Forms_ni+0x754598
00a59bc8 0996d41c System_Windows_Forms_ni+0x7547af
00a59c2c 0bc02e6d 0x996d41c
00a59c5c 0996b842 0xbc02e6d
00a59fb8 0fa8fa87 0x996b842
00a5a00c 0fa8f205 0xfa8fa87
00a5a040 0fa8f10b 0xfa8f205
00a5a058 02676666 0xfa8f10b
00a5a094 0fa8f09f 0x2676666
00a5a0a8 0fa8ed0c 0xfa8f09f
00a5a1b8 6dc355dc 0xfa8ed0c
00a5a238 6ca59703 mscorlib_ni+0x2355dc
00a5a2bc 6cd8c376 System_Windows_Forms_ni+0x729703
00a5a31c 6c529a00 System_Windows_Forms_ni+0xa5c376
00a5a324 6c529981 System_Windows_Forms_ni+0x1f9a00
00a5a338 6c52985a System_Windows_Forms_ni+0x1f9981
00a5a378 6cd8c587 System_Windows_Forms_ni+0x1f985a
00a5a3c8 6c511125 System_Windows_Forms_ni+0xa5c587
00a5a3f0 6c52985a System_Windows_Forms_ni+0x1e1125
00a5a454 75ec8e71 System_Windows_Forms_ni+0x1f985a
```

```
00a5a480 75ec90d1 user32!_InternalCallWinProc+0x2b
00a5a514 75eca66f user32!UserCallWinProcCheckWow+0x18e
00a5a580 75eca6e0 user32!DispatchMessageWorker+0x208
00a5a58c 0f1c6f4e user32!DispatchMessageW+0x10
00a5a5c0 0f1c58ed ModuleA+0x13c4e
[...]
```

We found Finalizer **Special Thread** (page 987):

```
0:002> k
ChildEBP RetAddr
0316ecc8 76432cc7 ntdll!NtWaitForSingleObject+0xc
0316ed3c 76432c02 KERNELBASE!WaitForSingleObjectEx+0x99
0316ed50 765b9839 KERNELBASE!WaitForSingleObject+0x12
(Inline) -------- combase!MTAThreadWaitForCall+0x43
0316ed80 7665d524 combase!MTAThreadDispatchCrossApartmentCall+0x1ed
(Inline) -------- combase!CRpcChannelBuffer::SwitchAptAndDispatchCall+0x33a2
0316eed4 7653caea combase!CRpcChannelBuffer::SendReceive2+0x62d
(Inline) -------- combase!ClientCallRetryContext::SendReceiveWithRetry+0x2e
(Inline) -------- combase!CAptRpcChnl::SendReceiveInRetryContext+0x81
0316ef34 76581789 combase!DefaultSendReceive+0x9e
(Inline) -------- combase!CAptRpcChnl::SendReceive+0x38
0316ef98 7665a010 combase!CCtxComChnl::SendReceive+0x248
0316efbc 76f85769 combase!NdrExtpProxySendReceive+0x5c
0316efd4 77006c1b rpcrt4!NdrpProxySendReceive+0x29
0316f400 76659e1e rpcrt4!NdrClientCall2+0x22b
0316f420 7653c46f combase!ObjectStublessClient+0x6c
0316f430 76581c07 combase!ObjectStubless+0xf
0316f4c4 76583024 combase!CObjectContext::InternalContextCallback+0x1e4
0316f518 6e6fcd4b combase!CObjectContext::ContextCallback+0xbc
0316f564 6e6fd936 mscorwks!CtxEntry::EnterContextOle32BugAware+0x2b
0316f684 6e7329cf mscorwks!CtxEntry::EnterContext+0x325
0316f6b8 6e732a74 mscorwks!RCWCleanupList::ReleaseRCWListInCorrectCtx+0xc4
0316f708 6e5908e3 mscorwks!RCWCleanupList::CleanupAllWrappers+0xdb
0316f74c 6e5907f3 mscorwks!SyncBlockCache::CleanupSyncBlocks+0xec
0316f910 6e589b7c mscorwks!Thread::DoExtraWorkForFinalizer+0x40
0316f920 6e54547f mscorwks!WKS::GCHeap::FinalizerThreadWorker+0x9a
0316f934 6e54541b mscorwks!Thread::DoADCallBack+0x32a
0316f9c8 6e54533a mscorwks!Thread::ShouldChangeAbortToUnload+0xe3
0316fa04 6e5b2763 mscorwks!Thread::ShouldChangeAbortToUnload+0x30a
0316fa2c 6e5b2774 mscorwks!ManagedThreadBase_NoADTransition+0x32
0316fa3c 6e5cb816 mscorwks!ManagedThreadBase::FinalizerBase+0xd
0316fa74 6e660ae9 mscorwks!WKS::GCHeap::FinalizerThreadStart+0xbb
0316fb10 76307c04 mscorwks!Thread::intermediateThreadProc+0x49
0316fb24 773fad1f kernel32!BaseThreadInitThunk+0x24
0316fb6c 773facea ntdll!__RtlUserThreadStart+0x2f
0316fb7c 00000000 ntdll!_RtlUserThreadStart+0x1b
```

We saw that it was blocked in an RPC call. Using the technique from *In Search of Lost CID* article[31] we found the destination thread:

```
0:002> kvL
ChildEBP RetAddr  Args to Child
0316ecc8 76432cc7 0000096c 00000000 00000000 ntdll!NtWaitForSingleObject+0xc
0316ed3c 76432c02 0000096c ffffffff 00000000 KERNELBASE!WaitForSingleObjectEx+0x99
0316ed50 765b9839 0000096c ffffffff 00ddfb88 KERNELBASE!WaitForSingleObject+0x12
(Inline) -------- -------- -------- -------- combase!MTAThreadWaitForCall+0x43
0316ed80 7665d524 00ddf298 0629fa10 0316efec combase!MTAThreadDispatchCrossApartmentCall+0x1ed
(Inline) -------- -------- -------- -------- combase!CRpcChannelBuffer::SwitchAptAndDispatchCall+0x33a2
0316eed4 7653caea 00ddfb88 0316efec 0316efb4 combase!CRpcChannelBuffer::SendReceive2+0x62d
(Inline) -------- -------- -------- -------- combase!ClientCallRetryContext::SendReceiveWithRetry+0x2e
(Inline) -------- -------- -------- -------- combase!CAptRpcChnl::SendReceiveInRetryContext+0x81
0316ef34 76581789 00ddfb88 0316efec 0316efb4 combase!DefaultSendReceive+0x9e
(Inline) -------- -------- -------- -------- combase!CAptRpcChnl::SendReceive+0x38
0316ef98 7665a010 00ddfb88 0316efec 0316efb4 combase!CCtxComChnl::SendReceive+0x248
0316efbc 76f85769 0628365c 0316f018 76f85740 combase!NdrExtpProxySendReceive+0x5c
0316efd4 77006c1b 6d6b47ca 0628365c 0316f438 rpcrt4!NdrpProxySendReceive+0x29
0316f400 76659e1e 7652d8f8 76532ff0 0316f438 rpcrt4!NdrClientCall2+0x22b
[...]

0:002> dpp 00ddfb88
00ddfb88  7652d400 7665bff0 combase!CRpcChannelBuffer::QueryInterface
00ddfb8c  76541e2c 76664690 combase![thunk]:CRpcChannelBuffer::QueryInterface`adjustor{4}'
00ddfb90  7653a65c 766646a0 combase![thunk]:CRpcChannelBuffer::QueryInterface`adjustor{8}'
00ddfb94  adb1682c
00ddfb98  429b3908
00ddfb9c  2b59b182
00ddfba0  e6a936e1
00ddfba4  00000003
00ddfba8  0000002a
00ddfbac  06268d68 00000000
00ddfbb0  00000000
00ddfbb4  00ddf298 00ddf330
00ddfbb8  00ddfe70 00000000
00ddfbbc  062d7660 00000044
00ddfbc0  00deb5f0 7652d280 combase!CStdIdentity::`vftable'
00ddfbc4  7652b2e0 76568760 combase!CDestObject::QueryInterface
00ddfbc8  00070005
00ddfbcc  00000003
00ddfbd0  000060b0
00ddfbd4  00000000
00ddfbd8  00000000
00ddfbdc  7652d400 7665bff0 combase!CRpcChannelBuffer::QueryInterface
00ddfbe0  76541e2c 76664690 combase![thunk]:CRpcChannelBuffer::QueryInterface`adjustor{4}'
00ddfbe4  7653a65c 766646a0 combase![thunk]:CRpcChannelBuffer::QueryInterface`adjustor{8}'
00ddfbe8  adb1682c
00ddfbec  429b3908
```

---

[31] Memory Dump Analysis Anthology, Volume 2, page 136

```
0:002> dd 00ddf298
00ddf298  00ddf330 7666ddd0 000070b8 000060b0
00ddf2a8  056aadfb 14bb2b53 a45b843e 2611fcc9
00ddf2b8  a45b843e 2611fcc9 00001800 60b070b8
00ddf2c8  66fb7794 88242aca 04000203 00020052
00ddf2d8  00dbfb20 00000000 00000000 00000000
00ddf2e8  00000001 ffffffff 00de5e48 0628365c
00ddf2f8  00000005 00000000 00000001 00000000
00ddf308  00000000 00070005 00000000 00000000
```

We saw that the finalizer thread #2 was waiting for the thread #0 that was waiting for the finalizer thread #2:

```
0:002> ~
#  0  Id: 70b8.60b0 Suspend: 0 Teb: 7ecaf000 Unfrozen
   1  Id: 70b8.26e8 Suspend: 0 Teb: 7ecac000 Unfrozen
.  2  Id: 70b8.5d2c Suspend: 0 Teb: 7eca9000 Unfrozen
   3  Id: 70b8.551c Suspend: 0 Teb: 7eb76000 Unfrozen
   4  Id: 70b8.7194 Suspend: 0 Teb: 7eb73000 Unfrozen
   5  Id: 70b8.465c Suspend: 0 Teb: 7eb0f000 Unfrozen
   6  Id: 70b8.64ac Suspend: 0 Teb: 7eb0c000 Unfrozen
   7  Id: 70b8.6200 Suspend: 0 Teb: 7eb09000 Unfrozen
   8  Id: 70b8.5790 Suspend: 0 Teb: 7eafa000 Unfrozen
   9  Id: 70b8.6c3c Suspend: 0 Teb: 7eaf4000 Unfrozen
  10  Id: 70b8.7320 Suspend: 0 Teb: 7eaeb000 Unfrozen
  11  Id: 70b8.1ebc Suspend: 0 Teb: 7eb06000 Unfrozen
  12  Id: 70b8.459c Suspend: 0 Teb: 7eb00000 Unfrozen
  13  Id: 70b8.74e8 Suspend: 0 Teb: 7eb7f000 Unfrozen
  14  Id: 70b8.6758 Suspend: 0 Teb: 7eafd000 Unfrozen
  15  Id: 70b8.72e8 Suspend: 0 Teb: 7eaf1000 Unfrozen
  16  Id: 70b8.5eec Suspend: 0 Teb: 7eaee000 Unfrozen
  17  Id: 70b8.4a74 Suspend: 0 Teb: 7e83f000 Unfrozen
  18  Id: 70b8.61b0 Suspend: 0 Teb: 7e83c000 Unfrozen
  19  Id: 70b8.3cc4 Suspend: 0 Teb: 7e839000 Unfrozen
  20  Id: 70b8.6554 Suspend: 0 Teb: 7e836000 Unfrozen
  21  Id: 70b8.5b5c Suspend: 0 Teb: 7e833000 Unfrozen
  22  Id: 70b8.6c48 Suspend: 0 Teb: 7e7ff000 Unfrozen
  23  Id: 70b8.12dc Suspend: 0 Teb: 7e7fc000 Unfrozen
  24  Id: 70b8.3a98 Suspend: 0 Teb: 7e7f9000 Unfrozen
  25  Id: 70b8.1cb4 Suspend: 0 Teb: 7e7f6000 Unfrozen
  26  Id: 70b8.5df8 Suspend: 0 Teb: 7e7f3000 Unfrozen
  27  Id: 70b8.287c Suspend: 0 Teb: 7e69f000 Unfrozen
  28  Id: 70b8.69b4 Suspend: 0 Teb: 7e69c000 Unfrozen
  29  Id: 70b8.159c Suspend: 0 Teb: 7e699000 Unfrozen
  30  Id: 70b8.1678 Suspend: 0 Teb: 7e696000 Unfrozen
  31  Id: 70b8.8a0 Suspend: 0 Teb: 7e693000 Unfrozen
  32  Id: 70b8.5984 Suspend: 0 Teb: 7e64f000 Unfrozen
  33  Id: 70b8.256c Suspend: 0 Teb: 7e649000 Unfrozen
```

This is a variant of **Deadlock** memory analysis pattern.

Critical Sections

For the high-level explanation of "deadlock" terminology, please refer to the discussion of "hangs" in Memory Dump Analysis Anthology[32]. **Deadlocks** do not only happen with synchronization primitives like mutexes, events or more complex objects (built upon primitives) like critical sections or executive resources (ERESOURCE). They can happen from a high level or systems perspective in inter-process or inter-component communication, for example, mutually waiting on messages: GUI window messages, LPC messages, RPC calls.

How can we see **Deadlocks** in memory dumps? Let us start with user dumps and critical sections.

First, we would recommend reading the following excellent MSDN article to understand various members of CRITICAL_SECTION structure[33].

WinDbg **!locks** command examines process critical section list and displays all locked critical sections, lock count and thread id of current critical section owner. This is the output from a memory dump of hanging Windows print spooler process (*spoolsv.exe*):

```
0:000> !locks
CritSec NTDLL!LoaderLock+0 at 784B0348
LockCount          4
RecursionCount     1
OwningThread       624
EntryCount         6c3
ContentionCount    6c3
*** Locked


CritSec LOCALSPL!SpoolerSection+0 at 76AB8070
LockCount          3
RecursionCount     1
OwningThread       1c48
EntryCount         646
ContentionCount    646
*** Locked
```

If we look at threads #624 and #1c48, we see them mutually waiting for each other:

- TID#**624** owns CritSec **784B0348** and is waiting for CritSec **76AB8070**
- TID#**1c48** owns CritSec **76AB8070** and is waiting for CritSec **784B0348**

```
0:000>~*kv
```

---

[32] Hangs Explained, Memory Dump Analysis Anthology, Volume 1, page 31

[33] Break Free of Code Deadlocks in Critical Sections Under Windows, https://docs.microsoft.com/en-us/archive/msdn-magazine/2003/december/break-free-of-code-deadlocks-in-critical-sections-under-windows

```
. 12 Id: bc0.624 Suspend: 1 Teb: 7ffd3000 Unfrozen
0000024c 00000000 00000000 NTDLL!ZwWaitForSingleObject+0xb
76ab8000 76a815ef 76ab8070 NTDLL!RtlpWaitForCriticalSection+0x9e
76ab8070 76a844f8 00cd1f38 NTDLL!RtlEnterCriticalSection+0x46
00cd1f38 76a8a1d7 00000000 LOCALSPL!EnterSplSem+0xb
00000000 00000000 00cd1f38 LOCALSPL!FindSpoolerByNameIncRef+0x1f
00000000 777f19bc 00000001 LOCALSPL!LocalGetPrinterDriverDirectory+0xe
00000000 777f19bc 00000001 spoolss!GetPrinterDriverDirectoryW+0x59
00000000 777f19bc 00000001 spoolsv!YGetPrinterDriverDirectory+0x27
00000000 777f19bc 00000001 WINSPOOL!GetPrinterDriverDirectoryW+0x7b
50000000 00000001 00000000 BRHLUI04+0x14ea
50002ea0 50000000 00000001 BRHLUI04!DllGetClassObject+0x1705
00000000 00000000 000cb570 NTDLL!LdrpRunInitializeRoutines+0x1df
000cc8f8 0288ea30 0288ea38 NTDLL!LdrpLoadDll+0x2e6
000cc8f8 0288ea30 0288ea38 NTDLL!LdrLoadDll+0x17)
000c1258 00000000 00000008 KERNEL32!LoadLibraryExW+0x231
000c150c 0288efd8 00000000 UNIDRVUI!PLoadCommonInfo+0x17e
000c150c 0288efd8 00000007 UNIDRVUI!DwDeviceCapabilities+0x1a
00070000 00071378 00000045 UNIDRVUI!DrvDeviceCapabilities+0x19


. 13 Id: bc0.1c48 Suspend: 1 Teb: 7ffd2000 Unfrozen
0000010c 00000000 00000000 NTDLL!ZwWaitForSingleObject+0xb
784b0301 78468d38 784b0348 NTDLL!RtlpWaitForCriticalSection+0x9e
784b0348 74fb4344 00000000 NTDLL!RtlEnterCriticalSection+0x46
74fb0000 02c0f2a8 00000000 NTDLL!LdrpGetProcedureAddress+0x122
74fb0000 02c0f2a8 00000000 NTDLL!LdrGetProcedureAddress+0x17
74fb0000 74fb4344 02c0f449 KERNEL32!GetProcAddress+0x41
017924b0 00000000 00000001 ws2_32!CheckForHookersOrChainers+0x1f
00000101 02c0f344 017924b0 ws2_32!WSAStartup+0x10f
00cdf79c 02c0f4f4 76a8c9bc LOCALSPL!GetDNSMachineName+0x1e
00000000 76a8c9bc 780276a2 LOCALSPL!GetPrinterUrl+0x2c
0176f570 ffffffff 01000000 LOCALSPL!UpdateDsSpoolerKey+0x322
0176f570 76a8c9bc 01792b90 LOCALSPL!RecreateDsKey+0x50
00000000 00000002 01792b90 LOCALSPL!SplAddPrinter+0x521
01791faa 0176a684 76a5cd34 WIN32SPL!InternalAddPrinterConnection+0x1b4
01791faa 02c0fa00 02c0fabc WIN32SPL!AddPrinterConnectionW+0x15
00076f1c 02c0fabc 01006873 spoolss!AddPrinterConnectionW+0x49
00076f1c 00000001 77107fb0 spoolsv!YAddPrinterConnection+0x17
00076f1c 02020202 00000001 spoolsv!RpcAddPrinterConnection+0xb
01006868 02c0fac0 00000001 rpcrt4!Invoke+0x30
00000000 00000000 000d22c8 rpcrt4!NdrStubCall2+0x655
000d22c8 00076fe0 000d22c8 rpcrt4!NdrServerCall2+0x17
010045fc 000d22c8 02c0fe0c rpcrt4!DispatchToStubInC+0x32
0000002b 00000000 02c0fe0c rpcrt4!RPC_INTERFACE::DispatchToStubWorker+0x100
000d22c8 00000000 02c0fe0c rpcrt4!RPC_INTERFACE::DispatchToStub+0x5e
000d3210 00076608 813b0013 rpcrt4!LRPC_SCALL::DealWithRequestMessage+0x1dd
000d21d0 02c0fe50 000d3210 rpcrt4!LRPC_ADDRESS::DealWithLRPCRequest+0x10c
770c9ad0 00076608 770cb6d8 rpcrt4!LRPC_ADDRESS::ReceiveLotsaCalls+0x229
00076608 770cb6d8 0288f9a8 rpcrt4!RecvLotsaCallsWrapper+0x9
00074a50 02c0ffec 77e7438b rpcrt4!BaseCachedThreadRoutine+0x11f
00076e68 770cb6d8 0288f9a8 rpcrt4!ThreadStartRoutine+0x18
770d1c54 00076e68 00000000 KERNEL32!BaseThreadStart+0x52
```

This analysis looks pretty simple and easy. What about the kernel and complete memory dumps? Of course, we cannot see user space critical sections in kernel memory dumps but we can see them in complete memory dumps after switching to the appropriate process context and using **!ntsdexts.locks**. This can be done via a simple script adapted from *debugger.chm* (see Deadlocks and Critical Sections section there).

Why is it so easy to see deadlocks when critical sections are involved? This is because their structures have a member that records their owner. So it is very easy to map them to corresponding threads. The same is with kernel ERESOURCE synchronization objects. Other objects do not have an owner, for example, in the case of events it is not so easy to find an owner just by looking at an event object. We need to examine thread call stacks, other structures or have access to source code.

There is also **!cs** WinDbg extension where **!cs -l** command lists all locked sections with stack traces and **!cs -t** shows critical section tree. For the latter we need to enable Application Verifier using *gflags.exe* or set 0x100 in the registry for your image[34]:

```
HKEY_LOCAL_MACHINE\SOFTWARE\Microsoft\Windows NT\CurrentVersion\Image File Execution Options\<executable>
GlobalFlag=0x00000100
```

Here is another **Deadlock** example in hanging IE process:

```
0:000> !locks

CritSec ntdll!LdrpLoaderLock+0 at 7c8877a0
WaiterWoken No
LockCount 3
RecursionCount 2
OwningThread d5a8
EntryCount 0
ContentionCount 5a
*** Locked

CritSec shell32!CMountPoint::_csDL+0 at 7cae42d0
WaiterWoken No
LockCount 1
RecursionCount 1
OwningThread b7b4
EntryCount 0
ContentionCount 7
*** Locked

Scanned 1024 critical sections
```

---

[34] https://docs.microsoft.com/en-gb/archive/blogs/mithuns/image-file-execution-options-ifeo

```
0:000> ~*kb 100

. 0 Id: c068.b7b4 Suspend: 1 Teb: 7ffdd000 Unfrozen
ChildEBP RetAddr Args to Child
0013bd0c 7c827d0b 7c83d236 000001d0 00000000 ntdll!KiFastSystemCallRet
0013bd10 7c83d236 000001d0 00000000 00000000 ntdll!NtWaitForSingleObject+0xc
0013bd4c 7c83d281 000001d0 00000004 00000001 ntdll!RtlpWaitOnCriticalSection+0x1a3
0013bd6c 7c82f20c 7c8877a0 00000000 0013be68 ntdll!RtlEnterCriticalSection+0xa8
0013bda0 7c82f336 00000000 00000000 0013bde8 ntdll!LdrLockLoaderLock+0x133
0013be1c 7c82f2a3 00000001 00000001 00000000 ntdll!LdrGetDllHandleEx+0x94
0013be38 77e65185 00000001 00000000 0013bea0 ntdll!LdrGetDllHandle+0x18
0013be84 77e6528f 0013bea0 00000000 7cae2f60 kernel32!GetModuleHandleForUnicodeString+0x20
0013c2fc 77e65155 00000001 00000002 7c8d8828 kernel32!BasepGetModuleHandleExW+0x17f
0013c314 7c91079e 7c8d8828 7c9107b8 0013c350 kernel32!GetModuleHandleW+0x29
0013c31c 7c9107b8 0013c350 7c91078d 00000001 shell32!IsProcessAnExplorer+0xb
0013c324 7c91078d 00000001 7c91373b 00000018 shell32!IsMainShellProcess2+0x46
0013c32c 7c91373b 00000018 00000000 7cae42d0 shell32!_Shell32LoadedInDesktop+0x7
0013c350 7c913776 00000018 00000000 7cae42d0 shell32!CMountPoint::_IsNetDriveLazyLoadNetDLLs+0x7b
0013c37c 7c9136dc 00000018 00000001 0013c634 shell32!CMountPoint::_GetMountPointDL+0x1c
0013c398 7c96dfd7 00000018 00000001 00000001 shell32!CMountPoint::GetMountPoint+0x46
0013c5e4 7c90f37d 0018e988 00000001 001a0ea8 shell32!CDrivesFolder::GetAttributesOf+0x7b
0013c624 779cc875 0018e9b0 00000001 04002000 shell32!CRegFolder::GetAttributesOf+0x122
0013c648 779cc917 0018e9b0 001e4dc8 04002000 shdocvw!SHGetAttributes+0x53
0013d728 779cd9c8 0013ddac 00193a50 80004005 shdocvw!CNscTree::_OnCDNotify+0x85
0013d754 779cd964 0013ddac 001a06c8 11281f2a shdocvw!CNscTree::_OnNotify+0x2e1
0013d768 779cd8ff 001a06c8 00010090 0000004e shdocvw!CNscTree::OnWinEvent+0x51
0013d798 75eba756 00193a50 00010090 0000004e shdocvw!CNSCBand::OnWinEvent+0x70
0013d7b8 75eba2a2 00193a50 00010090 0000004e browseui!_FwdWinEvent+0x1d
0013d7ec 75eba357 00010090 0000004e 00000064 browseui!CBandSite::_SendToToolband+0x44
0013d818 75ee2a72 0017de98 00010088 00000000 browseui!CBandSite::OnWinEvent+0x143
0013d864 75ee2b32 0017de98 00010088 0000004e browseui!CBrowserBandSite::OnWinEvent+0x14c
0013d890 75ee2a9a 0000004e 00000064 0013ddac browseui!CBaseBar::_CheckForwardWinEvent+0x88
0013d8ac 75ee29dc 0000004e 00000064 0013ddac browseui!CBaseBar::_OnNotify+0x1c
0013d8c8 75ee2965 00010088 0000004e 00000064 browseui!CBaseBar::v_WndProc+0xd4
0013d918 75ee28fa 00010088 0000004e 00000064 browseui!CDockingBar::v_WndProc+0x447
0013d948 75ee2880 00010088 0000004e 00000064 browseui!CBrowserBar::v_WndProc+0x99
0013d96c 7739b6e3 00010088 0000004e 00000064 browseui!CImpWndProc::s_WndProc+0x65
0013d998 7739b874 75ee2841 00010088 0000004e user32!InternalCallWinProc+0x28
0013da10 7739c2d3 00172e34 75ee2841 00010088 user32!UserCallWinProcCheckWow+0x151
0013da4c 7739c337 006172a0 00618f18 00000064 user32!SendMessageWorker+0x4bd
0013da6c 7743b07f 00010088 0000004e 00000064 user32!SendMessageW+0x7f
0013db04 7743b1ef 0013db1c fffffff4 0013ddac comctl32!CCSendNotify+0xc24
0013db40 774a5ab0 00010088 ffffffff fffffff4 comctl32!SendNotifyEx+0x57
0013dbac 774a652d 0001008a 0000004e 00000064 comctl32!CReBar::_WndProc+0x257
0013dbd0 7739b6e3 0001008a 0000004e 00000064 comctl32!CReBar::s_WndProc+0x2c
0013dbfc 7739b874 774a6501 0001008a 0000004e user32!InternalCallWinProc+0x28
0013dc74 7739c2d3 00172e34 774a6501 0001008a user32!UserCallWinProcCheckWow+0x151
0013dcb0 7739c337 00617350 0060a9c0 00000064 user32!SendMessageWorker+0x4bd
0013dcd0 7743b07f 0001008a 0000004e 00000064 user32!SendMessageW+0x7f
0013dd68 7743b10d 001c8900 fffffff4 0013ddac comctl32!CCSendNotify+0xc24
0013dd7c 7748a032 001c8900 00010001 0013ddac comctl32!CICustomDrawNotify+0x2c
0013e070 7748a8bb 001c8900 001d2aa8 01010060 comctl32!TV_DrawItem+0x356
0013e0f4 7748a9ac 00000154 01010060 00000000 comctl32!TV_DrawTree+0x136
0013e158 7745bdd0 001c8900 00000000 0013e21c comctl32!TV_Paint+0x65
0013e1a4 7739b6e3 00010090 0000000f 00000000 comctl32!TV_WndProc+0x6ea
0013e1d0 7739b874 7745b6e6 00010090 0000000f user32!InternalCallWinProc+0x28
```

```
0013e248  7739bfce  0015fce4  7745b6e6  00010090  user32!UserCallWinProcCheckWow+0x151
0013e278  7739bf74  7745b6e6  00010090  0000000f  user32!CallWindowProcAorW+0x98
0013e298  77431848  7745b6e6  00010090  0000000f  user32!CallWindowProcW+0x1b
0013e2b4  77431b9b  00010090  0000000f  00000000  comctl32!CallOriginalWndProc+0x1a
0013e310  77431d5d  001cf0f8  00010090  0000000f  comctl32!CallNextSubclassProc+0x3c
0013e334  779cd761  00010090  0000000f  00000000  comctl32!DefSubclassProc+0x46
0013e350  77431b9b  00010090  0000000f  00000000  shdocvw!CNotifySubclassWndProc::_SubclassWndProc+0xa7
0013e3ac  77431d5d  001cf0f8  00010090  0000000f  comctl32!CallNextSubclassProc+0x3c
0013e3d0  779cd86f  00010090  0000000f  00000000  comctl32!DefSubclassProc+0x46
0013e41c  779cd7e4  00010090  0000000f  00000000  shdocvw!CNscTree::_SubClassTreeWndProc+0x3ae
0013e43c  77431b9b  00010090  0000000f  00000000  shdocvw!CNscTree::s_SubClassTreeWndProc+0x34
0013e498  77431dc0  001cf0f8  00010090  0000000f  comctl32!CallNextSubclassProc+0x3c
0013e4ec  7739b6e3  00010090  0000000f  00000000  comctl32!MasterSubclassProc+0x54
0013e518  7739b874  77431d6c  00010090  0000000f  user32!InternalCallWinProc+0x28
0013e590  7739c8b8  0015fce4  77431d6c  00010090  user32!UserCallWinProcCheckWow+0x151
0013e5ec  7739c9c6  00617618  0000000f  00000000  user32!DispatchClientMessage+0xd9
0013e614  7c828536  0013e62c  00000018  0013e750  user32!__fnDWORD+0x24
0013e640  7739cbb2  7739cb75  00010090  0000005e  ntdll!KiUserCallbackDispatcher+0x2e
0013e654  77459d14  00010090  00000200  001c8900  user32!NtUserCallHwndLock+0xc
0013e66c  7745bd2d  00000004  016b0055  00000000  comctl32!TV_OnMouseMove+0x62
0013e6bc  7739b6e3  00010090  00000200  00000000  comctl32!TV_WndProc+0x647
0013e6e8  7739b874  7745b6e6  00010090  00000200  user32!InternalCallWinProc+0x28
0013e760  7739bfce  0015fce4  7745b6e6  00010090  user32!UserCallWinProcCheckWow+0x151
0013e790  7739bf74  7745b6e6  00010090  00000200  user32!CallWindowProcAorW+0x98
0013e7b0  77431848  7745b6e6  00010090  00000200  user32!CallWindowProcW+0x1b
0013e7cc  77431b9b  00010090  00000200  00000000  comctl32!CallOriginalWndProc+0x1a
0013e828  77431d5d  001cf0f8  00010090  00000200  comctl32!CallNextSubclassProc+0x3c
0013e84c  779cd761  00010090  00000200  00000000  comctl32!DefSubclassProc+0x46
0013e868  77431b9b  00010090  00000200  00000000  shdocvw!CNotifySubclassWndProc::_SubclassWndProc+0xa7
0013e8c4  77431d5d  001cf0f8  00010090  00000200  comctl32!CallNextSubclassProc+0x3c
0013e8e8  779cd86f  00010090  00000200  00000000  comctl32!DefSubclassProc+0x46
0013e934  779cd7e4  00010090  00000200  00000000  shdocvw!CNscTree::_SubClassTreeWndProc+0x3ae
0013e954  77431b9b  00010090  00000200  00000000  shdocvw!CNscTree::s_SubClassTreeWndProc+0x34
0013e9b0  77431dc0  001cf0f8  00010090  00000200  comctl32!CallNextSubclassProc+0x3c
0013ea04  7739b6e3  00010090  00000200  00000000  comctl32!MasterSubclassProc+0x54
0013ea30  7739b874  77431d6c  00010090  00000200  user32!InternalCallWinProc+0x28
0013eaa8  7739ba92  0015fce4  77431d6c  00010090  user32!UserCallWinProcCheckWow+0x151
0013eb10  7739bad0  0013eb50  00000000  0013eb38  user32!DispatchMessageWorker+0x327
0013eb20  75ed1410  0013eb50  00000000  00176388  user32!DispatchMessageW+0xf
0013eb38  75ed14fc  0013eb50  0013ee50  00000000  browseui!TimedDispatchMessage+0x33
0013ed98  75ec1c83  0015f7e8  0013ee50  0015f7e8  browseui!BrowserThreadProc+0x336
0013ee24  75ec61ef  0015f7e8  0015f7e8  00000000  browseui!BrowserProtectedThreadProc+0x44
0013fea8  779ba3a6  0015f7e8  00000001  00000000  browseui!SHOpenFolderWindow+0x22c
0013fec8  0040243d  00152552  00020d02  ffffffff  shdocvw!IEWinMain+0x129
0013ff1c  00402744  00400000  00000000  00152552  iexplore!WinMain+0x316
0013ffc0  77e6f23b  00000000  00000000  7ffde000  iexplore!WinMainCRTStartup+0x182
0013fff0  00000000  004025c2  00000000  78746341  kernel32!BaseProcessStart+0x23
```

```
1 Id: c068.d71c Suspend: 1 Teb: 7ffdc000 Unfrozen
ChildEBP RetAddr Args to Child
00d4fea0 7c827cfb 7c80e5bb 00000002 00d4fef0 ntdll!KiFastSystemCallRet
00d4fea4 7c80e5bb 00000002 00d4fef0 00000001 ntdll!NtWaitForMultipleObjects+0xc
00d4ff48 7c80e4a2 00000002 00d4ff70 00000000 ntdll!EtwpWaitForMultipleObjectsEx+0xf7
00d4ffb8 77e64829 00000000 00000000 00000000 ntdll!EtwpEventPump+0x27f
00d4ffec 00000000 7c80e1fa 00000000 00000000 kernel32!BaseThreadStart+0x34

2 Id: c068.cba4 Suspend: 1 Teb: 7ffdb000 Unfrozen
ChildEBP RetAddr Args to Child
012bfe18 7c82783b 77c885ac 000001c4 012bff74 ntdll!KiFastSystemCallRet
012bfe1c 77c885ac 000001c4 012bff74 00000000 ntdll!NtReplyWaitReceivePortEx+0xc
012bff84 77c88792 012bffac 77c8872d 00153cf0 rpcrt4!LRPC_ADDRESS::ReceiveLotsaCalls+0x198
012bff8c 77c8872d 00153cf0 00000000 00000000 rpcrt4!RecvLotsaCallsWrapper+0xd
012bffac 77c7b110 00167030 012bffec 77e64829 rpcrt4!BaseCachedThreadRoutine+0x9d
012bffb8 77e64829 00172088 00000000 00000000 rpcrt4!ThreadStartRoutine+0x1b
012bffec 00000000 77c7b0f5 00172088 00000000 kernel32!BaseThreadStart+0x34

3 Id: c068.8604 Suspend: 1 Teb: 7ffda000 Unfrozen
ChildEBP RetAddr Args to Child
013bfe28 7c827d0b 7c83d236 000001d0 00000000 ntdll!KiFastSystemCallRet
013bfe2c 7c83d236 000001d0 00000000 00000000 ntdll!NtWaitForSingleObject+0xc
013bfe68 7c83d281 000001d0 00000004 00000000 ntdll!RtlpWaitOnCriticalSection+0x1a3
013bfe88 7c839844 7c8877a0 00000000 77670000 ntdll!RtlEnterCriticalSection+0xa8
013bff90 77e52860 77670000 77670000 00171698 ntdll!LdrUnloadDll+0x35
013bffa4 776b171d 77670000 00000000 00000000 kernel32!FreeLibraryAndExitThread+0x38
013bffb8 77e64829 00171698 00000000 00000000 ole32!CRpcThreadCache::RpcWorkerThreadEntry+0x39
013bffec 00000000 776b16e4 00171698 00000000 kernel32!BaseThreadStart+0x34

4 Id: c068.d6dc Suspend: 1 Teb: 7ffd9000 Unfrozen
ChildEBP RetAddr Args to Child
016dfd24 7c827cfb 77e6202c 00000005 016dfd74 ntdll!KiFastSystemCallRet
016dfd28 77e6202c 00000005 016dfd74 00000001 ntdll!NtWaitForMultipleObjects+0xc
016dfdd0 7739bbd1 00000005 016dfdf8 00000000 kernel32!WaitForMultipleObjectsEx+0x11a
016dfe2c 7c919b2e 00000004 016dfe54 ffffffff user32!RealMsgWaitForMultipleObjectsEx+0x141
016dff50 7c8f7ada 77da3f12 00000000 00000000 shell32!CChangeNotify::_MessagePump+0x3b
016dff54 77da3f12 00000000 00000000 00000000 shell32!CChangeNotify::ThreadProc+0x1e
016dffb8 77e64829 00000000 00000000 00000000 shlwapi!WrapperThreadProc+0x94
016dffec 00000000 77da3ea5 0013dea8 00000000 kernel32!BaseThreadStart+0x34

5 Id: c068.caf4 Suspend: 1 Teb: 7ffd8000 Unfrozen
ChildEBP RetAddr Args to Child
01b1fdb4 7c827cfb 77e6202c 00000002 01b1fe04 ntdll!KiFastSystemCallRet
01b1fdb8 77e6202c 00000002 01b1fe04 00000001 ntdll!NtWaitForMultipleObjects+0xc
01b1fe60 7739bbd1 00000002 01b1fe88 00000000 kernel32!WaitForMultipleObjectsEx+0x11a
01b1febc 6c296601 00000001 01b1fef0 ffffffff user32!RealMsgWaitForMultipleObjectsEx+0x141
01b1fedc 6c29684b 000004ff ffffffff 00000001 duser!CoreSC::Wait+0x3a
01b1ff10 6c28f9e6 01b1ff50 00000000 00000000 duser!CoreSC::xwProcessNL+0xab
01b1ff30 6c28bce1 01b1ff50 00000000 00000000 duser!GetMessageExA+0x44
01b1ff84 77bcb530 00000000 00000000 00000000 duser!ResourceManager::SharedThreadProc+0xb6
01b1ffb8 77e64829 000385f0 00000000 00000000 msvcrt!_endthreadex+0xa3
01b1ffec 00000000 77bcb4bc 000385f0 00000000 kernel32!BaseThreadStart+0x34
```

```
6 Id: c068.d624 Suspend: 1 Teb: 7ffd7000 Unfrozen
ChildEBP RetAddr Args to Child
01c9ff9c 7c826f4b 7c83d424 00000001 01c9ffb0 ntdll!KiFastSystemCallRet
01c9ffa0 7c83d424 00000001 01c9ffb0 00000000 ntdll!NtDelayExecution+0xc
01c9ffb8 77e64829 00000000 00000000 00000000 ntdll!RtlpTimerThread+0x47
01c9ffec 00000000 7c83d3dd 00000000 00000000 kernel32!BaseThreadStart+0x34

7 Id: c068.b4e0 Suspend: 1 Teb: 7ffd6000 Unfrozen
ChildEBP RetAddr Args to Child
01d9fd58 7c827d0b 7c83d236 000001d0 00000000 ntdll!KiFastSystemCallRet
01d9fd5c 7c83d236 000001d0 00000000 00000000 ntdll!NtWaitForSingleObject+0xc
01d9fd98 7c83d281 000001d0 00000004 00000000 ntdll!RtlpWaitOnCriticalSection+0x1a3
01d9fdb8 7c839844 7c8877a0 75eb8b7c 75eb0000 ntdll!RtlEnterCriticalSection+0xa8
01d9fec0 77e6b1bb 75eb0000 75eb0000 001e2f98 ntdll!LdrUnloadDll+0x35
01d9fed4 77da4c1c 75eb0000 0020eec8 77da591b kernel32!FreeLibrary+0x41
01d9feec 7c83a827 0020eec8 7c889080 001e4ec0 shlwapi!ExecuteWorkItem+0x28
01d9ff44 7c83aa0b 77da591b 0020eec8 00000000 ntdll!RtlpWorkerCallout+0x71
01d9ff64 7c83aa82 00000000 0020eec8 001e4ec0 ntdll!RtlpExecuteWorkerRequest+0x4f
01d9ff78 7c839f60 7c83a9ca 00000000 0020eec8 ntdll!RtlpApcCallout+0x11
01d9ffb8 77e64829 00000000 00000000 00000000 ntdll!RtlpWorkerThread+0x61
01d9ffec 00000000 7c839efb 00000000 00000000 kernel32!BaseThreadStart+0x34

8 Id: c068.d5a8 Suspend: 1 Teb: 7ffd5000 Unfrozen
ChildEBP RetAddr Args to Child
01fbb41c 7c827d0b 7c83d236 00000468 00000000 ntdll!KiFastSystemCallRet
01fbb420 7c83d236 00000468 00000000 00000000 ntdll!NtWaitForSingleObject+0xc
01fbb45c 7c83d281 00000468 00000004 00000000 ntdll!RtlpWaitOnCriticalSection+0x1a3
01fbb47c 7c9136c9 7cae42d0 001c97b0 80070003 ntdll!RtlEnterCriticalSection+0xa8
01fbb494 7c913b75 0000000c 00000000 00000001 shell32!CMountPoint::GetMountPoint+0x33
01fbb4c8 7c91358d 01fbb4fc 0000000c 00000000 shell32!CDrivesFolder::_FillIDDrive+0x5c
01fbb52c 7c9109e7 0018e988 00000000 001c97b0 shell32!CDrivesFolder::ParseDisplayName+0x9f
01fbb594 7c9119ff 0018e9b0 00000000 001c97b0 shell32!CRegFolder::ParseDisplayName+0x93
01fbb5bc 7c910bb8 00000000 001a8e30 00000000 shell32!CDesktopFolder::_ChildParseDisplayName+0x22
01fbb60c 7c9109e7 0017cde0 00000000 001c97b0 shell32!CDesktopFolder::ParseDisplayName+0x7e
01fbb674 7c910a9b 0015f058 00000000 001c97b0 shell32!CRegFolder::ParseDisplayName+0x93
01fbb6ac 7c911ab4 00000000 00000000 00000000 shell32!SHParseDisplayName+0xa3
01fbb6d0 7c911a6e 01fbbe60 00000000 00000002 shell32!ILCreateFromPathEx+0x3d
01fbb6ec 7c911a4b 01fbbe60 01fbb700 00000000 shell32!SHILCreateFromPath+0x17
01fbb704 7c95e055 01fbbe60 00000104 01fbc0a0 shell32!ILCreateFromPathW+0x18
01fbbb84 7c9ef49d 01fbbe60 00000000 01fbbbac shell32!SHGetFileInfoW+0x117
01fbc06c 01b4d195 01fbc200 00000000 01fbc0a0 shell32!SHGetFileInfoA+0x6a
WARNING: Stack unwind information not available. Following frames may be wrong.
01fbc0a4 01b54a20 0000073c 02541f28 00000000 issftran!SSCopyFile+0x27ad
00000000 00000000 00000000 00000000 00000000 issftran!DllUnregisterServer+0x70ad

9 Id: c068.d750 Suspend: 1 Teb: 7ffd4000 Unfrozen
ChildEBP RetAddr Args to Child
0228ff7c 7c8277db 71b25914 000004b4 0228ffc0 ntdll!KiFastSystemCallRet
0228ff80 71b25914 000004b4 0228ffc0 0228ffb4 ntdll!ZwRemoveIoCompletion+0xc
0228ffb8 77e64829 71b259de 00000000 00000000 mswsock!SockAsyncThread+0x69
0228ffec 00000000 71b258ab 001fcd20 00000000 kernel32!BaseThreadStart+0x34

0:000> du 7c8d8828
7c8d8828  "EXPLORER.EXE"
```

```
0:000> da 01fbc200
01fbc200 "M:\WINDOWS"
```

Comments

Another example of the critical section analysis:

```
0:005> !locks

CritSec ModuleA!__onexitbegin+50cbc at 006f1da8
WaiterWoken No
LockCount 49
RecursionCount 1
OwningThread 19a4
EntryCount 0
ContentionCount 2a51
*** Locked

CritSec ModuleA!__onexitbegin+5131c at 006f2408
WaiterWoken No
LockCount 0
RecursionCount 1
OwningThread 10f4
EntryCount 0
ContentionCount 0
*** Locked

CritSec +6e8827c at 06e8827c
WaiterWoken No
LockCount 0
RecursionCount 1
OwningThread 19a4
EntryCount 0
ContentionCount 0
*** Locked

Scanned 2404 critical sections
```

In this example, we have only one critical section which blocks other threads according to this formula:

$$BlockedThreads = LockCount - (RecursionCount - 1) = 49 - (1 - 1)$$

```
CritSec Module!__onexitbegin+50cbc at 006f1da8
WaiterWoken No
LockCount 49
RecursionCount 1
OwningThread 19a4
EntryCount 0
ContentionCount 2a51
*** Locked
```

Then we can examine owner thread's call stack 19a4 by looking at **~*kv** output and find other waiting threads by searching for critical section address: 006f1da8.

All other two critical sections are being held by *OwningThread,* and there are no waiting threads for them:

BlockedThreads = LockCount - (RecursionCount - 1) = 0 - (1 - 1) = 0

Therefore, the rule of thumb is to look at *LockCount* values.

One of the questions asked is if there any way to see the stack trace if the thread-owner of a critical section is already dead?

```
0:022> !locks

CritSec ole32!g_mxsSingleThreadOle+18 at 76a40664
WaiterWoken No
LockCount 4
RecursionCount 1
OwningThread 1ec
EntryCount 0
ContentionCount 6
*** Locked
```

Virtual memory for TEB is decommitted already, and, therefore, no data for the stack start address and its limit is available. We might guess that stack region itself is decommitted during thread termination so we cannot use memory search here to find its raw stack data. Live debugging might help here with scripts to set conditional breakpoints and saving dumps automatically upon some condition.

Another example:

```
0:000> !locks

CritSec +83eb6d10 at 83eb6d10
WaiterWoken No
LockCount -452697857
RecursionCount 36294152
OwningThread a
EntryCount 1379620
ContentionCount 1379620
*** Locked

CritSec +840d6d10 at 840d6d10
WaiterWoken Yes
LockCount -60090439
RecursionCount 1093776890
OwningThread ffffffffadcb569d
EntryCount 0
ContentionCount 0
*** Locked

CritSec +840d6d10 at 840d6d10
WaiterWoken Yes
LockCount -60090439
RecursionCount 1093776890
OwningThread ffffffffadcb569d
EntryCount 0
ContentionCount 0
*** Locked
```

```
CritSec +86156d10 at 86156d10
WaiterWoken Yes
LockCount -278997059
RecursionCount 1224415142
OwningThread ffffffff9e8e4272
EntryCount 0
ContentionCount 0
*** Locked


CritSec +83c96d10 at 83c96d10
WaiterWoken Yes
LockCount 520027693
RecursionCount 1097194433
OwningThread ffffffff8c000036
EntryCount 0
ContentionCount 0
*** Locked


CritSec +83c96d10 at 83c96d10
WaiterWoken Yes
LockCount 520027693
RecursionCount 1097194433
OwningThread ffffffff8c000036
EntryCount 0
ContentionCount 0
*** Locked


Scanned 1223 critical sections
```

We can see here that *LockCount* and *RecursionCount* have strange numbers. Here we have **Critical Section Corruption** pattern (page 169). We can also try **!cs -l -o -s** command. Sometimes, if we dump all sections, we can see where corruption starts (**!locks -v** or **!cs**).

Example for **Virtualized Process** (page 1185):

```
0:000:x86> ~*kv

. 0 Id: 2e24.35f8 Suspend: 0 Teb: 7efdb000 Unfrozen
ChildEBP RetAddr Args to Child
0015cedc 77748e44 000004b8 00000000 00000000 ntdll_77710000!ZwWaitForSingleObject+0x15 (FPO: [3,0,0])
0015cf40 77748d28 00000000 00000000 000035f8 ntdll_77710000!RtlpWaitOnCriticalSection+0x13e (FPO: [Non-Fpo])
0015cf68 558f829b 00e531d8 d3c25775 058f0a0c ntdll_77710000!RtlEnterCriticalSection+0x150 (FPO: [Non-Fpo])
WARNING: Stack unwind information not available. Following frames may be wrong.
0015d4a4 558f9e66 d3c256e1 000000df 00000000 libdjvulibre!DJVU::DjVuDocument::process_threqs+0x6b
0015d530 558cdea5 0015d57c 00000001 00000001 libdjvulibre!DJVU::DjVuDocument::get_thumbnail+0x8c6
0015d594 0103d8d1 00c6a1e0 000000df 00000000 libdjvulibre!ddjvu_thumbnail_status+0x115
0015d604 55107cd9 00c3c5a8 00000000 00000006 djview+0x4d8d1
0015d658 53f3fc29 00000000 00c3c5a8 00b8ed18 QtCore4!QMetaCallEvent::placeMetaCall+0x19
0015d8a0 550f948d d3c25ad6 00eeb598 d3c25ad6 QtGui4!QApplicationPrivate::notify_helper+0xb9
0015d8e0 550fb07f 00b8e640 00eeb598 d3c25b12 QtCore4!QCoreApplication::notifyInternal+0x8d
0015d924 5511e835 00000000 00000000 00b8e640 QtCore4!QCoreApplicationPrivate::sendPostedEvents+0x1cf
00000000 00000000 00000000 00000000 00000000 QtCore4!QEventDispatcherWin32::event+0x555


1 Id: 2e24.1390 Suspend: 0 Teb: 7efd8000 Unfrozen
ChildEBP RetAddr Args to Child
0296f884 7344a41c 00000001 0296f8e4 00000001 ntdll_77710000!NtWaitForMultipleObjects+0x15 (FPO: [5,0,0])
0296f92c 7702338a 00000000 0296f978 77749f72 winmm!timeThread+0x3c (FPO: [Non-Fpo])
0296f938 77749f72 00000000 55277637 00000000 kernel32!BaseThreadInitThunk+0xe (FPO: [Non-Fpo])
0296f978 77749f45 7344a3e0 00000000 00000000 ntdll_77710000!__RtlUserThreadStart+0x70 (FPO: [Non-Fpo])
0296f990 00000000 7344a3e0 00000000 00000000 ntdll_77710000!_RtlUserThreadStart+0x1b (FPO: [Non-Fpo])
```

```
2 Id: 2e24.37a0 Suspend: 0 Teb: 7efd5000 Unfrozen
ChildEBP RetAddr Args to Child
02c3facc 77762f91 00000003 005fb610 00000001 ntdll_77710000!NtWaitForMultipleObjects+0x15 (FPO: [5,0,0])
02c3fc60 7702338a 00000000 02c3fcac 77749f72 ntdll_77710000!TppWaiterpThread+0x33d (FPO: [Non-Fpo])
02c3fc6c 77749f72 005fb5e0 557273e3 00000000 kernel32!BaseThreadInitThunk+0xe (FPO: [Non-Fpo])
02c3fcac 77749f45 77762e65 005fb5e0 00000000 ntdll_77710000!__RtlUserThreadStart+0x70 (FPO: [Non-Fpo])
02c3fcc4 00000000 77762e65 005fb5e0 00000000 ntdll_77710000!_RtlUserThreadStart+0x1b (FPO: [Non-Fpo])


3 Id: 2e24.2150 Suspend: 0 Teb: 7ef4a000 Unfrozen
ChildEBP RetAddr Args to Child
0300f940 77763392 0000039c 0300f9f4 54b175ef ntdll_77710000!NtWaitForWorkViaWorkerFactory+0x12 (FPO: [2,0,0])
0300faa0 7702338a 005fa788 0300faec 77749f72 ntdll_77710000!TppWorkerThread+0x216 (FPO: [Non-Fpo])
0300faac 77749f72 005fa788 54b175a3 00000000 kernel32!BaseThreadInitThunk+0xe (FPO: [Non-Fpo])
0300faec 77749f45 77763e85 005fa788 00000000 ntdll_77710000!__RtlUserThreadStart+0x70 (FPO: [Non-Fpo])
0300fb04 00000000 77763e85 005fa788 00000000 ntdll_77710000!_RtlUserThreadStart+0x1b (FPO: [Non-Fpo])


4 Id: 2e24.3478 Suspend: 0 Teb: 7ef4d000 Unfrozen
ChildEBP RetAddr Args to Child
0320f3bc 77748e44 000004c4 00000000 00000000 ntdll_77710000!ZwWaitForSingleObject+0x15 (FPO: [3,0,0])
0320f420 77748d28 00000000 00000000 058f0a18 ntdll_77710000!RtlpWaitOnCriticalSection+0x13e (FPO: [Non-Fpo])
0320f448 558f8750 04f3538c d0f77a55 058dbb18 ntdll_77710000!RtlEnterCriticalSection+0x150 (FPO: [Non-Fpo])
WARNING: Stack unwind information not available. Following frames may be wrong.
0320f984 558fa26c d0f77a41 058dbb18 04ffb618 libdjvulibre!DJVU::DjVuDocument::process_threqs+0x520
0320f9b0 5591ec70 058dbb18 00000042 00000001 libdjvulibre!DJVU::DjVuDocument::notify_file_flags_changed+0xdc
0320fa00 55900ac1 058dbb18 00000042 00000001 libdjvulibre!DJVU::DjVuPortcaster::notify_file_flags_changed+0x80
0320faf4 559005a7 d0f778f1 00000000 00000000 libdjvulibre!DJVU::DjVuFile::decode_func+0x4c1
0320fb20 55945bf2 058dbb18 d0f778b1 00000000 libdjvulibre!DJVU::DjVuFile::static_decode_func+0x87
0320fb60 55b4c556 04d95f90 d0f779b8 00000000 libdjvulibre!DJVU::GNativeString::setat+0x282
0320fb98 55b4c600 00000000 0320fbb0 7702338a msvcr100!_endthreadex+0x3f (FPO: [Non-Fpo])
0320fba4 7702338a 04ad13d8 0320fbf0 77749f72 msvcr100!_endthreadex+0xce (FPO: [Non-Fpo])
0320fbb0 77749f72 04ad13d8 549174bf 00000000 kernel32!BaseThreadInitThunk+0xe (FPO: [Non-Fpo])
0320fbf0 77749f45 55b4c59c 04ad13d8 00000000 ntdll_77710000!__RtlUserThreadStart+0x70 (FPO: [Non-Fpo])
0320fc08 00000000 55b4c59c 04ad13d8 00000000 ntdll_77710000!_RtlUserThreadStart+0x1b (FPO: [Non-Fpo])


0:000:x86> !cs -l -o -s
-----------------------------
DebugInfo = 0x00000000005f05c0
Critical section = 0x0000000000e531d8 (+0xE531D8)
LOCKED
LockCount = 0x1
WaiterWoken = No
OwningThread = 0x0000000000003478
RecursionCount = 0x1
LockSemaphore = 0x4B8
SpinCount = 0x0000000000000000
OwningThread DbgId = ~4s
OwningThread Stack =
ChildEBP RetAddr Args to Child
0320f3bc 77748e44 000004c4 00000000 00000000 ntdll_77710000!ZwWaitForSingleObject+0x15 (FPO: [3,0,0])
0320f420 77748d28 00000000 00000000 058f0a18 ntdll_77710000!RtlpWaitOnCriticalSection+0x13e (FPO: [Non-Fpo])
0320f448 558f8750 04f3538c d0f77a55 058dbb18 ntdll_77710000!RtlEnterCriticalSection+0x150 (FPO: [Non-Fpo])
0320f984 558fa26c d0f77a41 058dbb18 04ffb618 libdjvulibre!DJVU::DjVuDocument::process_threqs+0x520
0320f9b0 5591ec70 058dbb18 00000042 00000001 libdjvulibre!DJVU::DjVuDocument::notify_file_flags_changed+0xdc
0320fa00 55900ac1 058dbb18 00000042 00000001 libdjvulibre!DJVU::DjVuPortcaster::notify_file_flags_changed+0x80
0320faf4 559005a7 d0f778f1 00000000 00000000 libdjvulibre!DJVU::DjVuFile::decode_func+0x4c1
0320fb20 55945bf2 058dbb18 d0f778b1 00000000 libdjvulibre!DJVU::DjVuFile::static_decode_func+0x87
0320fb60 55b4c556 04d95f90 d0f779b8 00000000 libdjvulibre!DJVU::GNativeString::setat+0x282
0320fb98 55b4c600 00000000 0320fbb0 7702338a msvcr100!_endthreadex+0x3f (FPO: [Non-Fpo])
0320fba4 7702338a 04ad13d8 0320fbf0 77749f72 msvcr100!_endthreadex+0xce (FPO: [Non-Fpo])
0320fbb0 77749f72 04ad13d8 549174bf 00000000 kernel32!BaseThreadInitThunk+0xe (FPO: [Non-Fpo])
0320fbf0 77749f45 55b4c59c 04ad13d8 00000000 ntdll_77710000!__RtlUserThreadStart+0x70 (FPO: [Non-Fpo])
0320fc08 00000000 55b4c59c 04ad13d8 00000000 ntdll_77710000!_RtlUserThreadStart+0x1b (FPO: [Non-Fpo])
${$ntdllwsym}!RtlpStackTraceDataBase is NULL. Probably the stack traces are not enabled.
-----------------------------
DebugInfo = 0x0000000000625d80
Critical section = 0x0000000004f3538c (+0x4F3538C)
LOCKED
LockCount = 0x1
WaiterWoken = No
OwningThread = 0x00000000000035f8
RecursionCount = 0x1
LockSemaphore = 0x4C4
```

```
SpinCount = 0x0000000000000000
OwningThread DbgId = ~0s
OwningThread Stack =
ChildEBP RetAddr Args to Child
0015cedc 77748e44 000004b8 00000000 00000000 ntdll_77710000!ZwWaitForSingleObject+0x15 (FPO: [3,0,0])
0015cf40 77748d28 00000000 00000000 000035f8 ntdll_77710000!RtlpWaitOnCriticalSection+0x13e (FPO: [Non-Fpo])
0015cf68 558f829b 0e531d8 d3c25775 058f0a0c ntdll_77710000!RtlEnterCriticalSection+0x150 (FPO: [Non-Fpo])
0015d4a4 558f9e66 d3c256e1 000000df 00000000 libdjvulibre!DJVU::DjVuDocument::process_threqs+0x6b
0015d530 558cdea5 0015d57c 000000df 00000001 libdjvulibre!DJVU::DjVuDocument::get_thumbnail+0x8c6
0015d594 0103d8d1 00c6a1e0 000000df 00000000 libdjvulibre!ddjvu_thumbnail_status+0x115
0015d604 55107cd9 00c3c5a8 00000000 00000006 djview+0x4d8d1
0015d658 53f3fc29 00000000 00c3c5a8 00b8ed18 QtCore4!QMetaCallEvent::placeMetaCall+0x19
0015d8a0 550f948d 00c3c5a8 00eeb598 d3c25ad6 QtGui4!QApplicationPrivate::notify_helper+0xb9
0015d8e0 550fb07f 00b8e640 00eeb598 d3c25b12 QtCore4!QCoreApplication::notifyInternal+0x8d
0015d924 5511e835 00000000 00000000 00b8e640 QtCore4!QCoreApplicationPrivate::sendPostedEvents+0x1cf
00000000 00000000 00000000 00000000 00000000 QtCore4!QEventDispatcherWin32::event+0x555
${$ntdllwsym}!RtlpStackTraceDataBase is NULL. Probably the stack traces are not enabled.
```

Often, we can preliminary suppose a critical section deadlock if all locked critical section owner threads are waiting for critical sections (as seen from **!cs -l -o -s** WinDbg command output and corresponding stack traces, **k** or **!thread**).

Executive Resources

ERESOURCE (executive resource) is a Windows synchronization object that has ownership semantics.

An executive resource can be owned exclusively or can have a shared ownership. This is similar to the following file sharing analogy: when a file is opened for writing others can't write or read it; if we have that file opened for reading others can read it but can't write to it.

ERESOURCE structure is linked into a list and has threads as owners which allows us to quickly find deadlocks using **!locks** command in the kernel and complete memory dumps. Here is the definition of _ERESOURCE from x86 and x64 Windows:

```
0: kd> dt -r1 _ERESOURCE
   +0x000 SystemResourcesList : _LIST_ENTRY
      +0x000 Flink          : Ptr32 _LIST_ENTRY
      +0x004 Blink          : Ptr32 _LIST_ENTRY
   +0x008 OwnerTable      : Ptr32 _OWNER_ENTRY
      +0x000 OwnerThread    : Uint4B
      +0x004 OwnerCount     : Int4B
      +0x004 TableSize      : Uint4B
   +0x00c ActiveCount     : Int2B
   +0x00e Flag            : Uint2B
   +0x010 SharedWaiters   : Ptr32 _KSEMAPHORE
      +0x000 Header         : _DISPATCHER_HEADER
      +0x010 Limit          : Int4B
   +0x014 ExclusiveWaiters : Ptr32 _KEVENT
      +0x000 Header         : _DISPATCHER_HEADER
   +0x018 OwnerThreads    : [2] _OWNER_ENTRY
      +0x000 OwnerThread    : Uint4B
      +0x004 OwnerCount     : Int4B
      +0x004 TableSize      : Uint4B
   +0x028 ContentionCount  : Uint4B
   +0x02c NumberOfSharedWaiters : Uint2B
   +0x02e NumberOfExclusiveWaiters : Uint2B
   +0x030 Address         : Ptr32 Void
   +0x030 CreatorBackTraceIndex : Uint4B
   +0x034 SpinLock        : Uint4B


0: kd> dt -r1 _ERESOURCE
nt!_ERESOURCE
   +0x000 SystemResourcesList : _LIST_ENTRY
      +0x000 Flink          : Ptr64 _LIST_ENTRY
      +0x008 Blink          : Ptr64 _LIST_ENTRY
   +0x010 OwnerTable      : Ptr64 _OWNER_ENTRY
      +0x000 OwnerThread    : Uint8B
      +0x008 OwnerCount     : Int4B
      +0x008 TableSize      : Uint4B
   +0x018 ActiveCount     : Int2B
   +0x01a Flag            : Uint2B
   +0x020 SharedWaiters   : Ptr64 _KSEMAPHORE
      +0x000 Header         : _DISPATCHER_HEADER
      +0x018 Limit          : Int4B
```

```
+0x028 ExclusiveWaiters : Ptr64 _KEVENT
    +0x000 Header           : _DISPATCHER_HEADER
+0x030 OwnerThreads     : [2] _OWNER_ENTRY
    +0x000 OwnerThread      : Uint8B
    +0x008 OwnerCount       : Int4B
    +0x008 TableSize        : Uint4B
+0x050 ContentionCount  : Uint4B
+0x054 NumberOfSharedWaiters : Uint2B
+0x056 NumberOfExclusiveWaiters : Uint2B
+0x058 Address          : Ptr64 Void
+0x058 CreatorBackTraceIndex : Uint8B
+0x060 SpinLock         : Uint8B
```

If we have a list of resources from **!locks** output, we can start following threads that own these resources. Owner threads are marked with a star character (*):

```
0: kd> !locks
**** DUMP OF ALL RESOURCE OBJECTS ****
KD: Scanning for held locks......

Resource @ 0x8815b928    Exclusively owned
    Contention Count = 6234751
    NumberOfExclusiveWaiters = 53
     Threads: 89ab8db0-01<*>
    Threads Waiting On Exclusive Access:
        8810fa08      880f5b40      88831020      87e33020
        880353f0      88115020      88131678      880f5db0
        89295420      88255378      880f8b40      8940d020
        880f58d0      893ee500      880edac8      880f8db0
        89172938      879b3020      88091510      88038020
        880407b8      88051020      89511db0      8921f020
        880e9db0      87c33020      88064cc0      88044730
        8803f020      87a2a020      89529380      8802d330
        89a53020      89231b28      880285b8      88106b90
        8803cbc8      88aa3020      88093400      8809aab0
        880ea540      87d46948      88036020      8806e198
        8802d020      88038b40      8826b020      88231020
        890a2020      8807f5d0
```

We see that 53 threads are waiting for _KTHREAD 89ab8db0 to release _ERESOURCE 8815b928. Searching for this thread address reveals the following:

```
Resource @ 0x88159560    Exclusively owned
    Contention Count = 166896
    NumberOfExclusiveWaiters = 1
     Threads: 8802a790-01<*>
    Threads Waiting On Exclusive Access:
            89ab8db0
```

We see that the thread 89ab8db0 is waiting for 8802a790 to release the resource 88159560. We continue searching for the thread 8802a790 waiting for another thread, but we skip occurrences when this thread is not waiting:

```
Resource @ 0x881f7b60     Exclusively owned
      Threads: 8802a790-01<*>


Resource @ 0x8824b418     Exclusively owned
    Contention Count = 34
      Threads: 8802a790-01<*>


Resource @ 0x8825e5a0     Exclusively owned
      Threads: 8802a790-01<*>


Resource @ 0x88172428     Exclusively owned
    Contention Count = 5
    NumberOfExclusiveWaiters = 1
     Threads: 8802a790-01<*>
     Threads Waiting On Exclusive Access:
            880f5020
```

Searching further we see that the thread 8802a790 is waiting for the thread 880f5020 to release the resource 89bd7bf0:

```
Resource @ 0x89bd7bf0     Exclusively owned
    Contention Count = 1
    NumberOfExclusiveWaiters = 1
     Threads: 880f5020-01<*>
     Threads Waiting On Exclusive Access:
            8802a790
```

If we look carefully we see that we have already seen the thread 880f5020 above, and we repeat the fragment:

```
Resource @ 0x88172428     Exclusively owned
    Contention Count = 5
    NumberOfExclusiveWaiters = 1
     Threads: 8802a790-01<*>
     Threads Waiting On Exclusive Access:
            880f5020
```

We see that the thread 880f5020 is waiting for the thread 8802a790, and the thread 8802a790 is waiting for the thread 880f5020.

Therefore, we have identified the classical **Deadlock**. What we have to do now is to look at **Stack Traces** (page 1033) of these threads to see involved components.

LPC

Here is an example of **Deadlock** pattern involving LPC. In the stack trace below, *svchost.exe* thread (we call it thread A) receives an LPC call and dispatches it to *componentA* module which makes another LPC call (MessageId 000135b8) and then waiting for a reply:

```
THREAD 89143020  Cid 09b4.10dc  Teb: 7ff91000 Win32Thread: 00000000 WAIT: (Unknown) UserMode Non-
Alertable
    8914320c  Semaphore Limit 0x1
Waiting for reply to LPC MessageId 000135b8:
Current LPC port d64a5328
Not impersonating
DeviceMap              d64028f0
Owning Process         891b8b80      Image:         svchost.exe
Wait Start TickCount   237408        Ticks: 1890 (0:00:00:29.531)
Context Switch Count   866
UserTime               00:00:00.031
KernelTime             00:00:00.015
Win32 Start Address 0x000135b2
LPC Server thread working on message Id 135b2
Start Address kernel32!BaseThreadStartThunk (0x7c82b5f3)
Stack Init b91f9000 Current b91f8c08 Base b91f9000 Limit b91f6000 Call 0
Priority 9 BasePriority 8 PriorityDecrement 0
ChildEBP RetAddr
b91f8c20 8083e6a2 nt!KiSwapContext+0x26
b91f8c4c 8083f164 nt!KiSwapThread+0x284
b91f8c94 8093983f nt!KeWaitForSingleObject+0x346
b91f8d50 80834d3f nt!NtRequestWaitReplyPort+0x776
b91f8d50 7c94ed54 nt!KiFastCallEntry+0xfc
02bae928 7c941c94 ntdll!KiFastSystemCallRet
02bae92c 77c42700 ntdll!NtRequestWaitReplyPort+0xc
02bae984 77c413ba RPCRT4!LRPC_CCALL::SendReceive+0x230
02bae990 77c42c7f RPCRT4!I_RpcSendReceive+0x24
02bae9a4 77cb5d63 RPCRT4!NdrSendReceive+0x2b
02baec48 674825b6 RPCRT4!NdrClientCall+0x334
02baec5c 67486776 componentA!bar+0x16
...
...
...
02baf8d4 77c40f3b componentA!foo+0x157
02baf8f8 77cb23f7 RPCRT4!Invoke+0x30
02bafcf8 77cb26ed RPCRT4!NdrStubCall2+0x299
02bafd14 77c409be RPCRT4!NdrServerCall2+0x19
02bafd48 77c4093f RPCRT4!DispatchToStubInCNoAvrf+0x38
02bafd9c 77c40865 RPCRT4!RPC_INTERFACE::DispatchToStubWorker+0x117
02bafdc0 77c434b1 RPCRT4!RPC_INTERFACE::DispatchToStub+0xa3
02bafdfc 77c41bb3 RPCRT4!LRPC_SCALL::DealWithRequestMessage+0x42c
02bafe20 77c45458 RPCRT4!LRPC_ADDRESS::DealWithLRPCRequest+0x127
02baff84 77c2778f RPCRT4!LRPC_ADDRESS::ReceiveLotsaCalls+0x430
02baff8c 77c2f7dd RPCRT4!RecvLotsaCallsWrapper+0xd
02baffac 77c2de88 RPCRT4!BaseCachedThreadRoutine+0x9d
02baffb8 7c82608b RPCRT4!ThreadStartRoutine+0x1b
02baffec 00000000 kernel32!BaseThreadStart+0x34
```

We search for that LPC message to find the server thread:

```
1: kd> !lpc message 000135b8
Searching message 135b8 in threads ...
    Server thread 89115db0 is working on message 135b8
Client thread 89143020 waiting a reply from 135b8
...
...
...
```

It belongs to *Process.exe,* and we call it thread B (0x16 flags for **!thread** extension command are used to temporarily set the process context to the owning process and show the first three function call parameters):

```
1: kd> !thread 89115db0 0x16
THREAD 89115db0  Cid 098c.0384  Teb: 7ff79000 Win32Thread: 00000000 WAIT: (Unknown) UserMode Non-
Alertable
    8a114628  SynchronizationEvent
Not impersonating
DeviceMap               d64028f0
Owning Process          8a2c9d88    Image:        Process.exe
Wait Start TickCount    237408      Ticks: 1890 (0:00:00:29.531)
Context Switch Count    1590
UserTime                00:00:03.265
KernelTime              00:00:01.671
Win32 Start Address 0x000135b8
LPC Server thread working on message Id 135b8
Start Address kernel32!BaseThreadStartThunk (0x7c82b5f3)
Stack Init b952d000 Current b952cc60 Base b952d000 Limit b952a000 Call 0
Priority 9 BasePriority 8 PriorityDecrement 0
ChildEBP RetAddr  Args to Child
b952cc78 8083e6a2 89115e28 89115db0 89115e58 nt!KiSwapContext+0x26
b952cca4 8083f164 00000000 00000000 00000000 nt!KiSwapThread+0x284
b952ccec 8092db70 8a114628 00000006 ffffff01 nt!KeWaitForSingleObject+0x346
b952cd50 80834d3f 00000a7c 00000000 00000000 nt!NtWaitForSingleObject+0x9a
b952cd50 7c94ed54 00000a7c 00000000 00000000 nt!KiFastCallEntry+0xfc
22aceb48 7c942124 7c95970f 00000a7c 00000000 ntdll!KiFastSystemCallRet
22aceb4c 7c95970f 00000a7c 00000000 00000000 ntdll!NtWaitForSingleObject+0xc
22aceb88 7c959620 00000000 00000004 00002000 ntdll!RtlpWaitOnCriticalSection+0x19c
22aceba8 1b005744 06d30940 1b05ea80 06d30940 ntdll!RtlEnterCriticalSection+0xa8
22acebb0 1b05ea80 06d30940 feffffff 0cd410c0 componentB!bar+0xb
...
...
...
22acf8b0 77c40f3b 00080002 000800e2 00000001 componentB!foo+0xeb
22acf8e0 77cb23f7 0de110dc 22acfac8 00000007 RPCRT4!Invoke+0x30
22acfce0 77cb26ed 00000000 00000000 19f38f94 RPCRT4!NdrStubCall2+0x299
22acfcfc 77c409be 19f38f94 17316ef0 19f38f94 RPCRT4!NdrServerCall2+0x19
22acfd30 77c75e41 0de1dc58 19f38f94 22acfdec RPCRT4!DispatchToStubInCNoAvrf+0x38
22acfd48 77c4093f 0de1dc58 19f38f94 22acfdec RPCRT4!DispatchToStubInCAvrf+0x14
22acfd9c 77c40865 00000041 00000000 0de2b398 RPCRT4!RPC_INTERFACE::DispatchToStubWorker+0x117
22acfdc0 77c434b1 19f38f94 00000000 0de2b398 RPCRT4!RPC_INTERFACE::DispatchToStub+0xa3
22acfdfc 77c41bb3 1beeaec8 16b96f50 1baeef00 RPCRT4!LRPC_SCALL::DealWithRequestMessage+0x42c
22acfe20 77c45458 16b96f88 22acfe38 1beeaec8 RPCRT4!LRPC_ADDRESS::DealWithLRPCRequest+0x127
```

We see that the thread B is waiting for the critical section 06d30940, and we use user space **!locks** extension command to find who owns it after switching process context:

```
1: kd> .process /r /p 8a2c9d88
Implicit process is now 8a2c9d88
Loading User Symbols


1: kd> !ntsdexts.locks


CritSec +6d30940 at 06d30940
WaiterWoken        No
LockCount          1
RecursionCount     1
OwningThread       d6c
EntryCount         0
ContentionCount    1
*** Locked
```

Now we try to find a thread with TID d6c (thread C):

```
1: kd> !thread -t d6c
Looking for thread Cid = d6c ...
THREAD 890d8bb8  Cid 098c.0d6c  Teb: 7ff71000 Win32Thread: bc23cc20 WAIT: (Unknown) UserMode Non-
Alertable
    890d8da4  Semaphore Limit 0x1
Waiting for reply to LPC MessageId 000135ea:
Current LPC port d649a678
Not impersonating
DeviceMap              d64028f0
Owning Process         8a2c9d88       Image:          Process.exe
Wait Start TickCount   237641         Ticks: 1657 (0:00:00:25.890)
Context Switch Count   2102                   LargeStack
UserTime               00:00:00.734
KernelTime             00:00:00.234
Win32 Start Address msvcrt!_endthreadex (0x77b9b4bc)
Start Address kernel32!BaseThreadStartThunk (0x7c82b5f3)
Stack Init ba91d000 Current ba91cc08 Base ba91d000 Limit ba919000 Call 0
Priority 13 BasePriority 8 PriorityDecrement 0
ChildEBP RetAddr  Args to Child
ba91cc20 8083e6a2 890d8c30 890d8bb8 890d8c60 nt!KiSwapContext+0x26
ba91cc4c 8083f164 890d8da4 890d8d78 890d8bb8 nt!KiSwapThread+0x284
ba91cc94 8093983f 890d8da4 00000011 8a2c9d01 nt!KeWaitForSingleObject+0x346
ba91cd50 80834d3f 000008bc 19c94f00 19c94f00 nt!NtRequestWaitReplyPort+0x776
ba91cd50 7c94ed54 000008bc 19c94f00 19c94f00 nt!KiFastCallEntry+0xfc
2709ebf4 7c941c94 77c42700 000008bc 19c94f00 ntdll!KiFastSystemCallRet
2709ebf8 77c42700 000008bc 19c94f00 19c94f00 ntdll!NtRequestWaitReplyPort+0xc
2709ec44 77c413ba 2709ec80 2709ec64 77c42c7f RPCRT4!LRPC_CCALL::SendReceive+0x230
2709ec50 77c42c7f 2709ec80 779b2770 2709f06c RPCRT4!I_RpcSendReceive+0x24
2709ec64 77cb219b 2709ecac 1957cfe4 1957ab38 RPCRT4!NdrSendReceive+0x2b
2709f04c 779b43a3 779b2770 779b1398 2709f06c RPCRT4!NdrClientCall2+0x22e
...
...
...
2709ff84 77b9b530 26658fb0 00000000 00000000 ComponentC!foo+0x18d
```

```
2709ffb8 7c82608b 26d9af70 00000000 00000000 msvcrt!_endthreadex+0xa3
2709ffec 00000000 77b9b4bc 26d9af70 00000000 kernel32!BaseThreadStart+0x34
```

We see that the thread C makes another LPC call (MessageId 000135e) and waiting for a reply. Let's find the server thread processing the message (thread D):

```
1: kd> !lpc message 000135ea
Searching message 135ea in threads ...
Client thread 890d8bb8 waiting a reply from 135ea
    Server thread 89010020 is working on message 135ea
...
...
...


1: kd> !thread 89010020 16
THREAD 89010020  Cid 09b4.1530  Teb: 7ff93000 Win32Thread: 00000000 WAIT: (Unknown) UserMode Non-
Alertable
    8903ba28  Mutant - owning thread 89143020
Not impersonating
DeviceMap                 d64028f0
Owning Process            891b8b80       Image:         svchost.exe
Wait Start TickCount      237641         Ticks: 1657 (0:00:00:25.890)
Context Switch Count      8
UserTime                  00:00:00.000
KernelTime                00:00:00.000
Win32 Start Address 0x000135ea
LPC Server thread working on message Id 135ea
Start Address kernel32!BaseThreadStartThunk (0x7c82b5f3)
Stack Init b9455000 Current b9454c60 Base b9455000 Limit b9452000 Call 0
Priority 9 BasePriority 8 PriorityDecrement 0
ChildEBP RetAddr  Args to Child
b9454c78 8083e6a2 89010098 89010020 890100c8 nt!KiSwapContext+0x26
b9454ca4 8083f164 00000000 00000000 00000000 nt!KiSwapThread+0x284
b9454cec 8092db70 8903ba28 00000006 00000001 nt!KeWaitForSingleObject+0x346
b9454d50 80834d3f 00000514 00000000 00000000 nt!NtWaitForSingleObject+0x9a
b9454d50 7c94ed54 00000514 00000000 00000000 nt!KiFastCallEntry+0xfc
02b5f720 7c942124 75fdbe44 00000514 00000000 ntdll!KiFastSystemCallRet
02b5f724 75fdbe44 00000514 00000000 00000000 ntdll!NtWaitForSingleObject+0xc
02b5f744 75fdc57f 000e6014 000da62c 02b5fca0 ComponentD!bar+0x42
...
...
...
02b5f8c8 77c40f3b 000d0a48 02b5fc90 00000001 ComponentD!foo+0x49
02b5f8f8 77cb23f7 75fdf8f2 02b5fae0 00000007 RPCRT4!Invoke+0x30
02b5fcf8 77cb26ed 00000000 00000000 000d4f24 RPCRT4!NdrStubCall2+0x299
02b5fd14 77c409be 000d4f24 000b5d70 000d4f24 RPCRT4!NdrServerCall2+0x19
02b5fd48 77c4093f 75fff834 000d4f24 02b5fdec RPCRT4!DispatchToStubInCNoAvrf+0x38
02b5fd9c 77c40865 00000005 00000000 7600589c RPCRT4!RPC_INTERFACE::DispatchToStubWorker+0x117
02b5fdc0 77c434b1 000d4f24 00000000 7600589c RPCRT4!RPC_INTERFACE::DispatchToStub+0xa3
02b5fdfc 77c41bb3 000d3550 000a78d0 001054b8 RPCRT4!LRPC_SCALL::DealWithRequestMessage+0x42c
02b5fe20 77c45458 000a7908 02b5fe38 000d3550 RPCRT4!LRPC_ADDRESS::DealWithLRPCRequest+0x127
02b5ff84 77c2778f 02b5ffac 77c2f7dd 000a78d0 RPCRT4!LRPC_ADDRESS::ReceiveLotsaCalls+0x430
02b5ff8c 77c2f7dd 000a78d0 00000000 00000000 RPCRT4!RecvLotsaCallsWrapper+0xd
02b5ffac 77c2de88 0008ae00 02b5ffec 7c82608b RPCRT4!BaseCachedThreadRoutine+0x9d
```

```
02b5ffb8 7c82608b 000d5c20 00000000 00000000 RPCRT4!ThreadStartRoutine+0x1b
02b5ffec 00000000 77c2de6d 000d5c20 00000000 kernel32!BaseThreadStart+0x34
```

We see that the thread D is waiting for the mutant object owned by the thread A (89143020). Therefore we have **Deadlock** spanning 2 process boundaries via RPC/LPC calls with the following dependency graph:

A (svchost.exe) ^{LPC}-> B (Process.exe) ^{CritSec}-> C (Process.exe) ^{LPC}-> D (svchost.exe) ^{Obj}-> A (svchost.exe)

Managed Space

Now we illustrate a synchronization block **Deadlock** pattern in managed code. Here we can use either a manual **!syncblk** WinDbg command coupled with a stack trace and disassembly analysis or SOSEX[35] extension **!dlk** command (which automates the whole detection process).

```
0:011> !syncblk
Index SyncBlock MonitorHeld Recursion Owning Thread Info SyncBlock Owner
373 052cbf1c 3 1 08f69280 bc0 14 0a1ffd84 System.String
375 052cbd3c 3 1 08f68728 b6c 12 0a1ffd4c System.String


0:011> ~12s
[…]


0:012> k
ChildEBP RetAddr
WARNING: Stack unwind information not available. Following frames may be wrong.
09c8ebd0 79ed98fd ntdll!KiFastSystemCallRet
09c8ec38 79ed9889 mscorwks!WaitForMultipleObjectsEx_SO_TOLERANT+0x6f
09c8ec58 79ed9808 mscorwks!Thread::DoAppropriateAptStateWait+0x3c
09c8ecdc 79ed96c4 mscorwks!Thread::DoAppropriateWaitWorker+0x13c
09c8ed2c 79ed9a62 mscorwks!Thread::DoAppropriateWait+0x40
09c8ed88 79e78944 mscorwks!CLREvent::WaitEx+0xf7
09c8ed9c 79ed7b37 mscorwks!CLREvent::Wait+0x17
09c8ee28 79ed7a9e mscorwks!AwareLock::EnterEpilog+0x8c
09c8ee44 79ebd7e4 mscorwks!AwareLock::Enter+0x61
09c8eee4 074c1f38 mscorwks!JIT_MonEnterWorker_Portable+0xb3
09c8ef0c 793b0d1f 0x74c1f38
09c8ef14 79373ecd mscorlib_ni+0x2f0d1f
09c8ef28 793b0c68 mscorlib_ni+0x2b3ecd
09c8ef40 79e7c74b mscorlib_ni+0x2f0c68
09c8ef50 79e7c6cc mscorwks!CallDescrWorker+0x33
09c8efd0 79e7c8e1 mscorwks!CallDescrWorkerWithHandler+0xa3
09c8f110 79e7c783 mscorwks!MethodDesc::CallDescr+0x19c
09c8f12c 79e7c90d mscorwks!MethodDesc::CallTargetWorker+0x1f
09c8f140 79fc58cd mscorwks!MethodDescCallSite::Call_RetArgSlot+0x18
09c8f328 79ef3207 mscorwks!ThreadNative::KickOffThread_Worker+0x190
09c8f33c 79ef31a3 mscorwks!Thread::DoADCallBack+0x32a
09c8f3d0 79ef30c3 mscorwks!Thread::ShouldChangeAbortToUnload+0xe3
09c8f40c 79f01723 mscorwks!Thread::ShouldChangeAbortToUnload+0x30a
09c8f41c 79f02a5d mscorwks!Thread::RaiseCrossContextException+0x434
09c8f4cc 79f02ab7 mscorwks!Thread::DoADCallBack+0xda
09c8f4e8 79ef31a3 mscorwks!Thread::DoADCallBack+0x310
09c8f57c 79ef30c3 mscorwks!Thread::ShouldChangeAbortToUnload+0xe3
09c8f5b8 79ef4826 mscorwks!Thread::ShouldChangeAbortToUnload+0x30a
09c8f5e0 79fc57b1 mscorwks!Thread::ShouldChangeAbortToUnload+0x33e
09c8f5f8 79fc56ac mscorwks!ManagedThreadBase::KickOff+0x13
09c8f694 79f95a2e mscorwks!ThreadNative::KickOffThread+0x269
```

---

[35] http://www.stevestechspot.com/default.aspx

```
09c8fd34 76573833 mscorwks!Thread::intermediateThreadProc+0x49
09c8fd40 77c1a9bd kernel32!BaseThreadInitThunk+0xe
09c8fd80 00000000 ntdll!LdrInitializeThunk+0x4d


0:012> ub 074c1f38
074c1f11 eb10 jmp 074c1f23
074c1f13 8b0df8927b02 mov ecx,dword ptr ds:[27B92F8h]
074c1f19 e8367ef271 call mscorlib_ni+0x329d54 (793e9d54)
074c1f1e e89272a472 call mscorwks!JIT_EndCatch (79f091b5)
074c1f23 b9d0070000 mov ecx,7D0h
074c1f28 e8c432b072 call mscorwks!ThreadNative::Sleep (79fc51f1)
074c1f2d 8b0d88dc7b02 mov ecx,dword ptr ds:[27BDC88h]
074c1f33 e811389b72 call mscorwks!JIT_MonEnterWorker (79e75749)


0:012> dp 27BDC88h l1
027bdc88 0a1ffd84


0:012> ~14s


0:014> k
ChildEBP RetAddr
WARNING: Stack unwind information not available. Following frames may be wrong.
0b83ed04 79ed98fd ntdll!KiFastSystemCallRet
0b83ed6c 79ed9889 mscorwks!WaitForMultipleObjectsEx_SO_TOLERANT+0x6f
0b83ed8c 79ed9808 mscorwks!Thread::DoAppropriateAptStateWait+0x3c
0b83ee10 79ed96c4 mscorwks!Thread::DoAppropriateWaitWorker+0x13c
0b83ee60 79ed9a62 mscorwks!Thread::DoAppropriateWait+0x40
0b83eebc 79e78944 mscorwks!CLREvent::WaitEx+0xf7
0b83eed0 79ed7b37 mscorwks!CLREvent::Wait+0x17
0b83ef5c 79ed7a9e mscorwks!AwareLock::EnterEpilog+0x8c
0b83ef78 79ebd7e4 mscorwks!AwareLock::Enter+0x61
0b83f018 074c5681 mscorwks!JIT_MonEnterWorker_Portable+0xb3
0b83f01c 793b0d1f 0x74c5681
0b83f024 79373ecd mscorlib_ni+0x2f0d1f
0b83f038 793b0c68 mscorlib_ni+0x2b3ecd
0b83f050 79e7c74b mscorlib_ni+0x2f0c68
0b83f060 79e7c6cc mscorwks!CallDescrWorker+0x33
0b83f0e0 79e7c8e1 mscorwks!CallDescrWorkerWithHandler+0xa3
0b83f220 79e7c783 mscorwks!MethodDesc::CallDescr+0x19c
0b83f23c 79e7c90d mscorwks!MethodDesc::CallTargetWorker+0x1f
0b83f250 79fc58cd mscorwks!MethodDescCallSite::Call_RetArgSlot+0x18
0b83f438 79ef3207 mscorwks!ThreadNative::KickOffThread_Worker+0x190
0b83f44c 79ef31a3 mscorwks!Thread::DoADCallBack+0x32a
0b83f4e0 79ef30c3 mscorwks!Thread::ShouldChangeAbortToUnload+0xe3
0b83f51c 79f01723 mscorwks!Thread::ShouldChangeAbortToUnload+0x30a
0b83f52c 79f02a5d mscorwks!Thread::RaiseCrossContextException+0x434
0b83f5dc 79f02ab7 mscorwks!Thread::DoADCallBack+0xda
0b83f5f8 79ef31a3 mscorwks!Thread::DoADCallBack+0x310
0b83f68c 79ef30c3 mscorwks!Thread::ShouldChangeAbortToUnload+0xe3
0b83f6c8 79ef4826 mscorwks!Thread::ShouldChangeAbortToUnload+0x30a
0b83f6f0 79fc57b1 mscorwks!Thread::ShouldChangeAbortToUnload+0x33e
0b83f708 79fc56ac mscorwks!ManagedThreadBase::KickOff+0x13
0b83f7a4 79f95a2e mscorwks!ThreadNative::KickOffThread+0x269
0b83ff3c 76573833 mscorwks!Thread::intermediateThreadProc+0x49
```

```
0b83ff48 77c1a9bd kernel32!BaseThreadInitThunk+0xe
0b83ff88 00000000 ntdll!LdrInitializeThunk+0x4d


0:014> ub 074c5681
074c565c 080c54 or byte ptr [esp+edx*2],cl
074c565f 07 pop es
074c5660 8b0d88dc7b02 mov ecx,dword ptr ds:[27BDC88h]
074c5666 e8de009b72 call mscorwks!JIT_MonEnterWorker (79e75749)
074c566b a1240a5407 mov eax,dword ptr ds:[07540A24h]
074c5670 3105280a5407 xor dword ptr ds:[7540A28h],eax
074c5676 8b0d84dc7b02 mov ecx,dword ptr ds:[27BDC84h]
074c567c e8c8009b72 call mscorwks!JIT_MonEnterWorker (79e75749)


0:014> dp 27BDC84h l1
027bdc84 0a1ffd4c


0:014> !dlk
Examining SyncBlocks...
Scanning for ReaderWriterLock instances...
Scanning for holders of ReaderWriterLock locks...
Scanning for ReaderWriterLockSlim instances...
Scanning for holders of ReaderWriterLockSlim locks...
Examining CriticalSections...
Could not find symbol ntdll!RtlCriticalSectionList.
Scanning for threads waiting on SyncBlocks...
Scanning for threads waiting on ReaderWriterLock locks...
Scanning for threads waiting on ReaderWriterLocksSlim locks...
Scanning for threads waiting on CriticalSections...
*DEADLOCK DETECTED*
CLR thread 0xd holds the lock on SyncBlock 052cbd3c OBJ:0a1ffd4c[System.String] STRVAL=critical section 1
...and is waiting for the lock on SyncBlock 052cbf1c OBJ:0a1ffd84[System.String] STRVAL=critical section 2
CLR thread 0xb holds the lock on SyncBlock 052cbf1c OBJ:0a1ffd84[System.String] STRVAL=critical section 2
...and is waiting for the lock on SyncBlock 052cbd3c OBJ:0a1ffd4c[System.String] STRVAL=critical section 1
CLR Thread 0xd is waiting at UserQuery+ClassMain.thread_proc_1()(+0x42 IL)(+0x60 Native)
CLR Thread 0xb is waiting at UserQuery+ClassMain.thread_proc_2()(+0x19 IL)(+0x21 Native)


1 deadlock detected.
```

Mixed Objects

Kernel Space

Here is another pattern of a **Deadlock** variety involving mixed objects in kernel space. Let's look at a complete **Manual Dump** (page 705) file from a hanging system:

```
0: kd> !analyze -v

NMI_HARDWARE_FAILURE (80)
This is typically due to a hardware malfunction.  The hardware supplier should
be called.
Arguments:
Arg1: 004f4454
Arg2: 00000000
Arg3: 00000000
Arg4: 00000000
```

Here we have a problem to read all executive resource locks:

```
3: kd> !locks
**** DUMP OF ALL RESOURCE OBJECTS ****

Resource @ nt!CmpRegistryLock (0x808a48c0)    Shared 36 owning threads
    Contention Count = 48
      Threads: 86aecae0-01<*> 8b76db40-01<*> 8b76ddb0-01<*> 89773020-01<*>
               87222db0-01<*> 87024ba8-01<*> 89a324f0-01<*> 86b4e298-01<*>
               87925b40-01<*> 86b4db40-01<*> 8701f738-01<*> 86ffb198-01<*>
               86b492f0-01<*> 8701bad8-01<*> 86ae2db0-01<*> 86c85db0-01<*>
               86a9ddb0-01<*> 86a86db0-01<*> 86aa7db0-01<*> 86a9f5c0-01<*>
               86c5adb0-01<*> 8767ba38-01<*> 86afedb0-01<*> 89877960-01<*>
               8772cdb0-01<*> 87348628-01<*> 874d6748-01<*> 872365e0-01<*>
               87263970-01<*> 873bf020-01<*> 86c13db0-01<*> 893dcdb0-01<*>
               86afa020-01<*> 878e5020-01<*> 874959f8-01<*> 86b2dc70-01<*>
KD: Scanning for held locks…Error 1 in reading nt!_ERESOURCE.SystemResourcesList.Flink @ f76ee2a0
```

This is probably because the dump was **Truncated** (page 1130):

```
Loading Dump File [MEMORY.DMP]
Kernel Complete Dump File: Full address space is available

WARNING: Dump file has been truncated. Data may be missing.
```

However looking at the resource 808a48c0 closely we see that it is owned by the thread 86aecae0 (Cid 2810.2910) which is blocked on a mutant owned by the thread 86dcf3a8:

```
3: kd> !locks -v 0x808a48c0


Resource @ nt!CmpRegistryLock (0x808a48c0)     Shared 36 owning threads
    Contention Count = 48
      Threads: 86aecae0-01<*>


    THREAD 86aecae0  Cid 2810.2910  Teb: 7ffdd000 Win32Thread: bc54ab88 WAIT: (Unknown) KernelMode Non-
Alertable
          86dda264  Mutant - owning thread 86dcf3a8
      Not impersonating
      DeviceMap               da534618
      Owning Process          86f30b70      Image:          ApplicationA.exe
      Wait Start TickCount    1074481       Ticks: 51601 (0:00:13:26.265)
      Context Switch Count    9860                    LargeStack
      UserTime                00:00:01.125
      KernelTime              00:00:00.890
      Win32 Start Address 0x300019f0
      Start Address kernel32!BaseProcessStartThunk (0x7c8217f8)
      Stack Init b5342000 Current b5341150 Base b5342000 Limit b533d000 Call 0
      Priority 12 BasePriority 10 PriorityDecrement 0
      ChildEBP RetAddr
      b5341168 80833465 nt!KiSwapContext+0x26
      b5341194 80829a62 nt!KiSwapThread+0x2e5
      b53411dc b91f4c08 nt!KeWaitForSingleObject+0x346
WARNING: Stack unwind information not available. Following frames may be wrong.
      b5341200 b91ee770 driverA+0xec08
      b5341658 b91e9ca7 driverA+0x8770
      b5341af0 8088978c driverA+0x3ca7
      b5341af0 8082f829 nt!KiFastCallEntry+0xfc
      b5341b7c 808ce716 nt!ZwSetInformationFile+0x11
      b5341bbc 808dd8d8 nt!CmpDoFileSetSize+0x5e
      b5341bd4 808bd798 nt!CmpFileSetSize+0x16
      b5341bf4 808be23f nt!HvpGrowLog1+0x52
      b5341c18 808bfc6b nt!HvMarkDirty+0x453
      b5341c40 808c3fd4 nt!HvMarkCellDirty+0x255
      b5341cb4 808b7e2f nt!CmSetValueKey+0x390
      b5341d44 8088978c nt!NtSetValueKey+0x241
      b5341d44 7c9485ec nt!KiFastCallEntry+0xfc
      0013f5fc 00000000 ntdll!KiFastSystemCallRet


8b76db40-01<*>
```

```
THREAD 8b76db40  Cid 0004.00c8  Teb: 00000000 Win32Thread: 00000000 GATEWAIT
    Not impersonating
    DeviceMap               d6600900
    Owning Process          8b7772a8     Image:        System
    Wait Start TickCount    1074667      Ticks: 51415 (0:00:13:23.359)
    Context Switch Count    65106
    UserTime                00:00:00.000
    KernelTime              00:00:00.781
    Start Address nt!ExpWorkerThread (0x80880352)
    Stack Init bae35000 Current bae34c68 Base bae35000 Limit bae32000 Call 0
    Priority 12 BasePriority 12 PriorityDecrement 0
    ChildEBP RetAddr
    bae34c80 80833465 nt!KiSwapContext+0x26
    bae34cac 8082ffc0 nt!KiSwapThread+0x2e5
    bae34cd4 8087d6f6 nt!KeWaitForGate+0x152
    dbba6d78 00000000 nt!ExfAcquirePushLockExclusive+0x112
```

[...]

A reminder about **Cid**: it is the so-called **Client id** composed of **Process id** and **Thread id** (**Pid.Tid**). Also, a mutant is just another name for a mutex object which has ownership semantics:

```
0: kd> dt _KMUTANT 86dda264
nt!_KMUTANT
   +0x000 Header        : _DISPATCHER_HEADER
   +0x010 MutantListEntry : _LIST_ENTRY [ 0x86dcf3a8 - 0x86dcf3a8 ]
   +0x018 OwnerThread   : 86dcf3a8 _KTHREAD
   +0x01c Abandoned     : 0 "
   +0x01d ApcDisable    : 0x1 "
```

Now we look at that thread 86dcf3a8 and see that it belongs to *ApplicationB* (Cid 25a0.14b8):

```
3: kd> !thread 86dcf3a8
THREAD 86dcf3a8  Cid 25a0.14b8  Teb: 7ffa9000 Win32Thread: bc3e0d20 WAIT: (Unknown) UserMode Non-
Alertable
    8708b888  Thread
    86dcf420  NotificationTimer
Not impersonating
DeviceMap               da534618
Owning Process          87272d88     Image:        ApplicationB.exe
Wait Start TickCount    1126054      Ticks: 28 (0:00:00:00.437)
Context Switch Count    2291         LargeStack
UserTime                00:00:00.078
KernelTime              00:00:00.218
Win32 Start Address msvcrt!_endthreadex (0x77b9b4bc)
Start Address kernel32!BaseThreadStartThunk (0x7c8217ec)
Stack Init b550a000 Current b5509c60 Base b550a000 Limit b5507000 Call 0
Priority 8 BasePriority 8 PriorityDecrement 0
ChildEBP RetAddr  Args to Child
b5509c78 80833465 86dcf3a8 86dcf450 00000003 nt!KiSwapContext+0x26
b5509ca4 80829a62 00000000 b5509d14 00000000 nt!KiSwapThread+0x2e5
b5509cec 80938d0c 8708b888 00000006 00000001 nt!KeWaitForSingleObject+0x346
b5509d50 8088978c 00000960 00000000 b5509d14 nt!NtWaitForSingleObject+0x9a
b5509d50 7c9485ec 00000960 00000000 b5509d14 nt!KiFastCallEntry+0xfc
```

```
WARNING: Stack unwind information not available. Following frames may be wrong.
0454f3cc 00000000 00000000 00000000 00000000 ntdll!KiFastSystemCallRet
```

We see that it is waiting on 8708b888 object which is a thread itself, and it is waiting for the same mutant 86dda264 owned by the thread 86dcf3a8 (Cid 25a0.14b8):

```
3: kd> !thread 8708b888
THREAD 8708b888  Cid 25a0.1cb0  Teb: 7ffa6000 Win32Thread: bc3ecb20 WAIT: (Unknown) KernelMode Non-
Alertable
    86dda264  Mutant - owning thread 86dcf3a8
Not impersonating
DeviceMap               da534618
Owning Process          87272d88        Image:          ApplicationB.exe
Wait Start TickCount    1070470         Ticks: 55612 (0:00:14:28.937)
Context Switch Count    11                      LargeStack
UserTime                00:00:00.000
KernelTime              00:00:00.000
Win32 Start Address dll!_beginthread (0x1b1122a9)
Start Address kernel32!BaseThreadStartThunk (0x7c8217ec)
Stack Init b4d12000 Current b4d117fc Base b4d12000 Limit b4d0f000 Call 0
Priority 9 BasePriority 8 PriorityDecrement 0
ChildEBP RetAddr  Args to Child
b4d11814 80833465 8708b888 8708b930 00000003 nt!KiSwapContext+0x26
b4d11840 80829a62 0000096c b4d118c4 b91e8f08 nt!KiSwapThread+0x2e5
b4d11888 b91f4c08 86dda264 00000006 00000000 nt!KeWaitForSingleObject+0x346
WARNING: Stack unwind information not available. Following frames may be wrong.
b4d118ac b91ee818 86dda260 b4d11d64 86dda000 DriverA+0xec08
b4d11d04 b91e8f58 000025a0 0000096c b4d11d64 DriverA+0x8818
b4d11d58 8088978c 0000096c 0567f974 7c9485ec DriverA+0x2f58
b4d11d58 7c9485ec 0000096c 0567f974 7c9485ec nt!KiFastCallEntry+0xfc
0567f974 30cba6ad 0000096c 00000000 00000003 ntdll!KiFastSystemCallRet
```

We can summarize our findings in the following **Wait Chain** diagram (page 1221):

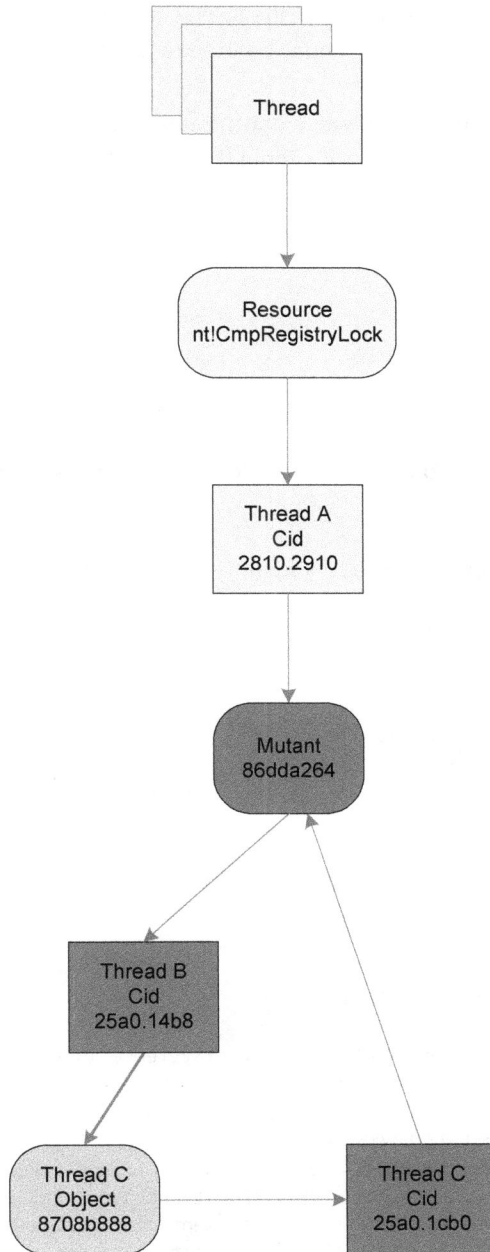

Looking from the component-object relationship perspective, it is *DriverA.sys* that is waiting on the mutant 86dda264 although both blocked threads B and C belong to *ApplicationB* process.

User Space

This is another variant of **Deadlock** pattern when we have mixed synchronization objects, for example, events, and critical sections. An event may be used to signal the availability of some work item for processing it, the fact that the queue is not empty, and a critical section may be used to protect some shared data.

The typical deadlock scenario here is when one thread resets an event by calling *WaitForSingleObject* and tries to acquire a critical section. In the meantime the second thread has already acquired that critical section and now is waiting for the event to be set:

```
Thread A       |   Thread B
..             |   ..
reset Event    |   ..
..             |   acquire CS
wait for CS    |   ..
               |   wait for Event
```

The classical fix to this bug is to acquire the critical section and wait for the event in the same order in both threads.

In our example crash dump, we can easily identify the second thread that acquired the critical section and is waiting for the event 0x480:

```
0:000> !locks

CritSec ntdll!LdrpLoaderLock+0 at 7c889d94
WaiterWoken        No
LockCount          9
RecursionCount     1
OwningThread       2038
EntryCount         0
ContentionCount    164
*** Locked


  13  Id: 590.2038 Suspend: 1 Teb: 7ffaa000 Unfrozen
ChildEBP RetAddr  Args to Child
0483fd5c 7c822124 77e6bad8 00000480 00000000 ntdll!KiFastSystemCallRet
0483fd60 77e6bad8 00000480 00000000 00000000 ntdll!NtWaitForSingleObject+0xc
0483fdd0 77e6ba42 00000480 ffffffff 00000000 kernel32!WaitForSingleObjectEx+0xac
0483fde4 776cfb30 00000480 ffffffff 777904f8 kernel32!WaitForSingleObject+0x12
0483fe00 776adfaa 00000480 00000000 00000080 ole32!CDllHost::ClientCleanupFinish+0x2a
0483fe2c 776adf1a 00000000 0483fe7c 77790828 ole32!DllHostProcessUninitialize+0x80
0483fe4c 776b063f 00000000 00000000 0c9ecee0 ole32!ApartmentUninitialize+0xf8
0483fe64 776b06e3 0483fe7c 00000000 00000001 ole32!wCoUninitialize+0x48
0483fe80 776e43f5 00000001 77670000 776afef0 ole32!CoUninitialize+0x65
0483fe8c 776afef0 0483feb4 776b5cb8 77670000 ole32!DoThreadSpecificCleanup+0x63
0483fe94 776b5cb8 77670000 00000003 00000000 ole32!ThreadNotification+0x37
0483feb4 776b5c1b 77670000 00000003 00000000 ole32!DllMain+0x176
0483fed4 7c82257a 77670000 00000003 00000000 ole32!_DllMainCRTStartup+0x52
0483fef4 7c83c195 776b5bd3 77670000 00000003 ntdll!LdrpCallInitRoutine+0x14
0483ffa8 77e661d6 00000000 00000000 0483ffec ntdll!LdrShutdownThread+0xd2
```

```
0483ffb8 77e66090 00000000 00000000 00000000 kernel32!ExitThread+0x2f
0483ffec 00000000 77c5de6d 0ab24f68 00000000 kernel32!BaseThreadStart+0x39


0:000> !handle 480 ff
Handle 00000480
  Type          Event
  Attributes    0
  GrantedAccess 0x1f0003:
        Delete,ReadControl,WriteDac,WriteOwner,Synch
        QueryState,ModifyState
  HandleCount   2
  PointerCount  4
  Name          <none>
No object specific information available
```

It is difficult to find the first thread, the one which has reset the event and is waiting for the critical section. In our dump we have 9 such threads from **!locks** command output:

```
LockCount          9
```

Event as a synchronization primitive does not have an owner. Despite this, we can try to find 0x480 and *WaitForSingleObject* address nearby on some other thread raw stack if that information wasn't overwritten. Let us do a virtual memory search:

```
0:000> s -d 0 L4000000 00000480
000726ec 00000480 00000022 000004a4 00000056
008512a0 00000480 00000480 00000000 00000000
008512a4 00000480 00000000 00000000 01014220
0085ab68 00000480 00000480 00000092 00000000
0085ab6c 00000480 00000092 00000000 01014234
00eb12a0 00000480 00000480 00000000 00000000
00eb12a4 00000480 00000000 00000000 0101e614
00ebeb68 00000480 00000480 00000323 00000000
00ebeb6c 00000480 00000323 00000000 0101e644
03ffb4fc 00000480 d772c13b ce753966 00fa840f
040212a0 00000480 00000480 00000000 00000000
040212a4 00000480 00000000 00000000 01063afc
0402ab68 00000480 00000480 00000fb6 00000000
0402ab6c 00000480 00000fb6 00000000 01063b5c
041312a0 00000480 00000480 00000000 00000000
041312a4 00000480 00000000 00000000 01065b28
0413eb68 00000480 00000480 00001007 00000000
0413eb6c 00000480 00001007 00000000 01065b7c
043412a0 00000480 00000480 00000000 00000000
043412a4 00000480 00000000 00000000 01066b44
0434ab68 00000480 00000480 00001033 00000000
0434ab6c 00000480 00001033 00000000 01066b9c
0483fd68 00000480 00000000 00000000 00000000
0483fdd8 00000480 ffffffff 00000000 0483fe00
0483fdec 00000480 ffffffff 777904f8 77790738
0483fe08 00000480 00000000 00000080 776b0070
0483fe20 00000480 00000000 00000000 0483fe4c
05296f58 00000480 ffffffff ffffffff ffffffff
```

```
05297eb0 00000480 00000494 000004a4 000004c0
0557cf9c 00000480 00000000 00000000 00000000
05580adc 00000480 00000000 00000000 00000000
0558715c 00000480 00000000 00000000 00000000
0558d3cc 00000480 00000000 00000000 00000000
0559363c 00000480 00000000 00000000 00000000
0559ee0c 00000480 00000000 00000000 00000000
055a507c 00000480 00000000 00000000 00000000
056768ec 00000480 00000000 00000000 00000000
0568ef14 00000480 00000000 00000000 00000000
0581ff88 00000480 07ca7ee0 0581ff98 776cf2a3
05ed1260 00000480 00000480 00000000 00000000
05ed1264 00000480 00000000 00000000 01276efc
05ed8b68 00000480 00000480 00005c18 00000000
05ed8b6c 00000480 00005c18 00000000 01276f74
08f112a0 00000480 00000480 00000000 00000000
08f112a4 00000480 00000000 00000000 00000000
08f1ab68 00000480 00000480 00007732 00000000
08f1ab6c 00000480 00007732 00000000 01352db0
```

In bold we highlighted the thread #13 raw stack occurrences and in italics bold, we highlighted memory locations that belong to another thread raw stack. In fact, these are the only memory locations from search results that make any sense from the code perspective. The only meaningful stack traces can be found in memory locations highlighted in bold above.

This can be seen if we feed search results to WinDbg **dds** command:

```
0:000> .foreach (place { s-[1]d 0 L4000000 00000480 }) { dds place -30; .printf "\n" }
000726bc  00000390
000726c0  00000022
000726c4  000003b4
000726c8  00000056
000726cc  00000004
000726d0  6dc3f6fd
000726d4  0000040c
000726d8  0000001e
000726dc  0000042c
000726e0  00000052
000726e4  00000004
000726e8  eacb0f6d
000726ec  00000480
000726f0  00000022
000726f4  000004a4
000726f8  00000056
000726fc  00000004
00072700  62b796d2
00072704  000004fc
00072708  0000001e
0007270c  0000051c
00072710  00000052
00072714  00000004
00072718  2a615cff
0007271c  00000570
00072720  00000024
```

```
00072724  00000598
00072728  00000058
0007272c  00000004
00072730  51913e59
00072734  000005f0
00072738  00000016
...
...
...
0568eee4  05680008 xpsp2res+0x1b0008
0568eee8  01200000
0568eeec  00001010
0568eef0  00200001
0568eef4  00000468
0568eef8  00000121
0568eefc  00000000
0568ef00  00000028
0568ef04  00000030
0568ef08  00000060
0568ef0c  00040001
0568ef10  00000000
0568ef14  00000480
0568ef18  00000000
0568ef1c  00000000
0568ef20  00000000
0568ef24  00000000
0568ef28  00000000
0568ef2c  00800000
0568ef30  00008000
0568ef34  00808000
0568ef38  00000080
0568ef3c  00800080
0568ef40  00008080
0568ef44  00808080
0568ef48  00c0c0c0
0568ef4c  00ff0000
0568ef50  0000ff00
0568ef54  00ffff00
0568ef58  000000ff
0568ef5c  00ff00ff
0568ef60  0000ffff


0581ff58  0581ff70
0581ff5c  776b063f ole32!wCoUninitialize+0x48
0581ff60  00000001
0581ff64  00007530
0581ff68  77790438 ole32!gATHost
0581ff6c  00000000
0581ff70  0581ff90
0581ff74  776cf370 ole32!CDllHost::WorkerThread+0xdd
0581ff78  0581ff8c
0581ff7c  00000001
0581ff80  77e6ba50 kernel32!WaitForSingleObjectEx
0581ff84  0657cfe8
0581ff88  00000480
0581ff8c  07ca7ee0
```

```
0581ff90    0581ff98
0581ff94    776cf2a3 ole32!DLLHostThreadEntry+0xd
0581ff98    0581ffb8
0581ff9c    776b2307 ole32!CRpcThread::WorkerLoop+0x1e
0581ffa0    77790438 ole32!gATHost
0581ffa4    00000000
0581ffa8    0657cfe8
0581ffac    77670000 ole32!_imp__InstallApplication <PERF> (ole32+0x0)
0581ffb0    776b2374 ole32!CRpcThreadCache::RpcWorkerThreadEntry+0x20
0581ffb4    00000000
0581ffb8    0581ffec
0581ffbc    77e6608b kernel32!BaseThreadStart+0x34
0581ffc0    0657cfe8
0581ffc4    00000000
0581ffc8    00000000
0581ffcc    0657cfe8
0581ffd0    3cfb5963
0581ffd4    0581ffc4


05ed1230    0101f070
05ed1234    05ed1274
05ed1238    05ed1174
05ed123c    05ed0000
05ed1240    05ed1280
05ed1244    00000000
05ed1248    00000000
05ed124c    00000000
05ed1250    05ed8b80
05ed1254    05ed8000
05ed1258    00002000
05ed125c    00001000
05ed1260    00000480
05ed1264    00000480
05ed1268    00000000
05ed126c    00000000
05ed1270    01276efc
05ed1274    05ed12b4
05ed1278    05ed1234
05ed127c    05ed0000
05ed1280    05ed2d00
05ed1284    05ed1240
05ed1288    05ed1400
05ed128c    00000000
05ed1290    05edade0
05ed1294    05eda000
05ed1298    00002000
05ed129c    00001000
05ed12a0    00000220
05ed12a4    00000220
05ed12a8    00000000
05ed12ac    00000000
...
...
...
08f1ab3c    00000000
08f1ab40    00000000
```

```
08f1ab44  00000000
08f1ab48  00000000
08f1ab4c  00000000
08f1ab50  00000000
08f1ab54  00000000
08f1ab58  00000000
08f1ab5c  00000000
08f1ab60  abcdbbbb
08f1ab64  08f11000
08f1ab68  00000480
08f1ab6c  00000480
08f1ab70  00007732
08f1ab74  00000000
08f1ab78  01352db0
08f1ab7c  dcbabbbb
08f1ab80  ffffffff
08f1ab84  c0c00ac1
08f1ab88  00000000
08f1ab8c  c0c0c0c0
08f1ab90  c0c0c0c0
08f1ab94  c0c0c0c0
08f1ab98  c0c0c0c0
08f1ab9c  c0c0c0c0
08f1aba0  c0c0c0c0
08f1aba4  ffffffff
08f1aba8  c0c00ac1
08f1abac  00000000
08f1abb0  c0c0c0c0
08f1abb4  c0c0c0c0
08f1abb8  c0c0c0c0
```

We see that the address 0581ff88 is the most meaningful and it also has *WaitForSingleObjectEx* nearby. This address belongs to the raw stack of the following thread #16:

```
 16  Id: 590.1a00 Suspend: 1 Teb: 7ffa9000 Unfrozen
ChildEBP RetAddr
0581fc98 7c822124 ntdll!KiFastSystemCallRet
0581fc9c 7c83970f ntdll!NtWaitForSingleObject+0xc
0581fcd8 7c839620 ntdll!RtlpWaitOnCriticalSection+0x19c
0581fcf8 7c83a023 ntdll!RtlEnterCriticalSection+0xa8
0581fe00 77e67bcd ntdll!LdrUnloadDll+0x35
0581fe14 776b46fb kernel32!FreeLibrary+0x41
0581fe20 776b470f ole32!CClassCache::CDllPathEntry::CFinishObject::Finish+0x2f
0581fe34 776b44a0 ole32!CClassCache::CFinishComposite::Finish+0x1d
0581ff0c 776b0bfd ole32!CClassCache::CleanUpDllsForApartment+0x1d0
0581ff38 776b0b1f ole32!FinishShutdown+0xd7
0581ff58 776b063f ole32!ApartmentUninitialize+0x94
0581ff70 776cf370 ole32!wCoUninitialize+0x48
0581ff90 776cf2a3 ole32!CDllHost::WorkerThread+0xdd
0581ff98 776b2307 ole32!DLLHostThreadEntry+0xd
0581ffac 776b2374 ole32!CRpcThread::WorkerLoop+0x1e
0581ffb8 77e6608b ole32!CRpcThreadCache::RpcWorkerThreadEntry+0x20
0581ffec 00000000 kernel32!BaseThreadStart+0x34
```

If we disassemble *ole32!CRpcThread::WorkerLoop* function which is found below *WaitForSingleObjectEx* function on both stack trace and raw stack data from search results, we see that the former function calls the latter function indeed:

```
0:000> uf ole32!CRpcThread::WorkerLoop
ole32!CRpcThread::WorkerLoop:
776b22e9 mov     edi,edi
776b22eb push    esi
776b22ec mov     esi,ecx
776b22ee cmp     dword ptr [esi+4],0
776b22f2 jne     ole32!CRpcThread::WorkerLoop+0x67 (776b234d)

ole32!CRpcThread::WorkerLoop+0xb:
776b22f4 push    ebx
776b22f5 push    edi
776b22f6 mov     edi,dword ptr [ole32!_imp__WaitForSingleObjectEx (77671304)]
776b22fc mov     ebx,7530h

ole32!CRpcThread::WorkerLoop+0x18:
776b2301 push    dword ptr [esi+0Ch]
776b2304 call    dword ptr [esi+8]
776b2307 call    dword ptr [ole32!_imp__GetCurrentThread (7767130c)]
776b230d push    eax

776b230e call    dword ptr [ole32!_imp__RtlCheckForOrphanedCriticalSections (77671564)]
776b2314 xor     eax,eax
776b2316 cmp     dword ptr [esi],eax
776b2318 mov     dword ptr [esi+8],eax
776b231b mov     dword ptr [esi+0Ch],eax
776b231e je      ole32!CRpcThread::WorkerLoop+0x65 (776b234b)

ole32!CRpcThread::WorkerLoop+0x37:
776b2320 push    esi
776b2321 mov     ecx,offset ole32!gRpcThreadCache (7778fc28)
776b2326 call    ole32!CRpcThreadCache::AddToFreeList (776de78d)

ole32!CRpcThread::WorkerLoop+0x55:
776b232b push    0
776b232d push    ebx
776b232e push    dword ptr [esi]
776b2330 call    edi
776b2332 test    eax,eax
776b2334 je      ole32!CRpcThread::WorkerLoop+0x60 (776cf3be)

ole32!CRpcThread::WorkerLoop+0x44:
776b233a push    esi
776b233b mov     ecx,offset ole32!gRpcThreadCache (7778fc28)
776b2340 call    ole32!CRpcThreadCache::RemoveFromFreeList (776e42de)
776b2345 cmp     dword ptr [esi+4],0
776b2349 je      ole32!CRpcThread::WorkerLoop+0x55 (776b232b)
```

```
ole32!CRpcThread::WorkerLoop+0x65:
776b234b pop       edi
776b234c pop       ebx

ole32!CRpcThread::WorkerLoop+0x67:
776b234d pop       esi
776b234e ret

ole32!CRpcThread::WorkerLoop+0x60:
776cf3be cmp       dword ptr [esi+4],eax
776cf3c1 je        ole32!CRpcThread::WorkerLoop+0x18 (776b2301)

ole32!CRpcThread::WorkerLoop+0x69:
776cf3c7 jmp       ole32!CRpcThread::WorkerLoop+0x65 (776b234b)
```

Therefore, we have possibly identified the thread #16 that resets the event by calling *WaitForSingleObjectEx* and tries to acquire the critical section. We also know the second thread #13 that has already acquired that critical section and now is waiting for the event to be signaled.

Comments

Regarding thread#16 we can see the module it was trying to free if we dump parameters for *FreeLibrary*:

```
0581fe14 776b46fb kernel32!FreeLibrary+0x41
```

In another memory dump, we had this:

```
16 Id: 13d0.2780 Suspend: 1 Teb: 7ffa8000 Unfrozen
ChildEBP RetAddr Args to Child
0210fc98 7c942124 7c95970f 00000100 00000000 ntdll!KiFastSystemCallRet
0210fc9c 7c95970f 00000100 00000000 00000000 ntdll!NtWaitForSingleObject+0xc
0210fcd8 7c959620 00000000 00000004 00000000 ntdll!RtlpWaitOnCriticalSection+0x19c
0210fcf8 7c95a023 7c9a9d94 0210fe78 0210fea8 ntdll!RtlEnterCriticalSection+0xa8
0210fe00 7c827bcd 02a10000 0210fea8 0210fee4 ntdll!LdrUnloadDll+0x35
0210fe14 775346eb 02a10000 0210ff0c 775346ff kernel32!FreeLibrary+0x41
[...]


0:000> lm
start end module name
[...]
02a10000 02a19000 DLL_A DLL_A.dll
```

Self

This is a variation of **Deadlock** pattern (page 214) where a thread that owns a resource (either in shared or exclusive mode) attempts to acquire it exclusively again. This results in a self-deadlock:

```
Resource @ 0x85d9c018    Shared 1 owning threads
    Contention Count = 2
    NumberOfExclusiveWaiters = 2
     Threads: 85db0030 02<*>
     Threads Waiting On Exclusive Access:
            85f07d78        85db0030
```

Comments

One of the users of Software Diagnostics Library commented that this could happen only if the resource had been first acquired as shared and then exclusively. According to WDK, resources support recursive locking. The only scenario which is not supported (and which may cause deadlocks) is acquiring a resource as shared and then exclusively.

Debugger Bug

When doing software behavior artifact collection, live debugging, or postmortem memory dump analysis we must also take into consideration the possibility of **Debugger Bugs.** We classify them into hard and soft bugs. The former are those software defects and behavioral problems that result in further abnormal software behavior incidents like crashes and hangs. Soft debugger bugs usually manifest themselves as glitches in data output, nonsense or false positive diagnostics, for example, the following excessive non-paged pool usage message in the output from **!vm** WinDbg command:

```
1: kd> !vm

*** Virtual Memory Usage ***
Physical Memory:      1031581 (     4126324 Kb)
Page File: \??\C:\pagefile.sys
Current:   4433524 Kb  Free Space:    4433520 Kb
Minimum:   4433524 Kb  Maximum:      12378972 Kb
Unimplemented error for MiSystemVaTypeCount
Available Pages:       817652 (     3270608 Kb)
ResAvail Pages:        965229 (     3860916 Kb)
Locked IO Pages:            0 (           0 Kb)
Free System PTEs:    33555714 (   134222856 Kb)
Modified Pages:         15794 (       63176 Kb)
Modified PF Pages:      15793 (       63172 Kb)
NonPagedPool Usage: 88079121 (   352316484 Kb)
NonPagedPoolNx Usage:   12885 (       51540 Kb)
NonPagedPool Max:      764094 (     3056376 Kb)
********** Excessive NonPaged Pool Usage *****
PagedPool 0 Usage:      35435 (      141740 Kb)
PagedPool 1 Usage:       3620 (       14480 Kb)
PagedPool 2 Usage:        573 (        2292 Kb)
PagedPool 3 Usage:        535 (        2140 Kb)
PagedPool 4 Usage:        538 (        2152 Kb)
PagedPool Usage:        40701 (      162804 Kb)
PagedPool Maximum:   33554432 (   134217728 Kb)
Session Commit:          9309 (       37236 Kb)
Shared Commit:           6460 (       25840 Kb)
Special Pool:               0 (           0 Kb)
Shared Process:          5760 (       23040 Kb)
PagedPool Commit:       40765 (      163060 Kb)
Driver Commit:           2805 (       11220 Kb)
Committed pages:       212472 (      849888 Kb)
Commit limit:         2139487 (     8557948 Kb)
```

Debugger Omission

If some false positives can be considered soft **Debugger Bugs** (page 239), false negatives can have more severe impact on software behavior analysis, especially in the malware analysis. A typical example here is the current **.imgscan** command which according to the documentation should by default scan virtual process space for MZ/PE signatures. Unfortunately it does not detect such signatures in resource pages (we have not checked stack regions yet):

```
0000000000fd0000 image base


SECTION HEADER #4
.rsrc name
6430 virtual size
4000 virtual address
6600 size of raw data
1600 file pointer to raw data
[...]
40000040 flags
Initialized Data
(no align specified)
Read Only


0:000> .imgscan /r 00000000`00fd4000 L200


0:000> s -[12]sa 00000000`00fd4000 1200
00000000`00fd40b0  "MZ"
00000000`00fd40fd  "!This program cannot be run in D"
00000000`00fd411d  "OS mode."
00000000`00fd4188  "Rich"
00000000`00fd4198  "PE"


0:000> !dh 00000000`00fd40b0


File Type: DLL
FILE HEADER VALUES
14C machine (i386)
3 number of sections
time date stamp Fri Jan 18 21:27:25 2013


0 file pointer to symbol table
0 number of symbols
E0 size of optional header
2102 characteristics
Executable
32 bit word machine
DLL
[...]
```

Other analysis scenarios include **!analyze -v** that shows us a breakpoint instead of an exception violation from a parallel thread.

Design Value

The pattern called **Small Value (**page 975) deals with easily recognizable values such as handles, timeouts, mouse pointer coordinates, enumeration values, and window messages. There is another kind of values, for example, 256 (+/- 1) or some other round value. Here we can also add some regular patterns in hex representation such as window handles or flags, for example, 0x10008000. Such designed values may fall into some module range, the so-called **Coincidental Symbolic Information** (page 145) pattern. They may not necessarily be stack trace parameters (which can also be **False Function Parameters**, page 414). If we see a design value in the output of WinDbg commands, especially related to abnormal behavior patterns, then it might point to some reached design limitations. For example, **Blocked** ALPC **Queue** (page 88) may have a limitation on I/O completion port[36]. We observed that when we had ALPC **Wait Chains** (page 1214) in one unresponsive system:

```
0: kd> !alpc /p <port_address>
[...]
512 thread(s) are registered with port IO completion object:
[...]
```

---

[36] Understanding I/O Completion Ports, Memory Dump Analysis Anthology, Volume 1, page 653

Deviant Module

When looking at the module list (**lmv**), searching for modules (**.imgscan**) or examining the particular module (**!address**, **!dh**) we may notice one of them as deviant. The deviation may be in (but not limited to as anything is possible):

- suspicious module name
- suspicious protection
- suspicious module load address

```
0:005> .imgscan
MZ at 00040000, prot 00000040, type 00020000 - size 1d000
MZ at 00340000, prot 00000002, type 01000000 - size 9c000
Name: iexplore.exe
MZ at 02250000, prot 00000002, type 00040000 - size 2000
MZ at 023b0000, prot 00000002, type 01000000 - size b000
Name: msimtf.dll
MZ at 03f80000, prot 00000002, type 00040000 - size 2000
MZ at 10000000, prot 00000004, type 00020000 - size 5000
Name: screens_dll.dll
MZ at 16080000, prot 00000002, type 01000000 - size 25000
Name: mdnsNSP.dll
MZ at 6ab50000, prot 00000002, type 01000000 - size 26000
Name: DSSENH.dll
MZ at 6b030000, prot 00000002, type 01000000 - size 5b0000
Name: MSHTML.dll
MZ at 6ba10000, prot 00000002, type 01000000 - size b4000
Name: JSCRIPT.dll
MZ at 6cec0000, prot 00000002, type 01000000 - size 1b000
Name: CRYPTNET.dll
MZ at 6d260000, prot 00000002, type 01000000 - size e000
Name: PNGFILTER.DLL
MZ at 6d2f0000, prot 00000002, type 01000000 - size 29000
Name: msls31.dll
MZ at 6d700000, prot 00000002, type 01000000 - size 30000
Name: MLANG.dll
MZ at 6d740000, prot 00000002, type 01000000 - size 4d000
Name: SSV.DLL
MZ at 6d7b0000, prot 00000002, type 01000000 - size c000
Name: ImgUtil.dll
MZ at 6ddb0000, prot 00000002, type 01000000 - size 2f000
Name: iepeers.DLL
MZ at 6df20000, prot 00000002, type 01000000 - size 33000
Name: IEShims.dll
MZ at 6eb80000, prot 00000002, type 01000000 - size a94000
Name: IEFRAME.dll
MZ at 703b0000, prot 00000002, type 01000000 - size 53000
Name: SWEEPRX.dll
MZ at 70740000, prot 00000002, type 01000000 - size 40000
Name: SWEEPRX.dll
MZ at 725a0000, prot 00000002, type 01000000 - size 12000
Name: PNRPNSP.dll
MZ at 725d0000, prot 00000002, type 01000000 - size 8000
```

```
Name: WINRNR.dll
MZ at 725e0000, prot 00000002, type 01000000 - size 136000
Name: MSXML3.dll
MZ at 72720000, prot 00000002, type 01000000 - size c000
Name: wshbth.dll
MZ at 72730000, prot 00000002, type 01000000 - size f000
Name: NAPINSP.dll
MZ at 72890000, prot 00000002, type 01000000 - size 6000
Name: SensApi.dll
MZ at 72ec0000, prot 00000002, type 01000000 - size 42000
Name: WINSPOOL.DRV
MZ at 734b0000, prot 00000002, type 01000000 - size 6000
Name: rasadhlp.dll
MZ at 736b0000, prot 00000002, type 01000000 - size 85000
Name: COMCTL32.dll
MZ at 73ac0000, prot 00000002, type 01000000 - size 7000
Name: MIDIMAP.dll
MZ at 73ae0000, prot 00000002, type 01000000 - size 14000
Name: MSACM32.dll
MZ at 73b00000, prot 00000002, type 01000000 - size 66000
Name: audioeng.dll
MZ at 73c30000, prot 00000002, type 01000000 - size 9000
Name: MSACM32.DRV
MZ at 73c60000, prot 00000002, type 01000000 - size 21000
Name: AudioSes.DLL
MZ at 73c90000, prot 00000002, type 01000000 - size 2f000
Name: WINMMDRV.dll
MZ at 74290000, prot 00000002, type 01000000 - size bb000
Name: PROPSYS.dll
MZ at 74390000, prot 00000002, type 01000000 - size f000
Name: nlaapi.dll
MZ at 743a0000, prot 00000002, type 01000000 - size 4000
Name: ksuser.dll
MZ at 74430000, prot 00000002, type 01000000 - size 15000
Name: Cabinet.dll
MZ at 74450000, prot 00000002, type 01000000 - size 3d000
Name: OLEACC.dll
MZ at 74490000, prot 00000002, type 01000000 - size 1ab000
Name: gdiplus.dll
MZ at 74640000, prot 00000002, type 01000000 - size 28000
Name: MMDevAPI.DLL
MZ at 74670000, prot 00000002, type 01000000 - size 32000
Name: WINMM.dll
MZ at 746b0000, prot 00000002, type 01000000 - size 31000
Name: TAPI32.dll
MZ at 749e0000, prot 00000002, type 01000000 - size 19e000
Name: COMCTL32.dll
MZ at 74b80000, prot 00000002, type 01000000 - size 7000
Name: AVRT.dll
MZ at 74ba0000, prot 00000002, type 01000000 - size 4a000
Name: RASAPI32.dll
MZ at 74ce0000, prot 00000002, type 01000000 - size 3f000
Name: UxTheme.dll
MZ at 74de0000, prot 00000002, type 01000000 - size 2d000
Name: WINTRUST.dll
MZ at 74ea0000, prot 00000002, type 01000000 - size 14000
```

```
Name: rasman.dll
MZ at 74f70000, prot 00000002, type 01000000 - size c000
Name: rtutils.dll
MZ at 74f80000, prot 00000002, type 01000000 - size 5000
Name: WSHTCPIP.dll
MZ at 74fb0000, prot 00000002, type 01000000 - size 21000
Name: NTMARTA.dll
MZ at 75010000, prot 00000002, type 01000000 - size 3b000
Name: RSAENH.dll
MZ at 75050000, prot 00000002, type 01000000 - size 5000
Name: MSIMG32.dll
MZ at 75060000, prot 00000002, type 01000000 - size 15000
Name: GPAPI.dll
MZ at 750a0000, prot 00000002, type 01000000 - size 46000
Name: SCHANNEL.dll
MZ at 752b0000, prot 00000002, type 01000000 - size 3b000
Name: MSWSOCK.dll
MZ at 75370000, prot 00000002, type 01000000 - size 45000
Name: bcrypt.dll
MZ at 753f0000, prot 00000002, type 01000000 - size 5000
Name: WSHIP6.dll
MZ at 75400000, prot 00000002, type 01000000 - size 8000
Name: VERSION.dll
MZ at 75420000, prot 00000002, type 01000000 - size 7000
Name: CREDSSP.dll
MZ at 75430000, prot 00000002, type 01000000 - size 35000
Name: ncrypt.dll
MZ at 75480000, prot 00000002, type 01000000 - size 22000
Name: dhcpcsvc6.DLL
MZ at 754b0000, prot 00000002, type 01000000 - size 7000
Name: WINNSI.DLL
MZ at 754c0000, prot 00000002, type 01000000 - size 35000
Name: dhcpcsvc.DLL
MZ at 75500000, prot 00000002, type 01000000 - size 19000
Name: IPHLPAPI.DLL
MZ at 75590000, prot 00000002, type 01000000 - size 3a000
Name: slc.dll
MZ at 755d0000, prot 00000002, type 01000000 - size f2000
Name: CRYPT32.dll
MZ at 75740000, prot 00000002, type 01000000 - size 12000
Name: MSASN1.dll
MZ at 75760000, prot 00000002, type 01000000 - size 11000
Name: SAMLIB.dll
MZ at 75780000, prot 00000002, type 01000000 - size 76000
Name: NETAPI32.dll
MZ at 75800000, prot 00000002, type 01000000 - size 2c000
Name: DNSAPI.dll
MZ at 75a70000, prot 00000002, type 01000000 - size 5f000
Name: sxs.dll
MZ at 75ad0000, prot 00000002, type 01000000 - size 2c000
Name: apphelp.dll
MZ at 75b30000, prot 00000002, type 01000000 - size 14000
Name: Secur32.dll
MZ at 75b50000, prot 00000002, type 01000000 - size 1e000
Name: USERENV.dll
MZ at 75c90000, prot 00000002, type 01000000 - size 7000
```

```
Name: PSAPI.DLL
MZ at 75ca0000, prot 00000002, type 01000000 - size c3000
Name: RPCRT4.dll
MZ at 75d70000, prot 00000002, type 01000000 - size 73000
Name: COMDLG32.dll
MZ at 75df0000, prot 00000002, type 01000000 - size 9000
Name: LPK.dll
MZ at 75e00000, prot 00000002, type 01000000 - size dc000
Name: KERNEL32.dll
MZ at 75ee0000, prot 00000002, type 01000000 - size aa000
Name: msvcrt.dll
MZ at 75f90000, prot 00000002, type 01000000 - size 1e8000
Name: iertutil.dll
MZ at 76180000, prot 00000002, type 01000000 - size 29000
Name: imagehlp.dll
MZ at 761b0000, prot 00000002, type 01000000 - size 6000
Name: NSI.dll
MZ at 761c0000, prot 00000002, type 01000000 - size 84000
Name: CLBCatQ.DLL
MZ at 76250000, prot 00000002, type 01000000 - size 49000
Name: WLDAP32.dll
MZ at 762a0000, prot 00000002, type 01000000 - size c6000
Name: ADVAPI32.dll
MZ at 76370000, prot 00000002, type 01000000 - size 4b000
Name: GDI32.dll
MZ at 763c0000, prot 00000002, type 01000000 - size 59000
Name: SHLWAPI.dll
MZ at 76420000, prot 00000002, type 01000000 - size e6000
Name: WININET.dll
MZ at 76510000, prot 00000002, type 01000000 - size b10000
Name: SHELL32.dll
MZ at 77020000, prot 00000002, type 01000000 - size 145000
Name: ole32.dll
MZ at 77170000, prot 00000002, type 01000000 - size 7d000
Name: USP10.dll
MZ at 771f0000, prot 00000002, type 01000000 - size 8d000
Name: OLEAUT32.dll
MZ at 77280000, prot 00000002, type 01000000 - size 18a000
Name: SETUPAPI.dll
MZ at 77410000, prot 00000002, type 01000000 - size 9d000
Name: USER32.dll
MZ at 774b0000, prot 00000002, type 01000000 - size 133000
Name: urlmon.dll
MZ at 775f0000, prot 00000002, type 01000000 - size 127000
Name: ntdll.dll
MZ at 77720000, prot 00000002, type 01000000 - size 3000
Name: Normaliz.dll
MZ at 77730000, prot 00000002, type 01000000 - size 2d000
Name: WS2_32.dll
MZ at 77760000, prot 00000002, type 01000000 - size 1e000
Name: IMM32.dll
MZ at 77780000, prot 00000002, type 01000000 - size c8000
Name: MSCTF.dll
MZ at 7c340000, prot 00000002, type 01000000 - size 56000
Name: MSVCR71.dll
```

```
0:005> !address 00040000
Usage:              <unclassified>
Allocation Base:    00040000
Base Address:       00040000
End Address:        0005d000
Region Size:        0001d000
Type:               00020000 MEM_PRIVATE
State:              00001000 MEM_COMMIT
Protect:            00000040 PAGE_EXECUTE_READWRITE


0:005> !address 10000000
Usage:              <unclassified>
Allocation Base:    10000000
Base Address:       10000000
End Address:        10001000
Region Size:        00001000
Type:               00020000 MEM_PRIVATE
State:              00001000 MEM_COMMIT
Protect:            00000004 PAGE_READWRITE
```

- suspicious text inside[37]
- suspicious import table (for example, screen grabbing) or its absence (dynamic imports)

```
0:005> !dh 10000000
[...]
2330 [       50] address [size] of Export Directory
20E0 [       78] address [size] of Import Directory
   0 [        0] address [size] of Resource Directory
   0 [        0] address [size] of Exception Directory
   0 [        0] address [size] of Security Directory
4000 [       34] address [size] of Base Relocation Directory
2060 [       1C] address [size] of Debug Directory
   0 [        0] address [size] of Description Directory
   0 [        0] address [size] of Special Directory
   0 [        0] address [size] of Thread Storage Directory
   0 [        0] address [size] of Load Configuration Directory
   0 [        0] address [size] of Bound Import Directory
2000 [       58] address [size] of Import Address Table Directory
   0 [        0] address [size] of Delay Import Directory
   0 [        0] address [size] of COR20 Header Directory
   0 [        0] address [size] of Reserved Directory
[...]
```

---

[37] Crash Dump Analysis of Defective Malware, Memory Dump Analysis Anthology, Volume 5, page 406

```
0:005> dps 10000000+2000 10000000+2000+58
10002000 76376101 gdi32!CreateCompatibleDC
10002004 763793d6 gdi32!StretchBlt
10002008 76377461 gdi32!CreateDIBSection
1000200c 763762a0 gdi32!SelectObject
10002010 00000000
10002014 75e4a411 kernel32!lstrcmpW
10002018 75e440aa kernel32!VirtualFree
1000201c 75e4ad55 kernel32!VirtualAlloc
10002020 00000000
10002024 77429ced user32!ReleaseDC
10002028 77423ba7 user32!NtUserGetWindowDC
1000202c 77430e21 user32!GetWindowRect
10002030 00000000
10002034 744a75e9 GdiPlus!GdiplusStartup
10002038 744976dd GdiPlus!GdipSaveImageToStream
1000203c 744cdd38 GdiPlus!GdipGetImageEncodersSize
10002040 744971cf GdiPlus!GdipDisposeImage
10002044 744a8591 GdiPlus!GdipCreateBitmapFromHBITMAP
10002048 744cdbae GdiPlus!GdipGetImageEncoders
1000204c 00000000
10002050 7707d51b ole32!CreateStreamOnHGlobal
10002054 00000000
10002058 00000000


0:000> !dh 012a0000
[...]
    0 [        0] address [size] of Export Directory
    0 [        0] address [size] of Import Directory
    0 [        0] address [size] of Resource Directory
    0 [        0] address [size] of Exception Directory
    0 [        0] address [size] of Security Directory
 8000 [       FC] address [size] of Base Relocation Directory
 4000 [       1C] address [size] of Debug Directory
    0 [        0] address [size] of Description Directory
    0 [        0] address [size] of Special Directory
    0 [        0] address [size] of Thread Storage Directory
    0 [        0] address [size] of Load Configuration Directory
    0 [        0] address [size] of Bound Import Directory
    0 [        0] address [size] of Import Address Table Directory
    0 [        0] address [size] of Delay Import Directory
    0 [        0] address [size] of COR20 Header Directory
    0 [        0] address [size] of Reserved Directory
[...]
```

- suspicious path names

```
Age: 7, Pdb: d:\work\BekConnekt\Client_src_code_New\Release\Blackjoe_new.pdb
```

```
Debug Directories(1)
Type Size Address Pointer
cv 46 2094 894 Format: RSDS, guid, 1, C:\MyWork\screens_dll\Release\screens_dll.pdb
```

- suspicious image path (although could be just dynamic code generation for .NET assemblies)
- uninitialized image resources

```
0:002> lmv m C6DC
start     end         module name
012a0000 012a9000   C6DC      C (no symbols)
Loaded symbol image file: C6DC.tmp
Image path: C:\Users\User\AppData\Local\Temp\C6DC.tmp
Image name: C6DC.tmp
Timestamp:        Sun May 30 20:18:32 2010 (4C02BA08)
CheckSum:         00000000
ImageSize:        00009000
File version:     0.0.0.0
Product version:  0.0.0.0
File flags:       0 (Mask 0)
File OS:          0 Unknown Base
File type:        0.0 Unknown
File date:        00000000.00000000
Translations:     0000.04b0 0000.04e4 0409.04b0 0409.04e4
```

Comments

.imgscan might not be able to find all hidden modules (**Debugger Omission** pattern, page 240).

Timestamps might be suspicious too.

Deviant Token

Sometimes we need to check what security principal or group we run a process under, or what privileges it has or whether it has impersonating threads. We may find an unexpected token with a different security identifier, for example, *Network Service* instead of *Local System* (SID: S-1-5-18):

```
PROCESS 8f218d88  SessionId: 0  Cid: 09c4    Peb: 7ffdf000  ParentCid: 0240
DirBase: bffd4260  ObjectTable: e10eae90  HandleCount:  93.
Image: ServiceA.exe
VadRoot 8f1f70e8 Vads 141 Clone 0 Private 477. Modified 2. Locked 0.
DeviceMap e10038d8
Token                        e10ff5d8
[...]


0: kd> !token e10ff5d8
_TOKEN e10ff5d8
TS Session ID: 0
User: S-1-5-20
[...]
```

Well-known SIDs can be found in MS KB article 243330[38].

---

[38] https://support.microsoft.com/en-gb/help/243330/well-known-security-identifiers-in-windows-operating-systems

Diachronic Module

When we have a performance issue, we may request a set of consecutive memory dump saved after some interval. In such memory dumps we may see the same thread(s) having similar stack trace(s). In this simple diagnostic scenario we may diagnose several patterns based on the stack traces: **Active Threads** (page 74) that can be **Spiking Threads** (page 989) with **Spike Intervals** (page 988) or stable, not changing, **Wait Chains** (for example, critical sections, page 1203). Here we may easily identify **Top** (page 1127) active and **Blocking** (page 107) modules based on **Module Wait Chain** (page 1220).

The more complex case arises when we have different **Active Threads** and/or **Wait Chains** with different thread IDs at different times. However, if their **Top Module** is the same, we may have found it as a performance root cause component especially in the case of **Active Threads** since it is statistically probable that such threads were active for considerable time deltas around the snapshot times (since threads are usually waiting). Such hypothesis may also be confirmed by inter-correlational analysis (**Inter-Correlation**[39]) with software traces and logs where we can see **Thread of Activity**[40] **Discontinuities**[41] and **Time Deltas**[42].

We call this analysis pattern **Diachronic Module** since we see the module component appears in different thread stack traces diachronically (at different times). The typical simplified scenario is illustrated in this diagram:

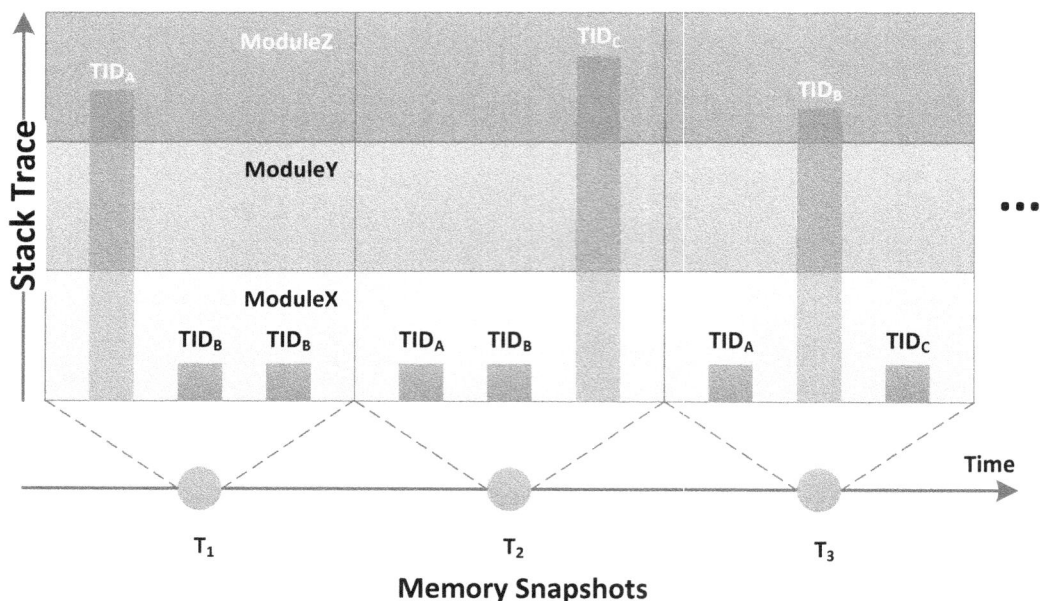

---

[39] Memory Dump Analysis Anthology, Volume 4, page 350
[40] Ibid., page 339
[41] Ibid., page 341
[42] Memory Dump Analysis Anthology, Volume 5, page 282

This analysis pattern is different from synchronous module case (the module component appears in different thread stack traces at the same time) which was named **Ubiquitous Component** (page 1135).

252 | D i a l o g   B o x

Dialog Box

Similar to **Message Box** (page 743) and **String Parameter** (page 1074) patterns we also have **Dialog Box** pattern where we can see dialog window caption and contents when we examine function parameters. Although in the examples below we know the dialog purpose from the friendly call stack function names, for many 3rd-party applications we either do not have symbols or such helper functions, but we want to know what was on the screen when screenshots were not collected.

The first two examples are from *Notepad* application, and the third is from IE:

```
0:000> kv
ChildEBP RetAddr Args to Child
0017f5c4 777b073f 777c3c9f 000d023c 00000001 ntdll!KiFastSystemCallRet
0017f5c8 777c3c9f 000d023c 00000001 00000000 user32!NtUserWaitMessage+0xc
0017f5fc 777c2dc0 00310778 000d023c 00000001 user32!DialogBox2+0x202
0017f624 777c2eec 76460000 02a6bc60 000d023c user32!InternalDialogBox+0xd0
0017f644 76489a65 76460000 02a6bc60 000d023c user32!DialogBoxIndirectParamAorW+0x37
0017f680 76489ccf 0017f68c 00000001 0017f6d4 comdlg32!ChooseFontX+0x1ba
0017f6bc 006741c7 0017f6d4 00000111 00000000 comdlg32!ChooseFontW+0x2e
0017f734 0067164a 000d023c 00000021 00000000 notepad!NPCommand+0x4c7
0017f758 777afd72 000d023c 00000111 00000021 notepad!NPWndProc+0x4cf
0017f784 777afe4a 0067146c 000d023c 00000111 user32!InternalCallWinProc+0x23
0017f7fc 777b018d 00000000 0067146c 000d023c user32!UserCallWinProcCheckWow+0x14b
0017f860 777b022b 0067146c 00000000 0017f8a4 user32!DispatchMessageWorker+0x322
0017f870 00671465 0017f888 00000000 0067a21c user32!DispatchMessageW+0xf
0017f8a4 0067195d 00670000 00000000 00231cfa notepad!WinMain+0xe3
0017f934 7652d0e9 7ffd9000 0017f980 77b019bb notepad!_initterm_e+0x1a1
0017f940 77b019bb 7ffd9000 78f7b908 00000000 kernel32!BaseThreadInitThunk+0xe
0017f980 77b0198e 006731ed 7ffd9000 00000000 ntdll!__RtlUserThreadStart+0x23
0017f998 00000000 006731ed 7ffd9000 00000000 ntdll!_RtlUserThreadStart+0x1b


0:000> dc 02a6bc60 150
02a6bc60 80c800c4 00000000 000d0014 011f0036 ............6...
02a6bc70 000000c4 00460000 006e006f 00000074 ......F.o.n.t...
02a6bc80 004d0008 00200053 00680053 006c0065 ..M.S. .S.h.e.l.
02a6bc90 0020006c 006c0044 00000067 50020000 l. .D.l.g....P
02a6bca0 00000000 00070007 00090028 ffff0440 ........(...@...
02a6bcb0 00260082 006f0046 0074006e 0000003a ..&.F.o.n.t.:...
02a6bcc0 00000000 50210b51 00000000 00100007 ....Q.!P........
02a6bcd0 004c0062 ffff0470 00000085 00000000 b.L.p..........
02a6bce0 50020000 00000000 0007006e 0009002c ...P....n...,...
02a6bcf0 ffff0441 00460082 006e006f 00200074 A.....F.o.n.t. .
02a6bd00 00740073 00790026 0065006c 0000003a s.t.&.y.l.e.:...
02a6bd10 00000000 50210041 00000000 0010006e ....A.!P....n...
02a6bd20 004c004a ffff0471 00000085 00000000 J.L.q..........
02a6bd30 50020000 00000000 000700bd 0009001e ...P...........
02a6bd40 ffff0442 00260082 00690053 0065007a B.....&.S.i.z.e.
02a6bd50 0000003a 00000000 50210b51 00000000 :.......Q.!P....
02a6bd60 001000be 004c0024 ffff0472 00000085 ....$.L.r.......
02a6bd70 00000000 50020007 00000000 00610007 ......P.......a.
02a6bd80 00480062 ffff0430 00450080 00660066 b.H.0.....E.f.f.
02a6bd90 00630065 00730074 00000000 50010003 e.c.t.s........P
```

```
0:000> kv
ChildEBP RetAddr  Args to Child
0017f5a8 777b073f 777c3c9f 000d023c 00000001 ntdll!KiFastSystemCallRet
0017f5ac 777c3c9f 000d023c 00000001 00000000 user32!NtUserWaitMessage+0xc
0017f5e0 777c2dc0 0044034a 000d023c 00000001 user32!DialogBox2+0x202
0017f608 777c2eec 768a0000 029030bc 000d023c user32!InternalDialogBox+0xd0
0017f628 777c10ef 768a0000 029030bc 000d023c user32!DialogBoxIndirectParamAorW+0x37
0017f64c 7695d877 768a0000 00003810 000d023c user32!DialogBoxParamW+0x3f
0017f670 76a744dc 768a0000 00003810 000d023c shell32!SHFusionDialogBoxParam+0x32
0017f6b0 00674416 000d023c 002530dc 00672fc4 shell32!ShellAboutW+0x4d
0017f734 0067164a 000d023c 00000041 00000000 notepad!NPCommand+0x718
0017f758 777afd72 000d023c 00000111 00000041 notepad!NPWndProc+0x4cf
0017f784 777afe4a 0067146c 000d023c 00000111 user32!InternalCallWinProc+0x23
0017f7fc 777b018d 00000000 0067146c 000d023c user32!UserCallWinProcCheckWow+0x14b
0017f860 777b022b 0067146c 00000000 0017f8a4 user32!DispatchMessageWorker+0x322
0017f870 00671465 0017f888 00000000 0067a21c user32!DispatchMessageW+0xf
0017f8a4 0067195d 00670000 00000000 00231cfa notepad!WinMain+0xe3
0017f934 7652d0e9 7ffd9000 0017f980 77b019bb notepad!_initterm_e+0x1a1
0017f940 77b019bb 7ffd9000 78f7b908 00000000 kernel32!BaseThreadInitThunk+0xe
0017f980 77b0198e 006731ed 7ffd9000 00000000 ntdll!__RtlUserThreadStart+0x23
0017f998 00000000 006731ed 7ffd9000 00000000 ntdll!_RtlUserThreadStart+0x1b


0:000> dc 029030bc 150
029030bc  ffff0001 00000000 00000000 80c800cc  ................
029030cc  0014000c 01130014 000000ee 00410000  ...............A.
029030dc  006f0062 00740075 00250020 00000073  b.o.u.t. .%.s...
029030ec  00000008 004d0000 00200053 00680053  ......M.S. .S.h.
029030fc  006c0065 0020006c 006c0044 00000067  e.l.l. .D.l.g...
0290310c  00000000 00000000 50000043 00370007  ........C..P..7.
0290311c  00140015 00003009 0082ffff 0000ffff  .....0..........
0290312c  00000000 00000000 00000000 5000008c  ...............P
0290313c  00370023 000a00c8 00003500 0082ffff  #.7......5......
0290314c  00000000 00000000 00000000 5000008c  ...............P
0290315c  00410023 000a00eb 0000350b 0082ffff  #.A......5......
0290316c  00000000 00000000 00000000 50000080  ...............P
0290317c  004b0023 000a00d2 0000350a 0082ffff  #.K......5......
0290318c  00000000 00000000 00000000 50000080  ...............P
0290319c  00550023 002800d2 00003513 0082ffff  #.U...(..5......
029031ac  00680054 00200065 00570025 004e0049  T.h.e. .%.W.I.N.
029031bc  004f0044 00530057 004c005f 004e004f  D.O.W.S._.L.O.N.
029031cc  00250047 006f0020 00650070 00610072  G.%. .o.p.e.r.a.
029031dc  00690074 0067006e 00730020 00730079  t.i.n.g. .s.y.s.
029031ec  00650074 0020006d 006e0061 00200064  t.e.m. .a.n.d. .
```

```
16 Id: 10fc.124c Suspend: 0 Teb: 7ffd7000 Unfrozen
ChildEBP RetAddr  Args to Child
053f8098 777b073f 777c3c9f 003d0650 00000001 ntdll!KiFastSystemCallRet
053f809c 777c3c9f 003d0650 00000001 00000000 user32!NtUserWaitMessage+0xc
053f80d0 777c2dc0 002e0378 003d0650 00000001 user32!DialogBox2+0x202
053f80f8 777c2eec 6f270000 03387bd4 003d0650 user32!InternalDialogBox+0xd0
053f8118 777c10ef 6f270000 03387bd4 003d0650 user32!DialogBoxIndirectParamAorW+0x37
053f813c 6f2c5548 6f270000 00005398 003d0650 user32!DialogBoxParamW+0x3f
053f8164 6f2c5743 6f270000 00005398 003d0650 ieframe!Detour_DialogBoxParamW+0x47
053f8188 6f2c56f5 6f270000 00005398 001905ea ieframe!SHFusionDialogBoxParam+0x32
053f9228 6f2c5378 001905ea 053fb540 00000104 ieframe!DoAddToFavDlgEx+0xcf
053fbb5c 6f2c58f9 001905ea 0e69a0c0 053fbff0 ieframe!AddToFavoritesEx+0x349
```

```
053fbdb8 6f2c57ee 00000000 053fbff0 00000000 ieframe!CBaseBrowser2::_AddToFavorites+0xe9
053fc0f4 6f2c3e5e 00000000 00000000 00000001 ieframe!CBaseBrowser2::_ExecAddToFavorites+0x123
053fc124 6f39ca4e 6f39c524 00000008 00000001 ieframe!CBaseBrowser2::_ExecExplorer+0xbe
053fc14c 6f39cee8 114ea39c 6f39c524 00000008 ieframe!CBaseBrowser2::Exec+0x12d
053fc17c 6f39cf17 6f39c524 00000008 00000001 ieframe!CShellBrowser2::_Exec_CCommonBrowser+0x80
053fc414 6f498284 114ea39c 6f39c524 00000008 ieframe!CShellBrowser2::Exec+0x626
053fc43c 6f49e5cd 0000a173 00000000 ffffff71 ieframe!CShellBrowser2::_FavoriteOnCommand+0x75
053fc458 6f3c5ea8 0000a173 00000000 00000111 ieframe!CShellBrowser2::_OnDefault+0x3e
053fd6f0 6f394194 0000a173 00000000 0000031a ieframe!CShellBrowser2::v_OnCommand+0xa7b
053fd70c 6f39898d 001905ea 00000111 0000a173 ieframe!CBaseBrowser2::v_WndProc+0x247
053fd770 6f3988db 001905ea 00000111 0000a173 ieframe!CShellBrowser2::v_WndProc+0x3fe
053fd794 777afd72 001905ea 00000111 0000a173 ieframe!CShellBrowser2::s_WndProc+0xfb
053fd7c0 777afe4a 6f39887a 001905ea 00000111 user32!InternalCallWinProc+0x23
053fd838 777b0943 00000000 6f39887a 001905ea user32!UserCallWinProcCheckWow+0x14b
053fd878 777b0b36 00252838 01223dc0 0000a173 user32!SendMessageWorker+0x4b7
053fd898 6f3cf032 001905ea 00000111 0000a173 user32!SendMessageW+0x7c
053fd8d0 6f396ead 0056049c 00000111 0000a173 ieframe!CInternetToolbarHost::v_WndProc+0xf8
053fd8f4 777afd72 0056049c 00000111 0000a173 ieframe!CImpWndProc::s_WndProc+0x65
053fd920 777afe4a 6f396e6e 0056049c 00000111 user32!InternalCallWinProc+0x23
053fd998 777b018d 00000000 6f396e6e 0056049c user32!UserCallWinProcCheckWow+0x14b
053fd9fc 777b022b 6f396e6e 00000000 053ffb14 user32!DispatchMessageWorker+0x322
053fda0c 6f39c1f5 053fda30 00000000 10eec4c0 user32!DispatchMessageW+0xf
053ffb14 6f34337f 0e7c3708 00000000 11bd8dc8 ieframe!CTabWindow::_TabWindowThreadProc+0x54c
053ffbcc 77525179 10eec4c0 00000000 053ffbe8 ieframe!LCIETab_ThreadProc+0x2c1
053ffbdc 7652d0e9 11bd8dc8 053ffc28 77b019bb iertutil!CIsoScope::RegisterThread+0xab
053ffbe8 77b019bb 11bd8dc8 7dd62326 00000000 kernel32!BaseThreadInitThunk+0xe
053ffc28 77b0198e 7752516b 11bd8dc8 00000000 ntdll!__RtlUserThreadStart+0x23
053ffc40 00000000 7752516b 11bd8dc8 00000000 ntdll!_RtlUserThreadStart+0x1b


0:000> dc 03387bd4 150
03387bd4 ffff0001 00000000 00000000 80c808c0 ................
03387be4 0000000a 011f0000 00000064 00410000 ........d.....A.
03387bf4 00640064 00610020 00460020 00760061 d.d. .a. .F.a.v.
03387c04 0072006f 00740069 00000065 00000008 o.r.i.t.e.......
03387c14 004d0000 00200053 00680053 006c0065 ..M.S. .S.h.e.l.
03387c24 0020006c 006c0044 00000067 00000000 l. .D.l.g.......
03387c34 00000000 50000003 0007000f 00140015 .......P........
03387c44 00009760 0082ffff 00bfffff 00000000 `...............
03387c54 00000000 00000000 50020000 00070035 ..........P5...
03387c64 000800db 000003f4 0082ffff 00640041 ............A.d.
03387c74 00200064 00200061 00610046 006f0076 d. .a. .F.a.v.o.
03387c84 00690072 00650074 00000000 00000000 r.i.t.e.........
03387c94 00000000 50020000 00110035 001000db .......P5.......
03387ca4 000003f5 0082ffff 00640041 00200064 ........A.d.d. .
03387cb4 00680074 00730069 00770020 00620065 t.h.i.s. .w.e.b.
03387cc4 00610070 00650067 00610020 00200073 p.a.g.e. .a.s. .
03387cd4 00200061 00610066 006f0076 00690072 a. .f.a.v.o.r.i.
03387ce4 00650074 0020002e 006f0054 00610020 t.e... .T.o. .a.
03387cf4 00630063 00730065 00200073 006f0079 c.c.e.s.s. .y.o.
```

Stack traces with *DialogBoxIndirectParam* call and x64 platform complicate the picture a bit. Please also note that a user may not see the dialog box that you see in a stack trace due to many reasons like terminal session problems or a process running in a non-interactive session.

Directing Module

In certain software behavior scenarios such as **Memory Leak** (page 732) when we see **Top Modules** (page 1127) calling OS API functions, we may suspect them having defects. However, this might not be the case when these modules were used from a directing module keeping references or handles preventing top modules from freeing memory or releasing resources.

For example, a memory dump from a process had two growing heap segments, and one of them had this recurrent stack trace saved in a user mode **Stack Trace** Database (page 1026):

```
38D2CE78: 02ba8 . 02ba8 [07] - busy (2b90), tail fill
Stack trace (38101) at 83e390:
7d6568be: ntdll!RtlAllocateHeapSlowly+0x00000041
7d62b846: ntdll!RtlAllocateHeap+0x00000E9F
337d0572: ModuleA!XHeapAlloc+0x00000115
[...]
338809e2: ModuleA!Execute+0x000002CD
488b3fc1: ModuleB!Execute+0x000000D3
679b8c64: ModuleC!ExecuteByHandle+0x00000074
[...]
67d241cb: ModuleD!Query+0x0000016B
67ba2ed4: ModuleE!Browse+0x000000E4
[...]
667122c6: ModuleF!Check+0x00000126
65e73826: ModuleG!Enum+0x00000406
[...]
```

Initially, we suspected *ModuleA* but found a different recurrent stack trace corresponding to another growing segment:

```
40C81688: 000c8 . 00058 [07] - busy (40), tail fill
Stack trace (38136) at 83f6a4:
7d6568be: ntdll!RtlAllocateHeapSlowly+0x00000041
7d62b846: ntdll!RtlAllocateHeap+0x00000E9F
7c3416b3: msvcr71!_heap_alloc+0x000000E0
7c3416db: msvcr71!_nh_malloc+0x00000010
67745875: ModuleX!BufAllocate+0x00000015
6775085e: ModuleY!QueryAttribute+0x0000008E
[...]
677502b5: ModuleY!Query+0x00000015
67ba2f19: ModuleE!Browser+0x00000129
[...]
667122c6: ModuleF!Check+0x00000126
65e73826: ModuleG!Enum+0x00000406
[...]
```

From the common stack trace fragment (highlighted in bold italics) we transferred our investigation to *ModuleE*, and indeed, the similar software incident (as per the latter stack trace) was found in a troubleshooting database.

Disassembly Ambiguity

Backward disassembling used in memory analysis patterns such as **Coincidental Symbolic Information** (page 148) may be ambiguous and can show **Wild Code** (page 1268) output. This may also be debugger disassembling algorithm dependent. For example, default 8-instruction backward disassembly shows this code:

```
0:011> ub 00007ff8`cdc9b4bf
00007ff8`cdc9b4ab 855948               test dword ptr [rcx+48h],ebx
00007ff8`cdc9b4ae b988bf03a8           mov  ecx,0A803BF88h
00007ff8`cdc9b4b3 f4                   hlt
00007ff8`cdc9b4b4 0100                 add  dword ptr [rax],eax
00007ff8`cdc9b4b6 00488b               add  byte ptr [rax-75h],cl
00007ff8`cdc9b4b9 09e8                 or   eax,ebp
00007ff8`cdc9b4bb 117236               adc  dword ptr [rdx+36h],esi
00007ff8`cdc9b4be 5f                   pop  rdi
```

However, if we specify the number of instructions to disassemble except 7 and 8, we get a different result (which is more correct from the forward code execution view since we disassembled the saved return address from the stack region):

```
0:011> ub 00007ff8`cdc9b4bf L1
00007ff8`cdc9b4ba e81172365f           call clr!JIT_MonEnter (00007ff9`2d0026d0)


0:011> ub 00007ff8`cdc9b4bf L2
00007ff8`cdc9b4b7 488b09               mov  rcx,qword ptr [rcx]
00007ff8`cdc9b4ba e81172365f           call clr!JIT_MonEnter (00007ff9`2d0026d0)


0:011> k L10
# Child-SP RetAddr Call Site
00 0000002a`fc23e308 00007ff9`53d06099 ntdll!NtWaitForMultipleObjects+0x14
01 0000002a`fc23e310 00007ff9`2d1a96be KERNELBASE!WaitForMultipleObjectsEx+0xf9
02 0000002a`fc23e610 00007ff9`2d1a951c clr!WaitForMultipleObjectsEx_SO_TOLERANT+0x62
03 0000002a`fc23e670 00007ff9`2d1a9315 clr!Thread::DoAppropriateWaitWorker+0x1e4
04 0000002a`fc23e770 00007ff9`2d0c2b7f clr!Thread::DoAppropriateWait+0x7d
05 0000002a`fc23e7f0 00007ff9`2d1aa491 clr!CLREventBase::WaitEx+0xc4
06 0000002a`fc23e880 00007ff9`2d1aa39e clr!AwareLock::EnterEpilogHelper+0xc2
07 0000002a`fc23e940 00007ff9`2d1c1a92 clr!AwareLock::EnterEpilog+0x62
08 0000002a`fc23e9a0 00007ff8`cdc9b4bf clr!JITutil_MonEnterWorker+0xe2
09 0000002a`fc23eb40 00007ff9`275231d3 0x00007ff8`cdc9b4bf
0a 0000002a`fc23eb80 00007ff9`27523064 mscorlib_ni+0x5031d3
[...]
```

We call this analysis pattern **Disassembly Ambiguity**.

The example dump is available for download[43].

---

[43] https://www.patterndiagnostics.com/SoftwareDiagnosticsCorpus/SDC1.zip

Disconnected Network Adapter

Sometimes we need to check network adapters (miniports) to see whether they are up, down, connected or disconnected. This can be done using **ndiskd** WinDbg extension and its commands. Here is an example from a kernel memory dump:

```
1: kd> !ndiskd.miniports
raspptp.sys, v0.0
  88453360 NetLuidIndex  1, IfIndex  3,  WAN Miniport (PPTP)
raspppoe.sys, v0.0
  884860e8 NetLuidIndex  0, IfIndex  4,  WAN Miniport (PPPOE)
ndiswan.sys, v0.0
  8842f0e8 NetLuidIndex  0, IfIndex  5,  WAN Miniport (IPv6)
  8842e0e8 NetLuidIndex  3, IfIndex  6,  WAN Miniport (IP)
rasl2tp.sys, v0.0
  8842b0e8 NetLuidIndex  0, IfIndex  2,  WAN Miniport (L2TP)
E1G60I32.sys, v8.1
  84b730e8 NetLuidIndex  4, IfIndex  8,  Intel(R) PRO/1000 MT Network Connection
tunnel.sys, v1.0
  84b370e8 NetLuidIndex  2, IfIndex  9,  isatap.{0DC6D9AD-70DC-41CE-9798-F71D1A8C899F}


1: kd> !ndiskd.miniport 84b730e8

MINIPORT

    Intel(R) PRO/1000 MT Network Connection


    Ndis Handle       84b730e8
    Ndis API Version  v6.0
    Adapter Context   88460008
    Miniport Driver   84b44938 - E1G60I32.sys  v8.1
    Ndis Verifier     [No flags set]


    Media Type        802.3
    Physical Medium   802.3
    Device Path       \??\PCI#VEN_8086&DEV_100F&SUBSYS_075015AD&REV_01#4&b70f118&0&0888#{ad498944-762f-
11d0-8dcb-00c04fc3358c}\{0DC6D9AD-70DC-41CE-9798-F71D1A8C899F}
    Device Object     84b73030
    MAC Address       00-0c-29-b1-7d-39

STATE

    Miniport          Running
    Device PnP        Started
    Datapath          00000002          ← DIVERTED_BECAUSE_MEDIA_DISCONNECTED
    NBL Status        NDIS_STATUS_MEDIA_DISCONNECTED
    Operational status DOWN
    Operational flags 00000002          ← DOWN_NOT_CONNECTED
    Admin status      ADMIN_UP
    Media             MediaDisconnected
    Power             D0
    References        6
```

```
User Handles        0
Total Resets        0
Pending OID         None
Flags               0c452218
    ↑ BUS_MASTER, 64BIT_DMA, SG_DMA, DEFAULT_PORT_ACTIVATED,
      SUPPORTS_MEDIA_SENSE, DOES_NOT_DO_LOOPBACK, NOT_MEDIA_CONNECTED
PnPFlags            00210021
    ↑ PM_SUPPORTED, DEVICE_POWER_ENABLED, RECEIVED_START, HARDWARE_DEVICE


BINDINGS


Filter List         Filter          Filter Driver       Context             _
QoS Packet Scheduler-0000
                    88e453d8        88e18938            88e1ed60


Open List           Open            Protocol            Context             _
RSPNDR              8bcbb470        8bd23ac8            8bcbb820
LLTDIO              8bcb8c00        8bd15980            8bd153f8
TCPIP6              88e528e8        88e02350            88e52c98
TCPIP               88e1c078        88e02aa8            88e1e6a8


MORE INFORMATION


    → Driver handlers               → Task offloads
    → Power management
    → Pending OIDs                  → Timers
                                    → Receive Side Throttling
    → Wake-on-LAN (WoL)             → Packet filter
    → NDIS ports
```

Another example from a different complete memory dump:

```
STATE


Device PnP          Started
Datapath            00000002            ← DIVERTED_BECAUSE_MEDIA_DISCONNECTED
Packet Status       NDIS_STATUS_NO_CABLE
Media               Not Connected
 [...]
```

Disk Packet Buildup

This is similar to **Network Packet Buildup** (page 818) pattern. It can be detectable either through SCSI WinDbg extension or using IRP **Object Distribution Anomaly** (page 842) pattern:

```
0: kd> .load scsikd

0: kd> !scsikd.classext
Storage class devices:

* !classext fffffa80026395b0 [1,2] SAMSUNG HS082HB Paging Disk

Usage: !classext <class device> <level [0-2]>

0: kd> !scsikd.classext fffffa80026395b0
Storage class device fffffa80026395b0 with extension at fffffa8002639700

Classpnp Internal Information at fffffa8002648010

-- dt classpnp!_CLASS_PRIVATE_FDO_DATA fffffa8002648010 --

Classpnp External Information at fffffa8002639700

SAMSUNG HS082HB NL100-01 S140JR0SA00025

Minidriver information at fffffa8002639bc0
Attached device object at fffffa80017ecda0
Physical device object at fffffa80024ab060

Media Geometry:

Bytes in a Sector = 512
Sectors per Track = 63
Tracks / Cylinder = 255
Media Length     = 80026361856 bytes = ~74 GB

-- dt classpnp!_FUNCTIONAL_DEVICE_EXTENSION fffffa8002639700 --
```

This is a normal case:

```
0: kd> !scsikd.classext fffffa80026395b0 2
Storage class device fffffa80026395b0 with extension at fffffa8002639700

Classpnp Internal Information at fffffa8002648010

Transfer Packet Engine:

Packet          Status DL Irp             Opcode  Sector/ListId   UL Irp
--------        ------ --------           ------  --------------- --------
```

```
fffffa8002648e80  Free  fffffa800249eac0
fffffa8002644220  Free  fffffa80024aa4f0
fffffa80026898a0  Free  fffffa80019d2b30
fffffa800267ad40  Free  fffffa8001801b90
fffffa800267aa60  Free  fffffa8001835e10
fffffa8002679010  Free  fffffa80019fac40
fffffa8002679770  Free  fffffa8002679500
fffffa80027659a0  Free  fffffa8002764e10
fffffa8002790e80  Free  fffffa800267a6a0
fffffa800278f5e0  Free  fffffa80019d53c0
fffffa8002599410  Free  fffffa8002785600
fffffa80027f7490  Free  fffffa800278ea00
fffffa80027f6e80  Free  fffffa80027f6c80
fffffa80027f69a0  Free  fffffa80027f67a0
fffffa80027f64c0  Free  fffffa80027f62c0
fffffa8002dd4440  Free  fffffa80027fc600
fffffa8002dced30  Free  fffffa8002dceb30
fffffa8002dce850  Free  fffffa8002ddc010
fffffa8002ddc530  Free  fffffa8002ddc330
fffffa8002de2d30  Free  fffffa8002de2b30
fffffa8002de2850  Free  fffffa8002de2650
fffffa8002de2370  Free  fffffa8002de2170
fffffa8002ddbe80  Free  fffffa8002ddbc80
fffffa8002ddb9a0  Free  fffffa8002ddb7a0
fffffa8002dda010  Free  fffffa8002ddae10
[...]
```

This is not:

```
0: kd> !scsikd.classext fffffa80026395b0 2

Storage class device fffffa80026395b0 with extension at fffffa8002639700

Classpnp Internal Information at fffffa8002648010

Transfer Packet Engine:

Packet            Status DL Irp           Opcode Sector   UL Irp
--------          ------ --------         ------ -------- --------
fffffa80c71d9560  Queued fffffa80c71d9360   2a   03cbb948 fffffa80c4f269d0 \FileName
fffffa80c77a3360  Queued fffffa80c77a3160   2a   0400f0a8 fffffa80c59c1010 \FileName
fffffa80c6cefe60  Queued fffffa80c6cefc60   2a   0400f128 fffffa80c59c1010 \FileName
fffffa80c6e92260  Queued fffffa80c4f80010   2a   0400f1e8 fffffa80c59c1010 \FileName
fffffa80c79dbca0  Queued fffffa80c79dbaa0   2a   0400c4e8 fffffa80c59c1010 \FileName
fffffa80c83f2d90  Queued fffffa80c3b23bc0   2a   0400f168 fffffa80c59c1010 \FileName
fffffa80c4a94640  Queued fffffa80c4a94440   2a   0400d5e8 fffffa80c59c1010 \FileName
fffffa80c7984010  Queued fffffa80c7984210   2a   0400d328 fffffa80c59c1010 \FileName
fffffa80c6e52be0  Queued fffffa80c6e529e0   2a   0400f1a8 fffffa80c59c1010 \FileName
fffffa80c7afada0  Queued fffffa80c7afaba0   2a   04010268 fffffa80c59c1010 \FileName
fffffa80c7c19d90  Queued fffffa80ca2c5e10   2a   0400c628 fffffa80c59c1010 \FileName
fffffa80c6182d60  Queued fffffa80c6182b60   2a   0400f9a8 fffffa80c59c1010 \FileName
fffffa80c8695ba0  Queued fffffa80c86959a0   2a   0400d128 fffffa80c59c1010 \FileName
fffffa80c6b42b40  Queued fffffa80c6b42940   2a   0400ed28 fffffa80c59c1010 \FileName
fffffa80c5e1ab00  Queued fffffa80c5e1a900   2a   0400eee8 fffffa80c59c1010 \FileName
```

```
fffffa80c5d80a30 Queued fffffa80c4841e10 2a 0400fba8 fffffa80c59c1010 \FileName
fffffa80c48255d0 Queued fffffa80c48253d0 2a 040119e8 fffffa80c59c1010 \FileName
fffffa80c718a270 Queued fffffa80c47d0010 2a 0400d1e8 fffffa80c59c1010 \FileName
fffffa80c51a94b0 Queued fffffa80c51a92b0 2a 0400bd28 fffffa80c59c1010 \FileName
fffffa80ca280990 Queued fffffa80c52b2930 2a 0400d268 fffffa80c59c1010 \FileName
fffffa80c586f280 Queued fffffa80c551fe10 2a 0400f068 fffffa80c59c1010 \FileName
fffffa80c8413540 Queued fffffa80c544ae10 2a 04011a68 fffffa80c59c1010 \FileName
fffffa80c544ac60 Queued fffffa80c535ba90 2a 0400e7e8 fffffa80c59c1010 \FileName
fffffa80c4678010 Queued fffffa80c4678230 2a 04011168 fffffa80c59c1010 \FileName
fffffa80c9d94be0 Queued fffffa80c59205e0 2a 0400d4a8 fffffa80c59c1010 \FileName
fffffa80c5920430 Queued fffffa80c59248f0 2a 0400ea68 fffffa80c59c1010 \FileName
fffffa80c737e8f0 Queued fffffa80c737e6f0 2a 0400fee8 fffffa80c59c1010 \FileName
fffffa80c4797c60 Queued fffffa80c5d31800 2a 0400f328 fffffa80c59c1010 \FileName
fffffa80c711d270 Queued fffffa80c76ee390 2a 0400eaa8 fffffa80c59c1010 \FileName
fffffa80c872dba0 Queued fffffa80c872d9a0 2a 0400eb28 fffffa80c59c1010 \FileName
fffffa80c9e67d10 Queued fffffa80c9e67b10 2a 04012168 fffffa80c59c1010 \FileName
fffffa80ca3bb350 Queued fffffa80c66e4370 2a 0400c928 fffffa80c59c1010 \FileName
fffffa80c5894ab0 Queued fffffa80c58948b0 2a 0400c368 fffffa80c59c1010 \FileName
fffffa80c305fe60 Queued fffffa80c305fc60 2a 04013168 fffffa80c59c1010 \FileName
fffffa80c496cce0 Queued fffffa80c496cae0 2a 0400d168 fffffa80c59c1010 \FileName
fffffa80c5e78c60 Queued fffffa80c905c7f0 2a 0400f8a8 fffffa80c59c1010 \FileName
fffffa80c905c640 Queued fffffa80c5c1c410 2a 0400f428 fffffa80c59c1010 \FileName
fffffa80c68ffc40 Queued fffffa80c68ffa40 2a 0400f468 fffffa80c59c1010 \FileName
fffffa80c3aa3e60 Queued fffffa80c3aa3c60 2a 0400c7a8 fffffa80c59c1010 \FileName
fffffa80c5e8dc60 Queued fffffa80c8852cf0 2a 0400f4a8 fffffa80c59c1010 \FileName
fffffa80c90082b0 Queued fffffa80c7907440 2a 04013428 fffffa80c59c1010 \FileName
fffffa80c7907290 Queued fffffa80c67aea80 2a 0400fe68 fffffa80c59c1010 \FileName
fffffa80c67ae8d0 Queued fffffa80c9383cf0 2a 0400f3a8 fffffa80c59c1010 \FileName
fffffa80c8497010 Queued fffffa80c8497270 2a 0400c5e8 fffffa80c59c1010 \FileName
fffffa80c78c7480 Queued fffffa80c78c7280 2a 0400c3e8 fffffa80c59c1010 \FileName
fffffa80c7f37d90 Queued fffffa80c618b480 2a 0400cce8 fffffa80c59c1010 \FileName
fffffa80c618b2d0 Queued fffffa80ca2e9e10 2a 0400ee28 fffffa80c59c1010 \FileName
fffffa80ca2e9c60 Queued fffffa80c5e783f0 2a 0400d8e8 fffffa80c59c1010 \FileName
fffffa80c64e1650 Queued fffffa80c64e1450 2a 0400d0e8 fffffa80c59c1010 \FileName
fffffa80c684dd60 Queued fffffa80c684db60 2a 0400c6a8 fffffa80c59c1010 \FileName
fffffa80c3b2bac0 Queued fffffa80c3b2b8c0 2a 040127a8 fffffa80c59c1010 \FileName
fffffa80c5ff64d0 Queued fffffa80c5ff62d0 2a 0400de68 fffffa80c59c1010 \FileName
fffffa80c99a84b0 Queued fffffa80c99a82b0 2a 0400cfe8 fffffa80c59c1010 \FileName
fffffa80ca300510 Queued fffffa80ca300310 2a 0400c168 fffffa80c59c1010 \FileName
[...]
```

Comments

For Windows 8 and higher there is **!storagekd.storclass 2** extension command.

Dispatch Level Spin

Spiking Thread pattern (page 1004) includes normal threads running at PASSIVE_LEVEL or APC_LEVEL IRQL that can be preempted by any other higher priority thread. Therefore, **Spiking Threads** are not necessarily ones that were in a RUNNING state when the memory dump was saved. They consumed much CPU, and this is reflected in their *User* and *Kernel* time values. The pattern also includes threads running at DISPATCH_LEVEL and higher IRQL. These threads cannot be preempted by another thread, so they usually remain in the RUNNING state all the time unless they lower their IRQL. Some of them can be trying to acquire a spinlock, and we need a more specialized pattern for them. We would see it when a spinlock for some data structure wasn't released or was corrupt, and some thread tries to acquire it and enters endless spinning loop unless interrupted by a higher IRQL interrupt. These infinite loops can also happen due to software defects in code running at dispatch level or higher IRQL.

Let's look at one example. The following running thread was interrupted by a keyboard interrupt apparently to save **Manual Dump** (page 705). We see that it spent almost 11 minutes in the kernel:

```
0: kd> !thread
THREAD 830c07c0  Cid 0588.0528  Teb: 7ffa3000 Win32Thread: e29546a8 RUNNING on processor 0
Not impersonating
DeviceMap               e257b7c8
Owning Process          831ec608         Image:        MyApp.EXE
Wait Start TickCount    122850           Ticks: 40796 (0:00:10:37.437)
Context Switch Count    191                      LargeStack
UserTime                00:00:00.000
KernelTime              00:10:37.406
Win32 Start Address MyApp!ThreadImpersonation (0x35f76821)
Start Address kernel32!BaseThreadStartThunk (0x7c810659)
Stack Init a07bf000 Current a07beca0 Base a07bf000 Limit a07bb000 Call 0
Priority 11 BasePriority 8 PriorityDecrement 2 DecrementCount 16
ChildEBP RetAddr
a07be0f8 f77777fa nt!KeBugCheckEx+0x1b
a07be114 f7777032 i8042prt!I8xProcessCrashDump+0x237
a07be15c 805448e5 i8042prt!I8042KeyboardInterruptService+0x21c
a07be15c 806e4a37 nt!KiInterruptDispatch+0x45 (FPO: [0,2] TrapFrame @ a07be180)
a07be220 a1342755 hal!KeAcquireInStackQueuedSpinLock+0x47
a07be220 a1342755 MyDriver!RcvData+0x98
```

To see the code and context we switch to the trap frame[44] and disassemble the interrupted function:

```
1: kd> .trap a07be180
ErrCode = 00000000
eax=a07be200 ebx=a07be228 ecx=831dabf5 edx=a07beb94 esi=831d02a8 edi=831dabd8
eip=806e4a37 esp=a07be1f4 ebp=a07be220 iopl=0 nv up ei pl nz na po nc
cs=0008 ss=0010 ds=0000 es=0000 fs=0000 gs=0000 efl=00000202
```

---

[44] Interrupt Frames and Stack Reconstruction, Memory Dump Analysis Anthology, Volume 1, page 83

```
hal!KeAcquireInStackQueuedSpinLock+0x47:
806e4a37 ebf3              jmp       hal!KeAcquireInStackQueuedSpinLock+0x3c (806e4a2c)

1: kd> uf hal!KeAcquireInStackQueuedSpinLock
hal!KeAcquireInStackQueuedSpinLock:
806e49f0 mov      eax,dword ptr ds:[FFFE0080h]
806e49f5 shr      eax,4
806e49f8 mov      al,byte ptr hal!HalpVectorToIRQL (806ef218)[eax]
806e49fe mov      dword ptr ds:[0FFFE0080h],41h
806e4a08 mov      byte ptr [edx+8],al
806e4a0b mov      dword ptr [edx+4],ecx
806e4a0e mov      dword ptr [edx],0
806e4a14 mov      eax,edx
806e4a16 xchg     edx,dword ptr [ecx]
806e4a18 cmp      edx,0
806e4a1b jne      hal!KeAcquireInStackQueuedSpinLock+0x34 (806e4a24)

[...]

hal!KeAcquireInStackQueuedSpinLock+0x34:
806e4a24 or       ecx,1
806e4a27 mov      dword ptr [eax+4],ecx
806e4a2a mov      dword ptr [edx],eax

hal!KeAcquireInStackQueuedSpinLock+0x3c:
806e4a2c test     dword ptr [eax+4],1
806e4a33 je       hal!KeAcquireInStackQueuedSpinLock+0x33 (806e4a23)

hal!KeAcquireInStackQueuedSpinLock+0x45:
806e4a35 pause
806e4a37 jmp      hal!KeAcquireInStackQueuedSpinLock+0x3c (806e4a2c)
```

JMP instruction transfers execution to the code that tests the first bit at [EAX+4] address. If it is not set, it falls through to the same JMP instruction. We know the value of EAX from the trap frame so we can dereference that address:

```
1: kd> dyd eax+4 l1
         3         2         1         0
       10987654 32109876 54321098 76543210
       -------- -------- -------- --------
a07be204  10000011 00011101 10101011 11110101   831dabf5
```

The value is odd: the first leftmost bit is set. Therefore, the code loops indefinitely unless a different thread running on another processor clears that bit. However the second processor is idle:

```
0: kd> ~0s

0: kd> k
ChildEBP RetAddr
f794cd54 00000000 nt!KiIdleLoop+0x14
```

Seems we have a problem. We need to examine *MyDriver.sys* code to understand how it uses queued spinlocks.

Note: In addition to user-defined there are internal system queued spinlocks we can check by using **!qlocks** WinDbg command.

Distributed Exception

Managed Code

Managed code **Nested Exceptions** (page 808) give us process virtual space bound stack traces. However, exception objects may be marshaled across processes and even computers. The remote stack trace return addresses do not have the same validity in different process contexts. Fortunately, there is a _remoteStackTraceString_ field in exception objects, and it contains the original stack trace. Default analysis command sometimes uses it:

```
0:013> !analyze -v

[...]

EXCEPTION_OBJECT: !pe 25203b0
Exception object: 00000000025203b0
Exception type: System.Reflection.TargetInvocationException
Message: Exception has been thrown by the target of an invocation.
InnerException: System.Management.Instrumentation.WmiProviderInstallationException, Use !PrintException
0000000002522cf0 to see more.
StackTrace (generated):
SP IP Function
000000001D39E720 0000000000000001 Component!Proxy.Start()+0x20
000000001D39E720 000007FEF503D0B6
mscorlib_ni!System.Threading.ExecutionContext.RunInternal(System.Threading.ExecutionContext,
System.Threading.ContextCallback, System.Object, Boolean)+0x286
000000001D39E880 000007FEF503CE1A
mscorlib_ni!System.Threading.ExecutionContext.Run(System.Threading.ExecutionContext,
System.Threading.ContextCallback, System.Object, Boolean)+0xa
000000001D39E8B0 000007FEF503CDD8
mscorlib_ni!System.Threading.ExecutionContext.Run(System.Threading.ExecutionContext,
System.Threading.ContextCallback, System.Object)+0x58
000000001D39E900 000007FEF4FB0302 mscorlib_ni!System.Threading.ThreadHelper.ThreadStart()+0x52

[...]

MANAGED_STACK_COMMAND: ** Check field _remoteStackTraceString **;!do 2522cf0;!do 2521900

[...]

0:013> !DumpObj 2522cf0
[...]
000007fef51b77f0 4000054 2c System.String 0 instance 2521900 _remoteStackTraceString
[...]

0:013> !DumpObj 2521900
Name: System.String
[...]
String: at System.Management.Instrumentation.InstrumentationManager.RegisterType(Type managementType)
at Component.Provider..ctor()
at Component.Start()
```

Checking this field may also be necessary for exceptions of interest from managed space **Execution Residue** (page 393). We call this pattern **Distributed Exception**. The basic idea is illustrated in the following diagram using the borrowed UML notation (not limited to just two computers):

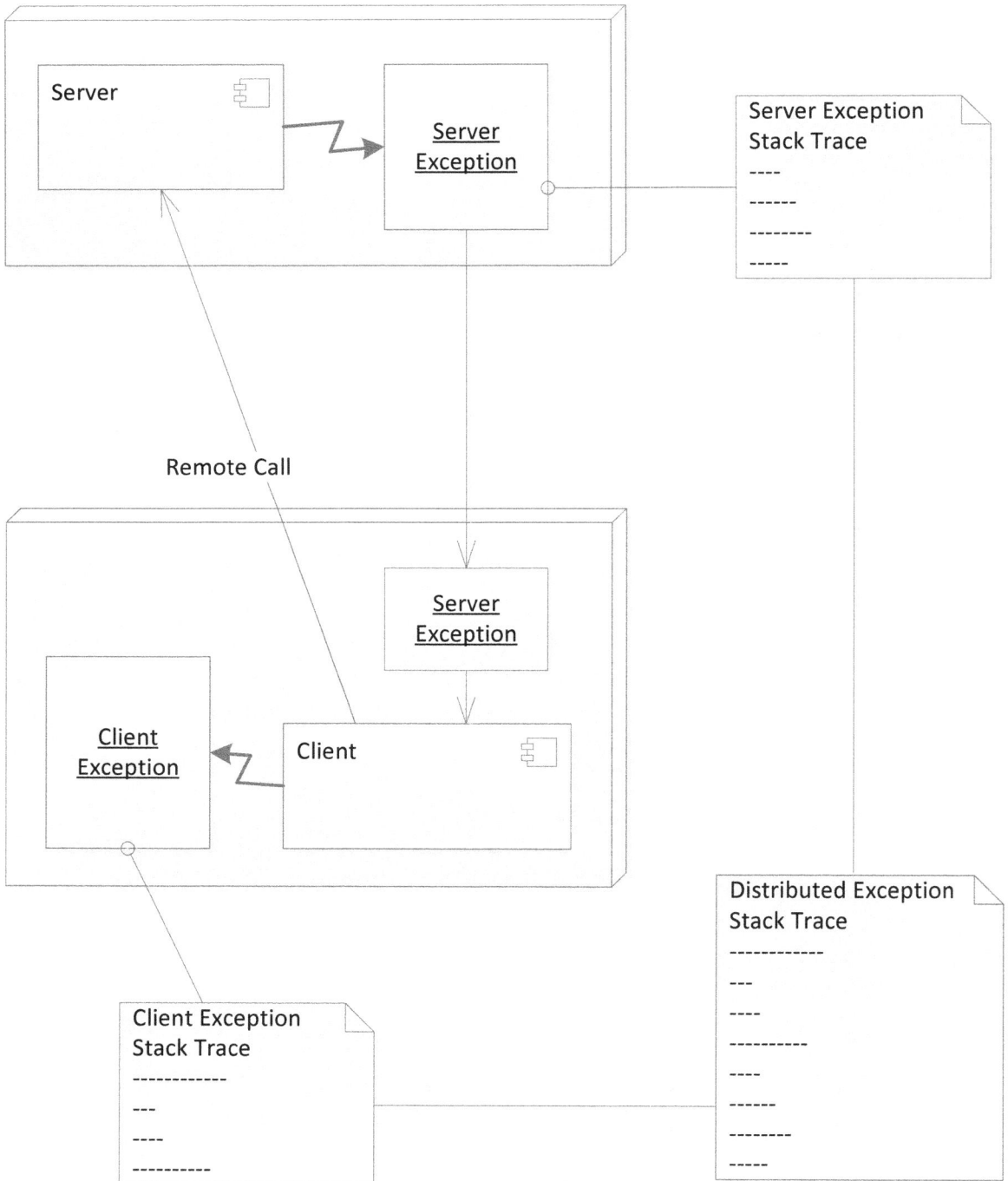

Distributed Spike

Abnormal CPU consumption detection usually goes at a process level when we detect it using Task Manager, for example. Sometimes that process has only one **Spiking Thread** (page 992) among many, but there are cases when CPU consumption is spread among many threads. We call this pattern **Distributed Spike**. Such behavior could be a consequence of weakly **Coupled Processes** (page 164), for example, in these two services (where, for simplicity, we highlight in bold threads with more than 1 second CPU time spent in user mode):

```
0:000> !runaway
 User Mode Time
  Thread       Time
  120:4e518    0 days 0:05:09.937
  126:531bc    0 days 0:03:56.546
   44:334c     0 days 0:03:40.765
  133:4fe1c    0 days 0:03:31.156
   45:42b4     0 days 0:03:27.328
  107:25ae0    0 days 0:03:19.921
   49:627c     0 days 0:02:48.250
  147:6b90c    0 days 0:02:33.046
  136:6620c    0 days 0:02:05.109
  127:4f2d0    0 days 0:02:04.046
  129:5bc30    0 days 0:02:02.171
   48:623c     0 days 0:02:01.796
  119:41f00    0 days 0:02:00.562
   74:cd18     0 days 0:01:59.453
   51:7a4c     0 days 0:01:54.234
   35:21d4     0 days 0:01:47.390
  148:326dc    0 days 0:01:32.640
  123:43c8c    0 days 0:01:32.515
  135:67b08    0 days 0:01:32.296
   11:aa8      0 days 0:01:30.906
  118:42f8c    0 days 0:01:20.265
   42:3a3c     0 days 0:01:20.000
   77:d024     0 days 0:01:19.734
  115:3a840    0 days 0:01:15.625
   89:145f4    0 days 0:01:10.500
  157:4e310    0 days 0:01:07.625
   80:d07c     0 days 0:01:07.468
   33:1ab0     0 days 0:01:00.593
  117:10bd4    0 days 0:00:59.421
  151:1aaa0    0 days 0:00:59.015
   28:17bc     0 days 0:00:58.796
   83:f3a4     0 days 0:00:55.828
  122:41964    0 days 0:00:55.578
  149:4101c    0 days 0:00:55.234
   10:aa4      0 days 0:00:52.453
  106:21b80    0 days 0:00:51.187
  132:62e5c    0 days 0:00:49.437
  160:3a3a8    0 days 0:00:48.875
  137:6bf90    0 days 0:00:48.687
  145:6f594    0 days 0:00:47.968
  143:58d60    0 days 0:00:45.703
   72:ba64     0 days 0:00:44.515
```

```
 41:19b0         0 days 0:00:44.000
130:5d480        0 days 0:00:43.750
139:6d090        0 days 0:00:42.062
138:6d578        0 days 0:00:40.406
 91:17974        0 days 0:00:40.359
152:37f80        0 days 0:00:39.781
 81:de68         0 days 0:00:39.265
150:65b2c        0 days 0:00:36.625
162:1f340        0 days 0:00:35.125
 85:10650        0 days 0:00:33.546
131:614e8        0 days 0:00:33.093
128:2eddc        0 days 0:00:33.000
146:6f690        0 days 0:00:32.015
161:3c4b4        0 days 0:00:30.421
167:3cde4        0 days 0:00:29.390
171:3979c        0 days 0:00:28.515
166:3cd40        0 days 0:00:28.312
168:68ef0        0 days 0:00:27.781
 65:aad0         0 days 0:00:26.593
109:267f4        0 days 0:00:26.390
 88:13624        0 days 0:00:26.000
173:5282c        0 days 0:00:24.640
153:71e14        0 days 0:00:23.390
112:322b4        0 days 0:00:22.812
110:9578         0 days 0:00:22.125
175:20230        0 days 0:00:20.250
 79:b458         0 days 0:00:20.218
 66:61b8         0 days 0:00:19.875
 62:9498         0 days 0:00:19.562
156:d900         0 days 0:00:19.015
121:5106c        0 days 0:00:18.687
142:6bb28        0 days 0:00:18.562
 46:2cbc         0 days 0:00:17.796
169:d920         0 days 0:00:16.875
154:720b4        0 days 0:00:16.484
170:4ac8c        0 days 0:00:15.968
 73:b010         0 days 0:00:13.609
 39:3224         0 days 0:00:13.406
172:722e4        0 days 0:00:12.375
 63:9780         0 days 0:00:12.203
177:8464         0 days 0:00:11.906
184:22908        0 days 0:00:10.234
140:5765c        0 days 0:00:09.750
174:2f484        0 days 0:00:08.390
 50:7230         0 days 0:00:07.125
187:3c324        0 days 0:00:06.765
125:46cf0        0 days 0:00:06.296
178:3a424        0 days 0:00:05.125
114:33d20        0 days 0:00:03.734
165:3ca74        0 days 0:00:01.203
189:3c358        0 days 0:00:01.000
164:3124c        0 days 0:00:00.578
 25:be4          0 days 0:00:00.515
 17:ba8          0 days 0:00:00.125
104:5cf8         0 days 0:00:00.109
 26:e4c          0 days 0:00:00.109
```

```
 96:5d44       0 days 0:00:00.093
 99:5b18       0 days 0:00:00.078
 56:8a6c       0 days 0:00:00.078
 55:8a68       0 days 0:00:00.078
  6:a08        0 days 0:00:00.078
  4:a00        0 days 0:00:00.062
103:5cfc       0 days 0:00:00.046
100:5ab8       0 days 0:00:00.046
 68:bf34       0 days 0:00:00.046
 37:29d4       0 days 0:00:00.046
101:5ab4       0 days 0:00:00.031
 98:5b44       0 days 0:00:00.031
 97:5d40       0 days 0:00:00.031
 57:8a70       0 days 0:00:00.031
 53:8a60       0 days 0:00:00.031
 36:29c0       0 days 0:00:00.031
 16:ac4        0 days 0:00:00.031
  1:9e4        0 days 0:00:00.031
 60:880c       0 days 0:00:00.015
 58:8a5c       0 days 0:00:00.015
 24:be0        0 days 0:00:00.015
 15:abc        0 days 0:00:00.015
188:13044      0 days 0:00:00.000
186:6530       0 days 0:00:00.000
185:2013c      0 days 0:00:00.000
183:6047c      0 days 0:00:00.000
182:65400      0 days 0:00:00.000
181:61560      0 days 0:00:00.000
180:2b7a4      0 days 0:00:00.000
179:56294      0 days 0:00:00.000
176:20300      0 days 0:00:00.000
163:2ab1c      0 days 0:00:00.000
159:276cc      0 days 0:00:00.000
158:72134      0 days 0:00:00.000
155:6a078      0 days 0:00:00.000
144:6ce98      0 days 0:00:00.000
141:5404       0 days 0:00:00.000
134:65718      0 days 0:00:00.000
124:4bed4      0 days 0:00:00.000
116:3c770      0 days 0:00:00.000
113:b08        0 days 0:00:00.000
111:28e54      0 days 0:00:00.000
108:25fbc      0 days 0:00:00.000
105:20504      0 days 0:00:00.000
102:5cf4       0 days 0:00:00.000
 95:5c70       0 days 0:00:00.000
 94:5ed4       0 days 0:00:00.000
 93:18c2c      0 days 0:00:00.000
 92:19fd8      0 days 0:00:00.000
 90:c870       0 days 0:00:00.000
 87:7994       0 days 0:00:00.000
 86:124cc      0 days 0:00:00.000
 84:eab8       0 days 0:00:00.000
 82:f2a4       0 days 0:00:00.000
 78:d5c0       0 days 0:00:00.000
 76:cfd0       0 days 0:00:00.000
```

```
75:cf64        0 days 0:00:00.000
71:b4f8        0 days 0:00:00.000
70:c628        0 days 0:00:00.000
69:c484        0 days 0:00:00.000
67:be84        0 days 0:00:00.000
64:aa00        0 days 0:00:00.000
61:93f0        0 days 0:00:00.000
59:89e4        0 days 0:00:00.000
54:8a64        0 days 0:00:00.000
52:89a8        0 days 0:00:00.000
47:4c64        0 days 0:00:00.000
43:3fa0        0 days 0:00:00.000
40:2c88        0 days 0:00:00.000
38:2a28        0 days 0:00:00.000
34:1928        0 days 0:00:00.000
32:1668        0 days 0:00:00.000
31:8dc         0 days 0:00:00.000
30:15d4        0 days 0:00:00.000
29:1044        0 days 0:00:00.000
27:fb4         0 days 0:00:00.000
23:bd8         0 days 0:00:00.000
22:bd4         0 days 0:00:00.000
21:bd0         0 days 0:00:00.000
20:bc8         0 days 0:00:00.000
19:bc4         0 days 0:00:00.000
18:bc0         0 days 0:00:00.000
14:ab8         0 days 0:00:00.000
13:ab4         0 days 0:00:00.000
12:ab0         0 days 0:00:00.000
 9:aa0         0 days 0:00:00.000
 8:a9c         0 days 0:00:00.000
 7:a98         0 days 0:00:00.000
 5:a04         0 days 0:00:00.000
 3:9f4         0 days 0:00:00.000
 2:9f0         0 days 0:00:00.000
 0:994         0 days 0:00:00.000
```

This is a real spike in the first service process as can be confirmed by a random non-waiting thread:

```
0:000> ~143k
ChildEBP RetAddr
050dfc68 7c82d6a4 ntdll!RtlEnterCriticalSection+0x1d
050dfc84 77c7bc50 ntdll!RtlInitializeCriticalSectionAndSpinCount+0x92
050dfc98 77c7bc7c rpcrt4!MUTEX::CommonConstructor+0x1b
050dfcac 77c7c000 rpcrt4!MUTEX::MUTEX+0x13
050dfcc8 77c6ff47 rpcrt4!BINDING_HANDLE::BINDING_HANDLE+0x2d
050dfcd8 77c6ff1f rpcrt4!SVR_BINDING_HANDLE::SVR_BINDING_HANDLE+0x10
050dfcfc 77c6d338 rpcrt4!RPC_ADDRESS::InquireBinding+0x8a
050dfd0c 77c6fd1d rpcrt4!LRPC_SCALL::ToStringBinding+0x16
050dfd1c 76554c83 rpcrt4!RpcBindingToStringBindingW+0x4d
050dfd5c 77c7c42a ServiceA!RpcSecurityCallback+0x1e
050dfdb4 77c7c4b0 rpcrt4!RPC_INTERFACE::CheckSecurityIfNecessary+0x6f
050dfdcc 77c7c46c rpcrt4!LRPC_SBINDING::CheckSecurity+0x4f
050dfdfc 77c812f0 rpcrt4!LRPC_SCALL::DealWithRequestMessage+0x2bb
050dfe20 77c88678 rpcrt4!LRPC_ADDRESS::DealWithLRPCRequest+0x127
050dff84 77c88792 rpcrt4!LRPC_ADDRESS::ReceiveLotsaCalls+0x430
```

```
050dff8c 77c8872d rpcrt4!RecvLotsaCallsWrapper+0xd
050dffac 77c7b110 rpcrt4!BaseCachedThreadRoutine+0x9d
050dffb8 77e64829 rpcrt4!ThreadStartRoutine+0x1b
050dffec 00000000 kernel32!BaseThreadStart+0x34


0:000> ~143r
eax=00000000 ebx=00000000 ecx=7c887784 edx=7c887780 esi=7c887784 edi=00163fb0
eip=7c81a37d esp=050dfc5c ebp=050dfc68 iopl=0 nv up ei ng nz na pe cy
cs=001b ss=0023 ds=0023 es=0023 fs=003b gs=0000 efl=00000287
ntdll!RtlEnterCriticalSection+0x1d:
7c81a37d 0f92c0          setb     al


0:000> .asm no_code_bytes
Assembly options: no_code_bytes


0:000> u 7c81a37d
ntdll!RtlEnterCriticalSection+0x1d:
7c81a37d setb     al
7c81a380 test     al,al
7c81a382 je       ntdll!RtlEnterCriticalSection+0x28 (7c82b096)
7c81a388 mov      ecx,dword ptr fs:[18h]
7c81a38f mov      eax,dword ptr [ecx+24h]
7c81a392 pop      edi
7c81a393 mov      dword ptr [edx+0Ch],eax
7c81a396 mov      dword ptr [edx+8],1


0:000> ub 7c81a37d
ntdll!RtlEnterCriticalSection+0x6:
7c81a366 mov      edx,dword ptr [ebp+8]
7c81a369 push     esi
7c81a36a lea      esi,[edx+4]
7c81a36d push     edi
7c81a36e mov      dword ptr [ebp-4],esi
7c81a371 mov      eax,0
7c81a376 mov      ecx,dword ptr [ebp-4]
7c81a379 lock btr dword ptr [ecx],eax
```

The second service is weakly (waiting for event notifications) coupled to the first service above:

```
0:000> !runaway
 User Mode Time
  Thread       Time
   5:dbec      0 days 0:01:50.031
   8:46008     0 days 0:01:46.062
  11:ad0c      0 days 0:01:13.921
  17:932c      0 days 0:01:03.234
  14:45d78     0 days 0:00:58.109
  15:6d4d0     0 days 0:00:00.015
   2:725a4     0 days 0:00:00.015
   0:6101c     0 days 0:00:00.015
  18:d1c4      0 days 0:00:00.000
  16:76bc      0 days 0:00:00.000
  13:456a8     0 days 0:00:00.000
  12:459e4     0 days 0:00:00.000
```

```
  10:3c768       0 days 0:00:00.000
   9:12d20       0 days 0:00:00.000
   7:46010       0 days 0:00:00.000
   6:4600c       0 days 0:00:00.000
   4:dbf0        0 days 0:00:00.000
   3:17ed4       0 days 0:00:00.000
   1:61024       0 days 0:00:00.000


0:000> ~11k
ChildEBP RetAddr
0223fa68 7c82787b ntdll!KiFastSystemCallRet
0223fa6c 77c80a6e ntdll!NtRequestWaitReplyPort+0xc
0223fab8 77c7fcf0 rpcrt4!LRPC_CCALL::SendReceive+0x230
0223fac4 77c80673 rpcrt4!I_RpcSendReceive+0x24
0223fad8 77ce315a rpcrt4!NdrSendReceive+0x2b
0223fec0 771f4fbd rpcrt4!NdrClientCall2+0x22e
0223fed8 771f4f60 ServiceB!RpcWaitEvent+0x1c
[...]


0:000> ~17k
ChildEBP RetAddr
0283fa68 7c82787b ntdll!KiFastSystemCallRet
0283fa6c 77c80a6e ntdll!NtRequestWaitReplyPort+0xc
0283fab8 77c7fcf0 rpcrt4!LRPC_CCALL::SendReceive+0x230
0283fac4 77c80673 rpcrt4!I_RpcSendReceive+0x24
0283fad8 77ce315a rpcrt4!NdrSendReceive+0x2b
0283fec0 771f4fbd rpcrt4!NdrClientCall2+0x22e
0283fed8 771f4f60 ServiceB!RpcWaitEvent+0x1c
[...]
```

Sometimes, semantically **Coupled Processes** (page 161) result in distributed spikes, and most often it is possible to predict another spiking process in such cases. In our example above, both spiking processes were semantically coupled with another service, and it was confirmed that it was spiking too:

```
0:000> !runaway
 User Mode Time
  Thread       Time
  89:10d4      0 days 0:03:03.500
  28:a94       0 days 0:00:39.562
  73:c10       0 days 0:00:37.531
  54:b88       0 days 0:00:37.140
  29:a98       0 days 0:00:35.906
  27:a90       0 days 0:00:35.500
  75:c2c       0 days 0:00:28.812
  90:10d8      0 days 0:00:27.000
  93:10e4      0 days 0:00:24.265
  32:aa4       0 days 0:00:12.906
  41:ac8       0 days 0:00:11.890
  35:ab0       0 days 0:00:11.875
  58:bc4       0 days 0:00:10.218
  42:acc       0 days 0:00:09.546
  85:e74       0 days 0:00:08.859
  36:ab4       0 days 0:00:08.578
  72:c0c       0 days 0:00:05.890
```

```
 70:c04        0 days 0:00:05.687
 33:aa8        0 days 0:00:05.046
 74:c14        0 days 0:00:04.953
 40:ac4        0 days 0:00:04.953
 38:abc        0 days 0:00:04.359
 39:ac0        0 days 0:00:04.312
 34:aac        0 days 0:00:04.140
 64:bec        0 days 0:00:03.812
 88:10d0       0 days 0:00:03.187
 30:a9c        0 days 0:00:02.859
  9:a10        0 days 0:00:01.968
 37:ab8        0 days 0:00:01.953
 92:10e0       0 days 0:00:01.718
 83:d00        0 days 0:00:01.125
 94:1150       0 days 0:00:01.031
 77:c54        0 days 0:00:00.890
 98:f2c0       0 days 0:00:00.265
 97:eb1c       0 days 0:00:00.265
 76:c50        0 days 0:00:00.265
 21:a48        0 days 0:00:00.187
 22:a4c        0 days 0:00:00.140
 63:be8        0 days 0:00:00.093
 23:a50        0 days 0:00:00.093
 53:af8        0 days 0:00:00.078
 24:a54        0 days 0:00:00.046
 71:c08        0 days 0:00:00.031
 65:bf0        0 days 0:00:00.031
 87:e8c        0 days 0:00:00.015
 57:bc0        0 days 0:00:00.015
104:6454c      0 days 0:00:00.000
103:63fb4      0 days 0:00:00.000
102:3c5ec      0 days 0:00:00.000
101:65178      0 days 0:00:00.000
100:5d0e4      0 days 0:00:00.000
 99:5bae4      0 days 0:00:00.000
 96:574        0 days 0:00:00.000
 95:b84        0 days 0:00:00.000
 91:10dc       0 days 0:00:00.000
 86:e88        0 days 0:00:00.000
 84:e70        0 days 0:00:00.000
 82:c84        0 days 0:00:00.000
 81:c68        0 days 0:00:00.000
 80:c64        0 days 0:00:00.000
 79:c60        0 days 0:00:00.000
 78:c5c        0 days 0:00:00.000
 69:c00        0 days 0:00:00.000
 68:bfc        0 days 0:00:00.000
 67:bf8        0 days 0:00:00.000
 66:bf4        0 days 0:00:00.000
 62:bd8        0 days 0:00:00.000
 61:bd4        0 days 0:00:00.000
 60:bd0        0 days 0:00:00.000
 59:bcc        0 days 0:00:00.000
 56:bbc        0 days 0:00:00.000
 55:bb8        0 days 0:00:00.000
 52:af4        0 days 0:00:00.000
```

```
51:af0     0 days 0:00:00.000
50:aec     0 days 0:00:00.000
49:ae8     0 days 0:00:00.000
48:ae4     0 days 0:00:00.000
47:ae0     0 days 0:00:00.000
46:adc     0 days 0:00:00.000
45:ad8     0 days 0:00:00.000
44:ad4     0 days 0:00:00.000
43:ad0     0 days 0:00:00.000
31:aa0     0 days 0:00:00.000
26:a8c     0 days 0:00:00.000
25:a64     0 days 0:00:00.000
20:a44     0 days 0:00:00.000
19:a40     0 days 0:00:00.000
18:a34     0 days 0:00:00.000
17:a30     0 days 0:00:00.000
16:a2c     0 days 0:00:00.000
15:a28     0 days 0:00:00.000
14:a24     0 days 0:00:00.000
13:a20     0 days 0:00:00.000
12:a1c     0 days 0:00:00.000
11:a18     0 days 0:00:00.000
10:a14     0 days 0:00:00.000
 8:a0c     0 days 0:00:00.000
 7:a08     0 days 0:00:00.000
 6:a04     0 days 0:00:00.000
 5:a00     0 days 0:00:00.000
 4:9fc     0 days 0:00:00.000
 3:9f8     0 days 0:00:00.000
 2:9f4     0 days 0:00:00.000
 1:9f0     0 days 0:00:00.000
 0:9e4     0 days 0:00:00.000
```

Comments

If timing information is not available, but the random process memory snapshots or snapshots by procdump tool reveal different spiking threads, then we may also have this pattern.

Distributed Wait Chain

Most **Wait Chain** patterns (page 1199) are about single wait chains. However, it is often a case when there are many different **Wait Chains** in a memory dump especially in terminal services environments. There can be **ALPC** (page 1214) and **Critical Section Wait Chains** (page 1203) at the same time. They can be related or completely disjoint. **Distributed Wait Chain** pattern covers a special case of several **Wait Chains** having the same structure (and possibly pointing in one direction). One such example we put below. In **Stack Trace Collection** (page 1052) from a complete memory dump from a hanging system we found several *explorer.exe* processes with **Critical Section Wait Chains** having the same structure and endpoint of **Top** (page 1127) and **Blocking** (page 107) *ModuleA*:

```
THREAD fffffa80137cf060  Cid 4884.4f9c  Teb: 000007fffffaa000 Win32Thread: fffff900c0fb98b0 WAIT:
(UserRequest) UserMode Non-Alertable
    fffffa8013570dc0  SynchronizationEvent
Not impersonating
DeviceMap                 fffff8a014e21d90
Owning Process            fffffa80131a75d0        Image:          explorer.exe
Attached Process          N/A          Image:          N/A
Wait Start TickCount      274752       Ticks: 212448 (0:00:55:19.500)
Context Switch Count      9889                      LargeStack
UserTime                  00:00:00.093
KernelTime                00:00:00.171
Win32 Start Address SHLWAPI!WrapperThreadProc (0x000007fefdafc608)
Stack Init fffff88013c25db0 Current fffff88013c25900
Base fffff88013c26000 Limit fffff88013c1b000 Call 0
Priority 11 BasePriority 9 UnusualBoost 0 ForegroundBoost 0 IoPriority 2 PagePriority 5
Kernel stack not resident.
Child-SP          RetAddr           Call Site
fffff880`13c25940 fffff800`01873652 nt!KiSwapContext+0x7a
fffff880`13c25a80 fffff800`01884a9f nt!KiCommitThreadWait+0x1d2
fffff880`13c25b10 fffff800`01b7768e nt!KeWaitForSingleObject+0x19f
fffff880`13c25bb0 fffff800`0187ced3 nt!NtWaitForSingleObject+0xde
fffff880`13c25c20 00000000`76d8135a nt!KiSystemServiceCopyEnd+0x13 (TrapFrame @ fffff880`13c25c20)
00000000`0489e518 00000000`76d7e4e8 ntdll!ZwWaitForSingleObject+0xa
00000000`0489e520 00000000`76d7e3db ntdll!RtlpWaitOnCriticalSection+0xe8
00000000`0489e5d0 000007fe`fdf8ff50 ntdll!RtlEnterCriticalSection+0xd1
00000000`0489e600 000007fe`fdf8fbd3 SHELL32!CFSFolder::GetIconOf+0x24b
00000000`0489f3a0 000007fe`fdf903d3 SHELL32!SHGetIconIndexFromPIDL+0x3f
00000000`0489f3d0 00000000`ff900328 SHELL32!SHMapIDListToSystemImageListIndexAsync+0x73
00000000`0489f470 00000000`ff8fff4b Explorer!SFTBarHost::AddImageForItem+0x9c
00000000`0489f4d0 00000000`ff8fd2f1 Explorer!SFTBarHost::_InternalRepopulateList+0x4ad
00000000`0489f5d0 00000000`ff8fd0b4 Explorer!SFTBarHost::_RepopulateList+0x1f3
00000000`0489f600 00000000`ff8fcccd Explorer!SFTBarHost::_OnBackgroundEnumDone+0xc1
00000000`0489f630 00000000`ff8fc9e2 Explorer!SFTBarHost::_WndProc+0x451
00000000`0489f680 00000000`76669bd1 Explorer!SFTBarHost::_WndProc_ProgramsMFU+0x1b
00000000`0489f6b0 00000000`766698da USER32!UserCallWinProcCheckWow+0x1ad
00000000`0489f770 00000000`ff8f1177 USER32!DispatchMessageWorker+0x3b5
00000000`0489f7f0 00000000`ff9130e9 Explorer!CTray::_MessageLoop+0x446
00000000`0489f880 000007fe`fdafc71e Explorer!CTray::MainThreadProc+0x8a
00000000`0489f8b0 00000000`76c2652d SHLWAPI!WrapperThreadProc+0x19b
00000000`0489f9b0 00000000`76d5c521 kernel32!BaseThreadInitThunk+0xd
00000000`0489f9e0 00000000`00000000 ntdll!RtlUserThreadStart+0x1d
```

```
0: kd> .process /r /p fffffa80131a75d0
Implicit process is now fffffa80`131a75d0
Loading User Symbols


0: kd> !cs -l -o -s
----------------------------------------
DebugInfo          = 0x0000000000499d90
Critical section   = 0x000007fefe3d5900 (SHELL32!g_csIconCache+0x0)
LOCKED
LockCount          = 0x2
WaiterWoken        = No
OwningThread       = 0x0000000000002b34
RecursionCount     = 0x1
LockSemaphore      = 0x7F8
SpinCount          = 0x0000000000000000
OwningThread       = .thread fffffa8013dc3b00


THREAD fffffa8013dc3b00  Cid 4884.2b34  Teb: 000007fffffac000 Win32Thread: fffff900c2bc1010 WAIT:
(Executive) KernelMode Non-Alertable
    fffff88011c03600  SynchronizationEvent
IRP List:
    fffffa800f8fc790: (0006,0430) Flags: 00000404  Mdl: 00000000
Not impersonating
DeviceMap                   fffff8a014e21d90
Owning Process              fffffa80131a75d0       Image:         explorer.exe
Attached Process            N/A            Image:         N/A
Wait Start TickCount        170052         Ticks: 317148 (0:01:22:35.437)
Context Switch Count        2                      LargeStack
UserTime                    00:00:00.000
KernelTime                  00:00:00.000
Win32 Start Address SHELL32!ShutdownThreadProc (0x000007fefe13ef54)
Stack Init fffff88011c03db0 Current fffff88011c03320
Base fffff88011c04000 Limit fffff88011bfd000 Call 0
Priority 11 BasePriority 8 UnusualBoost 0 ForegroundBoost 2 IoPriority 2 PagePriority 5
Child-SP          RetAddr          Call Site
fffff880`11c03360 fffff800`01873652 nt!KiSwapContext+0x7a
fffff880`11c034a0 fffff800`01884a9f nt!KiCommitThreadWait+0x1d2
fffff880`11c03530 fffff880`05c12383 nt!KeWaitForSingleObject+0x19f
fffff880`11c035d0 fffff880`012b9288 ModuleA+0x12468
fffff880`11c03750 fffff880`012b7d1b fltmgr!FltpPerformPostCallbacks+0x368
fffff880`11c03820 fffff880`012b66df fltmgr!FltpLegacyProcessingAfterPreCallbacksCompleted+0x39b
fffff880`11c038b0 fffff880`01b895ff fltmgr!FltpDispatch+0xcf
fffff880`11c03a30 fffff800`01b783b4 nt!IopCloseFile+0x11f
fffff880`11c03ac0 fffff800`01b78171 nt!ObpDecrementHandleCount+0xb4
fffff880`11c03b40 fffff800`01b78734 nt!ObpCloseHandleTableEntry+0xb1
fffff880`11c03bd0 fffff800`0187ced3 nt!ObpCloseHandle+0x94
fffff880`11c03c20 00000000`76d8140a nt!KiSystemServiceCopyEnd+0x13 (TrapFrame @ fffff880`11c03c20)
00000000`0754f348 000007fe`fd341873 ntdll!NtClose+0xa
00000000`0754f350 00000000`76c32f51 KERNELBASE!CloseHandle+0x13
00000000`0754f380 000007fe`fdaf9690 kernel32!CloseHandleImplementation+0x3d
00000000`0754f490 000007fe`fe191d7f SHLWAPI!CFileStream::Release+0x84
00000000`0754f4c0 000007fe`fe13ed57 SHELL32!IconCacheSave+0x2b7
00000000`0754f780 000007fe`fe13f0c6 SHELL32!CommonRestart+0x2f
00000000`0754f7f0 00000000`76c2652d SHELL32!ShutdownThreadProc+0x172
00000000`0754f820 00000000`76d5c521 kernel32!BaseThreadInitThunk+0xd
00000000`0754f850 00000000`00000000 ntdll!RtlUserThreadStart+0x1d
```

Divide by Zero

Kernel Mode

This is a kernel mode counterpart of **Divide by Zero** pattern in user mode (page 281). It manifests under different bugchecks, for example:

```
1: kd> !analyze -v

[...]

UNEXPECTED_KERNEL_MODE_TRAP (7f)
This means a trap occurred in kernel mode, and it's a trap of a kind that the kernel isn't allowed to
have/catch (bound trap) or that is always instant death (double fault).  The first number in the bugcheck
params is the number of the trap (8 = double fault, etc) Consult an Intel x86 family manual to learn more
about what these traps are. Here is a *portion* of those codes:
If kv shows a taskGate
        use .tss on the part before the colon, then kv.
Else if kv shows a trapframe
        use .trap on that value
Else
        .trap on the appropriate frame will show where the trap was taken
        (on x86, this will be the ebp that goes with the procedure KiTrap)
Endif
kb will then show the corrected stack.
Arguments:
Arg1: 00000000, EXCEPTION_DIVIDED_BY_ZERO
Arg2: 00000000
Arg3: 00000000
Arg4: 00000000

[...]

TRAP_FRAME: a8954c8c -- (.trap 0xffffffffa8954c8c)
ErrCode = 00000000
eax=ffffffff ebx=00000000 ecx=00000005 edx=00000000 esi=00000000 edi=00000000
eip=975c42cd esp=a8954d00 ebp=a8954d4c iopl=0 nv up ei pl zr na pe nc
cs=0008 ss=0010 ds=0023 es=0023 fs=0030 gs=0000 efl=00010246
win32k!NtGdiEnumObjects+0xc6:
975c42cd f7f6 div eax,esi
Resetting default scope

PROCESS_NAME: Application.EXE

[...]
```

```
STACK_TEXT:
a8954c2c 81ac2b76 0000007f 5317512a 975c42cd nt!KeBugCheck+0x14
a8954c80 81899808 a8954c8c a8954d4c 975c42cd nt!Ki386CheckDivideByZeroTrap+0x44
a8954c80 975c42cd a8954c8c a8954d4c 975c42cd nt!KiTrap00+0x88
a8954d4c 81898a7a 062102ce 00000001 00000000 Driver!EnumObjects+0xc6
a8954d4c 77a59a94 062102ce 00000001 00000000 nt!KiFastCallEntry+0x12a
WARNING: Frame IP not in any known module. Following frames may be wrong.
0012ca70 00000000 00000000 00000000 00000000 0x77a59a94


0: kd> !analyze -v


[...]


SYSTEM_SERVICE_EXCEPTION (3b)
An exception happened while executing a system service routine.
Arguments:
Arg1: 00000000c0000094, Exception code that caused the bugcheck
Arg2: fffff9600025ba6d, Address of the exception record for the exception that caused the bugcheck
Arg3: fffff8800ac361d0, Address of the context record for the exception that caused the bugcheck
Arg4: 0000000000000000, zero.


[...]


EXCEPTION_CODE: (NTSTATUS) 0xc0000094 - {EXCEPTION} Integer division by zero.


FAULTING_IP:
Driver!EnumObjects+e9
fffff960`0025ba6d f7f6 div eax,esi


CONTEXT: fffff8800ac361d0 -- (.cxr 0xfffff8800ac361d0)
rax=00000000ffffffff rbx=0000000000000000 rcx=0000000000000000
rdx=0000000000000000 rsi=0000000000000000 rdi=0000000000000000
rip=fffff9600025ba6d rsp=fffff8800ac36ba0 rbp=fffff8800ac36ca0
r8=0000000000000000 r9=0000000000000000 r10=0000000005892f18
r11=fffff900c28379e0 r12=0000000000000000 r13=0000000000000002
r14=0000000000000001 r15=0000000000000000
iopl=0         nv up ei ng nz na po nc
cs=0010 ss=0018 ds=002b es=002b fs=0053 gs=002b efl=00010286
Driver!EnumObjects+0xe9:
fffff960`0025ba6d f7f6 div eax,esi
Resetting default scope


[...]


STACK_TEXT:
fffff880`0ac36ba0 fffff800`01682993 Driver!EnumObjects+0xe9
fffff880`0ac36c20 00000000`748a1b3a nt!KiSystemServiceCopyEnd+0x13
00000000`001cdf08 00000000`00000000 0x748a1b3a
```

User Mode

Linux

This is a Linux variant of **Divide by Zero** (user mode) pattern previously described for Mac OS X (page 280) and Windows (page 281) platforms:

```
GNU gdb (GDB)
[...]
Program terminated with signal 8, Arithmetic exception.
#0  0x000000000040056f in procD ()

(gdb) x/i $rip
=> 0x40056f <procD+18>:  idivl  -0x8(%rbp)

(gdb) info r $rax
rax 0x1 1

(gdb) x/w $rbp-0x8
0x7f0f6806bd28:  0x00000000
```

Mac OS X

This is a Mac OS X / GDB counterpart to **Divide by Zero** (user mode) described for Windows platforms (page 281):

```
(gdb) bt
#0 0x000000010d3ebe9e in bar (a=1, b=0)
#1 0x000000010d3ebec3 in foo ()
#2 0x000000010d3ebeeb in main (argc=1, argv=0x7fff6cfeab18)


(gdb) x/i 0x000000010d3ebe9e
0x10d3ebe9e : idiv %esi


(gdb) info r rsi
rsi 0x0 0
```

The modeling application source code:

```
int bar(int a, int b)
{
        return a/b;
}

int foo()
{
        return bar(1,0);
}

int main(int argc, const char * argv[])
{
        return foo();
}
```

Windows

Integer division by zero is one of the most frequent exceptions[45]. It is easily recognizable in process crash dumps by the processor instruction that caused this exception type (DIV or IDIV):

```
FAULTING_IP:
DLL!FindHighestID+278
1b2713c4 f775e4 div dword ptr [ebp-0x1c]

EXCEPTION_RECORD: ffffffff -- (.exr ffffffffffffffff)
ExceptionAddress: 1b2713c4 (DLL!FindHighestID+0x00000278)
ExceptionCode: c0000094 (Integer divide-by-zero)
ExceptionFlags: 00000000
NumberParameters: 0
```

or

```
FAULTING_IP:
Application+263d8
004263d8 f7fe idiv eax,esi

EXCEPTION_RECORD: ffffffff -- (.exr 0xffffffffffffffff)
ExceptionAddress: 004263d8 (Application+0x000263d8)
ExceptionCode: c0000094 (Integer divide-by-zero)
ExceptionFlags: 00000000
NumberParameters: 0

ERROR_CODE: (NTSTATUS) 0xc0000094 - {EXCEPTION} Integer division by zero.
```

---

[45] Win32 Exception Frequencies, Memory Dump Analysis Anthology, Volume 2, page 427

Double Free

Kernel Pool

In contrast to **Double Free** pattern (page 289) in a user mode process heap double free in a kernel mode pool results in an immediate bugcheck in order to identify the driver causing the problem (BAD_POOL_CALLER bugcheck with Arg1 == 7):

```
2: kd> !analyze -v
...
...
...
BAD_POOL_CALLER (c2)
The current thread is making a bad pool request. Typically this is at a bad IRQL level or double freeing
the same allocation, etc.
Arguments:
Arg1: 00000007, Attempt to free pool which was already freed
Arg2: 0000121a, (reserved)
Arg3: 02140001, Memory contents of the pool block
Arg4: 89ba74f0, Address of the block of pool being deallocated
```

If we look at the block being deallocated we would see that it was marked as "Free" block:

```
2: kd> !pool 89ba74f0
Pool page 89ba74f0 region is Nonpaged pool
 89ba7000 size:   270 previous size:     0  (Allocated) Thre (Protected)
 89ba7270 size:     8 previous size:   270  (Free)      ....
 89ba7278 size:    18 previous size:     8  (Allocated) ReEv
 89ba7290 size:    80 previous size:    18  (Allocated) Mdl
 89ba7310 size:    80 previous size:    80  (Allocated) Mdl
 89ba7390 size:    30 previous size:    80  (Allocated) Vad
 89ba73c0 size:    98 previous size:    30  (Allocated) File (Protected)
 89ba7458 size:     8 previous size:    98  (Free)      Wait
 89ba7460 size:    28 previous size:     8  (Allocated) FSfm
 89ba74a0 size:    40 previous size:    18  (Allocated) Ntfr
 89ba74e0 size:     8 previous size:    40  (Free)      File
*89ba74e8 size:    a0 previous size:     8  (Free )     *ABCD
  Owning component : Unknown (update pooltag.txt)
 89ba7588 size:    38 previous size:    a0  (Allocated) Sema (Protected)
 89ba75c0 size:    38 previous size:    38  (Allocated) Sema (Protected)
 89ba75f8 size:    10 previous size:    38  (Free)      Nbtl
 89ba7608 size:    98 previous size:    10  (Allocated) File (Protected)
 89ba76a0 size:    28 previous size:    98  (Allocated) Ntfn
 89ba76c8 size:    40 previous size:    28  (Allocated) Ntfr
 89ba7708 size:    28 previous size:    40  (Allocated) NtFs
 89ba7730 size:    40 previous size:    28  (Allocated) Ntfr
 89ba7770 size:    40 previous size:    40  (Allocated) Ntfr
 89ba7a10 size:   270 previous size:   260  (Allocated) Thre (Protected)
 89ba7c80 size:    20 previous size:   270  (Allocated) VadS
```

The pool tag is a 4-byte character sequence used to associate drivers with pool blocks and is useful to identify a driver allocated or freed a block. In our case, the pool tag is ABCD, and it is associated with the driver that previously freed the block. All known pool tags corresponding to kernel components can be found in *pooltag.txt* located in triage subfolder where WinDbg is installed. However, our ABCD tag is not listed there. We can try to find the driver corresponding to ABCD tag using **findstr** CMD command:

```
C:\Windows\System32\drivers>findstr /m /l ABCD *.sys
```

The results of the search will help us to identify the driver which freed the block first. The driver that double freed the same block can be found on the call stack, and it may be the same driver or a different driver:

```
2: kd> k
ChildEBP RetAddr
f78be910 8089c8f4 nt!KeBugCheckEx+0x1b
f78be978 8089c622 nt!ExFreePoolWithTag+0x477
f78be988 f503968b nt!ExFreePool+0xf
WARNING: Stack unwind information not available. Following frames may be wrong.
f78be990 f5024a6e driver+0x1768b
f78be9a0 f50249e7 driver+0x2a6e
f78be9a4 84b430e0 driver+0x29e7
```

Because we do not have symbol files for *driver.sys* WinDbg warns us that it was unable to identify the correct stack trace and driver.sys might not have called *ExFreePool* or *ExFreePoolWithTag* function. To verify that *driver.sys* called *ExFreePool* function indeed we disassemble backward the return address of it:

```
2: kd> ub f503968b
driver+0x1767b:
f503967b 90              nop
f503967c 90              nop
f503967d 90              nop
f503967e 90              nop
f503967f 90              nop
f5039680 8b442404        mov     eax,dword ptr [esp+4]
f5039684 50              push    eax
f5039685 ff15202302f5    call    dword ptr [driver+0x320 (f5022320)]
```

Finally, we can get some info from the driver:

```
2: kd> lmv m driver
start    end       module name
f5022000 f503e400  driver   (no symbols)
    Loaded symbol image file: driver.sys
    Image path: \SystemRoot\System32\drivers\driver.sys
    Image name: driver.sys
    Timestamp:  Tue Aug 12 11:32:16 2007
```

If the company name developed the driver is absent, we could try techniques outlined in **Unknown Component** pattern (page 1150).

If we have symbols it is very easy to identify the code as can be seen from this 64-bit crash dump:

```
BAD_POOL_CALLER (c2)
The current thread is making a bad pool request. Typically this is at a bad IRQL level or double freeing
the same allocation, etc.
Arguments:
Arg1: 0000000000000007, Attempt to free pool which was already freed
Arg2: 000000000000121a, (reserved)
Arg3: 0000000000000080, Memory contents of the pool block
Arg4: fffffade6d54e270, Address of the block of pool being deallocated


0: kd> kL
fffffade`45517b08 fffff800`011ad905 nt!KeBugCheckEx
fffffade`45517b10 fffffade`5f5991ac nt!ExFreePoolWithTag+0x401
fffffade`45517bd0 fffffade`5f59a0b0 driver64!ProcessDataItem+0x198
fffffade`45517c70 fffffade`5f5885a6 driver64!OnDataArrival+0x2b4
fffffade`45517cd0 fffff800`01299cae driver64!ReaderThread+0x15a
fffffade`45517d70 fffff800`0102bbe6 nt!PspSystemThreadStartup+0x3e
fffffade`45517dd0 00000000`00000000 nt!KiStartSystemThread+0x16
```

Comments

One of the asked questions was: what happens if the block being deallocated can not be analyzed:

```
4: kd> !pool a4ef7920
Pool page a4ef7920 region is Nonpaged pool
a4ef7000 size:   e0 previous size:    0  (Allocated) MmCi
a4ef70e0 size:   68 previous size:   e0  (Allocated) TCIZ
a4ef7148 size:   e0 previous size:   68  (Allocated) MmCi
a4ef7228 size:   98 previous size:   e0  (Allocated) File (Protected)
a4ef72c0 size:   98 previous size:   98  (Allocated) File (Protected)
a4ef7358 size:  100 previous size:   98  (Allocated) MmCi
a4ef7458 size:   28 previous size:  100  (Allocated) NtFs
a4ef7480 size:   40 previous size:   28  (Allocated) Ntfr
a4ef74c0 size:   98 previous size:   40  (Allocated) File (Protected)
a4ef7558 size:    8 previous size:   98  (Free)      CcPL
a4ef7560 size:   40 previous size:    8  (Allocated) SevE
a4ef75a0 size:   40 previous size:   40  (Allocated) Ntfr
a4ef75e0 size:   10 previous size:   40  (Free)      TCI1
a4ef75f0 size:  180 previous size:   10  (Allocated) MmCi
a4ef7770 size:   98 previous size:  180  (Allocated) File (Protected)
a4ef7808 size:   88 previous size:   98  (Allocated) Adap (Protected)
a4ef7890 size:   88 previous size:   88  (Allocated) NEtd
a4ef7918 is not a valid large pool allocation, checking large session pool…
a4ef7918 is freed (or corrupt) pool
Bad allocation size @a4ef7918, zero is invalid


***
*** An error (or corruption) in the pool was detected;
*** Attempting to diagnose the problem.
***
*** Use !poolval a4ef7000 for more details.
***
```

```
Pool page [ a4ef7000 ] is __inVALID.

Analyzing linked list…
[ a4ef7890 -> a4ef7a10 (size = 0x180 bytes)]: Corrupt region

Scanning for single bit errors…

None found
```

The problem block start address can be calculated:

```
a4ef7890+88 = a4ef7918
```

We would try to see its contents, perhaps **dds** and **dps** would point to some symbolic data. Also, search for this address in kernel space might point to some other blocks as well. If we suspect some driver, we may want to enable Driver Verifier special pool.

Another asked question: the special pool is enabled, and it shows both free operation happening through the same thread and the stacks are exactly same:

```
2: kd> .bugcheck
Bugcheck code 000000C2
Arguments 00000000`00000007 00000000`00001097 00000000`00210007 fffff8a0`04b98e00


2: kd> !pool fffff8a0`04b98e00 2
Pool page fffff8a004b98e00 region is Paged pool
*fffff8a004b98df0 size: 210 previous size: 70 (Free) *MmSt
Pooltag MmSt : Mm section object prototype ptes, Binary : nt!mm


2: kd> !verifier 0x80 fffff8a0`04b98e00

Log of recent kernel pool Allocate and Free operations:

There are up to 0x10000 entries in the log.

Parsing 0x0000000000010000 log entries, searching for address 0xfffff8a004b98e00.

==================================
Pool block fffff8a004b98df0, Size 0000000000000210, Thread fffffa80122674f0
fffff80001b0bc9a nt!VfFreePoolNotification+0x4a
fffff800017a367c nt!ExDeferredFreePool+0x126d
fffff8000165b880 nt!MiDeleteSegmentPages+0x35c
fffff8000195cf2f nt!MiSegmentDelete+0x7b
fffff80001637e07 nt!MiCleanSection+0x2f7
fffff80001676754 nt!ObfDereferenceObject+0xd4
fffff80001661170 nt!CcDeleteSharedCacheMap+0x1bc
fffff80001699880 nt!CcUninitializeCacheMap+0x2f0
fffff880030ecfa6 ModuleA!ProcC+0x4b6
fffff880030ec840 ModuleA!ProcB+0x2a8
fffff880030ec994 ModuleA!ProcA+0x38
```

```
fffff80001b16750 nt!IovCallDriver+0xa0
fffff800019824bf nt!IopCloseFile+0x11f
===================================
Pool block fffff8a004b98df0, Size 0000000000000210, Thread fffffa80122674f0
fffff80001b0bc9a nt!VfFreePoolNotification+0x4a
fffff800017a367c nt!ExDeferredFreePool+0x126d
fffff8000165b880 nt!MiDeleteSegmentPages+0x35c
fffff8000195cf2f nt!MiSegmentDelete+0x7b
fffff80001637e07 nt!MiCleanSection+0x2f7
fffff80001676754 nt!ObfDereferenceObject+0xd4
fffff80001661170 nt!CcDeleteSharedCacheMap+0x1bc
fffff80001699880 nt!CcUninitializeCacheMap+0x2f0
fffff880030ecfa6 ModuleA!ProcC+0x4b6
fffff880030ec840 ModuleA!ProcB+0x2a8
fffff880030ec994 ModuleA!ProcA+0x38
fffff80001b16750 nt!IovCallDriver+0xa0
fffff800019824bf nt!IopCloseFile+0x11f
```

But current thread has no sign of *ModuleA.sys*:

```
2: kd> k
Child-SP RetAddr Call Site
fffff880`02378b28 fffff800`017a360e nt!KeBugCheckEx
fffff880`02378b30 fffff800`0178a53e nt!ExDeferredFreePool+0x11eb
fffff880`02378be0 fffff800`01798a0a nt!MiDeleteCachedSubsection+0x10ae
fffff880`02378c90 fffff800`01798b43 nt!MiRemoveUnusedSegments+0x8a
fffff880`02378cc0 fffff800`01910726 nt!MiDereferenceSegmentThread+0x103
fffff880`02378d40 fffff800`0164fae6 nt!PspSystemThreadStartup+0x5a
fffff880`02378d80 00000000`00000000 nt!KiStartSystemThread+0x16
```

Two logged free operations clearly show **Double Free**. But it was detected at a later time by a different thread.

If we see some leaking pool tag we can find its entries using this command **!poolfind** *ABCD* and then dump their memory contents.

Another example from a Software Diagnostics Library user:

```
Windows Server 2003 Kernel Version 3790 (Service Pack 2) MP (8 procs) Free x86 compatible
Product: Server, suite: Enterprise TerminalServer SingleUserTS
Built by: 3790.srv03_sp2_rtm.070216-1710
Kernel base = 0x80800000 PsLoadedModuleList = 0x808a6ea8
Debug session time: Wed May 21 23:55:16.743 2008 (GMT+8)
System Uptime: 1 days 5:48:24.125
Loading Kernel Symbols
Loading User Symbols
Loading unloaded module list
*
* Bugcheck Analysis
*

Use !analyze -v to get detailed debugging information.

BugCheck C2, {7, 121a, 0, 8b6e6d00}
```

```
Probably caused by : Fs_Rec.SYS ( Fs_Rec!UdfsRecFsControl+63 )


Followup: MachineOwner
___


3: kd> !analyze -v
*
* Bugcheck Analysis
*


BAD_POOL_CALLER (c2)
The current thread is making a bad pool request. Typically this is at a bad IRQL level or double freeing
the same allocation, etc.
Arguments:
Arg1: 00000007, Attempt to free pool which was already freed
Arg2: 0000121a, (reserved)
Arg3: 00000000, Memory contents of the pool block
Arg4: 8b6e6d00, Address of the block of pool being deallocated


Debugging Details:
_____


POOL_ADDRESS: 8b6e6d00

FREED_POOL_TAG: Thre

BUGCHECK_STR: 0xc2_7_Thre

CUSTOMER_CRASH_COUNT: 1

DEFAULT_BUCKET_ID: DRIVER_FAULT_SERVER_MINIDUMP

PROCESS_NAME: Rtvscan.exe

CURRENT_IRQL: 0

LAST_CONTROL_TRANSFER: from 808927bb to 80827c63

STACK_TEXT:
b86e18c0 808927bb 000000c2 00000007 0000121a nt!KeBugCheckEx+0x1b
b86e1928 8081e1b6 8b6e6d00 00000000 8b6e6af8 nt!ExFreePoolWithTag+0x477
b86e1954 f78037a1 8c8c8af8 8b95d030 b86e1988 nt!IopfCompleteRequest+0x180
b86e1964 f780309e 8c8c8af8 8a3aabd8 8c897730 Fs_Rec!UdfsRecFsControl+0x63
b86e1974 8081df65 8c8c8af8 8a3aabd8 8a3aabd8 Fs_Rec!FsRecFsControl+0x5a
b86e1988 808f785c 80a5a4d0 8b95d030 80a5a540 nt!IofCallDriver+0x45
b86e19d8 808220a4 8c8c8af8 b86e1c00 00000000 nt!IopMountVolume+0x1b4
b86e1a04 808f8910 b86e1c38 8b95d000 b86e1b40 nt!IopCheckVpbMounted+0x5c
b86e1afc 80937942 8b95d030 00000000 8a8d01e0 nt!IopParseDevice+0x3d4
b86e1b7c 80933a76 00000000 b86e1bbc 00000040 nt!ObpLookupObjectName+0x5b0
b86e1bd0 808ec76b 00000000 00000000 b86e1c01 nt!ObOpenObjectByName+0xea
b86e1d54 8088978c 05e7e2b4 05e7e28c 05e7e2d4 nt!NtQueryAttributesFile+0x11d
b86e1d54 7c8285ec 05e7e2b4 05e7e28c 05e7e2d4 nt!KiFastCallEntry+0xfc
```

```
WARNING: Frame IP not in any known module. Following frames may be wrong.
05e7e2d4 00000000 00000000 00000000 00000000 0x7c8285ec


STACK_COMMAND: kb


FOLLOWUP_IP:
Fs_Rec!UdfsRecFsControl+63
f78037a1 8bc6 mov eax,esi


SYMBOL_STACK_INDEX: 3


SYMBOL_NAME: Fs_Rec!UdfsRecFsControl+63


FOLLOWUP_NAME: MachineOwner


MODULE_NAME: Fs_Rec


IMAGE_NAME: Fs_Rec.SYS


DEBUG_FLR_IMAGE_TIMESTAMP: 3e800074


FAILURE_BUCKET_ID: 0xc2_7_Thre_Fs_Rec!UdfsRecFsControl+63


BUCKET_ID: 0xc2_7_Thre_Fs_Rec!UdfsRecFsControl+63


Followup: MachineOwner
```
———

An example involving special pool:

```
DRIVER_PAGE_FAULT_IN_FREED_SPECIAL_POOL (d5)
 Memory was referenced after it was freed.
 This cannot be protected by try-except.
 When possible, the guilty driver's name (Unicode string) is printed on
 the bugcheck screen and saved in KiBugCheckDriver.
```

Process Heap

Windows

Double-free bugs lead to **Dynamic Memory Corruption** pattern (page 330). The reason why **Double Free** deserves its own pattern name is the fact that either debug runtime libraries or even OS itself detect such bugs and save crash dumps immediately.

For some heap implementations, the double free operation does not lead to an immediate heap corruption and subsequent crash. For example, if we allocate 3 blocks in a row and then free the middle one twice there will be no crash as the second free call is able to detect that the block was already freed and does nothing. The following program loops forever and never crashes:

```
#include "stdafx.h"
#include <windows.h>

int _tmain(int argc, _TCHAR* argv[])
{
  while (true)
  {
    puts("Allocate: p1");
    void *p1 = malloc(100);
    puts("Allocate: p2");
    void *p2 = malloc(100);
    puts("Allocate: p3");
    void *p3 = malloc(100);

    puts("Free: p2");
    free(p2);
    puts("Double-Free: p2");
    free(p2);
    puts("Free: p1");
    free(p1);
    puts("Free: p3");
    free(p3);

    Sleep(100);
  }

  return 0;
}
```

The output of the program:

```
...
...
...
Allocate: p1
Allocate: p2
Allocate: p3
Free: p2
Double-Free: p2
Free: p1
Free: p3
Allocate: p1
Allocate: p2
Allocate: p3
Free: p2
Double-Free: p2
Free: p1
Free: p3
Allocate: p1
Allocate: p2
Allocate: p3
Free: p2
Double-Free: p2
...
...
...
```

However, if a free call triggered heap coalescence (adjacent free blocks form the bigger free block) then we have a heap corruption crash on the next double-free call because the coalescence triggered by the previous free call erased the free block information:

```
#include "stdafx.h"
#include <windows.h>

int _tmain(int argc, _TCHAR* argv[])
{
  while (true)
  {
    puts("Allocate: p1");
    void *p1 = malloc(100);
    puts("Allocate: p2");
    void *p2 = malloc(100);
    puts("Allocate: p3");
    void *p3 = malloc(100);

    puts("Free: p3");
    free(p3);
    puts("Free: p1");
    free(p1);
    puts("Free: p2");
    free(p2);
    puts("Double-Free: p2");
    free(p2);
```

```
    Sleep(100);
  }

  return 0;
}
```

The output of the program:

```
Allocate: p1
Allocate: p2
Allocate: p3
Free: p3
Free: p1
Free: p2
Double-Free: p2
Crash!
```

If we open a crash dump we will see the following **Stack Trace** (page 1033):

```
0:000> r
eax=00922130 ebx=00920000 ecx=10101010 edx=10101010 esi=00922128 edi=00921fc8
eip=76ee1ad5 esp=0012fd6c ebp=0012fd94 iopl=0 nv up ei pl zr na pe nc
cs=001b ss=0023 ds=0023 es=0023 fs=003b gs=0000 efl=00010246
ntdll!RtlpCoalesceFreeBlocks+0x6ef:
76ee1ad5 8b4904          mov     ecx,dword ptr [ecx+4] ds:0023:10101014=????????


0:000> kL
ChildEBP RetAddr
0012fd94 76ee1d37 ntdll!RtlpCoalesceFreeBlocks+0x6ef
0012fe8c 76ee1c21 ntdll!RtlpFreeHeap+0x1e2
0012fea8 758d7a7e ntdll!RtlFreeHeap+0x14e
0012febc 6cff4c39 kernel32!HeapFree+0x14
0012ff08 0040107b msvcr80!free+0xcd
0012ff5c 004011f1 DoubleFree!wmain+0x7b
0012ffa0 758d3833 DoubleFree!__tmainCRTStartup+0x10f
0012ffac 76eba9bd kernel32!BaseThreadInitThunk+0xe
0012ffec 00000000 ntdll!_RtlUserThreadStart+0x23
```

This is illustrated in the following picture where free calls result in heap coalescence, and the subsequent double-free call corrupts the heap:

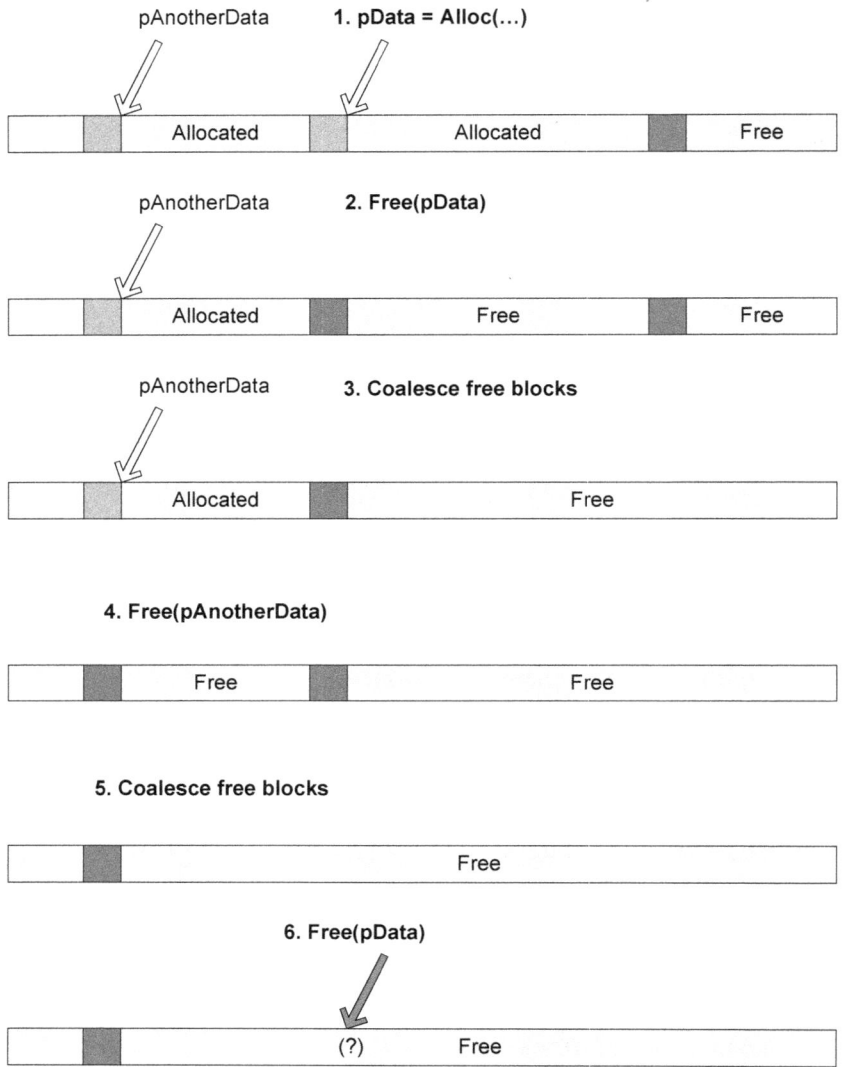

1. pData = Alloc(…)

2. Free(pData)

3. Coalesce free blocks

4. Free(pAnotherData)

5. Coalesce free blocks

6. Free(pData)

The problem here is that heap coalescence can be triggered sometime after the double free, so we need some solution to diagnose double-free bugs earlier, ideally at the first double-free call. For example, the following program crashes during the normal free operation long after the first double-free happened:

```
#include "stdafx.h"
#include <windows.h>

int _tmain(int argc, _TCHAR* argv[])
{
  while (true)
  {
    puts("Allocate: p1");
    void *p1 = malloc(100);
    puts("Allocate: p2");
    void *p2 = malloc(100);
```

```
    puts("Allocate: p3");
    void *p3 = malloc(100);

    puts("Free: p1");
    free(p1);
    puts("Free: p2");
    free(p2);
    puts("Double-Free: p2");
    free(p2);
    puts("Double-Free: p3");
    free(p3);

    Sleep(100);
  }

  return 0;
}
```

The output of the program:

```
Allocate: p1
Allocate: p2
Allocate: p3
Free: p1
Free: p2
Double-Free: p2
Free: p3
Allocate: p1
Allocate: p2
Allocate: p3
Free: p1
Free: p2
Double-Free: p2
Free: p3
Allocate: p1
Allocate: p2
Allocate: p3
Free: p1
Free: p2
Double-Free: p2
Free: p3
Allocate: p1
Allocate: p2
Allocate: p3
Free: p1
Free: p2
Double-Free: p2
Free: p3
Crash!
```

If we enable full page heap using *gflags.exe* from Debugging Tools for Windows the program crashes immediately on the double free call:

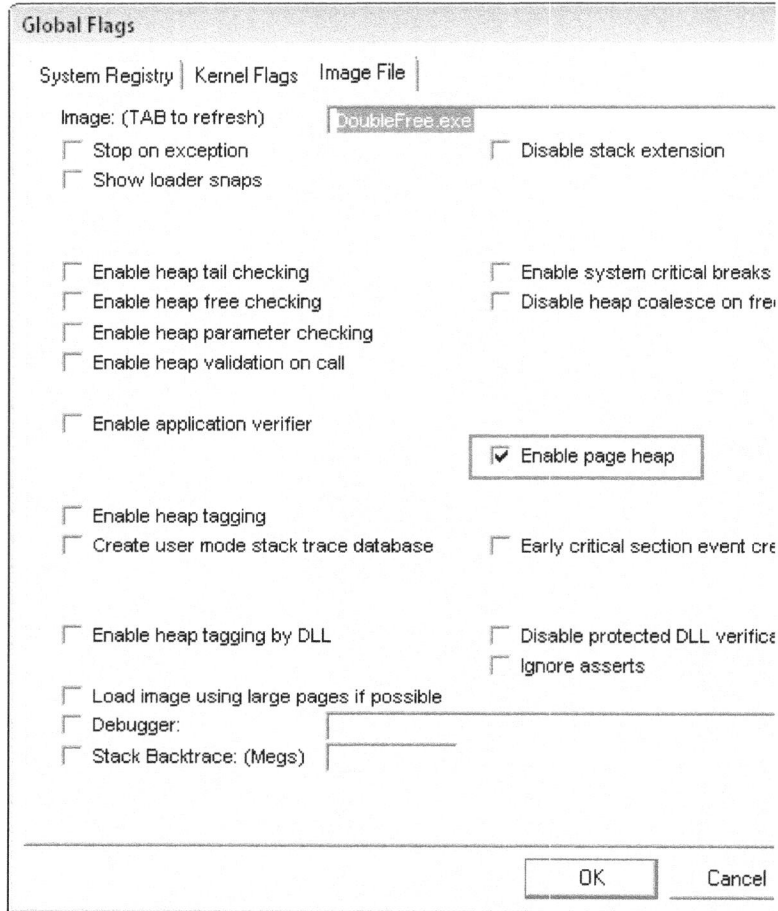

```
Allocate: p1
Allocate: p2
Allocate: p3
Free: p1
Free: p2
Double-Free: p2
Crash!
```

The crash dump shows the following **Stack Trace** (page 1033):

```
0:000> kL
ChildEBP RetAddr
0012f810 71aa4ced ntdll!DbgBreakPoint+0x1
0012f834 71aa9fc2 verifier!VerifierStopMessage+0x1fd
0012f890 71aaa4da verifier!AVrfpDphReportCorruptedBlock+0x102
0012f8a4 71ab2c98 verifier!AVrfpDphCheckNormalHeapBlock+0x18a
0012f8b8 71ab2a0e verifier!_EH4_CallFilterFunc+0x12
0012f8e0 76ee1039 verifier!_except_handler4+0x8e
0012f904 76ee100b ntdll!ExecuteHandler2+0x26
0012f9ac 76ee0e97 ntdll!ExecuteHandler+0x24
0012f9ac 71aaa3ad ntdll!KiUserExceptionDispatcher+0xf
0012fcf0 71aaa920 verifier!AVrfpDphCheckNormalHeapBlock+0x5d
0012fd0c 71aa879b verifier!AVrfpDphNormalHeapFree+0x20
0012fd60 76f31c8f verifier!AVrfDebugPageHeapFree+0x1cb
0012fda8 76efd9fa ntdll!RtlDebugFreeHeap+0x2f
0012fe9c 76ee1c21 ntdll!RtlpFreeHeap+0x5f
0012feb8 758d7a7e ntdll!RtlFreeHeap+0x14e
0012fecc 6cff4c39 kernel32!HeapFree+0x14
0012ff18 0040105f msvcr80!free+0xcd
0012ff5c 004011f1 DoubleFree!wmain+0x5f
0012ffa0 758d3833 DoubleFree!__tmainCRTStartup+0x10f
0012ffac 76eba9bd kernel32!BaseThreadInitThunk+0xe

0:000> !gflag
Current NtGlobalFlag contents: 0x02000000
    hpa - Place heap allocations at ends of pages
```

If we enable heap free checking instead of page heap we get our crash on the first double free call immediately too:

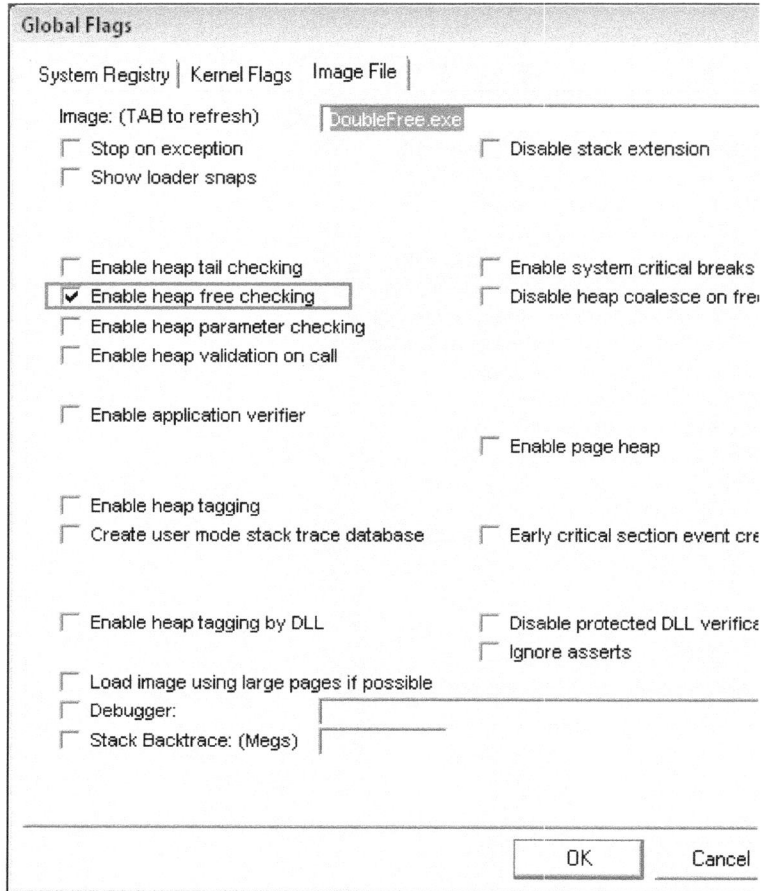

```
Allocate: p1
Allocate: p2
Allocate: p3
Free: p1
Free: p2
Double-Free: p2
Crash!
```

The crash dump shows the following **Stack Trace** (page 1033):

```
0:000> r
eax=feeefeee ebx=001b2040 ecx=001b0000 edx=001b2040 esi=d4476047 edi=001b2038
eip=76ee2086 esp=0012fe68 ebp=0012fe9c iopl=0   nv up ei ng nz na pe nc
cs=001b ss=0023 ds=0023 es=0023 fs=003b gs=0000             efl=00010286
ntdll!RtlpLowFragHeapFree+0x31:
76ee2086 8b4604          mov     eax,dword ptr [esi+4] ds:0023:d447604b=????????
```

```
0:000> kL
ChildEBP RetAddr
0012fe9c 76ee18c3 ntdll!RtlpLowFragHeapFree+0x31
0012feb0 758d7a7e ntdll!RtlFreeHeap+0x101
0012fec4 6cff4c39 kernel32!HeapFree+0x14
0012ff10 0040106d msvcr80!free+0xcd
0012ff5c 004011f1 DoubleFree!wmain+0x6d
0012ffa0 758d3833 DoubleFree!__tmainCRTStartup+0x10f
0012ffac 76eba9bd kernel32!BaseThreadInitThunk+0xe
0012ffec 00000000 ntdll!_RtlUserThreadStart+0x23


0:000> !gflag
Current NtGlobalFlag contents: 0x00000020
    hfc - Enable heap free checking
```

Comments

An example of **Double Free** detected in Windows 7:

```
0:048> k
ChildEBP RetAddr
206dee98 777f8567 ntdll!ZwWaitForSingleObject+0x15
206def1c 777f8695 ntdll!RtlReportExceptionEx+0x14b
206def74 7781e6e6 ntdll!RtlReportException+0x86
206def88 7781e763 ntdll!RtlpTerminateFailureFilter+0x14
206def94 777c73dc ntdll!RtlReportCriticalFailure+0x67
206defa8 777c7281 ntdll!_EH4_CallFilterFunc+0x12
206defd0 777ab499 ntdll!_except_handler4+0x8e
206deff4 777ab46b ntdll!ExecuteHandler2+0x26
206df018 777ab40e ntdll!ExecuteHandler+0x24
206df0a4 77760133 ntdll!RtlDispatchException+0x127
206df0a4 7781e753 ntdll!KiUserExceptionDispatcher+0xf
206df5e8 7781f659 ntdll!RtlReportCriticalFailure+0x57
206df5f8 7781f739 ntdll!RtlpReportHeapFailure+0x21
206df62c 777ce045 ntdll!RtlpLogHeapFailure+0xa1
206df65c 76aa6e6a ntdll!RtlFreeHeap+0x64
206df670 58110076 ole32!CRetailMalloc_Free+0x1c [d:\w7rtm\com\ole32\com\class\memapi.cxx @ 687]
WARNING: Stack unwind information not available. Following frames may be wrong.
206df6ac 581100e9 OUTLMIME!MimeOleInetDateToFileTime+0xd562
206df6b8 5811051d OUTLMIME!MimeOleInetDateToFileTime+0xd5d5
206df6e0 771562fa OUTLMIME!MimeOleInetDateToFileTime+0xda09
206df70c 77156d3a user32!InternalCallWinProc+0x23
206df784 771577c4 user32!UserCallWinProcCheckWow+0x109
206df7e4 77157bca user32!DispatchMessageWorker+0x3bc
206df7f4 581d74e6 user32!DispatchMessageA+0xf
206df830 581e04a3 OUTLPH!DllGetClassObject+0x5616
206df84c 581df9ac OUTLPH!DllGetClassObject+0xe5d3
206df880 6e558488 OUTLPH!DllGetClassObject+0xdadc
206df8a4 650fa17d OLMAPI32!HrCreateAsyncArgSet+0x479
206df8e8 650f8221 MSO!Ordinal381+0x48d
206df908 650f80a9 MSO!Ordinal19712+0x237
206df924 650f32d6 MSO!Ordinal19712+0xbf
206df958 650efe05 MSO!Ordinal5368+0x382
206df9b4 7725338a MSO!MsoFInitOffice+0x363
206df9c0 77789f72 kernel32!BaseThreadInitThunk+0xe
206dfa00 77789f45 ntdll!__RtlUserThreadStart+0x70
206dfa18 00000000 ntdll!_RtlUserThreadStart+0x1b
```

Because we have the stack unwind warning, we double check the return address to verify that *OUTLMIME* module called heap free function. The call involves a triple indirection of 58149f04 pointer address:

```
0:048> ub 58110076
OUTLMIME!MimeOleInetDateToFileTime+0xd550:
58110064 8b0f            mov     ecx,dword ptr [edi]
58110066 3bcb            cmp     ecx,ebx
58110068 740e            je      OUTLMIME!MimeOleInetDateToFileTime+0xd564 (58110078)
5811006a a1049f1458      mov     eax,dword ptr [OUTLMIME!HrGetMIMEStreamForMAPIMsg+0xe528 (58149f04)]
5811006f 8b10            mov     edx,dword ptr [eax]
58110071 51              push    ecx
58110072 50              push    eax
58110073 ff5214          call    dword ptr [edx+14h]

0:048> dps poi(poi(58149f04))+14 L1
76b97264  76aa6e4e ole32!CRetailMalloc_Free [d:\w7rtm\com\ole32\com\class\memapi.cxx @ 680]

0:048> !heap -s
*****************************************************************
*                                                               *
*                   HEAP ERROR DETECTED                         *
*                                                               *
*****************************************************************

Details:

Heap address:  00280000
Error address: 1cecd3e8
Error type: HEAP_FAILURE_BLOCK_NOT_BUSY
Details:    The caller performed an operation (such as a free
            or a size check) that is illegal on a free block.
Follow-up:  Check the error's stack trace to find the culprit.


Stack trace:
            777ce045: ntdll!RtlFreeHeap+0x00000064
            76aa6e6a: ole32!CRetailMalloc_Free+0x0000001c
            58110076: OUTLMIME!MimeOleInetDateToFileTime+0x0000d562
            581100e9: OUTLMIME!MimeOleInetDateToFileTime+0x0000d5d5
            5811051d: OUTLMIME!MimeOleInetDateToFileTime+0x0000da09
            771562fa: user32!InternalCallWinProc+0x00000023
            77156d3a: user32!UserCallWinProcCheckWow+0x00000109
            771577c4: user32!DispatchMessageWorker+0x000003bc
            77157bca: user32!DispatchMessageA+0x0000000f
            581d74e6: OUTLPH!DllGetClassObject+0x00005616
            581e04a3: OUTLPH!DllGetClassObject+0x0000e5d3
            581df9ac: OUTLPH!DllGetClassObject+0x0000dadc
            6e558488: OLMAPI32!HrCreateAsyncArgSet+0x00000479
            650fa17d: MSO!Ordinal381+0x0000048d
            650f8221: MSO!Ordinal19712+0x00000237
            650f80a9: MSO!Ordinal19712+0x000000bf
[...]

0:048> !heap -x 1cecd3e8
Entry    User      Heap      Segment     Size PrevSize Unused  Flags
-------------------------------------------------------------------------
1cecd3e8 1cecd3f0  00280000  0f945f18     20    -           0  LFH;free
```

Another example:

```
0:000> !heap -s -v

Details:

Heap address:    00cb0000
Error address:   103f4550
Error type:      HEAP_FAILURE_BLOCK_NOT_BUSY
Details:         The caller performed an operation (such as a free
or a size check) that is illegal on a free block.
Follow-up: Check the error's stack trace to find the culprit.

Stack trace:
772ec3bd: ntdll!RtlpFreeHeapInternal+0x000000db
772ac6dc: ntdll!RtlFreeHeap+0x0000002c
747a8eab: combase!CRetailMalloc_Free+0x0000001b
6a3537b1: hlink!CMalloc::Free+0x00000031
6a3536b3: hlink!HLNK_Unk::Release+0x000000f3
2e5933a8: PPCORE!PPMain+0x00406423
2e2847ba: PPCORE!PPMain+0x000f7835
2e26a9ec: PPCORE!PPMain+0x000dda67
2e26a8dd: PPCORE!PPMain+0x000dd958
2e26a76e: PPCORE!PPMain+0x000dd7e9
2e26a6e7: PPCORE!PPMain+0x000dd762
2e26a68c: PPCORE!PPMain+0x000dd707
2e26a616: PPCORE!PPMain+0x000dd691
2e26a5ec: PPCORE!PPMain+0x000dd667
54a6647e: OART!Ordinal834+0x00000057
54ade32c: OART!Ordinal971+0x00000094

0:000> !heap -x 103f4550
Entry User Heap Segment Size PrevSize Unused Flags
-----------------------------------

103f4550 103f4558 00cb0000 1010ffa8 e0 - 0 LFH;free
```

Mac OS X

This is a Mac OS X / GDB counterpart to **Double Free** pattern:

```
(gdb) bt
#0 0x00007fff8479582a in __kill ()
#1 0x00007fff8e0e0a9c in abort ()
#2 0x00007fff8e13f84c in free ()
#3 0x00000001035a8ef4 in main (argc=1, argv=0x7fff631a7b20)

(gdb) x/2i 0x00000001035a8ef4-8
0x1035a8eec : mov  -0x20(%rbp),%edi
0x1035a8eef : callq 0x1035a8f06

(gdb) frame 3
#3 0x00000001035a8ef4 in main (argc=1, argv=0x7fff631a7b20)
at .../DoubleFree/main.c:23
23 free(p2);
Current language: auto; currently minimal

(gdb) x/g $rbp-0x20
0x7fff631a7ae0: 0x00007fe6a8801400

(gdb) x/2w 0x00007fe6a8801400
0x7fe6a8801400: 0x00000000 0xb0000000
```

Here's the source code of the modeling application:

```c
int main(int argc, const char * argv[])
{
        char *p1 = (char *) malloc (1024);
        printf("p1 = %p\n", p1);

        char *p2 = (char *) malloc (1024);
        printf("p2 = %p\n", p2);

        free(p2);
        free(p1);
        free(p2);

        return 0;
}
```

Double IRP Completion

Similar to **Double Free** (process heap, page 289) and **Double Free** (kernel pool, page 282) that might be detected through **Instrumentation Information** (page 580) such as *gflags* and Driver Verifier there is also **Double IRP Completion** variant implemented through **Self-Diagnosis** (kernel mode, page 945). Here's a typical example:

```
0: kd> !analyze -v

[...]

MULTIPLE_IRP_COMPLETE_REQUESTS (44)
A driver has requested that an IRP be completed (IoCompleteRequest()), but the packet has already been completed. This
is a tough bug to find because the easiest case, a driver actually attempted to complete its own packet twice, is
generally not what happened. Rather, two separate drivers each believe that they own the packet, and each attempts to
complete it. The first actually works, and the second fails. Tracking down which drivers in the system actually did this
is difficult, generally because the trails of the first driver have been covered by the second. However, the driver
stack for the current request can be found by examining the DeviceObject fields in each of the stack locations.
Arguments:
Arg1: fffffa80104aa010, Address of the IRP
Arg2: 0000000000000eae
Arg3: 0000000000000000
Arg4: 0000000000000000


STACK_TEXT:
fffff880`0e322428 fffff800`01666224 : 00000000`00000044 fffffa80`104aa010 00000000`00000eae 00000000`00000000 :
nt!KeBugCheckEx
fffff880`0e322430 fffff880`03dd121f : fffffa80`0dc12c50 fffffa80`107750c8 fffffa80`104aa010 fffff880`0e322580 : nt! ??
::FNODOBFM::`string'+0x3eb3d
fffff880`0e322520 fffff880`03def17f : fffffa80`0dc12c50 fffffa80`104aa010 fffffa80`0cacb610 00000000`00000001 :
DriverA!DriverA::Create+0x3bf
[...]
fffff880`0e322740 fffff800`01972ba4 : fffffa80`0dc129f0 00000000`00000000 fffffa80`0fe7a010 00000000`00000001 :
nt!IopParseDevice+0x5a7
fffff880`0e3228d0 fffff800`01977b7d : fffffa80`0fe7a010 fffff880`0e322a30 fffffa80`00000040 fffffa80`0cae5080 :
nt!ObpLookupObjectName+0x585
fffff880`0e3229d0 fffff800`0197e647 : 00000000`000007ff 00000000`00000003 fffff8a0`05716d01 00000000`00000000 :
nt!ObOpenObjectByName+0x1cd
fffff880`0e322a80 fffff800`01988398 : 00000000`03f3e510 fffff8a0`c0100000 fffff8a0`0c26fe50 00000000`03f3e118 :
nt!IopCreateFile+0x2b7
fffff880`0e322b20 fffff800`0167b813 : fffffa80`0e10db30 00000000`00000001 fffffa80`1002b060 fffff800`0198f294 :
nt!NtCreateFile+0x78
fffff880`0e322bb0 00000000`772efc0a : 000007fe`f62c358f 00000000`03f3e1b0 00000000`7719fd72 000007fe`f62c6490 :
nt!KiSystemServiceCopyEnd+0x13
00000000`03f3e068 000007fe`f62c358f : 00000000`03f3e1b0 00000000`7719fd72 000007fe`f62c6490 00000000`00000005 :
ntdll!NtCreateFile+0xa

[...]


0: kd> !irp fffffa80104aa010
Irp is active with 1 stacks 3 is current (= 0xfffffa80104aa170)
No Mdl: No System Buffer: Thread fffffa801002b060: Irp is completed. Pending has been returned
cmd flg cl Device File Completion-Context
[ 0, 0] 0 2 fffffa800dc129f0 00000000 00000000-00000000
\Driver\DriverA
Args: 00000000 00000000 00000000 ffffffffc00a0006
```

Driver Device Collection

This pattern can be used to compare the current list of device and driver objects with some saved reference list to find out any changes. This listing can be done by using **!object** command:

```
0: kd> !object \Driver
[...]

0: kd> !object \FileSystem
[...]

0: kd> !object \Device
[...]
```

Note that the collection is called **Driver Device** and not Device Driver.

Dry Weight

Sometimes what looks like a memory leak when we install a new product version is not really a leak. With the previous version, we had 400 MB typical memory usage, but suddenly we get twice as more. We should not panic but collect a process memory dump to inspect it calmly offline. We may see **Dry Weight** increase: the size of all module images. For some products, the new release may mean complete redesign with a new more powerful framework or incorporation of the significant number of new 3rd-party components (**Module Variety**, page 787). Additional sign against the memory leak hypothesis is simultaneous memory usage increase for many product processes. Although, this may be some shared module with leaking code. For example, in the example below 50% of all committed memory was image memory:

```
0:000> !address -summary

--- Usage Summary ---------------- RgnCount ----------- Total Size -------- %ofBusy %ofTotal
[...]
Image                                 1806          0`19031000 ( 402.535 Mb)   4.29%   0.00%
Heap                                    72          0`02865000 (  40.395 Mb)   0.44%   0.00%
[...]


--- Type Summary (for busy) ------ RgnCount ----------- Total Size -------- %ofBusy %ofTotal
[...]
MEM_IMAGE                             2281          0`19AA8000 ( 413.000 Mb)   4.40%   0.00%
[...]


--- State Summary ---------------- RgnCount ----------- Total Size -------- %ofBusy %ofTotal
[...]
MEM_COMMIT                            2477          0`326e8000 ( 806.906 Mb)   8.76%   0.00%
[...]
```

WinDbg **lmt** command shows almost 50 new .NET components.

Dual Stack Trace

This is the kernel mode and space counterpart to a user mode and space stack trace and vice versa, for example:

```
25 Id: e8c.f20 Suspend: 1 Teb: 7ff9c000 Unfrozen
ChildEBP RetAddr
086acac4 7c90df5a ntdll!KiFastSystemCallRet
086acac8 7c8025db ntdll!ZwWaitForSingleObject+0xc
086acb2c 7c802542 kernel32!WaitForSingleObjectEx+0xa8
086acb40 00fbba3a kernel32!WaitForSingleObject+0x12
WARNING: Stack unwind information not available. Following frames may be wrong.
086ad3c8 00fbc139 ModuleA!DllCanUnloadNow+0x638b4a
[...]
086affb4 7c80b729 ModuleA!DllCanUnloadNow+0xc65c0
086affec 00000000 kernel32!BaseThreadStart+0x37


0: kd> !thread 88ec9020 1f
THREAD 88ec9020 Cid 17a0.2034 Teb: 7ffad000 Win32Thread: bc28c6e8 WAIT: (Unknown) UserMode Non-Alertable
89095f48 Semaphore Limit 0x10000
IRP List:
    89a5a370: (0006,0094) Flags: 00000900 Mdl: 00000000
Not impersonating
DeviceMap               d6c30c48
Owning Process  88fffd88        Image: iexplore.exe
Attached Process        N/A             Image: N/A
Wait Start TickCount    5632994 Ticks: 2980 (0:00:00:46.562)
Context Switch Count    2269            LargeStack
UserTime                00:00:00.000
KernelTime              00:00:00.000
Win32 Start Address 0x00a262d0
Start Address kernel32!BaseThreadStartThunk (0x77e617ec)
Stack Init b204c000 Current b204bc60 Base b204c000 Limit b2048000 Call 0
Priority 8 BasePriority 8 PriorityDecrement 0
ChildEBP RetAddr
b204bc78 80833ec5 nt!KiSwapContext+0x26
b204bca4 80829c14 nt!KiSwapThread+0x2e5
b204bcec 8093b174 nt!KeWaitForSingleObject+0x346
b204bd50 8088b41c nt!NtWaitForSingleObject+0x9a
b204bd50 7c82860c nt!KiFastCallEntry+0xfc (TrapFrame @ b204bd64)
058fcabc 7c827d29 ntdll!KiFastSystemCallRet
058fcac0 77e61d1e ntdll!ZwWaitForSingleObject+0xc
058fcb30 77e61c8d kernel32!WaitForSingleObjectEx+0xac
058fcb44 00f98b4a kernel32!WaitForSingleObject+0x12
WARNING: Stack unwind information not available. Following frames may be wrong.
058fd3cc 00f99249 ModuleA+0x638b4a
[...]
058fffb8 77e6482f ModuleA+0xc65c0
058fffec 00000000 kernel32!BaseThreadStart+0x34
```

This pattern is helpful when we have both process user space memory dumps and kernel and complete memory dumps and want to match stack traces of interest between them. See also patterns **Stack Trace** (page 1033) and **Stack Trace Collection** (page 1052).

Duplicate Extension

This pattern is **Duplicate Module** (page 310) equivalent for a debugger that uses loaded modules to extend its functionality. For example, in the case of WinDbg, there is a possibility that two different **Version-Specific Extensions** (page 1175) are loaded wreaking havoc on debugging process (Debugger DLL Hell). For example, we loaded a specific version of SOS extension and successfully got a stack trace:

```
0:000> lmv m mscorwks
start end module name
79e70000 7a3ff000 mscorwks (deferred)
Image path:      C:\Windows\Microsoft.NET\Framework\v2.0.50727\mscorwks.dll
Image name:      mscorwks.dll
Timestamp:       Wed Oct 24 08:41:29 2007 (471EF729)
CheckSum:        00597AA8
ImageSize:       0058F000
File version:    2.0.50727.1433
Product version: 2.0.50727.1433
File flags:      0 (Mask 3F)
File OS:         4 Unknown Win32
File type:       2.0 Dll
File date:       00000000.00000000
Translations:    0409.04b0
CompanyName:     Microsoft Corporation
ProductName:     Microsoft® .NET Framework
InternalName:    mscorwks.dll
OriginalFilename: mscorwks.dll
ProductVersion: 2.0.50727.1433
FileVersion:    2.0.50727.1433 (REDBITS.050727-1400)
FileDescription: Microsoft .NET Runtime Common Language Runtime - WorkStation
LegalCopyright: © Microsoft Corporation. All rights reserved.
Comments: Flavor=Retail

0:000> .chain
Extension DLL search Path:
[...]
Extension DLL chain:
dbghelp: image 6.12.0002.633, API 6.1.6, built Mon Feb 01 20:08:26 2010
[path: C:\Program Files (x86)\Debugging Tools for Windows (x86)\dbghelp.dll]
ext: image 6.12.0002.633, API 1.0.0, built Mon Feb 01 20:08:31 2010
[path: C:\Program Files (x86)\Debugging Tools for Windows (x86)\winext\ext.dll]
exts: image 6.12.0002.633, API 1.0.0, built Mon Feb 01 20:08:24 2010
[path: C:\Program Files (x86)\Debugging Tools for Windows (x86)\WINXP\exts.dll]
uext: image 6.12.0002.633, API 1.0.0, built Mon Feb 01 20:08:23 2010
[path: C:\Program Files (x86)\Debugging Tools for Windows (x86)\winext\uext.dll]
ntsdexts: image 6.1.7650.0, API 1.0.0, built Mon Feb 01 20:08:08 2010
[path: C:\Program Files (x86)\Debugging Tools for Windows (x86)\WINXP\ntsdexts.dll]
```

```
0:000> .load .load C:\Frameworks\32-bit\Framework.Updates\Microsoft.NET\Framework\v2.0.50727\sos

0:000> .chain
Extension DLL search Path:
[...]
Extension DLL chain:
C:\Frameworks\32-bit\Framework.Updates\Microsoft.NET\Framework\v2.0.50727\sos: image 2.0.50727.1433, API
1.0.0, built Wed Oct 24 04:41:30 2007
[path: C:\Frameworks\32-bit\Framework.Updates\Microsoft.NET\Framework\v2.0.50727\sos.dll]
dbghelp: image 6.12.0002.633, API 6.1.6, built Mon Feb 01 20:08:26 2010
[path: C:\Program Files (x86)\Debugging Tools for Windows (x86)\dbghelp.dll]
ext: image 6.12.0002.633, API 1.0.0, built Mon Feb 01 20:08:31 2010
[path: C:\Program Files (x86)\Debugging Tools for Windows (x86)\winext\ext.dll]
exts: image 6.12.0002.633, API 1.0.0, built Mon Feb 01 20:08:24 2010
[path: C:\Program Files (x86)\Debugging Tools for Windows (x86)\WINXP\exts.dll]
uext: image 6.12.0002.633, API 1.0.0, built Mon Feb 01 20:08:23 2010
[path: C:\Program Files (x86)\Debugging Tools for Windows (x86)\winext\uext.dll]
ntsdexts: image 6.1.7650.0, API 1.0.0, built Mon Feb 01 20:08:08 2010
[path: C:\Program Files (x86)\Debugging Tools for Windows (x86)\WINXP\ntsdexts.dll]


0:000> !CLRStack
OS Thread Id: 0xdd0 (0)
ESP       EIP
002eeaa8 77c40f34 [InlinedCallFrame: 002eeaa8] System.Windows.Forms.UnsafeNativeMethods.WaitMessage()
002eeaa4 7b08374f System.Windows.Forms.Application+ComponentManager.System.Windows.Forms.
UnsafeNativeMethods.IMsoComponentManager.FPushMessageLoop(Int32, Int32, Int32)
002eeb44 7b0831a5 System.Windows.Forms.Application+ThreadContext.RunMessageLoopInner(Int32,
System.Windows.Forms.ApplicationContext)
002eebbc 7b082fe3 System.Windows.Forms.Application+ThreadContext.RunMessageLoop(Int32,
System.Windows.Forms.ApplicationContext)
002eebec 7b0692c2 System.Windows.Forms.Application.Run(System.Windows.Forms.Form)
002eebfc 00833264 LINQPad.Program.Run(System.String, Boolean, System.String, Boolean, Boolean,
System.String)
002eec50 008311dc LINQPad.Program.Go(System.String[])
002eedac 00830545 LINQPad.Program.Start(System.String[])
002eede0 00830362 LINQPad.ProgramStarter.Run(System.String[])
002eede8 008300e3 LINQPad.Loader.Main(System.String[])
002ef00c 79e7c74b [GCFrame: 002ef00c]
```

Then we tried the default analysis command **!analyze -v -hang** and continued using SOS commands. Unfortunately, they no longer worked correctly:

```
0:000> !CLRStack
OS Thread Id: 0xdd0 (0)
ESP EIP
002eeaa8 77c40f34 [InlinedCallFrame: 002eeaa8]
002eeaa4 7b08374f
002eeb44 7b0831a5
002eebbc 7b082fe3
002eebec 7b0692c2
002eebfc 00833264
002eec50 008311dc
002eedac 00830545
002eede0 00830362
```

```
002eede8 008300e3
002ef00c 79e7c74b [GCFrame: 002ef00c]
```

Looking at loaded extensions list we see that an additional wrong version of SOS.DLL was loaded and that one gets all SOS commands:

```
0:000> .chain
Extension DLL search Path:
[...]
Extension DLL chain:
C:\Windows\Microsoft.NET\Framework\v2.0.50727\sos: image 2.0.50727.4963, API 1.0.0, built Thu Jul 07
03:08:08 2011
[path: C:\Windows\Microsoft.NET\Framework\v2.0.50727\sos.dll]
C:\Frameworks\32-bit\Framework.Updates\Microsoft.NET\Framework\v2.0.50727\sos: image 2.0.50727.1433, API
1.0.0, built Wed Oct 24 04:41:30 2007
[path: C:\Frameworks\32-bit\Framework.Updates\Microsoft.NET\Framework\v2.0.50727\sos.dll]
dbghelp: image 6.12.0002.633, API 6.1.6, built Mon Feb 01 20:08:26 2010
[path: C:\Program Files (x86)\Debugging Tools for Windows (x86)\dbghelp.dll]
ext: image 6.12.0002.633, API 1.0.0, built Mon Feb 01 20:08:31 2010
[path: C:\Program Files (x86)\Debugging Tools for Windows (x86)\winext\ext.dll]
exts: image 6.12.0002.633, API 1.0.0, built Mon Feb 01 20:08:24 2010
[path: C:\Program Files (x86)\Debugging Tools for Windows (x86)\WINXP\exts.dll]
uext: image 6.12.0002.633, API 1.0.0, built Mon Feb 01 20:08:23 2010
[path: C:\Program Files (x86)\Debugging Tools for Windows (x86)\winext\uext.dll]
ntsdexts: image 6.1.7650.0, API 1.0.0, built Mon Feb 01 20:08:08 2010
[path: C:\Program Files (x86)\Debugging Tools for Windows (x86)\WINXP\ntsdexts.dll]
```

If we specify the full path to the correct extension we get the right stack trace:

```
0:000> !C:\Frameworks\32-bit\Framework.Updates\Microsoft.NET\Framework\v2.0.50727\sos.CLRStack
OS Thread Id: 0xdd0 (0)
ESP      EIP
002eeaa8 77c40f34 [InlinedCallFrame: 002eeaa8] System.Windows.Forms.UnsafeNativeMethods.WaitMessage()
002eeaa4 7b08374f System.Windows.Forms.Application+ComponentManager.System.Windows.Forms.
UnsafeNativeMethods.IMsoComponentManager.FPushMessageLoop(Int32, Int32, Int32)
002eeb44 7b0831a5 System.Windows.Forms.Application+ThreadContext.RunMessageLoopInner(Int32,
System.Windows.Forms.ApplicationContext)
002eebbc 7b082fe3 System.Windows.Forms.Application+ThreadContext.RunMessageLoop(Int32,
System.Windows.Forms.ApplicationContext)
002eebec 7b0692c2 System.Windows.Forms.Application.Run(System.Windows.Forms.Form)
002eebfc 00833264 LINQPad.Program.Run(System.String, Boolean, System.String, Boolean, Boolean,
System.String)
002eec50 008311dc LINQPad.Program.Go(System.String[])
002eedac 00830545 LINQPad.Program.Start(System.String[])
002eede0 00830362 LINQPad.ProgramStarter.Run(System.String[])
002eede8 008300e3 LINQPad.Loader.Main(System.String[])
002ef00c 79e7c74b [GCFrame: 002ef00c]
```

To avoid confusion we unload the last loaded extension:

```
0:000> .unload C:\Windows\Microsoft.NET\Framework\v2.0.50727\sos
Unloading C:\Windows\Microsoft.NET\Framework\v2.0.50727\sos extension DLL
```

```
0:000> !CLRStack
OS Thread Id: 0xdd0 (0)
ESP      EIP
002eeaa8 77c40f34 [InlinedCallFrame: 002eeaa8] System.Windows.Forms.UnsafeNativeMethods.WaitMessage()
002eeaa4 7b08374f System.Windows.Forms.Application+ComponentManager.System.Windows.Forms.
UnsafeNativeMethods.IMsoComponentManager.FPushMessageLoop(Int32, Int32, Int32)
002eeb44 7b0831a5 System.Windows.Forms.Application+ThreadContext.RunMessageLoopInner(Int32,
System.Windows.Forms.ApplicationContext)
002eebbc 7b082fe3 System.Windows.Forms.Application+ThreadContext.RunMessageLoop(Int32,
System.Windows.Forms.ApplicationContext)
002eebec 7b0692c2 System.Windows.Forms.Application.Run(System.Windows.Forms.Form)
002eebfc 00833264 LINQPad.Program.Run(System.String, Boolean, System.String, Boolean, Boolean,
System.String)
002eec50 008311dc LINQPad.Program.Go(System.String[])
002eedac 00830545 LINQPad.Program.Start(System.String[])
002eede0 00830362 LINQPad.ProgramStarter.Run(System.String[])
002eede8 008300e3 LINQPad.Loader.Main(System.String[])
002ef00c 79e7c74b [GCFrame: 002ef00c]
```

Comments

There were a few questions asked:

Q. I thought the version of *sos.dll* that resides in the same folder as *mscorwks.dll* is always the correct one. It looks like, from your folder path names, that *mscorwks.dll* was updated, but *sos.dll* was not. If so, how did you get the correct version of *sos.dll*?

A. The dump came from another machine where *mscorwks* and *sos* were the same versions, of course. On the analysis machine, we have a different version of the framework installed with a different *sos*. So we have a discrepancy between the version of the *mscorwks* in the dump and *sos* on the analysis machine. We copy the correct version of the framework from the machine the dump came from. Please also check **Version-Specific Extension** pattern (page 1175).

Q. Yes, managed debugging requires that the analysis machine uses the same bitness and framework as the "dump" machine. When you say you "copy" the framework, what exactly do you copy? A subset of the binaries or all of them?

A. We usually request a copy of the whole folder just in case if there are any extra dependencies. However, we found out that *mscorwks* or *clr*, *mscordacwks*, and *sos* DLLs are sufficient.

Duplicated Module

In addition to **Module Variety** (page 787), this is another DLL Hell pattern. Here the same module is loaded at least twice, and we can detect this when we see the module load address appended to its name in the output of **lm** commands (this is done to make the name of the module unique):

```
0:000> lm
start     end         module name
00b20000 0147f000    MSO_b20000
30000000 309a7000    EXCEL
30c90000 31848000    mso
71c20000 71c32000    tsappcmp
745e0000 7489e000    msi
76290000 762ad000    imm32
76b70000 76b7b000    psapi
76f50000 76f63000    secur32
77380000 77411000    user32
77670000 777a9000    ole32
77ba0000 77bfa000    msvcrt
77c00000 77c48000    gdi32
77c50000 77cef000    rpcrt4
77da0000 77df2000    shlwapi
77e40000 77f42000    kernel32
77f50000 77feb000    advapi32
7c800000 7c8c0000    ntdll
```

Usually, this happens when the DLL is loaded from different locations. It can also be exactly the same DLL version. The problems usually surface when there are different DLL versions, and the new code loads the old version of the DLL and uses it. This may result in interface incompatibility issues and ultimately in application fault like an access violation.

In order to provide a dump to play with I created a small toy program called *2DLLS* to model the worst-case scenario similar to the one that I encountered in a production environment. The program periodically loads *MyDLL* module to call one of its functions. Unfortunately, in one place, it uses hard-coded relative path:

```
HMODULE hLib = LoadLibrary(L".\\DLL\\MyDLL.dll");
```

and in another place, it relies on DLL search order[46]:

```
hLib = LoadLibrary(L".\\MyDLL.dll");
```

PATH variable directories would be used for search if this DLL were not found in other locations specified by DLL search order. We see that the problem can happen when another application is installed which uses the old version of that DLL and modifies the PATH variable to point to its location. To model interface incompatibility,

---

[46] https://docs.microsoft.com/en-gb/windows/win32/dlls/dynamic-link-library-search-order

we compiled the version of *MyDLL* that causes NULL pointer access violation when the same function is called from it. The DLL was placed into a separate folder, and the PATH variable was modified to reference that folder:

```
C:\>set PATH=C:\OLD;%PATH%
```

The application crashes and the installed default postmortem debugger[47] saves its crash dump. If we open it, we see that it crashed in *MyDLL_1e60000* module which should trigger suspicion:

```
0:000> r
rax=0000000001e61010 rbx=0000000000000000 rcx=0000775dcac00000
rdx=0000000000000000 rsi=0000000000000006 rdi=0000000000001770
rip=0000000001e61010 rsp=000000000012fed8 rbp=0000000000000000
 r8=0000000000000000  r9=000000000012fd58 r10=0000000000000001
r11=000000000012fcc0 r12=0000000000000000 r13=0000000000000002
r14=0000000000000000 r15=0000000000000000
iopl=0 nv up ei pl nz na pe nc
cs=0033 ss=002b ds=002b es=002b fs=0053 gs=002b efl=00010200
MyDLL_1e60000!fnMyDLL:
00000000`01e61010 c704250000000000000000 mov dword ptr [0],0 ds:00000000`00000000=????????

0:000> kL
Child-SP          RetAddr           Call Site
00000000`0012fed8 00000001`40001093 MyDLL_1e60000!fnMyDLL
00000000`0012fee0 00000001`40001344 2DLLs+0x1093
00000000`0012ff10 00000000`773acdcd 2DLLs+0x1344
00000000`0012ff60 00000000`774fc6e1 kernel32!BaseThreadInitThunk+0xd
00000000`0012ff90 00000000`00000000 ntdll!RtlUserThreadStart+0x1d
```

Looking at the list of modules we see two versions of *MyDLL* loaded from two different folders:

```
0:000> lm
start            end              module name
00000000`01e60000 00000000`01e71000  MyDLL_1e60000
00000000`772a0000 00000000`7736a000  user32
00000000`77370000 00000000`774a1000  kernel32
00000000`774b0000 00000000`7762a000  ntdll
00000001`40000000 00000001`40010000  2DLLs
00000001`80000000 00000001`80011000  MyDLL
000007fe`fc9e0000 000007fe`fca32000  uxtheme
000007fe`fe870000 000007fe`fe9a9000  rpcrt4
000007fe`fe9b0000 000007fe`fe9bc000  lpk
000007fe`fea10000 000007fe`feae8000  oleaut32
000007fe`fecd0000 000007fe`fed6a000  usp10
000007fe`fedd0000 000007fe`fefb0000  ole32
000007fe`fefb0000 000007fe`ff0af000  advapi32
000007fe`ff0d0000 000007fe`ff131000  gdi32
000007fe`ff2e0000 000007fe`ff381000  msvcrt
000007fe`ff390000 000007fe`ff3b8000  imm32
000007fe`ff4b0000 000007fe`ff5b4000  msctf
```

---

[47] Custom Postmortem Debuggers in Vista, Memory Dump Analysis Anthology, Volume 1, page 618

```
0:000> lmv m MyDLL_1e60000
start             end               module name
00000000`01e60000 00000000`01e71000   MyDLL_1e60000
    Loaded symbol image file: MyDLL.dll
    Image path: C:\OLD\MyDLL.dll
    Image name: MyDLL.dll
    Timestamp:          Wed Jun 18 14:49:13 2008 (48591259)
...

0:000> lmv m MyDLL
start             end               module name
00000001`80000000 00000001`80011000   MyDLL
    Image path: C:\2DLLs\DLL\MyDLL.dll
    Image name: MyDLL.dll
    Timestamp:          Wed Jun 18 14:50:56 2008 (485912C0)
...
```

We can also see that the old version of MyDLL was the last loaded DLL:

```
0:000> !dlls -l

0x002c2680: C:\2DLLs\2DLLs.exe
    Base    0x140000000  EntryPoint  0x1400013b0  Size       0x00010000
    Flags   0x00004000   LoadCount   0x0000ffff   TlsIndex   0x00000000
            LDRP_ENTRY_PROCESSED

...

0x002ea9b0: C:\2DLLs\DLL\MyDLL.dll
    Base    0x180000000  EntryPoint  0x1800013d0  Size       0x00011000
    Flags   0x00084004   LoadCount   0x00000001   TlsIndex   0x00000000
            LDRP_IMAGE_DLL
            LDRP_ENTRY_PROCESSED
            LDRP_PROCESS_ATTACH_CALLED

...

0x002ec430: C:\OLD\MyDLL.dll
    Base    0x01e60000   EntryPoint  0x01e613e0   Size       0x00011000
    Flags   0x00284004   LoadCount   0x00000001   TlsIndex   0x00000000
            LDRP_IMAGE_DLL
            LDRP_ENTRY_PROCESSED
            LDRP_PROCESS_ATTACH_CALLED
            LDRP_IMAGE_NOT_AT_BASE
```

We can also see that the PATH variable points to its location, and this might explain why it was loaded:

```
0:000> !peb
PEB at 000007fffffd6000
...
Path=C:\OLD;C:\Windows\system32;C:\Windows;...
...
```

We might think that the module having an address in its name was loaded the last, but this is not true. If we save another copy of the dump from the existing one using **.dump** command and load the new dump file we would see that order of the module names is reversed:

```
0:000> kL
Child-SP          RetAddr           Call Site
00000000`0012fed8 00000001`40001093 MyDLL!fnMyDLL
00000000`0012fee0 00000001`40001344 2DLLs+0x1093
00000000`0012ff10 00000000`773acdcd 2DLLs+0x1344
00000000`0012ff60 00000000`774fc6e1 kernel32!BaseThreadInitThunk+0xd
00000000`0012ff90 00000000`00000000 ntdll!RtlUserThreadStart+0x1d

0:000> lm
start             end               module name
00000000`01e60000 00000000`01e71000 MyDLL
00000000`772a0000 00000000`7736a000 user32
00000000`77370000 00000000`774a1000 kernel32
00000000`774b0000 00000000`7762a000 ntdll
00000001`40000000 00000001`40010000 2DLLs
00000001`80000000 00000001`80011000 MyDLL_180000000
000007fe`fc9e0000 000007fe`fca32000 uxtheme
000007fe`fe870000 000007fe`fe9a9000 rpcrt4
000007fe`fe9b0000 000007fe`fe9bc000 lpk
000007fe`fea10000 000007fe`feae8000 oleaut32
000007fe`fecd0000 000007fe`fed6a000 usp10
000007fe`fedd0000 000007fe`fefb0000 ole32
000007fe`fefb0000 000007fe`ff0af000 advapi32
000007fe`ff0d0000 000007fe`ff131000 gdi32
000007fe`ff2e0000 000007fe`ff381000 msvcrt
000007fe`ff390000 000007fe`ff3b8000 imm32
000007fe`ff4b0000 000007fe`ff5b4000 msctf

0:000> !dlls -l

...

0x002ec430: C:\OLD\MyDLL.dll
        Base    0x01e60000  EntryPoint  0x01e613e0  Size       0x00011000
        Flags   0x00284004  LoadCount   0x00000001  TlsIndex   0x00000000
                LDRP_IMAGE_DLL
                LDRP_ENTRY_PROCESSED
                LDRP_PROCESS_ATTACH_CALLED
                LDRP_IMAGE_NOT_AT_BASE
```

The post-processed dump file used for this example can be downloaded to play with[48].

---

[48] https://www.dumpanalysis.org/pub/CDAPatternDuplicatedModule.zip

Comments

There were a few questions:

Q. We can also see that the old version of *MyDLL* was the last loaded DLL. That statement contradicts the following output where it's clear that the old DLL was loaded first:

```
0:000> lmv m MyDLL_1e60000
start end module name
00000000`01e60000 00000000`01e71000 MyDLL_1e60000
Loaded symbol image file: MyDLL.dll
Image path: C:\OLD\MyDLL.dll
Image name: MyDLL.dll
Timestamp: Wed Jun 18 14:49:13 2008 (48591259)
[...]


0:000> lmv m MyDLL
start end module name
00000001`80000000 00000001`80011000 MyDLL
Image path: C:\2DLLs\DLL\MyDLL.dll
Image name: MyDLL.dll
Timestamp: Wed Jun 18 14:50:56 2008 (485912C0)
[...]
```

A. We do not see the contradiction here: *Timestamp* is for the link time not the load time, and the loader is free to choose the base address.

Q. From the list of modules we are able to see two modules are duplicated. Is there any way to find out, who called the module to load into memory. We would like to see the calling function (the originator of duplication).

A. We suggest searching for module start address on thread raw stacks. Also, consider live debugging with enabled load modules event handling in WinDbg.

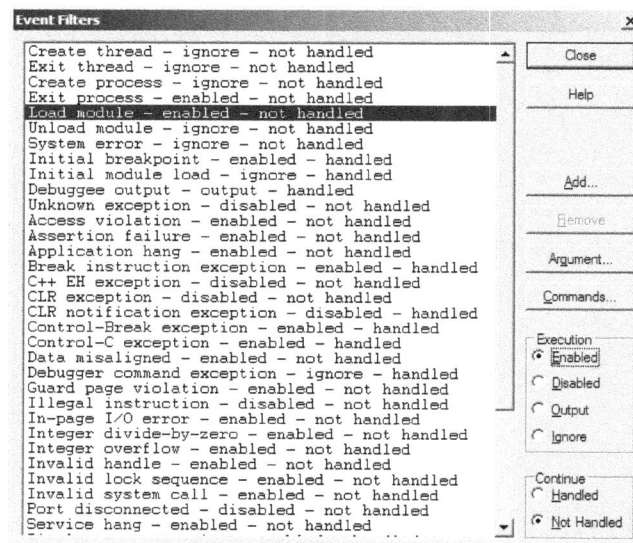

Dynamic Memory Corruption

Kernel Pool

If kernel pools are corrupt then calls that allocate or free memory result in bugchecks C2 or 19 and in other fewer frequent bugchecks (from Google stats[49]):

BugCheck C2: BAD_POOL_CALLER	1600
BugCheck 19: BAD_POOL_HEADER	434
BugCheck C5: DRIVER_CORRUPTED_EXPOOL	207
BugCheck DE: POOL_CORRUPTION_IN_FILE_AREA	106
BugCheck D0: DRIVER_CORRUPTED_MMPOOL	8
BugCheck D6: DRIVER_PAGE_FAULT_BEYOND_END_OF_ALLOCATION	3
BugCheck CD: PAGE_FAULT_BEYOND_END_OF_ALLOCATION	2
BugCheck C6: DRIVER_CAUGHT_MODIFYING_FREED_POOL	0

Bugchecks 0xC2 and 0x19 have parameters in their arguments that tell the type of detected pool corruption. We should refer to WinDbg help for details or use the variant of **!analyze** command where we can supply optional bugcheck arguments:

```
1: kd> !analyze -show c2
BAD_POOL_CALLER (c2)
The current thread is making a bad pool request.  Typically this is at a bad IRQL level or double freeing
the same allocation, etc.
Arguments:
Arg1: 00000000, The caller is requesting a zero byte pool allocation.
Arg2: 00000000, zero.
Arg3: 00000000, the pool type being allocated.
Arg4: 00000000, the pool tag being used.
```

<hr>

[49] Bugcheck Frequencies, Memory Dump Analysis Anthology, Volume 2, page 429

```
1: kd> !analyze -show 19 2 1 1 1
BAD_POOL_HEADER (19)
The pool is already corrupt at the time of the current request.
This may or may not be due to the caller.
The internal pool links must be walked to figure out a possible cause of
the problem, and then special pool applied to the suspect tags or the driver
verifier to a suspect driver.
Arguments:
Arg1: 00000002, the verifier pool pattern check failed.  The owner has likely corrupted the pool block
Arg2: 00000001, the pool entry being checked.
Arg3: 00000001, size of the block.
Arg4: 00000001, 0.
```

If we enable special pool on suspected drivers, we may get these bugchecks too with the following Google frequency:

BugCheck C1: SPECIAL_POOL_DETECTED_MEMORY_CORRUPTION	59
BugCheck D5: DRIVER_PAGE_FAULT_IN_FREED_SPECIAL_POOL	5
BugCheck CC: PAGE_FAULT_IN_FREED_SPECIAL_POOL	1

Here is one example of nonpaged pool corruption detected during *free* operation with the following **!analyze -v** output:

```
BAD_POOL_HEADER (19)
The pool is already corrupt at the time of the current request.
This may or may not be due to the caller.
The internal pool links must be walked to figure out a possible cause of
the problem, and then special pool applied to the suspect tags or the driver
verifier to a suspect driver.
Arguments:
Arg1: 00000020, a pool block header size is corrupt.
Arg2: a34583b8, The pool entry we were looking for within the page.
Arg3: a34584f0, The next pool entry.
Arg4: 0a270001, (reserved)

POOL_ADDRESS:  a34583b8 Nonpaged pool

PROCESS_NAME:  process.exe

CURRENT_IRQL:  2

STACK_TEXT:
b80a60cc 808927bb nt!KeBugCheckEx+0x1b
b80a6134 80892b6f nt!ExFreePoolWithTag+0x477
b80a6144 b9591400 nt!ExFreePool+0xf
WARNING: Stack unwind information not available. Following frames may be wrong.
b80a615c b957b954 driver+0x38400
b80a617c b957d482 driver+0x22954
b80a61c0 b957abf4 driver+0x24482
b80a6260 b957ccef driver+0x21bf4
b80a62a8 8081df65 driver+0x23cef
b80a62bc f721ac45 nt!IofCallDriver+0x45
b80a62e4 8081df65 fltMgr!FltpDispatch+0x6f
```

```
b80a62f8 b99de70b nt!IofCallDriver+0x45
b80a6308 b99da6ee filter!Dispatch+0xfb
b80a6318 8081df65 filter!dispatch+0x6e
b80a632c b9bdebfe nt!IofCallDriver+0x45
b80a6334 8081df65 2ndfilter!Redirect+0x7ea
b80a6348 b9bd1756 nt!IofCallDriver+0x45
b80a6374 b9bd1860 3rdfilter!PassThrough+0x136
b80a6384 8081df65 3rdfilter!Dispatch+0x80
b80a6398 808f5437 nt!IofCallDriver+0x45
b80a63ac 808ef963 nt!IopSynchronousServiceTail+0x10b
b80a63d0 8088978c nt!NtQueryDirectoryFile+0x5d
b80a63d0 7c8285ec nt!KiFastCallEntry+0xfc
00139524 7c8274eb ntdll!KiFastSystemCallRet
00139528 77e6ba40 ntdll!NtQueryDirectoryFile+0xc
00139830 77e6bb5f kernel32!FindFirstFileExW+0x3d5
00139850 6002665e kernel32!FindFirstFileW+0x16
00139e74 60026363 process+0x2665e
0013a328 60027852 process+0x26363
0013a33c 60035b58 process+0x27852
0013b104 600385ff process+0x35b58
0013b224 612cb643 process+0x385ff
0013b988 612cc109 dll!FileDialog+0xc53
0013bba0 612cb47b dll!FileDialog+0x1719
0013c2c0 7739b6e3 dll!FileDialog+0xa8b
0013c2ec 77395f82 USER32!InternalCallWinProc+0x28
0013c368 77395e22 USER32!UserCallDlgProcCheckWow+0x147
0013c3b0 7739c9c6 USER32!DefDlgProcWorker+0xa8
0013c3d8 7c828536 USER32!__fnDWORD+0x24
0013c3d8 808308f4 ntdll!KiUserCallbackDispatcher+0x2e
b80a66b8 8091d6d1 nt!KiCallUserMode+0x4
b80a6710 bf8a2622 nt!KeUserModeCallback+0x8f
b80a6794 bf8a2517 win32k!SfnDWORD+0xb4
b80a67dc bf8a13d9 win32k!xxxSendMessageToClient+0x133
b80a6828 bf85ae67 win32k!xxxSendMessageTimeout+0x1a6
b80a684c bf8847a1 win32k!xxxWrapSendMessage+0x1b
b80a6868 bf8c1459 win32k!NtUserfnNCDESTROY+0x27
b80a68a0 8088978c win32k!NtUserMessageCall+0xc0
b80a68a0 7c8285ec nt!KiFastCallEntry+0xfc
0013c3d8 7c828536 ntdll!KiFastSystemCallRet
0013c3d8 808308f4 ntdll!KiUserCallbackDispatcher+0x2e
b80a6b7c 8091d6d1 nt!KiCallUserMode+0x4
b80a6bd4 bf8a2622 nt!KeUserModeCallback+0x8f
b80a6c58 bf8a23a0 win32k!SfnDWORD+0xb4
b80a6ca0 bf8a13d9 win32k!xxxSendMessageToClient+0x118
b80a6cec bf85ae67 win32k!xxxSendMessageTimeout+0x1a6
b80a6d10 bf8c148c win32k!xxxWrapSendMessage+0x1b
b80a6d40 8088978c win32k!NtUserMessageCall+0x9d
b80a6d40 7c8285ec nt!KiFastCallEntry+0xfc
0013f474 7c828536 ntdll!KiFastSystemCallRet
0013f4a0 7739d1ec ntdll!KiUserCallbackDispatcher+0x2e
0013f4dc 7738cf29 USER32!NtUserMessageCall+0xc
0013f4fc 612d3276 USER32!SendMessageA+0x7f
0013f63c 611add41 dll!SubWindow+0x3dc6
0013f658 7739b6e3 dll!SetWindowText+0x37a1
0013f684 7739b874 USER32!InternalCallWinProc+0x28
0013f6fc 7739ba92 USER32!UserCallWinProcCheckWow+0x151
```

```
0013f764 7739bad0 USER32!DispatchMessageWorker+0x327
0013f774 61221ca8 USER32!DispatchMessageW+0xf
0013f7e0 0040156d dll!MainLoop+0x2c8
0013ff24 00401dfa process+0x156d
0013ffc0 77e6f23b process+0x1dfa
0013fff0 00000000 kernel32!BaseProcessStart+0x23


MODULE_NAME: driver

IMAGE_NAME:  driver.sys
```

We see that WinDbg pointed to *driver.sys* by using a procedure described in Component Identification article[50].

Any OS component could corrupt the pool prior to the detection as the bugcheck description says: "The pool is already corrupt at the time of the current request.". What other evidence can reinforce our belief in *driver.sys*? Let's look at our pool entry tag first:

```
1: kd> !pool a34583b8
Pool page a34583b8 region is Nonpaged pool
  a3458000 size:  270 previous size:    0  (Allocated)  Thre (Protected)
  a3458270 size:   10 previous size:  270  (Free)       RxIr
  a3458280 size:   40 previous size:   10  (Allocated)  Vadl
  a34582c0 size:   98 previous size:   40  (Allocated)  File (Protected)
  a3458358 size:    8 previous size:   98  (Free)       Vadl
  a3458360 size:   50 previous size:    8  (Allocated)  Gsem
  a34583b0 size:    8 previous size:   50  (Free)       CcSc
*a34583b8 size:  138 previous size:    8  (Allocated) *DRIV
  Owning component : Unknown (update pooltag.txt)
a34584f0 is not a valid large pool allocation, checking large session pool…
a34584f0 is freed (or corrupt) pool
Bad allocation size @a34584f0, zero is invalid

***
*** An error (or corruption) in the pool was detected;
*** Attempting to diagnose the problem.
***
*** Use !poolval a3458000 for more details.
***

Pool page [ a3458000 ] is __inVALID.

Analyzing linked list...
[ a34583b8 --> a34583d8 (size = 0x20 bytes)]: Corrupt region
[ a34583f8 --> a34585e8 (size = 0x1f0 bytes)]: Corrupt region

Scanning for single bit errors...

None found
```

---

[50] Component Identification, Memory Dump Analysis Anthology, Volume 1, page 46

We see that the tag is DRIV, and we know either from the association or from similar problems in the past that it belongs to *driver.sys*. Let's dump our pool entry contents to see if there are any symbolic hints in it:

```
1: kd> dps a34583b8
a34583b8  0a270001
a34583bc  5346574e
a34583c0  00000000
a34583c4  00000000
a34583c8  b958f532 driver+0x36532
a34583cc  a3471010
a34583d0  0000012e
a34583d4  00000001
a34583d8  00041457
a34583dc  05af0026
a34583e0  00068002
a34583e4  7b9ec6f5
a34583e8  ffffff00
a34583ec  73650cff
a34583f0  7461445c
a34583f4  97a10061
a34583f8  ff340004
a34583fc  c437862a
a3458400  6a000394
a3458404  00000038
a3458408  00000000
a345840c  bf000000
a3458410  bf0741b5
a3458414  f70741b5
a3458418  00000000
a345841c  00000000
a3458420  00000000
a3458424  00000000
a3458428  05000000
a345842c  34303220
a3458430  31323332
a3458434  ff322d36
```

Indeed we see that the possible code pointer *driver+0x36532* and the code around this address look normal:

```
3: kd> .asm no_code_bytes
Assembly options: no_code_bytes

3: kd> u b958f532
driver+0x36532:
b958f532 push    2Ch
b958f534 push    offset driver+0x68d08 (b95c1d08)
b958f539 call    driver+0x65c50 (b95bec50)
b958f53e mov     byte ptr [ebp-19h],0
b958f542 and     dword ptr [ebp-24h],0
b958f546 call    dword ptr [driver+0x65f5c (b95bef5c)]
b958f54c mov     ecx,dword ptr [ebp+0Ch]
b958f54f cmp     eax,ecx
```

```
3: kd> ub b958f532
driver+0x36528:
b958f528 leave
b958f529 ret      18h
b958f52c int      3
b958f52d int      3
b958f52e int      3
b958f52f int      3
b958f530 int      3
b958f531 int      3
```

Comments

Here is one of the asked questions.

Q. I have the same problem with BAD_POOL_HEADER; I see the pool header e173c1d8 is corrupt and marked as *Ppen. Could you help me to know what is that?

```
BAD_POOL_HEADER (19)
The pool is already corrupt at the time of the current request.
This may or may not be due to the caller.
The internal pool links must be walked to figure out a possible cause of
the problem, and then special pool applied to the suspect tags or the driver
verifier to a suspect driver.
Arguments:
Arg1: 00000020, a pool block header size is corrupt.
Arg2: e173c1d8, The pool entry we were looking for within the page.
Arg3: e173c1f8, The next pool entry.
Arg4: 0c040404, (reserved)


Debugging Details:
------


BUGCHECK_STR: 0x19_20


POOL_ADDRESS: e173c1d8


CUSTOMER_CRASH_COUNT: 6


DEFAULT_BUCKET_ID: COMMON_SYSTEM_FAULT


PROCESS_NAME: System


LOCK_ADDRESS: 8055b4e0 — (!locks 8055b4e0)


Resource @ nt!PiEngineLock (0x8055b4e0) Available


WARNING: SystemResourcesList->Flink chain invalid. Resource may be corrupted, or already deleted.


WARNING: SystemResourcesList->Blink chain invalid. Resource may be corrupted, or already deleted.
```

```
1 total locks

PNP_TRIAGE:
Lock address : 0x8055b4e0
Thread Count : 0
Thread address: 0x00000000
Thread wait : 0x0

LAST_CONTROL_TRANSFER: from 8054b583 to 804f9f33

STACK_TEXT:
f79f392c 8054b583 00000019 00000020 e173c1d8 nt!KeBugCheckEx+0x1b
f79f397c 8058fc05 e173c1e0 00000000 00000000 nt!ExFreePoolWithTag+0x2a3
f79f39dc 8059161d 85804dd0 e10f29a8 f79f3a48 nt!PipMakeGloballyUniqueId+0x3a9
f79f3ad0 8059222b 8593a7c8 861d33e8 8593a7c8 nt!PipProcessNewDeviceNode+0x185
f79f3d24 805927fa 8593a7c8 00000001 00000000 nt!PipProcessDevNodeTree+0x16b
f79f3d54 804f698e 00000003 8055b5c0 8056485c nt!PiRestartDevice+0x80
f79f3d7c 8053876d 00000000 00000000 863c1da8 nt!PipDeviceActionWorker+0x168
f79f3dac 805cff64 00000000 00000000 00000000 nt!ExpWorkerThread+0xef
f79f3ddc 805460de 8053867e 00000001 00000000 nt!PspSystemThreadStartup+0x34
00000000 00000000 00000000 00000000 00000000 nt!KiThreadStartup+0x16

STACK_COMMAND: kb

FOLLOWUP_IP:
nt!ExFreePoolWithTag+2a3
8054b583 8b45f8 mov eax,dword ptr [ebp-8]

SYMBOL_STACK_INDEX: 1

SYMBOL_NAME: nt!ExFreePoolWithTag+2a3

FOLLOWUP_NAME: MachineOwner

MODULE_NAME: nt

IMAGE_NAME: ntkrpamp.exe

DEBUG_FLR_IMAGE_TIMESTAMP: 4802516a

FAILURE_BUCKET_ID: 0x19_20_nt!ExFreePoolWithTag+2a3

BUCKET_ID: 0x19_20_nt!ExFreePoolWithTag+2a3

Followup: MachineOwner
---
```

```
0: kd> !pool e173c1d8
Pool page e173c1d8 region is Unknown
e173c000 size:   28 previous size:    0  (Allocated) CMVa
e173c028 size:    8 previous size:   28  (Free)      0…
e173c030 size:   10 previous size:    8  (Allocated) MmSt
e173c040 size:   48 previous size:   10  (Allocated) ScSh
e173c088 size:   68 previous size:   48  (Allocated) ScNc
e173c0f0 size:    8 previous size:   68  (Free)      Ntf0
e173c0f8 size:   10 previous size:    8  (Allocated) ObDi
e173c108 size:   28 previous size:   10  (Allocated) CMVa
e173c130 size:   80 previous size:   28  (Allocated) IoNm
e173c1b0 size:    8 previous size:   80  (Free)      Sect
e173c1b8 size:   20 previous size:    8  (Allocated) CMVa
*e173c1d8 size:   20 previous size:   20  (Allocated) *Ppen
Pooltag Ppen : routines to perform device enumeration, Binary : nt!pnp
GetUlongFromAddress: unable to read from 80565d50
e173c1f8 is not a valid small pool allocation, checking large pool…
unable to get pool big page table - either wrong symbols or pool tagging is disabled
e173c1f8 is freed (or corrupt) pool
Bad previous allocation size @e173c1f8, last size was 4


***
*** An error (or corruption) in the pool was detected;
*** Pool Region unknown (0xFFFFFFFFE173C1F8)
***
*** Use !poolval e173c000 for more details.
***


0: kd> !poolval e173c000
Pool page e173c000 region is Unknown


Validating Pool headers for pool page: e173c000


Pool page [ e173c000 ] is __inVALID.


Analyzing linked list…
[ e173c1d8 -> e173c2c0 (size = 0xe8 bytes)]: Corrupt region


Scanning for single bit errors…


None found


0: kd> dps e173c1d8
e173c1d8  0c040404
e173c1dc  6e657050
e173c1e0  00260032
e173c1e4  00370061
e173c1e8  00360035
e173c1ec  00370035
e173c1f0  00260032
e173c1f4  004e0030
e173c1f8  00520054
e173c1fc  004c004f
e173c200  002e0053
```

```
[...]
e173c214 00360032
e173c218 00300030
e173c21c 0c12040a
e173c220 e24e4d43
e173c224 00010001
e173c228 7224c689
e173c22c e17b53a4
e173c230 23230077
e173c234 4448233f
[...]
e173c24c 44264431
e173c250 375f5645
e173c254 26353036
```

A. Pooltag Ppen : routines to perform device enumeration, Binary : nt!pnp

Ppen is from PnP manager

If we search for this stack trace frame:

```
PipMakeGloballyUniqueId+0x3a9
```

we find the discussion of a similar BSOD and perhaps a solution[51].

Also, please note that the content of the address e173c1f8 and the content of nearby addresses are covered by UNICODE **Regular Data** (page 925). We may want to check these **String Hints** (page 1072).

Pool corruption may also cause access violations in pool management with general bugchecks such as KMODE_EXCEPTION_NOT_HANDLED (1e):

```
0: kd> k
# Child-SP RetAddr Call Site
00 fffff802`d2afe568 fffff802`d103db86 nt!KeBugCheckEx
01 fffff802`d2afe570 fffff802`d0fc652d nt!KiFatalExceptionHandler+0x22
02 fffff802`d2afe5b0 fffff802`d0e83139 nt!RtlpExecuteHandlerForException+0xd
03 fffff802`d2afe5e0 fffff802`d0e815a8 nt!RtlDispatchException+0x429
04 fffff802`d2afece0 fffff802`d0fcb0c2 nt!KiDispatchException+0x144
05 fffff802`d2aff3c0 fffff802`d0fc957d nt!KiExceptionDispatch+0xc2
06 fffff802`d2aff5a0 fffff802`d10af119 nt!KiGeneralProtectionFault+0xfd
*** ERROR: Module load completed but symbols could not be loaded for vmci.sys
07 fffff802`d2aff730 fffff800`84456159 nt!ExAllocatePoolWithTag+0x7c9
08 fffff802`d2aff810 fffff800`84457131 vmci+0x6159
09 fffff802`d2aff840 fffff800`8445398b vmci+0x7131
0a fffff802`d2aff890 fffff802`d0eec3c0 vmci+0x398b
0b fffff802`d2aff8c0 fffff802`d0eebad9 nt!KiExecuteAllDpcs+0x270
0c fffff802`d2affa10 fffff802`d0fc323a nt!KiRetireDpcList+0xe9
0d fffff802`d2affc60 00000000`00000000 nt!KiIdleLoop+0x5a
```

---

[51] http://social.microsoft.com/Forums/en/whssoftware/thread/98b381be-edff-43fb-b1d9-5307e6204733

Managed Heap

Here's **Managed Heap** counterpart to **Process Heap** (page 330) and **Kernel Pool** (page 315) **Dynamic Memory Corruption** patterns. It is usually detected by CLR during garbage collection phases. Here is a typical stack from CLR 2 (CLR 4 is similar):

```
0:000> kL
ChildEBP RetAddr
002baae0 779b06a0 ntdll!KiFastSystemCallRet
002baae4 772c77d4 ntdll!NtWaitForSingleObject+0xc
002bab54 772c7742 kernel32!WaitForSingleObjectEx+0xbe
002bab68 7a0c0a43 kernel32!WaitForSingleObject+0x12
002bab98 7a0c0e89 mscorwks!ClrWaitForSingleObject+0x24
002bb054 7a0c2bfd mscorwks!RunWatson+0x1df
002bb798 7a0c3171 mscorwks!DoFaultReportWorker+0xb62
002bb7d4 7a106b2d mscorwks!DoFaultReport+0xc3
002bb7fc 7a1061ac mscorwks!WatsonLastChance+0x43
002bbcb8 7a10624f mscorwks!EEPolicy::LogFatalError+0x3ae
002bbcd0 79ffee2f mscorwks!EEPolicy::HandleFatalError+0x36
002bbcf4 79f04f1f mscorwks!CLRVectoredExceptionHandlerPhase3+0xc1
002bbd28 79f04e98 mscorwks!CLRVectoredExceptionHandlerPhase2+0x20
002bbd5c 79f9149e mscorwks!CLRVectoredExceptionHandler+0x10a
002bbd70 779b1039 mscorwks!CLRVectoredExceptionHandlerShimX86+0x27
002bbd94 779b100b ntdll!ExecuteHandler2+0x26
002bbe3c 779b0e97 ntdll!ExecuteHandler+0x24
**002bbe3c 79f69360 ntdll!KiUserExceptionDispatcher+0xf**
**002bc13c 79f663f1 mscorwks!SVR::heap_segment_next_rw+0xf**
**002bc228 79f65d63 mscorwks!WKS::gc_heap::plan_phase+0x37c**
**002bc248 79f6614c mscorwks!WKS::gc_heap::gc1+0x6e**
**002bc25c 79f65f5d mscorwks!WKS::gc_heap::garbage_collect+0x261**
**002bc288 79f663c2 mscorwks!WKS::GCHeap::GarbageCollectGeneration+0x1a9**
**002bc314 79ef1566 mscorwks!WKS::gc_heap::try_allocate_more_space+0x12e**
**002bc328 79ef1801 mscorwks!WKS::gc_heap::allocate_more_space+0x11**
**002bc348 79e7510e mscorwks!WKS::GCHeap::Alloc+0x3b**
**002bc364 79e86713 mscorwks!Alloc+0x60**
002bc3a0 79e86753 mscorwks!SlowAllocateString+0x29
002bc3ac 79eb4efb mscorwks!UnframedAllocateString+0xc
002bc3e0 79e91f58 mscorwks!AllocateStringObject+0x2e
002bc424 79e82892 mscorwks!GlobalStringLiteralMap::AddStringLiteral+0x3f
002bc438 79e82810 mscorwks!GlobalStringLiteralMap::GetStringLiteral+0x43
002bc47c 79e82956 mscorwks!AppDomainStringLiteralMap::GetStringLiteral+0x72
002bc494 79e81b6f mscorwks!BaseDomain::GetStringObjRefPtrFromUnicodeString+0x31
002bc4cc 79ef4704 mscorwks!Module::ResolveStringRef+0x88
002bc4e4 79f23132 mscorwks!ConstructStringLiteral+0x39
002bc558 7908c351 mscorwks!CEEInfo::constructStringLiteral+0x108
002bc57c 7906276d mscorjit!Compiler::fgMorphConst+0xa3
002bc598 79065ea0 mscorjit!Compiler::fgMorphTree+0x63
002bc610 79062bb5 mscorjit!Compiler::fgMorphArgs+0x86
002bc63c 7906311f mscorjit!Compiler::fgMorphCall+0x2c1
002bc658 79065ea0 mscorjit!Compiler::fgMorphTree+0xa3
002bc6d0 79062bb5 mscorjit!Compiler::fgMorphArgs+0x86
002bc6fc 7906311f mscorjit!Compiler::fgMorphCall+0x2c1
002bc718 790650fa mscorjit!Compiler::fgMorphTree+0xa3
002bc738 79065026 mscorjit!Compiler::fgMorphStmts+0x63
```

```
002bc774 79064f9f mscorjit!Compiler::fgMorphBlocks+0x79
002bc788 79064e63 mscorjit!Compiler::fgMorph+0x60
002bc798 790614e6 mscorjit!Compiler::compCompile+0x5f
002bc7f0 79061236 mscorjit!Compiler::compCompile+0x2df
002bc884 7906118c mscorjit!jitNativeCode+0xb8
002bc8bc 79f0f9cf mscorjit!CILJit::compileMethod+0x3d
002bc928 79f0f945 mscorwks!invokeCompileMethodHelper+0x72
002bc96c 79f0f8da mscorwks!invokeCompileMethod+0x31
002bc9c4 79f0ea33 mscorwks!CallCompileMethodWithSEHWrapper+0x84
002bcd7c 79f0e795 mscorwks!UnsafeJitFunction+0x230
002bce20 79e87f52 mscorwks!MethodDesc::MakeJitWorker+0x1c1
002bce78 79e8809e mscorwks!MethodDesc::DoPrestub+0x486
002bcec8 00330836 mscorwks!PreStubWorker+0xeb
WARNING: Frame IP not in any known module. Following frames may be wrong.
002bcee0 79e7c74b 0x330836
002bcf10 79e7c6cc mscorwks!CallDescrWorker+0x33
002bcf90 79e7c8e1 mscorwks!CallDescrWorkerWithHandler+0xa3
002bd0d0 79e7c783 mscorwks!MethodDesc::CallDescr+0x19c
002bd0ec 79e7c90d mscorwks!MethodDesc::CallTargetWorker+0x1f
002bd100 79e8b983 mscorwks!MethodDescCallSite::Call_RetArgSlot+0x18
002bd1d8 79e8b8e6 mscorwks!MethodTable::RunClassInitWorker+0x8b
002bd260 79e8b7fa mscorwks!MethodTable::RunClassInitEx+0x11e
002bd724 79ebcee6 mscorwks!MethodTable::DoRunClassInitThrowing+0x2f0
002bd79c 79fc49db mscorwks!MethodTable::CheckRunClassInitNT+0x8c
002bd82c 790a2801 mscorwks!CEEInfo::initClass+0x19b
002bddcc 79062cdc mscorjit!Compiler::impExpandInline+0x2aaa
002bde24 79062b7c mscorjit!Compiler::fgMorphCallInline+0xf8
002bde50 7906311f mscorjit!Compiler::fgMorphCall+0x27b
002bde6c 790650fa mscorjit!Compiler::fgMorphTree+0xa3
002bde8c 79065026 mscorjit!Compiler::fgMorphStmts+0x63
002bdec8 79064f9f mscorjit!Compiler::fgMorphBlocks+0x79
002bdedc 79064e63 mscorjit!Compiler::fgMorph+0x60
002bdeec 790614e6 mscorjit!Compiler::compCompile+0x5f
002bdf44 79061236 mscorjit!Compiler::compCompile+0x2df
002bdfd8 7906118c mscorjit!jitNativeCode+0xb8
002be010 79f0f9cf mscorjit!CILJit::compileMethod+0x3d
002be07c 79f0f945 mscorwks!invokeCompileMethodHelper+0x72
002be0c0 79f0f8da mscorwks!invokeCompileMethod+0x31
002be118 79f0ea33 mscorwks!CallCompileMethodWithSEHWrapper+0x84
002be4d0 79f0e795 mscorwks!UnsafeJitFunction+0x230
002be574 79e87f52 mscorwks!MethodDesc::MakeJitWorker+0x1c1
002be5cc 79e8809e mscorwks!MethodDesc::DoPrestub+0x486
002be61c 00330836 mscorwks!PreStubWorker+0xeb
002be634 0570c859 0x330836
002be69c 0595bcc1 0x570c859
002be700 0595b954 0x595bcc1
002be704 099b66e0 0x595b954
002be708 002be728 0x99b66e0
002be70c 09589c90 0x2be728
002be728 099b67b8 0x9589c90
002be72c 00000000 0x99b67b8
```

Usually **!VerifyHeap** SOS WinDbg extension command helps to find the first invalid object on managed heap and shows the last valid one. Sometimes the corruption can deeply affect heap or when a crash happens during traversal GC state might not be valid for analysis:

```
0:000> !VerifyHeap
-verify will only produce output if there are errors in the heap
```
The garbage collector data structures are not in a valid state for traversal.
It is either in the "plan phase," where objects are being moved around, or
we are at the initialization or shutdown of the gc heap. Commands related to
displaying, finding or traversing objects as well as gc heap segments may not
work properly. !dumpheap and !verifyheap may incorrectly complain of heap
consistency errors.
```
Error requesting heap segment 80018001
Failed to retrieve segments for gc heap
Unable to build snapshot of the garbage collector state
```

```
0:000> !DumpHeap
```
The garbage collector data structures are not in a valid state for traversal.
It is either in the "plan phase," where objects are being moved around, or
we are at the initialization or shutdown of the gc heap. Commands related to
displaying, finding or traversing objects as well as gc heap segments may not
work properly. !dumpheap and !verifyheap may incorrectly complain of heap
consistency errors.
```
Error requesting heap segment 80018001
Failed to retrieve segments for gc heap
Unable to build snapshot of the garbage collector state
```

In such cases it is recommended to collect several dumps to catch more consistent heap state:

```
0:000> !VerifyHeap
-verify will only produce output if there are errors in the heap
```
object 0981f024: does not have valid MT
```
curr_object: 0981f024
```
Last good object: 0981f010

Then we can use **!DumpObj** (**!do**) command to check objects and **d*** WinDbg command variations to inspect raw memory.

Process Heap

Linux

This is a Linux variant of **Dynamic Memory Corruption** (process heap) pattern previously described for Mac OS X (page 328) and Windows (page 330) platforms.

The corruption may be internal to heap structures with subsequent memory access violation:

```
(gdb) bt
#0  0x000000000041482e in _int_malloc ()
#1  0x0000000000416d88 in malloc ()
#2  0x00000000004005dc in proc ()
#3  0x00000000004006ee in bar_three ()
#4  0x00000000004006fe in foo_three ()
#5  0x0000000000400716 in thread_three ()
#6  0x0000000000401760 in start_thread (arg=<optimized out>)
at pthread_create.c:304
#7  0x0000000000432609 in clone ()
#8  0x0000000000000000 in ?? ()


(gdb) x/i $rip
=> 0x41482e <_int_malloc+622>: mov    %rbx,0x10(%r12)


(gdb) x $r12+0x10
0x21687371: Cannot access memory at address 0x21687371


(gdb) p (char[4])0x21687371
$1 = "qsh!"
```

Or it may be detected with a diagnostic message (similar to double *free*):

```
(gdb) bt
#0  0x000000000043ef65 in raise ()
#1  0x0000000000409fc0 in abort ()
#2  0x0000000000040bf5b in __libc_message ()
#3  0x0000000000412042 in malloc_printerr ()
#4  0x0000000000416c27 in free ()
#5  0x0000000000400586 in proc ()
#6  0x000000000040067e in bar_four ()
#7  0x000000000040068e in foo_four ()
#8  0x00000000004006a6 in thread_four ()
#9  0x00000000004016c0 in start_thread (arg=<optimized out>)
at pthread_create.c:304
#10 0x0000000000432589 in clone ()
#11 0x0000000000000000 in ?? ()
```

Mac OS X

This is a Mac OS X / GDB counterpart to **Dynamic Memory Corruption** (process heap) pattern (page 330):

```
(gdb) bt
#0 0x00007fff8479582a in __kill ()
#1 0x00007fff8e0e0a9c in abort ()
#2 0x00007fff8e1024ac in szone_error ()
#3 0x00007fff8e1024e8 in free_list_checksum_botch ()
#4 0x00007fff8e102a7b in small_free_list_remove_ptr ()
#5 0x00007fff8e106bf7 in szone_free_definite_size ()
#6 0x00007fff8e13f789 in free ()
#7 0x000000010afafe23 in main (argc=1, argv=0x7fff6abaeb08)
```

Here's the source code of the modeling application:

```
int main(int argc, const char * argv[])
{
        char *p1 = (char *) malloc (1024);
        printf("p1 = %p\n", p1);

        char *p2 = (char *) malloc (1024);
        printf("p2 = %p\n", p2);

        char *p3 = (char *) malloc (1024);
        printf("p3 = %p\n", p3);

        char *p4 = (char *) malloc (1024);
        printf("p4 = %p\n", p4);

        char *p5 = (char *) malloc (1024);
        printf("p5 = %p\n", p5);

        char *p6 = (char *) malloc (1024);
        printf("p6 = %p\n", p6);

        char *p7 = (char *) malloc (1024);
        printf("p7 = %p\n", p7);

        free(p6);
        free(p4);
        free(p2);

        printf("Hello Crash!\n");
        strcpy(p2, "Hello Crash!");
        strcpy(p4, "Hello Crash!");
        strcpy(p6, "Hello Crash!");

        p2 = (char *) malloc (512);
        printf("p2 = %p\n", p2);
        p4 = (char *) malloc (1024);
        printf("p4 = %p\n", p4);

        6 = (char *) malloc (512);
```

```
    printf("p6 = %p\n", p6);

    free (p7);
    free (p6);
    free (p5);
    free (p4);
    free (p3);
    free (p2);
    free (p1);

    return 0;
}
```

Windows

This pattern is ubiquitous, its manifestations are random, and usually crashes happen far away from the original corruption point. In our user mode and space part of exception threads (we should not forget about **Multiple Exceptions** pattern, page 799) you would see something like this:

```
ntdll!RtlpCoalesceFreeBlocks+0x10c
ntdll!RtlFreeHeap+0x142
MSVCRT!free+0xda
componentA!xxx
```

or this stack trace fragment:

```
ntdll!RtlpCoalesceFreeBlocks+0x10c
ntdll!RtlpExtendHeap+0x1c1
ntdll!RtlAllocateHeap+0x3b6
componentA!xxx
```

or any similar variants and we need to know exact component that corrupted the application heap (which usually is not the same as *componentA.dll* we see in the crashed thread stack).

For this **common recurrent problem** we have a **general solution**: enable heap checking. This general solution has many variants applied in a **specific context**:

- parameter value checking for heap functions
- user space software heap checks before or after certain checkpoints (like "malloc"/"new" and/or "free"/"delete" calls): usually implemented by checking various fill patterns, etc.
- hardware/OS supported heap checks (like using guard and nonaccessible pages to trap buffer overruns)

The latter variant is the mostly used according to our experience and mainly due to the fact that usually heap corruptions originate from buffer overflows. And it is easier to rely on instant memory manager support than on checking fill patterns. Debugging TV episode 0x26 describes how we can enable full page heap[52]. There is an article on how to check in a user dump that full page heap was enabled[53].

The Windows kernel analog to user mode and space heap corruption is called page and nonpaged pool corruption. If we consider Windows kernel pools as variants of the heap, then exactly the same techniques are applicable there, for example, the so-called special pool enabled by Driver Verifier is implemented by nonaccessible pages[54].

---

[52] http://www.debugging.tv/Frames/0x26/DebuggingTV_Frame_0x26.pdf (https://www.youtube.com/watch?v=F4cCxHkJVCQ)

[53] http://support.citrix.com/article/CTX105955

[54] https://blogs.msdn.microsoft.com/ntdebugging/2013/08/22/understanding-pool-corruption-part-2-special-pool-for-buffer-overruns/

Comments

!heap -s -v WinDbg extension command verifies heap blocks:

```
0:001> !heap -s -v
*****************************************************************
* HEAP ERROR DETECTED                                          *
*                                                              *
*****************************************************************

Details:

Error address: 00740f28
Heap handle: 00740000
Error type heap_failure_multiple_entries_corruption (4)
Last known valid blocks: before - 007409e8, after - 007416b8
Stack trace:
77b6fc76: ntdll!RtlpAnalyzeHeapFailure+0x0000025b
77b29ef1: ntdll!RtlpCoalesceFreeBlocks+0x00000060
77ad2d07: ntdll!RtlpFreeHeap+0x000001f4
77ad2bf2: ntdll!RtlFreeHeap+0x00000142
752914d1: kernel32!HeapFree+0x00000014
010b11f0: Application+0x000011f0
010b1274: Application+0x00001274
010b1310: Application+0x00001310
75293677: kernel32!BaseThreadInitThunk+0x0000000e
77ad9f02: ntdll!__RtlUserThreadStart+0x00000070
77ad9ed5: ntdll!_RtlUserThreadStart+0x0000001b
LFH Key : 0x7c150f40
Termination on corruption : DISABLED
Heap Flags Reserv Commit Virt Free List UCR Virt Lock Fast
(k) (k) (k) (k) length blocks cont. heap
-------------------------------------------------------------------------
.004c0000 00000002 1024 104 104 2 1 1 0 0 LFH
.ERROR: Block 007416b8 previous size f2 does not match previous block size 44
HEAP 00740000 (Seg 00740000) At 007416b8 Error: invalid block Previous

00740000 00001002 64 12 64 3 2 1 0 0
-------------------------------------------------------------------------
```

Sometimes we may have a buffer underflow, and full page heap which places allocations at the end of pages will not catch the moment of corruption. Here we need to use backward full page heap:

```
gflags /p /enable ImageFile /full /backwards
```

Debugging TV frames episode 0x26 has full recording for such an example[55].

---

[55] http://www.debugging.tv

The new WinDbg 6.2.9200.20512 **!analyze -v** command detects invalid heap calls in case "heap termination on corruption" is not enabled (by default on legacy 32-bit apps). In the past, it was possible to see that only with the heap verification command such as **!heap -s -v** or via **dps** *ntdll!RtlpHeapFailureInfo*.

Visual C++ 2012 enables heap termination on corruption by default even for 32-bit targets according to SDL guidelines[56]:

```
0:001> !heap -s -v
[…]
Heap address: 00580000
Error address: 005c1a2a
Error type: HEAP_FAILURE_INVALID_ARGUMENT
Details: The caller tried to a free a block at an invalid
(unaligned) address.
Follow-up: Check the error's stack trace to find the culprit.


Stack trace:
7799dff5: ntdll!RtlFreeHeap+0x00000064
767514dd: kernel32!HeapFree+0x00000014
0138140f: AppD8!free+0x0000001a
0138134d: AppD8!StartModeling+0x0000001d
0138121a: AppD8!WndProc+0x0000007a
76f162fa: USER32!InternalCallWinProc+0x00000023
76f16d3a: USER32!UserCallWinProcCheckWow+0x00000109
76f177c4: USER32!DispatchMessageWorker+0x000003bc
76f1788a: USER32!DispatchMessageW+0x0000000f
0138109d: AppD8!wWinMain+0x0000009d
0138152a: AppD8!__tmainCRTStartup+0x000000fd
767533aa: kernel32!BaseThreadInitThunk+0x0000000e
77959ef2: ntdll!__RtlUserThreadStart+0x00000070
77959ec5: ntdll!_RtlUserThreadStart+0x0000001b


LFH Key : 0x3d43a3cb
Termination on corruption : DISABLED


0:001> !analyze -v
[…]
BUGCHECK_STR: APPLICATION_FAULT_ACTIONABLE_HEAP_CORRUPTION_heap_failure_invalid_argument
[…]
STACK_TEXT:
77a242a0 7799dff5 ntdll!RtlFreeHeap+0x64
77a242a4 767514dd kernel32!HeapFree+0x14
77a242a8 0138140f appd8!free+0x1a
77a242ac 0138134d appd8!StartModeling+0x1d
77a242b0 0138121a appd8!WndProc+0x7a
77a242b4 76f162fa user32!InternalCallWinProc+0x23
77a242b8 76f16d3a user32!UserCallWinProcCheckWow+0x109
77a242bc 76f177c4 user32!DispatchMessageWorker+0x3bc
```

---

[56] https://docs.microsoft.com/en-us/previous-versions/windows/desktop/cc307399(v=msdn.10)

```
77a242c0 76f1788a user32!DispatchMessageW+0xf
77a242c4 0138109d appd8!wWinMain+0x9d
77a242c8 0138152a appd8!__tmainCRTStartup+0xfd
77a242cc 767533aa kernel32!BaseThreadInitThunk+0xe
77a242d0 77959ef2 ntdll!__RtlUserThreadStart+0x70
77a242d4 77959ec5 ntdll!_RtlUserThreadStart+0x1b
[...]

0:001> dps ntdll!RtlpHeapFailureInfo
77a24268 00000000
77a2426c 00000000
77a24270 00000009
77a24274 00580000
77a24278 005c1a2a
77a2427c 00000000
77a24280 00000000
77a24284 00000000
77a24288 00000000
77a2428c 00000000
77a24290 00000000
77a24294 00000000
77a24298 00000000
77a2429c 00000000
77a242a0 7799dff5 ntdll!RtlFreeHeap+0x64
77a242a4 767514dd kernel32!HeapFree+0x14
77a242a8 0138140f AppD8!free+0x1a
77a242ac 0138134d AppD8!StartModeling+0x1d
77a242b0 0138121a AppD8!WndProc+0x7a
77a242b4 76f162fa USER32!InternalCallWinProc+0x23
77a242b8 76f16d3a USER32!UserCallWinProcCheckWow+0x109
77a242bc 76f177c4 USER32!DispatchMessageWorker+0x3bc
77a242c0 76f1788a USER32!DispatchMessageW+0xf
77a242c4 0138109d AppD8!wWinMain+0x9d
77a242c8 0138152a AppD8!__tmainCRTStartup+0xfd
77a242cc 767533aa kernel32!BaseThreadInitThunk+0xe
77a242d0 77959ef2 ntdll!__RtlUserThreadStart+0x70
77a242d4 77959ec5 ntdll!_RtlUserThreadStart+0x1b
77a242d8 00000000
77a242dc 00000000
77a242e0 00000000
77a242e4 00000000

0:001> ~*k

0 Id: 1d74.fd4 Suspend: 1 Teb: 7efdd000 Unfrozen
ChildEBP RetAddr
001cfa3c 76f1790d USER32!NtUserGetMessage+0x15
001cfa58 0138106f USER32!GetMessageW+0x33
001cfa90 0138152a AppD8!wWinMain+0x6f
001cfadc 767533aa AppD8!__tmainCRTStartup+0xfd
001cfae8 77959ef2 kernel32!BaseThreadInitThunk+0xe
001cfb28 77959ec5 ntdll!__RtlUserThreadStart+0x70
001cfb40 00000000 ntdll!_RtlUserThreadStart+0x1b
```

```
# 1 Id: 1d74.e98 Suspend: 1 Teb: 7efda000 Unfrozen
ChildEBP RetAddr
0118fbb4 779bf896 ntdll!DbgBreakPoint
0118fbe4 767533aa ntdll!DbgUiRemoteBreakin+0x3c
0118fbf0 77959ef2 kernel32!BaseThreadInitThunk+0xe
0118fc30 77959ec5 ntdll!__RtlUserThreadStart+0x70
0118fc48 00000000 ntdll!_RtlUserThreadStart+0x1b
```

Early Crash Dump

Some bugs are fixed using a brute-force approach via putting an exception handler to catch access violations and other exceptions. A long time ago I saw one such "incredible fix" when the image processing application was crashing after approximately N^{th} heap free runtime call. To ignore crashes, an SEH handler was put in place, but the application started to crash in different places. Therefore, the additional fix was to skip free calls when approaching N and resume afterward. The application started to crash less frequently.

Here getting **Early Crash Dump** when a first-chance exception happens can help in the component identification before corruption starts spreading across data. Recall that when an access violation happens in a process thread in user mode, the system generates the first-chance exception which can be caught by an attached debugger, and if there is no such debugger, the system tries to find an exception handler and if that exception handler catches and dismisses the exception the thread resumes its normal execution path. If there are no such handlers found, the system generates the so-called second-chance exception with the same exception context to notify the attached debugger and, if it is not attached, a default thread exception handler usually saves a postmortem user dump.

We can get first-chance exception memory dumps with:

- DebugDiag
- ADPlus in crash mode from Debugging Tools for Windows
- Exception Monitor from User Mode Process Dumper package
- ProcDump[57]

Here is an example configuration rule for crashes in one of the previous Debug Diagnostic tool versions for TestDefaultDebugger[58] process (Unconfigured First Chance Exceptions option is set to Full Userdump):

[57] https://docs.microsoft.com/en-gb/sysinternals/downloads/procdump
[58] TestDefaultDebugger, Memory Dump Analysis Anthology, Volume 1, page 641

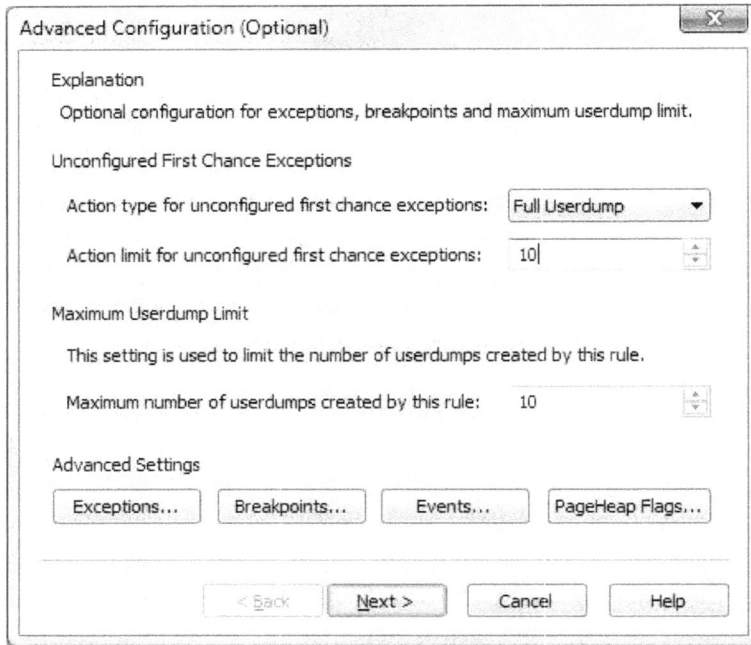

When we push the big crash button in TestDefaultDebugger dialog box, two crash dumps are saved, with the first and second-chance exceptions pointing to the same code:

```
Loading Dump File [C:\Program Files (x86)\DebugDiag\Logs\Crash rule for all instances of
TestDefaultDebugger.exe\TestDefaultDebugger__PID__4316__ Date__11_21_2007__Time_04_28_27PM__2__First
chance exception 0XC0000005.dmp]
User Mini Dump File with Full Memory: Only application data is available


Comment: 'Dump created by DbgHost. First chance exception 0XC0000005'
Symbol search path is: srv*c:\mss*http://msdl.microsoft.com/download/symbols
Executable search path is:
Windows Vista Version 6000 MP (2 procs) Free x86 compatible
Product: WinNt, suite: SingleUserTS
Debug session time: Wed Nov 21 16:28:27.000 2007 (GMT+0)
System Uptime: 0 days 23:45:34.711
Process Uptime: 0 days 0:01:09.000


This dump file has an exception of interest stored in it.
The stored exception information can be accessed via .ecxr.
(10dc.590): Access violation - code c0000005 (first/second chance not available)
eax=00000000 ebx=00000001 ecx=0017fe70 edx=00000000 esi=00425ae8 edi=0017fe70
eip=004014f0 esp=0017f898 ebp=0017f8a4 iopl=0         nv up ei ng nz ac pe cy
cs=0023 ss=002b ds=002b es=002b fs=0053 gs=002b          efl=00010297
TestDefaultDebugger!CTestDefaultDebuggerDlg::OnBnClickedButton1:
004014f0 c705000000000000000000 mov dword ptr ds:[0],0  ds:002b:00000000=????????
```

Loading Dump File [C:\Program Files (x86)\DebugDiag\Logs\Crash rule for all instances of
TestDefaultDebugger.exe\TestDefaultDebugger__PID__4316__ Date__11_21_2007__Time_04_28_34PM__693__
Second_Chance_Exception_C0000005.dmp]
User Mini Dump File with Full Memory: Only application data is available

Comment: 'Dump created by DbgHost. **Second_Chance_Exception_C0000005**'
Symbol search path is: srv*c:\mss*http://msdl.microsoft.com/download/symbols
Executable search path is:
Windows Vista Version 6000 MP (2 procs) Free x86 compatible
Product: WinNt, suite: SingleUserTS
Debug session time: Wed Nov 21 16:28:34.000 2007 (GMT+0)
System Uptime: 0 days 23:45:39.313
Process Uptime: 0 days 0:01:16.000

This dump file has an exception of interest stored in it.
The stored exception information can be accessed via .ecxr.
(10dc.590): Access violation - code c0000005 (first/second chance not available)
eax=00000000 ebx=00000001 ecx=0017fe70 edx=00000000 esi=00425ae8 edi=0017fe70
eip=004014f0 esp=0017f898 ebp=0017f8a4 iopl=0   nv up ei ng nz ac pe cy
cs=0023 ss=002b ds=002b es=002b fs=0053 gs=002b efl=00010297
TestDefaultDebugger!CTestDefaultDebuggerDlg::OnBnClickedButton1:
004014f0 c7050000000000000000 mov dword ptr ds:[0],0 ds:002b:00000000=????????

Effect Component

Some modules like drivers or runtime DLLs are always present after some action has happened. We call them **Effect Components**. It is the last thing to assume them to be the "Cause" components" or "Root Cause" or the so-called "culprit" components. Typical example is dump disk driver symbolic references found in **Execution Residue** (page 395) on the raw stack of a running bugchecking thread:

```
0: kd> !thread
THREAD fffffa8002bdebb0  Cid 03c4.03f0  Teb: 000007fffffde000 Win32Thread: fffff900c20f9810 RUNNING on
processor 0
IRP List:
    fffffa8002b986f0: (0006,0118) Flags: 00060000  Mdl: 00000000
Not impersonating
DeviceMap                   fffff88005346920
Owning Process              fffffa80035bec10        Image:         Application.exe
Attached Process            N/A         Image:         N/A
Wait Start TickCount        35246               Ticks: 7 (0:00:00:00.109)
Context Switch Count        1595                    LargeStack
UserTime                    00:00:00.000
KernelTime                  00:00:00.031
Win32 Start Address Application (0x0000000140002708)
Stack Init fffffa600495ddb0 Current fffffa600495d720
Base fffffa600495e000 Limit fffffa6004955000 Call 0
Priority 11 BasePriority 8 PriorityDecrement 1 IoPriority 2 PagePriority 5
Child-SP          RetAddr           : Call Site
fffffa60`0495d558 fffff800`0186e3ee : nt!KeBugCheckEx
fffffa60`0495d560 fffff800`0186d2cb : nt!KiBugCheckDispatch+0x6e
fffffa60`0495d6a0 fffffa60`03d5917a : nt!KiPageFault+0x20b (TrapFrame @ fffffa60`0495d6a0)
[...]


0: kd> dps fffffa6004955000 fffffa600495e000
fffffa60`04955000   00d4d0c8`00d4d0c8
fffffa60`04955008   00d4d0c8`00d4d0c8
fffffa60`04955010   00d4d0c8`00d4d0c8
[...]
fffffa60`0495c7e0   00000000`00000001
fffffa60`0495c7e8   fffffa60`02877f6f dump_SATA Driver!RecordExecutionHistory+0xcf
fffffa60`0495c7f0   fffffa80`024c05a8
fffffa60`0495c7f8   fffffa60`02869ad4 dump_dumpata!IdeDumpNotification+0x1a4
fffffa60`0495c800   fffffa60`0495cb00
fffffa60`0495c808   fffff800`0182ff34 nt!output_l+0x6c0
fffffa60`0495c810   fffffa60`02860110 crashdmp!StrBeginningDump
fffffa60`0495c818   fffffa60`0495cb00
fffffa60`0495c820   00000000`00000000
fffffa60`0495c828   fffffa60`02869b18 dump_dumpata!IdeDumpNotification+0x1e8
fffffa60`0495c830   00000000`00000000
fffffa60`0495c838   fffffa60`0495c8c0
fffffa60`0495c840   00000000`00000000
fffffa60`0495c848   fffffa60`00000024
fffffa60`0495c850   00000000`ffffffff
fffffa60`0495c858   00000000`00000000
fffffa60`0495c860   00000000`00000000
fffffa60`0495c868   fffffa60`0495cb00
fffffa60`0495c870   fffffa80`00000000
```

```
fffffa60`0495c878    00000000`00000000
fffffa60`0495c880    00000000`00000101
fffffa60`0495c888    fffffa60`02877f6f dump_SATA Driver!RecordExecutionHistory+0xcf
fffffa60`0495c890    fffffa60`0495cb0f
fffffa60`0495c898    fffff800`0182ff34 nt!output_l+0x6c0
fffffa60`0495c8a0    fffffa60`0495cb0f
fffffa60`0495c8a8    fffffa60`0495cb90
fffffa60`0495c8b0    00000000`00000040
fffffa60`0495c8b8    fffffa60`02877f6f dump_SATA Driver!RecordExecutionHistory+0xcf
fffffa60`0495c8c0    fffffa80`024c0728
fffffa60`0495c8c8    fffffa80`024c0728
fffffa60`0495c8d0    00000001`00000000
fffffa60`0495c8d8    fffffa60`00000026
fffffa60`0495c8e0    00000000`ffffffff
fffffa60`0495c8e8    00000000`00000000
fffffa60`0495c8f0    fffffa80`00000000
fffffa60`0495c8f8    fffffa60`0495cb90
fffffa60`0495c900    00000000`00000000
fffffa60`0495c908    fffffa60`02877f6f dump_SATA Driver!RecordExecutionHistory+0xcf
fffffa60`0495c910    00000000`00000000
fffffa60`0495c918    fffffa60`02877f6f dump_SATA Driver!RecordExecutionHistory+0xcf
fffffa60`0495c920    fffff880`05311010
fffffa60`0495c928    00000000`00000002
fffffa60`0495c930    fffffa60`02875094 dump_SATA_Driver!AhciAdapterControl
fffffa60`0495c938    fffffa80`024c6018
fffffa60`0495c940    fffffa80`024c0728
fffffa60`0495c948    fffffa60`02877f6f dump_SATA Driver!RecordExecutionHistory+0xcf
fffffa60`0495c950    fffffa80`024c0728
fffffa60`0495c958    00000000`00000000
fffffa60`0495c960    fffffa60`0495ca18
fffffa60`0495c968    00000000`00000000
fffffa60`0495c970    fffffa80`024c0728
fffffa60`0495c978    fffffa60`02876427 dump_SATA Driver!AhciHwInitialize+0x337
fffffa60`0495c980    fffffa80`024c0be6
fffffa60`0495c988    fffffa60`0286a459 dump_dumpata!IdeDumpWaitOnRequest+0x79
fffffa60`0495c990    00000000`00000000
fffffa60`0495c998    00000000`0000023a
fffffa60`0495c9a0    20474e55`534d4153
fffffa60`0495c9a8    204a4831`36314448
fffffa60`0495c9b0    20202020`20202020
fffffa60`0495c9b8    20202020`20202020
fffffa60`0495c9c0    fffffa80`024c05a8
fffffa60`0495c9c8    fffffa60`02869b18 dump_dumpata!IdeDumpNotification+0x1e8
fffffa60`0495c9d0    00000000`00000000
fffffa60`0495c9d8    fffffa60`0495ca60
fffffa60`0495c9e0    00000000`00000001
fffffa60`0495c9e8    fffffa60`02869396 dump_dumpata!IdeDumpMiniportChannelInitialize+0x236
fffffa60`0495c9f0    fffffa80`024c05a8
fffffa60`0495c9f8    fffffa60`02869ad4 dump_dumpata!IdeDumpNotification+0x1a4
fffffa60`0495ca00    00000000`00000000
fffffa60`0495ca08    fffffa60`0495ca90
fffffa60`0495ca10    00000000`00000001
fffffa60`0495ca18    00000001`00000038
fffffa60`0495ca20    00000000`10010000
fffffa60`0495ca28    00000000`00000003
fffffa60`0495ca30    fffffa80`024c05a8
```

```
fffffa60`0495ca38    fffffa60`0286a954 dump_dumpata!AtaPortGetPhysicalAddress+0x2c
fffffa60`0495ca40    fffffa80`024c0728
fffffa60`0495ca48    fffffa60`02877f6f dump_SATA Driver!RecordExecutionHistory+0xcf
fffffa60`0495ca50    00000000`00000001
fffffa60`0495ca58    0000003f`022a8856
fffffa60`0495ca60    fffffa80`0000000c
fffffa60`0495ca68    fffffa80`024c0728
fffffa60`0495ca70    00000000`00000200
fffffa60`0495ca78    fffffa60`02877f6f dump_SATA Driver!RecordExecutionHistory+0xcf
fffffa60`0495ca80    fffffa80`024c0728
fffffa60`0495ca88    ffff6226`4f5f3eb8
fffffa60`0495ca90    00000000`00000010
fffffa60`0495ca98    fffffa60`02860370 crashdmp!Context+0x30
fffffa60`0495caa0    fffffa80`024c05a8
fffffa60`0495caa8    fffffa60`02875a0d dump_SATA Driver!AhciHwStartIo+0x69d
fffffa60`0495cab0    fffffa80`024c0728
fffffa60`0495cab8    00000000`00000000
fffffa60`0495cac0    00000000`00000001
fffffa60`0495cac8    fffff800`018f3dfc nt!DisplayCharacter+0x5c
fffffa60`0495cad0    00000000`00000000
fffffa60`0495cad8    fffffa60`02877f6f dump_SATA Driver!RecordExecutionHistory+0xcf
fffffa60`0495cae0    00000000`00010000
fffffa60`0495cae8    00000000`00000000
fffffa60`0495caf0    fffffa60`0495cd10
fffffa60`0495caf8    fffffa60`0495cc00
fffffa60`0495cb00    fffffa80`024c01c0
fffffa60`0495cb08    fffffa60`02875c3f dump_SATA Driver!AhciHwInterrupt+0x2b
fffffa60`0495cb10    fffffa80`024c05a8
fffffa60`0495cb18    00000000`00000000
fffffa60`0495cb20    00000000`00000000
fffffa60`0495cb28    fffff800`01d406c9 hal!KeStallExecutionProcessor+0x25
fffffa60`0495cb30    00000000`00010000
fffffa60`0495cb38    00000000`00000000
fffffa60`0495cb40    fffffa60`0495cd10
fffffa60`0495cb48    fffffa60`0495cc00
fffffa60`0495cb50    00000000`00000000
fffffa60`0495cb58    fffffa60`0286a429 dump_dumpata!IdeDumpWaitOnRequest+0x49
fffffa60`0495cb60    fffffa60`02860370 crashdmp!Context+0x30
fffffa60`0495cb68    00000000`d8bda325
fffffa60`0495cb70    00000000`00000000
fffffa60`0495cb78    00000000`0000033e
fffffa60`0495cb80    00000000`00000000
fffffa60`0495cb88    fffffa60`028694d2 dump_dumpata!IdeDumpWritePending+0xee
fffffa60`0495cb90    fffffa80`024c0000
fffffa60`0495cb98    fffffa80`024c01c0
fffffa60`0495cba0    00000000`00000000
fffffa60`0495cba8    00000000`00000000
fffffa60`0495cbb0    fffffa80`024c01c0
fffffa60`0495cbb8    fffffa80`01e3c740
fffffa60`0495cbc0    00000000`00010000
fffffa60`0495cbc8    00000000`00000000
fffffa60`0495cbd0    00000000`0c01f000
fffffa60`0495cbd8    fffffa60`0285bca9 crashdmp!WritePageSpanToDisk+0x181
fffffa60`0495cbe0    00000000`83d81000
fffffa60`0495cbe8    00000000`00000000
fffffa60`0495cbf0    fffffa60`02860370 crashdmp!Context+0x30
```

```
fffffa60`0495cbf8  00000000`00000002
[...]
fffffa60`0495ccd0  00000000`0000c01d
fffffa60`0495ccd8  fffffa60`02860370 crashdmp!Context+0x30
fffffa60`0495cce0  00000000`0000bf80
fffffa60`0495cce8  00000000`00000001
fffffa60`0495ccf0  00000000`00000000
fffffa60`0495ccf8  fffffa80`01e353d0
fffffa60`0495cd00  fffffa80`01e353f8
fffffa60`0495cd08  fffffa60`0285bacc crashdmp!WriteFullDump+0x70
fffffa60`0495cd10  00000002`3a3d8000
fffffa60`0495cd18  00000000`0000c080
fffffa60`0495cd20  fffffa80`00000000
fffffa60`0495cd28  fffffa60`0285c9c0 crashdmp!CrashdmpWriteRoutine
fffffa60`0495cd30  fffff880`05311010
fffffa60`0495cd38  00000000`00000002
fffffa60`0495cd40  fffffa60`0495cf70
fffffa60`0495cd48  00000000`00000000
fffffa60`0495cd50  fffffa60`02860370 crashdmp!Context+0x30
fffffa60`0495cd58  fffffa60`0285b835 crashdmp!DumpWrite+0xc5
fffffa60`0495cd60  00000000`00000000
fffffa60`0495cd68  00000000`0000000f
fffffa60`0495cd70  00000000`00000001
fffffa60`0495cd78  fffffa60`00000001
fffffa60`0495cd80  fffffa80`02bdebb0
fffffa60`0495cd88  fffffa60`0285b153 crashdmp!CrashdmpWrite+0x57
fffffa60`0495cd90  00000000`00000000
fffffa60`0495cd98  fffffa60`028602f0 crashdmp!StrInitPortDriver
fffffa60`0495cda0  00000000`00000000
fffffa60`0495cda8  fffffa60`02860a00 crashdmp!ContextCopy
fffffa60`0495cdb0  00000000`00000000
fffffa60`0495cdb8  fffff800`01902764 nt!IoWriteCrashDump+0x3f4
fffffa60`0495cdc0  fffffa60`0495ce00
fffffa60`0495cdc8  00000028`00000025
fffffa60`0495cdd0  fffff800`018afd40 nt! ?? ::FNODOBFM::`string'
fffffa60`0495cdd8  00000000`000000d1
fffffa60`0495cde0  fffff880`05311010
fffffa60`0495cde8  00000000`00000002
fffffa60`0495cdf0  00000000`00000000
fffffa60`0495cdf8  fffffa60`03d5917a
fffffa60`0495ce00  202a2a2a`0a0d0a0d
fffffa60`0495ce08  7830203a`504f5453
fffffa60`0495ce10  31443030`30303030
fffffa60`0495ce18  46464646`78302820
fffffa60`0495ce20  31333530`30383846
fffffa60`0495ce28  fffff800`018f5f83 nt!VidDisplayString+0x143
fffffa60`0495ce30  30303030`30300030
fffffa60`0495ce38  2c323030`30303030
fffffa60`0495ce40  30303030`30307830
fffffa60`0495ce48  30303030`30303030
fffffa60`0495ce50  46464678`302c3030
fffffa60`0495ce58  fffff800`018fe040 nt!KiInvokeBugCheckEntryCallbacks+0x80
fffffa60`0495ce60  fffffa80`02bdebb0
fffffa60`0495ce68  fffff800`01921d52 nt!InbvDisplayString+0x72
fffffa60`0495ce70  fffff880`05311000
fffffa60`0495ce78  fffff800`01d406c9 hal!KeStallExecutionProcessor+0x25
```

```
fffffa60`0495ce80    00000000`00000001
fffffa60`0495ce88    00000000`0000000a
fffffa60`0495ce90    fffffa60`03d5917a
fffffa60`0495ce98    00000000`40000082
fffffa60`0495cea0    00000000`00000001
fffffa60`0495cea8    fffff800`01922c3e nt!KeBugCheck2+0x92e
fffffa60`0495ceb0    fffff800`000000d1
fffffa60`0495ceb8    00000000`000004d0
fffffa60`0495cec0    fffff800`01a43640 nt!KiProcessorBlock
fffffa60`0495cec8    00000000`0000000a
fffffa60`0495ced0    fffffa60`03d5917a
fffffa60`0495ced8    fffffa60`0495cf70
fffffa60`0495cee0    fffffa80`02bdebb0
fffffa60`0495cee8    00000000`00000000
fffffa60`0495cef0    00000000`00000000
fffffa60`0495cef8    fffffa80`02bdebb0
fffffa60`0495cf00    00000000`c21a6d00
fffffa60`0495cf08    00000000`00000000
fffffa60`0495cf10    fffff800`0198e7a0 nt!KiInitialPCR+0x2a0
fffffa60`0495cf18    fffff800`0198e680 nt!KiInitialPCR+0x180
fffffa60`0495cf20    fffffa80`02bb7320
fffffa60`0495cf28    00000000`00000000
fffffa60`0495cf30    00000000`00000000
fffffa60`0495cf38    fffff960`00000003
[...]
fffffa60`0495d050    00000000`00000001
fffffa60`0495d058    00000000`83360018
fffffa60`0495d060    fffffa80`02b3ee40
fffffa60`0495d068    fffff800`0186e650 nt!KeBugCheckEx
fffffa60`0495d070    00000000`00000000
fffffa60`0495d078    00000000`00000000
fffffa60`0495d080    00000000`00000000
fffffa60`0495d088    00000000`00000000
fffffa60`0495d090    00000000`00000000
fffffa60`0495d098    00000000`00000000
fffffa60`0495d0a0    00000000`00000000
[...]
```

If BSOD was reported after installing new drivers, we should not suspect *SATA_Driver* package here because its components would almost always be present on any bugcheck thread as referenced after a bugcheck cause. Their presence is the "effect". This example might seem trivial and pointless, but we have seen some memory dump analysis conclusions based on the reversal of causes and effects.

Embedded Comments

Such comments in dump files are useful to record external information like the reason for saving a memory dump, a tool used to do that, and some pre-analysis and monitoring data that might help or guide in the future analysis. Comments are not widely used, but some examples include **Manual Dump** (page 710), **False Positive Dump** (page 419) patterns, and process and thread CPU consumption comments in dump files saved by Sysinternals ProcDump[59] tool. Such comments may not be necessarily saved by *IDebugClient2 :: WriteDumpFile2* function but any buffer saved in memory that is accessible later from a dump file will do as was easily demonstrated by the SystemDump[60] tool that allowed embedding comments of arbitrary complexity.

---

[59] https://docs.microsoft.com/en-gb/sysinternals/downloads/procdump
[60] SystemDump, Memory Dump Analysis Anthology, Volume 1, page 646

Empty Stack Trace

Here we might need to do manual stack trace reconstruction[61] like shown in the following example:

```
0:002> ~2s
eax=00000070 ebx=0110fb94 ecx=00000010 edx=005725d8 esi=0110fe58 edi=00000d80
eip=7c82847c esp=0110efe0 ebp=0110eff0 iopl=0 nv up ei pl zr na pe nc
cs=001b ss=0023 ds=0023 es=0023 fs=003b gs=0000 efl=00000246
ntdll!KiFastSystemCallRet:
7c82847c c3 ret
```

```
0:002> kL
ChildEBP RetAddr
0110efdc 00000000 ntdll!KiFastSystemCallRet
```

```
0:002> !teb
TEB at   7ffdc000
ExceptionList:    0110f980
StackBase:              01110000
StackLimit:             0110d000
SubSystemTib:           00000000
FiberData:              00001e00
ArbitraryUserPointer:   00000000
Self:                   7ffdc000
EnvironmentPointer:     00000000
ClientId:               00000b04 . 00000bd0
RpcHandle:              00000000
Tls Storage:            00000000
PEB Address:            7ffda000
LastErrorValue: 87
LastStatusValue:        c000000d
Count Owned Locks:      0
HardErrorMode:   0
```

```
0:002> dps 0110d000 01110000
0110d000 00000000
0110d004 00000000
[...]
0110f640 0110f64c
0110f644 02b91ea8
0110f648 00001000
0110f64c 00000004
0110f650 0110f6f0
0110f654 0374669d DbgHelp!WriteFullMemory+0x3cd
0110f658 ffffffff
0110f65c 0110d000
0110f660 00000000
[...]
```

---

[61] Manual Stack Trace Reconstruction, Memory Dump Analysis Anthology, Volume 1, page 157

```
0110f6ac 00040004
0110f6b0 7ffe0000 SharedUserData
0110f6b4 00000000
0110f6b8 00001000
0110f6bc 00000000
0110f6c0 0480f5c0
0110f6c4 00000000
0110f6c8 04c4a000
0110f6cc 00000000
0110f6d0 000003c7
0110f6d4 00000000
0110f6d8 00023b17
0110f6dc 00000000
0110f6e0 01110000
0110f6e4 00000000
0110f6e8 0099f000
0110f6ec 00000000
0110f6f0 0110f704
0110f6f4 037469d6 DbgHelp!WriteDumpData+0x206
0110f6f8 0110f738
0110f6fc 0110f7b0
0110f700 00000000
0110f704 0110f868
0110f708 03747449 DbgHelp!MiniDumpProvideDump+0x359
0110f70c 0110f738
[...]
0110ff24 0000000a
0110ff28 33017f51 ModuleA!Run+0xde
0110ff2c 00000001
0110ff30 0110ff74
0110ff34 00f08898
0110ff38 00000000
0110ff3c 00f082a8
0110ff40 00000000
0110ff44 00000001
0110ff48 33017e33 ModuleA!ThreadProc+0x2c
0110ff4c a9b21e1e
0110ff50 00000000
0110ff54 00000000
0110ff58 00f08898
0110ff5c 0110ff4c
0110ff60 0110ffac
0110ff64 0110ff9c
0110ff68 33054245
0110ff6c 9ba52ad2
0110ff70 00000000
0110ff74 0110ffac
0110ff78 78543433 msvcr90!_endthreadex+0x44
0110ff7c 00f082a8
0110ff80 a9b2b0d3
0110ff84 00000000
0110ff88 00000000
0110ff8c 00f08898
0110ff90 0110ff80
0110ff94 0110ff80
0110ff98 0110ffdc
```

```
0110ff9c 0110ffdc
0110ffa0 7858cf5e msvcr90!_except_handler4
0110ffa4 d0f887df
0110ffa8 00000000
0110ffac 0110ffb8
0110ffb0 785434c7 msvcr90!_endthreadex+0xd8
0110ffb4 00000000
0110ffb8 0110ffec
0110ffbc 77e6482f kernel32!BaseThreadStart+0x34
0110ffc0 00f08898
0110ffc4 00000000
0110ffc8 00000000
0110ffcc 00f08898
0110ffd0 00000000
0110ffd4 0110ffc4
0110ffd8 80833bcc
0110ffdc ffffffff
0110ffe0 77e61a60 kernel32!_except_handler3
0110ffe4 77e64838 kernel32!`string'+0x98
0110ffe8 00000000
0110ffec 00000000
0110fff0 00000000
0110fff4 7854345e msvcr90!_endthreadex+0x6f
0110fff8 00f08898
0110fffc 00000000
01110000 00000130


0:002> k L=0110f650 0110f650 0110f650
ChildEBP RetAddr
WARNING: Frame IP not in any known module. Following frames may be wrong.
0110f650 0374669d 0x110f650
0110f6f0 037469d6 DbgHelp!WriteFullMemory+0x3cd
0110f704 03747449 DbgHelp!WriteDumpData+0x206
0110f868 03747662 DbgHelp!MiniDumpProvideDump+0x359
0110f8dc 33050dd9 DbgHelp!MiniDumpWriteDump+0x1b2
[...]
0110fdfc 33031726 ModuleA!WriteExceptionMiniDump+0x50
0110fea0 33018c81 ModuleA!ThreadHung+0x6c
[...]
0110ff44 33017e33 ModuleA!Run+0xde
00000000 00000000 ModuleA!ThreadProc+0x2c
```

Comments

One of the asked questions:

Q. Why does "**k**" even need the instruction pointer to walk the stack? I've always seen it set to EBP and ESP like this which does not make sense to me.

A. We think it needs EIP to show the top stack frame correctly pointing to the currently executing instruction. In our pattern example, it does not matter.

Environment Hint

This pattern is useful for inconsistent dumps or incomplete supporting information. It provides information about environment variables for troubleshooting suggestions such as product elimination for testing purposes and necessary upgrade, for example:

```
0: kd> !peb
PEB at 7ffd7000
InheritedAddressSpace:    No
ReadImageFileExecOptions:        Yes
BeingDebugged:            No
ImageBaseAddress:                01000000
Ldr 7c8897e0
Ldr.Initialized:                 Yes
Ldr.InInitializationOrderModuleList:     00081f18 . 000f9e88
Ldr.InLoadOrderModuleList:               00081eb0 . 000f9e78
Ldr.InMemoryOrderModuleList:             00081eb8 . 000f9e80
Base     TimeStamp                   Module
1000000  45d6a03c Feb 17 06:27:08 2007 C:\WINNT\system32\svchost.exe
7c800000 49900d60 Feb 09 11:02:56 2009 C:\WINNT\system32\ntdll.dll
[...]
SubSystemData:           00000000
ProcessHeap:                     00080000
ProcessParameters:               00020000
WindowTitle: 'C:\WINNT\system32\svchost.exe'
ImageFile: 'C:\WINNT\system32\svchost.exe'
CommandLine: 'C:\WINNT\system32\svchost.exe -k rpcss'
DllPath: [...]
Environment:                     00010000
ALLUSERSPROFILE=C:\Documents and Settings\All Users
[...]
PROTECTIONDIR=C:\Documents and Settings\All Users\Application Data\3rdPartyAntivirus\Protection
[...]
Path= [...]
```

Comments

We can get environment hints from all processes in a complete memory dump by using this command:

```
!for_each_process ".process /r /p @#Process; !peb"
```

Error Reporting Fault

This pattern is about faults in error reporting infrastructure. The latter should be guarded against such faults to avoid recursion. Here is a summary example of such a pattern on Windows platforms that involve Windows Error Reporting (WER).

In a complete memory dump, we notice thousands of *WerFault.exe* processes:

```
0: kd> !process 0 0
[...]
PROCESS fffffa8058010380
SessionId: 2 Cid: 488f0 Peb: 7efdf000 ParentCid: 27cb8
DirBase: 25640c000 ObjectTable: fffff8a06cd2ac50 HandleCount: 54.
Image: WerFault.exe

PROCESS fffffa805bbd5970
SessionId: 2 Cid: 4801c Peb: 7efdf000 ParentCid: 27cb8
DirBase: 2c3f69000 ObjectTable: fffff8a040563af0 HandleCount: 54.
Image: WerFault.exe

PROCESS fffffa8078aec060
SessionId: 2 Cid: 3feac Peb: 7efdf000 ParentCid: 488f0
DirBase: abd200000 ObjectTable: fffff8a07851a0a0 HandleCount: 59.
Image: WerFault.exe

PROCESS fffffa805bbe9a10
SessionId: 2 Cid: 3d8b8 Peb: 7efdf000 ParentCid: 4801c
DirBase: 261f91000 ObjectTable: fffff8a02d864d40 HandleCount: 56.
Image: WerFault.exe

PROCESS fffffa805bd29060
SessionId: 2 Cid: 1142c Peb: 7efdf000 ParentCid: 3feac
DirBase: 429fb3000 ObjectTable: fffff8a0355b42e0 HandleCount: 58.
Image: WerFault.exe

PROCESS fffffa8053d853d0
SessionId: 2 Cid: 1fc4c Peb: 7efdf000 ParentCid: 3d8b8
DirBase: 714371000 ObjectTable: fffff8a01cb6bba0 HandleCount: 58.
Image: WerFault.exe
[...]
```

Each process has only one thread running through WOW64 modules (**Virtualized Process** pattern, page 1185), so we get its 32-bit stack trace:

```
0: kd> !process fffffa8075c21b30 3f
[...]
THREAD fffffa807c183b60 Cid 2d3c8.4334c Teb: 000000007efdb000 Win32Thread: fffff900c3f71010 WAIT:
(UserRequest) UserMode Non-Alertable
[...]
```

```
0: kd> .load wow64exts

0: kd> .process /r /p fffffa8075c21b30
Implicit process is now fffffa80`75c21b30
Loading User Symbols
Loading Wow64 Symbols

0: kd> .thread /w fffffa807c183b60
Implicit thread is now fffffa80`7c183b60
x86 context set

0: kd:x86> k
*** Stack trace for last set context - .thread/.cxr resets it
ChildEBP RetAddr
000bf474 77080bdd ntdll!ZwWaitForMultipleObjects+0x15
000bf510 76bb1a2c KERNELBASE!WaitForMultipleObjectsEx+0x100
000bf558 76bb4208 kernel32!WaitForMultipleObjectsExImplementation+0xe0
000bf574 76bd80a4 kernel32!WaitForMultipleObjects+0x18
000bf5e0 76bd7f63 kernel32!WerpReportFaultInternal+0x186
000bf5f4 76bd7858 kernel32!WerpReportFault+0x70
000bf604 76bd77d7 kernel32!BasepReportFault+0x20
000bf690 776674df kernel32!UnhandledExceptionFilter+0x1af
000bf698 776673bc ntdll!__RtlUserThreadStart+0x62
000bf6ac 77667261 ntdll!_EH4_CallFilterFunc+0x12
000bf6d4 7764b459 ntdll!_except_handler4+0x8e
000bf6f8 7764b42b ntdll!ExecuteHandler2+0x26
000bf71c 7764b3ce ntdll!ExecuteHandler+0x24
000bf7a8 77600133 ntdll!RtlDispatchException+0x127
000bf7b4 000bf7c0 ntdll!KiUserExceptionDispatcher+0xf
WARNING: Frame IP not in any known module. Following frames may be wrong.
000bfb00 77629ef2 0xbf7c0
[...]
```

We find exception processing (**Exception Stack Trace** pattern, page 386) and the binary value in the stack trace (return address belongs to the stack region range). This thread is waiting for another process, and it is *WerFault.exe* too:

```
0: kd:x86> .effmach AMD64

0: kd> !process fffffa8075c21b30 3f
[...]
THREAD fffffa807c183b60 Cid 2d3c8.4334c Teb: 000000007efdb000 Win32Thread: fffff900c3f71010 WAIT:
(UserRequest) UserMode Non-Alertable
    fffffa80809c44e0 ProcessObject
[...]

0: kd> !process fffffa80809c44e0
PROCESS fffffa80809c44e0
SessionId: 2 Cid: 33844 Peb: 7efdf000 ParentCid: 2d3c8
DirBase: 9c53f000 ObjectTable: fffff8a0423d4170 HandleCount: 978.
Image: WerFault.exe
[...]
```

We go back to our original *WerFault* process, and in its PEB data we find it was called to report a fault from another process with PID 0n189240:

```
0: kd> !process fffffa8075c21b30 3f
[...]
CommandLine: 'C:\Windows\SysWOW64\WerFault.exe -u -p 189240 -s 3888'
[...]
```

And it is *WerFault.exe* too:

```
0: kd> !process 0n189240
Searching for Process with Cid == 2e338

PROCESS fffffa8078b659e0
SessionId: 2 Cid: 2e338 Peb: 7efdf000 ParentCid: 47608
DirBase: 201796000 ObjectTable: fffff8a02e664380 HandleCount: 974.
Image: WerFault.exe
[...]
```

So we see a chain of *WerFault.exe* processes each processing a fault in the previous one. So there should be the first fault somewhere which we can find in **Stack Trace Collection** (page 1052, including 32-bit stack traces for this example[62]) unless that exception stack trace data was **Paged Out** (page 864) due to insufficient memory occupied by *WerFault.exe* processes.

---

[62] Complete Stack Traces from x64 System, Memory Dump Analysis Anthology, Volume 5, page 30

Evental Dumps

One of the customers of Software Diagnostics Services[63] submitted memory dumps saved by DebugDiag to accompany software logs for the analysis of sudden process exit. We didn't request such memory dumps and initially dismissed them. However, during software log analysis we decided to look at **Adjoint Spaces**[64] to see whether there was some additional information in stack traces. We found out that those dumps were saved on each thread exit event. Since other threads were either waiting or **Active Threads** (page 69)**,** their analysis gave clues of process behavior before process exit. For example, we found ALPC **Wait Chain** (page 1214) to **Coupled Process** (page 162). The latter prompted us to analyze **Coupled Activities**[65] in the software log and diagnose the possible problem there. Since saving memory dumps on thread creation and exit can be a useful technique we decided to add **Evental Dumps** memory analysis pattern to our pattern catalog.

To illustrate this pattern we show **Stack Trace Collection** (page 1052) from *notepad.exe*. This process usually has just one thread. But, if we try to open a Print dialog the number of threads increases up to 12.

We attach WinDbg to *notepad.exe* process and set up debugging event filter (Debug \ Event Filters... menu) for Create Thread event with a command line as shown in this picture:

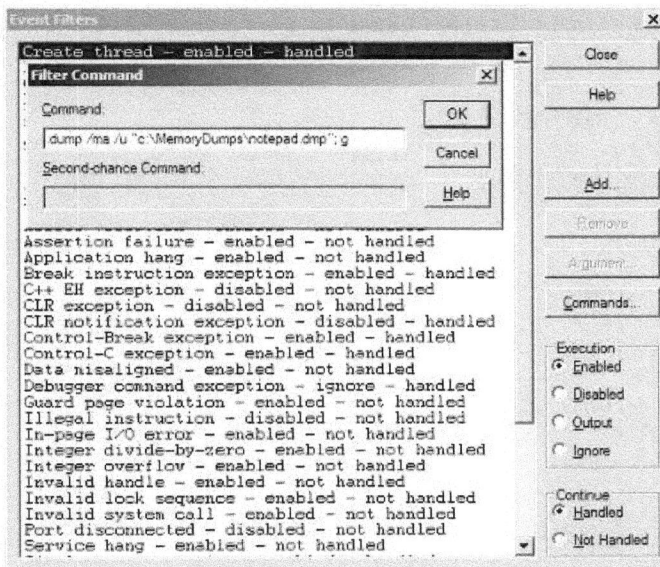

We then resume execution using **g** command and switch to Notepad. There we first open File \ Page Setup... dialog. We observe that a memory dump is saved. Then we open File \ Print... dialog and notice the creation 11 more process memory dumps:

[63] http://www.PatternDiagnostics.com/
[64] Memory Dump Analysis Anthology, Volume 8b, page 67
[65] Memory Dump Analysis Anthology, Volume 9a, page 92

notepad_09a8_2015-10-25_18-17-20-150_1344.dmp	25/10/2015 18:18	154,645 KB
notepad_09a8_2015-10-25_18-18-00-630_1344.dmp	25/10/2015 18:18	134,886 KB
notepad_09a8_2015-10-25_18-16-58-514_1344.dmp	25/10/2015 18:17	95,159 KB
notepad_09a8_2015-10-25_18-16-45-712_1344.dmp	25/10/2015 18:17	73,716 KB
notepad_09a8_2015-10-25_18-16-41-612_1344.dmp	25/10/2015 18:16	70,303 KB
notepad_09a8_2015-10-25_18-16-44-042_1344.dmp	25/10/2015 18:16	70,345 KB
notepad_09a8_2015-10-25_18-16-45-602_1344.dmp	25/10/2015 18:16	70,960 KB
notepad_09a8_2015-10-25_18-16-41-162_1344.dmp	25/10/2015 18:16	68,832 KB
notepad_09a8_2015-10-25_18-16-41-302_1344.dmp	25/10/2015 18:16	70,127 KB
notepad_09a8_2015-10-25_18-16-41-402_1344.dmp	25/10/2015 18:16	70,127 KB
notepad_09a8_2015-10-25_18-16-41-502_1344.dmp	25/10/2015 18:16	70,225 KB
notepad_09a8_2015-10-25_18-16-11-760_1344.dmp	25/10/2015 18:16	51,364 KB

We now show stack traces from these dumps where we use **~*kc** WinDbg command to minimize the amount of inessential for our purposes output:

// 1st dump

```
. 0 Id: 1344.1ca4 Suspend: 1 Teb: 000007ff`fffdd000 Unfrozen
# Call Site
00 ntdll!NtAlertThread
01 ntdll!TppWaiterEnqueueTransition
02 ntdll!TppWaitpSet
03 ntdll!TpSetWait
04 ntdll!TppTimerpInitTimerQueueQueue
05 ntdll!TppTimerpAllocTimerQueue
06 ntdll!TppTimerpAcquirePoolTimerQueue
07 ntdll!TppTimerAlloc
08 ntdll!TpAllocTimer
09 KERNELBASE!CreateThreadpoolTimer
0a rpcrt4!RPC_THREAD_POOL::CreateTimer
0b rpcrt4!GarbageCollectionNeeded
0c rpcrt4!LRPC_CASSOCIATION::RemoveReference
0d rpcrt4!LRPC_CCALL::`vector deleting destructor'
0e rpcrt4!LRPC_CCALL::FreeBuffer
0f rpcrt4!Ndr64pClientFinally
10 rpcrt4!NdrpClientCall3
11 rpcrt4!NdrClientCall3
12 sechost!LsaLookupClose
13 sechost!LookupAccountNameInternal
14 sechost!LookupAccountNameLocalW
15 rpcrt4!RpcpLookupAccountNameDirect
16 rpcrt4!RpcpLookupAccountName
17 rpcrt4!LRPC_BASE_BINDING_HANDLE::SetAuthInformation
18 rpcrt4!LRPC_BINDING_HANDLE::SetAuthInformation
19 rpcrt4!RpcBindingSetAuthInfoExW
1a winspool!STRING_HANDLE_bind
1b rpcrt4!GenericHandleMgr
1c rpcrt4!ExplicitBindHandleMgr
1d rpcrt4!Ndr64pClientSetupTransferSyntax
1e rpcrt4!NdrpClientCall3
1f rpcrt4!NdrClientCall3
20 winspool!RpcSplOpenPrinter
```

```
21 winspool!OpenPrinterRPC
22 winspool!OpenPrinter2W
23 comdlg32!PrintOpenPrinter
24 comdlg32!PrintDlgX
25 comdlg32!PageSetupDlgX
26 comdlg32!PageSetupDlgW
27 notepad!NPCommand
28 notepad!NPWndProc
29 user32!UserCallWinProcCheckWow
2a user32!DispatchMessageWorker
2b notepad!WinMain
2c notepad!DisplayNonGenuineDlgWorker
2d kernel32!BaseThreadInitThunk
2e ntdll!RtlUserThreadStart


1 Id: 1344.1ab0 Suspend: 1 Teb: 000007ff`fffdb000 Unfrozen
# Call Site
00 ntdll!RtlUserThreadStart
```

// 2nd dump

```
. 0 Id: 1344.1ca4 Suspend: 1 Teb: 000007ff`fffdd000 Unfrozen
# Call Site
00 ntdll!ZwOpenKeyEx
01 kernel32!LocalBaseRegOpenKey
02 kernel32!RegOpenKeyExInternalW
03 kernel32!RegOpenKeyExW
04 rpcrt4!Server2003NegotiateDisable
05 rpcrt4!IsBindTimeFeatureNegotiationDisabled
06 rpcrt4!OSF_CCONNECTION::SendBindPacket
07 rpcrt4!OSF_CCONNECTION::ActuallyDoBinding
08 rpcrt4!OSF_CCONNECTION::OpenConnectionAndBind
09 rpcrt4!OSF_CCALL::BindToServer
0a rpcrt4!OSF_BINDING_HANDLE::InitCCallWithAssociation
0b rpcrt4!OSF_BINDING_HANDLE::AllocateCCall
0c rpcrt4!OSF_BINDING_HANDLE::NegotiateTransferSyntax
0d rpcrt4!I_RpcNegotiateTransferSyntax
0e rpcrt4!Ndr64pClientSetupTransferSyntax
0f rpcrt4!NdrpClientCall3
10 rpcrt4!NdrClientCall3
11 srvcli!NetShareEnum
12 ntshrui!CShareCache::RefreshNoCritSec
13 ntshrui!CShareCache::Refresh
14 ntshrui!DllMain
15 ntdll!RtlRunOnceExecuteOnce
16 kernel32!InitOnceExecuteOnce
17 ntshrui!DllGetClassObject
18 ole32!CClassCache::CDllPathEntry::DllGetClassObject
19 ole32!CClassCache::CDllFnPtrMoniker::BindToObjectNoSwitch
1a ole32!CClassCache::GetClassObject
1b ole32!CServerContextActivator::CreateInstance
1c ole32!ActivationPropertiesIn::DelegateCreateInstance
1d ole32!CApartmentActivator::CreateInstance
1e ole32!CProcessActivator::CCICallback
1f ole32!CProcessActivator::AttemptActivation
```

```
20 ole32!CProcessActivator::ActivateByContext
21 ole32!CProcessActivator::CreateInstance
22 ole32!ActivationPropertiesIn::DelegateCreateInstance
23 ole32!CClientContextActivator::CreateInstance
24 ole32!ActivationPropertiesIn::DelegateCreateInstance
25 ole32!ICoCreateInstanceEx
26 ole32!CoCreateInstance
27 shell32!_SHCoCreateInstance
28 shell32!SHExtCoCreateInstance
29 shell32!DCA_SHExtCoCreateInstance
2a shell32!CFSIconOverlayManager::_s_LoadIconOverlayIdentifiers
2b shell32!CFSIconOverlayManager::CreateInstance
2c shell32!IconOverlayManagerInit
2d shell32!GetIconOverlayManager
2e shell32!FileIconInit
2f shell32!Shell_GetImageLists
30 comdlg32!CPrintDialog::CPrintDialog
31 comdlg32!Print_GeneralDlgProc
32 user32!UserCallDlgProcCheckWow
33 user32!DefDlgProcWorker
34 user32!InternalCreateDialog
35 user32!CreateDialogIndirectParamAorW
36 user32!CreateDialogIndirectParamW
37 comctl32!_CreatePageDialog
38 comctl32!_CreatePage
39 comctl32!PageChange
3a comctl32!InitPropSheetDlg
3b comctl32!PropSheetDlgProc
3c user32!UserCallDlgProcCheckWow
3d user32!DefDlgProcWorker
3e user32!InternalCreateDialog
3f user32!CreateDialogIndirectParamAorW
40 user32!CreateDialogIndirectParamW
41 comctl32!_RealPropertySheet
42 comctl32!_PropertySheet
43 comdlg32!Print_InvokePropertySheets
44 comdlg32!PrintDlgExX
45 comdlg32!PrintDlgExW
46 notepad!GetPrinterDCviaDialog
47 notepad!PrintIt
48 notepad!NPCommand
49 notepad!NPWndProc
4a user32!UserCallWinProcCheckWow
4b user32!DispatchMessageWorker
4c notepad!WinMain
4d notepad!DisplayNonGenuineDlgWorker
4e kernel32!BaseThreadInitThunk
4f ntdll!RtlUserThreadStart

1 Id: 1344.1ab0 Suspend: 1 Teb: 000007ff`fffdb000 Unfrozen
# Call Site
00 ntdll!NtWaitForMultipleObjects
01 ntdll!TppWaiterpThread
02 kernel32!BaseThreadInitThunk
03 ntdll!RtlUserThreadStart
```

```
2 Id: 1344.1638 Suspend: 1 Teb: 000007ff`fffd9000 Unfrozen
# Call Site
00 ntdll!RtlUserThreadStart
```

// 3rd dump: we see 2 threads start at the same time

```
. 0 Id: 1344.1ca4 Suspend: 1 Teb: 000007ff`fffdd000 Unfrozen
# Call Site
00 ntdll!RtlCompareMemoryUlong
01 ntdll!RtlpAllocateHeap
02 ntdll!RtlAllocateHeap
03 ntdll!RtlDebugAllocateHeap
04 ntdll! ?? ::FNODOBFM::`string'
05 ntdll!RtlAllocateHeap
06 ole32!CRpcResolver::GetThreadWinstaDesktop
07 ole32!CRpcResolver::GetConnection
08 ole32!CoInitializeSecurity
09 ole32!InitializeSecurity
0a ole32!ChannelProcessInitialize
0b ole32!CComApartment::InitRemoting
0c ole32!CGIPTable::RegisterInterfaceInGlobalHlp
0d ole32!CGIPTable::RegisterInterfaceInGlobal
0e shell32!MarshalToGIT
0f shell32!CBrowserProgressAggregator::BeginSession
10 shell32!IUnknown_BeginBrowserProgressSession
11 shell32!CDefView::CreateViewWindow3
12 shell32!CExplorerBrowser::_CreateViewWindow
13 shell32!CExplorerBrowser::_SwitchView
14 shell32!CExplorerBrowser::_BrowseToView
15 shell32!CExplorerBrowser::_BrowseObjectInternal
16 shell32!CExplorerBrowser::_OnBrowseObject
17 shell32!CExplorerBrowser::BrowseObject
18 comdlg32!CPrintDialog::CreatePrintBrowser
19 comdlg32!CPrintDialog::OnInitDialog
1a comdlg32!Print_GeneralDlgProc
1b user32!UserCallDlgProcCheckWow
1c user32!DefDlgProcWorker
1d user32!InternalCreateDialog
1e user32!CreateDialogIndirectParamAorW
1f user32!CreateDialogIndirectParamW
20 comctl32!_CreatePageDialog
21 comctl32!_CreatePage
22 comctl32!PageChange
23 comctl32!InitPropSheetDlg
24 comctl32!PropSheetDlgProc
25 user32!UserCallDlgProcCheckWow
26 user32!DefDlgProcWorker
27 user32!InternalCreateDialog
28 user32!CreateDialogIndirectParamAorW
29 user32!CreateDialogIndirectParamW
2a comctl32!_RealPropertySheet
2b comctl32!_PropertySheet
2c comdlg32!Print_InvokePropertySheets
2d comdlg32!PrintDlgExX
2e comdlg32!PrintDlgExW
2f notepad!GetPrinterDCviaDialog
```

```
30 notepad!PrintIt
31 notepad!NPCommand
32 notepad!NPWndProc
33 user32!UserCallWinProcCheckWow
34 user32!DispatchMessageWorker
35 notepad!WinMain
36 notepad!DisplayNonGenuineDlgWorker
37 kernel32!BaseThreadInitThunk
38 ntdll!RtlUserThreadStart


1 Id: 1344.1ab0 Suspend: 1 Teb: 000007ff`fffdb000 Unfrozen
# Call Site
00 ntdll!NtWaitForMultipleObjects
01 ntdll!TppWaiterpThread
02 kernel32!BaseThreadInitThunk
03 ntdll!RtlUserThreadStart


2 Id: 1344.1638 Suspend: 1 Teb: 000007ff`fffd9000 Unfrozen
# Call Site
00 ntdll!ZwAlpcSendWaitReceivePort
01 rpcrt4!LRPC_CCALL::SendReceive
02 rpcrt4!NdrpClientCall3
03 rpcrt4!NdrClientCall3
04 sechost!LsaLookupOpenLocalPolicy
05 sechost!LookupAccountNameInternal
06 sechost!LookupAccountNameLocalW
07 rpcrt4!RpcpLookupAccountNameDirect
08 rpcrt4!RpcpLookupAccountName
09 rpcrt4!LRPC_BASE_BINDING_HANDLE::SetAuthInformation
0a rpcrt4!LRPC_BINDING_HANDLE::SetAuthInformation
0b rpcrt4!RpcBindingSetAuthInfoExW
0c winspool!STRING_HANDLE_bind
0d rpcrt4!GenericHandleMgr
0e rpcrt4!ExplicitBindHandleMgr
0f rpcrt4!Ndr64pClientSetupTransferSyntax
10 rpcrt4!NdrpClientCall3
11 rpcrt4!NdrClientCall3
12 winspool!RpcSplOpenPrinter
13 winspool!OpenPrinterRPC
14 winspool!OpenPrinter2W
15 prncache!PrintCache::Listeners::Listener::Start
16 prncache!PrintCache::Listeners::Listener::StartCB
17 ntdll!TppWorkpExecuteCallback
18 ntdll!TppWorkerThread
19 kernel32!BaseThreadInitThunk
1a ntdll!RtlUserThreadStart


3 Id: 1344.830 Suspend: 1 Teb: 000007ff`fffd7000 Unfrozen
# Call Site
00 ntdll!RtlUserThreadStart


4 Id: 1344.1edc Suspend: 0 Teb: 000007ff`fffd5000 Unfrozen
# Call Site
00 ntdll!RtlUserThreadStart
```

// 4th dump

```
. 0 Id: 1344.1ca4 Suspend: 1 Teb: 000007ff`fffdd000 Unfrozen
# Call Site
00 ntdll!RtlCompareMemoryUlong
01 ntdll!RtlpAllocateHeap
02 ntdll!RtlAllocateHeap
03 ntdll!RtlDebugAllocateHeap
04 ntdll! ?? ::FNODOBFM::`string'
05 ntdll!RtlAllocateHeap
06 ole32!CRpcResolver::GetThreadWinstaDesktop
07 ole32!CRpcResolver::GetConnection
08 ole32!CoInitializeSecurity
09 ole32!InitializeSecurity
0a ole32!ChannelProcessInitialize
0b ole32!CComApartment::InitRemoting
0c ole32!CGIPTable::RegisterInterfaceInGlobalHlp
0d ole32!CGIPTable::RegisterInterfaceInGlobal
0e shell32!MarshalToGIT
0f shell32!CBrowserProgressAggregator::BeginSession
10 shell32!IUnknown_BeginBrowserProgressSession
11 shell32!CDefView::CreateViewWindow3
12 shell32!CExplorerBrowser::_CreateViewWindow
13 shell32!CExplorerBrowser::_SwitchView
14 shell32!CExplorerBrowser::_BrowseToView
15 shell32!CExplorerBrowser::_BrowseObjectInternal
16 shell32!CExplorerBrowser::_OnBrowseObject
17 shell32!CExplorerBrowser::BrowseObject
18 comdlg32!CPrintDialog::CreatePrintBrowser
19 comdlg32!CPrintDialog::OnInitDialog
1a comdlg32!Print_GeneralDlgProc
1b user32!UserCallDlgProcCheckWow
1c user32!DefDlgProcWorker
1d user32!InternalCreateDialog
1e user32!CreateDialogIndirectParamAorW
1f user32!CreateDialogIndirectParamW
20 comctl32!_CreatePageDialog
21 comctl32!_CreatePage
22 comctl32!PageChange
23 comctl32!InitPropSheetDlg
24 comctl32!PropSheetDlgProc
25 user32!UserCallDlgProcCheckWow
26 user32!DefDlgProcWorker
27 user32!InternalCreateDialog
28 user32!CreateDialogIndirectParamAorW
29 user32!CreateDialogIndirectParamW
2a comctl32!_RealPropertySheet
2b comctl32!_PropertySheet
2c comdlg32!Print_InvokePropertySheets
2d comdlg32!PrintDlgExX
2e comdlg32!PrintDlgExW
2f notepad!GetPrinterDCviaDialog
30 notepad!PrintIt
31 notepad!NPCommand
32 notepad!NPWndProc
33 user32!UserCallWinProcCheckWow
```

```
34 user32!DispatchMessageWorker
35 notepad!WinMain
36 notepad!DisplayNonGenuineDlgWorker
37 kernel32!BaseThreadInitThunk
38 ntdll!RtlUserThreadStart


1 Id: 1344.1ab0 Suspend: 1 Teb: 000007ff`fffdb000 Unfrozen
# Call Site
00 ntdll!NtWaitForMultipleObjects
01 ntdll!TppWaiterpThread
02 kernel32!BaseThreadInitThunk
03 ntdll!RtlUserThreadStart


2 Id: 1344.1638 Suspend: 1 Teb: 000007ff`fffd9000 Unfrozen
# Call Site
00 ntdll!ZwAlpcSendWaitReceivePort
01 rpcrt4!LRPC_CCALL::SendReceive
02 rpcrt4!NdrpClientCall3
03 rpcrt4!NdrClientCall3
04 sechost!LsaLookupOpenLocalPolicy
05 sechost!LookupAccountNameInternal
06 sechost!LookupAccountNameLocalW
07 rpcrt4!RpcpLookupAccountNameDirect
08 rpcrt4!RpcpLookupAccountName
09 rpcrt4!LRPC_BASE_BINDING_HANDLE::SetAuthInformation
0a rpcrt4!LRPC_BINDING_HANDLE::SetAuthInformation
0b rpcrt4!RpcBindingSetAuthInfoExW
0c winspool!STRING_HANDLE_bind
0d rpcrt4!GenericHandleMgr
0e rpcrt4!ExplicitBindHandleMgr
0f rpcrt4!Ndr64pClientSetupTransferSyntax
10 rpcrt4!NdrpClientCall3
11 rpcrt4!NdrClientCall3
12 winspool!RpcSplOpenPrinter
13 winspool!OpenPrinterRPC
14 winspool!OpenPrinter2W
15 prncache!PrintCache::Listeners::Listener::Start
16 prncache!PrintCache::Listeners::Listener::StartCB
17 ntdll!TppWorkpExecuteCallback
18 ntdll!TppWorkerThread
19 kernel32!BaseThreadInitThunk
1a ntdll!RtlUserThreadStart


3 Id: 1344.830 Suspend: 1 Teb: 000007ff`fffd7000 Unfrozen
# Call Site
00 ntdll!LdrpInitializeThread
01 ntdll!LdrpInitialize
02 ntdll!LdrInitializeThunk


4 Id: 1344.1edc Suspend: 1 Teb: 000007ff`fffd5000 Unfrozen
# Call Site
00 ntdll!RtlUserThreadStart
```

// 5th dump

```
. 0 Id: 1344.1ca4 Suspend: 1 Teb: 000007ff`fffdd000 Unfrozen
# Call Site
00 ntdll!ZwAlpcSendWaitReceivePort
01 rpcrt4!LRPC_CCALL::SendReceive
02 rpcrt4!NdrpClientCall3
03 rpcrt4!NdrClientCall3
04 sechost!LsaLookupClose
05 sechost!LookupAccountNameInternal
06 sechost!LookupAccountNameLocalW
07 rpcrt4!RpcpLookupAccountNameDirect
08 rpcrt4!RpcpLookupAccountName
09 rpcrt4!LRPC_BASE_BINDING_HANDLE::SetAuthInformation
0a rpcrt4!LRPC_FAST_BINDING_HANDLE::SetAuthInformation
0b rpcrt4!LRPC_FAST_BINDING_HANDLE::LRPC_FAST_BINDING_HANDLE
0c rpcrt4!LrpcCreateFastBindingHandle
0d rpcrt4!RpcBindingCreateW
0e ole32!CFastBH::CreateFromBindingString
0f ole32!CFastBH::GetOrCreate
10 ole32!CRpcResolver::GetConnection
11 ole32!CoInitializeSecurity
12 ole32!InitializeSecurity
13 ole32!ChannelProcessInitialize
14 ole32!CComApartment::InitRemoting
15 ole32!CGIPTable::RegisterInterfaceInGlobalHlp
16 ole32!CGIPTable::RegisterInterfaceInGlobal
17 shell32!MarshalToGIT
18 shell32!CBrowserProgressAggregator::BeginSession
19 shell32!IUnknown_BeginBrowserProgressSession
1a shell32!CDefView::CreateViewWindow3
1b shell32!CExplorerBrowser::_CreateViewWindow
1c shell32!CExplorerBrowser::_SwitchView
1d shell32!CExplorerBrowser::_BrowseToView
1e shell32!CExplorerBrowser::_BrowseObjectInternal
1f shell32!CExplorerBrowser::_OnBrowseObject
20 shell32!CExplorerBrowser::BrowseObject
21 comdlg32!CPrintDialog::CreatePrintBrowser
22 comdlg32!CPrintDialog::OnInitDialog
23 comdlg32!Print_GeneralDlgProc
24 user32!UserCallDlgProcCheckWow
25 user32!DefDlgProcWorker
26 user32!InternalCreateDialog
27 user32!CreateDialogIndirectParamAorW
28 user32!CreateDialogIndirectParamW
29 comctl32!_CreatePageDialog
2a comctl32!_CreatePage
2b comctl32!PageChange
2c comctl32!InitPropSheetDlg
2d comctl32!PropSheetDlgProc
2e user32!UserCallDlgProcCheckWow
2f user32!DefDlgProcWorker
30 user32!InternalCreateDialog
31 user32!CreateDialogIndirectParamAorW
32 user32!CreateDialogIndirectParamW
33 comctl32!_RealPropertySheet
```

```
34 comctl32!_PropertySheet
35 comdlg32!Print_InvokePropertySheets
36 comdlg32!PrintDlgExX
37 comdlg32!PrintDlgExW
38 notepad!GetPrinterDCviaDialog
39 notepad!PrintIt
3a notepad!NPCommand
3b notepad!NPWndProc
3c user32!UserCallWinProcCheckWow
3d user32!DispatchMessageWorker
3e notepad!WinMain
3f notepad!DisplayNonGenuineDlgWorker
40 kernel32!BaseThreadInitThunk
41 ntdll!RtlUserThreadStart


1 Id: 1344.1ab0 Suspend: 1 Teb: 000007ff`fffdb000 Unfrozen
# Call Site
00 ntdll!NtWaitForMultipleObjects
01 ntdll!TppWaiterpThread
02 kernel32!BaseThreadInitThunk
03 ntdll!RtlUserThreadStart


2 Id: 1344.1638 Suspend: 1 Teb: 000007ff`fffd9000 Unfrozen
# Call Site
00 ntdll!ZwAlpcSendWaitReceivePort
01 rpcrt4!LRPC_CCALL::SendReceive
02 rpcrt4!NdrpClientCall3
03 rpcrt4!NdrClientCall3
04 winspool!RpcSplOpenPrinter
05 winspool!OpenPrinterRPC
06 winspool!OpenPrinter2W
07 prncache!PrintCache::Listeners::Listener::Start
08 prncache!PrintCache::Listeners::Listener::StartCB
09 ntdll!TppWorkpExecuteCallback
0a ntdll!TppWorkerThread
0b kernel32!BaseThreadInitThunk
0c ntdll!RtlUserThreadStart


3 Id: 1344.830 Suspend: 1 Teb: 000007ff`fffd7000 Unfrozen
# Call Site
00 ntdll!NtWaitForMultipleObjects
01 KERNELBASE!WaitForMultipleObjectsEx
02 kernel32!WaitForMultipleObjects
03 prncache!PrintCache::Store::CacheStore::RegistryMonitor::MonitorRegistryChanges
04 prncache!PrintCache::Store::CacheStore::RegistryMonitor::MonitorRegistryChangesThreadProc
05 kernel32!BaseThreadInitThunk
06 ntdll!RtlUserThreadStart


4 Id: 1344.1edc Suspend: 1 Teb: 000007ff`fffd5000 Unfrozen
# Call Site
00 ntdll!ZwAlpcSendWaitReceivePort
01 rpcrt4!LRPC_CCALL::SendReceive
02 rpcrt4!NdrpClientCall3
03 rpcrt4!NdrClientCall3
04 winspool!RpcEnumPrinters
```

```
05 winspool!EnumPrintersW
06 prncache!PrintCache::Listeners::ConnectionListener::EnumConnectionsAndRegister
07 prncache!PrintCache::Listeners::ConnectionListener::UpdateCB
08 ntdll!TppWorkpExecuteCallback
09 ntdll!TppWorkerThread
0a kernel32!BaseThreadInitThunk
0b ntdll!RtlUserThreadStart


5 Id: 1344.1b44 Suspend: 1 Teb: 000007ff`fffd3000 Unfrozen
# Call Site
00 ntdll!RtlUserThreadStart
```

// 6th dump

```
. 0 Id: 1344.1ca4 Suspend: 1 Teb: 000007ff`fffdd000 Unfrozen
# Call Site
00 ntdll!NtAlpcConnectPort
01 rpcrt4!LRPC_CASSOCIATION::AlpcConnect
02 rpcrt4!LRPC_CASSOCIATION::Connect
03 rpcrt4!LRPC_BASE_BINDING_HANDLE::DriveStateForward
04 rpcrt4!LRPC_FAST_BINDING_HANDLE::Bind
05 rpcrt4!RpcBindingBind
06 ole32!CFastBH::CreateFromBindingString
07 ole32!CFastBH::GetOrCreate
08 ole32!CRpcResolver::GetConnection
09 ole32!CoInitializeSecurity
0a ole32!InitializeSecurity
0b ole32!ChannelProcessInitialize
0c ole32!CComApartment::InitRemoting
0d ole32!CGIPTable::RegisterInterfaceInGlobalHlp
0e ole32!CGIPTable::RegisterInterfaceInGlobal
0f shell32!MarshalToGIT
10 shell32!CBrowserProgressAggregator::BeginSession
11 shell32!IUnknown_BeginBrowserProgressSession
12 shell32!CDefView::CreateViewWindow3
13 shell32!CExplorerBrowser::_CreateViewWindow
14 shell32!CExplorerBrowser::_SwitchView
15 shell32!CExplorerBrowser::_BrowseToView
16 shell32!CExplorerBrowser::_BrowseObjectInternal
17 shell32!CExplorerBrowser::_OnBrowseObject
18 shell32!CExplorerBrowser::BrowseObject
19 comdlg32!CPrintDialog::CreatePrintBrowser
1a comdlg32!CPrintDialog::OnInitDialog
1b comdlg32!Print_GeneralDlgProc
1c user32!UserCallDlgProcCheckWow
1d user32!DefDlgProcWorker
1e user32!InternalCreateDialog
1f user32!CreateDialogIndirectParamAorW
20 user32!CreateDialogIndirectParamW
21 comctl32!_CreatePageDialog
22 comctl32!_CreatePage
23 comctl32!PageChange
24 comctl32!InitPropSheetDlg
25 comctl32!PropSheetDlgProc
26 user32!UserCallDlgProcCheckWow
```

```
27 user32!DefDlgProcWorker
28 user32!InternalCreateDialog
29 user32!CreateDialogIndirectParamAorW
2a user32!CreateDialogIndirectParamW
2b comctl32!_RealPropertySheet
2c comctl32!_PropertySheet
2d comdlg32!Print_InvokePropertySheets
2e comdlg32!PrintDlgExX
2f comdlg32!PrintDlgExW
30 notepad!GetPrinterDCviaDialog
31 notepad!PrintIt
32 notepad!NPCommand
33 notepad!NPWndProc
34 user32!UserCallWinProcCheckWow
35 user32!DispatchMessageWorker
36 notepad!WinMain
37 notepad!DisplayNonGenuineDlgWorker
38 kernel32!BaseThreadInitThunk
39 ntdll!RtlUserThreadStart


1 Id: 1344.1ab0 Suspend: 1 Teb: 000007ff`fffdb000 Unfrozen
# Call Site
00 ntdll!NtWaitForMultipleObjects
01 ntdll!TppWaiterpThread
02 kernel32!BaseThreadInitThunk
03 ntdll!RtlUserThreadStart


2 Id: 1344.1638 Suspend: 1 Teb: 000007ff`fffd9000 Unfrozen
# Call Site
00 ntdll!RtlEnterCriticalSection
01 ntdll!RtlDebugAllocateHeap
02 ntdll! ?? ::FNODOBFM::`string'
03 ntdll!RtlAllocateHeap
04 rpcrt4!AllocWrapper
05 rpcrt4!SID_CACHE::Query
06 rpcrt4!RpcpLookupAccountName
07 rpcrt4!LRPC_BASE_BINDING_HANDLE::SetAuthInformation
08 rpcrt4!LRPC_BINDING_HANDLE::SetAuthInformation
09 rpcrt4!RpcBindingSetAuthInfoExW
0a winspool!STRING_HANDLE_bind
0b rpcrt4!GenericHandleMgr
0c rpcrt4!ExplicitBindHandleMgr
0d rpcrt4!Ndr64pClientSetupTransferSyntax
0e rpcrt4!NdrpClientCall3
0f rpcrt4!NdrClientCall3
10 winspool!RpcSplOpenPrinter
11 winspool!OpenPrinterRPC
12 winspool!OpenPrinter2W
13 prncache!PrintCache::Listeners::Listener::Start
14 prncache!PrintCache::Listeners::Listener::StartCB
15 ntdll!TppWorkpExecuteCallback
16 ntdll!TppWorkerThread
17 kernel32!BaseThreadInitThunk
18 ntdll!RtlUserThreadStart
```

```
3 Id: 1344.830 Suspend: 1 Teb: 000007ff`fffd7000 Unfrozen
# Call Site
00 ntdll!NtWaitForMultipleObjects
01 KERNELBASE!WaitForMultipleObjectsEx
02 kernel32!WaitForMultipleObjects
03 prncache!PrintCache::Store::CacheStore::RegistryMonitor::MonitorRegistryChanges
04 prncache!PrintCache::Store::CacheStore::RegistryMonitor::MonitorRegistryChangesThreadProc
05 kernel32!BaseThreadInitThunk
06 ntdll!RtlUserThreadStart


4 Id: 1344.1edc Suspend: 1 Teb: 000007ff`fffd5000 Unfrozen
# Call Site
00 user32!NtUserAttachThreadInput
01 shell32!CWaitTask::s_WaitBeforeCursing
02 ntdll!RtlpTpWaitCallback
03 ntdll!TppWaitpExecuteCallback
04 ntdll!TppWorkerThread
05 kernel32!BaseThreadInitThunk
06 ntdll!RtlUserThreadStart


5 Id: 1344.1b44 Suspend: 1 Teb: 000007ff`fffd3000 Unfrozen
# Call Site
00 ntdll!NtWaitForWorkViaWorkerFactory
01 ntdll!TppWorkerThread
02 kernel32!BaseThreadInitThunk
03 ntdll!RtlUserThreadStart


6 Id: 1344.1d9c Suspend: 1 Teb: 000007ff`fffae000 Unfrozen
# Call Site
00 ntdll!RtlUserThreadStart
```

// 7th dump

```
. 0 Id: 1344.1ca4 Suspend: 1 Teb: 000007ff`fffdd000 Unfrozen
# Call Site
00 rpcrt4!RpcStringFreeW
01 ole32!CFastBH::CreateFromBindingString
02 ole32!CFastBH::GetOrCreate
03 ole32!CRpcResolver::GetConnection
04 ole32!CoInitializeSecurity
05 ole32!InitializeSecurity
06 ole32!ChannelProcessInitialize
07 ole32!CComApartment::InitRemoting
08 ole32!CGIPTable::RegisterInterfaceInGlobalHlp
09 ole32!CGIPTable::RegisterInterfaceInGlobal
0a shell32!MarshalToGIT
0b shell32!CBrowserProgressAggregator::BeginSession
0c shell32!IUnknown_BeginBrowserProgressSession
0d shell32!CDefView::CreateViewWindow3
0e shell32!CExplorerBrowser::_CreateViewWindow
0f shell32!CExplorerBrowser::_SwitchView
10 shell32!CExplorerBrowser::_BrowseToView
11 shell32!CExplorerBrowser::_BrowseObjectInternal
12 shell32!CExplorerBrowser::_OnBrowseObject
13 shell32!CExplorerBrowser::BrowseObject
```

```
14 comdlg32!CPrintDialog::CreatePrintBrowser
15 comdlg32!CPrintDialog::OnInitDialog
16 comdlg32!Print_GeneralDlgProc
17 user32!UserCallDlgProcCheckWow
18 user32!DefDlgProcWorker
19 user32!InternalCreateDialog
1a user32!CreateDialogIndirectParamAorW
1b user32!CreateDialogIndirectParamW
1c comctl32!_CreatePageDialog
1d comctl32!_CreatePage
1e comctl32!PageChange
1f comctl32!InitPropSheetDlg
20 comctl32!PropSheetDlgProc
21 user32!UserCallDlgProcCheckWow
22 user32!DefDlgProcWorker
23 user32!InternalCreateDialog
24 user32!CreateDialogIndirectParamAorW
25 user32!CreateDialogIndirectParamW
26 comctl32!_RealPropertySheet
27 comctl32!_PropertySheet
28 comdlg32!Print_InvokePropertySheets
29 comdlg32!PrintDlgExX
2a comdlg32!PrintDlgExW
2b notepad!GetPrinterDCviaDialog
2c notepad!PrintIt
2d notepad!NPCommand
2e notepad!NPWndProc
2f user32!UserCallWinProcCheckWow
30 user32!DispatchMessageWorker
31 notepad!WinMain
32 notepad!DisplayNonGenuineDlgWorker
33 kernel32!BaseThreadInitThunk
34 ntdll!RtlUserThreadStart


1 Id: 1344.1ab0 Suspend: 1 Teb: 000007ff`fffdb000 Unfrozen
# Call Site
00 ntdll!NtWaitForMultipleObjects
01 ntdll!TppWaiterpThread
02 kernel32!BaseThreadInitThunk
03 ntdll!RtlUserThreadStart


2 Id: 1344.1638 Suspend: 1 Teb: 000007ff`fffd9000 Unfrozen
# Call Site
00 ntdll!ZwAlpcSendWaitReceivePort
01 rpcrt4!LRPC_CCALL::SendReceive
02 rpcrt4!NdrpClientCall3
03 rpcrt4!NdrClientCall3
04 winspool!RpcSplOpenPrinter
05 winspool!OpenPrinterRPC
06 winspool!OpenPrinter2W
07 prncache!PrintCache::Listeners::Listener::Start
08 prncache!PrintCache::Listeners::Listener::StartCB
09 ntdll!TppWorkpExecuteCallback
0a ntdll!TppWorkerThread
0b kernel32!BaseThreadInitThunk
0c ntdll!RtlUserThreadStart
```

```
3 Id: 1344.830 Suspend: 1 Teb: 000007ff`fffd7000 Unfrozen
# Call Site
00 ntdll!NtWaitForMultipleObjects
01 KERNELBASE!WaitForMultipleObjectsEx
02 kernel32!WaitForMultipleObjects
03 prncache!PrintCache::Store::CacheStore::RegistryMonitor::MonitorRegistryChanges
04 prncache!PrintCache::Store::CacheStore::RegistryMonitor::MonitorRegistryChangesThreadProc
05 kernel32!BaseThreadInitThunk
06 ntdll!RtlUserThreadStart

4 Id: 1344.1edc Suspend: 1 Teb: 000007ff`fffd5000 Unfrozen
# Call Site
00 ntdll!NtWaitForMultipleObjects
01 KERNELBASE!WaitForMultipleObjectsEx
02 kernel32!WaitForMultipleObjectsExImplementation
03 user32!RealMsgWaitForMultipleObjectsEx
04 user32!MsgWaitForMultipleObjectsEx
05 user32!MsgWaitForMultipleObjects
06 shell32!SHProcessMessagesUntilEventsEx
07 shell32!CWaitTask::s_WaitBeforeCursing
08 ntdll!RtlpTpWaitCallback
09 ntdll!TppWaitpExecuteCallback
0a ntdll!TppWorkerThread
0b kernel32!BaseThreadInitThunk
0c ntdll!RtlUserThreadStart

5 Id: 1344.1b44 Suspend: 1 Teb: 000007ff`fffd3000 Unfrozen
# Call Site
00 ntdll!NtWaitForWorkViaWorkerFactory
01 ntdll!TppWorkerThread
02 kernel32!BaseThreadInitThunk
03 ntdll!RtlUserThreadStart

6 Id: 1344.1d9c Suspend: 1 Teb: 000007ff`fffae000 Unfrozen
# Call Site
00 ntdll!NtWaitForWorkViaWorkerFactory
01 ntdll!TppWorkerThread
02 kernel32!BaseThreadInitThunk
03 ntdll!RtlUserThreadStart

7 Id: 1344.139c Suspend: 1 Teb: 000007ff`fffac000 Unfrozen
# Call Site
00 ntdll!RtlUserThreadStart
```

// 8th dump

```
. 0 Id: 1344.1ca4 Suspend: 1 Teb: 000007ff`fffdd000 Unfrozen
# Call Site
00 user32!NtUserSetWindowLongPtr
01 user32!SetWindowLongPtr
02 ole32!OXIDEntry::StartServer
03 ole32!CGIPTable::RegisterInterfaceInGlobalHlp
04 ole32!CGIPTable::RegisterInterfaceInGlobal
05 shell32!MarshalToGIT
```

```
06 shell32!CBrowserProgressAggregator::BeginSession
07 shell32!IUnknown_BeginBrowserProgressSession
08 shell32!CDefView::CreateViewWindow3
09 shell32!CExplorerBrowser::_CreateViewWindow
0a shell32!CExplorerBrowser::_SwitchView
0b shell32!CExplorerBrowser::_BrowseToView
0c shell32!CExplorerBrowser::_BrowseObjectInternal
0d shell32!CExplorerBrowser::_OnBrowseObject
0e shell32!CExplorerBrowser::BrowseObject
0f comdlg32!CPrintDialog::CreatePrintBrowser
10 comdlg32!CPrintDialog::OnInitDialog
11 comdlg32!Print_GeneralDlgProc
12 user32!UserCallDlgProcCheckWow
13 user32!DefDlgProcWorker
14 user32!InternalCreateDialog
15 user32!CreateDialogIndirectParamAorW
16 user32!CreateDialogIndirectParamW
17 comctl32!_CreatePageDialog
18 comctl32!_CreatePage
19 comctl32!PageChange
1a comctl32!InitPropSheetDlg
1b comctl32!PropSheetDlgProc
1c user32!UserCallDlgProcCheckWow
1d user32!DefDlgProcWorker
1e user32!InternalCreateDialog
1f user32!CreateDialogIndirectParamAorW
20 user32!CreateDialogIndirectParamW
21 comctl32!_RealPropertySheet
22 comctl32!_PropertySheet
23 comdlg32!Print_InvokePropertySheets
24 comdlg32!PrintDlgExX
25 comdlg32!PrintDlgExW
26 notepad!GetPrinterDCviaDialog
27 notepad!PrintIt
28 notepad!NPCommand
29 notepad!NPWndProc
2a user32!UserCallWinProcCheckWow
2b user32!DispatchMessageWorker
2c notepad!WinMain
2d notepad!DisplayNonGenuineDlgWorker
2e kernel32!BaseThreadInitThunk
2f ntdll!RtlUserThreadStart


1 Id: 1344.1ab0 Suspend: 1 Teb: 000007ff`fffdb000 Unfrozen
# Call Site
00 ntdll!NtWaitForMultipleObjects
01 ntdll!TppWaiterpThread
02 kernel32!BaseThreadInitThunk
03 ntdll!RtlUserThreadStart


2 Id: 1344.1638 Suspend: 1 Teb: 000007ff`fffd9000 Unfrozen
# Call Site
00 ntdll!NtWaitForWorkViaWorkerFactory
01 ntdll!TppWorkerThread
02 kernel32!BaseThreadInitThunk
03 ntdll!RtlUserThreadStart
```

```
3 Id: 1344.830 Suspend: 1 Teb: 000007ff`fffd7000 Unfrozen
# Call Site
00 ntdll!NtWaitForMultipleObjects
01 KERNELBASE!WaitForMultipleObjectsEx
02 kernel32!WaitForMultipleObjects
03 prncache!PrintCache::Store::CacheStore::RegistryMonitor::MonitorRegistryChanges
04 prncache!PrintCache::Store::CacheStore::RegistryMonitor::MonitorRegistryChangesThreadProc
05 kernel32!BaseThreadInitThunk
06 ntdll!RtlUserThreadStart


4 Id: 1344.1edc Suspend: 1 Teb: 000007ff`fffd5000 Unfrozen
# Call Site
00 ntdll!NtWaitForMultipleObjects
01 KERNELBASE!WaitForMultipleObjectsEx
02 kernel32!WaitForMultipleObjectsExImplementation
03 user32!RealMsgWaitForMultipleObjectsEx
04 user32!MsgWaitForMultipleObjectsEx
05 user32!MsgWaitForMultipleObjects
06 shell32!SHProcessMessagesUntilEventsEx
07 shell32!CWaitTask::s_WaitBeforeCursing
08 ntdll!RtlpTpWaitCallback
09 ntdll!TppWaitpExecuteCallback
0a ntdll!TppWorkerThread
0b kernel32!BaseThreadInitThunk
0c ntdll!RtlUserThreadStart


5 Id: 1344.1b44 Suspend: 1 Teb: 000007ff`fffd3000 Unfrozen
# Call Site
00 ntdll!NtWaitForWorkViaWorkerFactory
01 ntdll!TppWorkerThread
02 kernel32!BaseThreadInitThunk
03 ntdll!RtlUserThreadStart


6 Id: 1344.1d9c Suspend: 1 Teb: 000007ff`fffae000 Unfrozen
# Call Site
00 ntdll!NtWaitForWorkViaWorkerFactory
01 ntdll!TppWorkerThread
02 kernel32!BaseThreadInitThunk
03 ntdll!RtlUserThreadStart


7 Id: 1344.139c Suspend: 1 Teb: 000007ff`fffac000 Unfrozen
# Call Site
00 ntdll!NtWaitForWorkViaWorkerFactory
01 ntdll!TppWorkerThread
02 kernel32!BaseThreadInitThunk
03 ntdll!RtlUserThreadStart


8 Id: 1344.1b80 Suspend: 1 Teb: 000007ff`fffaa000 Unfrozen
# Call Site
00 ntdll!RtlUserThreadStart
```

// 9th dump

```
. 0 Id: 1344.1ca4 Suspend: 1 Teb: 000007ff`fffdd000 Unfrozen
# Call Site
00 user32!NtUserPeekMessage
01 user32!PeekMessageW
02 shell32!PeekMessageWithWakeMask
03 shell32!SHProcessMessagesUntilEventsEx
04 shell32!CDefView::_SetItemCollection
05 shell32!CDefView::_CreateNewCollection
06 shell32!CDefView::CreateViewWindow3
07 shell32!CExplorerBrowser::_CreateViewWindow
08 shell32!CExplorerBrowser::_SwitchView
09 shell32!CExplorerBrowser::_BrowseToView
0a shell32!CExplorerBrowser::_BrowseObjectInternal
0b shell32!CExplorerBrowser::_OnBrowseObject
0c shell32!CExplorerBrowser::BrowseObject
0d comdlg32!CPrintDialog::CreatePrintBrowser
0e comdlg32!CPrintDialog::OnInitDialog
0f comdlg32!Print_GeneralDlgProc
10 user32!UserCallDlgProcCheckWow
11 user32!DefDlgProcWorker
12 user32!InternalCreateDialog
13 user32!CreateDialogIndirectParamAorW
14 user32!CreateDialogIndirectParamW
15 comctl32!_CreatePageDialog
16 comctl32!_CreatePage
17 comctl32!PageChange
18 comctl32!InitPropSheetDlg
19 comctl32!PropSheetDlgProc
1a user32!UserCallDlgProcCheckWow
1b user32!DefDlgProcWorker
1c user32!InternalCreateDialog
1d user32!CreateDialogIndirectParamAorW
1e user32!CreateDialogIndirectParamW
1f comctl32!_RealPropertySheet
20 comctl32!_PropertySheet
21 comdlg32!Print_InvokePropertySheets
22 comdlg32!PrintDlgExX
23 comdlg32!PrintDlgExW
24 notepad!GetPrinterDCviaDialog
25 notepad!PrintIt
26 notepad!NPCommand
27 notepad!NPWndProc
28 user32!UserCallWinProcCheckWow
29 user32!DispatchMessageWorker
2a notepad!WinMain
2b notepad!DisplayNonGenuineDlgWorker
2c kernel32!BaseThreadInitThunk
2d ntdll!RtlUserThreadStart


1 Id: 1344.1ab0 Suspend: 1 Teb: 000007ff`fffdb000 Unfrozen
# Call Site
00 ntdll!NtWaitForMultipleObjects
01 ntdll!TppWaiterpThread
```

```
02 kernel32!BaseThreadInitThunk
03 ntdll!RtlUserThreadStart

2 Id: 1344.1638 Suspend: 1 Teb: 000007ff`fffd9000 Unfrozen
# Call Site
00 ntdll!NtWaitForSingleObject
01 KERNELBASE!WaitForSingleObjectEx
02 shlwapi!CreateThreadWorker
03 shlwapi!SHCreateThread
04 shell32!CEnumThread::Run
05 shell32!CEnumTask::_StartEnumThread
06 shell32!CEnumTask::_IncrEnumFolder
07 shell32!CEnumTask::InternalResumeRT
08 shell32!CRunnableTask::Run
09 shell32!CShellTask::TT_Run
0a shell32!CShellTaskThread::ThreadProc
0b shell32!CShellTaskThread::s_ThreadProc
0c shlwapi!ExecuteWorkItemThreadProc
0d ntdll!RtlpTpWorkCallback
0e ntdll!TppWorkerThread
0f kernel32!BaseThreadInitThunk
10 ntdll!RtlUserThreadStart

3 Id: 1344.830 Suspend: 1 Teb: 000007ff`fffd7000 Unfrozen
# Call Site
00 ntdll!NtWaitForMultipleObjects
01 KERNELBASE!WaitForMultipleObjectsEx
02 kernel32!WaitForMultipleObjects
03 prncache!PrintCache::Store::CacheStore::RegistryMonitor::MonitorRegistryChanges
04 prncache!PrintCache::Store::CacheStore::RegistryMonitor::MonitorRegistryChangesThreadProc
05 kernel32!BaseThreadInitThunk
06 ntdll!RtlUserThreadStart

4 Id: 1344.1edc Suspend: 1 Teb: 000007ff`fffd5000 Unfrozen
# Call Site
00 ntdll!NtWaitForMultipleObjects
01 KERNELBASE!WaitForMultipleObjectsEx
02 kernel32!WaitForMultipleObjectsExImplementation
03 user32!RealMsgWaitForMultipleObjectsEx
04 user32!MsgWaitForMultipleObjectsEx
05 user32!MsgWaitForMultipleObjects
06 shell32!SHProcessMessagesUntilEventsEx
07 shell32!CWaitTask::s_WaitBeforeCursing
08 ntdll!RtlpTpWaitCallback
09 ntdll!TppWaitpExecuteCallback
0a ntdll!TppWorkerThread
0b kernel32!BaseThreadInitThunk
0c ntdll!RtlUserThreadStart

5 Id: 1344.1b44 Suspend: 1 Teb: 000007ff`fffd3000 Unfrozen
# Call Site
00 ntdll!NtWaitForWorkViaWorkerFactory
01 ntdll!TppWorkerThread
02 kernel32!BaseThreadInitThunk
03 ntdll!RtlUserThreadStart
```

```
 6 Id: 1344.1d9c Suspend: 1 Teb: 000007ff`fffae000 Unfrozen
# Call Site
00 ntdll!NtWaitForWorkViaWorkerFactory
01 ntdll!TppWorkerThread
02 kernel32!BaseThreadInitThunk
03 ntdll!RtlUserThreadStart


 7 Id: 1344.139c Suspend: 1 Teb: 000007ff`fffac000 Unfrozen
# Call Site
00 ntdll!NtWaitForWorkViaWorkerFactory
01 ntdll!TppWorkerThread
02 kernel32!BaseThreadInitThunk
03 ntdll!RtlUserThreadStart


 8 Id: 1344.1b80 Suspend: 1 Teb: 000007ff`fffaa000 Unfrozen
# Call Site
00 ntdll!ZwDelayExecution
01 KERNELBASE!SleepEx
02 ole32!CROIDTable::WorkerThreadLoop
03 ole32!CRpcThread::WorkerLoop
04 ole32!CRpcThreadCache::RpcWorkerThreadEntry
05 kernel32!BaseThreadInitThunk
06 ntdll!RtlUserThreadStart


 9 Id: 1344.1310 Suspend: 1 Teb: 000007ff`fffa8000 Unfrozen
# Call Site
00 ntdll!RtlUserThreadStart


// 10th dump


. 0 Id: 1344.1ca4 Suspend: 1 Teb: 000007ff`fffdd000 Unfrozen
# Call Site
00 kernel32!TlsGetValue
01 usp10!UspFreeMem
02 usp10!ScriptApplyDigitSubstitution
03 lpk!LpkCharsetDraw
04 lpk!LpkDrawTextEx
05 user32!DT_GetExtentMinusPrefixes
06 user32!NeedsEndEllipsis
07 user32!AddEllipsisAndDrawLine
08 user32!DrawTextExWorker
09 user32!DrawTextW
0a comctl32!CLVView::_ComputeLabelSizeWorker
0b comctl32!CLVView::v_RecomputeLabelSize
0c comctl32!CLVListView::v_DrawItem
0d comctl32!CLVDrawItemManager::DrawItem
0e comctl32!CLVDrawManager::_PaintItems
0f comctl32!CLVDrawManager::_PaintWorkArea
10 comctl32!CLVDrawManager::_OnPaintWorkAreas
11 comctl32!CLVDrawManager::_OnPaint
12 comctl32!CListView::WndProc
13 comctl32!CListView::s_WndProc
14 user32!UserCallWinProcCheckWow
15 user32!CallWindowProcAorW
16 user32!CallWindowProcW
```

```
17  comctl32!CallOriginalWndProc
18  comctl32!CallNextSubclassProc
19  comctl32!DefSubclassProc
1a  shell32!DefSubclassProc
1b  shell32!CListViewHost::s_ListViewSubclassWndProc
1c  comctl32!CallNextSubclassProc
1d  comctl32!MasterSubclassProc
1e  user32!UserCallWinProcCheckWow
1f  user32!DispatchClientMessage
20  user32!_fnDWORD
21  ntdll!KiUserCallbackDispatcherContinue
22  user32!NtUserDispatchMessage
23  user32!DispatchMessageWorker
24  user32!IsDialogMessageW
25  comctl32!Prop_IsDialogMessage
26  comctl32!_RealPropertySheet
27  comctl32!_PropertySheet
28  comdlg32!Print_InvokePropertySheets
29  comdlg32!PrintDlgExX
2a  comdlg32!PrintDlgExW
2b  notepad!GetPrinterDCviaDialog
2c  notepad!PrintIt
2d  notepad!NPCommand
2e  notepad!NPWndProc
2f  user32!UserCallWinProcCheckWow
30  user32!DispatchMessageWorker
31  notepad!WinMain
32  notepad!DisplayNonGenuineDlgWorker
33  kernel32!BaseThreadInitThunk
34  ntdll!RtlUserThreadStart

1 Id: 1344.1ab0 Suspend: 1 Teb: 000007ff`fffdb000 Unfrozen
# Call Site
00  ntdll!NtWaitForMultipleObjects
01  ntdll!TppWaiterpThread
02  kernel32!BaseThreadInitThunk
03  ntdll!RtlUserThreadStart

2 Id: 1344.1638 Suspend: 1 Teb: 000007ff`fffd9000 Unfrozen
# Call Site
00  ntdll!ZwCreateSection
01  KERNELBASE!BasepLoadLibraryAsDataFileInternal
02  KERNELBASE!LoadLibraryExW
03  user32!PrivateExtractIconsW
04  shell32!SHPrivateExtractIcons
05  shell32!SHDefExtractIconW
06  shell32!CExtractIcon::_ExtractW
07  shell32!CExtractIconBase::Extract
08  shell32!IExtractIcon_Extract
09  shell32!_GetILIndexGivenPXIcon
0a  shell32!_GetILIndexFromItem
0b  shell32!SHGetIconIndexFromPIDL
0c  shell32!MapIDListToIconILIndex
0d  shell32!CLoadSystemIconTask::InternalResumeRT
0e  shell32!CRunnableTask::Run
0f  shell32!CShellTask::TT_Run
```

```
10 shell32!CShellTaskThread::ThreadProc
11 shell32!CShellTaskThread::s_ThreadProc
12 shlwapi!ExecuteWorkItemThreadProc
13 ntdll!RtlpTpWorkCallback
14 ntdll!TppWorkerThread
15 kernel32!BaseThreadInitThunk
16 ntdll!RtlUserThreadStart


3 Id: 1344.830 Suspend: 1 Teb: 000007ff`fffd7000 Unfrozen
# Call Site
00 ntdll!NtWaitForMultipleObjects
01 KERNELBASE!WaitForMultipleObjectsEx
02 kernel32!WaitForMultipleObjects
03 prncache!PrintCache::Store::CacheStore::RegistryMonitor::MonitorRegistryChanges
04 prncache!PrintCache::Store::CacheStore::RegistryMonitor::MonitorRegistryChangesThreadProc
05 kernel32!BaseThreadInitThunk
06 ntdll!RtlUserThreadStart


4 Id: 1344.1edc Suspend: 1 Teb: 000007ff`fffd5000 Unfrozen
# Call Site
00 ntdll!ZwCreateSection
01 KERNELBASE!BasepLoadLibraryAsDataFileInternal
02 KERNELBASE!LoadLibraryExW
03 user32!PrivateExtractIconsW
04 shell32!SHPrivateExtractIcons
05 shell32!SHDefExtractIconW
06 shell32!CExtractIcon::_ExtractW
07 shell32!CExtractIconBase::Extract
08 shell32!IExtractIcon_Extract
09 shell32!_GetILIndexGivenPXIcon
0a shell32!_GetILIndexFromItem
0b shell32!SHGetIconIndexFromPIDL
0c shell32!MapIDListToIconILIndex
0d shell32!CLoadSystemIconTask::InternalResumeRT
0e shell32!CRunnableTask::Run
0f shell32!CShellTask::TT_Run
10 shell32!CShellTaskThread::ThreadProc
11 shell32!CShellTaskThread::s_ThreadProc
12 shlwapi!ExecuteWorkItemThreadProc
13 ntdll!RtlpTpWorkCallback
14 ntdll!TppWorkerThread
15 kernel32!BaseThreadInitThunk
16 ntdll!RtlUserThreadStart


5 Id: 1344.1b44 Suspend: 1 Teb: 000007ff`fffd3000 Unfrozen
# Call Site
00 ntdll!ZwCreateSection
01 KERNELBASE!BasepLoadLibraryAsDataFileInternal
02 KERNELBASE!LoadLibraryExW
03 user32!PrivateExtractIconsW
04 shell32!SHPrivateExtractIcons
05 shell32!SHDefExtractIconW
06 shell32!CExtractIcon::_ExtractW
07 shell32!CExtractIconBase::Extract
08 shell32!IExtractIcon_Extract
09 shell32!_GetILIndexGivenPXIcon
```

```
0a shell32!_GetILIndexFromItem
0b shell32!SHGetIconIndexFromPIDL
0c shell32!MapIDListToIconILIndex
0d shell32!CLoadSystemIconTask::InternalResumeRT
0e shell32!CRunnableTask::Run
0f shell32!CShellTask::TT_Run
10 shell32!CShellTaskThread::ThreadProc
11 shell32!CShellTaskThread::s_ThreadProc
12 shlwapi!ExecuteWorkItemThreadProc
13 ntdll!RtlpTpWorkCallback
14 ntdll!TppWorkerThread
15 kernel32!BaseThreadInitThunk
16 ntdll!RtlUserThreadStart

6 Id: 1344.1d9c Suspend: 1 Teb: 000007ff`fffae000 Unfrozen
# Call Site
00 ntdll!ZwCreateSection
01 KERNELBASE!BasepLoadLibraryAsDataFileInternal
02 KERNELBASE!LoadLibraryExW
03 user32!PrivateExtractIconsW
04 shell32!SHPrivateExtractIcons
05 shell32!SHDefExtractIconW
06 shell32!CExtractIcon::_ExtractW
07 shell32!CExtractIconBase::Extract
08 shell32!IExtractIcon_Extract
09 shell32!_GetILIndexGivenPXIcon
0a shell32!_GetILIndexFromItem
0b shell32!SHGetIconIndexFromPIDL
0c shell32!MapIDListToIconILIndex
0d shell32!CLoadSystemIconTask::InternalResumeRT
0e shell32!CRunnableTask::Run
0f shell32!CShellTask::TT_Run
10 shell32!CShellTaskThread::ThreadProc
11 shell32!CShellTaskThread::s_ThreadProc
12 shlwapi!ExecuteWorkItemThreadProc
13 ntdll!RtlpTpWorkCallback
14 ntdll!TppWorkerThread
15 kernel32!BaseThreadInitThunk
16 ntdll!RtlUserThreadStart

7 Id: 1344.139c Suspend: 1 Teb: 000007ff`fffac000 Unfrozen
# Call Site
00 ntdll!NtQueryKey
01 kernel32!BaseRegGetKeySemantics
02 kernel32!BaseRegGetUserAndMachineClass
03 kernel32!LocalBaseRegQueryValue
04 kernel32!RegQueryValueExW
05 shlwapi!SHRegQueryValueW
06 shlwapi!SHRegGetValueW
07 shlwapi!SHQueryValueExW
08 shell32!_GetServerInfo
09 shell32!_SHCoCreateInstance
0a shell32!CRegFolder::_CreateCachedRegFolder
0b shell32!CRegFolder::_BindToItem
0c shell32!CRegFolder::BindToObject
0d shell32!CRegFolder::_BindToItem
```

```
0e shell32!CRegFolder::BindToObject
0f shell32!SHBindToObject
10 shell32!CIconOverlayTask::InternalResumeRT
11 shell32!CRunnableTask::Run
12 shell32!CShellTask::TT_Run
13 shell32!CShellTaskThread::ThreadProc
14 shell32!CShellTaskThread::s_ThreadProc
15 shlwapi!ExecuteWorkItemThreadProc
16 ntdll!RtlpTpWorkCallback
17 ntdll!TppWorkerThread
18 kernel32!BaseThreadInitThunk
19 ntdll!RtlUserThreadStart


8 Id: 1344.1b80 Suspend: 1 Teb: 000007ff`fffaa000 Unfrozen
# Call Site
00 ntdll!ZwDelayExecution
01 KERNELBASE!SleepEx
02 ole32!CROIDTable::WorkerThreadLoop
03 ole32!CRpcThread::WorkerLoop
04 ole32!CRpcThreadCache::RpcWorkerThreadEntry
05 kernel32!BaseThreadInitThunk
06 ntdll!RtlUserThreadStart


9 Id: 1344.eb8 Suspend: 1 Teb: 000007ff`fffa8000 Unfrozen
# Call Site
00 ntdll!RtlUserThreadStart
```

// 11th dump

```
. 0 Id: 1344.1ca4 Suspend: 1 Teb: 000007ff`fffdd000 Unfrozen
# Call Site
00 usp10!GenericEngineGetGlyphs
01 usp10!ShlShape
02 usp10!ScriptShape
03 usp10!RenderItemNoFallback
04 usp10!RenderItemWithFallback
05 usp10!RenderItem
06 usp10!ScriptStringAnalyzeGlyphs
07 usp10!ScriptStringAnalyse
08 lpk!LpkCharsetDraw
09 lpk!LpkDrawTextEx
0a user32!DT_GetExtentMinusPrefixes
0b user32!NeedsEndEllipsis
0c user32!AddEllipsisAndDrawLine
0d user32!DrawTextExWorker
0e user32!DrawTextW
0f comctl32!CLVView::_ComputeLabelSizeWorker
10 comctl32!CLVView::v_RecomputeLabelSize
11 comctl32!CLVListView::v_DrawItem
12 comctl32!CLVDrawItemManager::DrawItem
13 comctl32!CLVDrawManager::_PaintItems
14 comctl32!CLVDrawManager::_PaintWorkArea
15 comctl32!CLVDrawManager::_OnPaintWorkAreas
16 comctl32!CLVDrawManager::_OnPaint
17 comctl32!CListView::WndProc
```

```
18 comctl32!CListView::s_WndProc
19 user32!UserCallWinProcCheckWow
1a user32!CallWindowProcAorW
1b user32!CallWindowProcW
1c comctl32!CallOriginalWndProc
1d comctl32!CallNextSubclassProc
1e comctl32!DefSubclassProc
1f shell32!DefSubclassProc
20 shell32!CListViewHost::s_ListViewSubclassWndProc
21 comctl32!CallNextSubclassProc
22 comctl32!MasterSubclassProc
23 user32!UserCallWinProcCheckWow
24 user32!DispatchClientMessage
25 user32!_fnDWORD
26 ntdll!KiUserCallbackDispatcherContinue
27 user32!NtUserDispatchMessage
28 user32!DispatchMessageWorker
29 user32!IsDialogMessageW
2a comctl32!Prop_IsDialogMessage
2b comctl32!_RealPropertySheet
2c comctl32!_PropertySheet
2d comdlg32!Print_InvokePropertySheets
2e comdlg32!PrintDlgExX
2f comdlg32!PrintDlgExW
30 notepad!GetPrinterDCviaDialog
31 notepad!PrintIt
32 notepad!NPCommand
33 notepad!NPWndProc
34 user32!UserCallWinProcCheckWow
35 user32!DispatchMessageWorker
36 notepad!WinMain
37 notepad!DisplayNonGenuineDlgWorker
38 kernel32!BaseThreadInitThunk
39 ntdll!RtlUserThreadStart

1 Id: 1344.1ab0 Suspend: 1 Teb: 000007ff`fffdb000 Unfrozen
# Call Site
00 ntdll!NtWaitForMultipleObjects
01 ntdll!TppWaiterpThread
02 kernel32!BaseThreadInitThunk
03 ntdll!RtlUserThreadStart

2 Id: 1344.1638 Suspend: 1 Teb: 000007ff`fffd9000 Unfrozen
# Call Site
00 ntdll!NtWaitForSingleObject
01 ntdll!RtlpWaitOnCriticalSection
02 ntdll!RtlEnterCriticalSection
03 user32!BitmapFromDIB
04 user32!ConvertDIBBitmap
05 user32!ConvertDIBIcon
06 user32!CreateIconFromResourceEx
07 user32!PrivateEnumProc
08 kernel32!EnumResourceNamesInternal
09 kernel32!EnumResourceNamesExW
0a user32!PrivateExtractIconsW
0b shell32!SHPrivateExtractIcons
```

```
0c shell32!SHDefExtractIconW
0d shell32!CExtractIcon::_ExtractW
0e shell32!CExtractIconBase::Extract
0f shell32!IExtractIcon_Extract
10 shell32!_GetILIndexGivenPXIcon
11 shell32!_GetILIndexFromItem
12 shell32!SHGetIconIndexFromPIDL
13 shell32!MapIDListToIconILIndex
14 shell32!CLoadSystemIconTask::InternalResumeRT
15 shell32!CRunnableTask::Run
16 shell32!CShellTask::TT_Run
17 shell32!CShellTaskThread::ThreadProc
18 shell32!CShellTaskThread::s_ThreadProc
19 shlwapi!ExecuteWorkItemThreadProc
1a ntdll!RtlpTpWorkCallback
1b ntdll!TppWorkerThread
1c kernel32!BaseThreadInitThunk
1d ntdll!RtlUserThreadStart


3 Id: 1344.830 Suspend: 1 Teb: 000007ff`fffd7000 Unfrozen
# Call Site
00 ntdll!NtWaitForMultipleObjects
01 KERNELBASE!WaitForMultipleObjectsEx
02 kernel32!WaitForMultipleObjects
03 prncache!PrintCache::Store::CacheStore::RegistryMonitor::MonitorRegistryChanges
04 prncache!PrintCache::Store::CacheStore::RegistryMonitor::MonitorRegistryChangesThreadProc
05 kernel32!BaseThreadInitThunk
06 ntdll!RtlUserThreadStart


4 Id: 1344.1edc Suspend: 1 Teb: 000007ff`fffd5000 Unfrozen
# Call Site
00 ntdll!NtWaitForSingleObject
01 ntdll!RtlpWaitOnCriticalSection
02 ntdll!RtlEnterCriticalSection
03 user32!BitmapFromDIB
04 user32!ConvertDIBBitmap
05 user32!ConvertDIBIcon
06 user32!CreateIconFromResourceEx
07 user32!PrivateEnumProc
08 kernel32!EnumResourceNamesInternal
09 kernel32!EnumResourceNamesExW
0a user32!PrivateExtractIconsW
0b shell32!SHPrivateExtractIcons
0c shell32!SHDefExtractIconW
0d shell32!CExtractIcon::_ExtractW
0e shell32!CExtractIconBase::Extract
0f shell32!IExtractIcon_Extract
10 shell32!_GetILIndexGivenPXIcon
11 shell32!_GetILIndexFromItem
12 shell32!SHGetIconIndexFromPIDL
13 shell32!MapIDListToIconILIndex
14 shell32!CLoadSystemIconTask::InternalResumeRT
15 shell32!CRunnableTask::Run
16 shell32!CShellTask::TT_Run
17 shell32!CShellTaskThread::ThreadProc
18 shell32!CShellTaskThread::s_ThreadProc
```

```
19 shlwapi!ExecuteWorkItemThreadProc
1a ntdll!RtlpTpWorkCallback
1b ntdll!TppWorkerThread
1c kernel32!BaseThreadInitThunk
1d ntdll!RtlUserThreadStart


5 Id: 1344.1b44 Suspend: 1 Teb: 000007ff`fffd3000 Unfrozen
# Call Site
00 user32!NtUserGetIconInfo
01 user32!CopyIcoCur
02 user32!InternalCopyImage
03 user32!CopyImage
04 comctl32!CImageList::_ReplaceIcon
05 comctl32!CImageList::ReplaceIcon
06 comctl32!CSparseImageList::ReplaceIcon
07 shell32!CIconCache::AddToBackIconTable
08 shell32!AddToBackIconTable
09 shell32!SHAddIconsToCache
0a shell32!_GetILIndexGivenPXIcon
0b shell32!_GetILIndexFromItem
0c shell32!SHGetIconIndexFromPIDL
0d shell32!MapIDListToIconILIndex
0e shell32!CLoadSystemIconTask::InternalResumeRT
0f shell32!CRunnableTask::Run
10 shell32!CShellTask::TT_Run
11 shell32!CShellTaskThread::ThreadProc
12 shell32!CShellTaskThread::s_ThreadProc
13 shlwapi!ExecuteWorkItemThreadProc
14 ntdll!RtlpTpWorkCallback
15 ntdll!TppWorkerThread
16 kernel32!BaseThreadInitThunk
17 ntdll!RtlUserThreadStart


6 Id: 1344.1d9c Suspend: 1 Teb: 000007ff`fffae000 Unfrozen
# Call Site
00 gdi32!NtUserSelectPalette
01 gdi32!SelectPalette
02 gdi32!SetDIBits
03 user32!BitmapFromDIB
04 user32!ConvertDIBBitmap
05 user32!ConvertDIBIcon
06 user32!CreateIconFromResourceEx
07 user32!PrivateEnumProc
08 kernel32!EnumResourceNamesInternal
09 kernel32!EnumResourceNamesExW
0a user32!PrivateExtractIconsW
0b shell32!SHPrivateExtractIcons
0c shell32!SHDefExtractIconW
0d shell32!CExtractIcon::_ExtractW
0e shell32!CExtractIconBase::Extract
0f shell32!IExtractIcon_Extract
10 shell32!_GetILIndexGivenPXIcon
11 shell32!_GetILIndexFromItem
12 shell32!SHGetIconIndexFromPIDL
13 shell32!MapIDListToIconILIndex
14 shell32!CLoadSystemIconTask::InternalResumeRT
```

```
15 shell32!CRunnableTask::Run
16 shell32!CShellTask::TT_Run
17 shell32!CShellTaskThread::ThreadProc
18 shell32!CShellTaskThread::s_ThreadProc
19 shlwapi!ExecuteWorkItemThreadProc
1a ntdll!RtlpTpWorkCallback
1b ntdll!TppWorkerThread
1c kernel32!BaseThreadInitThunk
1d ntdll!RtlUserThreadStart


7 Id: 1344.139c Suspend: 1 Teb: 000007ff`fffac000 Unfrozen
# Call Site
00 ntdll!NtWaitForMultipleObjects
01 KERNELBASE!WaitForMultipleObjectsEx
02 kernel32!WaitForMultipleObjectsExImplementation
03 user32!RealMsgWaitForMultipleObjectsEx
04 user32!MsgWaitForMultipleObjectsEx
05 user32!MsgWaitForMultipleObjects
06 shell32!CShellTaskScheduler::_TT_MsgWaitForMultipleObjects
07 shell32!CShellTaskScheduler::TT_TransitionThreadToRunningOrTerminating
08 shell32!CShellTaskThread::ThreadProc
09 shell32!CShellTaskThread::s_ThreadProc
0a shlwapi!ExecuteWorkItemThreadProc
0b ntdll!RtlpTpWorkCallback
0c ntdll!TppWorkerThread
0d kernel32!BaseThreadInitThunk
0e ntdll!RtlUserThreadStart


8 Id: 1344.1b80 Suspend: 1 Teb: 000007ff`fffaa000 Unfrozen
# Call Site
00 ntdll!ZwDelayExecution
01 KERNELBASE!SleepEx
02 ole32!CROIDTable::WorkerThreadLoop
03 ole32!CRpcThread::WorkerLoop
04 ole32!CRpcThreadCache::RpcWorkerThreadEntry
05 kernel32!BaseThreadInitThunk
06 ntdll!RtlUserThreadStart


9 Id: 1344.eb8 Suspend: 1 Teb: 000007ff`fffa8000 Unfrozen
# Call Site
00 ntdll!ZwAlpcSendWaitReceivePort
01 rpcrt4!LRPC_CCALL::SendReceive
02 rpcrt4!NdrpClientCall3
03 rpcrt4!NdrClientCall3
04 winspool!RpcFindNextPrinterChangeNotification
05 winspool!FindNextPrinterChangeNotification
06 prncache!PrintCache::Listeners::Listener::ProcessWait
07 prncache!PrintCache::Listeners::Listener::ProcessWaitCB
08 ntdll!TppWaitpExecuteCallback
09 ntdll!TppWorkerThread
0a kernel32!BaseThreadInitThunk
0b ntdll!RtlUserThreadStart
```

```
10 Id: 1344.f98 Suspend: 1 Teb: 000007ff`fffa6000 Unfrozen
# Call Site
00 ntdll!RtlUserThreadStart
```

// 12th dump

```
. 0 Id: 1344.1ca4 Suspend: 1 Teb: 000007ff`fffdd000 Unfrozen
# Call Site
00 usp10!otlChainingLookup::apply
01 usp10!ApplyLookup
02 usp10!ApplyFeatures
03 usp10!SubstituteOtlGlyphs
04 usp10!GenericEngineGetGlyphs
05 usp10!ShlShape
06 usp10!ScriptShape
07 usp10!RenderItemNoFallback
08 usp10!RenderItemWithFallback
09 usp10!RenderItem
0a usp10!ScriptStringAnalyzeGlyphs
0b usp10!ScriptStringAnalyse
0c lpk!LpkCharsetDraw
0d lpk!LpkDrawTextEx
0e user32!DT_DrawStr
0f user32!DT_DrawJustifiedLine
10 user32!DrawTextExWorker
11 user32!DrawTextW
12 comctl32!CLVView::_ComputeLabelSizeWorker
13 comctl32!CLVView::v_RecomputeLabelSize
14 comctl32!CLVListView::v_DrawItem
15 comctl32!CLVDrawItemManager::DrawItem
16 comctl32!CLVDrawManager::_PaintItems
17 comctl32!CLVDrawManager::_PaintWorkArea
18 comctl32!CLVDrawManager::_OnPaintWorkAreas
19 comctl32!CLVDrawManager::_OnPaint
1a comctl32!CListView::WndProc
1b comctl32!CListView::s_WndProc
1c user32!UserCallWinProcCheckWow
1d user32!CallWindowProcAorW
1e user32!CallWindowProcW
1f comctl32!CallOriginalWndProc
20 comctl32!CallNextSubclassProc
21 comctl32!DefSubclassProc
22 shell32!DefSubclassProc
23 shell32!CListViewHost::s_ListViewSubclassWndProc
24 comctl32!CallNextSubclassProc
25 comctl32!MasterSubclassProc
26 user32!UserCallWinProcCheckWow
27 user32!DispatchClientMessage
28 user32!_fnDWORD
29 ntdll!KiUserCallbackDispatcherContinue
2a user32!NtUserDispatchMessage
2b user32!DispatchMessageWorker
2c user32!IsDialogMessageW
2d comctl32!Prop_IsDialogMessage
2e comctl32!_RealPropertySheet
2f comctl32!_PropertySheet
```

```
30 comdlg32!Print_InvokePropertySheets
31 comdlg32!PrintDlgExX
32 comdlg32!PrintDlgExW
33 notepad!GetPrinterDCviaDialog
34 notepad!PrintIt
35 notepad!NPCommand
36 notepad!NPWndProc
37 user32!UserCallWinProcCheckWow
38 user32!DispatchMessageWorker
39 notepad!WinMain
3a notepad!DisplayNonGenuineDlgWorker
3b kernel32!BaseThreadInitThunk
3c ntdll!RtlUserThreadStart


1 Id: 1344.1ab0 Suspend: 1 Teb: 000007ff`fffdb000 Unfrozen
# Call Site
00 ntdll!NtWaitForMultipleObjects
01 ntdll!TppWaiterpThread
02 kernel32!BaseThreadInitThunk
03 ntdll!RtlUserThreadStart


2 Id: 1344.1638 Suspend: 1 Teb: 000007ff`fffd9000 Unfrozen
# Call Site
00 ntdll!NtUnmapViewOfSection
01 KERNELBASE!FreeLibrary
02 user32!PrivateExtractIconsW
03 shell32!SHPrivateExtractIcons
04 shell32!SHDefExtractIconW
05 shell32!CExtractIcon::_ExtractW
06 shell32!CExtractIconBase::Extract
07 shell32!IExtractIcon_Extract
08 shell32!_GetILIndexGivenPXIcon
09 shell32!_GetILIndexFromItem
0a shell32!SHGetIconIndexFromPIDL
0b shell32!MapIDListToIconILIndex
0c shell32!CLoadSystemIconTask::InternalResumeRT
0d shell32!CRunnableTask::Run
0e shell32!CShellTask::TT_Run
0f shell32!CShellTaskThread::ThreadProc
10 shell32!CShellTaskThread::s_ThreadProc
11 shlwapi!ExecuteWorkItemThreadProc
12 ntdll!RtlpTpWorkCallback
13 ntdll!TppWorkerThread
14 kernel32!BaseThreadInitThunk
15 ntdll!RtlUserThreadStart


3 Id: 1344.830 Suspend: 1 Teb: 000007ff`fffd7000 Unfrozen
# Call Site
00 ntdll!NtWaitForMultipleObjects
01 KERNELBASE!WaitForMultipleObjectsEx
02 kernel32!WaitForMultipleObjects
03 prncache!PrintCache::Store::CacheStore::RegistryMonitor::MonitorRegistryChanges
04 prncache!PrintCache::Store::CacheStore::RegistryMonitor::MonitorRegistryChangesThreadProc
05 kernel32!BaseThreadInitThunk
06 ntdll!RtlUserThreadStart
```

```
4 Id: 1344.1edc Suspend: 1 Teb: 000007ff`fffd5000 Unfrozen
# Call Site
00 ntdll!NtWaitForMultipleObjects
01 KERNELBASE!WaitForMultipleObjectsEx
02 kernel32!WaitForMultipleObjectsExImplementation
03 user32!RealMsgWaitForMultipleObjectsEx
04 user32!MsgWaitForMultipleObjectsEx
05 user32!MsgWaitForMultipleObjects
06 shell32!CShellTaskScheduler::_TT_MsgWaitForMultipleObjects
07 shell32!CShellTaskScheduler::TT_TransitionThreadToRunningOrTerminating
08 shell32!CShellTaskThread::ThreadProc
09 shell32!CShellTaskThread::s_ThreadProc
0a shlwapi!ExecuteWorkItemThreadProc
0b ntdll!RtlpTpWorkCallback
0c ntdll!TppWorkerThread
0d kernel32!BaseThreadInitThunk
0e ntdll!RtlUserThreadStart

5 Id: 1344.1b44 Suspend: 1 Teb: 000007ff`fffd3000 Unfrozen
# Call Site
00 ntdll!NtWaitForMultipleObjects
01 KERNELBASE!WaitForMultipleObjectsEx
02 kernel32!WaitForMultipleObjectsExImplementation
03 user32!RealMsgWaitForMultipleObjectsEx
04 user32!MsgWaitForMultipleObjectsEx
05 user32!MsgWaitForMultipleObjects
06 shell32!CShellTaskScheduler::_TT_MsgWaitForMultipleObjects
07 shell32!CShellTaskScheduler::TT_TransitionThreadToRunningOrTerminating
08 shell32!CShellTaskThread::ThreadProc
09 shell32!CShellTaskThread::s_ThreadProc
0a shlwapi!ExecuteWorkItemThreadProc
0b ntdll!RtlpTpWorkCallback
0c ntdll!TppWorkerThread
0d kernel32!BaseThreadInitThunk
0e ntdll!RtlUserThreadStart

6 Id: 1344.1d9c Suspend: 1 Teb: 000007ff`fffae000 Unfrozen
# Call Site
00 gdi32!ZwGdiSetDIBitsToDeviceInternal
01 gdi32!SetDIBitsToDevice
02 gdi32!SetDIBits
03 user32!BitmapFromDIB
04 user32!ConvertDIBBitmap
05 user32!ConvertDIBIcon
06 user32!CreateIconFromResourceEx
07 user32!PrivateEnumProc
08 kernel32!EnumResourceNamesInternal
09 kernel32!EnumResourceNamesExW
0a user32!PrivateExtractIconsW
0b shell32!SHPrivateExtractIcons
0c shell32!SHDefExtractIconW
0d shell32!CExtractIcon::_ExtractW
0e shell32!CExtractIconBase::Extract
0f shell32!IExtractIcon_Extract
10 shell32!_GetILIndexGivenPXIcon
11 shell32!_GetILIndexFromItem
```

```
12 shell32!SHGetIconIndexFromPIDL
13 shell32!MapIDListToIconILIndex
14 shell32!CLoadSystemIconTask::InternalResumeRT
15 shell32!CRunnableTask::Run
16 shell32!CShellTask::TT_Run
17 shell32!CShellTaskThread::ThreadProc
18 shell32!CShellTaskThread::s_ThreadProc
19 shlwapi!ExecuteWorkItemThreadProc
1a ntdll!RtlpTpWorkCallback
1b ntdll!TppWorkerThread
1c kernel32!BaseThreadInitThunk
1d ntdll!RtlUserThreadStart


7 Id: 1344.139c Suspend: 1 Teb: 000007ff`fffac000 Unfrozen
# Call Site
00 ntdll!ZwMapViewOfSection
01 KERNELBASE!BasepLoadLibraryAsDataFileInternal
02 KERNELBASE!LoadLibraryExW
03 user32!PrivateExtractIconsW
04 shell32!SHPrivateExtractIcons
05 shell32!SHDefExtractIconW
06 shell32!CExtractIcon::_ExtractW
07 shell32!CExtractIconBase::Extract
08 shell32!IExtractIcon_Extract
09 shell32!_GetILIndexGivenPXIcon
0a shell32!_GetILIndexFromItem
0b shell32!SHGetIconIndexFromPIDL
0c shell32!MapIDListToIconILIndex
0d shell32!CLoadSystemIconTask::InternalResumeRT
0e shell32!CRunnableTask::Run
0f shell32!CShellTask::TT_Run
10 shell32!CShellTaskThread::ThreadProc
11 shell32!CShellTaskThread::s_ThreadProc
12 shlwapi!ExecuteWorkItemThreadProc
13 ntdll!RtlpTpWorkCallback
14 ntdll!TppWorkerThread
15 kernel32!BaseThreadInitThunk
16 ntdll!RtlUserThreadStart


8 Id: 1344.1b80 Suspend: 1 Teb: 000007ff`fffaa000 Unfrozen
# Call Site
00 ntdll!ZwAlpcSendWaitReceivePort
01 rpcrt4!LRPC_CASSOCIATION::AlpcSendWaitReceivePort
02 rpcrt4!LRPC_BASE_CCALL::DoSendReceive
03 rpcrt4!LRPC_BASE_CCALL::SendReceive
04 rpcrt4!NdrpClientCall2
05 rpcrt4!NdrClientCall2
06 ole32!CRpcResolver::BulkUpdateOIDs
07 ole32!CROIDTable::ClientBulkUpdateOIDWithPingServer
08 ole32!CROIDTable::WorkerThreadLoop
09 ole32!CRpcThread::WorkerLoop
0a ole32!CRpcThreadCache::RpcWorkerThreadEntry
0b kernel32!BaseThreadInitThunk
0c ntdll!RtlUserThreadStart
```

```
 9 Id: 1344.eb8 Suspend: 1 Teb: 000007ff`fffa8000 Unfrozen
# Call Site
00 ntdll!NtWaitForWorkViaWorkerFactory
01 ntdll!TppWorkerThread
02 kernel32!BaseThreadInitThunk
03 ntdll!RtlUserThreadStart

10 Id: 1344.f98 Suspend: 1 Teb: 000007ff`fffa6000 Unfrozen
# Call Site
00 ntdll!NtWaitForWorkViaWorkerFactory
01 ntdll!TppWorkerThread
02 kernel32!BaseThreadInitThunk
03 ntdll!RtlUserThreadStart

11 Id: 1344.1fb0 Suspend: 1 Teb: 000007ff`fffa4000 Unfrozen
# Call Site
00 ntdll!RtlUserThreadStart
```

Exception Module

It is a module or component where the actual exception happened, for example, *ModuleA* from this **Exception Stack Trace** (page 386):

```
9 Id: 1df4.a08 Suspend: -1 Teb: 7fff4000 Unfrozen
ChildEBP RetAddr
1022f5a8 7c90df4a ntdll!KiFastSystemCallRet
1022f5ac 7c8648a2 ntdll!ZwWaitForMultipleObjects+0xc
1022f900 7c83ab50 kernel32!UnhandledExceptionFilter+0x8b9
1022f908 7c839b39 kernel32!BaseThreadStart+0x4d
1022f930 7c9032a8 kernel32!_except_handler3+0x61
1022f954 7c90327a ntdll!ExecuteHandler2+0x26
1022fa04 7c90e48a ntdll!ExecuteHandler+0x24
1022fa04 7c812afb ntdll!KiUserExceptionDispatcher+0xe
1022fd5c 0b82e680 kernel32!RaiseException+0x53
WARNING: Stack unwind information not available. Following frames may be wrong.
1022fd94 0b82d2f2 ModuleA+0x21e640
1022fde8 7753004f ModuleA+0x21d4f2
1022fdfc 7753032f ole32!CClassCache::CDllPathEntry::CanUnload_rl+0x3b
1022ff3c 7753028b ole32!CClassCache::FreeUnused+0x70
1022ff4c 775300b5 ole32!CoFreeUnusedLibrariesEx+0x36
1022ff58 77596af5 ole32!CoFreeUnusedLibraries+0x9
1022ff6c 77566ff9 ole32!CDllHost::MTAWorkerLoop+0x25
1022ff8c 7752687c ole32!CDllHost::WorkerThread+0xc1
1022ff94 774fe3ee ole32!DLLHostThreadEntry+0xd
1022ffa8 774fe456 ole32!CRpcThread::WorkerLoop+0x1e
1022ffb4 7c80b729 ole32!CRpcThreadCache::RpcWorkerThreadEntry+0x1b
1022ffec 00000000 kernel32!BaseThreadStart+0x37
```

Because we have **Software Exception** (page 977), we can use backward disassembly (**ub** WinDbg command) to check stack trace correctness in the case of stack unwind warnings (like in **Coincidental Symbolic Information** pattern, page 148). Here is another example, for recent MS Paint crash we observed, with *msvcrt* **Exception Module**. However, if we skip it as **Well-Tested Module** (page 1267), the next **Exception Module** candidate is *mspaint*.

```
0:000> kc
Call Site
ntdll!NtWaitForMultipleObjects
KERNELBASE!WaitForMultipleObjectsEx
kernel32!WaitForMultipleObjectsExImplementation
kernel32!WerpReportFaultInternal
kernel32!WerpReportFault
kernel32!BasepReportFault
kernel32!UnhandledExceptionFilter
ntdll! ?? ::FNODOBFM::`string'
ntdll!_C_specific_handler
ntdll!RtlpExecuteHandlerForException
ntdll!RtlDispatchException
ntdll!KiUserExceptionDispatch
msvcrt!memcpy
mspaint!CImgWnd::CmdCrop
```

```
mspaint!CPBView::OnImageCrop
mfc42u!_AfxDispatchCmdMsg
mfc42u!CCmdTarget::OnCmdMsg
mfc42u!CView::OnCmdMsg
mspaint!CPBView::OnCmdMsg
mfc42u!CFrameWnd::OnCmdMsg
mspaint!CGenericCommandSite::XGenericCommandSiteCommandHandler::Execute
UIRibbon!CControlUser::_ExecuteOnHandler
UIRibbon!CGenericControlUser::SetValueImpl
UIRibbon!CGenericDataSource::SetValue
UIRibbon!OfficeSpace::DataSource::SetValue
UIRibbon!OfficeSpace::FSControl::SetValue
UIRibbon!NetUI::DeferCycle::ProcessDataBindingPropertyChangeRecords
UIRibbon!NetUI::DeferCycle::HrAddDataBindingPropertyChangeRecord
UIRibbon!NetUI::Binding::SetDataSourceValue
UIRibbon!NetUI::Bindings::OnBindingPropertyChanged
UIRibbon!NetUI::Node::OnPropertyChanged
UIRibbon!FlexUI::Concept::OnPropertyChanged
UIRibbon!NetUI::Node::FExecuteCommand
UIRibbon!FlexUI::ExecuteAction::OnCommand
UIRibbon!NetUI::Node::FExecuteCommand
UIRibbon!NetUI::SimpleButton::OnEvent
UIRibbon!NetUI::Element::_DisplayNodeCallback
UIRibbon!GPCB::xwInvokeDirect
UIRibbon!GPCB::xwInvokeFull
UIRibbon!DUserSendEvent
UIRibbon!NetUI::Element::FireEvent
UIRibbon!NetUI::_FireClickEvent
UIRibbon!NetUI::SimpleButton::OnInput
UIRibbon!NetUI::Element::_DisplayNodeCallback
UIRibbon!GPCB::xwInvokeDirect
UIRibbon!GPCB::xwInvokeFull
UIRibbon!BaseMsgQ::xwProcessNL
UIRibbon!DelayedMsgQ::xwProcessDelayedNL
UIRibbon!ContextLock::~ContextLock
UIRibbon!HWndContainer::xdHandleMessage
UIRibbon!ExtraInfoWndProc
user32!UserCallWinProcCheckWow
user32!DispatchMessageWorker
mfc42u!CWinThread::PumpMessage
mfc42u!CWinThread::Run
mfc42u!AfxWinMain
mspaint!LDunscale
kernel32!BaseThreadInitThunk
ntdll!RtlUserThreadStart
```

Exception Reporting Thread

In addition to **Exception Thread** analysis pattern (or several threads when we have **Multiple Exceptions**, page 805) that we named **Exception Stack Trace** (page 387) there may be a separated thread that reports such exceptions (**Exception Reporting Thread**):

```
This dump file has an exception of interest stored in it.
The stored exception information can be accessed via .ecxr.
(4a0c.2ab4): Application hang - code cfffffff (first/second chance not available)
win32u!NtUserCreateWindowEx+0x14:

0:002> kc
# Call Site
00 win32u!NtUserCreateWindowEx
01 user32!VerNtUserCreateWindowEx
02 user32!CreateWindowInternal
03 user32!CreateWindowExW
04 CoreMessaging!Microsoft::CoreUI::Dispatch::UserAdapter::InitializeWindow
05 CoreMessaging!Microsoft::CoreUI::Dispatch::UserAdapter::Initialize
06 CoreMessaging!Microsoft::CoreUI::Dispatch::EventLoop::Callback_Run
07 CoreMessaging!Microsoft::CoreUI::Messaging::MessageSession$R::Microsoft__CoreUI__IExportMessageSession_Impl::Run
08 CoreMessaging!Microsoft::CoreUI::IExportMessageSession$X__ExportAdapter::Run
09 CoreMessaging!Windows::System::DispatcherQueue::RunLoop
0a CoreMessaging!Windows::System::DispatcherQueueController:: DispatcherQueueThreadProc
0b kernel32!BaseThreadInitThunk
0c ntdll!RtlUserThreadStart


0:002> ~42kc
# Call Site
00 ntdll!NtWaitForMultipleObjects
01 ntdll!WerpWaitForCrashReporting
02 ntdll!RtlReportExceptionEx
03 eModel!s_ReportAsyncBoundaryHangOnSuspendedThread
04 kernel32!BaseThreadInitThunk
05 ntdll!RtlUserThreadStart
```

We can spot such a thread in **Stack Trace Collection** (page 1053).

Although the example above is for application hang (**Blocked Thread**, page 93) and also illustrates **Self-Diagnosis** (page 949), similar threads may report **Handled Exceptions** (page 483). Usually, **Exception Threads** are also **Exception Reporting Threads** as shown in **Invalid Parameter** analysis pattern example (page 658).

Exception Stack Trace

This is a pattern that we see in many pattern interaction case studies published in Memory Dump Analysis Anthology volumes. We can also call it **Exception Thread**. It is **Stack Trace** (page 1033) that has exception processing functions, for example:

```
  9  Id: 1df4.a08 Suspend: -1 Teb: 7fff4000 Unfrozen
ChildEBP RetAddr
1022f5a8 7c90df4a ntdll!KiFastSystemCallRet
1022f5ac 7c8648a2 ntdll!ZwWaitForMultipleObjects+0xc
1022f900 7c83ab50 kernel32!UnhandledExceptionFilter+0x8b9
1022f908 7c839b39 kernel32!BaseThreadStart+0x4d
1022f930 7c9032a8 kernel32!_except_handler3+0x61
1022f954 7c90327a ntdll!ExecuteHandler2+0x26
1022fa04 7c90e48a ntdll!ExecuteHandler+0x24
1022fa04 7c812afb ntdll!KiUserExceptionDispatcher+0xe
1022fd5c 0b82e680 kernel32!RaiseException+0x53
1022fd94 0b82d2f2 DllA+0x21e640
1022fde8 7753004f DllA+0x21d4f2
1022fdfc 7753032f ole32!CClassCache::CDllPathEntry::CanUnload_rl+0x3b
1022ff3c 7753028b ole32!CClassCache::FreeUnused+0x70
1022ff4c 775300b5 ole32!CoFreeUnusedLibrariesEx+0x36
1022ff58 77596af5 ole32!CoFreeUnusedLibraries+0x9
1022ff6c 77566ff9 ole32!CDllHost::MTAWorkerLoop+0x25
1022ff8c 7752687c ole32!CDllHost::WorkerThread+0xc1
1022ff94 774fe3ee ole32!DLLHostThreadEntry+0xd
1022ffa8 774fe456 ole32!CRpcThread::WorkerLoop+0x1e
1022ffb4 7c80b729 ole32!CRpcThreadCache::RpcWorkerThreadEntry+0x1b
1022ffec 00000000 kernel32!BaseThreadStart+0x37
```

Such exceptions can be detected by the default analysis command (for example, **!analyze -v** WinDbg command) or by inspecting **Stack Trace Collection** (page 1052). However, if we do not see any exception thread, it does not mean there were no exceptions. There could be **Hidden Exceptions** (page 504) on raw stack data.

In our case we can get the exception information by looking at parameters to a unhandled exception filter:

```
0:009> kv 3
ChildEBP RetAddr Args to Child
1022f5a8 7c90df4a 7c8648a2 00000002 1022f730 ntdll!KiFastSystemCallRet
1022f5ac 7c8648a2 00000002 1022f730 00000001 ntdll!ZwWaitForMultipleObjects+0xc
1022f900 7c83ab50 1022f928 7c839b39 1022f930 kernel32!UnhandledExceptionFilter+0x8b9
```

```
0:009> .exptr 1022f928


----- Exception record at 1022fa1c:
ExceptionAddress: 7c812afb (kernel32!RaiseException+0x00000053)
  ExceptionCode: e06d7363 (C++ EH exception)
  ExceptionFlags: 00000001
NumberParameters: 3
  Parameter[0]: 19930520
  Parameter[1]: 1022fda4
  Parameter[2]: 0b985074
  pExceptionObject: 1022fda4
  _s_ThrowInfo : 0b985074


----- Context record at 1022fa3c:
eax=1022fd0c ebx=00000001 ecx=00000000 edx=1022fda4 esi=1022fd94 edi=77606068
eip=7c812afb esp=1022fd08 ebp=1022fd5c iopl=0 nv up ei pl nz na pe nc
cs=001b ss=0023 ds=0023 es=0023 fs=003b gs=0000 efl=00000206
kernel32!RaiseException+0x53:
7c812afb 5e pop esi
```

Comments

We can use Raymond Chen's technique to find out more about the type of C++ exception[66].

---

[66] https://devblogs.microsoft.com/oldnewthing/2010/07/30

Execution Residue

Linux

This is a Linux variant of **Execution Residue** pattern previously described for Mac OS X (page 391) and Windows (page 395) platforms. This is symbolic information left in a stack region including ASCII and UNICODE fragments or pointers to them, for example, return addresses from past function calls:

```
(gdb) bt
#0  0x00000000004431f1 in nanosleep ()
#1  0x00000000004430c0 in sleep ()
#2  0x0000000000400771 in procNE() ()
#3  0x00000000004007aa in bar_two() ()
#4  0x00000000004007b5 in foo_two() ()
#5  0x00000000004007c8 in thread_two(void*) ()
#6  0x00000000004140f0 in start_thread (arg=<optimized out>)
at pthread_create.c:304
#7  0x0000000000445879 in clone ()
#8  0x0000000000000000 in ?? ()

(gdb) x/512a $rsp-2000
0x7f4cacc42360: 0x0 0x0
0x7f4cacc42370: 0x0 0x0
0x7f4cacc42380: 0x0 0x0
0x7f4cacc42390: 0x0 0x0
[...]
0x7f4cacc42830: 0x0 0x0
0x7f4cacc42840: 0x0 0x0
0x7f4cacc42850: 0x0 0x0
0x7f4cacc42860: 0x7f4cacc42870 0x4005af <_Z6work_8v+9>
0x7f4cacc42870: 0x7f4cacc42880 0x4005ba <_Z6work_7v+9>
0x7f4cacc42880: 0x7f4cacc42890 0x4005c5 <_Z6work_6v+9>
0x7f4cacc42890: 0x7f4cacc428a0 0x4005d0 <_Z6work_5v+9>
0x7f4cacc428a0: 0x7f4cacc428b0 0x4005db <_Z6work_4v+9>
0x7f4cacc428b0: 0x7f4cacc428c0 0x4005e6 <_Z6work_3v+9>
0x7f4cacc428c0: 0x7f4cacc428d0 0x4005f1 <_Z6work_2v+9>
0x7f4cacc428d0: 0x7f4cacc428e0 0x4005fc <_Z6work_1v+9>
0x7f4cacc428e0: 0x7f4cacc42cf0 0x40060e <_Z4workv+16>
0x7f4cacc428f0: 0x0 0x0
0x7f4cacc42900: 0x0 0x0
0x7f4cacc42910: 0x0 0x0
[...]
0x7f4cacc42af0: 0x0 0x0
0x7f4cacc42b00: 0x0 0x0
0x7f4cacc42b10: 0x0 0x0
0x7f4cacc42b20: 0x0 0x4431e6 <nanosleep+38>
0x7f4cacc42b30: 0x0 0x4430c0 <sleep+224>
0x7f4cacc42b40: 0x0 0x0
0x7f4cacc42b50: 0x0 0x0
0x7f4cacc42b60: 0x0 0x0
0x7f4cacc42b70: 0x0 0x0
[...]
0x7f4cacc42cb0: 0x0 0x0
```

```
0x7f4cacc42cc0: 0x0 0x0
0x7f4cacc42cd0: 0x0 0x0
0x7f4cacc42ce0: 0xfffffed2 0x3ad3affa
0x7f4cacc42cf0: 0x7f4cacc42d00 0x0
0x7f4cacc42d00: 0x7f4cacc42d20 0x49c740 <default_attr>
0x7f4cacc42d10: 0x7f4cacc439c0 0x400771 <_Z6procNEv+19>
0x7f4cacc42d20: 0x7f4cacc42d30 0x4007aa <_Z7bar_twov+9>
0x7f4cacc42d30: 0x7f4cacc42d40 0x4007b5 <_Z7foo_twov+9>
0x7f4cacc42d40: 0x7f4cacc42d60 0x4007c8 <_Z10thread_twoPv+17>
0x7f4cacc42d50: 0x0 0x0
0x7f4cacc42d60: 0x0 0x4140f0 <start_thread+208>
0x7f4cacc42d70: 0x0 0x7f4cacc43700
0x7f4cacc42d80: 0x0 0x0
0x7f4cacc42d90: 0x0 0x0
[...]
```

However, supposed return addresses need to be checked for **Coincidental Symbolic Information** (page 145) pattern.

Mac OS X

This is a Mac OS X / GDB counterpart to **Execution Residue** pattern on Windows platforms (page 395):

```
(gdb) bt
#0  0x00007fff8616e82a in __kill ()
#1  0x00007fff8fab9a9c in abort ()
#2  0x000000010269dc29 in bar_5 ()
#3  0x000000010269dc39 in bar_4 ()
#4  0x000000010269dc49 in bar_3 ()
#5  0x000000010269dc59 in bar_2 ()
#6  0x000000010269dc69 in bar_1 ()
#7  0x000000010269dc79 in bar ()
#8  0x000000010269dca0 in main (argc=1, argv=0x7fff6229cb00)


(gdb) x $rsp
0x7fff6229ca38: 0x8fab9a9c


(gdb) x/1000a 0x7fff6229c000
0x7fff6229c000: 0x7fff8947b000 0x7fff8947b570
0x7fff6229c010: 0x4f3ee10c 0x7fff90cb0000
0x7fff6229c020: 0x7fff90cb04d0 0x4e938b16
[...]
0x7fff6229c5f0: 0x7fff622d8d80 0x10269d640
0x7fff6229c600: 0x7fff6229cad0 0x7fff622a460b
0x7fff6229c610: 0x100000000 0x269d000
0x7fff6229c620: 0x7fff6229c630 0x10269db59 <foo_8+9>
0x7fff6229c630: 0x7fff6229c640 0x10269db69 <foo_7+9>
0x7fff6229c640: 0x7fff6229c650 0x10269db79 <foo_6+9>
0x7fff6229c650: 0x7fff6229c660 0x10269db89 <foo_5+9>
0x7fff6229c660: 0x7fff6229c670 0x10269db99 <foo_4+9>
0x7fff6229c670: 0x7fff6229c680 0x10269dba9 <foo_3+9>
0x7fff6229c680: 0x7fff6229c690 0x10269dbb9 <foo_2+9>
0x7fff6229c690: 0x7fff6229c6a0 0x10269dbc9 <foo_1+9>
0x7fff6229c6a0: 0x7fff6229cac0 0x10269dbee <foo+30>
0x7fff6229c6b0: 0x0 0x0
0x7fff6229c6c0: 0x0 0x0
[...]
0x7fff6229c8d0: 0x7fff6229c960 0x7fff622b49cd
0x7fff6229c8e0: 0x10269f05c 0x0
0x7fff6229c8f0: 0x7fff622c465c 0x7fff8a31e5c0 <_Z21dyldGlobalLockReleasev>
0x7fff6229c900: 0x7fff8fab99eb <abort> 0x10269f05c
0x7fff6229c910: 0x101000000000000 0x7fff622d2110
0x7fff6229c920: 0x7fff622d8d80 0x10269f078
0x7fff6229c930: 0x7fff622daac8 0x18
0x7fff6229c940: 0x0 0x0
0x7fff6229c950: 0x10269e030 0x0
0x7fff6229c960: 0x7fff6229c980 0x7fff622a1922
0x7fff6229c970: 0x0 0x0
0x7fff6229c980: 0x7fff6229ca50 0x7fff8a31e716 <dyld_stub_binder_+13>
0x7fff6229c990: 0x1 0x7fff6229cb00
0x7fff6229c9a0: 0x7fff6229cb10 0xe223ea612ddc10b7
0x7fff6229c9b0: 0x8 0x0
0x7fff6229c9c0: 0xe223ea612ddc10b7 0x0
```

```
0x7fff6229c9d0: 0x0 0x0
0x7fff6229c9e0: 0x585f5f00474e414c 0x20435058005f4350
0x7fff6229c9f0: 0x0 0x0
0x7fff6229ca00: 0x0 0x0
0x7fff6229ca10: 0x0 0x0
0x7fff6229ca20: 0x0 0x0
0x7fff6229ca30: 0x7fff6229ca60 0x7fff8fab9a9c <abort+177>
0x7fff6229ca40: 0x0 0x0
0x7fff6229ca50: 0x7fffffffffdf 0x0
0x7fff6229ca60: 0x7fff6229ca70 0x10269dc29 <bar_5+9>
0x7fff6229ca70: 0x7fff6229ca80 0x10269dc39 <bar_4+9>
0x7fff6229ca80: 0x7fff6229ca90 0x10269dc49 <bar_3+9>
0x7fff6229ca90: 0x7fff6229caa0 0x10269dc59 <bar_2+9>
0x7fff6229caa0: 0x7fff6229cab0 0x10269dc69 <bar_1+9>
0x7fff6229cab0: 0x7fff6229cac0 0x10269dc79 <bar+9>
0x7fff6229cac0: 0x7fff6229cae0 0x10269dca0 <main+32>
0x7fff6229cad0: 0x7fff6229cb00 0x1
0x7fff6229cae0: 0x7fff6229caf0 0x10269db34 <start+52>
0x7fff6229caf0: 0x0 0x1
0x7fff6229cb00: 0x7fff6229cc48 0x0
0x7fff6229cb10: 0x7fff6229ccae 0x7fff6229ccca
[...]
```

Here's the source code of the modeling application:

```
#define def_call(name,x,y) void name##_##x() { name##_##y(); }
#define def_final(name,x) void name##_##x() { }
#define def_final_abort(name,x) void name##_##x() { abort(); }
#define def_init(name,y) void name() { name##_##y(); }
#define def_init_alloc(name,y,size) void name() { int arr[size]; name##_##y(); *arr=0; }

def_final(foo,9)
def_call(foo,8,9)
def_call(foo,7,8)
def_call(foo,6,7)
def_call(foo,5,6)
def_call(foo,4,5)
def_call(foo,3,4)
def_call(foo,2,3)
def_call(foo,1,2)
def_init_alloc(foo,1,256)
def_final_abort(bar,5)
def_call(bar,4,5)
def_call(bar,3,4)
def_call(bar,2,3)
def_call(bar,1,2)
def_init(bar,1)

int main(int argc, const char * argv[])
{
        foo();
        bar();
}
```

Windows

Managed Space

This is a .NET counterpart to unmanaged and native code **Execution Residue** pattern. Here we can use SOS extension **!DumpStack** command for call level execution residue (see **Caller-n-Callee** pattern example, page 122) and **!DumpStackObjects** (**!dso**) for managed object references found on a raw stack:

```
0:011> !DumpStackObjects
OS Thread Id: 0x8e0 (11)
ESP/REG Object Name
09efe4b8 0a2571bc System.Threading.Thread
09efe538 0a1ffddc System.Threading.Thread
09efe844 0a1ffba8 UserQuery
09efe974 0a1ffce0 System.Signature
09efea20 0a1ffd10 System.RuntimeTypeHandle[]
09efeae8 08985e14 System.Object[] (System.Reflection.AssemblyName[])
09efeaec 0a1ffa78 System.Diagnostics.Stopwatch
09efeaf0 0a1ffa6c LINQPad.Extensibility.DataContext.QueryExecutionManager
09efeafc 0a1ffba8 UserQuery
09efeb00 0a1ffa58 System.RuntimeType
09efeb04 08995474 LINQPad.ObjectGraph.Formatters.XhtmlWriter
09efeb08 08985dfc System.Reflection.Assembly
09efeb0c 08985dc8 LINQPad.ExecutionModel.ResultData
09efeb10 08984548 LINQPad.ExecutionModel.Server
09efebdc 0a1ffbe8 System.Reflection.RuntimeMethodInfo
09efebe0 0a1fcfc4 LINQPad.ExecutionModel.ConsoleTextReader
09efebe4 0a1fcddc System.IO.StreamReader+NullStreamReader
09efebe8 0899544c System.IO.TextWriter+SyncTextWriter
09efebec 08985efc System.Reflection.AssemblyName
09efebf0 08985d4c System.String C:\Users\Training\AppData\Local\Temp\LINQPad\fcamvgpa
09efec30 08984548 LINQPad.ExecutionModel.Server
09efeedc 08985910 System.Threading.ThreadStart


0:011> !DumpObj 0a2571bc
Name: System.Threading.Thread
MethodTable: 790fe704
EEClass: 790fe694
Size: 56(0x38) bytes
(C:\Windows\assembly\GAC_32\mscorlib\2.0.0.0__b77a5c561934e089\mscorlib.dll)
Fields:
MT Field Offset Type VT Attr Value Name
7910a5c4 4000634 4 ….Contexts.Context 0 instance 08980ee4 m_Context
79104de8 4000635 8 ….ExecutionContext 0 instance 00000000 m_ExecutionContext
790fd8c4 4000636 c System.String 0 instance 00000000 m_Name
790fe3b0 4000637 10 System.Delegate 0 instance 00000000 m_Delegate
79130084 4000638 14 System.Object[][] 0 instance 00000000 m_ThreadStaticsBuckets
7912d7c0 4000639 18 System.Int32[] 0 instance 00000000 m_ThreadStaticsBits
791028f4 400063a 1c …ation.CultureInfo 0 instance 00000000 m_CurrentCulture
791028f4 400063b 20 …ation.CultureInfo 0 instance 00000000 m_CurrentUICulture
790fd0f0 400063c 24 System.Object 0 instance 00000000 m_ThreadStartArg
791016bc 400063d 28 System.IntPtr 1 instance 8f69280 DONT_USE_InternalThread
79102290 400063e 2c System.Int32 1 instance 2 m_Priority
```

```
79102290 400063f 30 System.Int32 1 instance 11 m_ManagedThreadId
7910a7a8 4000640 168 …LocalDataStoreMgr 0 shared static s_LocalDataStoreMgr
>> Domain:Value 000710a8:06c42ef4 08e65d48:00000000 <<
790fd0f0 4000641 16c System.Object 0 shared static s_SyncObject
>> Domain:Value 000710a8:017b25d8 08e65d48:0898381c <<
```

Although unmanaged, CLR and JIT-code residue is useful for analysis, for example, as shown in **Handled Exception** (page 477) pattern examples.

Comments

Sometimes, if no exceptions are found on raw stack we can search all runtime types, for example:

```
0:000> !DumpRuntimeTypes
[...]
098b93e8 05179888 05622254 CustomException
[...]
09bcd368 ? 6969470c System.NullReferenceException
[...]
```

!DumpStackObjects can also accept the range, for example, the full stack region from **!teb** command (similar to **dps** or **dpS**).

Unmanaged Space

For the pattern about **NULL Code Pointer** (page 836), we created a simple program that crashes when we pass a NULL thread procedure pointer to *CreateThread* function. We might expect to see little in the raw stack data[67] because there was no user-supplied thread code. In reality, if we dump it we will see a lot of symbolic information for code and data including ASCII and UNICODE fragments that we call **Execution Residue** patterns, and one of them is **Exception Handling Residue**[68] we can use to check for **Hidden Exceptions** (page 506) and differentiate between 1st and 2nd chance exceptions[69]. Code residues are very powerful in reconstructing stack traces manually[70] or looking for partial stack traces and **Historical Information** (page 543).

To show typical execution residues we created another small program with two additional threads based on Visual Studio Win32 project. After we dismiss *About* box we create the first thread, and then we crash the process when creating the second thread because of the NULL thread procedure:

```
typedef DWORD (WINAPI *THREADPROC)(PVOID);

DWORD WINAPI ThreadProc(PVOID pvParam)
{
    for (unsigned int i = 0xFFFFFFFF; i; --i);
    return 0;
}

// Message handler for about box.
INT_PTR CALLBACK About(HWND hDlg, UINT message, WPARAM wParam, LPARAM lParam)
{
    UNREFERENCED_PARAMETER(lParam);
    switch (message)
    {
    case WM_INITDIALOG:
        return (INT_PTR)TRUE;

    case WM_COMMAND:
        if (LOWORD(wParam) == IDOK || LOWORD(wParam) == IDCANCEL)
        {
            EndDialog(hDlg, LOWORD(wParam));
            THREADPROC thProc = ThreadProc;
            HANDLE hThread = CreateThread(NULL, 0, ThreadProc, 0, 0, NULL);
            CloseHandle(hThread);
            Sleep(1000);
            hThread = CreateThread(NULL, 0, NULL, 0, 0, NULL);
            CloseHandle(hThread);
            return (INT_PTR)TRUE;
        }
        break;
    }
```

---

[67] Raw Stack Dump of All Threads (Process Dump), Memory Dump Analysis Anthology, Volume 1, page 231
[68] This is a pattern we may add in the future
[69] How to Distinguish Between 1st and 2nd Chances, Memory Dump Analysis Anthology, Volume 1, page 109
[70] Manual Stack Trace Reconstruction, Memory Dump Analysis Anthology, Volume 1, page 157

```
    return (INT_PTR)FALSE;
}
```

When we open the crash dump we see these threads:

```
0:002> ~*kL

   0  Id: cb0.9ac Suspend: 1 Teb: 7efdd000 Unfrozen
ChildEBP RetAddr
0012fdf4 00411554 user32!NtUserGetMessage+0x15
0012ff08 00412329 NullThread!wWinMain+0xa4
0012ffb8 0041208d NullThread!__tmainCRTStartup+0x289
0012ffc0 7d4e7d2a NullThread!wWinMainCRTStartup+0xd
0012fff0 00000000 kernel32!BaseProcessStart+0x28

   1  Id: cb0.8b4 Suspend: 1 Teb: 7efda000 Unfrozen
ChildEBP RetAddr
01eafea4 7d63f501 ntdll!NtWaitForMultipleObjects+0x15
01eaff48 7d63f988 ntdll!EtwpWaitForMultipleObjectsEx+0xf7
01eaffb8 7d4dfe21 ntdll!EtwpEventPump+0x27f
01eaffec 00000000 kernel32!BaseThreadStart+0x34

   2  Id: cb0.ca8 Suspend: 1 Teb: 7efd7000 Unfrozen
ChildEBP RetAddr
0222ffb8 7d4dfe21 NullThread!ThreadProc+0x34
0222ffec 00000000 kernel32!BaseThreadStart+0x34

#  3  Id: cb0.5bc Suspend: 1 Teb: 7efaf000 Unfrozen
ChildEBP RetAddr
WARNING: Frame IP not in any known module. Following frames may be wrong.
0236ffb8 7d4dfe21 0x0
0236ffec 00000000 kernel32!BaseThreadStart+0x34

   4  Id: cb0.468 Suspend: -1 Teb: 7efac000 Unfrozen
ChildEBP RetAddr
01f7ffb4 7d674807 ntdll!NtTerminateThread+0x12
01f7ffc4 7d66509f ntdll!RtlExitUserThread+0x26
01f7fff4 00000000 ntdll!DbgUiRemoteBreakin+0x41
```

We see our first created thread looping:

```
0:003> ~2s
eax=cbcf04b5 ebx=00000000 ecx=00000000 edx=00000000 esi=00000000 edi=0222ffb8
eip=00411aa4 esp=0222fee0 ebp=0222ffb8 iopl=0 nv up ei ng nz na po nc
cs=0023 ss=002b ds=002b es=002b fs=0053 gs=002b efl=00000282
NullThread!ThreadProc+0x34:
00411aa4 7402    je    NullThread!ThreadProc+0x38 (00411aa8)    [br=0]
```

```
0:002> u
NullThread!ThreadProc+0x34:
00411aa4 je          NullThread!ThreadProc+0x38 (00411aa8)
00411aa6 jmp         NullThread!ThreadProc+0x27 (00411a97)
00411aa8 xor         eax,eax
00411aaa pop         edi
00411aab pop         esi
00411aac pop         ebx
00411aad mov         esp,ebp
00411aaf pop         ebp
```

We might expect it is having very little in its raw stack data but what we see when we dump its stack range from **!teb** command is **Thread Startup Residue** (this is a pattern we may add in the future) where some symbolic information might be **Coincidental** too (**Coincidental Symbolic Information**, page 148):

```
0:002> dds 0222f000  02230000
0222f000  00000000
0222f004  00000000
0222f008  00000000
...
0222f104  00000000
0222f108  00000000
0222f10c  00000000
0222f110  7d621954 ntdll!RtlImageNtHeaderEx+0xee
0222f114  7efde000
0222f118  00000000
0222f11c  00000001
0222f120  000000e8
0222f124  004000e8 NullThread!_enc$textbss$begin <PERF>
(NullThread+0xe8)
0222f128  00000000
0222f12c  0222f114
0222f130  00000000
0222f134  0222fca0
0222f138  7d61f1f8 ntdll!_except_handler3
0222f13c  7d621958 ntdll!RtlpRunTable+0x4a0
0222f140  ffffffff
0222f144  7d621954 ntdll!RtlImageNtHeaderEx+0xee
0222f148  7d6218ab ntdll!RtlImageNtHeader+0x1b
0222f14c  00000001
0222f150  00400000 NullThread!_enc$textbss$begin <PERF>
(NullThread+0x0)
0222f154  00000000
0222f158  00000000
0222f15c  0222f160
0222f160  004000e8 NullThread!_enc$textbss$begin <PERF>
(NullThread+0xe8)
0222f164  0222f7bc
0222f168  7d4dfea3 kernel32!ConsoleApp+0xe
0222f16c  00400000 NullThread!_enc$textbss$begin <PERF>
(NullThread+0x0)
0222f170  7d4dfe77 kernel32!ConDllInitialize+0x1f5
0222f174  00000000
0222f178  7d4dfe8c kernel32!ConDllInitialize+0x20a
0222f17c  00000000
0222f180  00000000
...
0222f290  00000000
0222f294  0222f2b0
0222f298  7d6256e8 ntdll!bsearch+0x42
0222f29c  00180144
0222f2a0  0222f2b4
0222f2a4  7d625992 ntdll!ARRAY_FITS+0x29
0222f2a8  00000a8c
0222f2ac  00001f1c
0222f2b0  0222f2c0
0222f2b4  0222f2f4
0222f2b8  7d625944
ntdll!RtlpLocateActivationContextSection+0x1da
```

```
0222f2bc  00001f1c
0222f2c0  000029a8
...
0222f2e0  536cd652
0222f2e4  0222f334
0222f2e8  7d625b62 ntdll!RtlpFindUnicodeStringInSection+0x7b
0222f2ec  0222f418
0222f2f0  00000000
0222f2f4  0222f324
0222f2f8  7d6257f1
ntdll!RtlpFindNextActivationContextSection+0x64
0222f2fc  00181f1c
0222f300  c0150008
...
0222f320  7efd7000
0222f324  0222f344
0222f328  7d625cd2
ntdll!RtlFindNextActivationContextSection+0x46
0222f32c  0222f368
0222f330  0222f3a0
0222f334  0222f38c
0222f338  0222f340
0222f33c  00181f1c
0222f340  00000000
0222f344  0222f390
0222f348  7d625ad8
ntdll!RtlFindActivationContextSectionString+0xe1
0222f34c  0222f368
0222f350  0222f3a0
...
0222f38c  00000a8c
0222f390  0222f454
0222f394  7d626381
ntdll!CsrCaptureMessageMultiUnicodeStringsInPlace+0xa57
0222f398  00000003
0222f39c  00000000
0222f3a0  00181f1c
0222f3a4  0222f418
0222f3a8  0222f3b4
0222f3ac  7d6a0340 ntdll!LdrApiDefaultExtension
0222f3b0  7d6263df
ntdll!CsrCaptureMessageMultiUnicodeStringsInPlace+0xb73
0222f3b4  00000040
0222f3b8  00000000
...
0222f420  00000000
0222f424  0222f458
0222f428  7d625f9a
ntdll!CsrCaptureMessageMultiUnicodeStringsInPlace+0x4c1
0222f42c  00020000
0222f430  0222f44c
0222f434  0222f44c
0222f438  0222f44c
0222f43c  00000002
```

```
0222f440  00000002
0222f444  7d625f9a
ntdll!CsrCaptureMessageMultiUnicodeStringsInPlace+0x4c1
0222f448  00020000
0222f44c  00000000
0222f450  00003cfb
0222f454  0222f5bc
0222f458  0222f4f4
0222f45c  0222f5bc
0222f460  7d626290
ntdll!RtlDosApplyFileIsolationRedirection_Ustr+0x346
0222f464  0222f490
0222f468  00000000
0222f46c  0222f69c
0222f470  7d6262f5
ntdll!RtlDosApplyFileIsolationRedirection_Ustr+0x3de
0222f474  0222f510
0222f478  7d6a0340 ntdll!LdrApiDefaultExtension
0222f47c  7d626290
ntdll!RtlDosApplyFileIsolationRedirection_Ustr+0x346
0222f480  00000000
0222f484  00800000
...
0222f544  00000000
0222f548  00000001
0222f54c  7d6a0290 ntdll!LdrpHashTable+0x50
0222f550  00000000
0222f554  00500000
...
0222f59c  00000000
0222f5a0  0222f5d4
0222f5a4  7d6251d0 ntdll!LdrUnlockLoaderLock+0x84
0222f5a8  7d6251d7 ntdll!LdrUnlockLoaderLock+0xad
0222f5ac  00000000
0222f5b0  0222f69c
0222f5b4  00000000
0222f5b8  00003cfb
0222f5bc  0222f5ac
0222f5c0  7d626de0 ntdll!LdrGetDllHandleEx+0xbe
0222f5c4  0222f640
0222f5c8  7d61f1f8 ntdll!_except_handler3
0222f5cc  7d6251e0 ntdll!`string'+0x74
0222f5d0  ffffffff
0222f5d4  7d6251d7 ntdll!LdrUnlockLoaderLock+0xad
0222f5d8  7d626fb3 ntdll!LdrGetDllHandleEx+0x368
0222f5dc  00000001
0222f5e0  0ca80042
0222f5e4  7d626f76 ntdll!LdrGetDllHandleEx+0x329
0222f5e8  00000000
0222f5ec  7d626d0b ntdll!LdrGetDllHandle
0222f5f0  00000002
0222f5f4  001a0018
...
0222f640  0222f6a8
0222f644  7d61f1f8 ntdll!_except_handler3
0222f648  7d626e60 ntdll!`string'+0xb4
0222f64c  ffffffff
0222f650  7d626f76 ntdll!LdrGetDllHandleEx+0x329
0222f654  7d626d23 ntdll!LdrGetDllHandle+0x18
0222f658  00000001
...
0222f66c  0222f6b8
0222f670  7d4dff0e kernel32!GetModuleHandleForUnicodeString+0x20
0222f674  00000001
0222f678  00000000
0222f67c  0222f6d4
0222f680  7d4dff1e kernel32!GetModuleHandleForUnicodeString+0x97
0222f684  00000000
0222f688  7efd7c00
0222f68c  00000002
0222f690  00000001
0222f694  00000000
0222f698  0222f6f0
0222f69c  7d4c0000 kernel32!_imp__NtFsControlFile <PERF>
(kernel32+0x0)
0222f6a0  0222f684
0222f6a4  7efd7c00
0222f6a8  0222fb20
0222f6ac  7d4d89c4 kernel32!_except_handler3
0222f6b0  7d4dff28 kernel32!`string'+0x18
0222f6b4  ffffffff
0222f6b8  7d4dff1e kernel32!GetModuleHandleForUnicodeString+0x97
0222f6bc  7d4e001f kernel32!BasepGetModuleHandleExW+0x17f
0222f6c0  7d4e009f kernel32!BasepGetModuleHandleExW+0x23c
0222f6c4  00000000
0222f6c8  0222fc08
0222f6cc  00000001
0222f6d0  ffffffff
0222f6d4  001a0018
0222f6d8  7efd7c00
0222f6dc  0222fb50
0222f6e0  00000000
0222f6e4  00000000
0222f6e8  00000000
0222f6ec  02080000 oleaut32!_PictSaveEnhMetaFile+0x76
0222f6f0  0222f90c
0222f6f4  02080000 oleaut32!_PictSaveEnhMetaFile+0x76
0222f6f8  0222f704
0222f6fc  00000000
0222f700  7d4c0000 kernel32!_imp__NtFsControlFile <PERF>
(kernel32+0x0)
0222f704  00000000
0222f708  02080000 oleaut32!_PictSaveEnhMetaFile+0x76
0222f70c  0222f928
0222f710  02080000 oleaut32!_PictSaveEnhMetaFile+0x76
0222f714  0222f720
0222f718  00000000
0222f71c  7d4c0000 kernel32!_imp__NtFsControlFile <PERF>
(kernel32+0x0)
0222f720  00000000
0222f724  00000000
...
0222f7b8  0000f949
0222f7bc  0222fbf4
0222f7c0  7d4dfdd0 kernel32!_BaseDllInitialize+0x6b
0222f7c4  00000002
0222f7c8  00000000
0222f7cc  00000000
0222f7d0  7d4dfde4 kernel32!_BaseDllInitialize+0x495
0222f7d4  00000000
0222f7d8  7efde000
0222f7dc  7d4c0000 kernel32!_imp__NtFsControlFile <PERF>
(kernel32+0x0)
0222f7e0  00000000
0222f7e4  00000000
...
0222f894  01c58ae0
0222f898  0222fac0
0222f89c  7d62155b ntdll!RtlAllocateHeap+0x460
0222f8a0  7d61f78c ntdll!RtlAllocateHeap+0xee7
0222f8a4  00000000
0222f8a8  0222fc08
...
0222f8d8  00000000
0222f8dc  7d621954 ntdll!RtlImageNtHeaderEx+0xee
0222f8e0  0222f9a4
0222f8e4  7d614c88 ntdll!$$VProc_ImageExportDirectory+0x2c48
0222f8e8  0222f9a6
0222f8ec  7d612040 ntdll!$$VProc_ImageExportDirectory
0222f8f0  00000221
0222f8f4  0222f944
0222f8f8  7d627405 ntdll!LdrpSnapThunk+0xc0
0222f8fc  0222f9a6
0222f900  00000584
0222f904  7d600000 ntdll!RtlDosPathSeperatorsString <PERF>
(ntdll+0x0)
0222f908  7d613678 ntdll!$$VProc_ImageExportDirectory+0x1638
0222f90c  7d614c88 ntdll!$$VProc_ImageExportDirectory+0x2c48
0222f910  0222f9a4
0222f914  00000001
```

```
0222f918  0222f9a4
0222f91c  00000000
0222f920  0222f990
0222f924  7d6000f0 ntdll!RtlDosPathSeperatorsString <PERF>
(ntdll+0xf0)
0222f928  0222f968
0222f92c  00000001
0222f930  0222f9a4
0222f934  7d6000f0 ntdll!RtlDosPathSeperatorsString <PERF>
(ntdll+0xf0)
0222f938  0222f954
0222f93c  00000000
0222f940  00000000
0222f944  0222fa00
0222f948  7d62757a ntdll!LdrpGetProcedureAddress+0x189
0222f94c  0222f95c
0222f950  00000098
0222f954  00000005
0222f958  01c44f48
0222f95c  0222fb84
0222f960  7d62155b ntdll!RtlAllocateHeap+0x460
0222f964  7d61f78c ntdll!RtlAllocateHeap+0xee7
0222f968  00000000
0222f96c  0000008c
0222f970  00000000
0222f974  7d4d8472 kernel32!$$VProc_ImageExportDirectory+0x6d4e
0222f978  0222fa1c
0222f97c  7d627607 ntdll!LdrpGetProcedureAddress+0x274
0222f980  7d612040 ntdll!$$VProc_ImageExportDirectory
0222f984  002324f8
0222f988  7d600000 ntdll!RtlDosPathSeperatorsString <PERF>
(ntdll+0x0)
0222f98c  0222faa8
0222f990  0000a7bb
0222f994  00221f08
0222f998  0222f9a4
0222f99c  7d627c2e ntdll!RtlDecodePointer
0222f9a0  00000000
0222f9a4  74520000
0222f9a8  6365446c
0222f9ac  5065446f
0222f9b0  746e696f
0222f9b4  00007265
0222f9b8  7d627c2e ntdll!RtlDecodePointer
0222f9bc  00000000
...
0222f9f8  01c40640
0222f9fc  00000000
0222fa00  7d6275b2 ntdll!LdrpGetProcedureAddress+0xb3
0222fa04  7d627772 ntdll!LdrpSnapThunk+0x31c
0222fa08  7d600000 ntdll!RtlDosPathSeperatorsString <PERF>
(ntdll+0x0)
0222fa0c  0222fa44
0222fa10  00000000
0222fa14  0222faa8
0222fa18  00000000
0222fa1c  0222fab0
0222fa20  00000001
0222fa24  00000001
0222fa28  00000000
0222fa2c  0222fa9c
0222fa30  7d4c00e8 kernel32!_imp__NtFsControlFile <PERF>
(kernel32+0xe8)
0222fa34  01c44fe0
0222fa38  00000001
0222fa3c  01c401a0
0222fa40  7d4c00e8 kernel32!_imp__NtFsControlFile <PERF>
(kernel32+0xe8)
0222fa44  00110010
0222fa48  7d4d8478 kernel32!$$VProc_ImageExportDirectory+0x6d54
0222fa4c  00000000
0222fa50  0222fb0c
0222fa54  7d62757a ntdll!LdrpGetProcedureAddress+0x189
0222fa58  7d600000 ntdll!RtlDosPathSeperatorsString <PERF>
(ntdll+0x0)
0222fa5c  00000000
0222fa60  0022faa8
0222fa64  0222fab0
0222fa68  0222fb0c
0222fa6c  7d627607 ntdll!LdrpGetProcedureAddress+0x274
0222fa70  7d6a0180 ntdll!LdrpLoaderLock
0222fa74  7d6275b2 ntdll!LdrpGetProcedureAddress+0xb3
0222fa78  102ce1ac msvcr80d!`string'
0222fa7c  0222fc08
0222fa80  0000ffff
0222fa84  0022f8b0
0222fa88  0022f8a0
0222fa8c  00000003
0222fa90  0222fbd4
0222fa94  020215fc oleaut32!DllMain+0x2c
0222fa98  02020000 oleaut32!_imp__RegFlushKey <PERF>
(oleaut32+0x0)
0222fa9c  00000002
0222faa0  00000000
0222faa4  00000000
0222faa8  00000002
0222faac  0202162d oleaut32!DllMain+0x203
0222fab0  65440000
0222fab4  02020000 oleaut32!_imp__RegFlushKey <PERF>
(oleaut32+0x0)
0222fab8  00000001
0222fabc  00726574
0222fac0  0222facc
0222fac4  7d627c2e ntdll!RtlDecodePointer
0222fac8  00000000
0222facc  65440000
0222fad0  00000000
0222fad4  00000000
0222fad8  00726574
0222fadc  00000005
0222fae0  00000000
0222fae4  1021af95 msvcr80d!_heap_alloc_dbg+0x375
0222fae8  002322f0
0222faec  00000000
0222faf0  01c40238
0222faf4  0222fa78
0222faf8  7efd7bf8
0222fafc  00000020
0222fb00  7d61f1f8 ntdll!_except_handler3
0222fb04  7d6275b8 ntdll!`string'+0xc
0222fb08  ffffffff
0222fb0c  7d6275b2 ntdll!LdrpGetProcedureAddress+0xb3
0222fb10  00000000
0222fb14  00000000
0222fb18  0222fb48
0222fb1c  00000000
0222fb20  01000000
0222fb24  00000001
0222fb28  0222fb50
0222fb2c  7d4dac3a kernel32!GetProcAddress+0x44
0222fb30  0222fb50
0222fb34  7d4dac4c kernel32!GetProcAddress+0x5c
0222fb38  0222fc08
0222fb3c  00000013
0222fb40  00000000
0222fb44  01c44f40
0222fb48  01c4015c
0222fb4c  00000098
0222fb50  01c44f40
0222fb54  01c44f48
0222fb58  01c40238
0222fb5c  10204f9f msvcr80d!_initptd+0x10f
0222fb60  00000098
0222fb64  00000000
0222fb68  01c40000
0222fb6c  0222f968
0222fb70  7d4c0000 kernel32!_imp__NtFsControlFile <PERF>
(kernel32+0x0)
0222fb74  00000ca8
0222fb78  4b405064 msctf!g_timlist
```

```
0222fb7c  0222fbb8
0222fb80  4b3c384f msctf!CTimList::Leave+0x6
0222fb84  4b3c14d7 msctf!CTimList::IsThreadId+0x5a
0222fb88  00000ca8
0222fb8c  4b405064 msctf!g_timlist
0222fb90  4b3c0000 msctf!_imp__CheckTokenMembership <PERF>
(msctf+0x0)
0222fb94  01c70000
0222fb98  00000000
0222fb9c  4b405064 msctf!g_timlist
0222fba0  0222fb88
0222fba4  7d4dfd40 kernel32!FlsSetValue+0xc7
0222fba8  0222fca0
0222fbac  4b401dbd msctf!_except_handler3
0222fbb0  4b3c14e0 msctf!`string'+0x78
0222fbb4  0222fbd4
0222fbb8  0022f8a0
0222fbbc  00000001
0222fbc0  00000000
0222fbc4  00000000
0222fbc8  0222fc80
0222fbcc  0022f8a0
0222fbd0  0000156f
0222fbd4  0222fbf4
0222fbd8  020215a4 oleaut32!_DllMainCRTStartup+0x52
0222fbdc  02020000 oleaut32!_imp__RegFlushKey <PERF>
(oleaut32+0x0)
0222fbe0  00000002
0222fbe4  00000000
0222fbe8  00000000
0222fbec  0222fc08
0222fbf0  00000001
0222fbf4  0222fc14
0222fbf8  7d610024 ntdll!LdrpCallInitRoutine+0x14
0222fbfc  02020000 oleaut32!_imp__RegFlushKey <PERF>
(oleaut32+0x0)
0222fc00  00000001
0222fc04  00000000
0222fc08  00000001
0222fc0c  00000000
0222fc10  0022f8a0
0222fc14  00000001
0222fc18  00000000
0222fc1c  0222fcb0
0222fc20  7d62822e ntdll!LdrpInitializeThread+0x1a5
0222fc24  7d6a0180 ntdll!LdrpLoaderLock
0222fc28  7d62821c ntdll!LdrpInitializeThread+0x18f
0222fc2c  00000000
0222fc30  7efde000
0222fc34  00000000
...
0222fc6c  00000070
0222fc70  ffffffff
0222fc74  ffffffff
0222fc78  7d6281c7 ntdll!LdrpInitializeThread+0xd8
0222fc7c  7d6280d6 ntdll!LdrpInitializeThread+0x12c
0222fc80  00000000
```

```
0222fc84  00000000
0222fc88  0022f8a0
0222fc8c  0202155c oleaut32!_DllMainCRTStartup
0222fc90  7efde000
0222fc94  7d6a01f4 ntdll!PebLdr+0x14
0222fc98  0222fc2c
0222fc9c  00000000
0222fca0  0222fcfc
0222fca4  7d61f1f8 ntdll!_except_handler3
0222fca8  7d628148 ntdll!`string'+0xac
0222fcac  ffffffff
0222fcb0  7d62821c ntdll!LdrpInitializeThread+0x18f
0222fcb4  7d61e299 ntdll!ZwTestAlert+0x15
0222fcb8  7d628088 ntdll!_LdrpInitialize+0x1de
0222fcbc  0222fd20
0222fcc0  00000000
...
0222fcfc  0222ffec
0222fd00  7d61f1f8 ntdll!_except_handler3
0222fd04  7d628090 ntdll!`string'+0xfc
0222fd08  ffffffff
0222fd0c  7d628088 ntdll!_LdrpInitialize+0x1de
0222fd10  7d61ce0d ntdll!NtContinue+0x12
0222fd14  7d61e9b2 ntdll!KiUserApcDispatcher+0x3a
0222fd18  0222fd20
0222fd1c  00000001
0222fd20  0001002f
...
0222fdc8  00000000
0222fdcc  00000000
0222fdd0  00411032 NullThread!ILT+45(?ThreadProcYGKPAXZ)
0222fdd4  00000000
0222fdd8  7d4d1504 kernel32!BaseThreadStartThunk
0222fddc  00000023
0222fde0  00000202
...
0222ffb4  cccccccc
0222ffb8  0222ffec
0222ffbc  7d4dfe21 kernel32!BaseThreadStart+0x34
0222ffc0  00000000
0222ffc4  00000000
0222ffc8  00000000
0222ffcc  00000000
0222ffd0  00000000
0222ffd4  0222ffc4
0222ffd8  00000000
0222ffdc  ffffffff
0222ffe0  7d4d89c4 kernel32!_except_handler3
0222ffe4  7d4dfe28 kernel32!`string'+0x18
0222ffe8  00000000
0222ffec  00000000
0222fff0  00000000
0222fff4  00411032 NullThread!ILT+45(?ThreadProcYGKPAXZ)
0222fff8  00000000
0222fffc  00000000
02230000  ????????
```

The second crashed thread has much more symbolic information in it overwriting previous thread startup residue. It is mostly **Exception Handling Residue**[71] because exception handling consumes stack space as explained in the article[72]:

---

[71] We may add this pattern in the future.

[72] Who Calls the Postmortem Debugger?, Memory Dump Analysis Anthology, Volume 1, page 113

```
0:003> dds 0236a000 02370000                          0236a4ac  00230b98
0236a000  00000000                                    0236a4b0  0236a590
...                                                    0236a4b4  7d61f5d1 ntdll!RtlFreeHeap+0x20e
0236a060  00000000                                    0236a4b8  00221378
0236a064  0236a074                                    0236a4bc  7d61f5ed ntdll!RtlFreeHeap+0x70f
0236a068  00220000                                    0236a4c0  00000000
0236a06c  7d61f7b4 ntdll!RtlpAllocateFromHeapLookaside+0x13    0236a4c4  7d61f4ab ntdll!RtlFreeHeap
0236a070  00221378                                    0236a4c8  00000000
0236a074  0236a29c                                    0236a4cc  00000000
0236a078  7d61f748 ntdll!RtlAllocateHeap+0x1dd        ...
0236a07c  7d61f78c ntdll!RtlAllocateHeap+0xee7        0236a538  00000000
0236a080  0236a5f4                                    0236a53c  0236a678
0236a084  00000000                                    0236a540  7d61f1f8 ntdll!_except_handler3
...                                                    0236a544  7d624ba8 ntdll!`string'+0x1c
0236a1b4  0236a300                                    0236a548  ffffffff
0236a1b8  0236a1dc                                    0236a54c  7d624ba1
0236a1bc  7d624267 ntdll!RtlIsDosDeviceName_Ustr+0x2f ntdll!RtlpDosPathNameToRelativeNtPathName_Ustr+0x3cb
0236a1c0  0236a21c                                    0236a550  7d624c43
0236a1c4  7d624274 ntdll!RtlpDosSlashCONDevice        ntdll!RtlpDosPathNameToRelativeNtPathName_U+0x55
0236a1c8  00000001                                    0236a554  00000001
0236a1cc  0236a317                                    0236a558  0236a56c
0236a1d0  00000000                                    ...
0236a1d4  0236a324                                    0236a590  0236a5c0
0236a1d8  0236a290                                    0236a594  7d620304 ntdll!RtlNtStatusToDosError+0x38
0236a1dc  7d6248af ntdll!RtlGetFullPathName_Ustr+0x80b 0236a598  7d620309 ntdll!RtlNtStatusToDosError+0x3d
0236a1e0  7d6a00e0 ntdll!FastPebLock                  0236a59c  7d61c828 ntdll!ZwWaitForSingleObject+0x15
0236a1e4  7d62489d ntdll!RtlGetFullPathName_Ustr+0x15b 0236a5a0  7d4d8c82 kernel32!WaitForSingleObjectEx+0xac
0236a1e8  0236a5f4                                    0236a5a4  00000124
0236a1ec  00000208                                    0236a5a8  00000000
...                                                    0236a5ac  7d4d8ca7 kernel32!WaitForSingleObjectEx+0xdc
0236a224  00000000                                    0236a5b0  00000124
0236a228  00000038                                    0236a5b4  7d61f49c ntdll!RtlGetLastWin32Error
0236a22c  02080038 oleaut32!_PictSaveMetaFile+0x33    0236a5b8  80070000
0236a230  00000000                                    0236a5bc  00000024
...                                                    ...
0236a27c  00000000                                    0236a5f8  00000000
0236a280  0236a53c                                    0236a5fc  0236a688
0236a284  7d61f1f8 ntdll!_except_handler3             0236a600  7d4d89c4 kernel32!_except_handler3
0236a288  7d6245f0 ntdll!`string'+0x5c               0236a604  7d4d8cb0 kernel32!`string'+0x68
0236a28c  ffffffff                                    0236a608  ffffffff
0236a290  7d62489d ntdll!RtlGetFullPathName_Ustr+0x15b 0236a60c  7d4d8ca7 kernel32!WaitForSingleObjectEx+0xdc
0236a294  0236a5c8                                    0236a610  7d4d8bf1 kernel32!WaitForSingleObject+0x12
0236a298  00000008                                    0236a614  7d61f49c ntdll!RtlGetLastWin32Error
0236a29c  00000000                                    0236a618  7d61c92d ntdll!NtClose+0x12
0236a2a0  0236a54c                                    0236a61c  7d4d8e4f kernel32!CloseHandle+0x59
0236a2a4  7d624bcf                                    0236a620  00000124
ntdll!RtlpDosPathNameToRelativeNtPathName_Ustr+0x3d8  0236a624  0236a688
0236a2a8  7d6a00e0 ntdll!FastPebLock                  0236a628  69511753 <Unloaded_faultrep.dll>+0x11753
0236a2ac  7d624ba1                                    0236a62c  6951175b <Unloaded_faultrep.dll>+0x1175b
ntdll!RtlpDosPathNameToRelativeNtPathName_Ustr+0x3cb  0236a630  0236c6d0
0236a2b0  00000000                                    ...
0236a2b4  0236e6d0                                    0236a668  00000120
...                                                    0236a66c  00000000
0236a2e0  000a0008                                    0236a670  0236a630
0236a2e4  7d624be8 ntdll!`string'                     0236a674  7d94a2e9 user32!GetSystemMetrics+0x62
0236a2e8  00000000                                    0236a678  0236f920
0236a2ec  003a0038                                    0236a67c  69510078 <Unloaded_faultrep.dll>+0x10078
...                                                    0236a680  69503d10 <Unloaded_faultrep.dll>+0x3d10
0236a330  00650070                                    0236a684  ffffffff
0236a334  0050005c                                    0236a688  6951175b <Unloaded_faultrep.dll>+0x1175b
0236a338  00480043 advapi32!LsaGetQuotasForAccount+0x25 0236a68c  69506136 <Unloaded_faultrep.dll>+0x6136
0236a33c  00610046                                    0236a690  0236e6d0
0236a340  006c0075                                    0236a694  0236c6d0
0236a344  00520074                                    0236a698  0000009c
0236a348  00700065                                    0236a69c  0236a6d0
0236a34c  00780045                                    0236a6a0  00002000
0236a350  00630065                                    0236a6a4  0236eae4
0236a354  00690050                                    0236a6a8  695061ff <Unloaded_faultrep.dll>+0x61ff
0236a358  00650070                                    0236a6ac  00000000
0236a35c  00000000                                    0236a6b0  00000001
0236a360  00000000                                    0236a6b4  0236f742
...                                                    0236a6b8  69506210 <Unloaded_faultrep.dll>+0x6210
0236a4a0  0236a4b0                                    0236a6bc  00000028
0236a4a4  00000001                                    0236a6c0  0236c76c
0236a4a8  7d61f645 ntdll!RtlpFreeToHeapLookaside+0x22 ...
```

```
0236e6e0  0050005c
0236e6e4  00480043 advapi32!LsaGetQuotasForAccount+0x25
0236e6e8  00610046
...
0236e718  002204d8
0236e71c  0236e890
0236e720  77b940bb <Unloaded_VERSION.dll>+0x40bb
0236e724  77b91798 <Unloaded_VERSION.dll>+0x1798
0236e728  ffffffff
0236e72c  77b9178e <Unloaded_VERSION.dll>+0x178e
0236e730  69512587 <Unloaded_faultrep.dll>+0x12587
0236e734  0236e744
0236e738  00220000
0236e73c  7d61f7b4 ntdll!RtlpAllocateFromHeapLookaside+0x13
0236e740  00221378
0236e744  0236e96c
0236e748  7d61f748 ntdll!RtlAllocateHeap+0x1dd
0236e74c  7d61f78c ntdll!RtlAllocateHeap+0xee7
0236e750  0236eca4
0236e754  00000000
0236e758  0236ec94
0236e75c  7d620309 ntdll!RtlNtStatusToDosError+0x3d
0236e760  0236e7c8
0236e764  7d61c9db ntdll!NtQueryValueKey
0236e768  0236e888
0236e76c  0236e760
0236e770  7d61c9ed ntdll!NtQueryValueKey+0x12
0236e774  0236f920
0236e778  7d61f1f8 ntdll!_except_handler3
0236e77c  7d620310 ntdll!RtlpRunTable+0x490
0236e780  0236e790
0236e784  00220000
0236e788  7d61f7b4 ntdll!RtlpAllocateFromHeapLookaside+0x13
0236e78c  00221378
0236e790  0236e9b8
0236e794  7d61f748 ntdll!RtlAllocateHeap+0x1dd
0236e798  7d61f78c ntdll!RtlAllocateHeap+0xee7
0236e79c  0236ef18
0236e7a0  00000000
0236e7a4  00000000
0236e7a8  00220000
0236e7ac  0236e89c
0236e7b0  00000000
0236e7b4  00000128
0236e7b8  00000000
0236e7bc  0236e8c8
0236e7c0  0236e7c8
0236e7c4  c0000034
0236e7c8  0236e814
0236e7cc  7d61f1f8 ntdll!_except_handler3
0236e7d0  7d61f5f0 ntdll!CheckHeapFillPattern+0x64
0236e7d4  ffffffff
0236e7d8  7d61f5ed ntdll!RtlFreeHeap+0x70f
0236e7dc  7d4ded95 kernel32!FindClose+0x9b
0236e7e0  00220000
0236e7e4  00000000
0236e7e8  00220000
0236e7ec  00000000
0236e7f0  002314b4
0236e7f4  7d61ca1d ntdll!NtQueryInformationProcess+0x12
0236e7f8  7d4da465 kernel32!GetErrorMode+0x18
0236e7fc  ffffffff
0236e800  0000000c
0236e804  7d61ca65 ntdll!ZwSetInformationProcess+0x12
0236e808  7d4da441 kernel32!SetErrorMode+0x37
0236e80c  ffffffff
0236e810  0000000c
0236e814  0236e820
0236e818  00000004
0236e81c  00000000
0236e820  00000005
0236e824  0236eae8
0236e828  7d4e445f kernel32!GetLongPathNameW+0x38f
0236e82c  7d4e4472 kernel32!GetLongPathNameW+0x3a2
0236e830  00000001
```

```
0236e834  00000103
0236e838  00000000
0236e83c  0236f712
0236e840  7efaf000
0236e844  002316f0
0236e848  0000005c
0236e84c  7efaf000
0236e850  00000004
0236e854  002314b4
0236e858  0000ea13
0236e85c  0236e894
0236e860  00456b0d advapi32!RegQueryValueExW+0x96
0236e864  00000128
0236e868  0236e888
0236e86c  0236e8ac
0236e870  0236e8c8
0236e874  0236e8a4
0236e878  0236e89c
0236e87c  0236e88c
0236e880  7d635dc4 ntdll!iswdigit+0xf
0236e884  00000064
0236e888  00000000
0236e88c  7d624d81 ntdll!RtlpValidateCurrentDirectory+0xf6
0236e890  7d635d4e ntdll!RtlIsDosDeviceName_Ustr+0x1c0
0236e894  00000064
0236e898  0236e9d0
0236e89c  0236e9e7
0236e8a0  00000000
0236e8a4  0236e9f4
0236e8a8  0236e960
0236e8ac  7d6248af ntdll!RtlGetFullPathName_Ustr+0x80b
0236e8b0  7d6a00e0 ntdll!FastPebLock
0236e8b4  7d62489d ntdll!RtlGetFullPathName_Ustr+0x15b
0236e8b8  0236eca4
0236e8bc  00000208
0236e8c0  0236ec94
0236e8c4  00000000
0236e8c8  00220178
0236e8cc  00000004
0236e8d0  0236eb3c
0236e8d4  0236e8c8
0236e8d8  7d624d81 ntdll!RtlpValidateCurrentDirectory+0xf6
0236e8dc  0236e8f8
0236e8e0  7d6246c1 ntdll!RtlIsDosDeviceName_Ustr+0x14
0236e8e4  0236ea1c
0236e8e8  0236ea33
0236e8ec  00000000
0236e8f0  0236ea40
0236e8f4  0236e9ac
0236e8f8  7d6248af ntdll!RtlGetFullPathName_Ustr+0x80b
0236e8fc  7d6a00e0 ntdll!FastPebLock
0236e900  7d62489d ntdll!RtlGetFullPathName_Ustr+0x15b
0236e904  0236ef18
0236e908  00000208
...
0236e934  00000022
0236e938  00460044 advapi32!GetPerflibKeyValue+0x19e
0236e93c  0236ecd0
0236e940  00000000
0236e944  00000044
0236e948  02080044 oleaut32!_PictSaveMetaFile+0x3f
0236e94c  00000000
0236e950  4336ec0c
...
0236e9a8  0236ebd0
0236e9ac  7d62155b ntdll!RtlAllocateHeap+0x460
0236e9b0  7d61f78c ntdll!RtlAllocateHeap+0xee7
0236e9b4  00000000
0236e9b8  000003ee
0236e9bc  0236ed2c
0236e9c0  7d624bcf
ntdll!RtlpDosPathNameToRelativeNtPathName_Ustr+0x3d8
0236e9c4  7d6a00e0 ntdll!FastPebLock
0236e9c8  00000ab0
0236e9cc  00000381
```

```
0236e9d0  00233950
0236e9d4  0236ebfc
0236e9d8  7d62155b ntdll!RtlAllocateHeap+0x460
0236e9dc  7d61f78c ntdll!RtlAllocateHeap+0xee7
0236e9e0  00000003
0236e9e4  fffffffc
0236e9e8  00000aa4
0236e9ec  00230ba0
0236e9f0  00000004
0236e9f4  003a0043
0236e9f8  00000000
0236e9fc  000a0008
0236ea00  7d624be8 ntdll!`string'
0236ea04  00000000
0236ea08  00460044 advapi32!GetPerflibKeyValue+0x19e
0236ea0c  0236ecd0
0236ea10  00233948
...
0236ea44  00220640
0236ea48  7d62273d ntdll!RtlIntegerToUnicode+0x126
0236ea4c  0000000c
...
0236eab4  0236f79c
0236eab8  7d61f1f8 ntdll!_except_handler3
0236eabc  7d622758 ntdll!RtlpIntegerWChars+0x54
0236eac0  00220178
0236eac4  0236ed3c
0236eac8  00000005
0236eacc  0236ed00
0236ead0  7d622660 ntdll!RtlConvertSidToUnicodeString+0x1cb
0236ead4  00220178
0236ead8  0236eaf0
0236eadc  0236eaec
0236eae0  00000001
0236eae4  7d61f645 ntdll!RtlpFreeToHeapLookaside+0x22
0236eae8  00223620
0236eaec  00220178
0236eaf0  7d61f5d1 ntdll!RtlFreeHeap+0x20e
0236eaf4  002217f8
0236eaf8  7d61f5ed ntdll!RtlFreeHeap+0x70f
0236eafc  00000000
0236eb00  00220178
...
0236eb48  0236eb58
0236eb4c  7d635dc4 ntdll!iswdigit+0xf
0236eb50  00220178
0236eb54  00000381
0236eb58  002343f8
0236eb5c  0236eb78
0236eb60  7d620deb ntdll!RtlpCoalesceFreeBlocks+0x383
0236eb64  00000381
0236eb68  002343f8
0236eb6c  00220000
0236eb70  00233948
0236eb74  00220000
0236eb78  00000000
0236eb7c  00220000
0236eb80  0236ec60
0236eb84  7d620fbe ntdll!RtlFreeHeap+0x6b0
0236eb88  00220608
0236eb8c  7d61f5ed ntdll!RtlFreeHeap+0x70f
0236eb90  000000e8
0236eb94  7d61cd23 ntdll!ZwWriteVirtualMemory
0236eb98  7efde000
0236eb9c  000000e8
0236eba0  00233948
0236eba4  7efde000
0236eba8  000002e8
0236ebac  0000005d
0236ebb0  00220178
0236ebb4  00000156
0236ebb8  0236e9b4
0236ebbc  00233948
0236ebc0  7d61f1f8 ntdll!_except_handler3
0236ebc4  00000ab0
```

```
0236ebc8  00233948
0236ebcc  00233950
0236ebd0  00220178
0236ebd4  00220000
0236ebd8  00000ab0
0236ebdc  00220178
0236ebe0  00000000
0236ebe4  00233950
0236ebe8  7d4ddea8 kernel32!`string'+0x50
0236ebec  00000000
0236ebf0  00233950
0236ebf4  00220178
0236ebf8  00000aa4
0236ebfc  00000000
0236ec00  0236ec54
0236ec04  7d63668a ntdll!RtlCreateProcessParameters+0x375
0236ec08  7d63668f ntdll!RtlCreateProcessParameters+0x37a
0236ec0c  7d6369e9 ntdll!RtlCreateProcessParameters+0x35f
0236ec10  00000000
...
0236ec4c  0000007f
0236ec50  0236ef4c
0236ec54  7d61f1f8 ntdll!_except_handler3
0236ec58  7d61f5f0 ntdll!CheckHeapFillPattern+0x64
0236ec5c  ffffffff
0236ec60  7d61f5ed ntdll!RtlFreeHeap+0x70f
0236ec64  7d6365e2 ntdll!RtlDestroyProcessParameters+0x1b
0236ec68  00220000
0236ec6c  00000000
0236ec70  00233950
0236ec74  0236ef5c
0236ec78  7d4ec4bc kernel32!BasePushProcessParameters+0x806
0236ec7c  00233950
0236ec80  7d4ec478 kernel32!BasePushProcessParameters+0x7c5
0236ec84  7efde000
0236ec88  0236f748
0236ec8c  00000000
0236ec90  0236ed92
0236ec94  00000000
0236ec98  00000000
0236ec9c  01060104
0236eca0  0236f814
0236eca4  0020001e
0236eca8  7d535b50 kernel32!`string'
0236ecac  00780076
0236ecb0  002314e0
0236ecb4  00780076
0236ecb8  0236ed2c
0236ecbc  00020000
0236ecc0  7d4ddee4 kernel32!`string'
0236ecc4  0236efec
...
0236ed3c  006d0061
0236ed40  00460020 advapi32!GetPerflibKeyValue+0x17a
0236ed44  006c0069
0236ed48  00730065
0236ed4c  00280020
0236ed50  00380078
0236ed54  00290036
0236ed58  0044005c advapi32!CryptDuplicateHash+0x3
0236ed5c  00620065
0236ed60  00670075
...
0236ee7c  0236ee8c
0236ee80  00000001
0236ee84  7d61f645 ntdll!RtlpFreeToHeapLookaside+0x22
0236ee88  00230dc0
0236ee8c  0236ef6c
0236ee90  0236eea0
0236ee94  00000001
0236ee98  7d61f645 ntdll!RtlpFreeToHeapLookaside+0x22
0236ee9c  00223908
0236eea0  0236ef80
0236eea4  7d61f5d1 ntdll!RtlFreeHeap+0x20e
0236eea8  00221d38
```

```
0236eeac  7d61f5ed  ntdll!RtlFreeHeap+0x70f
0236eeb0  7d61f4ab  ntdll!RtlFreeHeap
0236eeb4  7d61c91b  ntdll!NtClose
0236eeb8  00000000
...
0236ef08  00000000
0236ef0c  7d621954  ntdll!RtlImageNtHeaderEx+0xee
0236ef10  7efde000
0236ef14  00001000
0236ef18  00000000
0236ef1c  000000e8
0236ef20  004000e8  NullThread!_enc$textbss$begin <PERF>
(NullThread+0xe8)
0236ef24  00000000
0236ef28  0236ef10
0236ef2c  00000000
0236ef30  0236f79c
0236ef34  7d61f1f8  ntdll!_except_handler3
0236ef38  7d621954  ntdll!RtlImageNtHeaderEx+0xee
0236ef3c  00220000
...
0236ef68  0236eeb0
0236ef6c  7d61f5ed  ntdll!RtlFreeHeap+0x70f
0236ef70  0236f79c
0236ef74  7d61f1f8  ntdll!_except_handler3
0236ef78  7d61f5f0  ntdll!CheckHeapFillPattern+0x64
0236ef7c  ffffffff
0236ef80  7d61f5ed  ntdll!RtlFreeHeap+0x70f
0236ef84  7d4ea183  kernel32!CreateProcessInternalW+0x21f5
0236ef88  00220000
0236ef8c  00000000
0236ef90  00223910
0236ef94  7d4ebc0b  kernel32!CreateProcessInternalW+0x1f26
0236ef98  00000000
0236ef9c  00000096
0236efa0  0236f814
0236efa4  00000103
0236efa8  7efde000
0236efac  00000001
0236efb0  0236effc
0236efb4  00000200
0236efb8  00000cb0
0236efbc  0236f00c
0236efc0  0236efdc
0236efc4  7d6256e8  ntdll!bsearch+0x42
0236efc8  00180144
0236efcc  0236efe0
0236efd0  7d625992  ntdll!ARRAY_FITS+0x29
0236efd4  00000a8c
0236efd8  00000000
0236efdc  00000000
0236efe0  00080000
0236efe4  00070000
0236efe8  00040000
0236efec  00000044
0236eff0  00000000
0236eff4  7d535b50  kernel32!`string'
0236eff8  00000000
0236effc  00000000
...
0236f070  00000001
0236f074  7d625ad8
ntdll!RtlFindActivationContextSectionString+0xe1
0236f078  004000e8  NullThread!_enc$textbss$begin <PERF>
(NullThread+0xe8)
0236f07c  0236f0cc
0236f080  00000000
0236f084  7d6256e8  ntdll!bsearch+0x42
0236f088  00180144
0236f08c  0236f0a0
0236f090  7d625992  ntdll!ARRAY_FITS+0x29
0236f094  00000a8c
...
0236f0d0  0236f120
0236f0d4  7d625b62  ntdll!RtlpFindUnicodeStringInSection+0x7b
```

```
0236f0d8  0236f204
0236f0dc  00000020
...
0236f190  000002a8
0236f194  7d625b62  ntdll!RtlpFindUnicodeStringInSection+0x7b
0236f198  00000001
0236f19c  00000000
0236f1a0  0236f1d0
0236f1a4  7d6257f1
ntdll!RtlpFindNextActivationContextSection+0x64
0236f1a8  00181f1c
...
0236f1f0  7efaf000
0236f1f4  7d625ad8
ntdll!RtlFindActivationContextSectionString+0xe1
0236f1f8  0236f214
0236f1fc  0236f24c
0236f200  00000000
0236f204  7d6256e8  ntdll!bsearch+0x42
0236f208  00180144
...
0236f24c  00000200
0236f250  00000734
0236f254  7d625b62  ntdll!RtlpFindUnicodeStringInSection+0x7b
0236f258  0236f384
...
0236f3f0  00000000
0236f3f4  00000000
0236f3f8  01034236
0236f3fc  00000000
0236f400  7d4d1510  kernel32!BaseProcessStartThunk
0236f404  00000018
0236f408  00003000
...
0236f62c  0236f63c
0236f630  00000001
0236f634  7d61f645  ntdll!RtlpFreeToHeapLookaside+0x22
0236f638  00231088
0236f63c  0236f71c
...
0236f70c  002333b8
0236f710  0236f720
0236f714  00000001
0236f718  7d61f645  ntdll!RtlpFreeToHeapLookaside+0x22
0236f71c  00228f20
0236f720  0236f800
0236f724  7d61f5d1  ntdll!RtlFreeHeap+0x20e
0236f728  00221318
0236f72c  7d61f5ed  ntdll!RtlFreeHeap+0x70f
0236f730  00000000
0236f734  00000096
0236f738  0236f814
0236f73c  00220608
0236f740  7d61f5ed  ntdll!RtlFreeHeap+0x70f
0236f744  0236f904
0236f748  008e0000
0236f74c  002334c2
...
0236f784  0236f7bc
0236f788  7d63d275  ntdll!_vsnwprintf+0x30
0236f78c  0236f79c
0236f790  0000f949
0236f794  0236ef98
0236f798  00000095
0236f79c  0236f7bc
0236f7a0  7d4d89c4  kernel32!_except_handler3
0236f7a4  7d4ed1d0  kernel32!`string'+0xc
0236f7a8  ffffffff
0236f7ac  7d4ebc0b  kernel32!CreateProcessInternalW+0x1f26
0236f7b0  7d4d14a2  kernel32!CreateProcessW+0x2c
0236f7b4  00000000
...
0236f7f0  0236f7bc
0236f7f4  7d61f1f8  ntdll!_except_handler3
0236f7f8  7d61d051  ntdll!NtWaitForMultipleObjects+0x15
```

```
0236f7fc  7d61c92d  ntdll!NtClose+0x12
0236f800  7d4d8e4f  kernel32!CloseHandle+0x59
0236f804  00000108
0236f808  0236fb8c
0236f80c  7d535b07  kernel32!UnhandledExceptionFilter+0x815
0236f810  00000108
0236f814  00430022  advapi32!_imp__OutputDebugStringW <PERF>
(advapi32+0x22)
0236f818  005c003a
0236f81c  00720050
...
0236f8ec  0055005c
0236f8f0  00650073
0236f8f4  00440072  advapi32!CryptDuplicateHash+0x19
0236f8f8  006d0075
0236f8fc  00730070
0236f900  006e005c
0236f904  00770065
0236f908  0064002e
0236f90c  0070006d
0236f910  0020003b
0236f914  00220071
0236f918  00000000
0236f91c  00000096
0236f920  7d4dda47  kernel32!DuplicateHandle+0xd0
0236f924  7d4dda47  kernel32!DuplicateHandle+0xd0
0236f928  0236fb8c
0236f92c  7d5358cb  kernel32!UnhandledExceptionFilter+0x5f1
0236f930  0236f9f0
0236f934  00000001
0236f938  00000000
0236f93c  7d535b43  kernel32!UnhandledExceptionFilter+0x851
0236f940  00000000
0236f944  00000000
0236f948  00000000
0236f94c  0236f95c
0236f950  00000098
0236f954  000001a2
0236f958  01c423b0
0236f95c  0236fb84
0236f960  7d62155b  ntdll!RtlAllocateHeap+0x460
0236f964  7d61f78c  ntdll!RtlAllocateHeap+0xee7
0236f968  00000000
0236f96c  0000008c
0236f970  00000000
0236f974  7d4d8472  kernel32!$$VProc_ImageExportDirectory+0x6d4e
0236f978  0236fa1c
0236f97c  00000044
0236f980  00000000
0236f984  7d535b50  kernel32!`string'
0236f988  00000000
0236f98c  00000000
0236f990  00000000
0236f994  00000000
0236f998  00000000
0236f99c  00000000
0236f9a0  00000000
0236f9a4  00000000
0236f9a8  00000000
0236f9ac  00000000
0236f9b0  00000000
0236f9b4  00000000
0236f9b8  00000000
0236f9bc  00000000
0236f9c0  0010000e
0236f9c4  7ffe0030  SharedUserData+0x30
0236f9c8  000000e8
0236f9cc  00000108
0236f9d0  00000200
0236f9d4  00000734
0236f9d8  00000018
0236f9dc  00000000
0236f9e0  7d5621d0  kernel32!ProgramFilesEnvironment+0x74
0236f9e4  00000040
0236f9e8  00000000
```

```
0236f9ec  00000000
0236f9f0  0000000c
0236f9f4  00000000
0236f9f8  00000001
0236f9fc  00000118
0236fa00  000000e8
0236fa04  c0000005
0236fa08  00000000
0236fa0c  00000008
0236fa10  00000000
0236fa14  00000110
0236fa18  0236f814
0236fa1c  6950878a  <Unloaded_faultrep.dll>+0x878a
0236fa20  00120010
0236fa24  7d51c5e4  kernel32!`string'
0236fa28  00000003
0236fa2c  05bc0047
...
0236fa74  0057005c
0236fa78  004b0032  advapi32!szPerflibSectionName <PERF>
(advapi32+0x80032)
0236fa7c  005c0033
0236fa80  00790073
...
0236fac8  0000002b
0236facc  00000000
0236fad0  7d61e3e6  ntdll!ZwWow64CsrNewThread+0x12
0236fad4  00000000
...
0236fb44  00000000
0236fb48  00000000
0236fb4c  7d61cb0d  ntdll!ZwQueryVirtualMemory+0x12
0236fb50  7d54eeb8  kernel32!_ValidateEH3RN+0xb6
0236fb54  ffffffff
0236fb58  7d4dfe28  kernel32!`string'+0x18
0236fb5c  00000000
0236fb60  0236fb78
0236fb64  0000001c
0236fb68  0000000f
0236fb6c  7d4dfe28  kernel32!`string'+0x18
0236fb70  0000f949
0236fb74  0236f814
0236fb78  7d4df000  kernel32!CheckForSameCurdir+0x39
0236fb7c  0236fbd4
0236fb80  7d4d89c4  kernel32!_except_handler3
0236fb84  7d535be0  kernel32!`string'+0xc
0236fb88  ffffffff
0236fb8c  7d535b43  kernel32!UnhandledExceptionFilter+0x851
0236fb90  7d508f4e  kernel32!BaseThreadStart+0x4a
0236fb94  0236fbb4
0236fb98  7d4d8a25  kernel32!_except_handler3+0x61
0236fb9c  0236fbbc
0236fba0  00000000
0236fba4  0236fbbc
0236fba8  00000000
0236fbac  00000000
0236fbb0  00000000
0236fbb4  0236fca0
0236fbb8  0236fcf0
0236fbbc  0236fbe0
0236fbc0  7d61ec2a  ntdll!ExecuteHandler2+0x26
0236fbc4  0236fca0
0236fbc8  0236ffdc
0236fbcc  0236fcf0
0236fbd0  0236fc7c
0236fbd4  0236ffdc
0236fbd8  7d61ec3e  ntdll!ExecuteHandler2+0x3a
0236fbdc  0236ffdc
0236fbe0  0236fc88
0236fbe4  7d61ebfb  ntdll!ExecuteHandler+0x24
0236fbe8  0236fca0
0236fbec  0236ffdc
0236fbf0  00000000
0236fbf4  0236fc7c
0236fbf8  7d4d89c4  kernel32!_except_handler3
```

```
0236fbfc  00000000
0236fc00  0036fca0
0236fc04  0236fc18
0236fc08  7d640ca6 ntdll!RtlCallVectoredContinueHandlers+0x15
0236fc0c  0236fca0
0236fc10  0236fcf0
0236fc14  7d6a0608 ntdll!RtlpCallbackEntryList
0236fc18  0236fc88
0236fc1c  7d6354c9 ntdll!RtlDispatchException+0x11f
0236fc20  0236fca0
0236fc24  0236fcf0
0236fc28  00000000
0236fc2c  00000000
...
0236fc88  0236ffec
0236fc8c  7d61dd26 ntdll!NtRaiseException+0x12
0236fc90  7d61ea51 ntdll!KiUserExceptionDispatcher+0x29
0236fc94  0236fca0
0236fc98  0236fcf0
0236fc9c  00000000
0236fca0  c0000005
0236fca4  00000000
0236fca8  00000000
0236fcac  00000000
0236fcb0  00000002
0236fcb4  00000008
0236fcb8  00000000
0236fcbc  00000000
0236fcc0  00000000
0236fcc4  6b021fa0
0236fcc8  78b83980
0236fccc  00000000
0236fcd0  00000000
0236fcd4  00000000
0236fcd8  7efad000
0236fcdc  023afd00
0236fce0  023af110
0236fce4  78b83980
0236fce8  010402e1
0236fcec  00000000
0236fcf0  0001003f
0236fcf4  00000000
0236fcf8  00000000
0236fcfc  00000000
0236fd00  00000000
0236fd04  00000000
0236fd08  00000000
0236fd0c  0000027f
0236fd10  00000000
0236fd14  0000ffff
0236fd18  00000000
0236fd1c  00000000
0236fd20  00000000
0236fd24  00000000
0236fd28  00000000
0236fd2c  00000000
0236fd30  00000000
0236fd34  00000000
0236fd38  00000000
0236fd3c  00000000
0236fd40  00000000
```

```
0236fd44  00000000
0236fd48  00000000
0236fd4c  00000000
0236fd50  00000000
0236fd54  00000000
0236fd58  00000000
0236fd5c  00000000
0236fd60  00000000
0236fd64  00000000
0236fd68  00000000
0236fd6c  00000000
0236fd70  00000000
0236fd74  00000000
0236fd78  00000000
0236fd7c  0000002b
0236fd80  00000053
0236fd84  0000002b
0236fd88  0000002b
0236fd8c  00000000
0236fd90  00000000
0236fd94  00000000
0236fd98  00000000
0236fd9c  47f30000
0236fda0  00000000
0236fda4  0236ffec
0236fda8  00000000
0236fdac  00000023
0236fdb0  00010246
0236fdb4  0236ffbc
0236fdb8  0000002b
0236fdbc  0000027f
0236fdc0  00000000
0236fdc4  00000000
0236fdc8  00000000
0236fdcc  00000000
0236fdd0  00000000
0236fdd4  00001f80
0236fdd8  00000000
0236fddc  00000000
...
0236ffb4  00000000
0236ffb8  00000000
0236ffbc  7d4dfe21 kernel32!BaseThreadStart+0x34
0236ffc0  00000000
0236ffc4  00000000
0236ffc8  00000000
0236ffcc  00000000
0236ffd0  c0000005
0236ffd4  0236ffc4
0236ffd8  0236fbb4
0236ffdc  ffffffff
0236ffe0  7d4d89c4 kernel32!_except_handler3
0236ffe4  7d4dfe28 kernel32!`string'+0x18
0236ffe8  00000000
0236ffec  00000000
0236fff0  00000000
0236fff4  00000000
0236fff8  00000000
0236fffc  00000000
02370000  ????????
```

Comments

!DumpStack and **!EEStack** SOS commands provide a summary of "call type" execution residue from the raw stack.

System Objects can shed extra light on past software behavior (page 1084).

We can also use **dpS** WinDbg command on a range to get all symbolic references only.

The undocumented **!ddstack** WinDbg extension (**ext**) command may save some time for listing **Execution Residue** symbols. It is equivalent to **!teb**, then **dpS**, but also gives stack addresses for mapped symbols like **dps** command but with less output (the command may give incorrect results for WOW64 process memory dumps saved as x64 memory dumps):

```
0:001> !ddstack
 Range: 0000000002ecf000->0000000002ee0000
 0x00000000`02edf4b0 0x00000000`775d0000 ntdll!RtlDeactivateActivationContext <PERF>
(ntdll+0x0)+0000000000000000
 0x00000000`02edf4c8 0x00000000`775fc454 ntdll!LdrpInitialize+00000000000000a4
 0x00000000`02edf538 0x00000000`775fc358 ntdll!LdrInitializeThunk+0000000000000018
 0x00000000`02edf5e0 0x00000000`776d4578 ntdll!`string'+0000000000000000
 0x00000000`02edf5e8 0x00000000`776d44e0 ntdll!`string'+0000000000000000
 0x00000000`02edf5f8 0x00000000`775f0f3b ntdll!TpPostTask+000000000000019b
 0x00000000`02edf658 0x00000000`775e6199 ntdll!TppWorkPost+0000000000000089
 0x00000000`02edf688 0x00000000`775fc520 ntdll!RtlUserThreadStart+0000000000000000
 0x00000000`02edf698 0x00000000`775e6b4d ntdll!TppWaitComplete+000000000000003d
 0x00000000`02edf6a8 0x00000000`775e6b4d ntdll!TppWaitComplete+000000000000003d
 0x00000000`02edf6c8 0x00000000`775eb828 ntdll!TppWaiterpDoTransitions+0000000000000154
 0x00000000`02edf6e8 0x00000000`775e6abe ntdll!TppWaiterpCompleteWait+000000000000004e
 0x00000000`02edf6f8 0x00000000`775d7858 ntdll!TppWaiterpWaitTimerExpired+0000000000000038
 0x00000000`02edf720 0x00000000`776d4578 ntdll!`string'+0000000000000000
 0x00000000`02edf728 0x00000000`776d44e0 ntdll!`string'+0000000000000000
 0x00000000`02edf738 0x00000000`776d4500 ntdll!`string'+0000000000000000
 0x00000000`02edf748 0x00000000`775eb037 ntdll!TppWaiterpThread+000000000000014d
 0x00000000`02edf768 0x00000000`776d4550 ntdll!`string'+0000000000000000
 0x00000000`02edf9e8 0x00000000`773c59ed kernel32!BaseThreadInitThunk+000000000000000d
 0x00000000`02edfa18 0x00000000`775fc541 ntdll!RtlUserThreadStart+000000000000001d

0:001> !teb
 TEB at 000007fffffdb000
 ExceptionList:        0000000000000000
 StackBase:            0000000002ee0000
 StackLimit:           0000000002ecf000
 SubSystemTib:         0000000000000000
 FiberData:            0000000000001e00
 ArbitraryUserPointer: 0000000000000000
 Self:                 000007fffffdb000
 EnvironmentPointer:   0000000000000000
 ClientId:             0000000000001344 . 0000000000001ab0
 RpcHandle:            0000000000000000
 Tls Storage:          0000000000000000
 PEB Address:          000007fffffdf000
 LastErrorValue: 0
 LastStatusValue: 0
 Count Owned Locks: 0
```

```
HardErrorMode:  0

0:001> dpS 0000000002ecf000 0000000002ee0000
 00000000`775d0000 ntdll!RtlDeactivateActivationContext <PERF> (ntdll+0x0)
 00000000`775fc454 ntdll!LdrpInitialize+0xa4
 00000000`775fc358 ntdll!LdrInitializeThunk+0x18
 00000000`776d4578 ntdll!`string'
 00000000`776d44e0 ntdll!`string'
 00000000`775f0f3b ntdll!TpPostTask+0x19b
 00000000`775e6199 ntdll!TppWorkPost+0x89
 00000000`775fc520 ntdll!RtlUserThreadStart
 00000000`775e6b4d ntdll!TppWaitComplete+0x3d
 00000000`775e6b4d ntdll!TppWaitComplete+0x3d
 00000000`775eb828 ntdll!TppWaiterpDoTransitions+0x154
 00000000`775e6abe ntdll!TppWaiterpCompleteWait+0x4e
 00000000`775d7858 ntdll!TppWaiterpWaitTimerExpired+0x38
 00000000`776d4578 ntdll!`string'
 00000000`776d44e0 ntdll!`string'
 00000000`776d4500 ntdll!`string'
 00000000`775eb037 ntdll!TppWaiterpThread+0x14d
 00000000`776d4550 ntdll!`string'
 00000000`773c59ed kernel32!BaseThreadInitThunk+0xd
 00000000`775fc541 ntdll!RtlUserThreadStart+0x1d
```

F

Fake Module

In **Fake Module** pattern, one of the loaded modules masquerades as a legitimate system DLL or a widely known value adding DLL from some popular 3rd-party product. To illustrate this pattern we modeled it as Victimware[73]: a process crashed after loading a malware module:

```
0:000> k
*** Stack trace for last set context - .thread/.cxr resets it
Child-SP          RetAddr           Call Site
00000000`0026f978 00000001`3f89103a 0x0
00000000`0026f980 00000001`3f8911c4 FakeModule!wmain+0x3a
00000000`0026f9c0 00000000`76e3652d FakeModule!__tmainCRTStartup+0x144
00000000`0026fa00 00000000`7752c521 kernel32!BaseThreadInitThunk+0xd
00000000`0026fa30 00000000`00000000 ntdll!RtlUserThreadStart+0x1d
```

When we inspected loaded modules we didn't find anything suspicious:

```
0:000> lmp
start             end               module name
00000000`76e20000 00000000`76f3f000 kernel32   <none>
00000000`77500000 00000000`776a9000 ntdll      <none>
00000001`3f890000 00000001`3f8a6000 FakeModule <none>
000007fe`f8cb0000 000007fe`f8cc7000 winspool   <none>
000007fe`fdb30000 000007fe`fdb9c000 KERNELBASE <none>
```

However, when checking module images for any modifications we find that *winspool* module was not compared with the corresponding existing binary from Microsoft symbol server:

```
0:000> !for_each_module "!chkimg -v -d @#ModuleName"
Searching for module with expression: kernel32
Will apply relocation fixups to file used for comparison
Will ignore NOP/LOCK errors
Will ignore patched instructions
Image specific ignores will be applied
Comparison image path: C:\WSDK8\Debuggers\x64\sym\kernel32.dll\503285C111f000\kernel32.dll
No range specified

Scanning section:    .text
Size: 633485
Range to scan: 76e21000-76ebba8d
Total bytes compared: 633485(100%)
Number of errors: 0
0 errors : kernel32
```

---

[73] http://www.dumpanalysis.org/victimware-book

```
Searching for module with expression: ntdll
Will apply relocation fixups to file used for comparison
Will ignore NOP/LOCK errors
Will ignore patched instructions
Image specific ignores will be applied
Comparison image path: C:\WSDK8\Debuggers\x64\sym\ntdll.dll\4EC4AA8E1a9000\ntdll.dll
No range specified


Scanning section:     .text
Size: 1049210
Range to scan: 77501000-7760127a
Total bytes compared: 1049210(100%)
Number of errors: 0


Scanning section:      RT
Size: 474
Range to scan: 77602000-776021da
Total bytes compared: 474(100%)
Number of errors: 0
0 errors : ntdll
Searching for module with expression: FakeModule
Error for FakeModule: Could not find image file for the module. Make sure binaries are included in the
symbol path.
```
Searching for module with expression: winspool
Error for winspool: Could not find image file for the module. Make sure binaries are included in the
symbol path.
```
Searching for module with expression: KERNELBASE
Will apply relocation fixups to file used for comparison
Will ignore NOP/LOCK errors
Will ignore patched instructions
Image specific ignores will be applied
Comparison image path: C:\WSDK8\Debuggers\x64\sym\KERNELBASE.dll\503285C26c000\KERNELBASE.dll
No range specified


Scanning section:     .text
Size: 302047
Range to scan: 7fefdb31000-7fefdb7abdf
Total bytes compared: 302047(100%)
Number of errors: 0
0 errors : KERNELBASE
```

Checking module data reveals that it was loaded not from *System32* folder and also does not have any version information:

```
0:000> lmv m winspool
start             end               module name
000007fe`f8cb0000 000007fe`f8cc7000   winspool   (deferred)
```
Image path: C:\Work\AWMA\FakeModule\x64\Release\winspool.drv
```
Image name: winspool.drv
Timestamp:        Fri Dec 28 22:22:42 2012 (50DE1BB2)
CheckSum:         00000000
ImageSize:        00017000
File version:     0.0.0.0
Product version:  0.0.0.0
```

```
File flags:          0 (Mask 0)
File OS:             0 Unknown Base
File type:           0.0 Unknown
File date:           00000000.00000000
Translations:        0000.04b0 0000.04e4 0409.04b0 0409.04e4
```

We could see that path by running the following command as well:

```
0:000> !for_each_module
00: 0000000076e20000  0000000076f3f000          kernel32
C:\Windows\System32\kernel32.dll                  kernel32.dll
01: 0000000077500000  00000000776a9000          ntdll
C:\Windows\System32\ntdll.dll                     ntdll.dll
02: 000000013f890000  000000013f8a6000          FakeModule
C:\Work\AWMA\FakeModule\x64\Release\FakeModule.exe  FakeModule.exe
03: 000007fef8cb0000  000007fef8cc7000          winspool C:\Work\AWMA\FakeModule\x64\Release\winspool.drv
04: 000007fefdb30000  000007fefdb9c000          KERNELBASE
C:\Windows\System32\KERNELBASE.dll                KERNELBASE.dll
```

Or from PEB:

```
0:000> !peb
PEB at 000007fffffdf000
[...]
7fef8cb0000 50de1bb2 Dec 28 22:22:42 2012 C:\Work\AWMA\FakeModule\x64\Release\winspool.drv
[...]
```

Another sign is the module size in memory which is much smaller than the real *winspool.drv*:

```
0:000> ? 000007fe`f8cc7000 - 000007fe`f8cb0000
Evaluate expression: 94208 = 00000000`0001700
```

Module size could help if legitimate module from the well-known folder was replaced. Module debug directory, and the size of export and import directories are also different with the original one revealing the development folder:

```
0:000> !dh 000007fe`f8cb0000
[...]
   0 [       0] address [size] of Export Directory
[...]
9000 [     208] address [size] of Import Address Table Directory
[...]
Debug Directories(2)
Type       Size    Address   Pointer
cv          49      e2c0      cac0 Format: RSDS, guid, 1,
C:\Work\AWMA\FakeModule\x64\Release\winspool.pdb
```

This can also be seen from the output of **!lmi** command:

```
0:000> !lmi 7fef8cb0000
Loaded Module Info: [7fef8cb0000]
Module: winspool
Base Address: 000007fef8cb0000
Image Name: winspool.drv
Machine Type:   34404 (X64)
Time Stamp:     50de1bb2 Fri Dec 28 22:22:42 2012
Size:           17000
CheckSum:       0
Characteristics: 2022
Debug Data Dirs: Type  Size      VA  Pointer
CODEVIEW    49, e2c0,    cac0 RSDS - GUID: {29D85193-1C9D-4997-95BA-DD190FA3C1BF}
Age: 1, Pdb: C:\Work\AWMA\FakeModule\x64\Release\winspool.pdb
??    10, e30c,    cb0c [Data not mapped]
Symbol Type:    DEFERRED - No error - symbol load deferred
Load Report:    no symbols loaded
```

False Effective Address

When calculating effective addresses such as [r10+10h] or [rax+rcx*12h+40h] to show their value in the output of some commands such as **.trap** or **.cxr** a debugger uses CPU register values from a saved trap frame or context structure. If such information is invalid, the reported effective address does not correspond to the real one during code execution. This analysis pattern is similar to **False Function Parameters** (page 414). Therefore, if a fault address is saved during bugcheck or exception processing, it may not correspond to the output of some commands where such calculation is necessary. For example, in a bugcheck parameter we have this referenced memory address:

```
Arg1: fffffadda17d001d, memory referenced
```

But the output of **.trap** command shows **NULL Pointer** (page 838) address:

```
NOTE: The trap frame does not contain all registers.
Some register values may be zeroed or incorrect.
rax=0000000000000000 rbx=0000000000000000 rcx=0000000000000000
[...]
movzx eax,word ptr [rax+10h] 0010=????
```

Usually, we are lucky, and an effective address is correct despite a warning such as in a pattern example on page 182 and a pattern interaction case study[74].

---

[74] "NULL Data Pointer, Stack Trace, Inline Function Optimization and Platformorphic Fault", Memory Dump Analysis Anthology, Volume 4, page 201

False Frame

Often a debugger is not able to reconstruct a stack trace correctly, for example, when symbols to guide the process are not available due to **Reduced Symbol Information** (page 921) or complete absence due to **Unloaded Module** (page 1156):

```
0:008> k
# ChildEBP RetAddr
00 0250f4b8 76d21775 ntdll!NtWaitForMultipleObjects+0x15
01 0250f554 75c419fc KERNELBASE!WaitForMultipleObjectsEx+0x100
02 0250f59c 75c4268c kernel32!WaitForMultipleObjectsExImplementation+0xe0
03 0250f5b8 75c681fc kernel32!WaitForMultipleObjects+0x18
04 0250f624 75c680bb kernel32!WerpReportFaultInternal+0x186
05 0250f638 75c679b0 kernel32!WerpReportFault+0x70
06 0250f648 75c6792f kernel32!BasepReportFault+0x20
07 0250f6d4 00e21e86 kernel32!UnhandledExceptionFilter+0x1af
08 0250f6f0 75c803cf ModuleA!UnhandledExceptionFilter+0x3d
09 0250f778 77e250d7 kernel32!UnhandledExceptionFilter+0x127
0a 0250f780 77e24fb4 ntdll!__RtlUserThreadStart+0x62
0b 0250f794 77e24e59 ntdll!_EH4_CallFilterFunc+0x12
0c 0250f7bc 77e134a1 ntdll!_except_handler4+0x8e
0d 0250f7e0 77e13473 ntdll!ExecuteHandler2+0x26
0e 0250f804 77e13414 ntdll!ExecuteHandler+0x24
0f 0250f890 77dc0133 ntdll!RtlDispatchException+0x127
10 0250f890 68a8e0ca ntdll!KiUserExceptionDispatcher+0xf
WARNING: Frame IP not in any known module. Following frames may be wrong.
11 0250fd58 02c45f58 <Unloaded_ModuleB.dll>+0x1e0ca
12 0250fd84 75c4343d 0x2c45f58
13 0250fd90 77de9812 kernel32!BaseThreadInitThunk+0xe
14 0250fdd0 77de97e5 ntdll!__RtlUserThreadStart+0x70
15 0250fde8 00000000 ntdll!_RtlUserThreadStart+0x1b
```

The address may be the valid return address from **Execution Residue** (page 395), but may also be completely random, non-executable:

```
0:008> ub 0x2c45f58
^ Unable to find valid previous instruction for 'ub 0x2c45f58'
```

```
0:008> !address 0x2c45f58
```

```
Usage: Free
Base Address: 02bb0000
End Address: 02cb0000
Region Size: 00100000 ( 1.000 MB)
State: 00010000 MEM_FREE
Protect: 00000001 PAGE_NOACCESS
Type: <info not present at the target>
```

In our case, we have symbol files for *ModuleB.dll* but they do not help.

```
0:008> .sympath+ C:\MemoryDumps\Modules\PDBs
```

If we have normal **Manual Dumps** (page 710) we can compare **Stack Trace Collections** (page 1053) and take the advantage of existing **Thread Posets** (page 1119) to get the correct stack trace.

Alternatively, we can either use manual stack trace reconstruction techniques[75] or use **Injected Symbols** (page 574):

```
0:008> lm
[...]
Unloaded modules:
[...]
68a70000 68ac0000 ModuleB.dll
[…]


0:008> .reload /f /i ModuleB.dll=68a70000
*** WARNING: Unable to verify timestamp for ModuleB.dll


0:008> kL
# ChildEBP RetAddr
00 0250f4b8 76d21775 ntdll!NtWaitForMultipleObjects+0x15
01 0250f554 75c419fc KERNELBASE!WaitForMultipleObjectsEx+0x100
02 0250f59c 75c4268c kernel32!WaitForMultipleObjectsExImplementation+0xe0
03 0250f5b8 75c681fc kernel32!WaitForMultipleObjects+0x18
04 0250f624 75c680bb kernel32!WerpReportFaultInternal+0x186
05 0250f638 75c679b0 kernel32!WerpReportFault+0x70
06 0250f648 75c6792f kernel32!BasepReportFault+0x20
07 0250f6d4 00e21e86 kernel32!UnhandledExceptionFilter+0x1af
08 0250f6f0 75c803cf ModuleA!UnhandledExceptionFilter+0x3d
09 0250f778 77e250d7 kernel32!UnhandledExceptionFilter+0x127
0a 0250f780 77e24fb4 ntdll!__RtlUserThreadStart+0x62
0b 0250f794 77e24e59 ntdll!_EH4_CallFilterFunc+0x12
0c 0250f7bc 77e134a1 ntdll!_except_handler4+0x8e
0d 0250f7e0 77e13473 ntdll!ExecuteHandler2+0x26
0e 0250f804 77e13414 ntdll!ExecuteHandler+0x24
0f 0250f890 77dc0133 ntdll!RtlDispatchException+0x127
10 0250f890 68a8e0ca ntdll!KiUserExceptionDispatcher+0xf
11 0250fd64 68a8f284 ModuleB!foo+0x5a
12 0250fd84 75c4343d ModuleB!bar+0xf4
13 0250fd90 77de9812 kernel32!BaseThreadInitThunk+0xe
14 0250fdd0 77de97e5 ntdll!__RtlUserThreadStart+0x70
15 0250fde8 00000000 ntdll!_RtlUserThreadStart+0x1b
```

We call this analysis pattern **False Frame**. Although we have **Incorrect Stack Trace** (page 563), just one stack trace frame is wrong. Sometimes, if there is **Coincidental Symbolic Information** (page 148) available we get **Coincidental Frames** (page 141).

---

[75] Memory Dump Analysis Anthology, Volume 1, page 157

False Function Parameters

Beginner users of WinDbg sometimes confuse the first 3 parameters (or 4 for x64) displayed by **kb** or **kv** commands with real function parameters:

```
0:000> kbnL
 # ChildEBP RetAddr  Args to Child
00 002df5f4 0041167b 002df97c 00000000 7efdf000 ntdll!DbgBreakPoint
01 002df6d4 004115c9 00000000 40000000 00000001 CallingConventions!A::thiscallFunction+0x2b
02 002df97c 004114f9 00000001 40001000 00000002 CallingConventions!fastcallFunction+0x69
03 002dfbf8 0041142b 00000000 40000000 00000001 CallingConventions!cdeclFunction+0x59
04 002dfe7c 004116e8 00000000 40000000 00000001 CallingConventions!stdcallFunction+0x5b
05 002dff68 00411c76 00000001 005a2820 005a28c8 CallingConventions!wmain+0x38
06 002dffb8 00411abd 002dfff0 7d4e7d2a 00000000 CallingConventions!__tmainCRTStartup+0x1a6
07 002dffc0 7d4e7d2a 00000000 00000000 7efdf000 CallingConventions!wmainCRTStartup+0xd
08 002dfff0 00000000 00411082 00000000 000000c8 kernel32!BaseProcessStart+0x28
```

The calling sequence for it is:

```
stdcallFunction(0, 0x40000000, 1, 0x40001000, 2, 0x40002000) ->
cdeclFunction(0, 0x40000000, 1, 0x40001000, 2, 0x40002000) ->
fastcallFunction(0, 0x40000000, 1, 0x40001000, 2, 0x40002000) ->
A::thiscallFunction(0, 0x40000000, 1, 0x40001000, 2, 0x40002000)
```

and we see that only in the case of **fastcall** calling convention we have a discrepancy due to the fact that the first two parameters are passed not via the stack but through ECX and EDX:

```
0:000> ub 004114f9
CallingConventions!cdeclFunction+0x45
004114e5 push     ecx
004114e6 mov      edx,dword ptr [ebp+14h]
004114e9 push     edx
004114ea mov      eax,dword ptr [ebp+10h]
004114ed push     eax
004114ee mov      edx,dword ptr [ebp+0Ch]
004114f1 mov      ecx,dword ptr [ebp+8]
004114f4 call     CallingConventions!ILT+475(?fastcallFunctionYIXHHHHHHZ) (004111e0)
```

However, if we have full symbols we can see all parameters:

```
0:000> .frame 2
02 002df97c 004114f9 CallingConventions!fastcallFunction+0x69

0:000> dv /i /V
prv param   002df974 @ebp-0x08              a = 0
prv param   002df968 @ebp-0x14              b = 1073741824
prv param   002df984 @ebp+0x08              c = 1
prv param   002df988 @ebp+0x0c              d = 1073745920
prv param   002df98c @ebp+0x10              e = 2
prv param   002df990 @ebp+0x14              f = 1073750016
prv local   002df7c7 @ebp-0x1b5            obj = class A
prv local   002df7d0 @ebp-0x1ac          dummy = int [100]
```

How does **dv** command know about values in ECX and EDX which were definitely overwritten by later code? This is because the called function prolog saved them as local variables which you can notice as negative offsets for EBP register in **dv** output above:

```
0:000> uf CallingConventions!fastcallFunction
CallingConventions!fastcallFunction
   32 00411560 push    ebp
   32 00411561 mov     ebp,esp
   32 00411563 sub     esp,27Ch
   32 00411569 push    ebx
   32 0041156a push    esi
   32 0041156b push    edi
   32 0041156c push    ecx
   32 0041156d lea     edi,[ebp-27Ch]
   32 00411573 mov     ecx,9Fh
   32 00411578 mov     eax,0CCCCCCCCh
   32 0041157d rep stos dword ptr es:[edi]
   32 0041157f pop     ecx
   32 00411580 mov     dword ptr [ebp-14h],edx
   32 00411583 mov     dword ptr [ebp-8],ecx
...
...
...
```

In order to spot the occurrences of this pattern, double checks and knowledge of calling conventions are required. Sometimes this pattern is a consequence of **Optimized Code** pattern (page 853).

x64 stack traces do not show any discrepancies except the fact that **thiscall** function parameters are shifted to the right:

```
0:000> kbL
RetAddr          : Args to Child                                         : Call Site
00000001`40001397 : cccccccc`cccccccc cccccccc`cccccccc cccccccc`cccccccc cccccccc`cccccccc : ntdll!DbgBreakPoint
00000001`40001233 : 00000000`0012fa94 cccccccc`00000000 cccccccc`40000000 cccccccc`00000001 : CallingConventions!A::thiscallFunction+0x37
00000001`40001177 : cccccccc`00000000 cccccccc`40000000 cccccccc`00000001 cccccccc`40001000 : CallingConventions!fastcallFunction+0x93
00000001`400010c7 : cccccccc`00000000 cccccccc`40000000 cccccccc`00000001 cccccccc`40001000 : CallingConventions!cdeclFunction+0x87
00000001`400012ae : cccccccc`00000000 cccccccc`40000000 cccccccc`00000001 cccccccc`40001000 : CallingConventions!stdcallFunction+0x87
00000001`400018ec : 00000001`00000001 00000000`00481a80 00000000`00000000 00000001`400026ee : CallingConventions!wmain+0x4e
00000001`4000173e : 00000000`00000000 00000000`00000000 00000000`00000000 00000000`00000000 : CallingConventions!__tmainCRTStartup+0x19c
00000000`77d5964c : 00000000`77d59620 00000000`00000000 00000000`00000000 00000000`0012ffa8 : CallingConventions!wmainCRTStartup+0xe
00000000`00000000 : 00000001`40001730 00000000`00000000 00000000`00000000 00000000`00000000 : kernel32!BaseProcessStart+0x29
```

How can this happen if the standard x64 calling convention passes the first 4 parameters via ECX, EDX, R8, and R9? This is because the called function prolog saved them on the stack (this might not be true in the case of optimized code):

```
0:000> uf CallingConventions!fastcallFunction
CallingConventions!fastcallFunction
   32 00000001`400011a0 44894c2420    mov     dword ptr [rsp+20h],r9d
   32 00000001`400011a5 4489442418    mov     dword ptr [rsp+18h],r8d
   32 00000001`400011aa 89542410      mov     dword ptr [rsp+10h],edx
   32 00000001`400011ae 894c2408      mov     dword ptr [rsp+8],ecx
...
...
...
```

A::thiscallFunction function passes **this** pointer via ECX too, and this explains the right shift of parameters.

Here is the C++ code we used for experimentation:

```
#include "stdafx.h"
#include <windows.h>

void __stdcall stdcallFunction (int, int, int, int, int, int);
void __cdecl cdeclFunction (int, int, int, int, int, int);
void __fastcall fastcallFunction (int, int, int, int, int, int);

class A
{
public:
 void thiscallFunction (int, int, int, int, int, int) { DebugBreak(); };
};

void __stdcall stdcallFunction (int a, int b, int c, int d, int e, int f)
{
 int dummy[100] = {0};

 cdeclFunction (a, b, c, d, e, f);
}

void __cdecl cdeclFunction (int a, int b, int c, int d, int e, int f)
{
 int dummy[100] = {0};

 fastcallFunction (a, b, c, d, e, f);
}

void __fastcall fastcallFunction (int a, int b, int c, int d, int e, int f)
{
 int dummy[100] = {0};

 A obj;

 obj.thiscallFunction (a, b, c, d, e, f);
}

int _tmain(int argc, _TCHAR* argv[])
{
 stdcallFunction (0, 0x40000000, 1, 0x40001000, 2, 0x40002000);

 return 0;
}
```

False Memory

When modeling **Invalid Pointer (Objects)** analysis pattern (see source code there, page 665), we noticed that if we use MEM_RELEASE instead of MEM_DECOMMIT in *VirtualFree* API call, we see page memory contents despite an access violation **Stored Exception** (page 1071) pointing to that page. Moreover, the page contents were not corresponding to what should have been expected from source code. We had to do live kernel debugging to verify what was going on.

We launched *InvalidPointerObject.exe* that displayed the committed address allocated via *VirtualAlloc* API call:

Then we broke into the system, found our process, and inspected that address:

```
Microsoft (R) Windows Debugger Version 10.0.18362.1 AMD64
Copyright (c) Microsoft Corporation. All rights reserved.

Opened \\.\pipe\com2
Waiting to reconnect...
Connected to Windows 10 18362 x64 target at (Fri May  1 22:46:00.982 2020 (UTC + 1:00)), ptr64 TRUE
Kernel Debugger connection established.
Symbol search path is: srv*
Executable search path is:
Windows 10 Kernel Version 18362 MP (1 procs) Free x64
Built by: 18362.1.amd64fre.19h1_release.190318-1202
Machine Name:
Kernel base = 0xfffff800`74800000 PsLoadedModuleList = 0xfffff800`74c48190
System Uptime: 0 days 0:00:00.000
KDTARGET: Refreshing KD connection
Break instruction exception - code 80000003 (first chance)
************************************************************************
*                                                                      *
*    You are seeing this message because you pressed either            *
*         CTRL+C (if you run console kernel debugger) or,              *
*         CTRL+BREAK (if you run GUI kernel debugger),                *
*    on your debugger machine's keyboard.                              *
*                                                                      *
*                   THIS IS NOT A BUG OR A SYSTEM CRASH                *
*                                                                      *
* If you did not intend to break into the debugger, press the "g" key, then *
```

```
* press the "Enter" key now.  This message might immediately reappear.  If it *
* does, press "g" and "Enter" again.                                         *
*                                                                            *
******************************************************************************
nt!DbgBreakPointWithStatus:
fffff800`749c93a0 cc                int     3

1: kd> !process 0 0
**** NT ACTIVE PROCESS DUMP ****
PROCESS ffffe00314e89300
    SessionId: none  Cid: 0004    Peb: 00000000  ParentCid: 0000
    DirBase: 001ad002  ObjectTable: ffffc90314806d40  HandleCount: 3136.
    Image: System

[...]


PROCESS ffffe00318d60080
    SessionId: 1  Cid: 1a90    Peb: 161ab73000  ParentCid: 1474
    DirBase: af7ee002  ObjectTable: ffffc9031c02a0c0  HandleCount:  33.
    Image: InvalidPointerObject.exe

[...]


1: kd> !process ffffe00318d60080 3f
PROCESS ffffe00318d60080
    SessionId: 1  Cid: 1a90    Peb: 161ab73000  ParentCid: 1474
    DirBase: af7ee002  ObjectTable: ffffc9031c02a0c0  HandleCount:  33.
    Image: InvalidPointerObject.exe
    VadRoot ffffe0031a78d1c0 Vads 22 Clone 0 Private 94. Modified 0. Locked 2.
    DeviceMap ffffc903193e9bf0
    Token                             ffffc9031c692060
    ElapsedTime                       00:01:13.571
    UserTime                          00:00:00.000
    KernelTime                        00:00:00.000
    QuotaPoolUsage[PagedPool]         20344
    QuotaPoolUsage[NonPagedPool]      3256
    Working Set Sizes (now,min,max)  (497, 50, 345) (1988KB, 200KB, 1380KB)
    PeakWorkingSetSize                465
    VirtualSize                       4139 Mb
    PeakVirtualSize                   4139 Mb
    PageFaultCount                    499
    MemoryPriority                    BACKGROUND
    BasePriority                      8
    CommitCharge                      107
    Job                               ffffe00317be8060

[...]


        THREAD ffffe003198ba0c0  Cid 1a90.18bc  Teb: 000000161ab74000 Win32Thread: 0000000000000000 WAIT:
(Executive) KernelMode Alertable
            ffffe0031a7b0238  NotificationEvent
        IRP List:
            ffffe00318a49510: (0006,0238) Flags: 00060900  Mdl: ffffe00319319470
        Not impersonating
        DeviceMap               ffffc903193e9bf0
```

```
       Owning Process        ffffe00318d60080      Image:         InvalidPointerObject.exe
       Attached Process      N/A              Image:         N/A
       Wait Start TickCount  6673             Ticks: 4692 (0:00:01:13.312)
       Context Switch Count  118              IdealProcessor: 1
       UserTime              00:00:00.000
       KernelTime            00:00:00.015
*** WARNING: Unable to verify checksum for InvalidPointerObject.exe
       Win32 Start Address InvalidPointerObject!wmainCRTStartup (0x00007ff66357e044)
       Stack Init ffff848c00a22c90 Current ffff848c00a22560
       Base ffff848c00a23000 Limit ffff848c00a1d000 Call 0000000000000000
       Priority 8 BasePriority 8 PriorityDecrement 0 IoPriority 2 PagePriority 5
       Child-SP          RetAddr           Call Site
       ffff848c`00a225a0 fffff800`7483c7bd nt!KiSwapContext+0x76
       ffff848c`00a226e0 fffff800`7483b644 nt!KiSwapThread+0xbfd
       ffff848c`00a22780 fffff800`7483ade5 nt!KiCommitThreadWait+0x144
       ffff848c`00a22820 fffff800`74de982a nt!KeWaitForSingleObject+0x255
       ffff848c`00a22900 fffff800`74de595f nt!IopSynchronousServiceTail+0x24a
       ffff848c`00a229a0 fffff800`749d2e15 nt!NtReadFile+0x59f
       ffff848c`00a22a90 00007ffb`0ed3c184 nt!KiSystemServiceCopyEnd+0x25 (TrapFrame @
ffff848c`00a22b00)
       00000016`1a96f338 00007ffb`0c405227 ntdll!NtReadFile+0x14
       00000016`1a96f340 00007ff6`6359b3b9 KERNELBASE!ReadFile+0x77
       00000016`1a96f3c0 00000000`00000001 InvalidPointerObject!_read_nolock+0x2f5
[minkernel\crts\ucrt\src\appcrt\lowio\read.cpp @ 566]
       00000016`1a96f3c8 00000000`00000000 0x1


1: kd> .thread /r /p ffffe003198ba0c0
Implicit thread is now ffffe003`198ba0c0
Implicit process is now ffffe003`18d60080
.cache forcedecodeuser done
Loading User Symbols
....


1: kd> kL
*** Stack trace for last set context - .thread/.cxr resets it
# Child-SP          RetAddr              Call Site
00 ffff848c`00a225a0 fffff800`7483c7bd nt!KiSwapContext+0x76
01 ffff848c`00a226e0 fffff800`7483b644 nt!KiSwapThread+0xbfd
02 ffff848c`00a22780 fffff800`7483ade5 nt!KiCommitThreadWait+0x144
03 ffff848c`00a22820 fffff800`74de982a nt!KeWaitForSingleObject+0x255
04 ffff848c`00a22900 fffff800`74de595f nt!IopSynchronousServiceTail+0x24a
05 ffff848c`00a229a0 fffff800`749d2e15 nt!NtReadFile+0x59f
06 ffff848c`00a22a90 00007ffb`0ed3c184 nt!KiSystemServiceCopyEnd+0x25
07 00000016`1a96f338 00007ffb`0c405227 ntdll!NtReadFile+0x14
*** WARNING: Unable to verify checksum for InvalidPointerObject.exe
08 00000016`1a96f340 00007ff6`6359b3b9 KERNELBASE!ReadFile+0x77
09 00000016`1a96f3c0 00000000`00000001 InvalidPointerObject!_read_nolock+0x2f5
0a 00000016`1a96f3c8 00000000`00000000 0x1
```

```
1: kd> !vad 146e3a70000 1


VAD @ ffffe0031a78eb10
  Start VPN           146e3a70  End VPN           146e3a70  Control Area  0000000000000000
  FirstProtoPte 0000000000000000  LastPte 0000000000000000  Commit Charge          1 (0n1)
  Secured.Flink              0  Blink                    0  Banked/Extend          0
  File Offset                0
      ViewUnmap MemCommit PrivateMemory READWRITE


1: kd> dc 146e3a70000
00000146`e3a70000 00000001 00000000 00000000 00000000 ..............
00000146`e3a70010 00000000 00000000 00000000 00000000 ..............
00000146`e3a70020 00000000 00000000 00000000 00000000 ..............
00000146`e3a70030 00000000 00000000 00000000 00000000 ..............
00000146`e3a70040 00000000 00000000 00000000 00000000 ..............
00000146`e3a70050 00000000 00000000 00000000 00000000 ..............
00000146`e3a70060 00000000 00000000 00000000 00000000 ..............
00000146`e3a70070 00000000 00000000 00000000 00000000 ..............
```

We see the page memory contents show the correct counter value (1):

```
struct Resource
{
    void DoSomething()
    {
        ++m_usageCounter;
    }
    std::size_t m_usageCounter{};
};
```

We resume system execution and hit a key. The program crashes in the second *DoSomething* call after releasing memory that contained Resource object:

```
        ::VirtualFree(pMem, 0, MEM_RELEASE);

        pResource->DoSomething();
```

We wait until WER dialog appears (we had to add DWORD DontShowUI (0) to \HKEY_LOCAL_MACHINE\SOFTWARE\Microsoft\Windows\Windows Error Reporting):

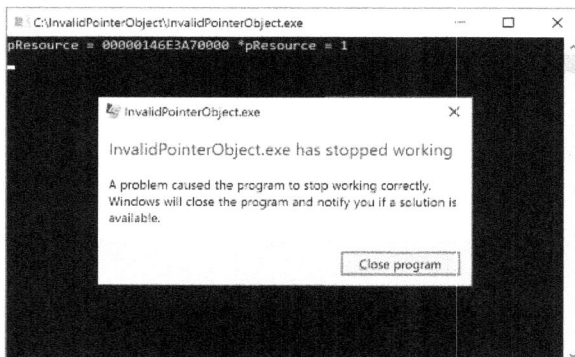

We then break in the system again and inspect the same address:

```
1: kd> g
Break instruction exception - code 80000003 (first chance)
***************************************************************************
*                                                                         *
*    You are seeing this message because you pressed either               *
*        CTRL+C (if you run console kernel debugger) or,                   *
*        CTRL+BREAK (if you run GUI kernel debugger),                      *
*    on your debugger machine's keyboard.                                  *
*                                                                         *
*                   THIS IS NOT A BUG OR A SYSTEM CRASH                    *
*                                                                         *
* If you did not intend to break into the debugger, press the "g" key, then *
* press the "Enter" key now.  This message might immediately reappear.  If it *
* does, press "g" and "Enter" again.                                      *
*                                                                         *
***************************************************************************
nt!DbgBreakPointWithStatus:
fffff800`749c93a0 cc              int     3

0: kd> .thread /r /p ffffe003198ba0c0
Implicit thread is now ffffe003`198ba0c0
Implicit process is now ffffe003`18d60080
.cache forcedecodeuser done
Loading User Symbols
....

0: kd> kL
*** Stack trace for last set context - .thread/.cxr resets it
# Child-SP          RetAddr           Call Site
00 ffff848c`00a21f70 fffff800`7483c7bd nt!KiSwapContext+0x76
01 ffff848c`00a220b0 fffff800`7483b644 nt!KiSwapThread+0xbfd
02 ffff848c`00a22150 fffff800`748884e7 nt!KiCommitThreadWait+0x144
03 ffff848c`00a221f0 fffff800`74e1ffe9 nt!KeWaitForMultipleObjects+0x287
04 ffff848c`00a22300 fffff800`74e1fd05 nt!ObWaitForMultipleObjects+0x2a9
05 ffff848c`00a22800 fffff800`749d2e15 nt!NtWaitForMultipleObjects+0x105
06 ffff848c`00a22a90 00007ffb`0ed3cc14 nt!KiSystemServiceCopyEnd+0x25
07 00000016`1a96e208 00007ffb`0c438027 ntdll!NtWaitForMultipleObjects+0x14
08 00000016`1a96e210 00007ffb`0c437f0e KERNELBASE!WaitForMultipleObjectsEx+0x107
09 00000016`1a96e510 00007ffb`0e0071fb KERNELBASE!WaitForMultipleObjects+0xe
0a 00000016`1a96e550 00007ffb`0e006ca8 KERNEL32!WerpReportFaultInternal+0x51b
0b 00000016`1a96e670 00007ffb`0c4df868 KERNEL32!WerpReportFault+0xac
0c 00000016`1a96e6b0 00007ffb`0ed44b32 KERNELBASE!UnhandledExceptionFilter+0x3b8
0d 00000016`1a96e7d0 00007ffb`0ed2c6d6 ntdll!RtlUserThreadStart$filt$0+0xa2
0e 00000016`1a96e810 00007ffb`0ed4121f ntdll!_C_specific_handler+0x96
0f 00000016`1a96e880 00007ffb`0ed0a289 ntdll!RtlpExecuteHandlerForException+0xf
10 00000016`1a96e8b0 00007ffb`0ed3fe8e ntdll!RtlDispatchException+0x219
11 00000016`1a96efc0 00007ff6`6357378a ntdll!KiUserExceptionDispatch+0x2e
*** WARNING: Unable to verify checksum for InvalidPointerObject.exe
12 00000016`1a96f6d8 00007ff6`63573875 InvalidPointerObject!Resource::DoSomething+0xa
13 00000016`1a96f6e0 00007ff6`6357dfd4 InvalidPointerObject!wmain+0xd5
14 (Inline Function) ---`--- InvalidPointerObject!invoke_main+0x22
15 00000016`1a96f730 00007ffb`0dfb7bd4 InvalidPointerObject!__scrt_common_main_seh+0x10c
```

```
16 00000016`1a96f770 00007ffb`0ed0ced1 KERNEL32!BaseThreadInitThunk+0x14
17 00000016`1a96f7a0 00000000`00000000 ntdll!RtlUserThreadStart+0x21


0: kd> .frame 0n18;dv /t /v
12 00000016`1a96f6d8 00007ff6`63573875 InvalidPointerObject!Resource::DoSomething+0xa
[C:\NewWork\InvalidPointerObject\InvalidPointerObject.cpp @ 10]
00000016`1a96f6e0 struct Resource * this = 0x00000146`e3a70000


0: kd> !vad 146e3a70000 1


VAD @ ffffe0031ab91080
   Start VPN            146e3a70  End VPN            146e3a70  Control Area  ffffe0031a66f780
   FirstProtoPte ffffc9031b8fdf50  LastPte ffffc9031b8fdf50  Commit Charge                  0 (0n0)
   Secured.Flink            0  Blink                  0  Banked/Extend                 0
   File Offset              0
       ViewShare READWRITE


ControlArea   @ ffffe0031a66f780
   Segment       ffffc9031c7d55d0  Flink       ffffe0031ab91f40  Blink       ffffe0031ab910e0
   Section Ref              1  Pfn Ref                0  Mapped Views                  3
   User Ref                 4  WaitForDel             0  Flush Count                   1
   File Object  0000000000000000  ModWriteCount          0  System Views                  0
   WritableRefs             0  PartitionId            0
   Flags (2000) Commit

      Pagefile-backed section


Segment @ ffffc9031c7d55d0
   ControlArea       ffffe0031a66f780  ExtendInfo       0000000000000000
   Total Ptes                   1
   Segment Size              1000  Committed                     1
   CreatingProcessId         1a90  FirstMappedVa       146e3a70000
   ProtoPtes         ffffc9031b8fdf50
   Flags (80000) ProtectionMask


0: kd> !ca ffffe0031a66f780 4


ControlArea   @ ffffe0031a66f780
   Segment       ffffc9031c7d55d0  Flink       ffffe0031ab91f40  Blink       ffffe0031ab910e0
   Section Ref              1  Pfn Ref                0  Mapped Views                  3
   User Ref                 4  WaitForDel             0  Flush Count                   1
   File Object  0000000000000000  ModWriteCount          0  System Views                  0
   WritableRefs             0  PartitionId            0
   Flags (2000) Commit

      Pagefile-backed section


3 mapped view(s):

ffffe0031ab91f40 - VAD ffffe0031ab91ee0, process ffffe0031a8d3080  WerFault.exe
ffffe0031ab93ca0 - VAD ffffe0031ab93c40, process ffffe0031acd3080  InvalidPointer
ffffe0031ab910e0 - VAD ffffe0031ab91080, process ffffe00318d60080  InvalidPointer
```

```
0: kd> dc 146e3a70000
00000146`e3a70000 000000f0 00001a90 000018bc 00000000 .............
00000146`e3a70010 00000000 00000000 00000000 00000000 .............
00000146`e3a70020 00000000 00000000 00000000 00000000 .............
00000146`e3a70030 00000000 00000000 00000000 00000000 .............
00000146`e3a70040 00000000 00000000 00000000 00000000 .............
00000146`e3a70050 00000000 00000000 00000000 00000000 .............
00000146`e3a70060 00000000 00000000 00000000 00000000 .............
00000146`e3a70070 00000000 00000000 00000000 00000000 .............
```

We see the page contents changed (it now contains PID and TID) and also its pagefile-backed section lists 3 mapped views including 2 new processes, one is **Zombie Process** (page 1278) duplicate of the original *InvalidPointerObject.exe* process and another is *WerFault.exe*:

```
0: kd> !process ffffe0031acd3080
PROCESS ffffe0031acd3080
    SessionId: 1  Cid: 06cc    Peb: 161ab73000  ParentCid: 1a90
    DirBase: 9d002002  ObjectTable: ffffc9031c03e5c0  HandleCount:   0.
    Image: InvalidPointerObject.exe
    VadRoot ffffe0031a789d90 Vads 21 Clone ffffe00318770810 Private 41. Modified 0. Locked 0.
    DeviceMap 0000000000000000
    Token                             ffffc9031d32a770
    ElapsedTime                       00:00:26.741
    UserTime                          00:00:00.000
    KernelTime                        00:00:00.000
    QuotaPoolUsage[PagedPool]         17776
    QuotaPoolUsage[NonPagedPool]      6024
    Working Set Sizes (now,min,max)   (28, 50, 345) (112KB, 200KB, 1380KB)
    PeakWorkingSetSize                10
    VirtualSize                       4138 Mb
    PeakVirtualSize                   4138 Mb
    PageFaultCount                    28
    MemoryPriority                    BACKGROUND
    BasePriority                      8
    CommitCharge                      51

No active threads

0: kd> !process 1a90
Searching for Process with Cid == 1a90
PROCESS ffffe00318d60080
    SessionId: 1  Cid: 1a90    Peb: 161ab73000  ParentCid: 1474
    DirBase: af7ee002  ObjectTable: ffffc9031c02a0c0  HandleCount:  39.
    Image: InvalidPointerObject.exe
    VadRoot ffffe0031a78d1c0 Vads 22 Clone ffffe00318770590 Private 43. Modified 18. Locked 0.
    DeviceMap ffffc903193e9bf0
    Token                             ffffc9031c692060
    ElapsedTime                       00:38:20.130
    UserTime                          00:00:00.000
    KernelTime                        00:00:00.000
    QuotaPoolUsage[PagedPool]         20352
    QuotaPoolUsage[NonPagedPool]      6328
    Working Set Sizes (now,min,max)   (547, 50, 345) (2188KB, 200KB, 1380KB)
    PeakWorkingSetSize                515
    VirtualSize                       4139 Mb
```

```
PeakVirtualSize              4139 Mb
PageFaultCount               552
MemoryPriority               BACKGROUND
BasePriority                 8
CommitCharge                 106
Job                          ffffe00317be8060
```

[...]

We resume system execution and collect the process crash dump. When we look at the crash address, we see the same unexpected **False Memory** contents:

```
This dump file has an exception of interest stored in it.
The stored exception information can be accessed via .ecxr.
(1a90.18bc): Access violation - code c0000005 (first/second chance not available)
For analysis of this file, run !analyze -v
ntdll!NtWaitForMultipleObjects+0x14:
00007ffb`0ed3cc14 c3              ret

0:000> kL
 # Child-SP          RetAddr           Call Site
00 00000016`1a96e208 00007ffb`0c438027 ntdll!NtWaitForMultipleObjects+0x14
01 00000016`1a96e210 00007ffb`0c437f0e KERNELBASE!WaitForMultipleObjectsEx+0x107
02 00000016`1a96e510 00007ffb`0e0071fb KERNELBASE!WaitForMultipleObjects+0xe
03 00000016`1a96e550 00007ffb`0e006ca8 kernel32!WerpReportFaultInternal+0x51b
04 00000016`1a96e670 00007ffb`0c4df868 kernel32!WerpReportFault+0xac
05 00000016`1a96e6b0 00007ffb`0ed44b32 KERNELBASE!UnhandledExceptionFilter+0x3b8
06 00000016`1a96e7d0 00007ffb`0ed2c6d6 ntdll!RtlUserThreadStart$filt$0+0xa2
07 00000016`1a96e810 00007ffb`0ed4121f ntdll!_C_specific_handler+0x96
08 00000016`1a96e880 00007ffb`0ed0a289 ntdll!RtlpExecuteHandlerForException+0xf
09 00000016`1a96e8b0 00007ffb`0ed3fe8e ntdll!RtlDispatchException+0x219
0a 00000016`1a96efc0 00007ff6`6357378a ntdLl!KiUserExceptionDispatch+0x2e
*** WARNING: Unable to verify checksum for InvalidPointerObject.exe -
0b 00000016`1a96f6d8 00007ff6`63573875 InvalidPointerObject!Resource::DoSomething+0xa
0c 00000016`1a96f6e0 00007ff6`6357dfd4 InvalidPointerObject!wmain+0xd5
0d (Inline Function) --------`-------- InvalidPointerObject!invoke_main+0x22
0e 00000016`1a96f730 00007ffb`0dfb7bd4 InvalidPointerObject!__scrt_common_main_seh+0x10c
0f 00000016`1a96f770 00007ffb`0ed0ced1 kernel32!BaseThreadInitThunk+0x14
10 00000016`1a96f7a0 00000000`00000000 ntdll!RtlUserThreadStart+0x21

0:000> dx Debugger.Sessions[0].Processes[6800].Threads[6332].Stack.Frames[11].SwitchTo();dv /t /v
Debugger.Sessions[0].Processes[6800].Threads[6332].Stack.Frames[11].SwitchTo()
00000016`1a96f6e0 struct Resource * this = 0x00000146`e3a70000


0:000> !address 0x00000146`e3a70000


Usage:               <unknown>
Base Address:        00000146`e3a70000
End Address:         00000146`e3a71000
Region Size:         00000000`00001000 (   4.000 kB)
State:               00001000            MEM_COMMIT
Protect:             00000004            PAGE_READWRITE
Type:                00040000            MEM_MAPPED
Allocation Base:     00000146`e3a70000
```

```
Allocation Protect:        00000004            PAGE_READWRITE


Content source: 1 (target), length: 1000


0:000> dc 0x00000146`e3a70000
00000146`e3a70000 000000f0 00001a90 000018bc 00000000  ..............
00000146`e3a70010 00000000 00000000 00000000 00000000  ..............
00000146`e3a70020 00000000 00000000 00000000 00000000  ..............
00000146`e3a70030 00000000 00000000 00000000 00000000  ..............
00000146`e3a70040 00000000 00000000 00000000 00000000  ..............
00000146`e3a70050 00000000 00000000 00000000 00000000  ..............
00000146`e3a70060 00000000 00000000 00000000 00000000  ..............
00000146`e3a70070 00000000 00000000 00000000 00000000  ..............


0:000> ~
. 0 Id: 1a90.18bc Suspend: 0 Teb: 00000016`1ab74000 Unfrozen


0:000> dx -r1 ((InvalidPointerObject!Resource *)0x146e3a70000)
((InvalidPointerObject!Resource *)0x146e3a70000) : 0x146e3a70000 [Type: Resource *]
[+0x000] m_usageCounter : 0x1a90000000f0 [Type: unsigned __int64]


0:000> .ecxr
rax=00000146e3a70000 rbx=00000146e3aa5bf0 rcx=00000146e3a70000
rdx=0000000000000000 rsi=0000000000000000 rdi=00000146e3aa5c70
rip=00007ff66357378a rsp=000000161a96f6d8 rbp=0000000000000000
r8=000000161a96f6a8 r9=0000000000000000 r10=0000000000000000
r11=0000000000000246 r12=0000000000000000 r13=0000000000000000
r14=0000000000000000 r15=0000000000000000
iopl=0 nv up ei pl nz na pe nc
cs=0033 ss=002b ds=002b es=002b fs=0053 gs=002b efl=00010202
InvalidPointerObject!Resource::DoSomething+0xa:
00007ff6`6357378a 488b00 mov rax,qword ptr [rax] ds:00000146`e3a70000=00001a90000000f0
```

Such **False Memory** may complicate the analysis of process crash dumps when we want to examine memory contents before exception.

The example memory dump, the application PDB file, and source code are available for download[76].

---

[76] http://www.patterndiagnostics.com/SoftwareDiagnosticsCorpus/SDC7.zip

False Positive Dump

Here we get crash dump files pointing to a wrong direction or not useful for analysis. This usually happens when a wrong tool was selected, or the right one was not properly configured for capturing crash dumps. Here is one example investigated in detail.

The customer experienced frequent spooler crashes on Windows Server 2003. The dump was sent for investigation to find an offending component. Usually, it is a printer driver. WinDbg revealed the following exception thread stack:

```
KERNEL32!RaiseException+0x56
KERNEL32!OutputDebugStringA+0x55
KERNEL32!OutputDebugStringW+0x39
PRINTER!ConvertTicket+0x3c90
PRINTER!DllGetClassObject+0x5d9b
PRINTER!DllGetClassObject+0x11bb
```

The immediate response is to point to *PRINTER.DLL,* but if we look at parameters to *OutputDebugStringA* we see that the string passed to it is a valid NULL-terminated string:

```
0:010> da 000d0040
000d0040  ".Lower DWORD of elapsed time = 3"
000d0060  "750000."
```

If we disassemble *OutputDebugStringA* up to *RaiseException* call we see:

```
0:010> u KERNEL32!OutputDebugStringA
KERNEL32!OutputDebugStringA+0x55
KERNEL32!OutputDebugStringA:
push    ebp
mov     ebp,esp
push    0FFFFFFFFh
push    offset KERNEL32!'string'+0x10
push    offset KERNEL32!_except_handler3
mov     eax,dword ptr fs:[00000000h]
push    eax
mov     dword ptr fs:[0],esp
push    ecx
push    ecx
sub     esp,228h
push    ebx
push    esi
push    edi
mov     dword ptr [ebp-18h],esp
and     dword ptr [ebp-4],0
mov     edx,dword ptr [ebp+8]
mov     edi,edx
or      ecx,0FFFFFFFFh
xor     eax,eax
repne scas byte ptr es:[edi]
not     ecx
```

```
mov      dword ptr [ebp-20h],ecx
mov      dword ptr [ebp-1Ch],edx
lea      eax,[ebp-20h]
push     eax
push     2
push     0
push     40010006h
call     KERNEL32!RaiseException
```

There are no jumps in the code prior to *RaiseException* call, and this means that raising an exception is expected. Also, MSDN documentation says:

> "If the application has no debugger, the system debugger displays the string. If the application has no debugger and the system debugger is not active, OutputDebugString does nothing."

So *spoolsv.exe* might have been monitored by a debugger which caught that exception and instead of dismissing it dumped the spooler process.

If we look at **!analyze -v** output we see the following:

```
Comment: 'Userdump generated complete user-mode minidump
with Exception Monitor function on WS002E0O-01-MFP'ERROR_CODE: (NTSTATUS) 0x40010006 -
Debugger printed exception on control C.
```

Fat Process Dump

During repeated execution either on one computer or in parallel on many computers with a uniform software and hardware the given process VM size tends to cluster around some value range, for example, 40 - 60 MB. If we get a collection of user process memory dumps taken from several production servers, say 20 files, we can either employ scripts to process all of them[77] or compare their file size and look for bigger ones for a starter, for example, 85 or 110 Mb. For certain processes, for example, a print spooler, after a software problem the process size tends to increase compared to normal execution. For other processes, certain error processing modules might be loaded increasing VM size, or in the case of incoming requests for a hung process, certain memory regions like heap could increase as well contributing to a dump file size increase. If we have fat and thin clients, we should also have thin and fat process dumps as well.

---

[77] Hundreds of Crash Dumps, Memory Dump Analysis Anthology, Volume 1, page 227

Fault Context

In the case of multiple different faults like bugchecks and different crash points, stack traces, and modules we can look at what is common among them. It could be their process context, which can easily be seen from the default analysis command:

```
1: kd> !analyze -v

[...]

PROCESS_NAME:  Application.exe
```

Then we can check whether an application is resource consumption intensive (could implicate hardware faults) like games and simulators or uses its own drivers (implicates latent corruption). In a production environment, it can also be removed if it is functionally non-critical and can be avoided or replaced.

First Fault Stack Trace

The case of **Error Reporting Fault** chain (page 348) led us to this pattern that corresponds to First Fault software diagnostics pattern proper[78]. Here the term *first fault* is used for an exception that was either ignored by surrounding code or led to other exceptions or error message boxes with stack traces that masked the first one. Typical examples where it is sometimes possible to get a first exception stack trace include but not limited to:

- Fault in error reporting (page 348) started as a fault in some other process
- **Hidden Exception** in user (page 506) or kernel (page 504) space
- Double fault (**Stack Overflow**, page 1004)
- **Nested Exception** in unmanaged (page 811) and managed (page 808) code
- **Nested Offender** (page 815)

It is also sometimes possible unless a stack region was **Paged Out** (page 864) to get partial stack traces from **Execution Residue** (page 395) when the sequence of return addresses was partially overwritten by subsequently executed code.

---

[78] Patterns of Software Diagnostics, First Fault, Memory Dump Analysis Anthology, Volume 7, page 406

Foreign Module Frame

Visio was freezing after saving a diagram as a picture after we tried to close it. It eventually crashed with WER saving a crash dump file in *LocalDumps* folder[79]. After a few such incidents, Visio suggested to disable a 3rd-party plugin. We did that, and double checked in Options \ Add-Ins dialog. Unfortunately, the same abnormal behavior continued. When we looked at the crash dump stack trace we noticed **Foreign Module Frame**:

```
0:000> k
# ChildEBP RetAddr
00 0019cbac 746b1556 ntdll!NtWaitForMultipleObjects+0xc
01 0019cd40 746b1408 KERNELBASE!WaitForMultipleObjectsEx+0x136
02 0019cd5c 747ea02a KERNELBASE!WaitForMultipleObjects+0x18
03 0019d198 747e9ac6 kernel32!WerpReportFaultInternal+0x545
04 0019d1a8 747ccf09 kernel32!WerpReportFault+0x7a
05 0019d1b0 746c9f53 kernel32!BasepReportFault+0x19
06 0019d244 76fc2de5 KERNELBASE!UnhandledExceptionFilter+0x1b3
07 0019d2e8 76f8acd6 ntdll!LdrpLogFatalUserCallbackException+0x4d
08 0019d2f4 76f9d572 ntdll!KiUserCallbackExceptionHandler+0x26
09 0019d318 76f9d544 ntdll!ExecuteHandler2+0x26
0a 0019d3e0 76f8ad8f ntdll!ExecuteHandler+0x24
0b 0019d3e0 55403000 ntdll!KiUserExceptionDispatcher+0xf
WARNING: Stack unwind information not available. Following frames may be wrong.
0c 0019d8d0 55402faa VISLIB!Ordinal1+0x24f3b
0d 0019d914 5b85c67e VISLIB!Ordinal1+0x24ee5
0e 0019d940 5b85c638 MSO!Ordinal2138+0x10a
0f 0019d950 5b8e7620 MSO!Ordinal2138+0xc4
10 0019d964 5b8e7602 MSO!Ordinal9998+0x3bc
11 0019d97c 5bc938a6 MSO!Ordinal9998+0x39e
12 0019dbb0 5c240add MSO!Ordinal7238+0x25bef
13 0019ddec 65598ed1 MSO!Ordinal2007+0x1766
14 0019de78 655c5eaa VisioPlugin!DllRegisterServer+0x43bf1
15 0019dfbc 555601db VisioPlugin!DllRegisterServer+0x70bca
16 0019dfe8 5555fe61 VISLIB!Ordinal1+0x182116
17 0019e028 55421b7c VISLIB!Ordinal1+0x181d9c
18 0019e070 5549f1a9 VISLIB!Ordinal1+0x43ab7
19 0019e090 5549ebba VISLIB!Ordinal1+0xc10e4
1a 0019e0c0 5540dd14 VISLIB!Ordinal1+0xc0af5
1b 0019e110 55426168 VISLIB!Ordinal1+0x2fc4f
1c 0019e134 55425446 VISLIB!Ordinal1+0x480a3
1d 0019e20c 5549eace VISLIB!Ordinal1+0x47381
1e 0019e264 5549e90e VISLIB!Ordinal1+0xc0a09
1f 0019e28c 6571fb03 VISLIB!Ordinal1+0xc0849
20 0019e334 6571f6cc mfc90u!CWnd::OnWndMsg+0x410
21 0019e354 553ef572 mfc90u!CWnd::WindowProc+0x24
22 0019e370 6571e2f2 VISLIB!Ordinal1+0x114ad
23 0019e3d8 6571e57e mfc90u!AfxCallWndProc+0xa3
24 0019e3fc 553ef518 mfc90u!AfxWndProc+0x37
25 0019e440 553ef4d9 VISLIB!Ordinal1+0x11453
```

[79] https://docs.microsoft.com/en-gb/windows/win32/wer/collecting-user-mode-dumps

```
26 0019e458 553ef49e VISLIB!Ordinal1+0x11414
27 0019e480 553ef338 VISLIB!Ordinal1+0x113d9
28 0019e49c 553ef2d6 VISLIB!Ordinal1+0x11273
29 0019e4c4 553ef107 VISLIB!Ordinal1+0x11211
2a 0019e528 75864923 VISLIB!Ordinal1+0x11042
2b 0019e554 75844790 user32!_InternalCallWinProc+0x2b
2c 0019e5fc 75844527 user32!UserCallWinProcCheckWow+0x1f0
2d 0019e638 71db7d40 user32!CallWindowProcW+0x97
2e 0019e6b8 71db7996 comctl32!CallNextSubclassProc+0x140
2f 0019e6d8 5b84d95a comctl32!DefSubclassProc+0x56
30 0019e720 5b84d7ad MSO!Ordinal6319+0x25e
31 0019e74c 71db7db8 MSO!Ordinal6319+0xb1
32 0019e7d0 71db7b61 comctl32!CallNextSubclassProc+0x1b8
33 0019e82c 75864923 comctl32!MasterSubclassProc+0xa1
34 0019e858 75844790 user32!_InternalCallWinProc+0x2b
35 0019e900 75844370 user32!UserCallWinProcCheckWow+0x1f0
36 0019e960 7584b179 user32!DispatchClientMessage+0xf0
37 0019e9a0 76f8ad66 user32!__fnDWORD+0x49
38 0019e9d8 75864dac ntdll!KiUserCallbackDispatcher+0x36
39 0019e9dc 75842ce8 user32!NtUserMessageCall+0xc
3a 0019ea68 758423ba user32!RealDefWindowProcWorker+0x148
3b 0019ea80 71f882ee user32!RealDefWindowProcW+0x5a
3c 0019eaa0 71f88145 uxtheme!DoMsgDefault+0x3a
3d 0019eab0 71f87bba uxtheme!OnDwpSysCommand+0x35
3e 0019eb1c 71f868d8 uxtheme!_ThemeDefWindowProc+0x6ca
3f 0019eb30 75842b66 uxtheme!ThemeDefWindowProcW+0x18
40 0019eb80 758415ee user32!DefWindowProcW+0x176
41 0019eb98 75851e3b user32!DefWindowProcWorker+0x2e
42 0019ec1c 758aa09b user32!DefFrameProcWorker+0xb7
43 0019ec34 55718ac5 user32!DefFrameProcW+0x1b
44 0019ec58 55708027 VISLIB!Ordinal1+0x33aa00
45 0019ec70 6571e3c1 VISLIB!Ordinal1+0x329f62
46 0019ec84 65725604 mfc90u!CWnd::Default+0x30
47 0019ec94 5549e617 mfc90u!CFrameWnd::OnSysCommand+0x50
48 0019ecb4 6571fd15 VISLIB!Ordinal1+0xc0552
49 0019ed64 6571f6cc mfc90u!CWnd::OnWndMsg+0x622
4a 0019ed84 553ef572 mfc90u!CWnd::WindowProc+0x24
4b 0019eda0 6571e2f2 VISLIB!Ordinal1+0x114ad
4c 0019ee08 6571e57e mfc90u!AfxCallWndProc+0xa3
4d 0019ee2c 553ef518 mfc90u!AfxWndProc+0x37
4e 0019ee70 553ef4d9 VISLIB!Ordinal1+0x11453
4f 0019ee88 553ef49e VISLIB!Ordinal1+0x11414
50 0019eeb0 553ef338 VISLIB!Ordinal1+0x113d9
51 0019eecc 553ef2d6 VISLIB!Ordinal1+0x11273
52 0019eef4 553ef107 VISLIB!Ordinal1+0x11211
53 0019ef58 75864923 VISLIB!Ordinal1+0x11042
54 0019ef84 75844790 user32!_InternalCallWinProc+0x2b
55 0019f02c 75844527 user32!UserCallWinProcCheckWow+0x1f0
56 0019f068 71db7d40 user32!CallWindowProcW+0x97
57 0019f0e8 71db7996 comctl32!CallNextSubclassProc+0x140
58 0019f108 5b84d95a comctl32!DefSubclassProc+0x56
59 0019f150 5b84d7ad MSO!Ordinal6319+0x25e
5a 0019f17c 71db7db8 MSO!Ordinal6319+0xb1
5b 0019f200 71db7b61 comctl32!CallNextSubclassProc+0x1b8
5c 0019f25c 75864923 comctl32!MasterSubclassProc+0xa1
5d 0019f288 75844790 user32!_InternalCallWinProc+0x2b
```

```
5e 0019f330 75844370 user32!UserCallWinProcCheckWow+0x1f0
5f 0019f390 7584b179 user32!DispatchClientMessage+0xf0
60 0019f3d0 76f8ad66 user32!__fnDWORD+0x49
61 0019f408 00000000 ntdll!KiUserCallbackDispatcher+0x36
```

Next, we applied **lmv** WinDbg command to the module name and followed its image path to rename it. After that, the problem disappeared. We call such modules **Foreign** because they were created not by the OS or the main process module vendors. Most likely these modules are either value-adding plugins or exposed **Message Hooks** (page 748).

FPU Exception

This pattern sometimes happens where we least expect it. Here's an extract from one crash dump raw stack analysis showing exception context and record, and the usage of **r** WinDbg command variant to display FPU registers:

```
0:002> dps 056c1000 057c0000
[...]
057bdee0 00000008
057bdee4 00000000
057bdee8 057bed6c
057bdeec 0d6e3130
057bdef0 057c0000
057bdef4 057b9000
057bdef8 006e3138
057bdefc 057be200
057bdf00 7c90e48a ntdll!KiUserExceptionDispatcher+0xe
057bdf04 057bed6c
057bdf08 057bdf2c
057bdf0c 057bdf14
057bdf10 057bdf2c
057bdf14 c0000090
057bdf18 00000010
057bdf1c 00000000
057bdf20 79098cc0 mscorjit!Compiler::FlatFPIsSameAsFloat+0xd
057bdf24 00000001
057bdf28 00000000
057bdf2c 0001003f
057bdf30 00000000
057bdf34 00000000
057bdf38 00000000
057bdf3c 00000000
057bdf40 00000000
057bdf44 00000000
057bdf48 ffff1372
057bdf4c fffffda1
057bdf50 ffffbfff
[...]

0:002> .cxr 057bdf2c
eax=c0000090 ebx=00000000 ecx=c0000090 edx=00000000 esi=057be244 edi=001d4388
eip=79f5236b esp=057be1f8 ebp=057be200 iopl=0         nv up ei ng nz ac pe cy
cs=001b ss=0023 ds=0023 es=0023 fs=003b gs=0000             efl=00010297
mscorwks!SOTolerantBoundaryFilter+0x22:
79f5236b d9059823f579 fld     dword ptr [mscorwks!_real (79f52398)] ds:0023:79f52398=40800000

0:002> .exr 057bdf14
ExceptionAddress: 79098cc0 (mscorjit!Compiler::FlatFPIsSameAsFloat+0x0000000d)
ExceptionCode: c0000090
ExceptionFlags: 00000010
NumberParameters: 1
Parameter[0]: 00000000
```

```
0:002> !error c0000090
Error code: (NTSTATUS) 0xc0000090 (3221225616) - {EXCEPTION} Floating-point invalid operation.

0:002> rMF
Last set context:
eax=c0000090 ebx=00000000 ecx=c0000090 edx=00000000 esi=057be244 edi=001d4388
eip=79f5236b esp=057be1f8 ebp=057be200 iopl=0 nv up ei ng nz ac pe cy
cs=001b ss=0023 ds=0023 es=0023 fs=003b gs=0000 efl=00010297
fpcw=1372: rn 64 pu-d- fpsw=FDA1: top=7 cc=1101 b-p--i fptw=BFFF
fopcode=045D fpip=001b:79098cc0 fpdp=0023:057bea7c
st0=-1.#IND00000000000000000e+0000 st1= 0.006980626232475338220e-4916
st2= 6.543831490564206840810e-4932 st3=-0.003025663186207448300e+2614
st4= 2.000000000000000000000e+0000 st5= 6.291456000000000000000e+0006
st6= 1.000000000000000000000e+0000 st7= 2.500000000000000000000e-0001
mscorwks!SOTolerantBoundaryFilter+0x22:
79f5236b d9059823f579 fld dword ptr [mscorwks!_real (79f52398)] ds:0023:79f52398=40800000
```

Frame Pointer Omission

This pattern is the most visible compiler optimization technique, and we can notice it in verbose stack traces:

```
0:000> kv
ChildEBP RetAddr
0012ee10 004737a7 application!MemCopy+0x17 (FPO: [3,0,2])
0012ef0c 35878c5b application!ProcessData+0x97 (FPO: [Uses EBP] [3,59,4])
WARNING: Frame IP not in any known module. Following frames may be wrong.
0012ef1c 72a0015b 0x35878c5b
0012ef20 a625e1b0 0x72a0015b
0012ef24 d938bcfe 0xa625e1b0
0012ef28 d4f91bb4 0xd938bcfe
0012ef2c c1c035ce 0xd4f91bb4
...
...
...
```

To recall, FPO is a compiler optimization where ESP register is used to address local variables and parameters instead of EBP. EBP may or may not be used for other purposes. When it is used, we notice

```
FPO: [Uses EBP]
```

as in the trace above. For a description of other FPO number triplets, please see Debugging Tools for Windows help section "k, kb, kd, kp, kP, kv (Display Stack Backtrace)".

Running the analysis command (**!analyze -v**) points to possible stack corruption:

```
PRIMARY_PROBLEM_CLASS:  STACK_CORRUPTION

BUGCHECK_STR:  APPLICATION_FAULT_STACK_CORRUPTION

FAULTING_IP:
application!MemCopy+17
00438637 f3a5 rep movs dword ptr es:[edi],dword ptr [esi]
```

Looking at EBP and ESP shows that they are mismatched:

```
0:000> r
eax=00000100 ebx=00a027f3 ecx=00000040 edx=0012ee58 esi=d938bcfe edi=0012ee58
eip=00438637 esp=0012ee0c ebp=00a02910 iopl=0         nv up ei pl nz na po nc
cs=001b  ss=0023  ds=0023  es=0023  fs=003b  gs=0000             efl=00000202
application!MemCopy+0x17:
00438637 f3a5 rep movs dword ptr es:[edi],dword ptr [esi] es:0023:0012ee58=00000010
ds:0023:d938bcfe=????????
```

We might think about **Local Buffer Overflow** pattern (page 691) here, but two top stack trace lines are in accordance with each other:

```
0:000> ub 004737a7
application!ProcessData+0x80:
00473790 cmp      eax,edi
00473792 jb       application!ProcessData+0x72 (00473782)
00473794 mov      ecx,dword ptr [esp+104h]
0047379b push     esi
0047379c lea      edx,[esp+38h]
004737a0 push     ecx
004737a1 push     edx
004737a2 call     application!MemCopy (00438620)
```

So perhaps EBP value differs greatly from ESP due to its usage as general purpose register and, in fact, there was no any stack corruption. Despite using public symbols, we have the instance of **Incorrect Stack Trace** pattern (page 563), and we might want to reconstruct it manually. Let's search for EBP value on the raw stack below the crash point:

```
0:000> !teb
TEB at 7ffdf000
    ExceptionList:        0012ffb0
    StackBase:            00130000
    StackLimit:           00126000
    SubSystemTib:         00000000
    FiberData:            00001e00
    ArbitraryUserPointer: 00000000
    Self:                 7ffdf000
    EnvironmentPointer:   00000000
    ClientId:             0000660c . 00005890
    RpcHandle:            00000000
    Tls Storage:          00000000
    PEB Address:          7ffd9000
    LastErrorValue:       0
    LastStatusValue:      0
    Count Owned Locks:    0
    HardErrorMode:        0

0:000> dds   00126000 00130000
00126000  00000000
00126004  00000000
00126008  00000000
...
...
...
0012eb0c  00a02910
0012eb10  7c90e25e ntdll!NtRaiseException+0xc
0012eb14  7c90eb15 ntdll!KiUserExceptionDispatcher+0x29
0012eb18  0012eb24
0012eb1c  0012eb40
0012eb20  00000000
0012eb24  c0000005
0012eb28  00000000
0012eb2c  00000000
0012eb30  00438637 application!MemCopy+0x17
0012eb34  00000002
0012eb38  00000000
0012eb3c  d938bcfe
```

```
...
...
...
0012ebf4  00a02910
0012ebf8  00438637 application!MemCopy+0x17
0012ebfc  0000001b
...
...
...
0012f134  00436323 application!ConstructInfo+0x113
0012f138  00a02910
0012f13c  0000011c
...
...
...
```

Let's see what functions *ConstructInfo* calls:

```
0:000> ub 00436323
application!ConstructInfo+0x103
00436313 lea      edx,[esp+10h]
00436317 push     edx
00436318 push     eax
00436319 push     30h
0043631b push     ecx
0043631c push     ebx
0043631d push     ebp
0043631e call     application!EnvelopeData (00438bf0)
```

We notice EBP was pushed prior to calling *EnvelopeData* function. If we disassemble this function, we see that it calls *ProcessData* function from our partial stack trace:

```
0:000> uf 00438bf0
application!EnvelopeData:
00438bf0 sub      esp,1F4h
00438bf6 push     ebx
00438bf7 mov      ebx,dword ptr [esp+20Ch]
00438bfe test     ebx,ebx
00438c00 push     ebp
...
...
...
00438c76 rep stos byte ptr es:[edi]
00438c78 lea      eax,[esp+14h]
00438c7c push     eax
00438c7d push     ebp
00438c7e call     application!ProcessData (00473710)
00438c83 pop      edi
00438c84 pop      esi
```

Let's try the elaborate form of **k** command and supply it with custom ESP and EBP values pointing to

```
0012f134  00436323 application!ConstructInfo+0x113
```

and also EIP of the fault:

```
0:000> k L=0012f134 0012f134 00438637
ChildEBP RetAddr
0012f1cc 00435a65 application!MemCopy+0x17
0012f28c 0043532e application!ClientHandleServerRequest+0x395
0012f344 00434fcd application!Accept+0x23
0012f374 0042e4f3 application!DataArrival+0x17d
0012f43c 0041aea9 application!ProcessInput+0x98
0012ff0c 0045b278 application!AppMain+0xda
0012ff24 0041900e application!WinMain+0x78
0012ffc0 7c816fd7 application!WinMainCRTStartup+0x134
0012fff0 00000000 kernel32!BaseProcessStart+0x23
```

We see that although it misses some initial frames after the *MemCopy* function, we aided WinDbg to walk to the bottom of the stack and reconstruct the plausible stack trace for us.

Frame Regularity

When the same API function is executed, it may leave the same data structure in its **Execution Residue** (page 395) inside raw stack regions of different threads. We call this analysis pattern **Frame Regularity**. It may be used to find and correctly interpret stack frame values from thread stack traces or regions based on values found in some other thread stack trace or region where we already know their meaning.

Consider the critical section **Wait Chain** (page 1203) below. We want to know what critical section the thread *F34* is waiting for. The backwards disassembly of 00007ffd`41894e14 return address does not show the critical section address explicitly. However, **00007ffd`43827e40** return address disassembly from a different critical section thread owner **D7C** shows critical section address **00007ffd`4391d8a8** which we can find as a 3rd "argument" to *ntdll!RtlpWaitOnCriticalSection* (which is just a value picked up from the stack region and not the real function argument passed by stack). Using **Frame Regularity** we try to see if the 3rd value for the same function from the thread *F34* under question is also a critical section address *00000071`3f08c488*. Indeed, we find that it is the address of the critical section owned by the thread *B18*.

```
0:000> !cs -l -o -s
----------------------------------------
DebugInfo           = 0x00007ffd4391dbe8
Critical section    = 0x00007ffd4391d8a8 (ntdll!LdrpLoaderLock+0x0)
LOCKED
LockCount           = 0x13
WaiterWoken         = No
OwningThread        = 0x0000000000000f34
RecursionCount      = 0x1
LockSemaphore       = 0x8B0
SpinCount           = 0x0000000004000000
OwningThread DbgId = ~14s
OwningThread Stack =
        Child-SP          RetAddr           : Args to Child                                                                    : Call Site
        00000071`40d4c618 00007ffd`43829a85 : 00000071`3f08c488 00000000`00000002 00000000`bd000200 00000000`00000000 :
ntdll!NtWaitForSingleObject+0xa
        00000071`40d4c620 00007ffd`43827f44 : 00000000`a90002ab 00007ffd`40d52eba 00000071`3f08c488 00000000`00000000 :
ntdll!RtlpWaitOnCriticalSection+0xe1
        00000071`40d4c6f0 00007ffd`41894e14 : 00000071`3f08c488 00007ffd`4229b3a8 00000000`00000000 00000071`3f08c470 :
ntdll!RtlpEnterCriticalSectionContended+0xa4
        00000071`40d4c730 00007ffd`41895d8d : 00000071`40c52ab0 00000000`00000000 00230022`00210020 00270026`00250024 :
shell32!kfapi::CFolderPathResolver::GetPath+0x168
        00000071`40d4dd50 00007ffd`41892d50 : 00000000`00000080 00000000`000000ce 00000000`00000104 00000000`000003ff :
shell32!kfapi::CFolderCache::GetPath+0x772
        00000071`40d4e0c0 00007ffd`41893540 : 00000000`00000000 20000020`00000000 00000000`000000ce 00000071`42141080 :
shell32!kfapi::CKFFacade::GetFolderPath+0x120
        00000071`40d4e220 00007ffd`4189368c : 00000000`00008023 00000000`000000ce 00000000`5307cc38 00000000`000000ce :
shell32!SHGetFolderPathEx+0x80
        00000071`40d4e290 00007ffd`40d61939 : 00000000`00000000 00000000`00000000 00000000`00000037 00000000`00008023 :
shell32!SHGetFolderPathWWorker+0xf9
        00000071`40d4e2f0 00007ffd`41a80fba : 00000000`00000000 00000000`00000000 00000071`40d4e400 00000071`42010000 :
KERNELBASE!SHGetFolderPathW+0x49
        00000071`40d4e330 00007ffd`40d7e60f : 00000000`00000001 00000000`00000020 00000000`00000035 00000071`42141080 :
shell32!SHGetSpecialFolderPathWWorker+0x23
        00000071`40d4e370 00000000`5317704d : 00000071`40d4e7d0 00000071`40d4ee68 00000000`00000000 00000000`53062b30 :
KERNELBASE!SHGetSpecialFolderPathW+0x3f
        00000071`40d4e3a0 00000000`530e72f1 : 00000000`5333fa10 00000000`00000001 00000000`5333fa10 00000000`530ab470 : ModuleA+0xccded
[...]
        00000071`40d4eba0 00007ffd`4380e82e : 00000071`40cc6780 00000000`53060000 00000071`00000001 00007ffd`40892421 :
ntdll!LdrpCallInitRoutine+0x4c
        00000071`40d4ec00 00007ffd`4380e624 : 00000071`40cb2790 00007ffd`4384ee00 00000071`40cb2790 00000000`53224dec :
ntdll!LdrpInitializeNode+0x176
ntdll!RtlpStackTraceDataBase is NULL. Probably the stack traces are not enabled.
----------------------------------------
DebugInfo           = 0x0000007140c52a70
Critical section    = 0x00007ffd31f41a88 (localspl!g_csBidiAccess+0x8)
LOCKED
LockCount           = 0x4
```

```
WaiterWoken      = No
OwningThread     = 0x0000000000000d7c
RecursionCount   = 0x1
LockSemaphore    = 0x1410
SpinCount        = 0x00000000020007d0
OwningThread DbgId = ~7s
OwningThread Stack =
        Child-SP          RetAddr           : Args to Child                                                          : Call Site
        00000071`4029e708 00007ffd`43829a85 : 0000a498`9a4b3f83 00000071`4029ec00 00000071`4029e880 00000071`4029e858 :
ntdll!NtWaitForSingleObject+0xa
        00000071`4029e710 00007ffd`43827f44 : 00000000`00000002 00007ffd`00000000 00007ffd`4391d8a8 00000071`4029e9d0 :
ntdll!RtlpWaitOnCriticalSection+0xe1
        00000071`4029e7e0 00007ffd`43827e40 : 00007ffd`41613750 00000071`3efa2a10 00007ffd`416b4d58 00007ffd`41686000 :
ntdll!RtlpEnterCriticalSectionContended+0xa4
        00000071`4029e820 00007ffd`4380ad5a : 00007ffd`41686000 00000071`4029e8e0 00007ffd`41613750 00000071`4029eeb8 :
ntdll!LdrpAcquireLoaderLock+0x2c
        00000071`4029e860 00007ffd`4386785f : 00000000`00000000 00007ffd`41685c64 00000000`00000000 00000071`4029e980 :
ntdll!LdrpGetDelayloadExportDll+0x7e
        00000071`4029e920 00007ffd`43826c8e : 00000000`00000000 00007ffd`41685c64 00000000`00000000 00007ffd`41613750 :
ntdll!LdrpHandleProtectedDelayload+0x3f
        00000071`4029ede0 00007ffd`4153763b : 00000071`4029ef50 00000000`00000000 00007ffd`2f4d3be0 00000000`00000003 :
ntdll!LdrResolveDelayLoadedAPI+0x8e
        00000071`4029ee40 00007ffd`415376df : 00000071`3ffe3020 00007ffd`2f4d2482 00000071`3ffe3020 00000071`3ffcb078 :
combase!__delayLoadHelper2+0x2b
        00000071`4029ee80 00007ffd`415239b6 : a4e9da62`d9130000 00000071`4029eed0 00000000`00000000 00000000`0000006c :
combase!_tailMerge_OLEAUT32_dll+0x3f
        00000071`4029eef0 00007ffd`41523883 : 00000071`40c22230 00000071`4029f029 00000000`80070015 00007ffd`3ffcf598 :
combase!wCoUninitialize+0xb6
        00000071`4029ef20 00007ffd`31e74e1a : 00000071`40c22230 00000000`00000000 00000000`80070015 00007ffd`2f4d3be0 :
combase!CoUninitialize+0xb3
        00000071`4029ef50 00007ffd`31e7459c : 00000000`00000000 00000071`4029f1d8 00007ffd`31f416d8 00000000`00000001 :
localspl!GetBidiStrings+0x3be
        00000071`4029f090 00007ffd`31e72150 : 00000000`00000000 00000071`4029f240 00007ffd`31f416d8 00000000`00000000 :
localspl!GetBidiPropertiesForDevnode+0x9c
        00000071`4029f140 00007ffd`31e7b03b : 00000000`00000008 00000071`403588e0 00000071`40a83130 00000000`00000001 :
localspl!GetPropertiesFromPrinter+0x1f4
        00000071`4029f750 00007ffd`31e7ae90 : 00000071`40aa6e40 00000000`00000000 00000000`00000001 00007ffd`ffff4b5e :
localspl!CreatePrintQueueDevnodeWorker+0xab
        00000071`4029f8a0 00007ffd`31eb475e : 00000000`00000000 00000000`00000000 00000071`3f05f470 00000000`00000000 :
localspl!CreatePrintQueueDevnode+0xb4
        00000071`4029f920 00007ffd`31eb46eb : 00000071`3ffe35c0 00000071`3f05f470 00007ffd`31eb4710 00000000`00000000 :
localspl!DevnodeCreationWorkItem::Run+0x4e
        00000071`4029f990 00007ffd`4386247e : 00007ffd`31eb46b0 00000071`3f05f3c0 00000071`4029fb78 00000071`3f05f470 :
localspl!NThreadingLibrary::TWorkCrew::tpSimpleCallback+0x3b
        00000071`4029f9c0 00007ffd`43824a5d : 00000071`3f05f470 00000071`3efd23f0 00000000`00000000 00000071`3f01e3e8 :
ntdll!TppSimplepExecuteCallback+0x7e
        00000071`4029fa00 00007ffd`410313d2 : 00000000`00000000 00007ffd`438245e0 00000071`3f01bf10 00000000`00000000 :
ntdll!TppWorkerThread+0x47d
ntdll!RtlpStackTraceDataBase is NULL. Probably the stack traces are not enabled.
----------------------------------------
DebugInfo        = 0x0000007140c52970
Critical section = 0x0000000001017600 (ModuleB+0x38F80)
LOCKED
LockCount        = 0x1
WaiterWoken      = No
OwningThread     = 0x0000000000000fe8
RecursionCount   = 0x1
LockSemaphore    = 0x14A0
SpinCount        = 0x00000000020007d0
OwningThread DbgId = ~22s
OwningThread Stack =
        Child-SP          RetAddr           : Args to Child                                                          : Call Site
        00000071`4102e6a8 00007ffd`43829a85 : 00000000`00000050 00007ffd`4381c937 00000071`3f110000 00000000`00000000 :
ntdll!NtWaitForSingleObject+0xa
        00000071`4102e6b0 00007ffd`43827f44 : 00000000`00000000 00000000`00000000 00007ffd`4391d8a8 00000000`00000000 :
ntdll!RtlpWaitOnCriticalSection+0xe1
        00000071`4102e780 00007ffd`43827e40 : 00000071`4102ebe8 00000000`00000000 00000071`4102ebb8 00000071`40cc5a00 :
ntdll!RtlpEnterCriticalSectionContended+0xa4
        00000071`4102e7c0 00007ffd`43818998 : 00007ff7`acadf000 00000000`00000000 00000071`4102e830 00000071`4102e830 :
ntdll!LdrpAcquireLoaderLock+0x2c
        00000071`4102e800 00007ffd`4380b229 : 00000000`00000000 00000071`4102ee40 00007ffd`437f4d38 00000000`00000000 :
ntdll!LdrpFindOrMapDll+0x4f8
        00000071`4102eb50 00007ffd`4380af29 : 00000000`00000000 00000000`00000000 00000071`4102ee40 00000071`4102ee40 :
ntdll!LdrpLoadDll+0x295
```

```
        00000071`4102ed80 00007ffd`40d58e4a : 00000000`00000000 00000071`4102ee50 00000000`010154a0 00000000`00000002 :
ntdll!LdrLoadDll+0x99
        00000071`4102ee00 00000000`00fd36ec : 00000000`00000000 00000000`010020a0 00000000`010154a0 00000000`00000000 :
KERNELBASE!LoadLibraryExW+0xca
        00000071`4102ee70 00000000`00fd3aa6 : 00000071`41147420 00000000`028424c0 00000000`00000001 00000071`411473dc : ModuleB+0x1f1c
[...]
        00000071`4102f5b0 00007ffd`3a9b5804 : 00000071`40c33ea8 00007ff7`00000008 00000000`00000008 00000071`3ffff190 :
winspool!SpoolerPrinterEventNative+0xb1
        00000071`4102f620 00007ffd`31a5566d : 00000071`40c33ea8 00000071`4102f719 00000000`00000008 00000000`00000000 :
winspool!SpoolerPrinterEvent+0x54
        00000071`4102f660 00007ffd`31e76682 : 00007ffd`31a55480 00000071`40c33ea8 00000071`4102f7c0 00000071`40aabcc0 :
PrintIsolationProxy!sandbox::PrintSandboxObject::SandboxDriverEvent+0x1ed
        00000071`4102f760 00007ffd`31e7659a : 00000071`3ffaf750 00007ffd`31e76610 00000071`40aabcc0 00000000`00000008 :
localspl!sandbox::SandboxObserver::SandboxDriverEvent+0x72
        00000071`4102f7b0 00007ffd`31e7621b : 00000071`40c33ea8 00000000`00000000 00000071`40c33ea8 00000000`00000000 :
localspl!sandbox::SandboxPrinterDriverEvent+0xda
        00000071`4102f820 00007ffd`31e76169 : 00000071`40aa6e40 00000000`00000001 00000000`00000000 00007ffd`31f40001 :
localspl!SplDriverEvent+0x5b
        00000071`4102f890 00007ffd`31f11c4b : 00000000`00000000 00000071`4102f940 00000071`40aa6e40 00007ffd`31f400c8 :
localspl!PrinterDriverEvent+0xbd
ntdll!RtlpStackTraceDataBase is NULL. Probably the stack traces are not enabled.
----------------------------------------
DebugInfo       = 0x0000007140c52630
Critical section = 0x000000713f08c488 (+0x713F08C488)
LOCKED
LockCount       = 0x1
WaiterWoken     = No
OwningThread    = 0x0000000000000b18
RecursionCount  = 0x1
LockSemaphore   = 0x14AC
SpinCount       = 0x00000000020007d0
OwningThread DbgId = ~1s
OwningThread Stack =
        Child-SP          RetAddr           : Args to Child                                                                          : Call Site
        00000071`3fe4b5e8 00007ffd`43829a85 : 00000001`00000000 00000000`00000000 00000071`41927fd0 00007ffd`43821067 :
ntdll!NtWaitForSingleObject+0xa
        00000071`3fe4b5f0 00007ffd`43827f44 : 00000000`00000000 00000000`0000017b 00007ffd`4391d8a8 00000000`00000000 :
ntdll!RtlpWaitOnCriticalSection+0xe1
        00000071`3fe4b6c0 00007ffd`43827e40 : 00007ffd`41c57850 00000071`3efe3700 00007ffd`4229bf90 00007ffd`42203380 :
ntdll!RtlpEnterCriticalSectionContended+0xa4
        00000071`3fe4b700 00007ffd`4380ad5a : 00007ffd`42203380 00000071`3fe4b7c0 00007ffd`41c57850 00007ffd`4381609c :
ntdll!LdrpAcquireLoaderLock+0x2c
        00000071`3fe4b740 00007ffd`4386785f : 00000000`00000000 00007ffd`422026f4 00000071`3ef01790 00000071`3fe4b860 :
ntdll!LdrpGetDelayloadExportDll+0x7e
        00000071`3fe4b800 00007ffd`43826c8e : 00000000`00000000 00007ffd`422026f4 00000000`00000000 00007ffd`41c57850 :
ntdll!LdrpHandleProtectedDelayload+0x3f
        00000071`3fe4bcc0 00007ffd`41a818eb : 00000071`3fe4c910 00000071`3fe4c8a0 00000000`00000000 ffffffff`ffffffff :
ntdll!LdrResolveDelayLoadedAPI+0x8e
        00000071`3fe4bd20 00007ffd`41896d9f : 00000071`40c52670 ffffffff`ffffffff 00000000`00000000 00000071`3fe4e201 :
shell32!_delayLoadHelper2+0x2b
        00000071`3fe4bd60 00007ffd`41894374 : 00000071`3fe4c8a0 00000071`3fe4bf10 00000000`00000027 00000071`3fe4bed0 :
shell32!_tailMerge_api_ms_win_core_com_l1_1_1_dll+0x3f
        00000071`3fe4bdd0 00007ffd`4189409a : 00000000`00000000 00000000`00000000 00000071`3fe4c910 00000000`00000000 :
shell32!kfapi::CFolderDefinitionStorage::_LoadRegistry+0xb4
        00000071`3fe4c440 00007ffd`41896943 : 00000000`00000031 00000000`00000000 00000071`3fe4c698 00000071`40c52670 :
shell32!kfapi::CFolderDefinitionStorage::Load+0x66
        00000071`3fe4c6a0 00007ffd`4189796a : 00000000`00000000 00000071`40c539a0 00000071`40c37700 00007ffd`41a80f90 :
shell32!kfapi::CFolderPathResolver::GetPath+0x242
        00000071`3fe4dcc0 00007ffd`41892d50 : 00000071`3fe4e050 00000071`3fe4e038 00000071`3fe4e038 00000000`00000200 :
shell32!kfapi::CFolderCache::GetPath+0xb74
        00000071`3fe4e030 00007ffd`41893540 : 00000071`3fe4e1c8 00000071`40cb16f0 00000071`40cb16f0 00000000`00000000 :
shell32!kfapi::CKFFacade::GetFolderPath+0x120
        00000071`3fe4e190 00007ffd`4189368c : 00000000`00008023 00007ffd`4382c0ae 00000000`00000000 00000071`3ef92bd0 :
shell32!SHGetFolderPathEx+0x80
        00000071`3fe4e200 00007ffd`40d61939 : 00000000`00000000 00000000`00000000 00007ffd`40dc3f80 00000000`00008023 :
shell32!SHGetFolderPathWWorker+0xf9
        00000071`3fe4e260 00007ffd`41a80fba : 00000000`00000000 00000000`00000000 00000071`3fe4e370 00000000`00000000 :
KERNELBASE!SHGetFolderPathW+0x49
        00000071`3fe4e2a0 00007ffd`40d7e60f : 00000071`3fe4e370 00000000`00000023 00000000`00000001 :
shell32!SHGetSpecialFolderPathWWorker+0x23
        00000071`3fe4e2e0 00000000`540b036d : 00000071`3fe4e630 00000000`00000001 00000000`00000000 00000071`3fe4e6b0 :
KERNELBASE!SHGetSpecialFolderPathW+0x3f
        00000071`3fe4e310 00000000`54096f45 : 00000071`3fe4e708 00000000`00000001 00000071`3fe4e6d8 00000000`53fd1903 : ModuleC+0xdca2d
ntdll!RtlpStackTraceDataBase is NULL. Probably the stack traces are not enabled.
```

```
0:000> ub 00007ffd`41894e14
shell32!kfapi::CFolderPathResolver::GetPath+0x145:
00007ffd`41894df1 498d5d30         lea     rbx,[r13+30h]
00007ffd`41894df5 48895c2468       mov     qword ptr [rsp+68h],rbx
00007ffd`41894dfa 4c897c2470       mov     qword ptr [rsp+70h],r15
00007ffd`41894dff 498bff           mov     rdi,r15
00007ffd`41894e02 4c897c2470       mov     qword ptr [rsp+70h],r15
00007ffd`41894e07 488975e0         mov     qword ptr [rbp-20h],rsi
00007ffd`41894e0b 488bce           mov     rcx,rsi
00007ffd`41894e0e ff159cbaa900     call    qword ptr [shell32!_imp_EnterCriticalSection (00007ffd`423308b0)]

0:000> ub 00007ffd`43827e40
ntdll!LdrpAcquireLoaderLock:
00007ffd`43827e14 4053             push    rbx
00007ffd`43827e16 4883ec30         sub     rsp,30h
00007ffd`43827e1a 488d0d4f8d0f00   lea     rcx,[ntdll!LdrpModuleEnumLock (00007ffd`43920b70)]
00007ffd`43827e21 e8ca040000       call    ntdll!RtlAcquireSRWLockShared (00007ffd`438282f0)
00007ffd`43827e26 803c258403fe7f00 cmp     byte ptr [SharedUserData+0x384 (00000000`7ffe0384)],0
00007ffd`43827e2e 0f85242c0700     jne     ntdll!LdrpAcquireLoaderLock+0x72c44 (00007ffd`4389aa58)
00007ffd`43827e34 488d0d6d5a0f00   lea     rcx,[ntdll!LdrpLoaderLock (00007ffd`4391d8a8)]
00007ffd`43827e3b e820000000       call    ntdll!RtlEnterCriticalSection (00007ffd`43827e60)
```

Frame Trace

When developers look at crash dumps, they are more interested in parameters and local variables in particular stack frames of interest. However, sometimes it is useful to look at all such frames, especially to gather the information that may be useful for technical support or to correlate to additional traces and logs (for example, **Historical Information**, page 543, to establish additional **Basic Facts**[80], and build **Vocabulary Index**[81]).

Listing the parameters can be done, for example, by using **Stack Trace** (page 1033) command variant (**kP** WinDbg command, but we use **kPL** to exclude source code references to reduce visual clutter):

```
0:000> kPL
# Child-SP          RetAddr           Call Site
00 000000e4`c0afe488 00007ffe`cc888037 ntdll!NtWaitForMultipleObjects+0x14
01 000000e4`c0afe490 00007ffe`cc887f1e KERNELBASE!WaitForMultipleObjectsEx+0x107
02 000000e4`c0afe790 00007ffe`cd8271fb KERNELBASE!WaitForMultipleObjects+0xe
03 000000e4`c0afe7d0 00007ffe`cd826ca8 kernel32!WerpReportFaultInternal+0x51b
04 000000e4`c0afe8f0 00007ffe`cc9300b8 kernel32!WerpReportFault+0xac
05 000000e4`c0afe930 00007ffe`cf6c4ab2 KERNELBASE!UnhandledExceptionFilter+0x3b8
06 000000e4`c0afea50 00007ffe`cf6ac656 ntdll!RtlUserThreadStart$filt$0+0xa2
07 000000e4`c0afea90 00007ffe`cf6c11cf ntdll!_C_specific_handler+0x96
08 000000e4`c0afeb00 00007ffe`cf68a209 ntdll!RtlpExecuteHandlerForException+0xf
09 000000e4`c0afeb30 00007ffe`cf6bfe3e ntdll!RtlDispatchException+0x219
0a 000000e4`c0aff240 00007ffe`cc8f0aa2 ntdll!KiUserExceptionDispatch+0x2e
0b 000000e4`c0aff948 00007ff6`c8ab1568 KERNELBASE!wil::details::DebugBreak+0x2
0c 000000e4`c0aff950 00007ff6`c8ab1560 FrameTrace!foo(
                         unsigned int64 num = 0,
                         class std::basic_string<wchar_t,std::char_traits<wchar_t>,std::allocator<wchar_t> > * str =
0x000000e4`c0aff9d0 "Hello World! Hello World! Hello World! Hello World! Hello World! Hello World! Hello World! Hello World! Hello World!
Hello World! Hello World! Hello World! Hello World! Hello World! Hello World! Hello World! Hello World! Hello World! Hello World! Hello
World! Hello World! Hello World! Hello World! Hello World! Hello World! Hello World! Hello World! Hello World! Hello World! Hello World!
Hello World! Hello World! ")+0x68
0d 000000e4`c0aff9b0 00007ff6`c8ab1560 FrameTrace!foo(
                         unsigned int64 num = 0,
                         class std::basic_string<wchar_t,std::char_traits<wchar_t>,std::allocator<wchar_t> > * str =
0x000000e4`c0affa30 "Hello World! Hello World! Hello World! Hello World! Hello World! Hello World! Hello World! Hello World! Hello World!
Hello World! Hello World! Hello World! Hello World! Hello World! Hello World! Hello World! ")+0x60
0e 000000e4`c0affa10 00007ff6`c8ab1560 FrameTrace!foo(
                         unsigned int64 num = 1,
                         class std::basic_string<wchar_t,std::char_traits<wchar_t>,std::allocator<wchar_t> > * str =
0x000000e4`c0affa90 "Hello World! Hello World! Hello World! Hello World! Hello World! Hello World! Hello World! Hello World! ")+0x60
0f 000000e4`c0affa70 00007ff6`c8ab1560 FrameTrace!foo(
                         unsigned int64 num = 2,
                         class std::basic_string<wchar_t,std::char_traits<wchar_t>,std::allocator<wchar_t> > * str =
0x000000e4`c0affaf0 "Hello World! Hello World! Hello World! Hello World! ")+0x60
10 000000e4`c0affad0 00007ff6`c8ab1560 FrameTrace!foo(
                         unsigned int64 num = 3,
                         class std::basic_string<wchar_t,std::char_traits<wchar_t>,std::allocator<wchar_t> > * str =
0x000000e4`c0affb50 "Hello World! Hello World! ")+0x60
11 000000e4`c0affb30 00007ff6`c8ab15b5 FrameTrace!foo(
                         unsigned int64 num = 4,
                         class std::basic_string<wchar_t,std::char_traits<wchar_t>,std::allocator<wchar_t> > * str =
0x000000e4`c0affbb0 "Hello World! ")+0x60
12 000000e4`c0affb90 00007ff6`c8ab2b14 FrameTrace!main(void)+0x25
13 (Inline Function) ---`--- FrameTrace!invoke_main+0x22
14 000000e4`c0affbe0 00007ffe`cd7d7bd4 FrameTrace!__scrt_common_main_seh(void)+0x10c
15 000000e4`c0affc20 00007ffe`cf68ce51 kernel32!BaseThreadInitThunk+0x14
16 000000e4`c0affc50 00000000`00000000 ntdll!RtlUserThreadStart+0x21
```

The stack trace comes from the following modeling application:

---

[80] Memory Dump Analysis Anthology, Volume 3, page 345

[81] Ibid., page 349

```
void foo(std::size_t num, const std::wstring& str)
{
        if (std::wstring concatStr{ str }; num)
        {
                concatStr += str;

                foo(-num, concatStr);
        }
        else
        {
                ::DebugBreak();
        }
}

int main()
{
        foo(5, L"Hello World! ");
}
```

To list local variable we need to use **!for_each_frame** WinDbg command:

```
0:000> !for_each_frame "dv"
- - - - - - - - - - - - - - - -
00 000000e4`c0afe488 00007ffe`cc888037 ntdll!NtWaitForMultipleObjects+0x14
Unable to enumerate locals, Win32 error 0n87
Private symbols (symbols.pri) are required for locals.
Type ".hh dbgerr005" for details.
- - - - - - - - - - - - - - - -
01 000000e4`c0afe490 00007ffe`cc887f1e KERNELBASE!WaitForMultipleObjectsEx+0x107
- - - - - - - - - - - - - - - -
02 000000e4`c0afe790 00007ffe`cd8271fb KERNELBASE!WaitForMultipleObjects+0xe
Unable to enumerate locals, Win32 error 0n87
Private symbols (symbols.pri) are required for locals.
Type ".hh dbgerr005" for details.
- - - - - - - - - - - - - - - -
03 000000e4`c0afe7d0 00007ffe`cd826ca8 kernel32!WerpReportFaultInternal+0x51b
Unable to enumerate locals, Win32 error 0n87
Private symbols (symbols.pri) are required for locals.
Type ".hh dbgerr005" for details.
- - - - - - - - - - - - - - - -
04 000000e4`c0afe8f0 00007ffe`cc9300b8 kernel32!WerpReportFault+0xac
Unable to enumerate locals, Win32 error 0n87
Private symbols (symbols.pri) are required for locals.
Type ".hh dbgerr005" for details.
- - - - - - - - - - - - - - - -
05 000000e4`c0afe930 00007ffe`cf6c4ab2 KERNELBASE!UnhandledExceptionFilter+0x3b8
Unable to enumerate locals, Win32 error 0n87
Private symbols (symbols.pri) are required for locals.
Type ".hh dbgerr005" for details.
- - - - - - - - - - - - - - - -
06 000000e4`c0afea50 00007ffe`cf6ac656 ntdll!RtlUserThreadStart$filt$0+0xa2
- - - - - - - - - - - - - - - -
07 000000e4`c0afea90 00007ffe`cf6c11cf ntdll!_C_specific_handler+0x96
Unable to enumerate locals, Win32 error 0n87
Private symbols (symbols.pri) are required for locals.
Type ".hh dbgerr005" for details.
- - - - - - - - - - - - - - - -
08 000000e4`c0afeb00 00007ffe`cf68a209 ntdll!RtlpExecuteHandlerForException+0xf
Unable to enumerate locals, Win32 error 0n87
Private symbols (symbols.pri) are required for locals.
Type ".hh dbgerr005" for details.
- - - - - - - - - - - - - - - -
09 000000e4`c0afeb30 00007ffe`cf6bfe3e ntdll!RtlDispatchException+0x219
- - - - - - - - - - - - - - - -
0a 000000e4`c0aff240 00007ffe`cc8f0aa2 ntdll!KiUserExceptionDispatch+0x2e
Unable to enumerate locals, Win32 error 0n87
Private symbols (symbols.pri) are required for locals.
```

```
Type ".hh dbgerr005" for details.
- - - - - - - - - - - - - - -
0b 000000e4`c0aff948 00007ff6`c8ab1568 KERNELBASE!wil::details::DebugBreak+0x2
Unable to enumerate locals, Win32 error 0n87
Private symbols (symbols.pri) are required for locals.
Type ".hh dbgerr005" for details.
- - - - - - - - - - - - - - -
0c 000000e4`c0aff950 00007ff6`c8ab1560 FrameTrace!foo+0x68 [C:\NewWork\FrameTrace\FrameTrace.cpp @ 14]
concatStr = "Hello World! Hello World! Hello World! Hello World! Hello World! Hello World! Hello World! Hello World! Hello World! Hello
World! Hello World! Hello World! Hello World! Hello World! Hello World! Hello World! Hello World! Hello World! Hello World! Hello World!
Hello World! Hello World! Hello World! Hello World! Hello World! Hello World! Hello World! Hello World! Hello World! Hello World! Hello
World! Hello World! "
num = 0
str = 0x000000e4`c0aff9d0 "Hello World! Hello World! Hello World! Hello World! Hello World! Hello World! Hello World! Hello World! Hello
World! Hello World! Hello World! Hello World! Hello World! Hello World! Hello World! Hello World! Hello World! Hello World! Hello World!
Hello World! Hello World! Hello World! Hello World! Hello World! Hello World! Hello World! Hello World! Hello World! Hello World! Hello
World! Hello World! Hello World! "
- - - - - - - - - - - - - - -
0d 000000e4`c0aff9b0 00007ff6`c8ab1560 FrameTrace!foo+0x60 [C:\NewWork\FrameTrace\FrameTrace.cpp @ 11]
concatStr = "Hello World! Hello World! Hello World! Hello World! Hello World! Hello World! Hello World! Hello World! Hello World! Hello
World! Hello World! Hello World! Hello World! Hello World! Hello World! Hello World! Hello World! Hello World! Hello World! Hello World!
Hello World! Hello World! Hello World! Hello World! Hello World! Hello World! Hello World! Hello World! Hello World! Hello World! Hello
World! Hello World! "
num = 0
str = 0x000000e4`c0affa30 "Hello World! Hello World! Hello World! Hello World! Hello World! Hello World! Hello World! Hello World! Hello
World! Hello World! Hello World! Hello World! Hello World! Hello World! Hello World! Hello World! "
- - - - - - - - - - - - - - -
0e 000000e4`c0affa10 00007ff6`c8ab1560 FrameTrace!foo+0x60 [C:\NewWork\FrameTrace\FrameTrace.cpp @ 11]
concatStr = "Hello World! Hello World! Hello World! Hello World! Hello World! Hello World! Hello World! Hello World! Hello World! Hello
World! Hello World! Hello World! Hello World! Hello World! Hello World! "
num = 1
str = 0x000000e4`c0affa90 "Hello World! Hello World! Hello World! Hello World! Hello World! Hello World! Hello World! Hello World! "
- - - - - - - - - - - - - - -
0f 000000e4`c0affa70 00007ff6`c8ab1560 FrameTrace!foo+0x60 [C:\NewWork\FrameTrace\FrameTrace.cpp @ 11]
concatStr = "Hello World! Hello World! Hello World! Hello World! Hello World! Hello World! Hello World! Hello World! "
num = 2
str = 0x000000e4`c0affaf0 "Hello World! Hello World! Hello World! Hello World! "
- - - - - - - - - - - - - - -
10 000000e4`c0affad0 00007ff6`c8ab1560 FrameTrace!foo+0x60 [C:\NewWork\FrameTrace\FrameTrace.cpp @ 11]
concatStr = "Hello World! Hello World! Hello World! Hello World! "
num = 3
str = 0x000000e4`c0affb50 "Hello World! Hello World! "
- - - - - - - - - - - - - - -
11 000000e4`c0affb30 00007ff6`c8ab15b5 FrameTrace!foo+0x60 [C:\NewWork\FrameTrace\FrameTrace.cpp @ 11]
concatStr = "Hello World! Hello World! "
num = 4
str = 0x000000e4`c0affbb0 "Hello World! "
- - - - - - - - - - - - - - -
12 000000e4`c0affb90 00007ff6`c8ab2b14 FrameTrace!main+0x25 [C:\NewWork\FrameTrace\FrameTrace.cpp @ 20]
- - - - - - - - - - - - - - -
13 (Inline Function) --------`-------- FrameTrace!invoke_main+0x22 [d:\A01\_work\6\s\src\vctools\crt\vcstartup\src\startup\exe_common.inl
@ 78]
- - - - - - - - - - - - - - -
14 000000e4`c0affbe0 00007ffe`cd7d7bd4 FrameTrace!__scrt_common_main_seh+0x10c
[d:\A01\_work\6\s\src\vctools\crt\vcstartup\src\startup\exe_common.inl @ 288]
has_cctor = false
main_result = <value unavailable>
tls_init_callback = <value unavailable>
is_nested = <value unavailable>
tls_dtor_callback = <value unavailable>
main_result = <value unavailable>
__scrt_current_native_startup_state = <value unavailable>
- - - - - - - - - - - - - - -
15 000000e4`c0affc20 00007ffe`cf68ce51 kernel32!BaseThreadInitThunk+0x14
Unable to enumerate locals, Win32 error 0n87
Private symbols (symbols.pri) are required for locals.
Type ".hh dbgerr005" for details.
- - - - - - - - - - - - - - -
16 000000e4`c0affc50 00000000`00000000 ntdll!RtlUserThreadStart+0x21
Unable to enumerate locals, Win32 error 0n87
Private symbols (symbols.pri) are required for locals.
Type ".hh dbgerr005" for details.
- - - - - - - - - - - - - - -
15 000000e4`c0affc20 00007ffe`cf68ce51 kernel32!BaseThreadInitThunk+0x14
```

We can also apply "**dv /i /V**" command to each frame to get additional low-level frame details:

```
[...]
11 000000e4`c0affb30 00007ff6`c8ab15b5 FrameTrace!foo+0x60 [C:\NewWork\FrameTrace\FrameTrace.cpp @ 11]
prv local  000000e4`c0affb50 @rsp+0x0020              concatStr = "Hello World! Hello World! "
prv param  000000e4`c0affb90 @rsp+0x0060              num = 4
prv param  000000e4`c0affb98 @rsp+0x0068              str = 0x000000e4`c0affbb0 "Hello World! "
[...]
```

We see this as a form of back tracing **Execution Residue** (page 395), for example:

```
0:000> !for_each_frame ".frame /c @$frame; dps rsp"
[...]
- - - - - - - - - - - - - - - - -
04 000000e4`c0afe8f0 00007ffe`cc9300b8 kernel32!WerpReportFault+0xac
04 000000e4`c0afe8f0 00007ffe`cc9300b8 kernel32!WerpReportFault+0xac
rax=000000000000005b rbx=0000000000000000 rcx=0000000000000003
rdx=000000e4c0afe888 rsi=0000000000000000 rdi=0000000000000003
rip=00007ffecd826ca8 rsp=000000e4c0afe8f0 rbp=0000000000000000
r8=0000000000000000  r9=00000000ffffffff r10=0000000000000000
r11=000000e4c0afdc30 r12=000000e4c0afeac0 r13=ffffffffffffffff
r14=000000e4c0afeac0 r15=0000000000001a38
iopl=0         nv up ei pl zr na po nc
cs=0033  ss=002b  ds=002b  es=002b  fs=0053  gs=002b            efl=00000246
kernel32!WerpReportFault+0xac:
00007ffe`cd826ca8 8bf8           mov     edi,eax
000000e4`c0afe8f0  00000000`00000000
000000e4`c0afe8f8  00000000`00000000
000000e4`c0afe900  00000000`00000003
000000e4`c0afe908  000000e4`c0afeac0
000000e4`c0afe910  00000000`00000004
000000e4`c0afe918  00000000`00000001
000000e4`c0afe920  00000000`00000000
000000e4`c0afe928  00007ffe`cc9300b8 KERNELBASE!UnhandledExceptionFilter+0x3b8
000000e4`c0afe930  00000000`00000000
000000e4`c0afe938  000000e4`c0affc50
000000e4`c0afe940  00007ffe`cd7c0000 kernel32!RtlVirtualUnwindStub <PERF> (kernel32+0x0)
000000e4`c0afe948  00000207`5d660000
000000e4`c0afe950  00000000`00000000
000000e4`c0afe958  00007ffe`cf6660b9 ntdll!RtlpFindEntry+0x4d
000000e4`c0afe960  00000004`00000006
000000e4`c0afe968  00000001`00000000

- - - - - - - - - - - - - - - - -
05 000000e4`c0afe930 00007ffe`cf6c4ab2 KERNELBASE!UnhandledExceptionFilter+0x3b8
05 000000e4`c0afe930 00007ffe`cf6c4ab2 KERNELBASE!UnhandledExceptionFilter+0x3b8
rax=000000000000005b rbx=0000000000000000 rcx=0000000000000003
rdx=000000e4c0afe888 rsi=00007ffecd7c0000 rdi=0000000000000000
rip=00007ffecc9300b8 rsp=000000e4c0afe930 rbp=000000e4c0affc50
r8=0000000000000000  r9=00000000ffffffff r10=0000000000000000
r11=000000e4c0afdc30 r12=000000e4c0afeac0 r13=ffffffffffffffff
r14=0000000000000001 r15=0000000000000004
iopl=0         nv up ei pl zr na po nc
cs=0033  ss=002b  ds=002b  es=002b  fs=0053  gs=002b            efl=00000246
KERNELBASE!UnhandledExceptionFilter+0x3b8:
00007ffe`cc9300b8 0f1f440000     nop     dword ptr [rax+rax]
000000e4`c0afe930  00000000`00000000
000000e4`c0afe938  000000e4`c0affc50
000000e4`c0afe940  00007ffe`cd7c0000 kernel32!RtlVirtualUnwindStub <PERF> (kernel32+0x0)
000000e4`c0afe948  00000207`5d660000
000000e4`c0afe950  00000000`00000000
000000e4`c0afe958  00007ffe`cf6660b9 ntdll!RtlpFindEntry+0x4d
000000e4`c0afe960  00000004`00000006
```

```
000000e4`c0afe968  00000001`00000000
000000e4`c0afe970  00000000`00000001
000000e4`c0afe978  00007ffe`cd7c0000 kernel32!RtlVirtualUnwindStub <PERF> (kernel32+0x0)
000000e4`c0afe980  00000207`5d662ff0
000000e4`c0afe988  00000000`00000000
000000e4`c0afe990  000000e4`c0afeac0
000000e4`c0afe998  00007ffe`cd7c0000 kernel32!RtlVirtualUnwindStub <PERF> (kernel32+0x0)
000000e4`c0afe9a0  00000000`005a0058
000000e4`c0afe9a8  00007ffe`cca6ff70 KERNELBASE!`string'
- - - - - - - - - - - - - - - -
06 000000e4`c0afea50 00007ffe`cf6ac656 ntdll!RtlUserThreadStart$filt$0+0xa2
06 000000e4`c0afea50 00007ffe`cf6ac656 ntdll!RtlUserThreadStart$filt$0+0xa2
rax=000000000000005b rbx=00007ffecf764420 rcx=0000000000000003
rdx=000000e4c0afe888 rsi=0000000000000000 rdi=0000000000000000
rip=00007ffecf6c4ab2 rsp=000000e4c0afea50 rbp=000000e4c0affc50
r8=0000000000000000  r9=00000000ffffffff r10=0000000000000000
r11=000000e4c0afdc30 r12=000000e4c0aff730 r13=000000e4c0affc50
r14=000000e4c0aff0c0 r15=00007ffecf620000
iopl=0         nv up ei pl zr na po nc
cs=0033  ss=002b  ds=002b  es=002b  fs=0053  gs=002b           efl=00000246
ntdll!RtlUserThreadStart$filt$0+0xa2:
00007ffe`cf6c4ab2 eb16            jmp     ntdll!RtlUserThreadStart$filt$0+0xba (00007ffe`cf6c4aca)
000000e4`c0afea50  00000000`00000000
000000e4`c0afea58  00007ffe`cf764420 ntdll!`string'+0x9aa8
000000e4`c0afea60  00000000`00000000
000000e4`c0afea68  000000e4`c0affbe0
000000e4`c0afea70  00000000`00000000
000000e4`c0afea78  00007ffe`cf6457d8 ntdll!LdrpAppendUnicodeStringToFilenameBuffer+0x50
000000e4`c0afea80  00000000`0006ce51
000000e4`c0afea88  00007ffe`cf6ac656 ntdll!_C_specific_handler+0x96
000000e4`c0afea90  000000e4`c0afeb40
000000e4`c0afea98  00007ffe`cf642930 ntdll!LdrpFindLoadedDllByNameLockHeld+0xe4
000000e4`c0afeaa0  000000e4`c0aff088
000000e4`c0afeaa8  000000e4`c0aff110
000000e4`c0afeab0  000000e4`c0aff240
000000e4`c0afeab8  00000000`00000000
000000e4`c0afeac0  000000e4`c0aff730
000000e4`c0afeac8  000000e4`c0aff240
- - - - - - - - - - - - - - - -
07 000000e4`c0afea90 00007ffe`cf6c11cf ntdll!_C_specific_handler+0x96
07 000000e4`c0afea90 00007ffe`cf6c11cf ntdll!_C_specific_handler+0x96
rax=000000000000005b rbx=00007ffecf764420 rcx=0000000000000003
rdx=000000e4c0afe888 rsi=0000000000000000 rdi=0000000000000000
rip=00007ffecf6ac656 rsp=000000e4c0afea90 rbp=000000000006ce51
r8=0000000000000000  r9=00000000ffffffff r10=0000000000000000
r11=000000e4c0afdc30 r12=000000e4c0aff730 r13=000000e4c0affc50
r14=000000e4c0aff0c0 r15=00007ffecf620000
iopl=0         nv up ei pl zr na po nc
cs=0033  ss=002b  ds=002b  es=002b  fs=0053  gs=002b           efl=00000246
ntdll!_C_specific_handler+0x96:
00007ffe`cf6ac656 85c0            test    eax,eax
000000e4`c0afea90  000000e4`c0afeb40
000000e4`c0afea98  00007ffe`cf642930 ntdll!LdrpFindLoadedDllByNameLockHeld+0xe4
000000e4`c0afeaa0  000000e4`c0aff088
000000e4`c0afeaa8  000000e4`c0aff110
000000e4`c0afeab0  000000e4`c0aff240
000000e4`c0afeab8  00000000`00000000
000000e4`c0afeac0  000000e4`c0aff730
000000e4`c0afeac8  000000e4`c0aff240
000000e4`c0afead0  00000000`00000000
000000e4`c0afead8  000000e4`c0afeb70
000000e4`c0afeae0  000000e4`c0aff240
000000e4`c0afeae8  00007ffe`cf6ac5c0 ntdll!_C_specific_handler
000000e4`c0afeaf0  00000000`00000000
000000e4`c0afeaf8  00007ffe`cf6c11cf ntdll!RtlpExecuteHandlerForException+0xf
```

```
000000e4`c0afeb00  00000000`00000000
000000e4`c0afeb08  000000e4`c0aff070

_ _ _ _ _ _ _ _ _ _ _ _ _ _ _ _ _
08 000000e4`c0afeb00 00007ffe`cf68a209 ntdll!RtlpExecuteHandlerForException+0xf
08 000000e4`c0afeb00 00007ffe`cf68a209 ntdll!RtlpExecuteHandlerForException+0xf
rax=000000000000005b rbx=0000000000000000 rcx=0000000000000003
rdx=000000e4c0afe888 rsi=000000e4c0aff730 rdi=0000000000000000
rip=00007ffecf6c11cf rsp=000000e4c0afeb00 rbp=000000e4c0aff070
r8=0000000000000000  r9=00000000ffffffff r10=0000000000000000
r11=000000e4c0afdc30 r12=00007ffecf6ac5c0 r13=000000e4c0aff240
r14=000000e4c0afeb70 r15=0000000000000000
iopl=0         nv up ei pl zr na po nc
cs=0033  ss=002b  ds=002b  es=002b  fs=0053  gs=002b                efl=00000246
ntdll!RtlpExecuteHandlerForException+0xf:
00007ffe`cf6c11cf 90              nop
000000e4`c0afeb00  00000000`00000000
000000e4`c0afeb08  000000e4`c0aff070
000000e4`c0afeb10  000000e4`c0aff730
000000e4`c0afeb18  000000e4`c0aff730
000000e4`c0afeb20  000000e4`c0aff0c0
000000e4`c0afeb28  00007ffe`cf68a209 ntdll!RtlDispatchException+0x219
000000e4`c0afeb30  000000e4`00000001
000000e4`c0afeb38  00007ffe`cf620000 ntdll!RtlStringCchCopyW <PERF> (ntdll+0x0)
000000e4`c0afeb40  00000000`00000000
000000e4`c0afeb48  00007ffe`cf78e9f0 ntdll!__PchSym_ <PERF> (ntdll+0x16e9f0)
000000e4`c0afeb50  000000e4`c0afeb70
000000e4`c0afeb58  000000e4`c0aff090
000000e4`c0afeb60  000000e4`c0aff080
000000e4`c0afeb68  00000000`00000000
000000e4`c0afeb70  000000e4`00000000
000000e4`c0afeb78  00007ffe`cc8300f0 KERNELBASE!UrlHashW <PERF> (KERNELBASE+0xf0)

_ _ _ _ _ _ _ _ _ _ _ _ _ _ _ _
09 000000e4`c0afeb30 00007ffe`cf6bfe3e ntdll!RtlDispatchException+0x219
09 000000e4`c0afeb30 00007ffe`cf6bfe3e ntdll!RtlDispatchException+0x219
rax=000000000000005b rbx=0000000000000000 rcx=0000000000000003
rdx=000000e4c0afe888 rsi=000000e4c0aff730 rdi=0000000000000000
rip=00007ffecf68a209 rsp=000000e4c0afeb30 rbp=000000e4c0aff070
r8=0000000000000000  r9=00000000ffffffff r10=0000000000000000
r11=000000e4c0afdc30 r12=00007ffecf6ac5c0 r13=000000e4c0aff240
r14=000000e4c0afeb70 r15=0000000000000000
iopl=0         nv up ei pl zr na po nc
cs=0033  ss=002b  ds=002b  es=002b  fs=0053  gs=002b                efl=00000246
ntdll!RtlDispatchException+0x219:
00007ffe`cf68a209 8bd0            mov     edx,eax
000000e4`c0afeb30  000000e4`00000001
000000e4`c0afeb38  00007ffe`cf620000 ntdll!RtlStringCchCopyW <PERF> (ntdll+0x0)
000000e4`c0afeb40  00000000`00000000
000000e4`c0afeb48  00007ffe`cf78e9f0 ntdll!__PchSym_ <PERF> (ntdll+0x16e9f0)
000000e4`c0afeb50  000000e4`c0afeb70
000000e4`c0afeb58  000000e4`c0aff090
000000e4`c0afeb60  000000e4`c0aff080
000000e4`c0afeb68  00000000`00000000
000000e4`c0afeb70  000000e4`00000000
000000e4`c0afeb78  00007ffe`cc8300f0 KERNELBASE!UrlHashW <PERF> (KERNELBASE+0xf0)
000000e4`c0afeb80  00000001`00000000
000000e4`c0afeb88  00000012`00000018
000000e4`c0afeb90  00000000`00000000
000000e4`c0afeb98  00360030`00300030
000000e4`c0afeba0  00001f80`0010000f
000000e4`c0afeba8  00000000`00000033

_ _ _ _ _ _ _ _ _ _ _ _ _ _ _ _
0a 000000e4`c0aff240 00007ffe`cc8f0aa2 ntdll!KiUserExceptionDispatch+0x2e
0a 000000e4`c0aff240 00007ffe`cc8f0aa2 ntdll!KiUserExceptionDispatch+0x2e
rax=000000000000005b rbx=000002075d662a10 rcx=0000000000000003
rdx=000000e4c0afe888 rsi=0000000000000000 rdi=000002075d666e40
```

```
rip=00007ffecf6bfe3e rsp=000000e4c0aff240 rbp=0000000000000000
r8=0000000000000000  r9=00000000ffffffff r10=0000000000000000
r11=000000e4c0afdc30 r12=0000000000000000 r13=0000000000000000
r14=0000000000000000 r15=0000000000000000
iopl=0         nv up ei pl zr na po nc
cs=0033  ss=002b  ds=002b  es=002b  fs=0053  gs=002b              efl=00000246
ntdll!KiUserExceptionDispatch+0x2e:
00007ffe`cf6bfe3e 84c0                    test    al,al
000000e4`c0aff240  00007ff6`c8ac32f0 FrameTrace!`string'
000000e4`c0aff248  00000000`000a0008
000000e4`c0aff250  00000207`5d662a10
000000e4`c0aff258  00007ff6`00200000
000000e4`c0aff260  000000e4`c0aff2f0
000000e4`c0aff268  000000e4`c0aff2f0
000000e4`c0aff270  00001f80`0010005f
000000e4`c0aff278  0053002b`002b0033
000000e4`c0aff280  00000246`002b002b
000000e4`c0aff288  00000000`00000000
000000e4`c0aff290  00000000`00000000
000000e4`c0aff298  00000000`00000000
000000e4`c0aff2a0  00000000`00000000
000000e4`c0aff2a8  00000000`00000000
000000e4`c0aff2b0  00000000`00000000
000000e4`c0aff2b8  000000e4`c0aff970

 _ _ _ _ _ _ _ _ _ _ _ _ _ _ _ _
0b 000000e4`c0aff948 00007ff6`c8ab1568 KERNELBASE!wil::details::DebugBreak+0x2
0b 000000e4`c0aff948 00007ff6`c8ab1568 KERNELBASE!wil::details::DebugBreak+0x2
rax=000000000000005b rbx=000002075d662a10 rcx=0000000000000003
rdx=000000e4c0afe888 rsi=0000000000000000 rdi=000002075d666e40
rip=00007ffecc8f0aa2 rsp=000000e4c0aff948 rbp=0000000000000000
r8=0000000000000000  r9=00000000ffffffff r10=0000000000000000
r11=000000e4c0afdc30 r12=0000000000000000 r13=0000000000000000
r14=0000000000000000 r15=0000000000000000
iopl=0         nv up ei pl zr na po nc
cs=0033  ss=002b  ds=002b  es=002b  fs=0053  gs=002b              efl=00000246
KERNELBASE!wil::details::DebugBreak+0x2:
00007ffe`cc8f0aa2 cc                    int     3
000000e4`c0aff948  00007ff6`c8ab1568 FrameTrace!foo+0x68 [C:\NewWork\FrameTrace\FrameTrace.cpp @ 14]
000000e4`c0aff950  000000e4`c0aff970
000000e4`c0aff958  000000e4`c0aff9d0
000000e4`c0aff960  00000000`000000d0
000000e4`c0aff968  00000207`5d66a990
000000e4`c0aff970  00000207`5d66b070
000000e4`c0aff978  00007ff6`c8ab15ed FrameTrace!std::basic_string<wchar_t,std::char_traits<wchar_t>,
std::allocator<wchar_t> >::operator+=+0x1d [C:\Program Files (x86)\Microsoft Visual
Studio\2019\Professional\VC\Tools\MSVC\14.26.28801\include\xstring @ 2821]
000000e4`c0aff980  00000000`000001a0
000000e4`c0aff988  00000000`000001a7
000000e4`c0aff990  0000e8d4`e5494150
000000e4`c0aff998  0000e8d4`e5494150
000000e4`c0aff9a0  000000e4`c0affa30
000000e4`c0aff9a8  00007ff6`c8ab1560 FrameTrace!foo+0x60 [C:\NewWork\FrameTrace\FrameTrace.cpp @ 11]
000000e4`c0aff9b0  00000000`00000000
000000e4`c0aff9b8  000000e4`c0aff9d0
000000e4`c0aff9c0  00000000`00000068

 _ _ _ _ _ _ _ _ _ _ _ _ _ _ _ _
0c 000000e4`c0aff950 00007ff6`c8ab1560 FrameTrace!foo+0x68 [C:\NewWork\FrameTrace\FrameTrace.cpp @ 14]
0c 000000e4`c0aff950 00007ff6`c8ab1560 FrameTrace!foo+0x68 [C:\NewWork\FrameTrace\FrameTrace.cpp @ 14]
rax=000000000000005b rbx=000002075d662a10 rcx=0000000000000003
rdx=000000e4c0afe888 rsi=0000000000000000 rdi=000002075d666e40
rip=00007ff6c8ab1568 rsp=000000e4c0aff950 rbp=0000000000000000
r8=0000000000000000  r9=00000000ffffffff r10=0000000000000000
r11=000000e4c0afdc30 r12=0000000000000000 r13=0000000000000000
r14=0000000000000000 r15=0000000000000000
iopl=0         nv up ei pl zr na po nc
```

```
cs=0033  ss=002b  ds=002b  es=002b  fs=0053  gs=002b            efl=00000246
FrameTrace!foo+0x68:
00007ff6`c8ab1568 90                   nop
000000e4`c0aff950  000000e4`c0aff970
000000e4`c0aff958  000000e4`c0aff9d0
000000e4`c0aff960  00000000`000000d0
000000e4`c0aff968  00000207`5d66a990
000000e4`c0aff970  00000207`5d66b070
000000e4`c0aff978  00007ff6`c8ab15ed FrameTrace!std::basic_string<wchar_t,std::char_traits<wchar_t>,
std::allocator<wchar_t> >::operator+=+0x1d [C:\Program Files (x86)\Microsoft Visual
Studio\2019\Professional\VC\Tools\MSVC\14.26.28801\include\xstring @ 2821]
000000e4`c0aff980  00000000`000001a0
000000e4`c0aff988  00000000`000001a7
000000e4`c0aff990  0000e8d4`e5494150
000000e4`c0aff998  0000e8d4`e5494150
000000e4`c0aff9a0  000000e4`c0affa30
000000e4`c0aff9a8  00007ff6`c8ab1560 FrameTrace!foo+0x60 [C:\NewWork\FrameTrace\FrameTrace.cpp @ 11]
000000e4`c0aff9b0  00000000`00000000
000000e4`c0aff9b8  000000e4`c0aff9d0
000000e4`c0aff9c0  00000000`00000068
000000e4`c0aff9c8  00000207`5d66a8a0
_ _ _ _ _ _ _ _ _ _ _ _ _ _ _ _
[...]
```

We need to reset the current context after the command above since the last frame becomes the current:

```
0:000> kc
*** Stack trace for last set context - .thread/.cxr resets it
# Call Site
15 ntdll!RtlUserThreadStart

0:000> .cxr
Resetting default scope

0:000> kc
# Call Site
00 ntdll!NtWaitForMultipleObjects
01 KERNELBASE!WaitForMultipleObjectsEx
02 KERNELBASE!WaitForMultipleObjects
03 kernel32!WerpReportFaultInternal
04 kernel32!WerpReportFault
05 KERNELBASE!UnhandledExceptionFilter
06 ntdll!RtlUserThreadStart$filt$0
07 ntdll!_C_specific_handler
08 ntdll!RtlpExecuteHandlerForException
09 ntdll!RtlDispatchException
0a ntdll!KiUserExceptionDispatch
0b KERNELBASE!wil::details::DebugBreak
0c FrameTrace!foo
0d FrameTrace!foo
0e FrameTrace!foo
0f FrameTrace!foo
10 FrameTrace!foo
11 FrameTrace!foo
12 FrameTrace!main
13 FrameTrace!invoke_main
14 FrameTrace!__scrt_common_main_seh
```

```
15 kernel32!BaseThreadInitThunk
16 ntdll!RtlUserThreadStart
```

We call this analysis pattern **Frame Trace**.

The example memory dump, the application PDB file, and source code are available for download[82].

---

[82] https://www.patterndiagnostics.com/SoftwareDiagnosticsCorpus/SDC8.zip

Frozen Process

It looks like Windows 8 reuses a frozen thread debugging concept for the so-called a "deeply frozen" process:

```
0: kd> !sprocess 2
Dumping Session 2
[...]
PROCESS fffffa8002cb2940
SessionId: 2 Cid: 0c80 Peb: 7f6c41dd000 ParentCid: 0288
DeepFreeze
DirBase: 2ef45000 ObjectTable: fffff8a002f215c0 HandleCount: <Data Not Accessible>
Image: iexplore.exe
[...]

0: kd> dt nt!_KPROCESS fffffa8002cb2940
+0x000 Header             : _DISPATCHER_HEADER
+0x018 ProfileListHead    : _LIST_ENTRY [ 0xfffffa80`02cb2958 - 0xfffffa80`02cb2958 ]
+0x028 DirectoryTableBase : 0x2ef45000
+0x030 ThreadListHead     : _LIST_ENTRY [ 0xfffffa80`01e4edf8 - 0xfffffa80`01f5bbf8 ]
+0x040 ProcessLock        : 0
+0x044 Spare0             : 0
+0x048 Affinity           : _KAFFINITY_EX
+0x0f0 ReadyListHead      : _LIST_ENTRY [ 0xfffffa80`02cb2a30 - 0xfffffa80`02cb2a30 ]
+0x100 SwapListEntry      : _SINGLE_LIST_ENTRY
+0x108 ActiveProcessors   : _KAFFINITY_EX
+0x1b0 AutoAlignment      : 0y0
+0x1b0 DisableBoost       : 0y0
+0x1b0 DisableQuantum     : 0y0
+0x1b0 AffinitySet        : 0y0
+0x1b0 DeepFreeze         : 0y1
+0x1b0 TimerVirtualization : 0y1
+0x1b0 ActiveGroupsMask   : 0y00000000000000000001 (0x1)
+0x1b0 ReservedFlags      : 0y000000 (0)
+0x1b0 ProcessFlags       : 0n112
+0x1b4 BasePriority       : 8 ”
+0x1b5 QuantumReset       : 6 ”
+0x1b6 Visited            : 0 ”
+0x1b7 Flags              : _KEXECUTE_OPTIONS
+0x1b8 ThreadSeed         : [20] 0
+0x208 IdealNode          : [20] 0
+0x230 IdealGlobalNode    : 0
+0x232 Spare1             : 0
+0x234 StackCount         : _KSTACK_COUNT
+0x238 ProcessListEntry   : _LIST_ENTRY [ 0xfffffa80`03816b78 - 0xfffffa80`02cc2b78 ]
+0x248 CycleTime          : 0x225078
+0x250 ContextSwitches    : 0x22
+0x258 SchedulingGroup    : (null)
+0x260 FreezeCount        : 0
+0x264 KernelTime         : 0
+0x268 UserTime           : 0
+0x26c LdtFreeSelectorHint : 0
+0x26e LdtTableLength     : 0
+0x270 LdtSystemDescriptor : _KGDTENTRY64
+0x280 LdtBaseAddress     : (null)
```

```
+0x288 LdtProcessLock    : _FAST_MUTEX
+0x2c0 InstrumentationCallback : (null)
```

We also see that all its threads have a freeze count 1:

```
0: kd> !process fffffa8002cb2940 2
[...]
THREAD fffffa8001e4eb00 Cid 0c80.0514 Teb: 000007f6c41de000 Win32Thread: fffff901000e5b90 WAIT:
(Suspended) KernelMode Non-Alertable
FreezeCount 1
fffffa8001e4ede0 NotificationEvent


THREAD fffffa800219c080 Cid 0c80.0d88 Teb: 000007f6c41db000 Win32Thread: fffff90103f206e0 WAIT:
(Suspended) KernelMode Non-Alertable
FreezeCount 1
fffffa800219c360 NotificationEvent
[...]


0: kd> dt _KTHREAD fffffa800219c080
nt!_KTHREAD
+0x000 Header            : _DISPATCHER_HEADER
+0x018 SListFaultAddress : (null)
+0x020 QuantumTarget     : 0x18c26200
+0x028 InitialStack      : 0xfffff880`1548ddd0 Void
+0x030 StackLimit        : 0xfffff880`15488000 Void
+0x038 StackBase         : 0xfffff880`1548e000 Void
+0x040 ThreadLock        : 0
+0x048 CycleTime         : 0x15ca97c8
+0x050 CurrentRunTime    : 0
+0x054 ExpectedRunTime   : 0xd77e
+0x058 KernelStack       : 0xfffff880`1548d430 Void
+0x060 StateSaveArea     : 0xfffff880`1548de00 _XSAVE_FORMAT
+0x068 SchedulingGroup   : (null)
+0x070 WaitRegister      : _KWAIT_STATUS_REGISTER
+0x071 Running           : 0 ''
+0x072 Alerted           : [2]   ""
+0x074 KernelStackResident : 0y1
+0x074 ReadyTransition   : 0y0
+0x074 ProcessReadyQueue : 0y0
+0x074 WaitNext          : 0y0
+0x074 SystemAffinityActive : 0y0
+0x074 Alertable         : 0y0
+0x074 CodePatchInProgress : 0y0
+0x074 UserStackWalkActive : 0y0
+0x074 ApcInterruptRequest : 0y0
+0x074 QuantumEndMigrate : 0y0
+0x074 UmsDirectedSwitchEnable : 0y0
+0x074 TimerActive       : 0y0
+0x074 SystemThread      : 0y0
+0x074 ProcessDetachActive : 0y0
+0x074 CalloutActive     : 0y0
+0x074 ScbReadyQueue     : 0y0
+0x074 ApcQueueable      : 0y1
+0x074 ReservedStackInUse : 0y0
+0x074 UmsPerformingSyscall : 0y0
```

```
+0x074 Reserved            : 0y0000000000000 (0)
+0x074 MiscFlags           : 0n65537
+0x078 AutoAlignment       : 0y0
+0x078 DisableBoost        : 0y0
+0x078 UserAffinitySet     : 0y0
+0x078 AlertedByThreadId   : 0y0
+0x078 QuantumDonation     : 0y0
+0x078 EnableStackSwap     : 0y1
+0x078 GuiThread           : 0y1
+0x078 DisableQuantum      : 0y0
+0x078 ChargeOnlyGroup     : 0y0
+0x078 DeferPreemption     : 0y0
+0x078 QueueDeferPreemption : 0y0
+0x078 ForceDeferSchedule  : 0y0
+0x078 ExplicitIdealProcessor : 0y0
+0x078 FreezeCount         : 0y1
+0x078 EtwStackTraceApcInserted : 0y00000000 (0)
+0x078 ReservedFlags       : 0y0000000000 (0)
+0x078 ThreadFlags         : 0n8288
+0x07c Spare0              : 0
+0x080 SystemCallNumber    : 0x87
+0x084 Spare1              : 0
+0x088 FirstArgument       : 0x00000000`0000017c Void
+0x090 TrapFrame           : (null)
+0x098 ApcState            : _KAPC_STATE
+0x098 ApcStateFill        : [43]  "???"
+0x0c3 Priority            : 8 "
+0x0c4 UserIdealProcessor  : 1
+0x0c8 WaitStatus          : 0n256
+0x0d0 WaitBlockList       : 0xffffffa80`0219c1c0 _KWAIT_BLOCK
+0x0d8 WaitListEntry       : _LIST_ENTRY [ 0xffffffa80`0418a458 - 0xffffff880`009eb300 ]
+0x0d8 SwapListEntry       : _SINGLE_LIST_ENTRY
+0x0e8 Queue               : 0xffffffa80`03da4bc0 _KQUEUE
+0x0f0 Teb                 : 0x000007f6`c41db000 Void
+0x0f8 RelativeTimerBias   : 0x00000001`8b165f54
+0x100 Timer               : _KTIMER
+0x140 WaitBlock           : [4] _KWAIT_BLOCK
+0x140 WaitBlockFill4      : [20]  "h???"
+0x154 ContextSwitches     : 0x1817
+0x140 WaitBlockFill5      : [68]  "h???"
+0x184 State               : 0x5 "
+0x185 NpxState            : 1 "
+0x186 WaitIrql            : 0 "
+0x187 WaitMode            : 0 "
+0x140 WaitBlockFill6      : [116]  "h???"
+0x1b4 WaitTime            : 0xf0172e
+0x140 WaitBlockFill7      : [164]  "h???"
+0x1e4 KernelApcDisable    : 0n0
+0x1e6 SpecialApcDisable   : 0n0
+0x1e4 CombinedApcDisable  : 0
+0x140 WaitBlockFill8      : [40]  "h???"
+0x168 ThreadCounters      : (null)
+0x140 WaitBlockFill9      : [88]  "h???"
+0x198 XStateSave          : (null)
+0x140 WaitBlockFill10     : [136]  "h???"
+0x1c8 Win32Thread         : 0xffffff901`03f206e0 Void
```

```
+0x140 WaitBlockFill11  : [176]  "h???"
+0x1f0 Ucb              : (null)
+0x1f8 Uch              : (null)
+0x200 TebMappedLowVa   : (null)
+0x208 QueueListEntry   : _LIST_ENTRY [ 0xfffffa80`02ccf408 - 0xfffffa80`03da4bf0 ]
+0x218 NextProcessor    : 0
+0x21c DeferredProcessor : 1
+0x220 Process          : 0xfffffa80`02cb2940 _KPROCESS
+0x228 UserAffinity     : _GROUP_AFFINITY
+0x228 UserAffinityFill : [10]  "???"
+0x232 PreviousMode     : 1 "
+0x233 BasePriority     : 8 "
+0x234 PriorityDecrement : 0 "
+0x234 ForegroundBoost  : 0y0000
+0x234 UnusualBoost     : 0y0000
+0x235 Preempted        : 0 "
+0x236 AdjustReason     : 0 "
+0x237 AdjustIncrement  : 0 "
+0x238 Affinity         : _GROUP_AFFINITY
+0x238 AffinityFill     : [10]  "???"
+0x242 ApcStateIndex    : 0 "
+0x243 WaitBlockCount   : 0x1 "
+0x244 IdealProcessor   : 1
+0x248 ApcStatePointer  : [2] 0xfffffa80`0219c118 _KAPC_STATE
+0x258 SavedApcState    : _KAPC_STATE
+0x258 SavedApcStateFill : [43]  "???"
+0x283 WaitReason       : 0x5 "
+0x284 SuspendCount     : 0 "
+0x285 Saturation       : 0 "
+0x286 SListFaultCount  : 0
+0x288 SchedulerApc     : _KAPC
+0x288 SchedulerApcFill0 : [1]  "??????"
+0x289 ResourceIndex    : 0x1 "
+0x288 SchedulerApcFill1 : [3]  "???"
+0x28b QuantumReset     : 0x6 "
+0x288 SchedulerApcFill2 : [4]  "???"
+0x28c KernelTime       : 7
+0x288 SchedulerApcFill3 : [64]  "???"
+0x2c8 WaitPrcb         : (null)
+0x288 SchedulerApcFill4 : [72]  "???"
+0x2d0 LegoData         : (null)
[...]
```

This is different when a process is under a debugger, and all its threads are frozen except the one that communicates to the debugger like in the case study[83]. In Windows 8 this happens, for example, when we switch to a desktop from IE launched from the start page. Then we would see shortly that iexplore.exe process changes from *Running* to *Suspended* in Task Manager *Details* page. This pattern covers both the new feature and a debugged process case.

---

[83] "Stack Trace Collection, Suspended Threads, Not My Version, Special Process, Main Thread and Blocked LPC Chain Threads", Memory Dump Analysis Anthology, Volume 4, page 204

Ghost Thread

Sometimes **Wait Chains** (page 1209) such as involving critical sections (page 1203) may have **Missing Thread** (page 768) endpoint. However, in some cases, we might see **Ghost Thread** whose TID was reused by subsequent thread creation in a different process. For example, critical section structure may refer to such TID as in the example below.

```
// Critical section from LSASS process

THREAD fffffa803431cb50 Cid 03e8.2718 Teb: 000007fffff80000 Win32Thread: 0000000000000000 WAIT:
(UserRequest) UserMode Non-Alertable
    fffffa80330e0500 SynchronizationEvent
Impersonation token: fffff8a00b807060 (Level Impersonation)
Owning Process            fffffa8032354c40      Image: lsass.exe
Attached Process          N/A            Image:        N/A
Wait Start TickCount      107175         Ticks: 19677 (0:00:05:06.963)
Context Switch Count      2303           IdealProcessor: 1
UserTime                  00:00:00.218
KernelTime                00:00:00.109
Win32 Start Address ntdll!TppWorkerThread (0x0000000076e1f2e0)
Stack Init fffff88008e5fdb0 Current fffff88008e5f900
Base fffff88008e60000 Limit fffff88008e5a000 Call 0
Priority 10 BasePriority 10 UnusualBoost 0 ForegroundBoost 0 IoPriority 2 PagePriority 5
Kernel stack not resident.
Child-SP RetAddr Call Site
fffff880`08e5f940 fffff800`01c7cf72 nt!KiSwapContext+0x7a
fffff880`08e5fa80 fffff800`01c8e39f nt!KiCommitThreadWait+0x1d2
fffff880`08e5fb10 fffff800`01f7fe3e nt!KeWaitForSingleObject+0x19f
fffff880`08e5fbb0 fffff800`01c867d3 nt!NtWaitForSingleObject+0xde
fffff880`08e5fc20 00000000`76e5067a nt!KiSystemServiceCopyEnd+0x13 (TrapFrame @ fffff880`08e5fc20)
00000000`0427cca8 00000000`76e4d808 ntdll!NtWaitForSingleObject+0xa
00000000`0427ccb0 00000000`76e4d6fb ntdll!RtlpWaitOnCriticalSection+0xe8
00000000`0427cd60 000007fe`f46a4afe ntdll!RtlEnterCriticalSection+0xd1
[...]

1: kd> .process /r /p fffffa8032354c40
Implicit process is now fffffa80`32353b30
Loading User Symbols
```

```
1: kd> !cs -l -o -s
-----------------------------------------
DebugInfo          = 0x0000000003475220
Critical section   = 0x0000000003377740 (+0x3377740)
LOCKED
LockCount          = 0x10
WaiterWoken        = No
OwningThread       = 0x00000000000004e4
RecursionCount     = 0x0
LockSemaphore      = 0x0
SpinCount          = 0x0000000000000000
OwningThread       = .thread fffffa80344e4c00
[...]


// The "owner" thread is from winlogon.exe


1: kd> !thread fffffa80344e4c00 1f
THREAD fffffa80344e4c00 Cid 21d0.14e4 Teb: 000007fffffae000 Win32Thread: fffff900c0998c20 WAIT:
(WrUserRequest) UserMode Non-Alertable
fffffa80355817d0 SynchronizationEvent
Not impersonating
DeviceMap          fffff8a0000088f0
Owning Process     fffffa8034ff77c0          Image: winlogon.exe
[...]
```

A PML (Process Monitor) log was recorded before the complete memory dump was forced, and it clearly shows **Glued Activity** trace analysis pattern[84]. LSASS owned the thread but then the thread exited, and 2 other processes subsequently reused its TID.

---

[84] Glued Activity, Memory Dump Analysis Anthology, Volume 6, page 250

Glued Stack Trace

Sometimes we have **Truncated Stack Trace** (page 1130) and need to perform manual stack trace reconstruction[85] of the missing part to get approximate full stack trace. Often we are only able to reconstruct some parts and glue them together perhaps with some missing intermediate frames:

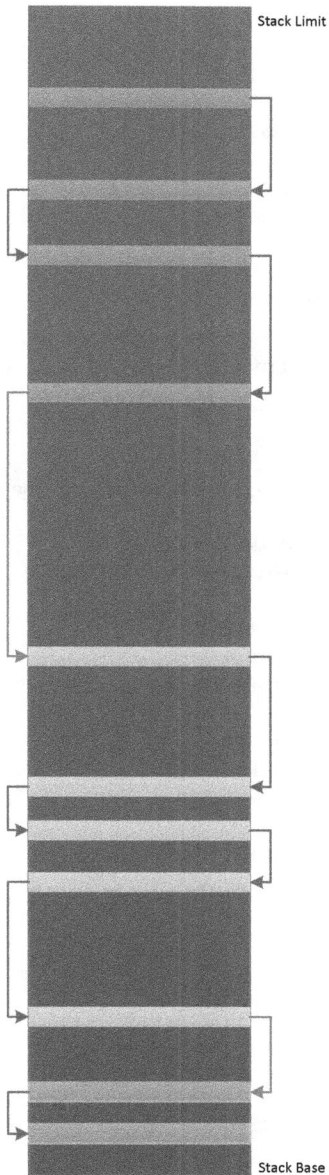

---

[85] Manual Stack Trace Reconstruction, Memory Dump Analysis Anthology, Volume 1, page 157

For example, we have this truncated stack trace due to the lack of symbols:

```
1: kd> k
ChildEBP RetAddr
97543b6c 85adf579 nt!KiTrap0E+0x2ac
WARNING: Stack unwind information not available. Following frames may be wrong.
97543be8 85adf770 myfault+0x579
97543bf4 85adf7fc myfault+0x770
97543c2c 81827ecf myfault+0x7fc
97543c44 81988f65 nt!IofCallDriver+0x63
97543c64 81989f25 nt!IopSynchronousServiceTail+0x1e0
97543d00 8198ee8d nt!IopXxxControlFile+0x6b7
97543d34 8188c96a nt!NtDeviceIoControlFile+0x2a
97543d34 77510f34 nt!KiFastCallEntry+0x12a
0012f9a0 7750f850 ntdll!KiFastSystemCallRet
0012f9a4 77417c92 ntdll!NtDeviceIoControlFile+0xc
0012fa04 00401a5b kernel32!DeviceIoControl+0x14a
0012fa94 7700becf NotMyfault+0x1a5b
0012facc 00000000 USER32!xxxDrawButton+0xc1
```

Manual stack reconstruction brings this fragment:

```
1: kd> k L=0012fb94 0012fb94 0012fb94
ChildEBP RetAddr
WARNING: Frame IP not in any known module. Following frames may be wrong.
0012fb94 77001ae8 0x12fb94
0012fc0c 7700286a USER32!UserCallWinProcCheckWow+0x14b
0012fc4c 77002bba USER32!SendMessageWorker+0x4b7
0012fc6c 7700c6b4 USER32!SendMessageW+0x7c
0012fc84 7700c7c9 USER32!xxxButtonNotifyParent+0x41
0012fca0 7700c7e8 USER32!xxxBNReleaseCapture+0xf7
0012fd24 7701632e USER32!ButtonWndProcWorker+0x910
0012fd44 77001a10 USER32!ButtonWndProcA+0x4c
0012fd70 77001ae8 USER32!InternalCallWinProc+0x23
0012fde8 77002a47 USER32!UserCallWinProcCheckWow+0x14b
0012fe4c 77002a98 USER32!DispatchMessageWorker+0x322
0012fe5c 76ff11fc USER32!DispatchMessageW+0xf
0012fe80 76fe98d2 USER32!IsDialogMessageW+0x586
0012fea0 00401cc9 USER32!IsDialogMessageA+0xff
0012ff10 004022ec NotMyfault+0x1cc9
00000000 00000000 NotMyfault+0x22ec
```

And finally we get the 3rd usual thread start fragment:

```
1: kd> k L=0012ffa0 0012ffa0 0012ffa0
ChildEBP RetAddr
WARNING: Frame IP not in any known module. Following frames may be wrong.
0012ffa0 77413833 0x12ffa0
0012ffac 774ea9bd kernel32!BaseThreadInitThunk+0xe
0012ffec 00000000 ntdll!_RtlUserThreadStart+0x23
```

Gluing them together, we get this approx. stack trace:

```
97543b6c 85adf579 nt!KiTrap0E+0x2ac
WARNING: Stack unwind information not available. Following frames may be wrong.
97543be8 85adf770 myfault+0x579
97543bf4 85adf7fc myfault+0x770
97543c2c 81827ecf myfault+0x7fc
97543c44 81988f65 nt!IofCallDriver+0x63
97543c64 81989f25 nt!IopSynchronousServiceTail+0x1e0
97543d00 8198ee8d nt!IopXxxControlFile+0x6b7
97543d34 8188c96a nt!NtDeviceIoControlFile+0x2a
97543d34 77510f34 nt!KiFastCallEntry+0x12a
0012f9a0 7750f850 ntdll!KiFastSystemCallRet
0012f9a4 77417c92 ntdll!NtDeviceIoControlFile+0xc
0012fa04 00401a5b kernel32!DeviceIoControl+0x14a
0012fa94 7700becf NotMyfault+0x1a5b
0012fc0c 7700286a USER32!UserCallWinProcCheckWow+0x14b
0012fc4c 77002bba USER32!SendMessageWorker+0x4b7
0012fc6c 7700c6b4 USER32!SendMessageW+0x7c
0012fc84 7700c7c9 USER32!xxxButtonNotifyParent+0x41
0012fca0 7700c7e8 USER32!xxxBNReleaseCapture+0xf7
0012fd24 7701632e USER32!ButtonWndProcWorker+0x910
0012fd44 77001a10 USER32!ButtonWndProcA+0x4c
0012fd70 77001ae8 USER32!InternalCallWinProc+0x23
0012fde8 77002a47 USER32!UserCallWinProcCheckWow+0x14b
0012fe4c 77002a98 USER32!DispatchMessageWorker+0x322
0012fe5c 76ff11fc USER32!DispatchMessageW+0xf
0012fe80 76fe98d2 USER32!IsDialogMessageW+0x586
0012fea0 00401cc9 USER32!IsDialogMessageA+0xff
0012ff10 004022ec NotMyfault+0x1cc9
0012ffac 774ea9bd kernel32!BaseThreadInitThunk+0xe
0012ffec 00000000 ntdll!_RtlUserThreadStart+0x23
```

H

Handle Leak

Although **Handle Leak** may lead to **Insufficient Memory** (page 590), it is not always the case especially if pool structures are small such as events. So **Handle Leak** pattern covers high memory usage (including fat structures), high handle counts and also abnormal differences in allocations and deallocations. As an example of the latter here is a nonpaged pool leak of Event objects and correlated pooltag ABCD. Although memory usage footprint is small compared with other nonleaking pooltags we see that the difference between *Allocs* and *Frees* is surely abnormal and correlating with high handle counts:

```
0: kd> !poolused 3
Sorting by  NonPaged Pool Consumed

Pool Used:
NonPaged                      Paged
Tag    Allocs    Frees     Diff     Used   Allocs   Frees    Diff     Used
[...]
ABCD  1778517  1704538    73979  4734656        0       0       0        0 UNKNOWN pooltag 'ABCD',
please update pooltag.txt
Even  6129633  6063728    65905  4224528        0       0       0        0 Event objects
[...]


0: kd> !process 0 0

[...]


PROCESS d2b85360  SessionId: 2  Cid: 1bf4    Peb: 7ffdf000  ParentCid: 1688
DirBase: 7d778dc0  ObjectTable: e53dda08  HandleCount: 18539.
Image: AppA.exe

PROCESS b2fcd670  SessionId: 2  Cid: 0818    Peb: 7ffd4000  ParentCid: 1688
DirBase: 7d778400  ObjectTable: b3ffd8c0  HandleCount: 36252.
Image: AppB.exe

[...]
```

Comments

In process memory dumps we can also see high handle counts for leak cases:

```
0:000> !handle
[...]
273020   Handles
Type           Count
None           93
Event          222742
Section        26
File           33
Directory      3
Mutant         8
WindowStation  2
Semaphore      23
Key            24
Process        2
Thread         50042
Desktop        1
IoCompletion   7
Timer          1
TpWorkerFactory 2
ALPC Port      5
WaitCompletionPacket 6
```

Handle Limit

GDI

Kernel Space

Among various memory leaks leading to **Insufficient Memory** pattern (page 587), there is so-called session pool leak briefly touched in the pattern about kernel pool leaks (page 599). It also involves GDI handles and structures allocated per user session that has the limit on how many of them can be created and this pattern should rather be called **Handle Limit**. Such leaks can result in poor visual application behavior after some time when drawing requests are not satisfied anymore. In severe cases, when the same bugs are present in a display driver, it can result in bugchecks like

```
BugCheck AB: SESSION_HAS_VALID_POOL_ON_EXIT
```

or, if a handle allocation request was not satisfied, it may result in a NULL pointer stored somewhere with the subsequent **Invalid Pointer** access (page 661):

```
SYSTEM_THREAD_EXCEPTION_NOT_HANDLED (7e)

CONTEXT:  b791e010 -- (.cxr 0xffffffffb791e010)
eax=00000000 ebx=bc43d004 ecx=a233add8 edx=00000000 esi=bc430fff edi=00000000
eip=bfe7d380 esp=b791e3dc ebp=b791e480 iopl=0 nv up ei pl zr na pe nc
cs=0008 ss=0010 ds=0023 es=0023 fs=0030 gs=0000 efl=00010246
DisplayDriver+0x3e380:
bfe7d380 8a4702    mov     al,byte ptr [edi+2]       ds:0023:00000002=??
```

We can write three Win32 applications in Visual C++ that simulate GDI leaks. All of them create GDI objects in a loop and select them into their current graphics device context (DC) on Windows Server 2003 x64 SP2. Before running them, we get the following session paged pool statistics:

```
lkd> !poolused c

  Sorting by Session Paged Pool Consumed

  Pool Used:
            NonPaged            Paged
  Tag     Allocs     Used     Allocs     Used
  NV_x       0         0        5   14024704 UNKNOWN pooltag 'NV_x', please update pooltag.txt
  BIG        0         0      257    3629056 Large session pool allocations (ntos\ex\pool.c) , Binary:
nt!mm
  NV         0         0      203    1347648 nVidia video driver
  Ttfd       0         0      233    1053152 TrueType Font driver
  Gh05       0         0      391    1050400 Gdi Handle manager specific object types: defined in
w32\ntgdi\inc\ntgdistr.h , Binary: win32k.sys
  Gla1       0         0      348     785088 Gdi handle manager specific object types allocated from
lookaside memory: defined in w32\ntgdi\inc\ntgdistr.h , Binary: win32k.sys
  Gcac       0         0       25     640880 Gdi glyph cache
  Gla5       0         0      631     323072 Gdi handle manager specific object types allocated from
```

```
lookaside memory: defined in w32\ntgdi\inc\ntgdistr.h , Binary: win32k.sys
  Gdrs        0        0       33     172288 Gdi GDITAG_DRVSUP
  Gla:        0        0      212     139072 Gdi handle manager specific object types allocated from
lookaside memory: defined in w32\ntgdi\inc\ntgdistr.h , Binary: win32k.sys
  Gla4        0        0      487     116880 Gdi handle manager specific object types allocated from
lookaside memory: defined in w32\ntgdi\inc\ntgdistr.h , Binary: win32k.sys
  Usti        0        0      148      97088 THREADINFO , Binary: win32k!AllocateW32Thread
  Gla8        0        0      383      91920 Gdi handle manager specific object types allocated from
lookaside memory: defined in w32\ntgdi\inc\ntgdistr.h , Binary: win32k.sys
  Gla@        0        0      339      70512 Gdi handle manager specific object types allocated from
lookaside memory: defined in w32\ntgdi\inc\ntgdistr.h , Binary: win32k.sys
  Gbaf        0        0       48      67584 UNKNOWN pooltag 'Gbaf', please update pooltag.txt
  knlf        0        0       20      66496 UNKNOWN pooltag 'knlf', please update pooltag.txt
  GDev        0        0        7      57344 Gdi pdev
  Usqu        0        0      152      53504 Q , Binary: win32k!InitQEntryLookaside
  Uscu        0        0      334      53440 CURSOR , Binary: win32k!_CreateEmptyCursorObject
  Bmfd        0        0       21      50224 Font related stuff
  Uspi        0        0      153      40000 PROCESSINFO , Binary: win32k!MapDesktop
  Gfnt        0        0       47      39856 UNKNOWN pooltag 'Gfnt', please update pooltag.txt
  Ggb         0        0       34      39088 Gdi glyph bits
  Gh08        0        0       33      38656 Gdi Handle manager specific object types: defined in
w32\ntgdi\inc\ntgdistr.h , Binary: win32k.sys
  Ghab        0        0      228      32832 Gdi Handle manager specific object types: defined in
w32\ntgdi\inc\ntgdistr.h , Binary: win32k.sys
  Ovfl        0        0        1      32768 The internal pool tag table has overflowed - usually this is a
result of nontagged allocations being made
  Gpff        0        0       88      27712 Gdi physical font file
  Gpfe        0        0       88      27600 UNKNOWN pooltag 'Gpfe', please update pooltag.txt
  thdd        0        0        1      20480 DirectDraw/3D handle manager table
  Gebr        0        0       17      19776 Gdi ENGBRUSH
  Gh0@        0        0       86      19264 Gdi Handle manager specific object types: defined in
w32\ntgdi\inc\ntgdistr.h , Binary: win32k.sys
  Gsp         0        0       79      18960 Gdi sprite
  HT40        0        0        2      16384 UNKNOWN pooltag 'HT40', please update pooltag.txt
  Gpat        0        0        4      16192 UNKNOWN pooltag 'Gpat', please update pooltag.txt
  Ggls        0        0      169      12944 Gdi glyphset
  Glnk        0        0      371      11872 Gdi PFELINK
  Gldv        0        0        9      11248 Gdi Ldev
  Gffv        0        0       84       9408 Gdi FONTFILEVIEW
  Gfsb        0        0        1       8192 Gdi font sustitution list
  Uskt        0        0        2       7824 KBDTABLE , Binary: win32k!ReadLayoutFile
  Gh04        0        0        7       5856 Gdi Handle manager specific object types: defined in
w32\ntgdi\inc\ntgdistr.h , Binary: win32k.sys
  Gdcf        0        0       51       5712 UNKNOWN pooltag 'Gdcf', please update pooltag.txt
  Gh0<        0        0       88       5632 Gdi Handle manager specific object types: defined in
w32\ntgdi\inc\ntgdistr.h , Binary: win32k.sys
  Gglb        0        0        1       4096 Gdi temp buffer
  Ustm        0        0       30       3360 TIMER , Binary: win32k!InternalSetTimer
  Gspm        0        0       39       3120 UNKNOWN pooltag 'Gspm', please update pooltag.txt
  Usac        0        0       16       3056 ACCEL , Binary: win32k!_CreateAcceleratorTable
  Usqm        0        0       25       2800 QMSG , Binary: win32k!InitQEntryLookaside
  Ghas        0        0        3       2592 Gdi Handle manager specific object types: defined in
w32\ntgdi\inc\ntgdistr.h , Binary: win32k.sys
  Uscl        0        0       20       2128 CLASS , Binary: win32k!ClassAlloc
  Uswl        0        0        1       2032 WINDOWLIST , Binary: win32k!BuildHwndList
  Gmul        0        0       19       1520 UNKNOWN pooltag 'Gmul', please update pooltag.txt
```

```
Dddp       0        0        8     1472 UNKNOWN pooltag 'Dddp', please update pooltag.txt
Ggdv       0        0        8     1472 Gdi GDITAG_GDEVICE
UsDI       0        0        4     1408 DEVICEINFO , Binary: win32k!CreateDeviceInfo
Vtfd       0        0        4     1312 Font file/context
Ushk       0        0       20     1280 HOTKEY , Binary: win32k!_RegisterHotKey
Gspr       0        0        3     1264 Gdi sprite grow range
Gtmw       0        0       13     1248 Gdi TMW_INTERNAL
Gxlt       0        0        8     1152 Gdi Xlate
Gpft       0        0        2      944 Gdi font table
Uspp       0        0        5      944 PNP , Binary: win32k!AllocateAndLinkHidTLCInf
Ussm       0        0        7      896 SMS , Binary: win32k!InitSMSLookaside
Gdbr       0        0       10      800 Gdi driver brush realization
Usdc       0        0        8      768 DCE , Binary: win32k!CreateCacheDC
Usct       0        0       12      768 CHECKPT , Binary: win32k!CkptRestore
Usim       0        0        2      736 IME , Binary: win32k!CreateInputContext
Usci       0        0        3      720 CLIENTTHREADINFO , Binary: win32k!InitSystemThread
Gh09       0        0        1      640 Gdi Handle manager specific object types: defined in
w32\ntgdi\inc\ntgdistr.h , Binary: win32k.sys
Ussy       1       80        4      608 SYSTEM , Binary: win32k!xxxDesktopThread
Urdr       0        0        9      576 REDIRECT , Binary: win32k!SetRedirectionBitmap
Uswd       0        0        2      576 WINDOW , Binary: win32k!xxxCreateWindowEx
Uscb       0        0        3      544 CLIPBOARD , Binary: win32k!_ConvertMemHandle
Gcsl       0        0        1      496 Gdi string resource script names
Ustx       0        0       10      496 TEXT , Binary: win32k!NtUserDrawCaptionTemp
Ussw       0        0        1      496 SWP , Binary: win32k!_BeginDeferWindowPos
Gdev       0        0        2      480 Gdi GDITAG_DEVMODE
Usih       0        0       10      480 IMEHOTKEY , Binary: win32k!SetImeHotKey
Gdrv       0        0        1      368 UNKNOWN pooltag 'Gdrv', please update pooltag.txt
GVdv       0        0        1      320 UNKNOWN pooltag 'GVdv', please update pooltag.txt
Gmap       0        0        1      320 Gdi font map signature table
Uskb       0        0        2      288 KBDLAYOUT , Binary: win32k!xxxLoadKeyboardLayoutEx
Uskf       0        0        2      288 KBDFILE , Binary: win32k!LoadKeyboardLayoutFile
Uswe       0        0        2      224 WINEVENT , Binary: win32k!_SetWinEventHook
Gddf       0        0        2      224 Gdi ddraw driver heaps
Gddv       0        0        2      192 Gdi ddraw driver video memory list
GFil       0        0        2      192 Gdi engine descriptor list
Gdwd       0        0        2       96 Gdi watchdog support objects , Binary: win32k.sys
Usd9       0        0        1       80 DDE9 , Binary: win32k!xxxCsDdeInitialize
Gvds       0        0        1       64 UNKNOWN pooltag 'Gvds', please update pooltag.txt
GreA       0        0        1       64 UNKNOWN pooltag 'GreA', please update pooltag.txt
Usse       0        0        1       48 SECURITY , Binary: win32k!SetDisconnectDesktopSecu
Usvl       0        0        1       48 VWPL , Binary: win32k!VWPLAdd
Mdxg       1      112        0        0 UNKNOWN pooltag 'Mdxg', please update pooltag.txt
Gini       3      128        0        0 Gdi fast mutex
Usev       1       64        0        0 EVENT , Binary: win32k!xxxPollAndWaitForSingleO
Gdde       3      240        0        0 Gdi ddraw event
TOTAL      9      624            6256 24408704
```

The first application leaks fonts:

```
LRESULT CALLBACK WndProc(HWND hWnd, UINT message, WPARAM wParam, LPARAM lParam)
{
 int wmId, wmEvent;
 PAINTSTRUCT ps;
 HDC hdc;

 switch (message)
 {
   case WM_PAINT:
     hdc = BeginPaint(hWnd, &ps);
     while (true)
     {
         HFONT hf = CreateFont(10, 10, 0, 0, 0, 0, 0, 0, 0, 0, 0, 0, 0, L"Arial");
         SelectObject(ps.hdc, hf);
     }
     EndPaint(hWnd, &ps);
     break;
```

We clearly see the leak as the greatly increased the number of allocations for "Gla:" pool tag:

```
 Pool Used:
             NonPaged           Paged
Tag    Allocs    Used    Allocs      Used
NV_x      0       0         5  14024704 UNKNOWN pooltag 'NV_x', please update pooltag.txt
Gla:      0       0     10194   6687264 Gdi handle manager specific object types allocated from
Lookaside memory: defined in w32\ntgdi\inc\ntgdistr.h , Binary: win32k.sys
 BIG      0       0       248   3690496 Large session pool allocations (ntos\ex\pool.c) , Binary:
nt!mm
 NV       0       0       203   1347648 nVidia video driver
 Gh05     0       0       396   1057888 Gdi Handle manager specific object types: defined in
w32\ntgdi\inc\ntgdistr.h , Binary: win32k.sys
 Ttfd     0       0       226   1043264 TrueType Font driver
```

The second application leaks fonts and pens:

```
LRESULT CALLBACK WndProc(HWND hWnd, UINT message, WPARAM wParam, LPARAM lParam)
{
 int wmId, wmEvent;
 PAINTSTRUCT ps;
 HDC hdc;

 switch (message)
 {
   case WM_PAINT:
     hdc = BeginPaint(hWnd, &ps);
     while (true)
     {
       HFONT hf = CreateFont(10, 10, 0, 0, 0, 0, 0, 0, 0, 0, 0, 0, 0, L"Arial");
       HPEN hp = CreatePen(0, 10, RGB(10, 20, 30));
       SelectObject(ps.hdc, hf);
       SelectObject(ps.hdc, hp);
     }
```

```
        EndPaint(hWnd, &ps);
        break;
```

We see that roughly the same number of allocations is split between "Gla:" and "Gh0@" pool tags:

```
 Pool Used:
             NonPaged              Paged
 Tag     Allocs      Used      Allocs      Used
 NV_x        0         0           5  14024704 UNKNOWN pooltag 'NV_x', please update pooltag.txt
 BIG         0         0         262   3874816 Large session pool allocations (ntos\ex\pool.c) , Binary:
nt!mm
 Gla:        0         0        5203   3413168 Gdi handle manager specific object types allocated from
lookaside memory: defined in w32\ntgdi\inc\ntgdistr.h , Binary: win32k.sys
 NV          0         0         203   1347648 nVidia video driver
 Gh0@        0         0        5077   1137248 Gdi Handle manager specific object types: defined in
w32\ntgdi\inc\ntgdistr.h , Binary: win32k.sys
 Ttfd        0         0         233   1053152 TrueType Font driver
```

The third program leaks fonts, pens, and brushes:

```
LRESULT CALLBACK WndProc(HWND hWnd, UINT message, WPARAM wParam, LPARAM lParam)
{
 int wmId, wmEvent;
 PAINTSTRUCT ps;
 HDC hdc;

 switch (message)
 {
   case WM_PAINT:
   hdc = BeginPaint(hWnd, &ps);
   while (true)
   {
     HFONT hf = CreateFont(10, 10, 0, 0, 0, 0, 0, 0, 0, 0, 0, 0, 0, L"Arial");
     HPEN hp = CreatePen(0, 10, RGB(10, 20, 30));
     HBRUSH hb = CreateSolidBrush(RGB(10, 20, 30));
     SelectObject(ps.hdc, hf);
     SelectObject(ps.hdc, hp);
     SelectObject(ps.hdc, hb);
   }
   EndPaint(hWnd, &ps);
   break;
```

Now we see that the same number of allocations is almost equally split between "Gla:", "Gh0@", and "Gla@" pool tags:

```
Pool Used:
                NonPaged            Paged
Tag      Allocs      Used     Allocs      Used
NV_x          0         0          5 14024704 UNKNOWN pooltag 'NV_x', please update pooltag.txt
BIG           0         0        262  3874816 Large session pool allocations (ntos\ex\pool.c) , Binary:
nt!mm
Gla:          0         0       3539  2321584 Gdi handle manager specific object types allocated from
lookaside memory: defined in w32\ntgdi\inc\ntgdistr.h , Binary: win32k.sys
NV            0         0        203  1347648 nVidia video driver
Ttfd          0         0        233  1053152 TrueType Font driver
Gh05          0         0        392  1052768 Gdi Handle manager specific object types: defined in
w32\ntgdi\inc\ntgdistr.h , Binary: win32k.sys
Gla1          0         0        353   796368 Gdi handle manager specific object types allocated from
lookaside memory: defined in w32\ntgdi\inc\ntgdistr.h , Binary: win32k.sys
Gh0@          0         0       3414   764736 Gdi Handle manager specific object types: defined in
w32\ntgdi\inc\ntgdistr.h , Binary: win32k.sys
Gla@          0         0       3665   762320 Gdi handle manager specific object types allocated from
lookaside memory: defined in w32\ntgdi\inc\ntgdistr.h , Binary: win32k.sys
Gcac          0         0         25   640880 Gdi glyph cache
```

When the certain amount of handles is reached, all subsequent GDI *Create* calls fail, and other applications start showing various visual defects. Print screen operation also fails with insufficient memory message.

User Space

Windows imposes a restriction on the number of GDI handles per process, and by default, it is approx. 10,000. If this number is reached, we can have abnormal software behavior symptoms such as hangs, glitches in visual appearance, and out-of-memory exceptions resulted in error messages and crashes. We already documented this analysis pattern for kernel and complete memory dumps that we called **Handle Limit** (**GDI**, **Kernel Space**, page 466). However, one of Software Diagnostics Services' training customers reported an out-of-memory exception with trace analysis diagnostics pointing to 10,000 leaked GDI objects. The process memory dump was saved, and the customer asked whether it was possible to analyze it, or similar memory dumps to find out from the dump itself whether we have GDI leak and what GDI objects were involved.

We recreated one of the applications from the kernel pattern variant (the one that leaks fonts) with one modification that it just stops after 10,000 font creation attempts. After launch, we tried to open *About* dialog box, but the whole application became unresponsive, and no dialog box was visible. We save the process memory dump and found out that its **Main Thread** (page 694) was inside **Dialog Box** (page 252) processing:

```
0:000> kc
# Call Site
00 user32!NtUserWaitMessage
01 user32!DialogBox2
02 user32!InternalDialogBox
03 user32!DialogBoxIndirectParamAorW
04 user32!DialogBoxParamW
05 GUIHandleLeak!WndProc
06 user32!UserCallWinProcCheckWow
07 user32!DispatchMessageWorker
08 GUIHandleLeak!wWinMain
09 GUIHandleLeak!invoke_main
0a GUIHandleLeak!__scrt_common_main_seh
0b kernel32!BaseThreadInitThunk
0c ntdll!RtlUserThreadStart
```

In order to look at GDI handle table we studied the relevant chapters in Feng Yuan's book "Windows Graphics Programming" and the post[86] which has all necessary structure definitions.

We get the current process GDI table address from the disassembly:

```
0:000> .asm no_code_bytes
Assembly options: no_code_bytes

0:000> uf gdi32!GdiQueryTable
gdi32!GdiQueryTable:
00007ffc`7f172610 sub      rsp,38h
00007ffc`7f172614 or       qword ptr [rsp+20h],0FFFFFFFFFFFFFFFFh
```

---

[86] http://stackoverflow.com/questions/13905661/how-to-get-list-of-gdi-handles

```
00007ffc`7f17261a lea      rdx,[rsp+20h]
00007ffc`7f17261f mov      ecx,0Eh
00007ffc`7f172624 mov      byte ptr [rsp+28h],0
00007ffc`7f172629 call     qword ptr [gdi32!_imp_NtVdmControl (00007ffc`7f1ba5a8)]
00007ffc`7f17262f test     eax,eax
00007ffc`7f172631 js       gdi32!GdiQueryTable+0x33 (00007ffc`7f172643)  Branch

gdi32!GdiQueryTable+0x23:
00007ffc`7f172633 cmp      byte ptr [rsp+28h],0
00007ffc`7f172638 je       gdi32!GdiQueryTable+0x33 (00007ffc`7f172643)  Branch

gdi32!GdiQueryTable+0x2a:
00007ffc`7f17263a mov      rax,qword ptr [gdi32!pGdiSharedHandleTable (00007ffc`7f2541b8)]
00007ffc`7f172641 jmp      gdi32!GdiQueryTable+0x35 (00007ffc`7f172645)  Branch

gdi32!GdiQueryTable+0x33:
00007ffc`7f172643 xor      eax,eax

gdi32!GdiQueryTable+0x35:
00007ffc`7f172645 add      rsp,38h
00007ffc`7f172649 ret

0:000> dp 00007ffc`7f2541b8 L1
00007ffc`7f2541b8  000000db`56a50000
```

We dump the first 0x1000 qword values:

```
0:000> dq 000000db`56a50000 L1000
000000db`56a50000  00000000`00000000 40000000`00000000
000000db`56a50010  00000000`00000000 00000000`00000000
000000db`56a50020  40000000`00000000 00000000`00000000
000000db`56a50030  00000000`00000000 00000000`00000000
000000db`56a50040  00000000`00000000 00000000`00000000
000000db`56a50050  00000000`00000000 00000000`00000000
000000db`56a50060  00000000`00000000 00000000`00000000
000000db`56a50070  00000000`00000000 00000000`00000000
000000db`56a50080  00000000`00000000 00000000`00000000
000000db`56a50090  00000000`00000000 00000000`00000000
000000db`56a500a0  00000000`00000000 00000000`00000000
000000db`56a500b0  00000000`00000000 00000000`00000000
000000db`56a500c0  00000000`00000000 00000000`00000000
000000db`56a500d0  00000000`00000000 00000000`00000000
000000db`56a500e0  00000000`00000000 00000000`00000000
000000db`56a500f0  fffff901`40000e60 40040104`00000000
000000db`56a50100  00000000`00000000 fffff901`40000d60
000000db`56a50110  40080188`00000000 00000000`00000000
000000db`56a50120  fffff901`400008b0 40080108`00000000
000000db`56a50130  00000000`00000000 fffff901`400007c0
000000db`56a50140  40080108`00000000 00000000`00000000
000000db`56a50150  fffff901`400006d0 40080108`00000000
[...]
000000db`56a57ce0  fffff901`429d24f0 400aee0a`00002c30
000000db`56a57cf0  000000db`564f3b20 fffff901`42910570
000000db`56a57d00  400a360a`00002c30 000000db`564e57b0
```

```
000000db`56a57d10  fffff901`40700420 40105310`000002b4
000000db`56a57d20  00000089`39410fc0 fffff901`407ec4a0
000000db`56a57d30  400a010a`000002b4 00000089`3900ae70
000000db`56a57d40  fffff901`407036d0 400a010a`000002b4
000000db`56a57d50  00000089`3900ae60 fffff901`440b56e0
000000db`56a57d60  400a030a`00002c30 000000db`564f0e90
000000db`56a57d70  fffff901`43e7fd50 40040104`00000000
000000db`56a57d80  00000000`00000000 fffff901`42c0f010
000000db`56a57d90  400a4b0a`00003190 0000003a`1a30b670
000000db`56a57da0  fffff901`440deaf0 400a6d0a`00002c30
000000db`56a57db0  000000db`564f3b00 fffff901`407f2010
000000db`56a57dc0  40100510`00001704 000000d8`d6230f60
000000db`56a57dd0  fffff901`40714180 40100210`00001704
000000db`56a57de0  000000d8`d6230f48 fffff901`4009d840
000000db`56a57df0  40100210`00001704 000000d8`d6230f78
000000db`56a57e00  fffff901`43e50950 40100230`00001704
000000db`56a57e10  00000000`00000000 fffff901`43e30010
000000db`56a57e20  40100230`00001704 00000000`00000000
000000db`56a57e30  fffff901`44f1d010 4005a105`0000168c
000000db`56a57e40  00000000`00000000 fffff901`440ded80
000000db`56a57e50  400a2e0a`00002c30 000000db`564f3b10
000000db`56a57e60  fffff901`4070b3b0 40050405`00000000
000000db`56a57e70  00000000`00000000 fffff901`42a0a010
000000db`56a57e80  400a870a`00002c30 000000db`564e7160
000000db`56a57e90  fffff901`407a7450 4008cd08`00000000
000000db`56a57ea0  00000000`00000000 fffff901`400c49c0
000000db`56a57eb0  40046904`000002b4 00000089`39410f90
000000db`56a57ec0  fffff901`41fb8010 4005c705`00000000
000000db`56a57ed0  00000000`00000000 fffff901`423dc790
000000db`56a57ee0  40086708`00000000 00000000`00000000
000000db`56a57ef0  fffff901`40699620 40010301`0000168c
000000db`56a57f00  00000000`01100000 fffff901`43e54510
000000db`56a57f10  40050305`0000168c 00000000`00000000
000000db`56a57f20  fffff901`407164c0 40100610`00001448
000000db`56a57f30  000000fe`4d8d0cf0 fffff901`407eee50
000000db`56a57f40  40100410`00001448 000000fe`4d8d0cd8
000000db`56a57f50  fffff901`43e2abb0 40080508`00000000
000000db`56a57f60  00000000`00000000 fffff901`40715010
000000db`56a57f70  40050305`0000168c 00000000`00000000
000000db`56a57f80  fffff901`42872b80 40084e08`00000000
000000db`56a57f90  00000000`00000000 fffff901`407175a0
000000db`56a57fa0  410f080f`00000000 00000000`00000000
000000db`56a57fb0  fffff901`407f4000 40050605`00000000
000000db`56a57fc0  00000000`00000000 fffff901`406d6bb0
000000db`56a57fd0  40080508`00000000 00000000`00000000
000000db`56a57fe0  fffff901`43e3a4c0 40120812`00000000
000000db`56a57ff0  00000000`00000000 fffff901`44fe1010
```

We see that typical cell value has 3 qwords (8-byte or 4-word sized values for both x64 and **Virtualized Process**, page 1185). The non-zeroed data starts from **000000db`56a500f0** address. Clearly, some entries have *wProcessId* equal to the PID from our dump:

```
0:000> ~
.  0  Id: 2c30.292c Suspend: 0 Teb: 00007ff7`1bf3e000 Unfrozen
```

Let's look at one of such entries (the first and the last qword values are pointers):

```
0:000> dq 000000db`56a57da0 L3
000000db`56a57da0  fffff901`440deaf0 400a6d0a`00002c30
000000db`56a57db0  000000db`564f3b00

0:000> dw 000000db`56a57da0 L3*4
000000db`56a57da0  eaf0 440d f901 ffff 2c30 0000 6d0a 400a
000000db`56a57db0  3b00 564f 00db 0000
```

Applying 7f to wType word 400a gives us 0xa or 10 which is a font handle:

```
0:000> ? 400a & 7f
Evaluate expression: 10 = 00000000`0000000a
```

Since there are entries from other processes from the same session in this table assessing the handle leak visually is difficult so we wrote a WinDbg script that goes from the first non-zero *pKernelAddress* ($t0) to the first zero entry and for the given *wProcessId* ($tpid) counts the number of entries ($t1) and the number of entries ($t3) for the given wType ($t2). The script also counts the total entries till the first zero one ($t4):

```
.while (qwo(@$t0)) { .if (wo(@$t0+8) == @$tpid) {r $t1 = @$t1+1; .if (((qwo(@$t0+8) >> 0n48) & 7f) ==
@$t2) {r $t3 = @$t3+1} }; r $t0 = @$t0+3*8; r $t4 = @$t4+1}
```

To execute it we prepare the variables:

```
0:000> r $t0=000000db`56a500f0

0:000> r $t1=0

0:000> r $t2=a

0:000> r $t3=0

0:000> r $t4=0

0:000> .while (qwo(@$t0)) { .if (wo(@$t0+8) == @$tpid) {r $t1 = @$t1+1; .if (((qwo(@$t0+8) >> 0n48) & 7f)
== @$t2) {r $t3 = @$t3+1} }; r $t0 = @$t0+3*8; r $t4 = @$t4+1}
```

After execution we get the modified variables that show us that the total consecutive non-zero handle table entries is 21464, the total number of entries for the current process is 9990, and the total number of fonts is 9982:

```
0:000> ? $t0
Evaluate expression: 942052007216 = 000000db`56acdd30

0:000> ? $t1
Evaluate expression: 9990 = 00000000`00002706
```

```
0:000> ? $t2
Evaluate expression: 10 = 00000000`0000000a

0:000> ? $t3
Evaluate expression: 9982 = 00000000`000026fe

0:000> ? $t4
Evaluate expression: 21464 = 00000000`000053d8
```

If we repeat the same script for device contexts (*wType* is 1) we get only 2 entries for our PID:

```
0:000> r $t0=000000db`56a500f0

0:000> r $t1=0

0:000> r $t2=1

0:000> r $t3=0

0:000> r $t4=0

0:000> .while (qwo(@$t0)) { .if (wo(@$t0+8) == @$tpid) {r $t1 = @$t1+1; .if (((qwo(@$t0+8) >> 0n48)  &
7f) == @$t2) {r $t3 = @$t3+1} }; r $t0 = @$t0+3*8; r $t4 = @$t4+1}

0:000> ? $t3
Evaluate expression: 2 = 00000000`00000002
```

Of course, this script may be further improved, for example, to process all possible *wType* values and print their statistics. It can also be made as a textual WinDbg script procedure with arguments.

Handled Exception

.NET CLR

Similar to unmanaged user space **Handled Exceptions** (page 483) residue we can see a similar one on raw stacks of .NET CLR threads. Here are some typical fragments (x86, CLR 4 has similar residue):

```
[...]
09c8e1e0 79ef2dee mscorwks!ExInfo::Init+0x41
09c8e1e4 00004000
09c8e1e8 79f088cc mscorwks!`string'
09c8e1ec 79f088c2 mscorwks!ExInfo::UnwindExInfo+0x14d
09c8e1f0 08f68728
09c8e1f4 95f5b898
09c8e1f8 09c8e1a4
09c8e1fc 09c8e92c
09c8e200 7a34d0d8 mscorwks!GetManagedNameForTypeInfo+0x22b02
09c8e204 79f091ee mscorwks!COMPlusCheckForAbort+0x15
09c8e208 00000000
09c8e20c 0aada664
09c8e210 0aaabff4
09c8e214 00000000
09c8e218 09c8eeec
09c8e21c 074c1f23
09c8e220 09c8ef0c
09c8e224 79f091cb mscorwks!JIT_EndCatch+0x16
09c8e228 09c8ef0c
09c8e22c 09c8eeec
09c8e230 074c1f23
09c8e234 09c8e25c
09c8e238 0009c108
09c8e23c 09c8e460
09c8e240 09c8e5c4
09c8e244 00071d88
09c8e248 08f68728
09c8e24c 79e734c4 mscorwks!ClrFlsSetValue+0x57
09c8e250 95f5b8e4
09c8e254 0aada634
09c8e258 08f68728
09c8e25c 0aada90c
09c8e260 0aaabff4
09c8e264 00000002
09c8e268 09c8e304
09c8e26c 0aada664
09c8e270 00000000
09c8e274 09c8ef0c
09c8e278 09c8e234
09c8e27c 074c1f13
09c8e280 00000000
09c8e284 08f688a0
09c8e288 09c8e234
09c8e28c 79f00c0b mscorwks!Thread::ReturnToContext+0x4e2
09c8e290 0aada90c
09c8e294 09c8eef4
```

```
09c8e298 09c8e2bc
09c8e29c 79f08eb8 mscorwks!EEJitManager::ResumeAtJitEH+0x28
09c8e2a0 09c8e460
09c8e2a4 074c1ed8
09c8e2a8 074b41a8
09c8e2ac 00000000
09c8e2b0 08f68728
09c8e2b4 00000000
09c8e2b8 09c8e410
09c8e2bc 09c8e3c8
09c8e2c0 79f08df5 mscorwks!COMPlusUnwindCallback+0x7c3
09c8e2c4 09c8e460
09c8e2c8 074b41a8
09c8e2cc 00000000
09c8e2d0 08f68728
09c8e2d4 00000000
09c8e2d8 0009c108
09c8e2dc 09c8e410
09c8e2e0 09c8e5c4
09c8e2e4 074b41a8
09c8e2e8 09c8e3a4
09c8e2ec 79e734c4 mscorwks!ClrFlsSetValue+0x57
09c8e2f0 95f5b984
09c8e2f4 0009c128
09c8e2f8 09c8e3a4
09c8e2fc 00000000
09c8e300 00000000
09c8e304 00000002
[...]
09c8e4e4 00000000
09c8e4e8 79f09160 mscorwks!_CT??_R0H+0x34b4
09c8e4ec ffffffff
09c8e4f0 73792e2f msvcr80!_getptd+0x6
09c8e4f4 ffffffff
09c8e4f8 737b7a78 msvcr80!__FrameUnwindToState+0xd9
09c8e4fc 737b7a5e msvcr80!__FrameUnwindToState+0xbf
09c8e500 95f5bc05
09c8e504 e06d7363
09c8e508 1fffffff
09c8e50c 19930522
09c8e510 ffffffff
09c8e514 ffffffff
09c8e518 09c8e500
09c8e51c 09c8e554
09c8e520 09c8e5a8
09c8e524 73798cd9 msvcr80!_except_handler4
09c8e528 efbc0d3d
09c8e52c fffffffe
09c8e530 737b7a5e msvcr80!__FrameUnwindToState+0xbf
09c8e534 737b89cb msvcr80!__InternalCxxFrameHandler+0x6d
09c8e538 09c8eab0
09c8e53c 09c8e6a0
09c8e540 79f09160 mscorwks!_CT??_R0H+0x34b4
09c8e544 ffffffff
09c8e548 00000000
09c8e54c 00000000
```

```
09c8e550  00000000
09c8e554  09c8e590
09c8e558  737b8af1 msvcr80!__CxxFrameHandler3+0x26
09c8e55c  09c8e600
09c8e560  09c8eab0
09c8e564  01010101
09c8e568  09000000
09c8e56c  09c8f160
09c8e570  07540c00
09c8e574  00071d88
09c8e578  08e65d48
09c8e57c  09c8e5ec
09c8e580  074c1ec8
09c8e584  00000024
09c8e588  00000001
09c8e58c  0009c108
09c8e590  08f68728
09c8e594  00000000
09c8e598  00000000
09c8e59c  09c8eb38
09c8e5a0  00000000
09c8e5a4  09c8e6a0
09c8e5a8  09c8f15c
09c8e5ac  09c8f15c
09c8e5b0  09c8eb38
09c8e5b4  95f5bf28
09c8e5b8  09c8e8f4
09c8e5bc  79e84bf2 mscorwks!Thread::StackWalkFrames+0xb8
09c8e5c0  08f68728
09c8e5c4  09c8ea40
09c8e5c8  79e84bf2 mscorwks!Thread::StackWalkFrames+0xb8
09c8e5cc  09c8e5ec
09c8e5d0  79f07d64 mscorwks!COMPlusUnwindCallback
09c8e5d4  09c8ea40
09c8e5d8  00000005
09c8e5dc  00000000
09c8e5e0  08f68728
09c8e5e4  08f688a0
09c8e5e8  08f68728
09c8e5ec  09c8ec20
09c8e5f0  00000000
09c8e5f4  09c8ecbc
09c8e5f8  09c8ecc0
09c8e5fc  09c8ecc4
09c8e600  09c8ecc8
09c8e604  09c8eccc
09c8e608  09c8ecd0
09c8e60c  09c8ecd4
09c8e610  09c8eeec
09c8e614  09c8ecd8
09c8e618  09c8ecd8
09c8e61c  00000024
09c8e620  00000000
09c8e624  0009c108
09c8e628  08f68728
09c8e62c  00000000
```

```
09c8e630 00000000
09c8e634 79e71ba4 mscorwks!Thread::CatchAtSafePoint
09c8e638 00000000
09c8e63c 79e71ba4 mscorwks!Thread::CatchAtSafePoint
09c8e640 09c8f15c
09c8e644 09c8f15c
09c8e648 00000000
09c8e64c 95f5bcc0
09c8e650 09c8e988
09c8e654 79e84bf2 mscorwks!Thread::StackWalkFrames+0xb8
09c8e658 09c8ea40
09c8e65c 79e84bf2 mscorwks!Thread::StackWalkFrames+0xb8
09c8e660 09c8e680
09c8e664 79f07957 mscorwks!COMPlusThrowCallback
09c8e668 09c8ea40
09c8e66c 00000000
09c8e670 00000000
09c8e674 0aada90c
09c8e678 09c8ea40
09c8e67c 79e84bff mscorwks!Thread::StackWalkFrames+0xc5
09c8e680 09c8ec20
09c8e684 00000000
09c8e688 09c8ecbc
09c8e68c 09c8ecc0
09c8e690 09c8ecc4
09c8e694 09c8ecc8
[...]
09c8e8f0 95f5b264
09c8e8f4 09c8e914
09c8e8f8 79f07d5e mscorwks!UnwindFrames+0x62
09c8e8fc 79f07d64 mscorwks!COMPlusUnwindCallback
09c8e900 09c8ea40
09c8e904 00000005
09c8e908 00000000
09c8e90c 09c8ef6c
09c8e910 08f68728
09c8e914 09c8e9a4
09c8e918 79f089cc mscorwks!COMPlusAfterUnwind+0x97
09c8e91c 08f68728
09c8e920 09c8ea40
09c8e924 00000001
09c8e928 00000000
09c8e92c 09c8ef6c
09c8e930 79f0a3d9 mscorwks!COMPlusNestedExceptionHandler
09c8e934 09c8f160
09c8e938 00000000
09c8e93c 00000000
09c8e940 cccccccc
[...]
```

Sometimes we can see *'ExecuteHandler'* calls if they were not overwritten:

```
[...]
09d2e6e0 00000000
09d2e6e4 00000720
09d2e6e8 77c41039 ntdll!ExecuteHandler2+0x26
09d2e6ec 09d2e7c8
09d2e6f0 09d2eb60
09d2e6f4 09d2e7e4
09d2e6f8 09d2e7a4
09d2e6fc 09d2eb60
09d2e700 77c4104d ntdll!ExecuteHandler2+0x3a
09d2e704 09d2eb60
09d2e708 09d2e7b0
09d2e70c 77c4100b ntdll!ExecuteHandler+0x24
09d2e710 09d2e7c8
09d2e714 00000001
09d2e718 09d2e6b0
09d2e71c 09d2e7a4
09d2e720 09d2e784
09d2e724 76545ac9 kernel32!_except_handler4
[...]
```

If there are such traces they can be visible as **Caller-n-Callee** (page 122) pattern:

```
0:011> !DumpStack
OS Thread Id: 0x3cc (11)
Current frame: ntdll!KiFastSystemCallRet
ChildEBP RetAddr Caller, Callee
09d2e690 77c40690 ntdll!ZwWaitForMultipleObjects+0xc
09d2e694 76577e09 kernel32!WaitForMultipleObjectsEx+0x11d, calling ntdll!NtWaitForMultipleObjects
09d2e6d8 76578101 kernel32!WaitForMultipleObjectsEx+0x33, calling ntdll! 09d2e6e4 77c41039 ntdll!ExecuteHandler2+0x26
09d2e708 77c4100b ntdll!ExecuteHandler+0x24, calling ntdll!ExecuteHandler2
09d2e730 6baa516a clr!WaitForMultipleObjectsEx_SO_TOLERANT+0x56, calling RtlActivateActivationContextUnsafeFast
kernel32!WaitForMultipleObjectsEx
09d2e794 6baa4f98 clr!Thread::DoAppropriateAptStateWait+0x4d, calling clr!WaitForMultipleObjectsEx_SO_TOLERANT
09d2e7b4 6baa4dd8 clr!Thread::DoAppropriateWaitWorker+0x17d, calling clr!Thread::DoAppropriateAptStateWait
09d2e848 6baa4e99 clr!Thread::DoAppropriateWait+0x60, calling clr!Thread::DoAppropriateWaitWorker
09d2e8b4 6baa4f17 clr!CLREvent::WaitEx+0x106, calling clr!Thread::DoAppropriateWait
09d2e8e0 6baa484b clr!CLRGetTickCount64+0x6b, calling clr!_allmul
09d2e908 6baa4409 clr!CLREvent::Wait+0x19, calling clr!CLREvent::WaitEx
[...]
```

Comments

x64 example:

```
0000002afc23d480 00007ff92d0c950b clr!ProcessCLRException+0x2e9, calling clr!ClrUnwindEx
00007ff9577beced ntdll!RtlpExecuteHandlerForException+0xd
```

!DumpStack also accepts the range parameter, for example, from **!teb** (like **dps** or **dpS**).

Kernel Space

This is a variant of **Handled Exception** pattern in kernel space similar to the user (page 483) and managed spaces (page 477). The crash dump was the same as in **Hidden Exception** in kernel space pattern (page 504):

```
fffff880`0a83d910 00000000`00000000
fffff880`0a83d918 fffff6fc`40054fd8
fffff880`0a83d920 fffff880`0a83dca0
fffff880`0a83d928 fffff800`016bcc1c nt!_C_specific_handler+0xcc
fffff880`0a83d930 00000000`00000000
fffff880`0a83d938 00000000`00000000
fffff880`0a83d940 00000000`00000000
fffff880`0a83d948 00000000`00000000
fffff880`0a83d950 fffff800`0189ee38 nt!BBTBuffer <PERF> (nt+0x280e38)
fffff880`0a83d958 fffff880`0a83e940
fffff880`0a83d960 fffff800`016ad767 nt!IopCompleteRequest+0x147
fffff880`0a83d968 fffff880`0a83de40
fffff880`0a83d970 fffff800`01665e40 nt!_GSHandlerCheck_SEH
fffff880`0a83d978 fffff800`017e5338 nt!_imp_NtOpenSymbolicLinkObject+0xfe30
fffff880`0a83d980 fffff880`0a83e310
fffff880`0a83d988 00000000`00000000
fffff880`0a83d990 00000000`00000000
fffff880`0a83d998 fffff800`016b42dd nt!RtlpExecuteHandlerForException+0xd
fffff880`0a83d9a0 fffff800`017d7d0c nt!_imp_NtOpenSymbolicLinkObject+0x2804
fffff880`0a83d9a8 fffff880`0a83eab0
fffff880`0a83d9b0 00000000`00000000


0: kd> ub fffff800`016b42dd
nt!RtlpExceptionHandler+0x24:
fffff800`016b42c4 cc              int 3
fffff800`016b42c5 cc              int 3
fffff800`016b42c6 cc              int 3
fffff800`016b42c7 cc              int 3
fffff800`016b42c8 0f1f840000000000 nop dword ptr [rax+rax]
nt!RtlpExecuteHandlerForException:
fffff800`016b42d0 4883ec28        sub rsp,28h
fffff800`016b42d4 4c894c2420      mov qword ptr [rsp+20h],r9
fffff800`016b42d9 41ff5130        call qword ptr [r9+30h]
```

User Space

If we do not see exception codes when we inspect raw stack data we, nevertheless, in some cases may see execution residue left after calling exception handlers. For example, we can see that when we launch TestWER[87] tool and select *'Handled Exception'* checkbox:

If we then click on a button and then save a process memory dump using Task Manager we find the following traces on a raw stack:

```
0:000> !teb
TEB at 7efdd000
ExceptionList:           0018fe20
StackBase:               00190000
StackLimit:              0018d000
SubSystemTib:            00000000
FiberData:               00001e00
ArbitraryUserPointer:    00000000
Self:                    7efdd000
EnvironmentPointer:      00000000
ClientId:                00000b38 . 00000f98
RpcHandle:               00000000
Tls Storage:             7efdd02c
PEB Address:             7efde000
LastErrorValue:          0
LastStatusValue:         c0000034
Count Owned Locks:       0
HardErrorMode:           0
```

```
0:000> dps 0018d000 00190000
[...]
0018f414 00000000
0018f418 0018f840
0018f41c 0018f4cc
0018f420 77726a9b ntdll!ExecuteHandler+0x24
0018f424 0018f4e4
0018f428 0018f840
0018f42c 0018f534
0018f430 0018f4b8
0018f434 00412600 TestWER!_except_handler4
0018f438 00000001
0018f43c 00000000
[...]


0:000> ub 77726a9b
ntdll!ExecuteHandler+0x7:
77726a7e 33f6 xor esi,esi
77726a80 33ff xor edi,edi
77726a82 ff742420 push dword ptr [esp+20h]
77726a86 ff742420 push dword ptr [esp+20h]
77726a8a ff742420 push dword ptr [esp+20h]
77726a8e ff742420 push dword ptr [esp+20h]
77726a92 ff742420 push dword ptr [esp+20h]
77726a96 e808000000 call ntdll!ExecuteHandler2 (77726aa3)
```

If we compare the output above with the raw stack fragment from the second chance exception memory dump (after we relaunch TestWER, do not select *'Handled Exception'* checkbox and click on the big lightning button) we would see the similar call fragment:

```
[...]
0018f3f4 00dd0aa7
0018f3f8 0018f41c
0018f3fc 77726ac9 ntdll!ExecuteHandler2+0x26
0018f400 fffffffe
0018f404 0018ffc4
0018f408 0018f534
0018f40c 0018f4b8
0018f410 0018f840
0018f414 77726add ntdll!ExecuteHandler2+0x3a
0018f418 0018ffc4
0018f41c 0018f4cc
0018f420 77726a9b ntdll!ExecuteHandler+0x24
0018f424 0018f4e4
0018f428 0018ffc4
0018f42c 0018f534
0018f430 0018f4b8
0018f434 77750ae5 ntdll!_except_handler4
0018f438 00000000
0018f43c 0018f4e4
0018f440 0018ffc4
0018f444 77726a3d ntdll!RtlDispatchException+0x127
0018f448 0018f4e4
0018f44c 0018ffc4
0018f450 0018f534
```

```
0018f454 0018f4b8
0018f458 77750ae5 ntdll!_except_handler4
0018f45c 00000111
0018f460 0018f4e4
[...]
```

Sometimes, we can also see *"Unwind"*, *"StackWalk"*, *"WalkFrames"*, *"EH"*, *"Catch"* functions too. Sometimes we do not see anything because such residue was overwritten by subsequent function calls after **Handled Exceptions** happened sometime in the past.

Comments

If we get several same first chance exception dumps for the same process, it means that it was handled. Otherwise, we would not see the subsequent dumps.

Hardware Activity

Sometimes, when a high number of interrupts is reported, but there are no signs of an interrupt storm[88] or pending DPCs in a memory dump file it is useful to search for this pattern in running and / or suspected threads. This can be done by examining execution residue left on a thread raw stack. Although the found driver activity may not be related to reported problems, it can be a useful start for a driver elimination procedure for a general recommendation to check suspected drivers for any updates. Here is an example of a thread raw stack with a network card doing "Scatter-Gather" DMA:

```
1: kd> !thread
THREAD f7732090 Cid 0000.0000 Teb: 00000000 Win32Thread: 00000000 RUNNING on processor 1
Not impersonating
Owning Process 8089db40 Image: Idle
Attached Process N/A Image: N/A
Wait Start TickCount 0 Ticks: 24437545 (4:10:03:56.640)
Context Switch Count 75624870
UserTime 00:00:00.000
KernelTime 4 Days 08:56:05.125
Stack Init f78b3000 Current f78b2d4c Base f78b3000 Limit f78b0000 Call 0
Priority 0 BasePriority 0 PriorityDecrement 0
ChildEBP RetAddr Args to Child
f3b30c5c 00000000 00000000 00000000 00000000 LiveKdD+0x1c07


1: kd> dds f78b0000 f78b3000
f78b0000 00000000
f78b0004 00000000
f78b0008 00000000
f78b000c 00000000
f78b0010 00000000
[...]
f78b2870 8b3de0d0
f78b2874 80887b75 nt!KiFlushTargetSingleTb+0xd
f78b2878 8b49032c
f78b287c 00000000
f78b2880 2d003202
f78b2884 00000000
f78b2888 00000000
f78b288c 2d003202
f78b2890 8b490302
f78b2894 f78b28a4
f78b2898 80a61456 hal!KfLowerIrql+0x62
f78b289c 2d00320a
f78b28a0 00000000
f78b28a4 8b3de0d0
f78b28a8 8b3e3730
f78b28ac 00341eb0
f78b28b0 f78b2918
```

---

[88] https://docs.microsoft.com/en-us/windows-hardware/drivers/debugger/debugging-an-interrupt-storm

```
f78b28b4 f63fbf78 NetworkAdapterA!SendWithScatterGather+0x318
f78b28b8 8b3de0d0
f78b28bc 8b341eb0
f78b28c0 f78b28d4
f78b28c4 00000000
f78b28c8 80a5f3c0 hal!KfAcquireSpinLock
f78b28cc 00000000
f78b28d0 8b3de0d0
f78b28d4 00000000
f78b28d8 8b3de0d0
f78b28dc 8b3eb730
f78b28e0 005a7340
f78b28e4 f78b294c
f78b28e8 f63fbf78 NetworkAdapterA!SendWithScatterGather+0x318
f78b28ec 8b3de0d0
f78b28f0 8a5a7340
f78b28f4 f78b2908
f78b28f8 00000000
f78b28fc 8b3de0d0
f78b2900 8b0f5158
f78b2904 001e2340
f78b2908 f78b2970
f78b290c f63fbf78 NetworkAdapterA!SendWithScatterGather+0x318
f78b2910 8b3de0d0
f78b2914 8b1e2340
f78b2918 f78b292c
f78b291c 00000000
f78b2920 80a5f3c0 hal!KfAcquireSpinLock
f78b2924 00000000
f78b2928 8b3de0d0
f78b292c 00000000
f78b2930 8b3eb700
f78b2934 00000000
f78b2938 00000000
f78b293c 00000000
f78b2940 00000000
f78b2944 00000000
f78b2948 00000000
f78b294c 0a446aa2
f78b2950 f78b29b8
f78b2954 8b0f5158
f78b2958 8b01ce10
f78b295c 00000001
f78b2960 8b3de0d0
f78b2964 80a5f302 hal!HalpPerfInterrupt+0x32
f78b2968 00000001
f78b296c 8b3de0d0
f78b2970 80a5f302 hal!HalpPerfInterrupt+0x32
f78b2974 8b3de302
f78b2978 f78b2988
f78b297c 80a61456 hal!KfLowerIrql+0x62
f78b2980 80a5f3c0 hal!KfAcquireSpinLock
f78b2984 8b3de302
f78b2988 f78b29a4
f78b298c 80a5f44b hal!KfReleaseSpinLock+0xb
f78b2990 f63fbbbf NetworkAdapterA!SendPackets+0x1b3
```

```
f78b2994 8a446a90
f78b2998 8b0e8ab0
f78b299c 00000000
f78b29a0 008b29d0
f78b29a4 f78b29bc
f78b29a8 f7163790 NDIS!ndisMProcessSGList+0x90
f78b29ac 8b3de388
f78b29b0 f78b29d0
f78b29b4 00000001
f78b29b8 00000000
f78b29bc f78b29e8
f78b29c0 80a60147 hal!HalBuildScatterGatherList+0x1c7
f78b29c4 8b0e89b0
f78b29c8 00000000
f78b29cc 8a44cde8
f78b29d0 8b1e2340
f78b29d4 8a446aa2
f78b29d8 8b026ca0
f78b29dc 8b1e2340
f78b29e0 8b0e8ab0
f78b29e4 8b0e8ab0
f78b29e8 f78b2a44
f78b29ec f716369f NDIS!ndisMAllocSGList+0xda
f78b29f0 8a44cde8
f78b29f4 8b0e89b0
f78b29f8 8a446a70
f78b29fc 00000000
f78b2a00 00000036
f78b2a04 f7163730 NDIS!ndisMProcessSGList
f78b2a08 8b1e2340
f78b2a0c 00000000
f78b2a10 8a44cde8
f78b2a14 00000218
f78b2a18 8b1e2308
[...]
f78b2a40 029a9e02
f78b2a44 f78b2a60
f78b2a48 f71402ff NDIS!ndisMSendX+0x1dd
f78b2a4c 8b490310
f78b2a50 8b1e2340
f78b2a54 8a446a70
f78b2a58 8a9a9e02
f78b2a5c 8a9a9e02
f78b2a60 f78b2a88
f78b2a64 f546c923 tcpip!ARPSendData+0x1a9
f78b2a68 8b3e76c8
f78b2a6c 8b1e2340
f78b2a70 8a9a9ea8
f78b2a74 8b490310
f78b2a78 80888b00 nt!RtlBackoff+0x68
f78b2a7c 8a446a70
f78b2a80 8a446aa2
f78b2a84 8a446a70
f78b2a88 f78b2ab4
f78b2a8c f546ba5d tcpip!ARPTransmit+0x112
f78b2a90 8b490310
```

```
f78b2a94 8b1e2340
f78b2a98 8a9a9ea8
f78b2a9c 00000103
f78b2aa0 8a446a70
f78b2aa4 00000000
f78b2aa8 8b342398
f78b2aac 8a47e1f8
f78b2ab0 8b1e2340
f78b2ab4 f78b2bf0
f78b2ab8 f546c4fc tcpip!_IPTransmit+0x866
f78b2abc 8a9a9ebc
f78b2ac0 f78b2b02
f78b2ac4 00000001
[...]
```

We also do a sanity check for **Coincidental Symbolic Information** (page 145):

```
1: kd> ub f63fbf78
NetworkAdapterA!SendWithScatterGather+0x304:
f63fbf64 push     eax
f63fbf65 push     edi
f63fbf66 push     esi
f63fbf67 mov      dword ptr [ebp-44h],ecx
f63fbf6a mov      dword ptr [ebp-3Ch],ecx
f63fbf6d mov      dword ptr [ebp-34h],ecx
f63fbf70 mov      dword ptr [ebp-2Ch],ecx
f63fbf73 call     NetworkAdapterA!PacketRetrieveNicActions (f63facd2)

1: kd> ub f63fbbbf
NetworkAdapterA!SendPackets+0x190:
f63fbb9c cmp      dword ptr [esi+0Ch],2
f63fbba0 jl       NetworkAdapterA!SendPackets+0x19e (f63fbbaa)
f63fbba2 mov      dword ptr [ecx+3818h],eax
f63fbba8 jmp      NetworkAdapterA!SendPackets+0x1a4 (f63fbbb0)
f63fbbaa mov      dword ptr [ecx+438h],eax
f63fbbb0 mov      dl,byte ptr [esi+2BCh]
f63fbbb6 mov      ecx,dword ptr [ebp+8]
f63fbbb9 call     dword ptr [NetworkAdapterA!_imp_KfReleaseSpinLock (f640ca18)]

1: kd> ub 80a60147
hal!HalBuildScatterGatherList+0x1b0:
80a60130 je       hal!HalBuildScatterGatherList+0x1b9 (80a60139)
80a60132 mov      dword ptr [eax+4],1
80a60139 push     dword ptr [ebp+20h]
80a6013c push     eax
80a6013d mov      eax,dword ptr [ebp+0Ch]
80a60140 push     dword ptr [eax+14h]
80a60143 push     eax
80a60144 call     dword ptr [ebp+1Ch]
```

Hardware Error

This pattern occurs frequently. It can be internal CPU malfunction due to overheating, RAM or hard disk I/O problem that usually results in the appropriate bugcheck. The most frequent one is the 6th from the top of bugcheck frequency table[89]:

- BUGCHECK 9C: MACHINE_CHECK_EXCEPTION

Other relevant bugchecks include:

- BUGCHECK 7B: INACCESSIBLE_BOOT_DEVICE
- BUGCHECK 77: KERNEL_STACK_INPAGE_ERROR
- BUGCHECK 7A: KERNEL_DATA_INPAGE_ERROR

Another bugcheck from this category can be triggered on purpose to get a crash dump of a hanging or slow system[90]:

- BUGCHECK 80: NMI_HARDWARE_FAILURE

Please also note that other popular bugchecks like

- BUGCHECK 7F: UNEXPECTED_KERNEL_MODE_TRAP
- BUGCHECK 50: PAGE_FAULT_IN_NONPAGED_AREA

can result from RAM problems but we should try to find a software cause first.

Sometimes the following bugchecks like

- BUGCHECK 7E: SYSTEM_THREAD_EXCEPTION_NOT_HANDLED

report EXCEPTION_DOESNOT_MATCH_CODE, where read or write address does not correspond to faulted instruction at EIP:

---

[89] Bugcheck Frequencies, Memory Dump Analysis Anthology, Volume 2, page 429
[90] NMI_HARDWARE_FAILURE, Memory Dump Analysis Anthology, Volume 1, page 135

```
SYSTEM_THREAD_EXCEPTION_NOT_HANDLED (7e)
This is a very common bugcheck. Usually the exception address pinpoints
the driver/function that caused the problem. Always note this address
as well as the link date of the driver/image that contains this address.
Arguments:
Arg1: c0000005, The exception code that was not handled
Arg2: bf802671, The address that the exception occurred at
Arg3: f10b8c74, Exception Record Address
Arg4: f10b88c4, Context Record Address

FAULTING_IP:
driver!AcquireSemaphoreShared+4
bf802671 90 nop

EXCEPTION_RECORD: f10b8c74 -- (.exr ffffffff10b8c74)
ExceptionAddress: bf802671 (driver!AcquireSemaphoreShared+0x00000004)
ExceptionCode: c0000005 (Access violation)
ExceptionFlags: 00000000
NumberParameters: 2
Parameter[0]: 00000001
Parameter[1]: 0000000c
Attempt to write to address 0000000c

CONTEXT: f10b88c4 -- (.cxr ffffffff10b88c4)
eax=884d2d01 ebx=0000000c ecx=00000000 edx=80010031 esi=8851ef60 edi=bc3846d4
eip=bf802671 esp=f10b8d3c ebp=f10b8d70 iopl=0 nv up ei pl nz na po nc
cs=0008 ss=0010 ds=0023 es=0023 fs=0030 gs=0000 efl=00010206
driver!AcquireSemaphoreShared+0x4:
```
bf802671 90 nop
```
Resetting default scope

WRITE_ADDRESS: 0000000c
```

EXCEPTION_DOESNOT_MATCH_CODE: This indicates a hardware error.
Instruction at bf802671 does not read/write to 0000000c

Code mismatch can also happen in user mode but from my experience it usually results from improper **Hooked Function** (page 548) or similar corruption:

```
EXCEPTION_RECORD: ffffffff -- (.exr 0xffffffffffffffff)
ExceptionAddress: 7c848768 (ntdll!_LdrpInitialize+0x00000184)
ExceptionCode: c0000005 (Access violation)
ExceptionFlags: 00000001
NumberParameters: 0

DEFAULT_BUCKET_ID: CODE_ADDRESS_MISMATCH

WRITE_ADDRESS: f774f120
```

```
FAULTING_IP:
ntdll!_LdrpInitialize+184
7c848768 cc int 3
```

EXCEPTION_DOESNOT_MATCH_CODE: This indicates a hardware error.
Instruction at 7c848768 does not read/write to f774f120

```
STACK_TEXT:
0012fd14 7c8284c5 0012fd28 7c800000 00000000 ntdll!_LdrpInitialize+0x184
00000000 00000000 00000000 00000000 00000000 ntdll!KiUserApcDispatcher+0x25
```

In such cases, EIP might point to the middle of the expected instruction (see also **Wild Code**, page 1268):

```
FAULTING_IP:
+59c3659
059c3659 86990508f09b xchg bl,byte ptr [ecx-640FF7FBh]
```

Here is another example of the real hardware error (note the concatenated error code for bugcheck 0x9C):

```
MACHINE_CHECK_EXCEPTION (9c)
A fatal Machine Check Exception has occurred.
KeBugCheckEx parameters;
    x86 Processors
        If the processor has ONLY MCE feature available (For example Intel
        Pentium), the parameters are:
        1 - Low  32 bits of P5_MC_TYPE MSR
        2 - Address of MCA_EXCEPTION structure
        3 - High 32 bits of P5_MC_ADDR MSR
        4 - Low  32 bits of P5_MC_ADDR MSR
        If the processor also has MCA feature available (For example Intel
        Pentium Pro), the parameters are:
        1 - Bank number
        2 - Address of MCA_EXCEPTION structure
        3 - High 32 bits of MCi_STATUS MSR for the MCA bank that had the error
        4 - Low  32 bits of MCi_STATUS MSR for the MCA bank that had the error
    IA64 Processors
        1 - Bugcheck Type
            1 - MCA_ASSERT
            2 - MCA_GET_STATEINFO
                SAL returned an error for SAL_GET_STATEINFO while processing MCA.
            3 - MCA_CLEAR_STATEINFO
                SAL returned an error for SAL_CLEAR_STATEINFO while processing MCA.
            4 - MCA_FATAL
                FW reported a fatal MCA.
            5 - MCA_NONFATAL
                SAL reported a recoverable MCA and we don't support currently
                support recovery or SAL generated an MCA and then couldn't
                produce an error record.
            0xB - INIT_ASSERT
            0xC - INIT_GET_STATEINFO
                SAL returned an error for SAL_GET_STATEINFO while processing INIT event.
            0xD - INIT_CLEAR_STATEINFO
                SAL returned an error for SAL_CLEAR_STATEINFO while processing INIT event.
            0xE - INIT_FATAL
                Not used.
```

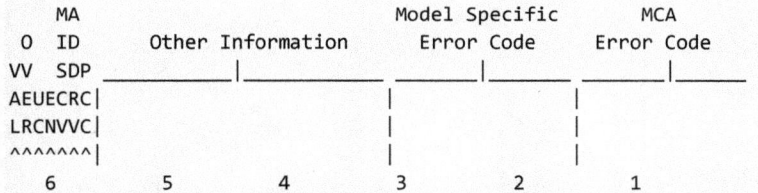

```
        2 - Address of log
        3 - Size of log
        4 - Error code in the case of x_GET_STATEINFO or x_CLEAR_STATEINFO
    AMD64 Processors
        1 - Bank number
        2 - Address of MCA_EXCEPTION structure
        3 - High 32 bits of MCi_STATUS MSR for the MCA bank that had the error
        4 - Low  32 bits of MCi_STATUS MSR for the MCA bank that had the error
Arguments:
Arg1: 00000000
Arg2: 808a07a0
Arg3: be000300
Arg4: 1008081f

Debugging Details:
------------------


    NOTE:  This is a hardware error.  This error was reported by the CPU
    via Interrupt 18.  This analysis will provide more information about
    the specific error.  Please contact the manufacturer for additional
    information about this error and troubleshooting assistance.

    This error is documented in the following publication:

        - IA-32 Intel(r) Architecture Software Developer's Manual
          Volume 3: System Programming Guide

    Bit Mask:

     MA                      Model Specific       MCA
  O  ID    Other Information    Error Code      Error Code
 VV  SDP _____|_____ _____|_____ _____|_____
 AEUECRC|                    |              |
 LRCNVVC|                    |              |
 ^^^^^^^|                    |              |
    6        5        4        3        2        1
 3210987654321098765432109876543210987654321098765432109876543210
 ----------------------------------------------------------------
 1011111000000000000000011000000000001000000001000000010000011111

VAL    - MCi_STATUS register is valid
         Indicates that the information contained within the IA32_MCi_STATUS
         register is valid.  When this flag is set, the processor follows the
         rules given for the OVER flag in the IA32_MCi_STATUS register when
         overwriting previously valid entries.  The processor sets the VAL
         flag and software is responsible for clearing it.

UC     - Error Uncorrected
         Indicates that the processor did not or was not able to correct the
         error condition.  When clear, this flag indicates that the processor
         was able to correct the error condition.

EN     - Error Enabled
         Indicates that the error was enabled by the associated EEj bit of the
         IA32_MCi_CTL register.
```

MISCV - IA32_MCi_MISC Register Valid
        Indicates that the IA32_MCi_MISC register contains additional
        information regarding the error. When clear, this flag indicates
        that the IA32_MCi_MISC register is either not implemented or does
        not contain additional information regarding the error.

ADDRV - IA32_MCi_ADDR register valid
        Indicates that the IA32_MCi_ADDR register contains the address where
        the error occurred.

PCC   - Processor Context Corrupt
        Indicates that the state of the processor might have been corrupted
        by the error condition detected and that reliable restarting of the
        processor may not be possible.

BUSCONNERR - Bus and Interconnect Error   BUS{LL}_{PP}_{RRRR}_{II}_{T}_err
        These errors match the format 0000 1PPT RRRR IILL

    Concatenated Error Code:

    _VAL_UC_EN_MISCV_ADDRV_PCC_BUSCONNERR_1F

    This error code can be reported back to the manufacturer.
    They may be able to provide additional information based upon
    this error. All questions regarding STOP 0x9C should be
    directed to the hardware manufacturer.

BUGCHECK_STR: 0x9C_IA32_GenuineIntel

DEFAULT_BUCKET_ID: DRIVER_FAULT

PROCESS_NAME: Idle

CURRENT_IRQL: 2

LAST_CONTROL_TRANSFER: from 80a7fbd8 to 8087b6be

STACK_TEXT:
f773d280 80a7fbd8 0000009c 00000000 f773d2b0 nt!KeBugCheckEx+0x1b
f773d3b4 80a7786f f7737fe0 00000000 00000000 hal!HalpMcaExceptionHandler+0x11e
f773d3b4 f75a9ca2 f7737fe0 00000000 00000000 hal!HalpMcaExceptionHandlerWrapper+0x77
f78c6d50 8083abf2 00000000 0000000e 00000000 intelppm!AcpiC1Idle+0x12
f78c6d54 00000000 0000000e 00000000 00000000 nt!KiIdleLoop+0xa

Comments

Another possibility of a hardware error: frequent multiple unrelated bugchecks and bugchecks in memory dumps with valid instructions at faulting IP. Beware also about misaligned IP that can look like a valid instruction.

Additional examples:

```
WHEA_UNCORRECTABLE_ERROR (124)
A fatal hardware error has occurred. Parameter 1 identifies the type of error
source that reported the error. Parameter 2 holds the address of the
WHEA_ERROR_RECORD structure that describes the error condition.
Arguments:
Arg1: 0000000000000000, Machine Check Exception
Arg2: fffffa8004b46748, Address of the WHEA_ERROR_RECORD structure.
Arg3: 0000000000000000, High order 32-bits of the MCi_STATUS value.
Arg4: 0000000000000000, Low order 32-bits of the MCi_STATUS value.

1: kd> dt -r _WHEA_ERROR_RECORD fffffa8004b46748
hal!_WHEA_ERROR_RECORD
   +0x000 Header             : _WHEA_ERROR_RECORD_HEADER
      +0x000 Signature          : 0x52455043
      +0x004 Revision           : _WHEA_REVISION
         +0x000 MinorRevision     : 0x10 ''
         +0x001 MajorRevision     : 0x2 ''
         +0x000 AsUSHORT          : 0x210
      +0x006 SignatureEnd       : 0xffffffff
      +0x00a SectionCount       : 3
      +0x00c Severity           : 1 ( WheaErrSevFatal )
      +0x010 ValidBits          : _WHEA_ERROR_RECORD_HEADER_VALIDBITS
         +0x000 PlatformId        : 0y0
         +0x000 Timestamp         : 0y1
         +0x000 PartitionId       : 0y0
         +0x000 Reserved          : 0y000000000000000000000000000000000 (0)
         +0x000 AsULONG           : 2
      +0x014 Length             : 0x3a0
      +0x018 Timestamp          : _WHEA_TIMESTAMP
         +0x000 Seconds           : 0y00100010 (0x22)
         +0x000 Minutes           : 0y00101011 (0x2b)
         +0x000 Hours             : 0y00001100 (0xc)
         +0x000 Precise           : 0y0
         +0x000 Reserved          : 0y0000000 (0)
         +0x000 Day               : 0y00010110 (0x16)
         +0x000 Month             : 0y00000100 (0x4)
         +0x000 Year              : 0y00001010 (0xa)
         +0x000 Century           : 0y00010100 (0x14)
         +0x000 AsLARGE_INTEGER   : _LARGE_INTEGER 0x140a0416`000c2b22
      +0x020 PlatformId         : _GUID {00000000-0000-0000-0000-000000000000}
         +0x000 Data1             : 0
         +0x004 Data2             : 0
         +0x006 Data3             : 0
         +0x008 Data4             : [8]  ""
      +0x030 PartitionId        : _GUID {00000000-0000-0000-0000-000000000000}
         +0x000 Data1             : 0
         +0x004 Data2             : 0
         +0x006 Data3             : 0
         +0x008 Data4             : [8]  ""
      +0x040 CreatorId          : _GUID {cf07c4bd-b789-4e18-b3c4-1f732cb57131}
         +0x000 Data1             : 0xcf07c4bd
         +0x004 Data2             : 0xb789
         +0x006 Data3             : 0x4e18
         +0x008 Data4             : [8]  "???"
      +0x050 NotifyType         : _GUID {e8f56ffe-919c-4cc5-ba88-65abe14913bb}
```

```
      +0x000 Data1                : 0xe8f56ffe
      +0x004 Data2                : 0x919c
      +0x006 Data3                : 0x4cc5
      +0x008 Data4                : [8]  "???"
   +0x060 RecordId        : 0x01cae219`673474d3
   +0x068 Flags           : _WHEA_ERROR_RECORD_HEADER_FLAGS
      +0x000 Recovered            : 0y0
      +0x000 PreviousError        : 0y1
      +0x000 Simulated            : 0y0
      +0x000 Reserved             : 0y00000000000000000000000000000 (0)
      +0x000 AsULONG              : 2
   +0x06c PersistenceInfo : _WHEA_PERSISTENCE_INFO
      +0x000 Signature            : 0y0000000000000000 (0)
      +0x000 Length               : 0y00000000000000000000000000 (0)
      +0x000 Identifier           : 0y0000000000000000 (0)
      +0x000 Attributes           : 0y00
      +0x000 DoNotLog             : 0y0
      +0x000 Reserved             : 0y00000 (0)
      +0x000 AsULONGLONG          : 0
   +0x074 Reserved        : [12]  ""
+0x080 SectionDescriptor : [1] _WHEA_ERROR_RECORD_SECTION_DESCRIPTOR
   +0x000 SectionOffset   : 0x158
   +0x004 SectionLength   : 0xc0
   +0x008 Revision        : _WHEA_REVISION
      +0x000 MinorRevision        : 0x1 ''
      +0x001 MajorRevision        : 0x2 ''
      +0x000 AsUSHORT             : 0x201
   +0x00a ValidBits       : _WHEA_ERROR_RECORD_SECTION_DESCRIPTOR_VALIDBITS
      +0x000 FRUId                : 0y0
      +0x000 FRUText              : 0y0
      +0x000 Reserved             : 0y000000 (0)
      +0x000 AsUCHAR              : 0 ''
   +0x00b Reserved        : 0 ''
   +0x00c Flags           : _WHEA_ERROR_RECORD_SECTION_DESCRIPTOR_FLAGS
      +0x000 Primary              : 0y1
      +0x000 ContainmentWarning   : 0y0
      +0x000 Reset                : 0y0
      +0x000 ThresholdExceeded    : 0y0
      +0x000 ResourceNotAvailable : 0y0
      +0x000 LatentError          : 0y0
      +0x000 Reserved             : 0y00000000000000000000000000 (0)
      +0x000 AsULONG              : 1
   +0x010 SectionType     : _GUID {9876ccad-47b4-4bdb-b65e-16f193c4f3db}
      +0x000 Data1                : 0x9876ccad
      +0x004 Data2                : 0x47b4
      +0x006 Data3                : 0x4bdb
      +0x008 Data4                : [8]  "???"
   +0x020 FRUId           : _GUID {00000000-0000-0000-0000-000000000000}
      +0x000 Data1                : 0
      +0x004 Data2                : 0
      +0x006 Data3                : 0
      +0x008 Data4                : [8]  ""
   +0x030 SectionSeverity : 1 ( WheaErrSevFatal )
   +0x034 FRUText         : [20]  ""
```

```
KERNEL_STACK_INPAGE_ERROR (77)
The requested page of kernel data could not be read in. Caused by
bad block in paging file or disk controller error.
In the case when the first arguments is 0 or 1, the stack signature
in the kernel stack was not found. Again, bad hardware.
An I/O status of c000009c (STATUS_DEVICE_DATA_ERROR) or
C000016AL (STATUS_DISK_OPERATION_FAILED) normally indicates
the data could not be read from the disk due to a bad
block. Upon reboot autocheck will run and attempt to map out the bad
sector. If the status is C0000185 (STATUS_IO_DEVICE_ERROR) and the paging
file is on a SCSI disk device, then the cabling and termination should be
checked. See the knowledge base article on SCSI termination.
Arguments:
Arg1: 0000000000000001, (page was retrieved from disk)
Arg2: fffffa800818e870, value found in stack where signature should be
Arg3: 0000000000000000, 0
Arg4: fffff8800c6e5e80, address of signature on kernel stack


2: kd> k
Child-SP RetAddr Call Site
fffff880`0371da18 fffff800`03110b01 nt!KeBugCheckEx
fffff880`0371da20 fffff800`030c8c54 nt! ?? ::FNODOBFM::`string'+0x51e31
fffff880`0371db30 fffff800`030c8bef nt!MmInPageKernelStack+0x40
fffff880`0371db90 fffff800`030c8928 nt!KiInSwapKernelStacks+0x1f
fffff880`0371dbc0 fffff800`0332be5a nt!KeSwapProcessOrStack+0x84
fffff880`0371dc00 fffff800`03085d26 nt!PspSystemThreadStartup+0x5a
fffff880`0371dc40 00000000`00000000 nt!KiStartSystemThread+0x16
```

For WHEA_UNCORRECTABLE_ERROR (124) we have additional WinDbg commands **!whea**, **!errrec**, and **!errpkt**:

```
2: kd> !whea
 Error Source Table @ fffff8004bbd4a90
 4 Error Sources
 Error Source 0 @ ffffe00014376bd0
 Notify Type : {14374010-e000-ffff-984a-bd4b00f8ffff}
 Type : 0x0 (MCE)
 Error Count : 1
 Record Count : 4
 Record Length : 728
 Error Records : wrapper @ ffffe000110e0000 record @ ffffe000110e0028
 : wrapper @ ffffe000110e0728 record @ ffffe000110e0750
 : wrapper @ ffffe000110e0e50 record @ ffffe000110e0e78
 : wrapper @ ffffe000110e1578 record @ ffffe000110e15a0
 Descriptor : @ ffffe00014376c29
 Length : 3cc
 Max Raw Data Length : 141
 Num Records To Preallocate : 4
 Max Sections Per Record : 4
 Error Source ID : 0
 Flags : 00000000
 [...]

2: kd> !errrec ffffe000110e0028
 ===========================================
 Common Platform Error Record @ ffffe000110e0028
 -------------------------------------------
 Record Id : 01d21a1a7e5fffd1
 Severity : Fatal (1)
 Length : 928
```

```
Creator : Microsoft
Notify Type : Machine Check Exception
Timestamp : 9/30/2016 9:05:50 (UTC)
Flags : 0x00000000


==========================================
Section 0 : Processor Generic
────────────────────────────--

Descriptor @ ffffe000110e00a8
Section @ ffffe000110e0180
Offset : 344
Length : 192
Flags : 0x00000001 Primary
Severity : Fatal


Proc. Type : x86/x64
 Instr. Set : x64
 Error Type : Micro-Architectural Error
 Flags : 0x00
 CPU Version : 0x00000000000306a9
 Processor ID : 0x0000000000000002


==========================================
Section 1 : x86/x64 Processor Specific
────────────────────────────--

Descriptor @ ffffe000110e00f0
Section @ ffffe000110e0240
Offset : 536
Length : 128
Flags : 0x00000000
Severity : Fatal


Local APIC Id : 0x0000000000000002
 CPU Id : a9 06 03 00 00 08 10 02 - bf e3 ba 7f ff fb eb bf
 00 00 00 00 00 00 00 00 - 00 00 00 00 00 00 00 00
 00 00 00 00 00 00 00 00 - 00 00 00 00 00 00 00 00


Proc. Info 0 @ ffffe000110e0240


==========================================
Section 2 : x86/x64 MCA
────────────────────────────--

Descriptor @ ffffe000110e0138
Section @ ffffe000110e02c0
Offset : 664
Length : 264
Flags : 0x00000000
Severity : Fatal


Error : Internal unclassified (Proc 2 Bank 4)
 Status : 0xb200000000100402
```

We also observed internal errors in Visual C++ compiler followed by memory management bugchecks a few seconds later.

Hidden Call

Sometimes, due to optimization or indeterminate stack trace reconstruction, we may not see all stack trace frames. In some cases, it is possible to reconstruct such **Hidden Calls**. For example, we have the following unmanaged **Stack Trace** (page 1033) of **CLR Thread** (page 135):

```
0:000> k
ChildEBP RetAddr
0011d6b8 66fdee7c mscorwks!JIT_IsInstanceOfClass+0xd
0011d6cc 67578500 PresentationCore_ni!`string'+0x4a2bc
0011d6e0 67578527 PresentationCore_ni!`string' <PERF> (PresentationCore_ni+0x778500)
0011d6f4 6757850d PresentationCore_ni!`string' <PERF> (PresentationCore_ni+0x778527)
0011d708 6757850d PresentationCore_ni!`string' <PERF> (PresentationCore_ni+0x77850d)
0011d71c 6757850d PresentationCore_ni!`string' <PERF> (PresentationCore_ni+0x77850d)
0011d730 6757850d PresentationCore_ni!`string' <PERF> (PresentationCore_ni+0x77850d)
0011d744 6757850d PresentationCore_ni!`string' <PERF> (PresentationCore_ni+0x77850d)
0011d758 6757850d PresentationCore_ni!`string' <PERF> (PresentationCore_ni+0x77850d)
0011d76c 67578527 PresentationCore_ni!`string' <PERF> (PresentationCore_ni+0x77850d)
0011d780 6757850d PresentationCore_ni!`string' <PERF> (PresentationCore_ni+0x778527)
0011d794 6757850d PresentationCore_ni!`string' <PERF> (PresentationCore_ni+0x77850d)
0011d7a8 6757850d PresentationCore_ni!`string' <PERF> (PresentationCore_ni+0x77850d)
0011d7bc 6757850d PresentationCore_ni!`string' <PERF> (PresentationCore_ni+0x77850d)
0011d7d0 6757850d PresentationCore_ni!`string' <PERF> (PresentationCore_ni+0x77850d)
0011d7e4 6757850d PresentationCore_ni!`string' <PERF> (PresentationCore_ni+0x77850d)
0011d7f8 6757850d PresentationCore_ni!`string' <PERF> (PresentationCore_ni+0x77850d)
0011d80c 6757850d PresentationCore_ni!`string' <PERF> (PresentationCore_ni+0x77850d)
0011d820 6757850d PresentationCore_ni!`string' <PERF> (PresentationCore_ni+0x77850d)
0011d834 6757850d PresentationCore_ni!`string' <PERF> (PresentationCore_ni+0x77850d)
0011d848 6757850d PresentationCore_ni!`string' <PERF> (PresentationCore_ni+0x77850d)
0011d85c 6757850d PresentationCore_ni!`string' <PERF> (PresentationCore_ni+0x77850d)
0011d870 6757850d PresentationCore_ni!`string' <PERF> (PresentationCore_ni+0x77850d)
0011d884 6757850d PresentationCore_ni!`string' <PERF> (PresentationCore_ni+0x77850d)
0011d898 6757850d PresentationCore_ni!`string' <PERF> (PresentationCore_ni+0x77850d)
0011d8ac 6757850d PresentationCore_ni!`string' <PERF> (PresentationCore_ni+0x77850d)
0011d8c0 6757850d PresentationCore_ni!`string' <PERF> (PresentationCore_ni+0x77850d)
0011d8d4 6757850d PresentationCore_ni!`string' <PERF> (PresentationCore_ni+0x77850d)
0011d8e8 67578527 PresentationCore_ni!`string' <PERF> (PresentationCore_ni+0x77850d)
0011d8fc 6757850d PresentationCore_ni!`string' <PERF> (PresentationCore_ni+0x778527)
0011d910 6757850d PresentationCore_ni!`string' <PERF> (PresentationCore_ni+0x77850d)
0011d924 6757850d PresentationCore_ni!`string' <PERF> (PresentationCore_ni+0x77850d)
0011d938 6757850d PresentationCore_ni!`string' <PERF> (PresentationCore_ni+0x77850d)
0011d94c 6757850d PresentationCore_ni!`string' <PERF> (PresentationCore_ni+0x77850d)
0011d960 6757850d PresentationCore_ni!`string' <PERF> (PresentationCore_ni+0x77850d)
0011d974 6757850d PresentationCore_ni!`string' <PERF> (PresentationCore_ni+0x77850d)
0011d988 6757850d PresentationCore_ni!`string' <PERF> (PresentationCore_ni+0x77850d)
0011d99c 6757850d PresentationCore_ni!`string' <PERF> (PresentationCore_ni+0x77850d)
0011d9b0 6757850d PresentationCore_ni!`string' <PERF> (PresentationCore_ni+0x77850d)
0011d9c4 6757850d PresentationCore_ni!`string' <PERF> (PresentationCore_ni+0x77850d)
0011d9d8 67578527 PresentationCore_ni!`string' <PERF> (PresentationCore_ni+0x77850d)
0011d9ec 6757850d PresentationCore_ni!`string' <PERF> (PresentationCore_ni+0x778527)
0011da00 6757850d PresentationCore_ni!`string' <PERF> (PresentationCore_ni+0x77850d)
0011da14 6757850d PresentationCore_ni!`string' <PERF> (PresentationCore_ni+0x77850d)
0011da28 6757850d PresentationCore_ni!`string' <PERF> (PresentationCore_ni+0x77850d)
0011da3c 6757850d PresentationCore_ni!`string' <PERF> (PresentationCore_ni+0x77850d)
```

```
0011da50 6757850d PresentationCore_ni!`string' <PERF> (PresentationCore_ni+0x77850d)
0011da64 6757850d PresentationCore_ni!`string' <PERF> (PresentationCore_ni+0x77850d)
0011da78 6757850d PresentationCore_ni!`string' <PERF> (PresentationCore_ni+0x77850d)
0011da8c 6757850d PresentationCore_ni!`string' <PERF> (PresentationCore_ni+0x77850d)
0011daa0 6757850d PresentationCore_ni!`string' <PERF> (PresentationCore_ni+0x77850d)
0011dab4 6757850d PresentationCore_ni!`string' <PERF> (PresentationCore_ni+0x77850d)
0011dac8 6757850d PresentationCore_ni!`string' <PERF> (PresentationCore_ni+0x77850d)
0011dadc 6757850d PresentationCore_ni!`string' <PERF> (PresentationCore_ni+0x77850d)
0011daf0 6757850d PresentationCore_ni!`string' <PERF> (PresentationCore_ni+0x77850d)
0011db04 6757850d PresentationCore_ni!`string' <PERF> (PresentationCore_ni+0x77850d)
0011db18 6757850d PresentationCore_ni!`string' <PERF> (PresentationCore_ni+0x77850d)
0011db2c 67578527 PresentationCore_ni!`string' <PERF> (PresentationCore_ni+0x77850d)
0011db40 6757850d PresentationCore_ni!`string' <PERF> (PresentationCore_ni+0x778527)
0011db54 6757850d PresentationCore_ni!`string' <PERF> (PresentationCore_ni+0x77850d)
0011db68 6757850d PresentationCore_ni!`string' <PERF> (PresentationCore_ni+0x77850d)
0011db7c 6757850d PresentationCore_ni!`string' <PERF> (PresentationCore_ni+0x77850d)
0011db90 6757850d PresentationCore_ni!`string' <PERF> (PresentationCore_ni+0x77850d)
0011dba4 6757850d PresentationCore_ni!`string' <PERF> (PresentationCore_ni+0x77850d)
0011dbb8 6757850d PresentationCore_ni!`string' <PERF> (PresentationCore_ni+0x77850d)
0011dbcc 6757850d PresentationCore_ni!`string' <PERF> (PresentationCore_ni+0x77850d)
0011dbe0 6757850d PresentationCore_ni!`string' <PERF> (PresentationCore_ni+0x77850d)
0011dbf4 6757850d PresentationCore_ni!`string' <PERF> (PresentationCore_ni+0x77850d)
0011dc08 6757850d PresentationCore_ni!`string' <PERF> (PresentationCore_ni+0x77850d)
0011dc1c 6757850d PresentationCore_ni!`string' <PERF> (PresentationCore_ni+0x77850d)
0011dc30 6757850d PresentationCore_ni!`string' <PERF> (PresentationCore_ni+0x77850d)
0011dc44 6757850d PresentationCore_ni!`string' <PERF> (PresentationCore_ni+0x77850d)
0011dc58 66fc3282 PresentationCore_ni!`string' <PERF> (PresentationCore_ni+0x77850d)
*** WARNING: Unable to verify checksum for PresentationFramework.ni.dll
0011dd28 662a75e6 PresentationCore_ni!`string'+0x2e6c2
0011de08 662190a0 PresentationFramework_ni+0x2675e6
0011dffc 66fc35e2 PresentationFramework_ni+0x1d90a0
0011e0ec 66fd9dad PresentationCore_ni!`string'+0x2ea22
0011e214 66fe0459 PresentationCore_ni!`string'+0x451ed
0011e238 66fdfd40 PresentationCore_ni!`string'+0x4b899
0011e284 66fdfc9b PresentationCore_ni!`string'+0x4b180
*** WARNING: Unable to verify checksum for WindowsBase.ni.dll
0011e2b0 723ca31a PresentationCore_ni!`string'+0x4b0db
0011e2cc 723ca20a WindowsBase_ni+0x9a31a
0011e30c 723c8384 WindowsBase_ni+0x9a20a
0011e330 723cd26d WindowsBase_ni+0x98384
0011e368 723cd1f8 WindowsBase_ni+0x9d26d
0011e380 72841b4c WindowsBase_ni+0x9d1f8
0011e390 728589ec mscorwks!CallDescrWorker+0x33
0011e410 72865acc mscorwks!CallDescrWorkerWithHandler+0xa3
0011e54c 72865aff mscorwks!MethodDesc::CallDescr+0x19c
0011e568 72865b1d mscorwks!MethodDesc::CallTargetWorker+0x1f
0011e580 728bd9c8 mscorwks!MethodDescCallSite::CallWithValueTypes+0x1a
0011e74c 728bdb1e mscorwks!ExecuteCodeWithGuaranteedCleanupHelper+0x9f
*** WARNING: Unable to verify checksum for mscorlib.ni.dll
0011e7fc 68395887 mscorwks!ReflectionInvocation::ExecuteCodeWithGuaranteedCleanup+0x10f
0011e818 683804b5 mscorlib_ni+0x235887
0011e830 723cd133 mscorlib_ni+0x2204b5
0011e86c 723c7a27 WindowsBase_ni+0x9d133
0011e948 723c7d13 WindowsBase_ni+0x97a27
0011e984 723ca4fe WindowsBase_ni+0x97d13
0011e9d0 723ca42a WindowsBase_ni+0x9a4fe
```

```
0011e9f0 723ca31a WindowsBase_ni+0x9a42a
0011ea0c 723ca20a WindowsBase_ni+0x9a31a
0011ea4c 723c8384 WindowsBase_ni+0x9a20a
0011ea70 723c74e1 WindowsBase_ni+0x98384
0011eaac 723c7430 WindowsBase_ni+0x974e1
0011eadc 723c9b6c WindowsBase_ni+0x97430
0011eb2c 757462fa WindowsBase_ni+0x99b6c
0011eb58 75746d3a user32!InternalCallWinProc+0x23
0011ebd0 757477c4 user32!UserCallWinProcCheckWow+0x109
0011ec30 7574788a user32!DispatchMessageWorker+0x3bc
0011ec40 0577304e user32!DispatchMessageW+0xf
WARNING: Frame IP not in any known module. Following frames may be wrong.
0011ec5c 723c7b24 0x577304e
0011eccc 723c71f9 WindowsBase_ni+0x97b24
0011ecd8 723c719c WindowsBase_ni+0x971f9
0011ece4 6620f07e WindowsBase_ni+0x9719c
0011ecf0 6620e37f PresentationFramework_ni+0x1cf07e
0011ed14 661f56d6 PresentationFramework_ni+0x1ce37f
0011ed24 661f5699 PresentationFramework_ni+0x1b56d6
0011ed80 72841b4c PresentationFramework_ni+0x1b5699
0011eda0 72841b4c mscorwks!CallDescrWorker+0x33
0011edb0 728589ec mscorwks!CallDescrWorker+0x33
0011ee30 72865acc mscorwks!CallDescrWorkerWithHandler+0xa3
0011ef6c 72865aff mscorwks!MethodDesc::CallDescr+0x19c
0011ef88 72865b1d mscorwks!MethodDesc::CallTargetWorker+0x1f
0011efa0 728fef01 mscorwks!MethodDescCallSite::CallWithValueTypes+0x1a
0011f104 728fee21 mscorwks!ClassLoader::RunMain+0x223
0011f36c 728ff33e mscorwks!Assembly::ExecuteMainMethod+0xa6
0011f83c 728ff528 mscorwks!SystemDomain::ExecuteMainMethod+0x45e
0011f88c 728ff458 mscorwks!ExecuteEXE+0x59
0011f8d4 70aef4f3 mscorwks!_CorExeMain+0x15c
0011f90c 70b77efd mscoreei!_CorExeMain+0x10a
0011f924 70b74de3 mscoree!ShellShim__CorExeMain+0x7d
0011f92c 754c338a mscoree!_CorExeMain_Exported+0x8
0011f938 77659f72 kernel32!BaseThreadInitThunk+0xe
0011f978 77659f45 ntdll!__RtlUserThreadStart+0x70
0011f990 00000000 ntdll!_RtlUserThreadStart+0x1b
```

Its **Managed Stack Trace** (page 704) is the following:

```
0:000> !CLRStack
OS Thread Id: 0x1520 (0)
ESP       EIP
0011e7a0 728493a4 [HelperMethodFrame_PROTECTOBJ: 0011e7a0]
System.Runtime.CompilerServices.RuntimeHelpers.ExecuteCodeWithGuaranteedCleanup(TryCode, CleanupCode, System.Object)
0011e808 68395887 System.Threading.ExecutionContext.RunInternal(System.Threading.ExecutionContext,
System.Threading.ContextCallback, System.Object)
0011e824 683804b5 System.Threading.ExecutionContext.Run(System.Threading.ExecutionContext,
System.Threading.ContextCallback, System.Object)
0011e83c 723cd133 System.Windows.Threading.DispatcherOperation.Invoke()
0011e874 723c7a27 System.Windows.Threading.Dispatcher.ProcessQueue()
0011e950 723c7d13 System.Windows.Threading.Dispatcher.WndProcHook(IntPtr, Int32, IntPtr, IntPtr, Boolean ByRef)
0011e99c 723ca4fe MS.Win32.HwndWrapper.WndProc(IntPtr, Int32, IntPtr, IntPtr, Boolean ByRef)
0011e9e8 723ca42a MS.Win32.HwndSubclass.DispatcherCallbackOperation(System.Object)
0011e9f8 723ca31a System.Windows.Threading.ExceptionWrapper.InternalRealCall(System.Delegate, System.Object, Boolean)
0011ea1c 723ca20a System.Windows.Threading.ExceptionWrapper.TryCatchWhen(System.Object, System.Delegate, System.Object,
Boolean, System.Delegate)
0011ea64 723c8384 System.Windows.Threading.Dispatcher.WrappedInvoke(System.Delegate, System.Object, Boolean,
```

```
System.Delegate)
0011ea84 723c74e1 System.Windows.Threading.Dispatcher.InvokeImpl(System.Windows.Threading.DispatcherPriority,
System.TimeSpan, System.Delegate, System.Object, Boolean)
0011eac8 723c7430 System.Windows.Threading.Dispatcher.Invoke(System.Windows.Threading.DispatcherPriority,
System.Delegate, System.Object)
0011eaec 723c9b6c MS.Win32.HwndSubclass.SubclassWndProc(IntPtr, Int32, IntPtr, IntPtr)
0011ec74 00270b04 [NDirectMethodFrameStandalone: 0011ec74]
MS.Win32.UnsafeNativeMethods.DispatchMessage(System.Windows.Interop.MSG ByRef)
0011ec84 723c7b24 System.Windows.Threading.Dispatcher.PushFrameImpl(System.Windows.Threading.DispatcherFrame)
0011ecd4 723c71f9 System.Windows.Threading.Dispatcher.PushFrame(System.Windows.Threading.DispatcherFrame)
0011ece0 723c719c System.Windows.Threading.Dispatcher.Run()
0011ecec 6620f07e System.Windows.Application.RunDispatcher(System.Object)
0011ecf8 6620e37f System.Windows.Application.RunInternal(System.Windows.Window)
0011ed1c 661f56d6 System.Windows.Application.Run(System.Windows.Window)
0011ed2c 661f5699 System.Windows.Application.Run()
[...]
```

Caller-n-Callee (page 122) traces also do not reveal anything more:

```
Thread   0
Current frame: mscorwks!JIT_IsInstanceOfClass+0xd
ChildEBP RetAddr  Caller,Callee
0011d6b8 66fdee7c (MethodDesc 0x66ee2954 +0x3c
MS.Internal.DeferredElementTreeState.GetLogicalParent(System.Windows.DependencyObject,
MS.Internal.DeferredElementTreeState)), calling mscorwks!JIT_IsInstanceOfClass
0011d6cc 67578500 (MethodDesc 0x66ee1270 +0x110
MS.Internal.UIElementHelper.InvalidateAutomationAncestors(System.Windows.DependencyObject)), calling (MethodDesc
0x66ee2954 +0 MS.Internal.DeferredElementTreeState.GetLogicalParent(System.Windows.DependencyObject,
MS.Internal.DeferredElementTreeState))
0011d6e0 67578527 (MethodDesc 0x66ee1270 +0x137
MS.Internal.UIElementHelper.InvalidateAutomationAncestors(System.Windows.DependencyObject)), calling (MethodDesc
0x66ee1270 +0 MS.Internal.UIElementHelper.InvalidateAutomationAncestors(System.Windows.DependencyObject))
0011d6f4 6757850d (MethodDesc 0x66ee1270 +0x11d
MS.Internal.UIElementHelper.InvalidateAutomationAncestors(System.Windows.DependencyObject)), calling (MethodDesc
0x66ee1270 +0 MS.Internal.UIElementHelper.InvalidateAutomationAncestors(System.Windows.DependencyObject))
0011d708 6757850d (MethodDesc 0x66ee1270 +0x11d
MS.Internal.UIElementHelper.InvalidateAutomationAncestors(System.Windows.DependencyObject)), calling (MethodDesc
0x66ee1270 +0 MS.Internal.UIElementHelper.InvalidateAutomationAncestors(System.Windows.DependencyObject))
0011d71c 6757850d (MethodDesc 0x66ee1270 +0x11d
MS.Internal.UIElementHelper.InvalidateAutomationAncestors(System.Windows.DependencyObject)), calling (MethodDesc
0x66ee1270 +0 MS.Internal.UIElementHelper.InvalidateAutomationAncestors(System.Windows.DependencyObject))
[...]
```

However, if we check the return address for **Top Module** (page 1127) *mscorwks* (66fdee7c) we will see a call possibly related to 3D processing:

```
0:000> k
ChildEBP RetAddr
0011d6b8 66fdee7c mscorwks!JIT_IsInstanceOfClass+0xd
0011d6cc 67578500 PresentationCore_ni!`string'+0x4a2bc
0011d6e0 67578527 PresentationCore_ni!`string' <PERF> (PresentationCore_ni+0x778500)
0011d6f4 6757850d PresentationCore_ni!`string' <PERF> (PresentationCore_ni+0x778527)
[...]
```

```
0:000> ub 66fdee7c
PresentationCore_ni!`string'+0x4a2a2:
66fdee62 740c            je      PresentationCore_ni!`string'+0x4a2b0 (66fdee70)
66fdee64 8bc8            mov     ecx,eax
66fdee66 8b01            mov     eax,dword ptr [ecx]
66fdee68 ff90d8030000    call    dword ptr [eax+3D8h]
66fdee6e 8bf0            mov     esi,eax
66fdee70 8bd7            mov     edx,edi
66fdee72 b998670467      mov     ecx,offset PresentationCore_ni!`string'+0xb1bd8 (67046798)
66fdee77 e82c7afaff      call    PresentationCore_ni!?System.Windows.Media.Media3D.Viewport3DVisual.
PrecomputeContent@@200001+0x3c (66f868a8)
```

The call structure seems to be valid when we check the next return address from the stack trace (67578500):

```
0:000> ub 67578500
PresentationCore_ni!`string' <PERF> (PresentationCore_ni+0x7784e7):
675784e7 e8f4a2a0ff      call    PresentationCore_ni!?System.Windows.Media.Media3D.ScaleTransform3D.
UpdateResource@@2002011280M802+0x108 (66f827e0)
PresentationCore_ni!`string' <PERF> (PresentationCore_ni+0x7784ec):
675784ec eb05            jmp     PresentationCore_ni!`string' <PERF> (PresentationCore_ni+0x7784f3)
(675784f3)
PresentationCore_ni!`string' <PERF> (PresentationCore_ni+0x7784ee):
675784ee b801000000      mov     eax,1
PresentationCore_ni!`string' <PERF> (PresentationCore_ni+0x7784f3):
675784f3 85c0            test    eax,eax
PresentationCore_ni!`string' <PERF> (PresentationCore_ni+0x7784f5):
675784f5 74b1            je      PresentationCore_ni!`string' <PERF> (PresentationCore_ni+0x7784a8)
(675784a8)
PresentationCore_ni!`string' <PERF> (PresentationCore_ni+0x7784f7):
675784f7 8bcb            mov     ecx,ebx
PresentationCore_ni!`string' <PERF> (PresentationCore_ni+0x7784f9):
675784f9 33d2            xor     edx,edx
PresentationCore_ni!`string' <PERF> (PresentationCore_ni+0x7784fb):
675784fb e84069a6ff      call    PresentationCore_ni!`string'+0x4a280 (66fdee40)
```

Hidden Exception

> ### Kernel Space

This is an example of **Hidden Exception** (page 506) pattern in kernel space:

```
0: kd> !thread
THREAD ffffffa800d4bf9c0  Cid 0e88.56e0  Teb: 000007fffffd8000 Win32Thread: 0000000000000000 RUNNING on
processor 0
Not impersonating
DeviceMap                ffffff8a001e91950
Owning Process           ffffffa800b33cb30        Image:          svchost.exe
Attached Process         N/A             Image:          N/A
Wait Start TickCount     13154529        Ticks: 0
Context Switch Count     1426
UserTime                 00:00:00.015
KernelTime               00:00:00.124
Win32 Start Address 0x0000000077728d20
Stack Init fffff8800a83fdb0 Current fffff8800a83eb90
Base fffff8800a840000 Limit fffff8800a83a000 Call 0
Priority 10 BasePriority 10 UnusualBoost 0 ForegroundBoost 0 IoPriority 2 PagePriority 5
[...]


0: kd> dps fffff8800a83a000 fffff8800a840000
[...]
fffff880`0a83e180 fffff880`0a83ea10
fffff880`0a83e188 fffff880`0a83e6d0
fffff880`0a83e190 fffff880`0a83e968
fffff880`0a83e198 fffff800`016c88cf nt!KiDispatchException+0x16f
fffff880`0a83e1a0 fffff880`0a83e968
fffff880`0a83e1a8 fffff880`0a83e1d0
fffff880`0a83e1b0 fffff880`00000000
fffff880`0a83e1b8 00000000`00000000
fffff880`0a83e1c0 00000000`00000000
fffff880`0a83e1c8 00000000`00000000
[...]


0: kd> .cxr fffff880`0a83e1d0
rax=0000000000000009 rbx=ffffffa800d4c1de0 rcx=0000000000000000
rdx=fffff8800a83ece0 rsi=0000000000000000 rdi=0000000000000000
rip=fffff800016ad74f rsp=fffff8800a83eba0 rbp=00000000a000000c
r8=fffff8800a83ecd8 r9=fffff8800a83ecc0 r10=0000000000000000
r11=fffff8800a83ed58 r12=0000000000000000 r13=0000000000000000
r14=ffffffa800d4bf9c0 r15=ffffffa800d4c1ea0
iopl=0         nv up ei pl zr na po nc
cs=0010  ss=0018  ds=002b  es=002b  fs=0053  gs=002b             efl=00010246
nt!IopCompleteRequest+0x12f:
fffff800`016ad74f 48894108 mov qword ptr [rcx+8],rax ds:002b:00000000`00000008=??????????????????
```

Comments

Another example:

```
0: kd> k
# ChildEBP RetAddr
00 8078aefc 8281db8c hal!READ_PORT_USHORT+0x8
01 8078af0c 8281dcf5 hal!HalpCheckPowerButton+0x2e
02 8078af10 8292cdde hal!HaliHaltSystem+0x7
03 8078af5c 8292dc79 nt!KiBugCheckDebugBreak+0x73
04 8078b320 8292cc24 nt!KeBugCheck2+0xa7f
05 8078b340 82a5a49b nt!KeBugCheckEx+0x1e
06 8078bc90 828fe9c9 nt!PspSystemThreadStartup+0xde
07 00000000 00000000 nt!KiThreadStartup+0x19

0: kd> !thread
 THREAD 863475f8 Cid 0004.0008 Teb: 00000000 Win32Thread: 00000000 RUNNING on processor 0
 Not impersonating
 DeviceMap 8d6080c0
 Owning Process 863478d0 Image: System
 Attached Process N/A Image: N/A
 Wait Start TickCount 2624 Ticks: 7 (0:00:00:00.109)
 Context Switch Count 1025 IdealProcessor: 0
 UserTime 00:00:00.000
 KernelTime 00:00:03.962
 Win32 Start Address nt!Phase1Initialization (0x829dd53b)
 Stack Init 8078bed0 Current 8078b890 Base 8078c000 Limit 80789000 Call 0
 Priority 31 BasePriority 8 UnusualBoost 0 ForegroundBoost 0 IoPriority 2 PagePriority 5
 ChildEBP RetAddr Args to Child
 8078aefc 8281db8c 00001000 00000000 8078af5c hal!READ_PORT_USHORT+0x8 (FPO: [1,0,0])
 8078af0c 8281dcf5 8292cdde 2b2952aa 807c960c hal!HalpCheckPowerButton+0x2e (FPO: [Non-Fpo])
 8078af10 8292cdde 2b2952aa 807c960c 00000000 hal!HaliHaltSystem+0x7 (FPO: [0,0,0])
 8078af5c 8292dc79 00000004 00000000 00000000 nt!KiBugCheckDebugBreak+0x73
 8078b320 8292cc24 0000007e c0000005 8cc14540 nt!KeBugCheck2+0xa7f
 8078b340 82a5a49b 0000007e c0000005 8cc14540 nt!KeBugCheckEx+0x1e
 8078bc90 828fe9c9 829dd53b 80806cb0 00000000 nt!PspSystemThreadStartup+0xde
 00000000 00000000 00000000 00000000 00000000 nt!KiThreadStartup+0x19

0: kd> dps 80789000 8078c000
 80789000 00000000
 80789004 00000000
 ...
 8078b470 8078b880
 8078b474 82902277 nt!KiDispatchException+0x17c
 8078b478 8078b89c
 8078b47c 8078b480
 8078b480 00010017
 ...

0: kd> .cxr 8078b480
 eax=00000000 ebx=87428554 ecx=8078b998 edx=00000000 esi=871121d0 edi=0000008c
 eip=8cc11340 esp=8078b964 ebp=8078ba28 iopl=0 nv up ei ng nz ac po nc
 cs=0008 ss=0010 ds=0023 es=0023 fs=0030 gs=0000 efl=00210292
 Driver+0x1340:
 8cc11340 ff5000 call dword ptr [eax] ds:0023:00000000=????????
```

Managed Space

For completion, we introduce a managed space version of **Hidden Exception** in addition to user (page 509) and kernel (page 504) space variants.

```
0:000> ~*kL
[...]
13 Id: 1b70.1c2c Suspend: 0 Teb: 00446000 Unfrozen
# ChildEBP RetAddr
00 08e7ec4c 755e1cf3 ntdll!NtWaitForMultipleObjects+0xc
01 08e7ede0 6ef8bc6e KERNELBASE!WaitForMultipleObjectsEx+0x133
02 08e7ee30 6ef8b9b3 clr!WaitForMultipleObjectsEx_SO_TOLERANT+0x3c
03 08e7eebc 6ef8baa4 clr!Thread::DoAppropriateWaitWorker+0x237
04 08e7ef28 6ef8bc14 clr!Thread::DoAppropriateWait+0x64
05 08e7ef74 6eef648b clr!CLREventBase::WaitEx+0x128
06 08e7ef8c 6f0058f6 clr!CLREventBase::Wait+0x1a
07 08e7f018 6f005834 clr!AwareLock::EnterEpilogHelper+0xa8
08 08e7f060 6f005980 clr!AwareLock::EnterEpilog+0x48
09 08e7f078 6f00662c clr!AwareLock::Enter+0x4a
0a 08e7f104 08d71d79 clr!JITutil_MonEnterWorker+0x9c
WARNING: Frame IP not in any known module. Following frames may be wrong.
0b 08e7f120 6dd9608d 0x8d71d79
0c 08e7f12c 6ddc2925 mscorlib_ni+0x3c608d
0d 08e7f190 6ddc2836 mscorlib_ni+0x3f2925
0e 08e7f1a4 6ddc27f1 mscorlib_ni+0x3f2836
0f 08e7f1c0 6dd95fe8 mscorlib_ni+0x3f27f1
10 08e7f1d8 6ee6eaf6 mscorlib_ni+0x3c5fe8
11 08e7f1e4 6ee71d50 clr!CallDescrWorkerInternal+0x34
12 08e7f238 6ee77764 clr!CallDescrWorkerWithHandler+0x6b
13 08e7f2a0 6eef4d2d clr!MethodDescCallSite::CallTargetWorker+0x16a
14 08e7f414 6efae269 clr!ThreadNative::KickOffThread_Worker+0x173
15 08e7f428 6efae2d3 clr!ManagedThreadBase_DispatchInner+0x71
16 08e7f4cc 6efae3a0 clr!ManagedThreadBase_DispatchMiddle+0x7e
17 08e7f528 6ee7af05 clr!ManagedThreadBase_DispatchOuter+0x5b
18 08e7f534 6ee7aea2 clr!ManagedThreadBase_DispatchInCorrectAD+0x15
19 08e7f600 6ee7af4d clr!Thread::DoADCallBack+0x328
1a 08e7f624 6efae2d3 clr!ManagedThreadBase_DispatchInner+0x4e
1b 08e7f6c8 6efae3a0 clr!ManagedThreadBase_DispatchMiddle+0x7e
1c 08e7f724 6efae40f clr!ManagedThreadBase_DispatchOuter+0x5b
1d 08e7f748 6eef4be2 clr!ManagedThreadBase_FullTransitionWithAD+0x2f
1e 08e7f7c4 6eef62d1 clr!ThreadNative::KickOffThread+0x256
1f 08e7fbe4 76c28484 clr!Thread::intermediateThreadProc+0x55
20 08e7fbf8 77842fea kernel32!BaseThreadInitThunk+0x24
21 08e7fc40 77842fba ntdll!__RtlUserThreadStart+0x2f
22 08e7fc50 00000000 ntdll!_RtlUserThreadStart+0x1b
[...]

0:000> ~13s
eax=00000000 ebx=00000001 ecx=00000000 edx=00000000 esi=00000001 edi=00000001
eip=7784a7bc esp=08e7ec50 ebp=08e7ede0 iopl=0 nv up ei pl nz ac pe nc
cs=0023 ss=002b ds=002b es=002b fs=0053 gs=002b efl=00000216
ntdll!NtWaitForMultipleObjects+0xc:
7784a7bc c21400 ret 14h
```

```
0:013> !CLRStack
OS Thread Id: 0x1c2c (13)
Child SP IP       Call Site
08e7efb4 7784a7bc [GCFrame: 08e7efb4]
08e7f094 7784a7bc [HelperMethodFrame_1OBJ: 08e7f094] System.Threading.Monitor.Enter(System.Object)
08e7f10c 08d71d79 UserQuery+ClassMain.thread_proc_1()
08e7f128 6dd9608d *** ERROR: Module load completed but symbols could not be loaded for mscorlib.ni.dll
System.Threading.ThreadHelper.ThreadStart_Context(System.Object)
08e7f134 6ddc2925 System.Threading.ExecutionContext.RunInternal(System.Threading.ExecutionContext,
System.Threading.ContextCallback, System.Object, Boolean)
08e7f1a0 6ddc2836 System.Threading.ExecutionContext.Run(System.Threading.ExecutionContext,
System.Threading.ContextCallback, System.Object, Boolean)
08e7f1b4 6ddc27f1 System.Threading.ExecutionContext.Run(System.Threading.ExecutionContext,
System.Threading.ContextCallback, System.Object)
08e7f1cc 6dd95fe8 System.Threading.ThreadHelper.ThreadStart()
08e7f308 6ee6eaf6 [GCFrame: 08e7f308]
08e7f4e8 6ee6eaf6 [DebuggerU2MCatchHandlerFrame: 08e7f4e8]
08e7f554 6ee6eaf6 [ContextTransitionFrame: 08e7f554]
08e7f6e4 6ee6eaf6 [DebuggerU2MCatchHandlerFrame: 08e7f6e4]


0:013> !teb
TEB at 00446000
ExceptionList:     08e7edd0
StackBase:                 08e80000
StackLimit:                08e7a000
SubSystemTib:              00000000
FiberData:                 00001e00
ArbitraryUserPointer:      00000000
Self:                      00446000
EnvironmentPointer:        00000000
ClientId:                  00001b70 . 00001c2c
RpcHandle:                 00000000
Tls Storage:               008eb8e8
PEB Address:               0040a000
LastErrorValue: 0
LastStatusValue:           c0000034
Count Owned Locks:         0
HardErrorMode:   0


0:013> !DumpStackObjects 08e7a000 08e80000
OS Thread Id: 0x1c2c (13)
ESP/REG Object Name
08E7DD18 0270f714 LINQPad.ExecutionModel.OutPipe
08E7DD20 02736ca8 LINQPad.Disposable
08E7DD2C 0270f714 LINQPad.ExecutionModel.OutPipe
08E7DD3C 02736ca8 LINQPad.Disposable
08E7DD40 02736c88 System.Action
08E7DD44 02736ca8 LINQPad.Disposable
08E7DD64 0270f714 LINQPad.ExecutionModel.OutPipe
08E7DD98 02736ca8 LINQPad.Disposable
08E7DDB8 0270f714 LINQPad.ExecutionModel.OutPipe
08E7DE78 0270f9ec System.Object
08E7DE7C 0270f990 LINQPad.ObjectGraph.Formatters.HtmlWriter
08E7DEAC 0270f990 LINQPad.ObjectGraph.Formatters.HtmlWriter
08E7DEE4 0262e16c System.String
08E7DEF8 026aa9d0 System.String
```

```
08E7DF04 0270f990 LINQPad.ObjectGraph.Formatters.HtmlWriter
08E7E054 02724ecc System.Threading.ThreadHelper
08E7E058 026fad7c System.Threading.ContextCallback
08E7E06C 026fad7c System.Threading.ContextCallback
08E7E074 02724ecc System.Threading.ThreadHelper
08E7E0A8 0272fb68 System.NullReferenceException
08E7E0AC 026fad7c System.Threading.ContextCallback
08E7E0B8 02724ecc System.Threading.ThreadHelper
08E7E340 0272fcc0 System.Runtime.CompilerServices.RuntimeHelpers+TryCode
08E7E344 0272fce0 System.Runtime.CompilerServices.RuntimeHelpers+CleanupCode
08E7E348 0272fca4 System.Environment+ResourceHelper+GetResourceStringUserData
08E7E35C 0272fce0 System.Runtime.CompilerServices.RuntimeHelpers+CleanupCode
08E7E378 0272fca4 System.Environment+ResourceHelper+GetResourceStringUserData
08E7E37C 0272fc0c System.Environment+ResourceHelper
08E7E964 0272fb68 System.NullReferenceException
08E7EB3C 02724ecc System.Threading.ThreadHelper
08E7ECCC 02724ecc System.Threading.ThreadHelper
08E7ECD0 026fad7c System.Threading.ContextCallback
08E7ECD8 0272fa88 System.String critical section 1
08E7EFE8 0272fabc System.String critical section 2
08E7F034 026fad7c System.Threading.ContextCallback
08E7F088 02724ecc System.Threading.ThreadHelper
08E7F08C 026fad7c System.Threading.ContextCallback
08E7F0B8 02724ecc System.Threading.ThreadHelper
08E7F0C0 026fad7c System.Threading.ContextCallback
08E7F0F0 0272fabc System.String critical section 2
08E7F11C 026fad7c System.Threading.ContextCallback
08E7F128 02724f00 System.Threading.ExecutionContext
08E7F134 02724e98 System.Threading.Thread
08E7F144 02724e98 System.Threading.Thread
[...]
08E7F244 02724ee0 System.Threading.ThreadStart
08E7F2C4 02724ee0 System.Threading.ThreadStart
08E7F2D8 02724ee0 System.Threading.ThreadStart
```

The example dump is available for download[91].

---

[91] http://www.patterndiagnostics.com/SoftwareDiagnosticsCorpus/SDC2.zip

User Space

This pattern occurs frequently. It manifests itself when we run **!analyze -v** command, and we do not see an exception, or see only a breakpoint hit. In this case, manual analysis is required. Sometimes this happens because of another pattern: **Multiple Exceptions** (page 799). In other cases an exception happens, and it is handled by an exception handler dismissing it, and a process continues its execution slowly accumulating corruption inside its data leading to a new crash or hang. Sometimes we see a process hanging during its termination like the case shown below.

We have a process dump with only one thread:

```
0:000> kv
ChildEBP RetAddr
0096fcdc 7c822124 ntdll!KiFastSystemCallRet
0096fce0 77e6baa8 ntdll!NtWaitForSingleObject+0xc
0096fd50 77e6ba12 kernel32!WaitForSingleObjectEx+0xac
0096fd64 67f016ce kernel32!WaitForSingleObject+0x12
0096fd78 7c82257a component!DllInitialize+0xc2
0096fd98 7c8118b0 ntdll!LdrpCallInitRoutine+0x14
0096fe34 77e52fea ntdll!LdrShutdownProcess+0x130
0096ff20 77e5304d kernel32!_ExitProcess+0x43
0096ff34 77bcade4 kernel32!ExitProcess+0x14
0096ff40 77bcaefb msvcrt!__crtExitProcess+0x32
0096ff70 77bcaf6d msvcrt!_cinit+0xd2
0096ff84 77bcb555 msvcrt!_exit+0x11
0096ffb8 77e66063 msvcrt!_endthreadex+0xc8
0096ffec 00000000 kernel32!BaseThreadStart+0x34
```

We can look at its raw stack and try to find the symbol address for *KiUserExceptionDispatcher*. This function calls *RtlDispatchException*:

```
0:000> !teb
TEB at 7ffdc000
    ExceptionList:        0096fd40
    StackBase:            00970000
    StackLimit:           0096a000
    SubSystemTib:         00000000
    FiberData:            00001e00
    ArbitraryUserPointer: 00000000
    Self:                 7ffdc000
    EnvironmentPointer:   00000000
    ClientId:             00000858 . 000008c0
    RpcHandle:            00000000
    Tls Storage:          00000000
    PEB Address:          7ffdd000
    LastErrorValue:       0
    LastStatusValue:      c0000135
    Count Owned Locks:    0
    HardErrorMode:        0
```

```
0:000> dds 0096a000 00970000
...
...
...
0096c770  7c8140cc ntdll!RtlDispatchException+0x91
0096c774  0096c808
0096c778  0096ffa8
0096c77c  0096c824
0096c780  0096c7e4
0096c784  77bc6c74 msvcrt!_except_handler3
0096c788  00000000
0096c78c  0096c808
0096c790  01030064
0096c794  00000000
0096c798  00000000
0096c79c  00000000
0096c7a0  00000000
0096c7a4  00000000
0096c7a8  00000000
0096c7ac  00000000
0096c7b0  00000000
0096c7b4  00000000
0096c7b8  00000000
0096c7bc  00000000
0096c7c0  00000000
0096c7c4  00000000
0096c7c8  00000000
0096c7cc  00000000
0096c7d0  00000000
0096c7d4  00000000
0096c7d8  00000000
0096c7dc  00000000
0096c7e0  00000000
0096c7e4  00000000
0096c7e8  00970000
0096c7ec  00000000
0096c7f0  0096caf0
0096c7f4  7c82ecc6 ntdll!KiUserExceptionDispatcher+0xe
0096c7f8  0096c000
0096c7fc  0096c824 ; a pointer to an exception context
0096c800  0096c808
0096c804  0096c824
0096c808  c0000005
0096c80c  00000000
0096c810  00000000
0096c814  77bd8df3 msvcrt!wcschr+0x15
0096c818  00000002
0096c81c  00000000
0096c820  01031000
0096c824  0001003f
0096c828  00000000
0096c82c  00000000
0096c830  00000000
0096c834  00000000
0096c838  00000000
0096c83c  00000000
```

A second parameter to both functions is a pointer to the so-called exception context (processor state when an exception occurred). We can use **.cxr** command to change thread execution context to what it was at exception time:

```
0:000> .cxr 0096c824
[...]
msvcrt!wcschr+0x15:
77bd8df3 668b08 mov cx, word ptr [eax] ds:0023:01031000=????
```

After changing the context, we can see the thread stack prior to that exception:

```
0:000> kL
ChildEBP RetAddr
0096caf0 67b11808 msvcrt!wcschr+0x15
0096cb10 67b1194d component2!function1+0x50
0096cb24 67b11afb component2!function2+0x1a
0096eb5c 67b11e10 component2!function3+0x39
0096ed94 67b14426 component2!function4+0x155
0096fdc0 67b164b7 component2!function5+0x3b
0096fdcc 00402831 component2!function6+0x5b
0096feec 0096ff14 program!function+0x1d1
0096ffec 00000000 kernel32!BaseThreadStart+0x34
```

We see that the exception happened when *component2* was searching a Unicode string for a character (*wcschr*). Most likely the string was not zero terminated.

To summarize and show the common exception handling path in user space here is another thread stack taken from a different dump:

```
ntdll!KiFastSystemCallRet
ntdll!NtWaitForMultipleObjects+0xc
kernel32!UnhandledExceptionFilter+0x746
kernel32!_except_handler3+0x61
ntdll!ExecuteHandler2+0x26
ntdll!ExecuteHandler+0x24
ntdll!RtlDispatchException+0x91
ntdll!KiUserExceptionDispatcher+0xe
ntdll!RtlpCoalesceFreeBlocks+0x36e ; crash is here
ntdll!RtlFreeHeap+0x38e
msvcrt!free+0xc3
msvcrt!_freefls+0x124
msvcrt!_freeptd+0x27
msvcrt!__CRTDLL_INIT+0x1da
ntdll!LdrpCallInitRoutine+0x14
ntdll!LdrShutdownThread+0xd2
kernel32!ExitThread+0x2f
kernel32!BaseThreadStart+0x39
```

When *RtlpCoalesceFreeBlocks* (this function compacts a heap, and it is called from *RtlFreeHeap*) does an illegal memory access, then this exception is first processed in kernel, and because it happened in user space and mode the execution is transferred to *RtlDispatchException* which searches for exception handlers, and in this case there is a default one installed: *UnhandledExceptionFilter*. If we see the latter function on a call stack we can manually get exception context, and from it, a thread stack leading to it, like in this example:

```
0:000> ~*kv
...
...
...
. 0 Id: 1568.68c Suspend: 1 Teb: 7ffde000 Unfrozen
ChildEBP RetAddr  Args to Child
...
...
...
0012a984 715206e0 0012a9ac 7800bdb5 0012a9b4 KERNEL32!UnhandledExceptionFilter+0x140 (FPO: [Non-Fpo])
...
...
...
0:000> dt _EXCEPTION_POINTERS 0012a9ac
+0x000 ep_xrecord : 0x12aa78
+0x004 ep_context : 0x12aa94

0:000> .cxr 0012aa94
eax=00000000 ebx=00000000 ecx=00000000 edx=7283e058 esi=0271a60c edi=00000000
eip=35c5f973 esp=0012ad60 ebp=0012ad7c iopl=0 nv up ei pl zr na pe nc
cs=001b ss=0023 ds=0023 es=0023 fs=0038 gs=0000 efl=00010246
componentA!InternalFoo+0x21:
35c5f973 8b01 mov eax,dword ptr [ecx] ds:0023:00000000=????????
```

We can also search for exception codes like c0000005 using scripts to dump raw stack data[92]. For example:

```
007cfa40 017d0000
007cfa44 007cfd90
007cfa48 7c82855e ntdll!KiUserExceptionDispatcher+0xe
007cfa4c 7c826d9b ntdll!NtContinue+0xc
007cfa50 7c82856c ntdll!KiUserExceptionDispatcher+0x1c
007cfa54 007cfa78
007cfa58 00000000
007cfa5c c0000005
007cfa60 00000000
007cfa64 00000000
007cfa68 0100e076 component!foo+0x1c4
007cfa6c 00000002
007cfa70 00000001
007cfa74 00000000
007cfa78 0001003f
007cfa7c 00000003
```

---

[92] WinDbg Scripts, Memory Dump Analysis Anthology, Volume 1, pages 231-240

```
007cfa80 000000b0
007cfa84 00000001
007cfa88 00000000
[...]

1: kd> .cxr 007cfa78
eax=01073bb0 ebx=7ffd9000 ecx=00000050 edx=01073bb0 esi=000003e5 edi=00000000
eip=0100e076 esp=007cfd44 ebp=007cfd90 iopl=0 nv up ei pl zr na pe nc
cs=001b ss=0023 ds=0023 es=0023 fs=003b gs=0000 efl=00000246
component!foo+0x1c4:
001b:0100e076 891a mov dword ptr [edx],ebx ds:0023:01073bb0=????????
```

The presence of unloaded fault handling modules can be the sign of **Hidden Exceptions** too:

```
Unloaded modules:
697b0000 697c7000 faultrep.dll
Timestamp: Fri Mar 25 02:11:44 2005 (42437360)
Checksum: 0001DC38
```

Comments

Sometimes we can spot 0001003f and its address can be the beginning of a context record (x86):

```
[...]
 0070f678 00000000
 0070f67c 0001003f
[...]
```

We can also search for it, for example, in the first 256MB of the process address space:

```
0:000> s-d 0 L10000000/4 0001003f
0070f67c 0001003f 00000000 00000000 00000000 ?..............
```

On Windows 10 RSP below KiUserExceptionDispatch can be used as an address for **.cxr** command:

```
[...]
 00000023`d432f4f0 00000000`00000000
 00000023`d432f4f8 00007ffa`e5c5577a ntdll!KiUserExceptionDispatch+0x3a
 00000023`d432f500 00000000`00000000
[...]

0:001> .cxr 00000023`d432f500
 rax=0000000000000000 rbx=0000000000000000 rcx=00007ff676f399b0
 rdx=0000000000000000 rsi=00000023d3e3c190 rdi=00007ff676f211e0
 rip=00007ff676f2120d rsp=00000023d432fc30 rbp=0000000000000000
 r8=00006f6d5c4f5ead r9=0000000000000032 r10=0000000000000032
 r11=00000023d432f960 r12=0000000000000000 r13=0000000000000000
 r14=0000000000000000 r15=0000000000000000
 iopl=0 nv up ei pl nz na po nc
 cs=0033 ss=002b ds=002b es=002b fs=0053 gs=002b efl=00010206
 Application+0x120d:
 00007ff6`76f2120d c70000000000 mov dword ptr [rax],0 ds:00000000`00000000=????????
```

Hidden IRP

Sometimes we suspect a particular thread is doing I/O, but IRP is missing in the output of **!thread** WinDbg command. The way to proceed is to examine the list of IRPs and associated threads from the output of **!irpfind** command. Here is a synthesized example from a few **Virtualized** (page 1192) **Young System** (page 1276) crash dumps:

```
0: kd> !thread fffffa8004e2d280


THREAD fffffa8004e2d280 Cid 0004.0020 Teb: 0000000000000000 Win32Thread: 0000000000000000 WAIT:
(Executive) KernelMode Non-Alertable
fffff880009ec440 NotificationEvent
Not impersonating
[...]

0: kd> !irpfind


Irp [ Thread ] irpStack: (Mj,Mn) DevObj [Driver] MDL Process
[...]
fffffa800424e4e0 [fffffa8004e2d280] irpStack: (3, 0) fffffa8004ed6d40 [ \Driver\DriverA]
[...]
```

Now we can inspect the found IRP (**!irp** command) and device object (for example, by using **!devobj** and **!devstack** commands). Sometimes we can see the same IRP address as **Execution Residue** (page 395) among "*Args to Child*" values in the output of **!thread** command or **kv** (if the thread is current).

Hidden Module

Sometimes we look for modules that were loaded and unloaded at some time. **lm** command lists unloaded modules, but some of them could be mapped to address space without using the runtime loader. The latter case is common for drm-type protection tools, rootkits, malware or crimeware which can influence a process execution. In such cases, we can hope that they still remain in virtual memory and search for them. WinDbg **.imgscan** command greatly helps in identifying MZ/PE module headers. The following example illustrates this command without implying that the found module did any harm:

```
0:000> .imgscan
MZ at 000d0000, prot 00000002, type 01000000 - size 6000
  Name: usrxcptn.dll
MZ at 00350000, prot 00000002, type 01000000 - size 9b000
  Name: ADVAPI32.dll
MZ at 00400000, prot 00000002, type 01000000 - size 23000
  Name: javaw.exe
MZ at 01df0000, prot 00000002, type 01000000 - size 8b000
  Name: OLEAUT32.dll
MZ at 01e80000, prot 00000002, type 01000000 - size 52000
  Name: SHLWAPI.dll
...
```

We do not see *usrxcptn* in either loaded or unloaded module lists:

```
0:002> lm
start    end        module name
00350000 003eb000   advapi32
00400000 00423000   javaw
01df0000 01e7b000   oleaut32
01e80000 01ed2000   shlwapi
...

Unloaded modules:
```

Then we can use **Unknown Component** pattern (page 1150) to see the module resources if present in memory:

```
0:002> !dh 000d0000

...

SECTION HEADER #4
   .rsrc name
    418 virtual size
   4000 virtual address
    600 size of raw data
   1600 file pointer to raw data
      0 file pointer to relocation table
      0 file pointer to line numbers
      0 number of relocations
      0 number of line numbers
40000040 flags
```

```
          Initialized Data
          (no align specified)
          Read Only

...

0:002> dc 000d0000+4000 L418
...
000d4140  ... n…z.)…F.i.l.
000d4150  ... e.D.e.s.c.r.i.p.
000d4160  ... t.i.o.n…..U.s.
000d4170  ...    e.r. .D.u.m.p. .
000d4180  ... U.s.e.r. .M.o.d.
000d4190  ... e. .E.x.c.e.p.t.
000d41a0  ... i.o.n. .D.i.s.p.
000d41b0  ... a.t.c.h.e.r…..

0:002> du 000d416C
000d416c  "User Dump User Mode Exception Di"
000d41ac  "spatcher"
```

This component seems to be loaded or mapped only if the userdump package is fully installed: *usrxcptn.dll* is a part of its redistribution package, and the application is added to Process Dumper applet in Control Panel. Although from the memory dump comment we also see that the dump was taken manually using command line userdump.exe, we see that the full userdump package was additionally installed and that was probably not necessary[93]:

```
Loading Dump File [javaw.dmp]
User Mini Dump File with Full Memory: Only application data is available

Comment: 'Userdump generated complete user-mode minidump with Standalone function on COMPUTER-NAME'
```

Comments

.imgscan may not be able to find all hidden modules (**Debugger Omission** pattern, page 240).

---

[93] Correcting Microsoft Article about userdump.exe, Memory Dump Analysis Anthology, Volume 1, page 612

Hidden Parameter

This pattern is a variant of **Execution Residue** (page 395) and **String Parameter** (page 1074) where we have parameters left out from a stack trace due to register calling conventions and compiler optimizations. However, using raw stack analysis of a region around stack frames of interest we find what we are looking for. Here's an example from an x64 system blocked thread waiting for data from a named pipe:

```
0: kd> kL
*** Stack trace for last set context - .thread/.cxr resets it
Child-SP          RetAddr           Call Site
fffffa60`2c3627d0 fffff800`018b90fa nt!KiSwapContext+0x7f
fffffa60`2c362910 fffff800`018add3b nt!KiSwapThread+0x13a
fffffa60`2c362980 fffff800`01b2121f nt!KeWaitForSingleObject+0x2cb
fffffa60`2c362a10 fffff800`01b319b6 nt!IopXxxControlFile+0xdeb
fffffa60`2c362b40 fffff800`018b68f3 nt!NtFsControlFile+0x56
fffffa60`2c362bb0 00000000`778d6eaa nt!KiSystemServiceCopyEnd+0x13
00000000`11f4da68 00000000`77767b6e ntdll!ZwFsControlFile+0xa
00000000`11f4da70 000007fe`ff94abc8 kernel32!WaitNamedPipeW+0x22f
00000000`11f4db60 000007fe`ff98a32d RPCRT4!NdrProxyForwardingFunction255+0x814d
00000000`11f4dc30 000007fe`ff98918b RPCRT4!OSF_CCONNECTION::TransOpen+0xcd
00000000`11f4dcc0 000007fe`ff988f9b RPCRT4!OSF_CCONNECTION::OpenConnectionAndBind+0x17b
00000000`11f4dd90 000007fe`ff988ec6 RPCRT4!OSF_CCALL::BindToServer+0xbb
00000000`11f4de40 000007fe`ff983368 RPCRT4!OSF_BINDING_HANDLE::InitCCallWithAssociation+0xa5
00000000`11f4dea0 000007fe`ff983220 RPCRT4!OSF_BINDING_HANDLE::AllocateCCall+0x118
00000000`11f4dfd0 000007fe`ffa1f740 RPCRT4!OSF_BINDING_HANDLE::NegotiateTransferSyntax+0x30
00000000`11f4e020 000007fe`ffa1fecb RPCRT4!Ndr64pClientSetupTransferSyntax+0x200
00000000`11f4e080 000007fe`ffa20281 RPCRT4!NdrpClientCall3+0x6b
00000000`11f4e2d0 000007fe`fe087c8c RPCRT4!NdrClientCall3+0xdd
[...]
```

Even if we disassemble the return address of a caller of *WaitNamedPipeW* function we won't easily find the passed first string parameter (named pipe name) unless we do a substantial reverse engineering and data flow analysis:

```
0: kd> ub 000007fe`ff94abc8
RPCRT4!_imp_load_getaddrinfo+0x7:
000007fe`ff94ab9f jmp RPCRT4!_tailMerge_WS2_32_dll (000007fe`ff94cef8)
000007fe`ff94aba4 call qword ptr [RPCRT4!_imp_GetLastError (000007fe`ffa2d528)]
000007fe`ff94abaa mov r12d,eax
000007fe`ff94abad cmp r12d,0E7h
000007fe`ff94abb4 jne RPCRT4!NdrProxyForwardingFunction255+0x8193 (000007fe`ff99c8fb)
000007fe`ff94abba mov edx,3E8h
000007fe`ff94abbf mov rcx,rsi
000007fe`ff94abc2 call qword ptr [RPCRT4!_imp_WaitNamedPipeW (000007fe`ffa2d3f8)]
```

However, dumping raw stack data around corresponding frames gives us pipe name clue and possible service name to look further:

```
0: kd> dpu 00000000`11f4da70
00000000`11f4da70 00000000`11f4dba8 "\\.\PIPE\ServiceArpc"
00000000`11f4da78 00000000`00000000
00000000`11f4da80 00000000`00000000
00000000`11f4da88 00000000`000003e8
00000000`11f4da90 00000000`11f4db30
00000000`11f4da98 00000000`00110018
00000000`11f4daa0 00000000`0d9001a0
00000000`11f4daa8 00000000`0000001a
00000000`11f4dab0 00000000`00000000
00000000`11f4dab8 00000000`00000000
00000000`11f4dac0 00000000`0020000c
00000000`11f4dac8 00000000`0d9001e2 "ServiceArpc"
00000000`11f4dad0 00000000`00000000
00000000`11f4dad8 00000000`00000000
00000000`11f4dae0 00000000`00240022
```

Hidden Process

Not all processes are linked into a list that some commands traverse such as **!process 0 0**. A process may unlink itself or be in an initialization stage. However, a process structure is allocated from the nonpaged pool, and such pool can be searched for "*Proc*" pool tag (unless a process changes that in memory). For example:

```
0: kd> !poolfind Proc

Searching NonPaged pool (83c3c000 : 8bc00000) for Tag: Proc

*87b15000 size:   298 previous size:    0 (Free)        Pro.
*87b18370 size:   298 previous size:   98 (Allocated) Proc (Protected)
[...]
*8a35e900 size:   298 previous size:   30 (Allocated) Proc (Protected)
*8a484000 size:   298 previous size:    0 (Allocated) Proc (Protected)
*8a4a2d68 size:   298 previous size:   28 (Allocated) Proc (Protected)
[...]
```

One such structure is missing from the active process linked list (note that it has a parent PID):

```
0: kd> !process 8a484000+20
PROCESS 8a484020  SessionId: 0  Cid: 05a0    Peb: 00000000  ParentCid: 0244
DirBase: bffc2200  ObjectTable: e17e6a78  HandleCount:   0.
Image: AppChild.exe
VadRoot 8a574f80 Vads 4 Clone 0 Private 3. Modified 0. Locked 0.
DeviceMap e1002898
Token                             e1a36030
ElapsedTime                       00:00:00.000
UserTime                          00:00:00.000
KernelTime                        419 Days 13:24:16.625
QuotaPoolUsage[PagedPool]         7580
QuotaPoolUsage[NonPagedPool]      160
Working Set Sizes (now,min,max)  (12, 50, 345) (48KB, 200KB, 1380KB)
PeakWorkingSetSize                12
VirtualSize                       1 Mb
PeakVirtualSize                   1 Mb
PageFaultCount                    5
MemoryPriority                    BACKGROUND
BasePriority                      8
CommitCharge                      156

    No active threads
```

We may think that this process is a zombie (note that unlike terminated processes it has a non-zero data such as VAD and object table and zero PEB and elapsed time) but inspection of its parent process thread stacks reveals that it was in the process of creation (note an attached process field):

```
THREAD 8a35dad8  Cid 0244.0248  Teb: 7ffdd000 Win32Thread: bc3aa688 WAIT: (Unknown) KernelMode Non-
Alertable
ba971608  NotificationEvent
Impersonation token:  e2285030 (Level Impersonation)
DeviceMap                 e1a31a58
Owning Process            8a35e920        Image:         AppParent.exe
Attached Process          8a484020        Image:         AppChild.exe
Wait Start TickCount      2099            Ticks: 1 (0:00:00:00.015)
Context Switch Count      279                     LargeStack
UserTime                  00:00:00.046
KernelTime                00:00:00.046
Win32 Start Address AppParent!mainCRTStartup (0x0100d303)
Start Address kernel32!BaseProcessStartThunk (0x77e617f8)
Stack Init ba972000 Current ba971364 Base ba972000 Limit ba96e000 Call 0
Priority 8 BasePriority 8 PriorityDecrement 0
ChildEBP RetAddr
ba97137c 80833f2d nt!KiSwapContext+0x26
ba9713a8 80829c72 nt!KiSwapThread+0x2e5
ba9713f0 bad3c9db nt!KeWaitForSingleObject+0x346
[...]
ba971b94 8094cfc3 nt!MmCreatePeb+0x2cc
ba971ce4 8094d42d nt!PspCreateProcess+0x5a9
ba971d38 8088b4ac nt!NtCreateProcessEx+0x77
ba971d38 7c82845c nt!KiFastCallEntry+0xfc (TrapFrame @ ba971d64)
0006f498 7c826d09 ntdll!KiFastSystemCallRet
0006f49c 77e6cf95 ntdll!ZwCreateProcessEx+0xc
0006fcc0 7d1ec670 kernel32!CreateProcessInternalW+0x15e5
0006fd0c 01008bcf ADVAPI32!CreateProcessAsUserW+0x108
[...]
```

Hidden Stack

Sometimes, when we have **One-Thread Process** (page 851) memory dumps, it is possible to get other stack regions indirectly through the analysis of virtual memory regions. Consider, for example, this dump that has only one process exit thread:

```
0:000> kL
# Child-SP          RetAddr           Call Site
00 000000f1`828ff848 00007ff9`d29aa9b8 ntdll!NtTerminateProcess+0x14
01 000000f1`828ff850 00007ff9`d113cd8a ntdll!RtlExitUserProcess+0xb8
02 000000f1`828ff880 00007ff7`fbb91231 kernel32!ExitProcessImplementation+0xa
03 000000f1`828ff8b0 00007ff7`fbb9125f HiddenStack!bar1+0x41
04 000000f1`828ffa80 00007ff7`fbb91cb5 HiddenStack!foo1+0x1f
05 000000f1`828ffc40 00007ff7`fbb91b1b HiddenStack!std::_Invoker_functor::_Call<void (__cdecl*)(void)>+0x15
06 000000f1`828ffc70 00007ff7`fbb917c4 HiddenStack!std::invoke<void (__cdecl*)(void)>+0x1b
07 000000f1`828ffca0 00007ff7`fbb99728 HiddenStack!std::thread::_Invoke<std::tuple<void (__cdecl*)(void)>,0>+0x64
08 000000f1`828ffcf0 00007ff9`d1137bd4 HiddenStack!thread_start<unsigned int (__cdecl*)(void *),1>+0x50
09 000000f1`828ffd20 00007ff9`d29aced1 kernel32!BaseThreadInitThunk+0x14
0a 000000f1`828ffd50 00000000`00000000 ntdll!RtlUserThreadStart+0x21
```

There are no more thread stack traces:

```
0:000> ~
. 0 Id: 27d4.22a4 Suspend: -1 Teb: 000000f1`8266a000 Unfrozen
```

However, in addition to thread #0, we can find several regions having *PAGE_GUARD* protection:

```
0:000> !address
[...]
+ f1`82800000   f1`828fb000    0`000fb000 MEM_PRIVATE MEM_RESERVE                            Stack     [~0; 27d4.22a4]
  f1`828fb000   f1`828fe000    0`00003000 MEM_PRIVATE MEM_COMMIT  PAGE_READWRITE|PAGE_GUARD Stack     [~0; 27d4.22a4]
  f1`828fe000   f1`82900000    0`00002000 MEM_PRIVATE MEM_COMMIT  PAGE_READWRITE            Stack     [~0; 27d4.22a4]
+ f1`82900000   f1`829fb000    0`000fb000 MEM_PRIVATE MEM_RESERVE                            <unknown>
  f1`829fb000   f1`829fe000    0`00003000 MEM_PRIVATE MEM_COMMIT  PAGE_READWRITE|PAGE_GUARD <unknown>
  f1`829fe000   f1`82a00000    0`00002000 MEM_PRIVATE MEM_COMMIT  PAGE_READWRITE            <unknown> [..........]
+ f1`82a00000   f1`82afc000    0`000fc000 MEM_PRIVATE MEM_RESERVE                            <unknown>
  f1`82afc000   f1`82aff000    0`00003000 MEM_PRIVATE MEM_COMMIT  PAGE_READWRITE|PAGE_GUARD <unknown>
  f1`82aff000   f1`82b00000    0`00001000 MEM_PRIVATE MEM_COMMIT  PAGE_READWRITE            <unknown> [..........]
+ f1`82b00000   f1`82bfb000    0`000fb000 MEM_PRIVATE MEM_RESERVE                            <unknown>
  f1`82bfb000   f1`82bfe000    0`00003000 MEM_PRIVATE MEM_COMMIT  PAGE_READWRITE|PAGE_GUARD <unknown>
  f1`82bfe000   f1`82c00000    0`00002000 MEM_PRIVATE MEM_COMMIT  PAGE_READWRITE            <unknown> [..........]
+ f1`82c00000   1fe`828f0000  10c`ffcf0000 MEM_FREE     PAGE_NOACCESS                         Free
[...]
```

We then can get **Rough Stack Traces** (page 940) out of them:

```
0:000> .lines -d
Line number information will not be loaded

0:000> dpS f1`829fe000 f1`82a00000
00007ff9`d2986139 ntdll!RtlpFindEntry+0x4d
00007ff9`d297dbea ntdll!RtlpAllocateHeap+0xcfa
00007ff9`d297babb ntdll!RtlpAllocateHeapInternal+0x1cb
00007ff9`d297babb ntdll!RtlpAllocateHeapInternal+0x1cb
00007ff9`d2a463fa ntdll!RtlpValidateHeap+0x32
00007ff9`d2a44b25 ntdll!RtlDebugAllocateHeap+0x35d
00007ff9`d29f49d6 ntdll!RtlpAllocateHeap+0x77ae6
00007ff9`d29f49d6 ntdll!RtlpAllocateHeap+0x77ae6
```

```
00007ff9`d0070000 KERNELBASE!UrlHashW <PERF> (KERNELBASE+0x0)
00007ff9`d007b4b1 KERNELBASE!SetTEBLangID+0x2d
00007ff9`d007ac70 KERNELBASE!_KernelBaseBaseDllInitialize+0x90
00007ff9`d297babb ntdll!RtlpAllocateHeapInternal+0x1cb
00007ff9`d297babb ntdll!RtlpAllocateHeapInternal+0x1cb
00007ff9`d19e7890 msvcrt!CRTDLL_INIT
00007ff9`d29db5a3 ntdll!RTL_BINARY_ARRAY<RTLP_FLS_SLOT,8,4>::ChunkAllocate+0x67
00007ff9`d19e0000 msvcrt!`dynamic initializer for '__ExceptionPtr::m_badAllocExceptionPtr" <PERF> (msvcrt+0x0)
00007ff9`d29db65d ntdll!RTL_BINARY_ARRAY<RTLP_FLS_SLOT,8,4>::SetValue+0x39
00007ff9`d2964ef7 ntdll!RtlDeactivateActivationContextUnsafeFast+0xc7
00007ff9`d299439c ntdll!RtlFlsSetValue+0xec
00007ff9`d2986139 ntdll!RtlpFindEntry+0x4d
00000000`7ffe0301 SharedUserData+0x301
00007ff9`d297dbea ntdll!RtlpAllocateHeap+0xcfa
00000000`7ffe0358 SharedUserData+0x358
00007ff7`fbb923ca HiddenStack!std::chrono::duration_cast<std::chrono::duration<double,
std::ratio<1,1000000000> >,__int64,std::ratio<1,1000000000>,void>+0x4a
00000000`7ffe0358 SharedUserData+0x358
00007ff9`d294bb47 ntdll!RtlGetSystemTimePrecise+0x57
00007ff9`d00b6931 KERNELBASE!SleepEx+0xa1
00007ff9`d00d3890 KERNELBASE!GetSystemTimePreciseAsFileTime+0x10
00007ff7`fbb931b4 HiddenStack!_Thrd_sleep+0x3c
00007ff7`fbb916c5 HiddenStack!std::this_thread::sleep_until<std::chrono::steady_clock,
std::chrono::duration<__int64,std::ratio<1,1000000000> > >+0x65
00007ff7`fbb91651
HiddenStack!std::chrono::operator+<std::chrono::steady_clock,std::chrono::duration<__int64,std::ratio<1,1000000000>
>,__int64,std::ratio<1,1> >+0x41
00007ff7`fbb913fd HiddenStack!std::this_thread::sleep_for<__int64,std::ratio<1,1> >+0x2d
00007ff7`fbb912a9 HiddenStack!bar2+0x39
00007ff7`fbb912df HiddenStack!foo2+0x1f
00007ff7`fbb91cb5 HiddenStack!std::_Invoker_functor::_Call<void (__cdecl*)(void)>+0x15
00007ff7`fbb91aec HiddenStack!std::unique_ptr<std::tuple<void (__cdecl*)(void)>,std::default_delete<std::tuple<void
(__cdecl*)(void)> > >::unique_ptr<std::tuple<void (__cdecl*)(void)>,std::default_delete<std::tuple<void
(__cdecl*)(void)> > ><std::default_delete<std::tuple<void (__cdecl*)(void)> >,0>+0x2c
00007ff7`fbb91b1b HiddenStack!std::invoke<void (__cdecl*)(void)>+0x1b
00007ff7`fbb917c4 HiddenStack!std::thread::_Invoke<std::tuple<void (__cdecl*)(void)>,0>+0x64
00007ff7`fbb9c1d7 HiddenStack!__acrt_getptd+0xb3
00007ff7`fbb99728 HiddenStack!thread_start<unsigned int (__cdecl*)(void *),1>+0x50
00007ff9`d1137bd4 kernel32!BaseThreadInitThunk+0x14
00007ff9`d29aced1 ntdll!RtlUserThreadStart+0x21


0:000> dpS f1`82aff000 f1`82b00000
00007ff9`d2986139 ntdll!RtlpFindEntry+0x4d
00007ff9`d297dbea ntdll!RtlpAllocateHeap+0xcfa
00007ff9`d297dbea ntdll!RtlpAllocateHeap+0xcfa
00007ff9`d297babb ntdll!RtlpAllocateHeapInternal+0x1cb
00007ff9`d2a463fa ntdll!RtlpValidateHeap+0x32
00007ff9`d2a463fa ntdll!RtlpValidateHeap+0x32
00007ff9`d2a44b25 ntdll!RtlDebugAllocateHeap+0x35d
00007ff9`d29f49d6 ntdll!RtlpAllocateHeap+0x77ae6
00007ff9`d2962da8 ntdll!LdrpInitializeThread+0x40
00007ff9`d297562f ntdll!TppCallbackCheckThreadAfterCallback+0x9f
00007ff9`d29700e5 ntdll!RtlRegisterThreadWithCsrss+0x35
00007ff9`d29b18f5 ntdll!_LdrpInitialize+0x89
00007ff9`d2975394 ntdll!TppCallbackEpilog+0x144
00007ff9`d29701d6 ntdll!TppCritSetThread+0x7a
00007ff9`d2973155 ntdll!TppWorkCallbackPrologRelease+0x1c9
00007ff9`d296e2c3 ntdll!LdrpWorkCallback+0x63
00007ff9`d2aa52f0 ntdll!LdrpWorkQueue
00007ff9`d29708a2 ntdll!TppWorkpExecuteCallback+0xb2
00000000`7ffe0386 SharedUserData+0x386
```

```
00007ff9`d2974060 ntdll!TppWorkerThread+0x300
00007ff9`d1137bd4 kernel32!BaseThreadInitThunk+0x14
00007ff9`d29aced1 ntdll!RtlUserThreadStart+0x21


0:000> dpS f1`82bfe000 f1`82c00000
00007ff9`d2986139 ntdll!RtlpFindEntry+0x4d
00007ff9`d297dbea ntdll!RtlpAllocateHeap+0xcfa
00007ff9`d297dbea ntdll!RtlpAllocateHeap+0xcfa
00007ff9`d297babb ntdll!RtlpAllocateHeapInternal+0x1cb
00007ff9`d2a463fa ntdll!RtlpValidateHeap+0x32
00007ff9`d2a463fa ntdll!RtlpValidateHeap+0x32
00007ff9`d2a44b25 ntdll!RtlDebugAllocateHeap+0x35d
00007ff9`d29f49d6 ntdll!RtlpAllocateHeap+0x77ae6
00007ff9`d2962da8 ntdll!LdrpInitializeThread+0x40
00007ff9`d29700e5 ntdll!RtlRegisterThreadWithCsrss+0x35
00007ff9`d29b18f5 ntdll!_LdrpInitialize+0x89
00007ff9`d297babb ntdll!RtlpAllocateHeapInternal+0x1cb
00007ff9`d29701d6 ntdll!TppCritSetThread+0x7a
00007ff9`d2970098 ntdll!TppPoolAddWorker+0x68
00007ff9`d2974060 ntdll!TppWorkerThread+0x300
00007ff9`d1137bd4 kernel32!BaseThreadInitThunk+0x14
00007ff9`d29aced1 ntdll!RtlUserThreadStart+0x21
```

We call such analysis pattern **Hidden Stack** as another way to get **Historical Information** (page 543) from memory dumps.

The example memory dump, the application PDB file, and source code are available for download[94].

---

[94] http://www.patterndiagnostics.com/SoftwareDiagnosticsCorpus/SDC5.zip

Hidden Stack Trace

Sometimes, a stack trace from **Stack Trace Collection** (page 1052) may look well-formed at first sight, for example, having an expected start frames:

```
0:000> ~*k

[...]

# 19 Id: 16a4.21f4 Suspend: 0 Teb: 7e95b000 Unfrozen
ChildEBP RetAddr
0c2de6b0 74eb112f ntdll!NtWaitForMultipleObjects+0xc
0c2de83c 76ca7b89 KERNELBASE!WaitForMultipleObjectsEx+0xcc
0c2de858 76d007bf kernel32!WaitForMultipleObjects+0x19
0c2dec98 76d00295 kernel32!WerpReportFaultInternal+0x50b
0c2deca8 76ce1709 kernel32!WerpReportFault+0x74
0c2decb0 74f5f705 kernel32!BasepReportFault+0x19
0c2ded3c 76fb4f84 KERNELBASE!UnhandledExceptionFilter+0x1f4
0c2ded54 76fb5728 ntdll!TppExceptionFilter+0x30
0c2ded64 76f5c95a ntdll!TppWorkerpInnerExceptionFilter+0xe
0c2df914 76ca7c04 ntdll!TppWorkerThread+0x87f5a
0c2df928 76f1ad1f kernel32!BaseThreadInitThunk+0x24
0c2df970 76f1acea ntdll!__RtlUserThreadStart+0x2f
0c2df980 00000000 ntdll!_RtlUserThreadStart+0x1b

[...]
```

So, we may think something wrong happened in *ntdll!TppWorkerThread* code (although 0x87f5a offset looks suspicious). However, in reality, in this case, due to exception filter logic (or some other reason in different cases), we have **Hidden Stack Trace**. When looking at *UnhandledExceptionFilter* parameters (or raw stack as in the case of **Hidden Exceptions**, page 504), we find an exception context:

```
0:019> kv
ChildEBP RetAddr Args to Child
0c2de6b0 74eb112f 00000003 0c2de880 00000001 ntdll!NtWaitForMultipleObjects+0xc
0c2de83c 76ca7b89 00000003 0c2de880 00000000 KERNELBASE!WaitForMultipleObjectsEx+0xcc
0c2de858 76d007bf 00000003 0c2de880 00000000 kernel32!WaitForMultipleObjects+0x19
0c2dec98 76d00295 00000000 00000001 00000000 kernel32!WerpReportFaultInternal+0x50b
0c2deca8 76ce1709 0c2ded3c 74f5f705 0c2ded94 kernel32!WerpReportFault+0x74
0c2decb0 74f5f705 0c2ded94 00000001 a79b7895 kernel32!BasepReportFault+0x19
0c2ded3c 76fb4f84 0c2ded94 0c2ded94 00000000 KERNELBASE!UnhandledExceptionFilter+0x1f4
0c2ded54 76fb5728 00000000 00000000 0c2df914 ntdll!TppExceptionFilter+0x30
0c2ded64 76f5c95a 0c2df8d0 76f00a70 0c2df914 ntdll!TppWorkerpInnerExceptionFilter+0xe
0c2df914 76ca7c04 0f79e380 76ca7be0 a5b45024 ntdll!TppWorkerThread+0x87f5a
0c2df928 76f1ad1f 0f79e380 a59141d7 00000000 kernel32!BaseThreadInitThunk+0x24
0c2df970 76f1acea ffffffff 76f00233 00000000 ntdll!__RtlUserThreadStart+0x2f
0c2df980 00000000 76ed4a00 0f79e380 00000000 ntdll!_RtlUserThreadStart+0x1b

0:019> dd 0c2ded94 L2
0c2ded94 0c2deef8 0c2def48
```

```
0:019> .cxr 0c2def48
eax=15f237e5 ebx=15f235e9 ecx=15f237e1 edx=7e95b000 esi=15f237e1 edi=09724b10
eip=76f00fb2 esp=0c2df3ac ebp=0c2df3ac iopl=0 nv up ei pl nz na po nc
cs=0023 ss=002b ds=002b es=002b fs=0053 gs=002b efl=00010202
ntdll!RtlEnterCriticalSection+0x12:
76f00fb2 f00fba3000 lock btr dword ptr [eax],0 ds:002b:15f237e5=????????


0:019> k
*** Stack trace for last set context - .thread/.cxr resets it
ChildEBP RetAddr
0c2df3ac 7407999c ntdll!RtlEnterCriticalSection+0x12
0c2df3cc 7407acd6 ModuleA!DoWork+0x1b
[...]
0c2df73c 76ee3aa7 ModuleA!ThreadPoolWorkCallback+0xa9
0c2df77c 76ee1291 ntdll!TppWorkpExecuteCallback+0x137
0c2df914 76ca7c04 ntdll!TppWorkerThread+0x48e
0c2df928 76f1ad1f kernel32!BaseThreadInitThunk+0x24
0c2df970 76f1acea ntdll!__RtlUserThreadStart+0x2f
0c2df980 00000000 ntdll!_RtlUserThreadStart+0x1b
```

We consider this a different pattern than **Hidden Call** (page 499) because an entire stack (sub)trace is missing between *UnhandledExceptionFilter* and thread start frames:

```
ntdll!NtWaitForMultipleObjects
KERNELBASE!WaitForMultipleObjectsEx
kernel32!WaitForMultipleObjects
kernel32!WerpReportFaultInternal
kernel32!WerpReportFault
kernel32!BasepReportFault
KERNELBASE!UnhandledExceptionFilter
[...]
ntdll!TppWorkerThread
kernel32!BaseThreadInitThunk
ntdll!__RtlUserThreadStart
ntdll!_RtlUserThreadStart
```

This pattern is also different from **Past Stack Trace** (page 886) pattern because **Hidden Stack Trace** belongs to PRESENT time zone. Our example is also different from **Hidden Exception** (page 504) analysis pattern and its recovered stack trace because exception processing is not hidden and shows **Exception Stack Trace** (page 386) albeit with a hidden part.

We were also fortunate to have **Stored Exception** (page 1071, accessible by **!analyze -v** command):

```
0:019> .exr -1
ExceptionAddress: 76f00fb2 (ntdll!RtlEnterCriticalSection+0x00000012)
ExceptionCode: c0000005 (Access violation)
ExceptionFlags: 00000000
NumberParameters: 2
Parameter[0]: 00000001
Parameter[1]: 15f237e5
Attempt to write to address 15f237e5
```

```
0:019> .ecxr
eax=15f237e5 ebx=15f235e9 ecx=15f237e1 edx=7e95b000 esi=15f237e1 edi=09724b10
eip=76f00fb2 esp=0c2df3ac ebp=0c2df3ac iopl=0 nv up ei pl nz na po nc
cs=0023 ss=002b ds=002b es=002b fs=0053 gs=002b efl=00010202
ntdll!RtlEnterCriticalSection+0x12:
76f00fb2 f00fba3000 lock btr dword ptr [eax],0 ds:002b:15f237e5=????????
```

So this **Hidden Stack Trace** is detected straightforwardly. But in other cases, such as when we have **Multiple Exceptions** (page 799) in a process dump or **Stack Trace Collection** (page 1052) from a complete memory dump, we need to pay attention to such a possibility.

High Contention

.NET CLR Monitors

This is a high contention pattern variant where the contention is around a monitor object. For example, we have a **Distributed** CPU **Spike** (page 265) for some threads:

```
0:000> !runaway
 User Mode Time
  Thread       Time
    9:6ff4      0 days 0:07:39.019
   12:6b88      0 days 0:06:19.786
   11:6bf0      0 days 0:06:13.889
   10:6930      0 days 0:06:09.240
   16:3964      0 days 0:05:44.483
   17:6854      0 days 0:05:35.326
   13:668c      0 days 0:05:35.123
   14:5594      0 days 0:05:34.858
   15:7248      0 days 0:05:23.111
    2:c54       0 days 0:00:41.215
    4:1080      0 days 0:00:00.349
    7:10f0      0 days 0:00:00.302
    0:c3c       0 days 0:00:00.271
[...]
```

If we look at their stack traces, we find them all blocked trying to enter a monitor[95], for example:

```
0:000> ~*k

[...]

12 Id: d50.6b88 Suspend: 0 Teb: 000007ff`fffd8000 Unfrozen
Child-SP RetAddr Call Site
00000000`1a98e798 000007fe`fd0c1420 ntdll!ZwWaitForMultipleObjects+0xa
00000000`1a98e7a0 00000000`76e82cf3 KERNELBASE!WaitForMultipleObjectsEx+0xe8
00000000`1a98e8a0 000007fe`f82e0669 kernel32!WaitForMultipleObjectsExImplementation+0xb3
00000000`1a98e930 000007fe`f82dbec9 mscorwks!WaitForMultipleObjectsEx_SO_TOLERANT+0xc1
00000000`1a98e9d0 000007fe`f82a0569 mscorwks!Thread::DoAppropriateAptStateWait+0x41
00000000`1a98ea30 000007fe`f82beaec mscorwks!Thread::DoAppropriateWaitWorker+0x191
00000000`1a98eb30 000007fe`f81f1b9a mscorwks!Thread::DoAppropriateWait+0x5c
00000000`1a98eba0 000007fe`f82fd3c9 mscorwks!CLREvent::WaitEx+0xbe
00000000`1a98ec50 000007fe`f81ac6be mscorwks!AwareLock::EnterEpilog+0xc9
00000000`1a98ed20 000007fe`f81c7b2b mscorwks!AwareLock::Enter+0x72
00000000`1a98ed50 000007fe`f87946af mscorwks!AwareLock::Contention+0x1fb
00000000`1a98ee20 000007ff`00161528 mscorwks!JITutil_MonContention+0xdf
00000000`1a98efd0 000007ff`0016140e 0x7ff`00161528
00000000`1a98f040 000007ff`00167271 0x7ff`0016140e
```

---

[95] http://en.wikipedia.org/wiki/Monitor_(synchronization)

```
00000000`1a98f0a0 000007fe`f74e2bbb 0x7ff`00167271
00000000`1a98f130 000007fe`f753ed76 mscorlib_ni+0x2f2bbb
00000000`1a98f180 000007fe`f8390282 mscorlib_ni+0x34ed76
00000000`1a98f1d0 000007fe`f8274363 mscorwks!CallDescrWorker+0x82
00000000`1a98f220 000007fe`f8274216 mscorwks!CallDescrWorkerWithHandler+0xd3
00000000`1a98f2c0 000007fe`f81c96a7 mscorwks!DispatchCallDebuggerWrapper+0x3e
00000000`1a98f320 000007fe`f830ae42 mscorwks!DispatchCallNoEH+0x5f
00000000`1a98f3a0 000007fe`f81bdc00 mscorwks!AddTimerCallback_Worker+0x92
00000000`1a98f430 000007fe`f82a41a5 mscorwks!ManagedThreadCallState::IsAppDomainEqual+0x4c
00000000`1a98f480 000007fe`f82df199 mscorwks!SVR::gc_heap::make_heap_segment+0x155
00000000`1a98f550 000007fe`f82ececa mscorwks!DoOpenIAssemblyStress::DoOpenIAssemblyStress+0x99
00000000`1a98f590 000007fe`f830c0db mscorwks!AddTimerCallbackEx+0xba
00000000`1a98f650 000007fe`f81ebb37 mscorwks!ThreadpoolMgr::AsyncTimerCallbackCompletion+0x53
00000000`1a98f6b0 000007fe`f81fe92a mscorwks!UnManagedPerAppDomainTPCount::DispatchWorkItem+0x157
00000000`1a98f750 000007fe`f81bb1fc mscorwks!ThreadpoolMgr::WorkerThreadStart+0x1ba
00000000`1a98f7f0 00000000`76e7652d mscorwks!Thread::intermediateThreadProc+0x78
00000000`1a98fcc0 00000000`76fac521 kernel32!BaseThreadInitThunk+0xd
00000000`1a98fcf0 00000000`00000000 ntdll!RtlUserThreadStart+0x1d


[...]


15 Id: d50.7248 Suspend: 0 Teb: 000007ff`ffee6000 Unfrozen
Child-SP RetAddr Call Site
00000000`1c16e6f0 000007fe`f87946af mscorwks!AwareLock::Contention+0x13b
00000000`1c16e7c0 000007ff`0016135e mscorwks!JITutil_MonContention+0xdf
00000000`1c16e970 000007ff`0016726b 0x7ff`0016135e
00000000`1c16e9c0 000007fe`f74e2bbb 0x7ff`0016726b
00000000`1c16ea50 000007fe`f753ed76 mscorlib_ni+0x2f2bbb
00000000`1c16eaa0 000007fe`f8390282 mscorlib_ni+0x34ed76
00000000`1c16eaf0 000007fe`f8274363 mscorwks!CallDescrWorker+0x82
00000000`1c16eb40 000007fe`f8274216 mscorwks!CallDescrWorkerWithHandler+0xd3
00000000`1c16ebe0 000007fe`f81c96a7 mscorwks!DispatchCallDebuggerWrapper+0x3e
00000000`1c16ec40 000007fe`f830ae42 mscorwks!DispatchCallNoEH+0x5f
00000000`1c16ecc0 000007fe`f81bdc00 mscorwks!AddTimerCallback_Worker+0x92
00000000`1c16ed50 000007fe`f82a41a5 mscorwks!ManagedThreadCallState::IsAppDomainEqual+0x4c
00000000`1c16eda0 000007fe`f82df199 mscorwks!SVR::gc_heap::make_heap_segment+0x155
00000000`1c16ee70 000007fe`f82ececa mscorwks!DoOpenIAssemblyStress::DoOpenIAssemblyStress+0x99
00000000`1c16eeb0 000007fe`f830c0db mscorwks!AddTimerCallbackEx+0xba
00000000`1c16ef70 000007fe`f81ebb37 mscorwks!ThreadpoolMgr::AsyncTimerCallbackCompletion+0x53
00000000`1c16efd0 000007fe`f81fe92a mscorwks!UnManagedPerAppDomainTPCount::DispatchWorkItem+0x157
00000000`1c16f070 000007fe`f81bb1fc mscorwks!ThreadpoolMgr::WorkerThreadStart+0x1ba
00000000`1c16f110 00000000`76e7652d mscorwks!Thread::intermediateThreadProc+0x78
00000000`1c16f9e0 00000000`76fac521 kernel32!BaseThreadInitThunk+0xd
00000000`1c16fa10 00000000`00000000 ntdll!RtlUserThreadStart+0x1d


[...]
```

Thread #15 seems was caught at the time when it was trying to enter and not waiting yet. If we check a monitor object the thread #12 tries to enter we see it has an address 01af0be8:

```
0:000> !u 000007ff`00161528
Normal JIT generated code
[...]
000007ff`00161505 90                      nop
000007ff`00161506 48b8f089ae1100000000 mov rax,11AE89F0h
000007ff`00161510 488b00           mov    rax,qword ptr [rax]
000007ff`00161513 48894528         mov    qword ptr [rbp+28h],rax
000007ff`00161517 488b4528         mov    rax,qword ptr [rbp+28h]
000007ff`0016151b 48894518         mov    qword ptr [rbp+18h],rax
000007ff`0016151f 488b4d28         mov    rcx,qword ptr [rbp+28h]
000007ff`00161523 e8b8d422f8       call   mscorwks!JIT_MonEnter (000007fe`f838e9e0)
>>> 000007ff`00161528 90                      nop
000007ff`00161529 90                      nop
000007ff`0016152a 90                      nop
[...]
000007ff`001615d2 4883c430         add    rsp,30h
000007ff`001615d6 5d               pop    rbp
000007ff`001615d7 f3c3             rep ret


0:000> dps 11AE89F0h l1
00000000`11ae89f0  00000000`01af0be8
```

This object seems to be owned by the thread #17:

```
0:000> !syncblk
Index         SyncBlock MonitorHeld Recursion Owning Thread Info    SyncBlock Owner
 1362 000000001ba7b6c0          15         1 000000001c0173b0  6854 17  0000000001af0be8 System.Object
[...]
```

This thread seems to be blocked in ALPC:

```
0:017> k
Child-SP RetAddr Call Site
00000000`1d55c9e8 000007fe`fee1a776 ntdll!NtAlpcSendWaitReceivePort+0xa
00000000`1d55c9f0 000007fe`fee14e42 rpcrt4!LRPC_CCALL::SendReceive+0x156
00000000`1d55cab0 000007fe`ff0828c0 rpcrt4!I_RpcSendReceive+0x42
00000000`1d55cae0 000007fe`ff08282f ole32!ThreadSendReceive+0x40
00000000`1d55cb30 000007fe`ff08265b ole32!CRpcChannelBuffer::SwitchAptAndDispatchCall+0xa3
00000000`1d55cbd0 000007fe`fef3daaa ole32!CRpcChannelBuffer::SendReceive2+0x11b
00000000`1d55cd90 000007fe`fef3da0c ole32!CAptRpcChnl::SendReceive+0x52
00000000`1d55ce60 000007fe`ff08205d ole32!CCtxComChnl::SendReceive+0x68
00000000`1d55cf10 000007fe`feebfd61 ole32!NdrExtpProxySendReceive+0x45
00000000`1d55cf40 000007fe`ff07f82f rpcrt4!NdrpClientCall2+0x9ea
00000000`1d55d6b0 000007fe`fef3d8a2 ole32!ObjectStublessClient+0x1ad
00000000`1d55da40 000007fe`fa511ba8 ole32!ObjectStubless+0x42
[...]
```

.NET Heap

This is **High Contention** pattern variant for .NET heap where we can see *gc_heap* functions in unmanaged **Stack Trace Collection** (page 1053), **Spiking Threads** (page 992) doing garbage collection, and threads waiting for object allocation:

```
0:000> ~*k

[...]

 4  Id: ad8.1338 Suspend: 0 Teb: 00007ff5`ff774000 Unfrozen
# Child-SP          RetAddr           Call Site
00 00000030`f9dff1c8 00007ff9`f4121118 ntdll!NtWaitForSingleObject+0xa
01 00000030`f9dff1d0 00007ff9`ee3594fb KERNELBASE!WaitForSingleObjectEx+0x94
02 00000030`f9dff270 00007ff9`ee3594a7 clr!CLREventWaitHelper2+0x38
03 00000030`f9dff2b0 00007ff9`ee359430 clr!CLREventWaitHelper+0x1f
04 00000030`f9dff310 00007ff9`ee533c96 clr!CLREventBase::WaitEx+0x63
05 00000030`f9dff3a0 00007ff9`ee85849a clr!SVR::gc_heap::user_thread_wait+0x58
06 00000030`f9dff3d0 00007ff9`ee74073f clr!SVR::gc_heap::background_gc_wait+0x4a
07 00000030`f9dff400 00007ff9`ee740cfd clr!SVR::GCHeap::GarbageCollect+0x2998df
08 00000030`f9dff440 00007ff9`ee4ccdf9 clr!SVR::WaitForFinalizerEvent+0x3272ed
09 00000030`f9dff480 00007ff9`ee35c481 clr!SVR::GCHeap::FinalizerThreadWorker+0x4a
0a 00000030`f9dff4c0 00007ff9`ee35c408 clr!ManagedThreadBase_DispatchInner+0x2d
0b 00000030`f9dff500 00007ff9`ee35c379 clr!ManagedThreadBase_DispatchMiddle+0x6c
0c 00000030`f9dff600 00007ff9`ee46c477 clr!ManagedThreadBase_DispatchOuter+0x75
0d 00000030`f9dff690 00007ff9`ee417de6 clr!SVR::GCHeap::FinalizerThreadStart+0xd7
0e 00000030`f9dff730 00007ff9`f60413d2 clr!Thread::intermediateThreadProc+0x7d
0f 00000030`f9dff7f0 00007ff9`f6ea54e4 kernel32!BaseThreadInitThunk+0x22
10 00000030`f9dff820 00000000`00000000 ntdll!RtlUserThreadStart+0x34

[...]

 8  Id: ad8.1960 Suspend: 0 Teb: 00007ff5`ff58c000 Unfrozen
# Child-SP          RetAddr           Call Site
00 00000030`fb90b898 00007ff9`f4121118 ntdll!NtWaitForSingleObject+0xa
01 00000030`fb90b8a0 00007ff9`ee3594fb KERNELBASE!WaitForSingleObjectEx+0x94
02 00000030`fb90b940 00007ff9`ee3594a7 clr!CLREventWaitHelper2+0x38
03 00000030`fb90b980 00007ff9`ee359430 clr!CLREventWaitHelper+0x1f
04 00000030`fb90b9e0 00007ff9`ee533c96 clr!CLREventBase::WaitEx+0x63
05 00000030`fb90ba70 00007ff9`ee85849a clr!SVR::gc_heap::user_thread_wait+0x58
06 00000030`fb90baa0 00007ff9`ee780417 clr!SVR::gc_heap::background_gc_wait+0x4a
07 00000030`fb90bad0 00007ff9`ee4c41e8 clr!SVR::gc_heap::wait_for_bgc_high_memory+0x2b8907
08 00000030`fb90bb60 00007ff9`ee355272 clr!SVR::GCHeap::Alloc+0x257
09 00000030`fb90bbc0 00007ff9`eb524a1d clr!JIT_New+0x142
0a 00000030`fb90be70 00007ff9`e8bd8ec8 System_Xml_ni+0x154a1d
0b 00000030`fb90bed0 00007ff9`e8d6ec7c System_Runtime_Serialization_ni+0xa8ec8
0c 00000030`fb90bf20 00007ff9`e9ed637b System_Runtime_Serialization_ni+0x23ec7c
0d 00000030`fb90bf80 00007ff9`ea6df472 System_ServiceModel_ni+0xdd637b
0e 00000030`fb90bfe0 00000030`fb90bfc0 System_ServiceModel_ni+0x15df472
0f 00000030`fb90bfe8 00000000`00000000 0x00000030`fb90bfc0

[...]
```

```
14  Id: ad8.11d4 Suspend: 0 Teb: 00007ff5`ff586000 Unfrozen
# Child-SP          RetAddr           Call Site
00 00000031`4a42eb10 00007ff9`ee4a3a76 clr!SVR::gc_heap::background_mark_simple1+0xcd9
01 00000031`4a42eba0 00007ff9`ee4a458b clr!SVR::gc_heap::background_mark_simple+0x99
02 00000031`4a42ebd0 00007ff9`ee52e68c clr!SVR::gc_heap::background_promote+0x15d
03 00000031`4a42ec40 00007ff9`ee538836 clr!PinObject+0x2c
04 00000031`4a42ec80 00007ff9`ee532fc8 clr!ScanConsecutiveHandlesWithoutUserData+0x62
05 00000031`4a42ecb0 00007ff9`ee5338f2 clr!BlockScanBlocksWithoutUserData+0x44
06 00000031`4a42ece0 00007ff9`ee5339fc clr!ProcessScanQNode+0x3d
07 00000031`4a42ed10 00007ff9`ee53397d clr!ProcessScanQueue+0x3d
08 00000031`4a42ed40 00007ff9`ee533bcf clr!xxxTableScanQueuedBlocksAsync+0x5d
09 00000031`4a42ed70 00007ff9`ee5353a5 clr!xxxAsyncSegmentIterator+0x2d
0a 00000031`4a42eda0 00007ff9`ee533ab6 clr!TableScanHandles+0x79
0b 00000031`4a42ee50 00007ff9`ee535607 clr!xxxTableScanHandlesAsync+0x9b
0c 00000031`4a42eff0 00007ff9`ee53795d clr!HndScanHandlesForGC+0x137
0d 00000031`4a42f090 00007ff9`ee535769 clr!Ref_TracePinningRoots+0xfd
0e 00000031`4a42f110 00007ff9`ee4a4351 clr!CNameSpace::GcScanHandles+0x4d
0f 00000031`4a42f150 00007ff9`ee55cbe9 clr!SVR::gc_heap::background_mark_phase+0x331
10 00000031`4a42f1e0 00007ff9`ee4a32ed clr!SVR::gc_heap::gc1+0xcd
11 00000031`4a42f240 00007ff9`ee417de6 clr!SVR::gc_heap::bgc_thread_function+0x177
12 00000031`4a42f280 00007ff9`f60413d2 clr!Thread::intermediateThreadProc+0x7d
13 00000031`4a42fcc0 00007ff9`f6ea54e4 kernel32!BaseThreadInitThunk+0x22
14 00000031`4a42fcf0 00000000`00000000 ntdll!RtlUserThreadStart+0x34

15  Id: ad8.f9c Suspend: 0 Teb: 00007ff5`ff648000 Unfrozen
# Child-SP          RetAddr           Call Site
00 00000030`f4eddb58 00007ff9`f4121118 ntdll!NtWaitForSingleObject+0xa
01 00000030`f4eddb60 00007ff9`ee3594fb KERNELBASE!WaitForSingleObjectEx+0x94
02 00000030`f4eddc00 00007ff9`ee3594a7 clr!CLREventWaitHelper2+0x38
03 00000030`f4eddc40 00007ff9`ee359430 clr!CLREventWaitHelper+0x1f
04 00000030`f4eddca0 00007ff9`ee533c96 clr!CLREventBase::WaitEx+0x63
05 00000030`f4eddd30 00007ff9`ee85849a clr!SVR::gc_heap::user_thread_wait+0x58
06 00000030`f4eddd60 00007ff9`ee780417 clr!SVR::gc_heap::background_gc_wait+0x4a
07 00000030`f4eddd90 00007ff9`ee4c41e8 clr!SVR::gc_heap::wait_for_bgc_high_memory+0x2b8907
08 00000030`f4edde20 00007ff9`ee355272 clr!SVR::GCHeap::Alloc+0x257
09 00000030`f4edde80 00007ff9`e9f72cfe clr!JIT_New+0x142
0a 00000030`f4ede130 00007ff9`e6e1bf11 System_ServiceModel_ni+0xe72cfe
0b 00000030`f4ede1b0 00007ff9`e6e1be90 System_ServiceModel_Internals_ni+0x4bf11
0c 00000030`f4ede210 00007ff9`ed205156 System_ServiceModel_Internals_ni+0x4be90
0d 00000030`f4ede270 00007ff9`ee35ab53 mscorlib_ni+0x545156
0e 00000030`f4ede2d0 00007ff9`ee35aa3e clr!CallDescrWorkerInternal+0x83
0f 00000030`f4ede310 00007ff9`ee395b80 clr!CallDescrWorkerWithHandler+0x4a
10 00000030`f4ede350 00007ff9`ee9160b8 clr!DispatchCallSimple+0x60
11 00000030`f4ede3e0 00007ff9`ee35c481 clr!BindIoCompletionCallBack_Worker+0xb8
12 00000030`f4ede470 00007ff9`ee35c408 clr!ManagedThreadBase_DispatchInner+0x2d
13 00000030`f4ede4b0 00007ff9`ee35c379 clr!ManagedThreadBase_DispatchMiddle+0x6c
14 00000030`f4ede5b0 00007ff9`ee35c4bb clr!ManagedThreadBase_DispatchOuter+0x75
15 00000030`f4ede640 00007ff9`ee916219 clr!ManagedThreadBase_FullTransitionWithAD+0x2f
16 00000030`f4ede6a0 00007ff9`ee916129 clr!BindIoCompletionCallbackStubEx+0xb9
17 00000030`f4ede720 00007ff9`ee4da72d clr!BindIoCompletionCallbackStub+0x9
18 00000030`f4ede750 00007ff9`ee417de6 clr!ThreadpoolMgr::CompletionPortThreadStart+0x23d
19 00000030`f4ede7f0 00007ff9`f60413d2 clr!Thread::intermediateThreadProc+0x7d
1a 00000030`f4edf7b0 00007ff9`f6ea54e4 kernel32!BaseThreadInitThunk+0x22
1b 00000030`f4edf7e0 00000000`00000000 ntdll!RtlUserThreadStart+0x34
```

```
16  Id: ad8.d50 Suspend: 0 Teb: 00007ff5`ff64a000 Unfrozen
# Child-SP          RetAddr           Call Site
00 00000030`f4cde038 00007ff9`f4121118 ntdll!NtWaitForSingleObject+0xa
01 00000030`f4cde040 00007ff9`ee3594fb KERNELBASE!WaitForSingleObjectEx+0x94
02 00000030`f4cde0e0 00007ff9`ee3594a7 clr!CLREventWaitHelper2+0x38
03 00000030`f4cde120 00007ff9`ee359430 clr!CLREventWaitHelper+0x1f
04 00000030`f4cde180 00007ff9`ee533c96 clr!CLREventBase::WaitEx+0x63
05 00000030`f4cde210 00007ff9`ee85849a clr!SVR::gc_heap::user_thread_wait+0x58
06 00000030`f4cde240 00007ff9`ee780417 clr!SVR::gc_heap::background_gc_wait+0x4a
07 00000030`f4cde270 00007ff9`ee4c41e8 clr!SVR::gc_heap::wait_for_bgc_high_memory+0x2b8907
08 00000030`f4cde300 00007ff9`ee355272 clr!SVR::GCHeap::Alloc+0x257
09 00000030`f4cde360 00007ff9`e9f72cfe clr!JIT_New+0x142
0a 00000030`f4cde610 00007ff9`e6e1bf11 System_ServiceModel_ni+0xe72cfe
0b 00000030`f4cde690 00007ff9`e6e1be90 System_ServiceModel_Internals_ni+0x4bf11
0c 00000030`f4cde6f0 00007ff9`ed205156 System_ServiceModel_Internals_ni+0x4be90
0d 00000030`f4cde750 00007ff9`ee35ab53 mscorlib_ni+0x545156
0e 00000030`f4cde7b0 00007ff9`ee35aa3e clr!CallDescrWorkerInternal+0x83
0f 00000030`f4cde7f0 00007ff9`ee395b80 clr!CallDescrWorkerWithHandler+0x4a
10 00000030`f4cde830 00007ff9`ee9160b8 clr!DispatchCallSimple+0x60
11 00000030`f4cde8c0 00007ff9`ee35c481 clr!BindIoCompletionCallBack_Worker+0xb8
12 00000030`f4cde950 00007ff9`ee35c408 clr!ManagedThreadBase_DispatchInner+0x2d
13 00000030`f4cde990 00007ff9`ee35c379 clr!ManagedThreadBase_DispatchMiddle+0x6c
14 00000030`f4cdea90 00007ff9`ee35c4bb clr!ManagedThreadBase_DispatchOuter+0x75
15 00000030`f4cdeb20 00007ff9`ee916219 clr!ManagedThreadBase_FullTransitionWithAD+0x2f
16 00000030`f4cdeb80 00007ff9`ee916129 clr!BindIoCompletionCallbackStubEx+0xb9
17 00000030`f4cdec00 00007ff9`ee4da72d clr!BindIoCompletionCallbackStub+0x9
18 00000030`f4cdec30 00007ff9`ee417de6 clr!ThreadpoolMgr::CompletionPortThreadStart+0x23d
19 00000030`f4cdecd0 00007ff9`f60413d2 clr!Thread::intermediateThreadProc+0x7d
1a 00000030`f4cdfd10 00007ff9`f6ea54e4 kernel32!BaseThreadInitThunk+0x22
1b 00000030`f4cdfd40 00000000`00000000 ntdll!RtlUserThreadStart+0x34

17  Id: ad8.1584 Suspend: 0 Teb: 00007ff5`ff644000 Unfrozen
# Child-SP          RetAddr           Call Site
00 00000030`f4dde9e8 00007ff9`f4121118 ntdll!NtWaitForSingleObject+0xa
01 00000030`f4dde9f0 00007ff9`ee3594fb KERNELBASE!WaitForSingleObjectEx+0x94
02 00000030`f4ddea90 00007ff9`ee3594a7 clr!CLREventWaitHelper2+0x38
03 00000030`f4ddead0 00007ff9`ee359430 clr!CLREventWaitHelper+0x1f
04 00000030`f4ddeb30 00007ff9`ee533c96 clr!CLREventBase::WaitEx+0x63
05 00000030`f4ddebc0 00007ff9`ee85849a clr!SVR::gc_heap::user_thread_wait+0x58
06 00000030`f4ddebf0 00007ff9`ee780417 clr!SVR::gc_heap::background_gc_wait+0x4a
07 00000030`f4ddec20 00007ff9`ee4c41e8 clr!SVR::gc_heap::wait_for_bgc_high_memory+0x2b8907
08 00000030`f4ddecb0 00007ff9`ee35579d clr!SVR::GCHeap::Alloc+0x257
09 00000030`f4dded10 00007ff9`ee355f32 clr!AllocateArrayEx+0x1a6
0a 00000030`f4ddee40 00007ff9`ed204d4f clr!JIT_NewArr1+0x252
0b 00000030`f4ddf0f0 00007ff9`e6e13574 mscorlib_ni+0x544d4f
0c 00000030`f4ddf150 00007ff9`e6e1bf11 System_ServiceModel_Internals_ni+0x43574
0d 00000030`f4ddf1c0 00007ff9`e6e1be90 System_ServiceModel_Internals_ni+0x4bf11
0e 00000030`f4ddf220 00007ff9`ed205156 System_ServiceModel_Internals_ni+0x4be90
0f 00000030`f4ddf280 00007ff9`ee35ab53 mscorlib_ni+0x545156
10 00000030`f4ddf2e0 00007ff9`ee35aa3e clr!CallDescrWorkerInternal+0x83
11 00000030`f4ddf320 00007ff9`ee395b80 clr!CallDescrWorkerWithHandler+0x4a
12 00000030`f4ddf360 00007ff9`ee9160b8 clr!DispatchCallSimple+0x60
13 00000030`f4ddf3f0 00007ff9`ee35c481 clr!BindIoCompletionCallBack_Worker+0xb8
14 00000030`f4ddf480 00007ff9`ee35c408 clr!ManagedThreadBase_DispatchInner+0x2d
15 00000030`f4ddf4c0 00007ff9`ee35c379 clr!ManagedThreadBase_DispatchMiddle+0x6c
16 00000030`f4ddf5c0 00007ff9`ee35c4bb clr!ManagedThreadBase_DispatchOuter+0x75
```

```
17 00000030`f4ddf650 00007ff9`ee916219 clr!ManagedThreadBase_FullTransitionWithAD+0x2f
18 00000030`f4ddf6b0 00007ff9`ee916129 clr!BindIoCompletionCallbackStubEx+0xb9
19 00000030`f4ddf730 00007ff9`ee4da72d clr!BindIoCompletionCallbackStub+0x9
1a 00000030`f4ddf760 00007ff9`ee417de6 clr!ThreadpoolMgr::CompletionPortThreadStart+0x23d
1b 00000030`f4ddf800 00007ff9`f60413d2 clr!Thread::intermediateThreadProc+0x7d
1c 00000030`f4ddf840 00007ff9`f6ea54e4 kernel32!BaseThreadInitThunk+0x22
1d 00000030`f4ddf870 00000000`00000000 ntdll!RtlUserThreadStart+0x34


[...]


20  Id: ad8.fcc Suspend: 0 Teb: 00007ff5`ff64c000 Unfrozen
# Child-SP          RetAddr           Call Site
00 00000030`f4fde938 00007ff9`f4121118 ntdll!NtWaitForSingleObject+0xa
01 00000030`f4fde940 00007ff9`ee3594fb KERNELBASE!WaitForSingleObjectEx+0x94
02 00000030`f4fde9e0 00007ff9`ee3594a7 clr!CLREventWaitHelper2+0x38
03 00000030`f4fdea20 00007ff9`ee359430 clr!CLREventWaitHelper+0x1f
04 00000030`f4fdea80 00007ff9`ee533c96 clr!CLREventBase::WaitEx+0x63
05 00000030`f4fdeb10 00007ff9`ee85849a clr!SVR::gc_heap::user_thread_wait+0x58
06 00000030`f4fdeb40 00007ff9`ee780417 clr!SVR::gc_heap::background_gc_wait+0x4a
07 00000030`f4fdeb70 00007ff9`ee4c41e8 clr!SVR::gc_heap::wait_for_bgc_high_memory+0x2b8907
08 00000030`f4fdec00 00007ff9`ee3555f0 clr!SVR::GCHeap::Alloc+0x257
09 00000030`f4fdec60 00007ff9`ee41963a clr!AllocateObject+0x68
0a 00000030`f4fdecf0 00007ff9`ee41983d clr!Thread::GetExposedObject+0x4e
0b 00000030`f4fded90 00007ff9`ee355a3a clr!GetCurrentThreadHelper+0x99
0c 00000030`f4fdeef0 00007ff9`ed162b87 clr!ThreadNative::GetCurrentThread+0x22
0d 00000030`f4fdef20 00007ff9`ed162ab9 mscorlib_ni+0x4a2b87
0e 00000030`f4fdf080 00007ff9`ed1e49c2 mscorlib_ni+0x4a2ab9
0f 00000030`f4fdf0b0 00007ff9`ed1e47ae mscorlib_ni+0x5249c2
10 00000030`f4fdf140 00007ff9`ed18c084 mscorlib_ni+0x5247ae
11 00000030`f4fdf1b0 00007ff9`ee35ab53 mscorlib_ni+0x4cc084
12 00000030`f4fdf250 00007ff9`ee35aa3e clr!CallDescrWorkerInternal+0x83
13 00000030`f4fdf290 00007ff9`ee35b1d2 clr!CallDescrWorkerWithHandler+0x4a
14 00000030`f4fdf2d0 00007ff9`ee40e053 clr!MethodDescCallSite::CallTargetWorker+0x251
15 00000030`f4fdf480 00007ff9`ee35c481 clr!AppDomainTimerCallback_Worker+0x23
16 00000030`f4fdf570 00007ff9`ee35c408 clr!ManagedThreadBase_DispatchInner+0x2d
17 00000030`f4fdf5b0 00007ff9`ee35c379 clr!ManagedThreadBase_DispatchMiddle+0x6c
18 00000030`f4fdf6b0 00007ff9`ee35c4bb clr!ManagedThreadBase_DispatchOuter+0x75
19 00000030`f4fdf740 00007ff9`ee40dfe5 clr!ManagedThreadBase_FullTransitionWithAD+0x2f
1a 00000030`f4fdf7a0 00007ff9`ee40df59 clr!AppDomainTimerCallback+0x66
1b 00000030`f4fdf800 00007ff9`ee40db62 clr!ThreadpoolMgr::AsyncTimerCallbackCompletion+0x36
1c 00000030`f4fdf850 00007ff9`ee540af6 clr!UnManagedPerAppDomainTPCount::DispatchWorkItem+0x122
1d 00000030`f4fdf8f0 00007ff9`ee5409ea clr!ThreadpoolMgr::ExecuteWorkRequest+0x46
1e 00000030`f4fdf920 00007ff9`ee417de6 clr!ThreadpoolMgr::WorkerThreadStart+0xf4
1f 00000030`f4fdf9b0 00007ff9`f60413d2 clr!Thread::intermediateThreadProc+0x7d
20 00000030`f4fdfbf0 00007ff9`f6ea54e4 kernel32!BaseThreadInitThunk+0x22
21 00000030`f4fdfc20 00000000`00000000 ntdll!RtlUserThreadStart+0x34


0:000> !runaway
User Mode Time
Thread       Time
8:1960       0 days 1:09:12.218
14:11d4      0 days 0:03:31.937
2:9e8        0 days 0:03:03.250
3:e34        0 days 0:02:41.562
13:f54        0 days 0:02:38.718
4:1338       0 days 0:00:07.984
```

```
0:1014        0 days 0:00:00.046
11:1534        0 days 0:00:00.015
7:1798        0 days 0:00:00.015
20:fcc         0 days 0:00:00.000
19:f48         0 days 0:00:00.000
18:1a60        0 days 0:00:00.000
17:1584        0 days 0:00:00.000
16:d50         0 days 0:00:00.000
15:f9c         0 days 0:00:00.000
12:1988        0 days 0:00:00.000
10:14fc        0 days 0:00:00.000
9:1ae0        0 days 0:00:00.000
6:14cc        0 days 0:00:00.000
5:1a50        0 days 0:00:00.000
1:1258        0 days 0:00:00.000
```

Critical Sections

Similar to kernel mode involving executive resources (page 537), **High Contention** pattern can be observed in user space involving critical sections guarding shared regions like serialized process heap or a memory database, for example, in one Windows service process during increased workload:

```
0:000> !locks

CritSec +310608 at 00310608
WaiterWoken       No
LockCount         6
RecursionCount    1
OwningThread      d9c
EntryCount        0
ContentionCount   453093
*** Locked

CritSec +8f60f78 at 08f60f78
WaiterWoken       No
LockCount         8
RecursionCount    1
OwningThread      d9c
EntryCount        0
ContentionCount   af7f0
*** Locked

CritSec +53bf8f10 at 53bf8f10
WaiterWoken       No
LockCount         0
RecursionCount    1
OwningThread      1a9c
EntryCount        0
ContentionCount   e
*** Locked

Scanned 7099 critical sections
```

When looking at the owning thread, we see that the contention involves process heap:

```
0:000> ~~[d9c]kL
ChildEBP RetAddr
0e2ff9d4 7c81e845 ntdll!RtlpFindAndCommitPages+0x14e
0e2ffa0c 7c81e4ef ntdll!RtlpExtendHeap+0xa6
0e2ffc38 7c3416b3 ntdll!RtlAllocateHeap+0x645
0e2ffc78 7c3416db msvcr71!_heap_alloc+0xe0
0e2ffc80 7c3416f8 msvcr71!_nh_malloc+0x10
0e2ffc8c 672e14fd msvcr71!malloc+0xf
0e2ffc98 0040bc28 dll!MemAlloc+0xd
...
0e2fff84 7c349565 dll!WorkItemThread+0x152
0e2fffb8 77e6608b msvcr71!_endthreadex+0xa0
0e2fffec 00000000 kernel32!BaseThreadStart+0x34
```

However, two critical section addresses belong to the same heap:

```
0:000> !address 00310608
    00310000 : 00310000 - 00010000
                    Type       00020000 MEM_PRIVATE
                    Protect    00000004 PAGE_READWRITE
                    State      00001000 MEM_COMMIT
                    Usage      RegionUsageHeap
                    Handle     00310000

0:000> !address 08f60f78
    08f30000 : 08f30000 - 00200000
                    Type       00020000 MEM_PRIVATE
                    Protect    00000004 PAGE_READWRITE
                    State      00001000 MEM_COMMIT
                    Usage      RegionUsageHeap
                    Handle     00310000
```

Lock contention is confirmed by heap statistics as well:

```
0:000> !heap -s
LFH Key                  : 0x07262959
  Heap      Flags    Reserv  Commit   Virt    Free  List    UCR  Virt  Lock  Fast
                      (k)     (k)      (k)     (k) length        blocks cont. heap
00140000 00000002     8192    2876    3664     631   140     46    0     1e   L
    External fragmentation   21 % (140 free blocks)
00240000 00008000       64      12      12      10     1      1    0      0
Virtual block: 0ea20000 - 0ea20000 (size 00000000)
Virtual block: 0fa30000 - 0fa30000 (size 00000000)
00310000 00001002 1255320 961480 1249548 105378       0 16830    2 453093   L
    Virtual address fragmentation   23 % (16830 uncommited ranges)
    Lock contention   4534419
003f0000 00001002       64      36      36       0     0      1    0      0   L
00610000 00001002       64      16      16       4     2      1    0      0   L
...
```

Executive Resources

Some Windows synchronization objects like executive resources and critical sections have a struct member called *ContentionCount*. This is the number of times a resource was accessed or, in other words, it is the accumulated number of threads waiting for an object: when a thread tries to acquire an object and is put into a waiting state the count is incremented. Hence the name of this pattern: **High Contention**.

Here is an example. In a kernel memory dump, we have just one exclusively owned lock, and it seems that no other threads were blocked by it at the time the dump was saved. However, the high contention count reveals CPU spike (**Spiking Thread**, page 992):

```
3: kd> !locks
**** DUMP OF ALL RESOURCE OBJECTS ****
KD: Scanning for held locks...

Resource @ 0x8abc11f0    Exclusively owned
    Contention Count = 19648535
       Threads: 896395f8-01<*>
KD: Scanning for held locks…

Resource @ 0x896fab88    Shared 1 owning threads
       Threads: 88c78608-01<*>
KD: Scanning for held locks...
15464 total locks, 2 locks currently held


3: kd> !thread 896395f8
THREAD 896395f8  Cid 04c0.0138  Teb: 7ffde000 Win32Thread: bc922d20 RUNNING on processor 1
Not impersonating
DeviceMap                 e3d4c008
Owning Process            8a035020        Image:          MyApp.exe
Wait Start TickCount      36969283        Ticks: 0
Context Switch Count      1926423                  LargeStack
UserTime                  00:00:53.843
KernelTime                00:13:10.703
Win32 Start Address 0x00401478
Start Address 0x77e617f8
Stack Init ba14b000 Current ba14abf8 Base ba14b000 Limit ba146000 Call 0
Priority 11 BasePriority 6 PriorityDecrement 5
ChildEBP RetAddr
ba14ac94 bf8c6505 001544c8 bf995948 000c000a nt!_wcsicmp+0x3a
ba14ace0 bf8c6682 00000000 00000000 00000000 win32k!_FindWindowEx+0xfb
ba14ad48 8088978c 00000000 00000000 0012f8d4 win32k!NtUserFindWindowEx+0xef
ba14ad48 7c8285ec 00000000 00000000 0012f8d4 nt!KiFastCallEntry+0xfc
```

```
3: kd> !process 8a035020
PROCESS 8a035020  SessionId: 9  Cid: 04c0    Peb: 7ffdf000  ParentCid: 10e8
    DirBase: cffaf7a0  ObjectTable: e4ba30a0  HandleCount:  73.
    Image: MyApp.exe
    VadRoot 88bc1bf8 Vads 82 Clone 0 Private 264. Modified 0. Locked 0.
    DeviceMap e3d4c008
    Token                             e5272028
    ElapsedTime                       00:14:19.360
    UserTime                          00:00:53.843
    KernelTime                        00:13:10.703
    QuotaPoolUsage[PagedPool]         40660
    QuotaPoolUsage[NonPagedPool]      3280
    Working Set Sizes (now,min,max)   (1139, 50, 345) (4556KB, 200KB, 1380KB)
    PeakWorkingSetSize                1141
    VirtualSize                       25 Mb
    PeakVirtualSize                   27 Mb
    PageFaultCount                    1186
    MemoryPriority                    BACKGROUND
    BasePriority                      6
    CommitCharge                      315
```

Comments

High Contention may also be visible from non-locked objects too:

```
0: kd> !locks -v
**** DUMP OF ALL RESOURCE OBJECTS ****

Resource @ nt!ExpFirmwareTableResource (0xfffff80001a315c0) Available

Resource @ nt!PsLoadedModuleResource (0xfffff80001a596a0) Available

Resource @ nt!MmSectionExtendResource (0xfffff80001a59440) Available

Resource @ nt!MmSectionExtendSetResource (0xfffff80001a594c0) Available
Contention Count = 68

Resource @ nt!SepRmDbLock (0xfffff80001a2e340) Available
Contention Count = 1710

Resource @ nt!SepRmDbLock (0xfffff80001a2e3a8) Available
Contention Count = 387

Resource @ nt!SepRmDbLock (0xfffff80001a2e410) Available
Contention Count = 256

Resource @ nt!SepRmDbLock (0xfffff80001a2e478) Available
Contention Count = 212

Resource @ nt!SepRmGlobalSaclLock (0xfffff80001a2e4e0) Available

Resource @ nt!SepLsaAuditQueueInfo (0xfffff80001a2e240) Available

Resource @ nt!SepLsaDeletedLogonQueueInfo (0xfffff80001a2e0e0) Available

Resource @ 0xfffffa804dc09920 Available

Resource @ nt!PnpRegistryDeviceResource (0xfffff80001a8f9e0) Available
Contention Count = 23562

Resource @ nt!PopPolicyLock (0xfffff80001a3b9e0) Available
Contention Count = 19

Resource @ CI!g_StoreLock (0xfffff88000c05cc0) Available

Resource @ nt!CmpRegistryLock (0xfffff80001a10000) Available
Contention Count = 21297917

[...]
```

Processors

This is a variant of **High Contention** pattern for processors where we have more threads at the same priority than the available processors. All these threads share the same notification event (or any other similar synchronization mechanism) and rush once it is signaled. If this happens often, the system becomes sluggish, or even appears frozen.

```
0: kd> !running

System Processors 3 (affinity mask)
  Idle Processors 0


Prcbs  Current   Next
  0    ffdff120  89a92020          O...............
  1    f7737120  89275020          W...............


0: kd> !ready
Processor 0: Ready Threads at priority 8
    THREAD 894a1db0  Cid 1a98.25c0  Teb: 7ffde000 Win32Thread: bc19cea8 READY
    THREAD 897c4818  Cid 11d8.1c5c  Teb: 7ffa2000 Win32Thread: bc2c5ba8 READY
    THREAD 8911fd18  Cid 2730.03f4  Teb: 7ffd9000 Win32Thread: bc305830 READY
Processor 1: Ready Threads at priority 8
    THREAD 89d89db0  Cid 1b10.20ac  Teb: 7ffd7000 Win32Thread: bc16e680 READY
    THREAD 891f24a8  Cid 1e2c.20d0  Teb: 7ffda000 Win32Thread: bc1b9ea8 READY
    THREAD 89214db0  Cid 1e2c.24d4  Teb: 7ffd7000 Win32Thread: bc24ed48 READY
    THREAD 89a28020  Cid 1b10.21b4  Teb: 7ffa7000 Win32Thread: bc25b3b8 READY
    THREAD 891e03b0  Cid 1a98.05c4  Teb: 7ffdb000 Win32Thread: bc228bb0 READY
    THREAD 891b0020  Cid 1cd0.0144  Teb: 7ffde000 Win32Thread: bc205ea8 READY
```

All these threads have the common stack trace (we show only a few threads here):

```
0: kd> !thread 89a92020 1f
THREAD 89a92020  Cid 11d8.27d8  Teb: 7ffd9000 Win32Thread: bc1e6860 RUNNING on processor 0
Not impersonating
DeviceMap               e502b248
Owning Process          89e2a020       Image:         ProcessA.exe
Attached Process        N/A            Image:         N/A
Wait Start TickCount    336581         Ticks: 0
Context Switch Count    61983                    LargeStack
UserTime                00:00:00.156
KernelTime              00:00:00.281
Win32 Start Address ntdll!RtlpWorkerThread (0x7c839f2b)
Start Address kernel32!BaseThreadStartThunk (0x77e617ec)
Stack Init f3730000 Current f372f7e0 Base f3730000 Limit f372c000 Call 0
Priority 8 BasePriority 8 PriorityDecrement 0
ChildEBP RetAddr
f3cc98e8 f6e21915 DriverA+0x1e4d
[...]
f3cc9ac0 f67f05dc nt!IofCallDriver+0x45
[...]
02e7ff44 7c83aa3b ntdll!RtlpWorkerCallout+0x71
02e7ff64 7c83aab2 ntdll!RtlpExecuteWorkerRequest+0x4f
```

```
02e7ff78 7c839f90 ntdll!RtlpApcCallout+0x11
02e7ffb8 77e6482f ntdll!RtlpWorkerThread+0x61
02e7ffec 00000000 kernel32!BaseThreadStart+0x34


0: kd> !thread 89275020 1f
THREAD 89275020  Cid 1cd0.2510  Teb: 7ffa9000 Win32Thread: bc343180 RUNNING on processor 1
Not impersonating
DeviceMap                e1390978
Owning Process           89214708     Image:         ProcessB.exe
Attached Process         N/A          Image:         N/A
Wait Start TickCount     336581       Ticks: 0
Context Switch Count     183429                   LargeStack
UserTime                 00:00:00.171
KernelTime               00:00:00.484
Win32 Start Address ntdll!RtlpWorkerThread (0x7c839f2b)
Start Address kernel32!BaseThreadStartThunk (0x77e617ec)
Stack Init b9f6e000 Current b9f6d7e0 Base b9f6e000 Limit b9f6a000 Call 0
Priority 8 BasePriority 8 PriorityDecrement 0
ChildEBP RetAddr
b9f6d87c f6e22d4b nt!KeWaitForSingleObject+0x497
b9f6d8e8 f6e21915 DriverA+0x1e4d
[...]
b9f6dac0 f67f05dc nt!IofCallDriver+0x45
[...]
0507ff44 7c83aa3b ntdll!RtlpWorkerCallout+0x71
0507ff64 7c83aab2 ntdll!RtlpExecuteWorkerRequest+0x4f
0507ff78 7c839f90 ntdll!RtlpApcCallout+0x11
0507ffb8 77e6482f ntdll!RtlpWorkerThread+0x61
0507ffec 00000000 kernel32!BaseThreadStart+0x34


0: kd> !thread 89d89db0 1f
THREAD 89d89db0  Cid 1b10.20ac  Teb: 7ffd7000 Win32Thread: bc16e680 READY
Not impersonating
DeviceMap                e4e3a0b8
Owning Process           898cb020     Image:         ProcessC.exe
Attached Process         N/A          Image:         N/A
Wait Start TickCount     336581       Ticks: 0
Context Switch Count     159844                   LargeStack
UserTime                 00:00:00.234
KernelTime               00:00:00.484
Win32 Start Address ntdll!RtlpWorkerThread (0x7c839f2b)
Start Address kernel32!BaseThreadStartThunk (0x77e617ec)
Stack Init b9e1e000 Current b9e1d7e0 Base b9e1e000 Limit b9e1a000 Call 0
Priority 8 BasePriority 8 PriorityDecrement 0
ChildEBP RetAddr
b9e1d7f8 80831292 nt!KiSwapContext+0x26
b9e1d818 80828c73 nt!KiExitDispatcher+0xf8
b9e1d830 80829c72 nt!KiAdjustQuantumThread+0x109
b9e1d87c f6e22d4b nt!KeWaitForSingleObject+0x536
b9e1d8e8 f6e21915 DriverA+0x1e4d
[...]
b9e1dac0 f67f05dc nt!IofCallDriver+0x45
[...]
014dff44 7c83aa3b ntdll!RtlpWorkerCallout+0x71
014dff64 7c83aab2 ntdll!RtlpExecuteWorkerRequest+0x4f
```

```
014dff78 7c839f90 ntdll!RtlpApcCallout+0x11
014dffb8 77e6482f ntdll!RtlpWorkerThread+0x61
```

These threads also share the same synchronization object:

```
0: kd> .thread 89275020
Implicit thread is now 89275020


0: kd> kv 1
ChildEBP RetAddr  Args to Child
b9f6d87c f6e22d4b f6e25130 00000006 00000001 nt!KeWaitForSingleObject+0x497


0: kd> .thread 89d89db0
Implicit thread is now 89d89db0


0: kd> kv 4
ChildEBP RetAddr  Args to Child
b9e1d7f8 80831292 f7737120 f7737b50 f7737a7c nt!KiSwapContext+0x26
b9e1d818 80828c73 00000000 89d89db0 89d89e58 nt!KiExitDispatcher+0xf8
b9e1d830 80829c72 f7737a7c 00000102 00000001 nt!KiAdjustQuantumThread+0x109
b9e1d87c f6e22d4b f6e25130 00000006 00000001 nt!KeWaitForSingleObject+0x536


0: kd> dt _DISPATCHER_HEADER f6e25130
ntdll!_DISPATCHER_HEADER
   +0x000 Type          : 0 ”
   +0x001 Absolute      : 0 ”
   +0x001 NpxIrql       : 0 ”
   +0x002 Size          : 0x4 ”
   +0x002 Hand          : 0x4 ”
   +0x003 Inserted      : 0 ”
   +0x003 DebugActive   : 0 ”
   +0x000 Lock          : 262144
   +0x004 SignalState   : 1
   +0x008 WaitListHead  : _LIST_ENTRY [ 0xf6e25138 - 0xf6e25138 ]
```

Historical Information

Although crash dumps are static in nature, they contain **Historical Information** about past system dynamics that might give clues to a problem and help with troubleshooting and debugging.

For example, IRP flow between user processes and drivers is readily available in any kernel or complete memory dump. WinDbg **!irpfind** command will show the list of currently present I/O request packets. **!irp** command will give individual packet details.

Recent Driver Verifier improvements allow embedding stack traces associated with IRP allocation, completion, and cancellation[96].

Other information that can be included in the process, kernel, and complete memory dumps may reveal some history of function calls beyond the current snapshot of thread stacks:

- Heap allocation stack traces that are usually used for debugging memory leaks (**Stack Trace** Database, page 1026).
- Handle traces that are used to debug handle leaks (**!htrace** command).
- Raw stack data interpreted symbolically. Some examples include dumping stack data from all process threads and dumping kernel mode stack data.
- LPC and ALPC messages (**!lpc thread** or **!alpc /lpp**).
- **Waiting Thread Time** pattern (page 1257).

Comments

Unloaded module list (**lm**) is another example of **Historical Information** pattern.

Last error values for all threads make another good example of historical info (**Last Error Collection** pattern, page 672).

!obtrace command monitors more than **!htrace** command[97].

Debugging TV Frames episode 0x29 shows an example for *notepad.exe*[98].

---

[96] https://docs.microsoft.com/en-gb/windows-hardware/drivers/devtest/driver-verifier
[97] Windows Internals, 5th edition, p. 156
[98] http://www.debugging.tv

Hooked Functions

Kernel Space

This is a variation of **Hooked Functions** pattern for kernel space. In addition to trampoline patching, we also see a modified service table:

```
0: kd> !chkimg -lo 50 -d !nt -v
Searching for module with expression: !nt
Will apply relocation fixups to file used for comparison
Will ignore NOP/LOCK errors
Will ignore patched instructions
Image specific ignores will be applied
Comparison image path: c:\symdownstream\ntkrnlmp.exe\4B7A8E62280000\ntkrnlmp.exe
No range specified


Scanning section:    .text
Size: 625257
Range to scan: 80801000-80899a69
    808373e3-808373e9  7 bytes - nt!KeAcquireQueuedSpinLockAtDpcLevel+1b
  [ f7 41 04 01 00 00 00:e9 00 0d b2 76 cc cc ]
    8083e6c8-8083e6cb  4 bytes - nt!KiServiceTable+440 (+0x72e5)
  [ 98 4e 98 80:d0 66 e9 f4 ]
    80840605-8084060a  6 bytes - nt!KxFlushEntireTb+9 (+0x1f3d)
  [ ff 15 1c 10 80 80:e9 a5 7a b1 76 cc ]
Total bytes compared: 625257(100%)
Number of errors: 17


Scanning section: MISYSPTE
Size: 1906
Range to scan: 8089a000-8089a772
Total bytes compared: 1906(100%)
Number of errors: 0


Scanning section:    POOLMI
Size: 7868
Range to scan: 8089b000-8089cebc
Total bytes compared: 7868(100%)
Number of errors: 0


Scanning section: POOLCODE
Size: 7754
Range to scan: 8089d000-8089ee4a
Total bytes compared: 7754(100%)
Number of errors: 0


Scanning section:    PAGE
Size: 1097281
Range to scan: 808bc000-809c7e41
Total bytes compared: 1097281(100%)
Number of errors: 0
```

```
Scanning section:   PAGELK
Size: 63633
Range to scan: 809c8000-809d7891
Total bytes compared: 63633(100%)
Number of errors: 0


Scanning section:  PAGEWMI
Size: 7095
Range to scan: 809ef000-809f0bb7
Total bytes compared: 7095(100%)
Number of errors: 0


Scanning section:   PAGEKD
Size: 16760
Range to scan: 809f1000-809f5178
Total bytes compared: 16760(100%)
Number of errors: 0


Scanning section: PAGEHDLS
Size: 7508
Range to scan: 809f7000-809f8d54
Total bytes compared: 7508(100%)
Number of errors: 0
17 errors : !nt (808373e3-8084060a)


0: kd> dds 8083e6c8
8083e6c8   f4e966d0 DriverA+0x20d8
8083e6cc   80983436 nt!NtUnloadKey2
8083e6d0   809837b5 nt!NtUnloadKeyEx
8083e6d4   8091cec8 nt!NtUnlockFile
8083e6d8   80805d80 nt!NtUnlockVirtualMemory
8083e6dc   80937630 nt!NtUnmapViewOfSection
8083e6e0   808e7154 nt!NtVdmControl
8083e6e4   809c6ba3 nt!NtWaitForDebugEvent
8083e6e8   8092dc24 nt!NtWaitForMultipleObjects
8083e6ec   8092ccf4 nt!NtWaitForSingleObject
8083e6f0   809c132f nt!NtWaitHighEventPair
8083e6f4   809c12c3 nt!NtWaitLowEventPair
8083e6f8   80925c8d nt!NtWriteFile
8083e6fc   80901790 nt!NtWriteFileGather
8083e700   8091214c nt!NtWriteRequestData
8083e704   8093e63b nt!NtWriteVirtualMemory
8083e708   80822751 nt!NtYieldExecution
8083e70c   808c7c46 nt!NtCreateKeyedEvent
8083e710   8093eee3 nt!NtOpenKeyedEvent
8083e714   809c1ee8 nt!NtReleaseKeyedEvent
8083e718   809c2183 nt!NtWaitForKeyedEvent
8083e71c   809a610b nt!NtQueryPortInformationProcess
8083e720   809a6123 nt!NtGetCurrentProcessorNumber
8083e724   809a1849 nt!NtWaitForMultipleObjects32
8083e728   90909090
8083e72c   1c0d3b90
8083e730   0f8089f1
8083e734   037aaa85
8083e738   00c1f700
```

```
8083e73c  0fffff00
8083e740  037a9e85
8083e744  9090c300


0: kd> u 808373e3
nt!KeAcquireQueuedSpinLockAtDpcLevel+0x1b:
808373e3 jmp      DriverB+0x10e8 (f73580e8)
808373e8 int      3
808373e9 int      3
808373ea je       nt!KeAcquireQueuedSpinLockAtDpcLevel+0x12 (808373da)
808373ec pause
808373ee jmp      nt!KeAcquireQueuedSpinLockAtDpcLevel+0x1b (808373e3)
nt!KeReleaseInStackQueuedSpinLockFromDpcLevel:
808373f0 lea      ecx,[ecx]
nt!KeReleaseQueuedSpinLockFromDpcLevel:
808373f2 mov      eax,ecx


0: kd> u 80840605
nt!KxFlushEntireTb+0x9:
80840605 jmp      DriverB+0x10af (f73580af)
8084060a int      3
8084060b mov      byte ptr [ebp-1],al
8084060e mov      ebx,offset nt!KiTbFlushTimeStamp (808a7100)
80840613 mov      ecx,dword ptr [nt!KiTbFlushTimeStamp (808a7100)]
80840619 test     cl,1
8084061c jne      nt!KxFlushEntireTb+0x19 (8082cd8d)
80840622 mov      eax,ecx
```

Comments

Another example:

```
4: kd> !chkimg -lo 50 -d !nt
8083351c-80833520 5 bytes - nt!NtYieldExecution
[ 8b ff 55 8b ec:e9 5c 03 e6 73 ]
808345d0-808345d3 4 bytes - nt!KiServiceTable+440 (+0x10b4)
[ 9c c2 8b 80:5c d7 f1 f4 ]
808eeb1e-808eeb22 5 bytes - nt!NtCreateFile
[ 8b ff 55 8b ec:e9 1c 4d da 73 ]
809233b0-809233b4 5 bytes - nt!NtUnmapViewOfSection (+0x34892)
[ 8b ff 55 8b ec:e9 f2 04 d7 73 ]
8092d3ae-8092d3b4 7 bytes - nt!NtMapViewOfSection (+0x9ffe)
[ 6a 38 68 b8 41 80 80:e9 de 64 d6 73 90 90 ]
80931c90-80931c96 7 bytes - nt!NtProtectVirtualMemory (+0x48e2)
[ 6a 44 68 d8 43 80 80:e9 be 1b d6 73 90 90 ]
8094af32-8094af36 5 bytes - nt!NtCreateProcess (+0x192a2)
[ 8b ff 55 8b ec:e9 32 89 d4 73 ]
8094c714-8094c718 5 bytes - nt!NtTerminateProcess (+0x17e2)
[ 8b ff 55 8b ec:e9 12 71 d4 73 ]
43 errors : !nt (8083351c-8094c718)


4: kd> u 8094af32
nt!NtCreateProcess:
*** ERROR: Symbol file could not be found. Defaulted to export symbols for 3rdPartyAVDriver.sys -
8094af32 e93289d473 jmp 3rdPartyAVDriver+0x13869 (f4693869)
8094af37 33c0     xor eax,eax
8094af39 f6451c01 test byte ptr [ebp+1Ch],1
8094af3d 7401     je nt!NtCreateProcess+0xe (8094af40)
8094af3f 40       inc eax
8094af40 f6452001 test byte ptr [ebp+20h],1
8094af44 7403     je nt!NtCreateProcess+0x17 (8094af49)
8094af46 83c802   or eax,2
```

The simplified version of the command:

```
!chkimg -db -v ModuleName
```

For example:

```
!chkimg -db -v nt
```

This allows to use **!for_each_module** command

To include the mismatch summary use this simplified version of the command:

```
!chkimg -db -d -v ModuleName
```

For example:

```
!chkimg -db -d -v ntdll
```

User Space

Hooking functions using trampoline method is so common on Windows that sometimes we need to check **Hooked Functions** in specific modules and determine which module hooked them for troubleshooting or memory forensic analysis needs. If original unhooked modules are available (via symbol server, for example) this can be done by using **!chkimg** WinDbg extension command:

```
0:002> !chkimg -lo 50 -d !kernel32 -v
Searching for module with expression: !kernel32
Will apply relocation fixups to file used for comparison
Will ignore NOP/LOCK errors
Will ignore patched instructions
Image specific ignores will be applied
Comparison image path: c:\symdownstream\kernel32.dll\44C60F39102000\kernel32.dll
No range specified


Scanning section:    .text
Size: 564445
Range to scan: 77e41000-77ecacdd
  77e44004-77e44008  5 bytes - kernel32!GetDateFormatA
 [ 8b ff 55 8b ec:e9 f7 bf 08 c0 ]
   77e4412e-77e44132  5 bytes - kernel32!GetTimeFormatA (+0x12a)
 [ 8b ff 55 8b ec:e9 cd be 06 c0 ]
   77e4e857-77e4e85b  5 bytes - kernel32!FileTimeToLocalFileTime (+0xa729)
 [ 8b ff 55 8b ec:e9 a4 17 00 c0 ]
   77e56b5f-77e56b63  5 bytes - kernel32!GetTimeZoneInformation (+0x8308)
 [ 8b ff 55 8b ec:e9 9c 94 00 c0 ]
   77e579a9-77e579ad  5 bytes - kernel32!GetTimeFormatW (+0xe4a)
 [ 8b ff 55 8b ec:e9 52 86 06 c0 ]
   77e57fc8-77e57fcc  5 bytes - kernel32!GetDateFormatW (+0x61f)
 [ 8b ff 55 8b ec:e9 33 80 08 c0 ]
   77e6f32b-77e6f32f  5 bytes - kernel32!GetLocalTime (+0x17363)
 [ 8b ff 55 8b ec:e9 d0 0c 00 c0 ]
   77e6f891-77e6f895  5 bytes - kernel32!LocalFileTimeToFileTime (+0x566)
 [ 8b ff 55 8b ec:e9 6a 07 01 c0 ]
   77e83499-77e8349d  5 bytes - kernel32!SetLocalTime (+0x13c08)
 [ 8b ff 55 8b ec:e9 62 cb 00 c0 ]
   77e88c32-77e88c36  5 bytes - kernel32!SetTimeZoneInformation (+0x5799)
 [ 8b ff 55 8b ec:e9 c9 73 01 c0 ]
Total bytes compared: 564445(100%)
Number of errors: 50
50 errors : !kernel32 (77e44004-77e88c36)


0:002> u 77e44004
kernel32!GetDateFormatA:
77e44004 e9f7bf08c0      jmp     37ed0000
77e44009 81ec18020000    sub     esp,218h
77e4400f a148d1ec77      mov     eax,dword ptr [kernel32!__security_cookie (77ecd148)]
77e44014 53              push    ebx
77e44015 8b5d14          mov     ebx,dword ptr [ebp+14h]
77e44018 56              push    esi
77e44019 8b7518          mov     esi,dword ptr [ebp+18h]
77e4401c 57              push    edi
```

```
0:002> u 37ed0000
*** ERROR: Symbol file could not be found.  Defaulted to export symbols for MyDateTimeHooks.dll -
37ed0000 e99b262f2d      jmp         MyDateTimeHooks+0x26a0 (651c26a0)
37ed0005 8bff            mov         edi,edi
37ed0007 55              push        ebp
37ed0008 8bec            mov         ebp,esp
37ed000a e9fa3ff73f      jmp         kernel32!GetDateFormatA+0x5 (77e44009)
37ed000f 0000            add         byte ptr [eax],al
37ed0011 0000            add         byte ptr [eax],al
37ed0013 0000            add         byte ptr [eax],al
```

Comments

The simplified version of the command:

```
!chkimg -db -v ModuleName
```

For example:

```
!chkimg -db -v ntdll
```

To include the mismatch summary use this version:

```
!chkimg -db -d -v ModuleName
```

For example:

```
!chkimg -db -d -v ntdll
```

Sometimes, several different modules from different products may patch different functions from the DLL. So, in general, we need to check all reported hooked functions.

Hooked Modules

In **Hooked Functions** pattern (page 544) we used **!chkimg** WinDbg command. To check all modules, we can use this simple command:

```
!for_each_module !chkimg -lo 50 -d !${@#ModuleName} -v
```

For example:

```
0:000:x86> !for_each_module !chkimg -lo 50 -d !${@#ModuleName} -v
...
Scanning section:    .text
Size: 74627
Range to scan: 71c01000-71c13383
    71c02430-71c02434  5 bytes - WS2_32!WSASend
 [ 8b ff 55 8b ec:e9 cb db 1c 0d ]
    71c0279b-71c0279f  5 bytes - WS2_32!select (+0x36b)
 [ 6a 14 68 58 28:e9 60 d8 15 0d ]
    71c0290e-71c02912  5 bytes - WS2_32!WSASendTo (+0x173)
 [ 8b ff 55 8b ec:e9 ed d6 1b 0d ]
    71c02cb2-71c02cb6  5 bytes - WS2_32!closesocket (+0x3a4)
 [ 8b ff 55 8b ec:e9 49 d3 19 0d ]
    71c02e12-71c02e16  5 bytes - WS2_32!WSAIoctl (+0x160)
 [ 8b ff 55 8b ec:e9 e9 d1 1e 0d ]
    71c02ec2-71c02ec6  5 bytes - WS2_32!send (+0xb0)
 [ 8b ff 55 8b ec:e9 39 d1 14 0d ]
    71c02f7f-71c02f83  5 bytes - WS2_32!recv (+0xbd)
 [ 8b ff 55 8b ec:e9 7c d0 17 0d ]
    71c03c04-71c03c08  5 bytes - WS2_32!WSAGetOverlappedResult (+0xc85)
 [ 8b ff 55 8b ec:e9 f7 c3 1f 0d ]
    71c03c75-71c03c79  5 bytes - WS2_32!recvfrom (+0x71)
 [ 8b ff 55 8b ec:e9 86 c3 16 0d ]
    71c03d14-71c03d18  5 bytes - WS2_32!sendto (+0x9f)
 [ 8b ff 55 8b ec:e9 e7 c2 13 0d ]
    71c03da8-71c03dac  5 bytes - WS2_32!WSACleanup (+0x94)
 [ 8b ff 55 8b ec:e9 53 c2 25 0d ]
    71c03f38-71c03f3c  5 bytes - WS2_32!WSASocketW (+0x190)
 [ 6a 20 68 08 40:e9 c3 c0 11 0d ]
    71c0446a-71c0446e  5 bytes - WS2_32!connect (+0x532)
 [ 8b ff 55 8b ec:e9 91 bb 18 0d ]
    71c04f3b-71c04f3f  5 bytes - WS2_32!WSAStartup (+0xad1)
 [ 6a 14 68 60 50:e9 c0 b0 29 0d ]
    71c06162-71c06166  5 bytes - WS2_32!shutdown (+0x1227)
 [ 8b ff 55 8b ec:e9 99 9e 12 0d ]
    71c069e9-71c069ed  5 bytes - WS2_32!WSALookupServiceBeginW (+0x887)
 [ 8b ff 55 8b ec:e9 12 96 0f 0d ]
    71c06c91-71c06c95  5 bytes - WS2_32!WSALookupServiceNextW (+0x2a8)
 [ 8b ff 55 8b ec:e9 6a 93 10 0d ]
    71c06ecd-71c06ed1  5 bytes - WS2_32!WSALookupServiceEnd (+0x23c)
 [ 8b ff 55 8b ec:e9 2e 91 0e 0d ]
    71c090be-71c090c2  5 bytes - WS2_32!WSAEventSelect (+0x21f1)
 [ 8b ff 55 8b ec:e9 3d 6f 20 0d ]
    71c09129-71c0912d  5 bytes - WS2_32!WSACreateEvent (+0x6b)
```

```
[ 33 c0 50 50 6a:e9 d2 6e 22 0d ]
   71c0938e-71c09392  5 bytes - WS2_32!WSACloseEvent (+0x265)
[ 6a 0c 68 c8 93:e9 6d 6c 24 0d ]
   71c093d9-71c093dd  5 bytes - WS2_32!WSAWaitForMultipleEvents (+0x4b)
[ 8b ff 55 8b ec:e9 22 6c 1a 0d ]
   71c093ea-71c093ee  5 bytes - WS2_32!WSAEnumNetworkEvents (+0x11)
[ 8b ff 55 8b ec:e9 11 6c 21 0d ]
   71c09480-71c09484  5 bytes - WS2_32!WSARecv (+0x96)
[ 8b ff 55 8b ec:e9 7b 6b 1d 0d ]
   71c0eecb-71c0eecf  5 bytes - WS2_32!WSACancelAsyncRequest (+0x5a4b)
[ 8b ff 55 8b ec:e9 30 11 26 0d ]
   71c10d39-71c10d3d  5 bytes - WS2_32!WSAAsyncSelect (+0x1e6e)
[ 8b ff 55 8b ec:e9 c2 f2 26 0d ]
   71c10ee3-71c10ee7  5 bytes - WS2_32!WSAConnect (+0x1aa)
[ 8b ff 55 8b ec:e9 18 f1 22 0d ]
   71c10f9f-71c10fa3  5 bytes - WS2_32!WSAAccept (+0xbc)
[ 8b ff 55 8b ec:e9 5c f0 27 0d ]
Total bytes compared: 74627(100%)
Number of errors: 140
140 errors : !WS2_32 (71c02430-71c10fa3)
...
```

Comments

We can also use these variants:

```
!for_each_module !chkimg -db -d -v ${@#ModuleName}
```

```
!for_each_module !chkimg -db -d -v @#ModuleName
```

Hooking Level

In addition to **Hooked Functions** (page 544) pattern, we should also pay attention a number of patched functions. Often value-added hooksware[99] (see also **Hooksware** patterns, page 1295) has configuration options that fine-tune hooking behavior. For example, an application with the less number of patched functions behaved incorrectly, and two process user dumps were saved from the working and non-working environment:

Problem behavior

```
0:000> !chkimg -lo 50 -d !user32 -v
Searching for module with expression: !user32
Will apply relocation fixups to file used for comparison
Will ignore NOP/LOCK errors
Will ignore patched instructions
Image specific ignores will be applied
Comparison image path: c:\mss\user32.dll\49E0380E9d000\user32.dll
No range specified


Scanning section: .text
Size: 422527
Range to scan: 76e31000-76e9827f
76e3d6f8-76e3d6fc 5 bytes - user32!NtUserSetThreadDesktop
[ b8 30 12 00 00:e9 03 29 13 09 ]
76e3dc2a-76e3dc2e 5 bytes - user32!CreateWindowExA (+0x532)
[ 8b ff 55 8b ec:e9 d1 23 15 09 ]
76e3f8f8-76e3f8fc 5 bytes - user32!PostMessageA (+0x1cce)
[ 8b ff 55 8b ec:e9 03 07 fa 08 ]
76e41305-76e41309 5 bytes - user32!CreateWindowExW (+0x1a0d)
[ 8b ff 55 8b ec:e9 f6 ec 13 09 ]
76e435e3-76e435e7 5 bytes - user32!NtUserSetWindowPos (+0x22de)
[ b8 38 12 00 00:e9 18 ca 11 09 ]
76e48343-76e48347 5 bytes - user32!PeekMessageA (+0x4d60)
[ 8b ff 55 8b ec:e9 b8 7c fb 08 ]
76e48ab3-76e48ab7 5 bytes - user32!GetMessageA (+0x770)
[ 8b ff 55 8b ec:e9 48 75 fd 08 ]
76e4a175-76e4a179 5 bytes - user32!PostMessageW (+0x16c2)
[ 8b ff 55 8b ec:e9 86 5e f8 08 ]
76e4fef7-76e4fefb 5 bytes - user32!GetMessageW (+0x5d82)
[ 8b ff 55 8b ec:e9 04 01 fc 08 ]
76e5045a-76e5045e 5 bytes - user32!PeekMessageW (+0x563)
[ 8b ff 55 8b ec:e9 a1 fb f9 08 ]
76e8d37d-76e8d381 5 bytes - user32!MessageBoxTimeoutW (+0x3cf23)
[ 8b ff 55 8b ec:e9 7e 2c fd 08 ]
76e8d4d9-76e8d4dd 5 bytes - user32!MessageBoxIndirectA (+0x15c)
[ 8b ff 55 8b ec:e9 22 2b ff 08 ]
76e8d5d3-76e8d5d7 5 bytes - user32!MessageBoxIndirectW (+0xfa)
[ 8b ff 55 8b ec:e9 28 2a fe 08 ]
```

---

[99] Hooksware, Memory Dump Analysis Anthology, Volume 2, page 63

```
76e8d65d-76e8d661 5 bytes - user32!MessageBoxExW (+0x8a)
[ 8b ff 55 8b ec:e9 9e 29 00 09 ]
Total bytes compared: 422527(100%)
```
Number of errors: 70
```
70 errors : !user32 (76e3d6f8-76e8d661)


0:000> u EnumDisplayDevicesW
user32!EnumDisplayDevicesW:
76e3ba5b 8bff               mov edi,edi
76e3ba5d 55                 push ebp
76e3ba5e 8bec               mov ebp,esp
76e3ba60 81ec54030000       sub esp,354h
76e3ba66 a1c090e976         mov eax,dword ptr [user32!__security_cookie (76e990c0)]
76e3ba6b 33c5               xor eax,ebp
76e3ba6d 8945fc mov dword ptr [ebp-4],eax
76e3ba70 53                 push ebx
```

Expected behavior

```
0:000> !chkimg -lo 50 -d !user32 -v
Searching for module with expression: !user32
Will apply relocation fixups to file used for comparison
Will ignore NOP/LOCK errors
Will ignore patched instructions
Image specific ignores will be applied
Comparison image path: c:\mss\user32.dll\49E0380E9d000\user32.dll
No range specified


Scanning section: .text
Size: 422527
Range to scan: 76e31000-76e9827f
76e39c11-76e39c15 5 bytes - user32!MonitorFromPoint
[ 6a 08 68 50 9c:e9 ea 63 10 09 ]
76e3b8ea-76e3b8ee 5 bytes - user32!GetMonitorInfoA (+0x1cd9)
[ 8b ff 55 8b ec:e9 11 47 12 09 ]
```
76e3ba5b-76e3ba5f 5 bytes - user32!EnumDisplayDevicesW (+0x171)
[8b ff 55 8b ec:e9 a0 45 0b 09]
```
76e3d6f8-76e3d6fa 3 bytes - user32!NtUserSetThreadDesktop (+0x1c9d)
[ b8 30 12:e9 03 29 ]
76e3d6fc - user32!NtUserSetThreadDesktop+4 (+0x04)
[ 00:09 ]
76e3dc2a-76e3dc2e 5 bytes - user32!CreateWindowExA (+0x52e)
[ 8b ff 55 8b ec:e9 d1 23 15 09 ]
76e3e7cd-76e3e7d1 5 bytes - user32!SetWindowLongA (+0xba3)
[ 8b ff 55 8b ec:e9 2e 18 03 09 ]
76e3f8f8-76e3f8fc 5 bytes - user32!PostMessageA (+0x112b)
[ 8b ff 55 8b ec:e9 03 07 e7 08 ]
76e41305-76e41309 5 bytes - user32!CreateWindowExW (+0x1a0d)
[ 8b ff 55 8b ec:e9 f6 ec 13 09 ]
76e413b4-76e413b8 5 bytes - user32!SetWindowLongW (+0xaf)
[ 8b ff 55 8b ec:e9 47 ec 03 09 ]
76e41709-76e4170d 5 bytes - user32!MonitorFromRect (+0x355)
[ 6a 08 68 48 17:e9 f2 e8 0e 09 ]
76e435e3-76e435e7 5 bytes - user32!NtUserSetWindowPos (+0x1eda)
[ b8 38 12 00 00:e9 18 ca fe 08 ]
```

```
76e440c5-76e440c9 5 bytes - user32!EnumDisplaySettingsExW (+0xae2)
[ 8b ff 55 8b ec:e9 36 bf 06 09 ]
76e441a1-76e441a5 5 bytes - user32!EnumDisplaySettingsW (+0xdc)
[ 8b ff 55 8b ec:e9 5a be 08 09 ]
76e46d4a-76e46d4e 5 bytes - user32!EnumDisplayDevicesA (+0x2ba9)
[ 8b ff 55 8b ec:e9 b1 92 0b 09 ]
76e46fe6-76e46fea 5 bytes - user32!EnumDisplaySettingsA (+0x29c)
[ 8b ff 55 8b ec:e9 15 90 09 09 ]
76e47010-76e47014 5 bytes - user32!EnumDisplaySettingsExA (+0x2a)
[ 8b ff 55 8b ec:e9 eb 8f 07 09 ]
76e47d12-76e47d16 5 bytes - user32!GetMonitorInfoW (+0xd02)
[ 8b ff 55 8b ec:e9 e9 82 10 09 ]
76e48343-76e48347 5 bytes - user32!PeekMessageA (+0x631)
[ 8b ff 55 8b ec:e9 b8 7c e8 08 ]
76e4844c-76e48450 5 bytes - user32!NtUserEnumDisplayMonitors (+0x109)
[ b8 81 11 00 00:e9 af 7b 0c 09 ]
76e488d4-76e488d8 5 bytes - user32!MonitorFromWindow (+0x488)
[ 6a 08 68 28 89:e9 27 77 0d 09 ]
76e48ab3-76e48ab7 5 bytes - user32!GetMessageA (+0x1df)
[ 8b ff 55 8b ec:e9 48 75 ea 08 ]
76e49994-76e49998 5 bytes - user32!GetWindowLongA (+0xee1)
[ 6a 08 68 d0 99:e9 67 66 00 09 ]
76e49af1-76e49af5 5 bytes - user32!GetSystemMetrics (+0x15d)
[ 6a 0c 68 58 9b:e9 0a 65 12 09 ]
76e4a175-76e4a179 5 bytes - user32!PostMessageW (+0x684)
[ 8b ff 55 8b ec:e9 86 5e e5 08 ]
76e4f8bf-76e4f8c3 5 bytes - user32!GetWindowLongW (+0x574a)
[ 6a 08 68 00 f9:e9 3c 07 01 09 ]
76e4fef7-76e4fefb 5 bytes - user32!GetMessageW (+0x638)
[ 8b ff 55 8b ec:e9 04 01 e9 08 ]
76e5045a-76e5045e 5 bytes - user32!PeekMessageW (+0x563)
[ 8b ff 55 8b ec:e9 a1 fb e6 08 ]
76e8d37d-76e8d381 5 bytes - user32!MessageBoxTimeoutW (+0x3cf23)
[ 8b ff 55 8b ec:e9 7e 2c ea 08 ]
76e8d4d9-76e8d4dd 5 bytes - user32!MessageBoxIndirectA (+0x15c)
[ 8b ff 55 8b ec:e9 22 2b ec 08 ]
76e8d5d3-76e8d5d7 5 bytes - user32!MessageBoxIndirectW (+0xfa)
[ 8b ff 55 8b ec:e9 28 2a eb 08 ]
76e8d65d-76e8d661 5 bytes - user32!MessageBoxExW (+0x8a)
[ 8b ff 55 8b ec:e9 9e 29 ed 08 ]
Total bytes compared: 422527(100%)
Number of errors: 154
154 errors : !user32 (76e39c11-76e8d661)


0:000> u EnumDisplayDevicesW
user32!EnumDisplayDevicesW:
76e3ba5b e9a0450b09      jmp 7fef0000
76e3ba60 81ec54030000    sub esp,354h
76e3ba66 a1c090e976      mov eax,dword ptr [user32!__security_cookie (76e990c0)]
76e3ba6b 33c5            xor eax,ebp
76e3ba6d 8945fc mov dword ptr [ebp-4],eax
76e3ba70 53 push         ebx
76e3ba71 56 push         esi
76e3ba72 8b7510 mov esi,dword ptr [ebp+10h]
```

Hyperdump

Virtual memory may contain regions that are memories of some other processes or systems. We do not consider the ordinary case of memory-mapped regions here but the case of type 2 hypervisor[100]. In such a case, memory regions may be "physical memories" of **Virtualized Systems** (page 1193). For example, we discovered such a region in crashed *vmware-vmx.exe* process memory dump:

```
0:007> !address -summary

--- Usage Summary ---------------- RgnCount ----------- Total Size -------- %ofBusy %ofTotal
Free                              231 7ffe`d009b000 ( 127.995 TB)  100.00%
<unknown>                         518 1`2508e000 ( 4.579 GB)        96.41%    0.00%
Image                             547 0`07056000 ( 112.336 MB)       2.31%    0.00%
Heap                               73 0`0216a000 ( 33.414 MB)        0.69%    0.00%
Stack                              81 0`01b00000 ( 27.000 MB)        0.56%    0.00%
Other                              11 0`001d0000 ( 1.813 MB)         0.04%    0.00%
TEB                                27 0`00036000 ( 216.000 kB)       0.00%    0.00%
PEB                                 1 0`00001000 ( 4.000 kB)         0.00%    0.00%

--- Type Summary (for busy) ------ RgnCount ----------- Total Size -------- %ofBusy %ofTotal
MEM_MAPPED                         88 1`0e25a000 ( 4.221 GB)         88.88%    0.00%
MEM_PRIVATE                       623 0`1aca5000 ( 428.645 MB)        8.81%    0.00%
MEM_IMAGE                         547 0`07056000 ( 112.336 MB)        2.31%    0.00%

--- State Summary ---------------- RgnCount ----------- Total Size -------- %ofBusy %ofTotal
MEM_FREE                          231 7ffe`d009b000 ( 127.995 TB)             100.00%
MEM_COMMIT                       1185 1`27657000 ( 4.616 GB)         97.18%    0.00%
MEM_RESERVE                        73 0`088fe000 ( 136.992 MB)        2.82%    0.00%

--- Protect Summary (for commit) - RgnCount ----------- Total Size -------- %ofBusy %ofTotal
PAGE_READWRITE                    473 1`1f38b000 ( 4.488 GB)         94.49%    0.00%
PAGE_READONLY                     400 0`04a05000 ( 74.020 MB)         1.52%    0.00%
PAGE_EXECUTE_READ                 196 0`0367a000 ( 54.477 MB)         1.12%    0.00%
PAGE_WRITECOPY                     59 0`001de000 ( 1.867 MB)          0.04%    0.00%
PAGE_READWRITE|PAGE_GUARD          27 0`00051000 ( 324.000 kB)        0.01%    0.00%
PAGE_NOACCESS                      27 0`0001b000 ( 108.000 kB)        0.00%    0.00%
PAGE_EXECUTE_READWRITE              3 0`00003000 ( 12.000 kB)         0.00%    0.00%

--- Largest Region by Usage ----------- Base Address -------- Region Size ----------
Free                290`ffe50000        7d66`9b210000 ( 125.401 TB)
<unknown>           28f`f8f90000        1`00000000 ( 4.000 GB)
Image               7ffa`9969f000       0`00e47000 ( 14.277 MB)
Heap                28f`95c7b000        0`00ae4000 ( 10.891 MB)
Stack               b8`f7b00000         0`000fc000 (1008.000 kB)
Other               28f`f2050000        0`00181000 ( 1.504 MB)
TEB                 b8`f7147000         0`00002000 ( 8.000 kB)
PEB                 b8`f7146000         0`00001000 ( 4.000 kB)
```

---

[100] https://en.wikipedia.org/wiki/Hypervisor

The size of the region is 4 GB which coincides with the size of Windows VM:

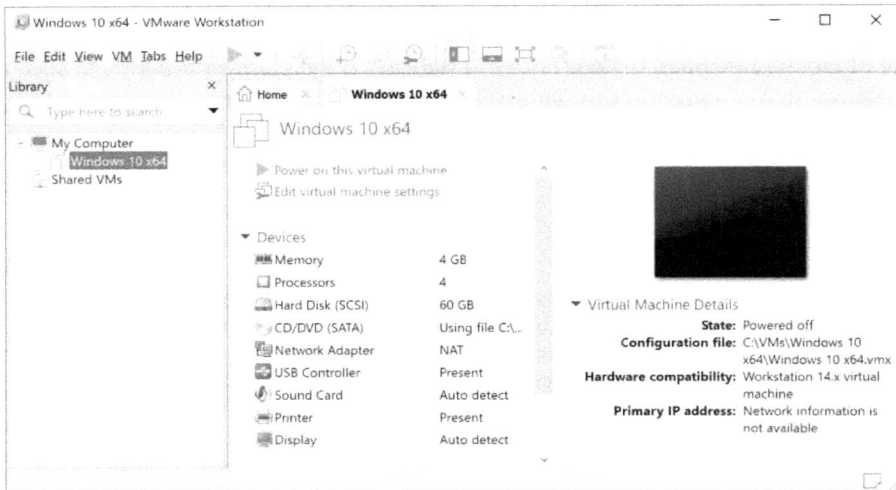

We assume that the whole VM physical space was placed there, and we had an instance of a physical memory dump inside a process memory dump. Whatever is such a physical memory dump internal organization, most likely the pages correspond to 4 KB memory chunks inside. We can employ WinDbg commands that allow the address parameter. For example, we can look for **Hidden Modules** (page 515):

```
0:007> .imgscan /r 28f`f8f90000 L?1`00000000
[...]
MZ at 00000290`f5867000 - size 7f000
Name: HAL.dll
[...]
MZ at 00000290`a089b000 - size 3000
Name: TDI.SYS
[...]


0:007> !dh 00000290`a089b000


File Type: DLL
FILE HEADER VALUES
14C machine (i386)
2 number of sections
592AD310 time date stamp Sun May 28 06:39:28 2017

0 file pointer to symbol table
0 number of symbols
E0 size of optional header
2122 characteristics
Executable
App can handle >2gb addresses
32 bit word machine
DLL
```

```
OPTIONAL HEADER VALUES
10B magic #
9.00 linker version
A00 size of code
400 size of initialized data
0 size of uninitialized data
0 address of entry point
1000 base of code
----- new -----
ffffffff8a7d0000 image base
1000 section alignment
200 file alignment
3 subsystem (Windows CUI)
10.00 operating system version
10.00 image version
5.01 subsystem version
3000 size of image
400 size of headers
10F33 checksum
0000000000040000 size of stack reserve
0000000000001000 size of stack commit
0000000000100000 size of heap reserve
0000000000001000 size of heap commit
540 DLL characteristics
Dynamic base
NX compatible
No structured exception handler
1140 [ 73A] address [size] of Export Directory
0    [ 0]   address [size] of Import Directory
2000 [ 3E8] address [size] of Resource Directory
0    [ 0]   address [size] of Exception Directory
0    [ 0]   address [size] of Security Directory
0    [ 0]   address [size] of Base Relocation Directory
1000 [ 1C]  address [size] of Debug Directory
0    [ 0]   address [size] of Description Directory
0    [ 0]   address [size] of Special Directory
0    [ 0]   address [size] of Thread Storage Directory
0    [ 0]   address [size] of Load Configuration Directory
0    [ 0]   address [size] of Bound Import Directory
0    [ 0]   address [size] of Import Address Table Directory
0    [ 0]   address [size] of Delay Import Directory
0    [ 0]   address [size] of COR20 Header Directory
0    [ 0]   address [size] of Reserved Directory


SECTION HEADER #1
.text name
87A virtual size
1000 virtual address
A00 size of raw data
400 file pointer to raw data
0 file pointer to relocation table
0 file pointer to line numbers
0 number of relocations
0 number of line numbers
60000020 flags
Code
```

```
(no align specified)
Execute Read

Debug Directories(1)
Type Size Address Pointer
cv 20 101c 41c Format: RSDS, guid, 1, tdi.pdb

SECTION HEADER #2
.rsrc name
3E8 virtual size
2000 virtual address
400 size of raw data
E00 file pointer to raw data
0 file pointer to relocation table
0 file pointer to line numbers
0 number of relocations
0 number of line numbers
40000040 flags
Initialized Data
(no align specified)
Read Only
[...]
```

We call such pattern **Hyperdump**:

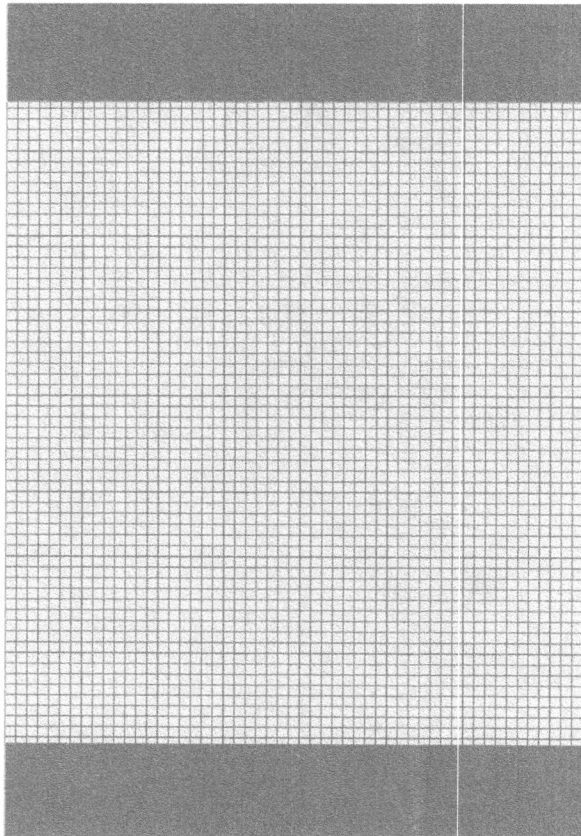

Incomplete Stack Trace

GDB

Users of WinDbg debugger accustomed to full thread stack traces will wonder whether a thread starts from *main*:

```
(gdb) where
#0 0x000000010d3b0e90 in bar () at main.c:15
#1 0x000000010d3b0ea9 in foo () at main.c:20
#2 0x000000010d3b0ec4 in main (argc=1,
argv=0x7fff6cfafbf8) at main.c:25
```

Of course, it does not, and a stack trace is shown starting from *main* function by default. We can change this behavior by using the following command:

```
(gdb) set backtrace past-main
```

Now we see the additional frame:

```
(gdb) where
#0 0x000000010d3b0e90 in bar () at main.c:15
#1 0x000000010d3b0ea9 in foo () at main.c:20
#2 0x000000010d3b0ec4 in main (argc=1,
argv=0x7fff6cfafbf8) at main.c:25
#3 0x000000010d3b0e74 in start ()
```

For Linux we have:

```
(gdb) set backtrace past-main

(gdb) bt
 #0 0x000000000042fed1 in nanosleep ()
 #1 0x000000000042fda0 in sleep ()
 #2 0x000000000040078a in main ()
 #3 0x0000000000405283 in __libc_start_main ()
 #4 0x00000000004003e9 in _start ()
```

Incomplete Session

It is a useful pattern for the analysis of memory dumps from terminal services environments. Normally, session processes include *csrss.exe*, *winlogon.exe*, *wfshell.exe* (in the case of some Citrix products), *explorer.exe* and a few user defined processes such as *winword.exe*, for example:

```
0: kd> !session
Sessions on machine: 6
Valid Sessions: 0 1 3 5 6 8

0: kd> !sprocess 6
Dumping Session 6

_MM_SESSION_SPACE fffffa6009447000
_MMSESSION fffffa6009447b40
PROCESS fffffa800fcee630
SessionId: 6 Cid: 1974 Peb: 7fffffd5000 ParentCid: 147c
DirBase: 158baf000 ObjectTable: fffff8801ef13b00 HandleCount: 532.
Image: csrss.exe

PROCESS fffffa800fc77040
SessionId: 6 Cid: 1ae4 Peb: 7fffffde000 ParentCid: 147c
DirBase: 15d2b4000 ObjectTable: fffff8802084b570 HandleCount: 238.
Image: winlogon.exe

PROCESS fffffa800fe61040
SessionId: 6 Cid: 1edc Peb: 7efdf000 ParentCid: 1ec8
DirBase: 14df74000 ObjectTable: fffff88020f486e0 HandleCount: 313.
Image: wfshell.exe

PROCESS fffffa800ff5a660
SessionId: 6 Cid: 2054 Peb: 7fffffdf000 ParentCid: 1dbc
DirBase: 201a81000 ObjectTable: fffff88020dd56e0 HandleCount: 447.
Image: explorer.exe

PROCESS fffffa800fe28040
SessionId: 6 Cid: 1ce4 Peb: 7efdf000 ParentCid: 13a8
DirBase: 11f552000 ObjectTable: fffff8801fe96990 HandleCount: 1842.
Image: WINWORD.EXE

PROCESS fffffa800f119c10
SessionId: 6 Cid: 2074 Peb: 7efdf000 ParentCid: 2054
DirBase: 2d994f000 ObjectTable: fffff8801e76aec0 HandleCount: 673.
Image: iexplore.exe
```

If we compare with the last session #8 we see that the latter has only two processes:

```
0: kd> !sprocess 8
Dumping Session 8

_MM_SESSION_SPACE fffffa600bafc000
_MMSESSION fffffa600bafcb40
PROCESS fffffa80103a4480
SessionId: 8 Cid: 2858 Peb: 7fffffdf000 ParentCid: 2660
DirBase: a04bb000 ObjectTable: fffff8801cb926a0 HandleCount: 534.
Image: csrss.exe

PROCESS fffffa801065b770
SessionId: 8 Cid: 2878 Peb: 7fffffdf000 ParentCid: 2660
DirBase: 5da40000 ObjectTable: fffff8801ce5e440 HandleCount: 235.
Image: winlogon.exe
```

Such anomalies may point to a disconnected session that failed to terminate due to some unresponsive session process, or a session that is stuck in session initialization process launch sequence due to threads blocked in wait chains. Here process threads need to be analyzed.

Comments

Terminal session management systems may also preallocate sessions to make logon faster.

In the case of many terminal sessions on Windows we can dump processes sorted by session via **!sprocess -4** to spot **Incomplete Sessions** (page 560).

Inconsistent Dump

We have to live with tools that produce inconsistent dumps. For example, LiveKd.exe from sysinternals.com which was widely used in the past by Microsoft and Citrix technical support to save complete memory dumps without a server reboot. Here we reproduce a note from one of the past articles[101]:

> LiveKd.exe-generated dumps are always inconsistent and cannot be a reliable source for certain types of dump analysis, for example, looking at resource contention. This is because it takes a considerable amount of time to save a dump on a live system, and the system is being changed during that process. The instantaneous traditional CrashOnCtrlScroll method or SystemDump tool always save a reliable and consistent dump because the system is frozen first (any process or kernel activity is disabled), then a dump is saved to a page file.

If we look at such inconsistent dump, we will find that many useful kernel structures such as ERESOURCE list (**!locks**) are broken and even circular referenced, and therefore, WinDbg commands display "strange" output.

Easy and painless (for customers) crash dump generation using such "Live" tools means that it is widely used, and we have to analyze memory dumps saved by these tools and sent from customers. This brings us to the next crash dump analysis pattern called **Inconsistent Dump**.

If we have such a memory dump, we should look at it in order to extract maximum useful information that helps in identifying the root cause or give us further directions. Not all information is inconsistent in such dumps. For example, drivers, processes, thread stacks and IRP lists can give us some clues about activities. Even some information not visible in a consistent dump can surface in the inconsistent dump.

For example, we had a LiveKd memory dump from Windows Server 2003 where we looked at process stacks and found that for some processes in addition to their own threads there were additional terminated threads belonging to a completely different process (never seen in the consistent memory dumps).

Comments

Newer versions of LiveKd pause a VM while saving a memory dump[102]. There are even more options added recently for consistency. When using LiveKd for child Hyper-V partitions (-hv) we should use -p option to pause the partition. Please also see **Mirror Dump Set** analysis pattern (page 751).

---

[101] Inconsistent Dump, Memory Dump Analysis Anthology, Volume 1, page 269
[102] https://docs.microsoft.com/en-gb/sysinternals/downloads/livekd

Incorrect Stack Trace

One of the mistakes beginners make is trusting WinDbg **!analyze** or **kv** commands displaying a stack trace. WinDbg is only a tool, sometimes information necessary to get correct stack trace is missing, and, therefore, some critical thought is required to distinguish between correct and incorrect stack traces. We call this pattern **Incorrect Stack Trace**. **Incorrect Stack Traces** usually

- Have a WinDbg warning: *"Following frames may be wrong."*
- Do not have the correct bottom frame like *kernel32!BaseThreadStart* (in user-mode)
- Have function calls that do not make any sense
- Have strange looking disassembled function code or code that does not make any sense from compiler perspective
- Have ChildEBP and RetAddr addresses that do not make any sense

Consider the following **Stack Trace** (page 1033):

```
0:011> k
ChildEBP RetAddr
WARNING: Frame IP not in any known module. Following frames may be wrong.
0184e434 7c830b10 0x184e5bf
0184e51c 7c81f832 ntdll!RtlGetFullPathName_Ustr+0x15b
0184e5f8 7c83b1dd ntdll!RtlpLowFragHeapAlloc+0xc6a
00099d30 00000000 ntdll!RtlpLowFragHeapFree+0xa7
```

Here we have almost all attributes of a wrong stack trace. At first glance it looks like some heap corruption happened (runtime heap *alloc* and *free* functions are present) but if we give it a second thought we see that the low fragmentation heap *Free* function shouldn't call the low fragmentation heap *Alloc* function and the latter shouldn't query the full path name. That does not make any sense.

What should we do here? Look at the raw stack and try to build the correct stack trace ourselves. In our case, this is very easy. We need to traverse stack frames from *BaseThreadStart+0x34* until we do not find any function call or reach the top. When functions are called (no optimization, most compilers) EBP registers are linked together as explained on the following slide from Practical Foundations of Debugging seminars[103]:

---

[103] Windows Debugging: Practical Foundations, http://www.dumpanalysis.org/windows-debugging-practical-foundations

func() { func2(1); }   func2(int i) { int var; }

push 1   push ebp
call func2   mov ebp, esp   sub esp, 4

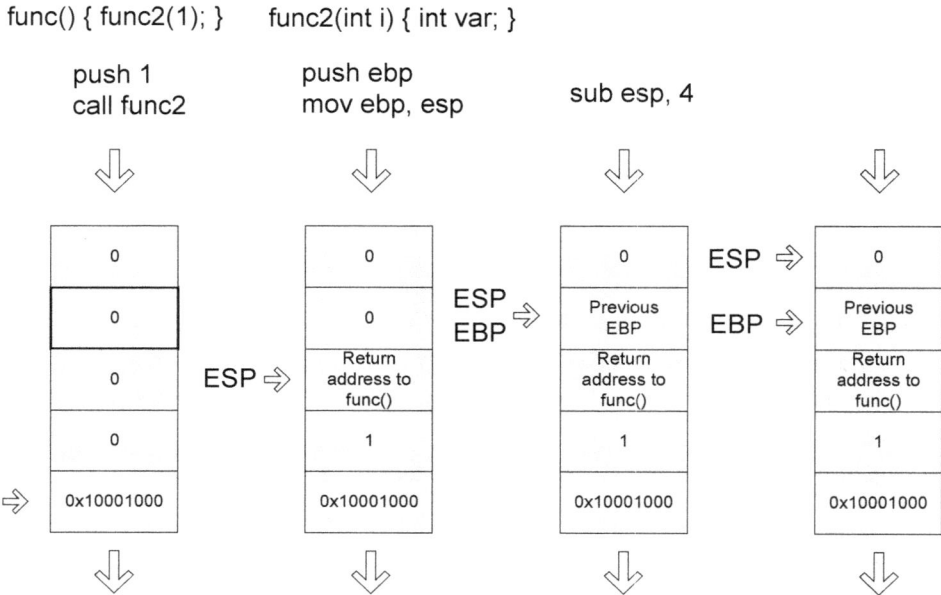

```
0:011> !teb
TEB at 7ffd8000
    ExceptionList:         0184ebdc
    StackBase:             01850000
    StackLimit:            01841000
    SubSystemTib:          00000000
    FiberData:             00001e00
    ArbitraryUserPointer:  00000000
    Self:                  7ffd8000
    EnvironmentPointer:    00000000
    ClientId:              0000061c . 00001b60
    RpcHandle:             00000000
    Tls Storage:           00000000
    PEB Address:           7ffdf000
    LastErrorValue:        0
    LastStatusValue:       c0000034
    Count Owned Locks:     0
    HardErrorMode:         0


0:011> dds 01841000 01850000
01841000  00000000
...
...
...
0184eef0  0184ef0c
0184eef4  7615dff2 localspl!SplDriverEvent+0x21
0184eef8  00bc3e08
0184eefc  00000003
0184ef00  00000001
0184ef04  00000000
0184ef08  0184efb0
0184ef0c  0184ef30
```

```
0184ef10  7615f9d0  localspl!PrinterDriverEvent+0x46
0184ef14  00bc3e08
0184ef18  00000003
0184ef1c  00000000
0184ef20  0184efb0
0184ef24  00b852a8
0184ef28  00c3ec58
0184ef2c  00bafcc0
0184ef30  0184f3f8
0184ef34  7614a9b4  localspl!SplAddPrinter+0x5f3
0184ef38  00c3ec58
0184ef3c  00000003
0184ef40  00000000
0184ef44  0184efb0
0184ef48  00c117f8
...
...
...
0184ff28  00000000
0184ff2c  00000000
0184ff30  0184ff84
0184ff34  77c75286  RPCRT4!LRPC_ADDRESS::ReceiveLotsaCalls+0x3a
0184ff38  0184ff4c
0184ff3c  77c75296  RPCRT4!LRPC_ADDRESS::ReceiveLotsaCalls+0x4a
0184ff40  7c82f2fc  ntdll!RtlLeaveCriticalSection
0184ff44  000de378
0184ff48  00097df0
0184ff4c  4d2fa200
0184ff50  ffffffff
0184ff54  ca5b1700
0184ff58  ffffffff
0184ff5c  8082d821
0184ff60  0184fe38
0184ff64  00097df0
0184ff68  000000aa
0184ff6c  80020000
0184ff70  0184ff54
0184ff74  80020000
0184ff78  000b0c78
0184ff7c  00a50180
0184ff80  0184fe38
0184ff84  0184ff8c
0184ff88  77c5778f  RPCRT4!RecvLotsaCallsWrapper+0xd
0184ff8c  0184ffac
0184ff90  77c5f7dd  RPCRT4!BaseCachedThreadRoutine+0x9d
0184ff94  0009c410
0184ff98  00000000
0184ff9c  00000000
0184ffa0  00097df0
0184ffa4  00097df0
0184ffa8  00015f90
0184ffac  0184ffb8
0184ffb0  77c5de88  RPCRT4!ThreadStartRoutine+0x1b
0184ffb4  00088258
0184ffb8  0184ffec
0184ffbc  77e6608b  kernel32!BaseThreadStart+0x34
```

```
0184ffc0  00097df0
0184ffc4  00000000
0184ffc8  00000000
0184ffcc  00097df0
0184ffd0  8ad84818
0184ffd4  0184ffc4
0184ffd8  8980a700
0184ffdc  ffffffff
0184ffe0  77e6b7d0 kernel32!_except_handler3
0184ffe4  77e66098 kernel32!`string'+0x98
0184ffe8  00000000
0184ffec  00000000
0184fff0  00000000
77c5de6d  RPCRT4!ThreadStartRoutine
0184fff8  00097df0
0184fffc  00000000
01850000  00000008
```

Next, we need to use custom **k** command and specify the base pointer. In our case, the last found stack address that links EBP pointers is 0184eef0:

```
0:011> k L=0184eef0
ChildEBP RetAddr
WARNING: Frame IP not in any known module. Following frames may be wrong.
0184eef0 7615dff2 0x184e5bf
0184ef0c 7615f9d0 localspl!SplDriverEvent+0x21
0184ef30 7614a9b4 localspl!PrinterDriverEvent+0x46
0184f3f8 761482de localspl!SplAddPrinter+0x5f3
0184f424 74067c8f localspl!LocalAddPrinterEx+0x2e
0184f874 74067b76 SPOOLSS!AddPrinterExW+0x151
0184f890 01007e29 SPOOLSS!AddPrinterW+0x17
0184f8ac 01006ec3 spoolsv!YAddPrinter+0x75
0184f8d0 77c70f3b spoolsv!RpcAddPrinter+0x37
0184f8f8 77ce23f7 RPCRT4!Invoke+0x30
0184fcf8 77ce26ed RPCRT4!NdrStubCall2+0x299
0184fd14 77c709be RPCRT4!NdrServerCall2+0x19
0184fd48 77c7093f RPCRT4!DispatchToStubInCNoAvrf+0x38
0184fd9c 77c70865 RPCRT4!RPC_INTERFACE::DispatchToStubWorker+0x117
0184fdc0 77c734b1 RPCRT4!RPC_INTERFACE::DispatchToStub+0xa3
0184fdfc 77c71bb3 RPCRT4!LRPC_SCALL::DealWithRequestMessage+0x42c
0184fe20 77c75458 RPCRT4!LRPC_ADDRESS::DealWithLRPCRequest+0x127
0184ff84 77c5778f RPCRT4!LRPC_ADDRESS::ReceiveLotsaCalls+0x430
0184ff8c 77c5f7dd RPCRT4!RecvLotsaCallsWrapper+0xd
```

Stack traces make more sense now, but we do not see *BaseThreadStart+0x34*. By default, WinDbg displays only 20 (0x14) function calls (stack frames), so we need to specify stack frame count in hexadecimal format, for example, 0x100 (0n256):

```
0:011> k L=0184eef0 100
ChildEBP RetAddr
WARNING: Frame IP not in any known module. Following frames may be wrong.
0184eef0 7615dff2 0x184e5bf
0184ef0c 7615f9d0 localspl!SplDriverEvent+0x21
0184ef30 7614a9b4 localspl!PrinterDriverEvent+0x46
0184f3f8 761482de localspl!SplAddPrinter+0x5f3
0184f424 74067c8f localspl!LocalAddPrinterEx+0x2e
0184f874 74067b76 SPOOLSS!AddPrinterExW+0x151
0184f890 01007e29 SPOOLSS!AddPrinterW+0x17
0184f8ac 01006ec3 spoolsv!YAddPrinter+0x75
0184f8d0 77c70f3b spoolsv!RpcAddPrinter+0x37
0184f8f8 77ce23f7 RPCRT4!Invoke+0x30
0184fcf8 77ce26ed RPCRT4!NdrStubCall2+0x299
0184fd14 77c709be RPCRT4!NdrServerCall2+0x19
0184fd48 77c7093f RPCRT4!DispatchToStubInCNoAvrf+0x38
0184fd9c 77c70865 RPCRT4!RPC_INTERFACE::DispatchToStubWorker+0x117
0184fdc0 77c734b1 RPCRT4!RPC_INTERFACE::DispatchToStub+0xa3
0184fdfc 77c71bb3 RPCRT4!LRPC_SCALL::DealWithRequestMessage+0x42c
0184fe20 77c75458 RPCRT4!LRPC_ADDRESS::DealWithLRPCRequest+0x127
0184ff84 77c5778f RPCRT4!LRPC_ADDRESS::ReceiveLotsaCalls+0x430
0184ff8c 77c5f7dd RPCRT4!RecvLotsaCallsWrapper+0xd
0184ffac 77c5de88 RPCRT4!BaseCachedThreadRoutine+0x9d
0184ffb8 77e6608b RPCRT4!ThreadStartRoutine+0x1b
0184ffec 00000000 kernel32!BaseThreadStart+0x34
```

Now our stack trace looks much better. For another complete example, please see the article[104].

Sometimes **Incorrect Stack Trace** is reported when symbols were not applied. Non-symbol gaps in stack traces can be the sign of this pattern too:

```
STACK_TEXT:
WARNING: Stack unwind information not available. Following frames may be wrong.
00b2f42c 091607aa mydll!foo+0x8338
00b2f4cc 7c83ab9e mydll!foo+0x8fe3
00b2f4ec 7c832d06 ntdll!RtlFindNextActivationContextSection+0x46
00b2f538 001a5574 ntdll!RtlFindActivationContextSectionString+0xe1
00b2f554 7c8302b3 0x1a5574
00b2f560 7c82f9c1 ntdll!RtlpFreeToHeapLookaside+0x22
00b2f640 7c832b7f ntdll!RtlFreeHeap+0x20e
001dd000 00080040 ntdll!LdrUnlockLoaderLock+0xad
001dd00c 0052005c 0x80040
001dd010 00470045 0x52005c
0052005c 00000000 0x470045
```

---

[104] Manual Stack Trace Reconstruction, Memory Dump Analysis Anthology, Volume 1, page 157

Comments

To check the correctness of some frames, we can use the same method as described in **Coincidental Symbolic Information** pattern (page 148). We use backward disassembly on a return address:

```
0286f430 690e6daa mshtml!CBase::PrivateInvokeEx+0x6d
WARNING: Stack unwind information not available. Following frames may be wrong.
0286f494 6915f5c5 jscript9!DllGetClassObject+0x18bb1


0:005> ub 690e6daa
jscript9!DllGetClassObject+0x18b9e:
690e6d97 ff7514 push dword ptr [ebp+14h]
690e6d9a ff7510 push dword ptr [ebp+10h]
690e6d9d 8b06   mov eax,dword ptr [esi]
690e6d9f 53     push ebx
690e6da0 ff75ec push dword ptr [ebp-14h]
690e6da3 ff7508 push dword ptr [ebp+8]
690e6da6 56     push esi
690e6da7 ff5020 call dword ptr [eax+20h]
```

Incorrect Symbolic Information

Most of the time this pattern is associated with function names and offsets, for example, *module!foo* vs. *module!foo+100*. In some cases, the module name is incorrect itself or absent altogether. This can happen in complete memory dumps when we forget to reload user space symbols after changing the process context, for example:

```
; previous process context of firefox.exe
; switching to winlogon.exe context

kd> .process fffffadfe718c040
Implicit process is now fffffadf`e718c040


kd> !process fffffadfe718c040
PROCESS fffffadfe718c040
    SessionId: 0  Cid: 017c    Peb: 7fffffd9000  ParentCid: 0130
    DirBase: 01916000  ObjectTable: fffffa800099a890  HandleCount: 754.
    Image: winlogon.exe
    VadRoot fffffadfe75e91f0 Vads 190 Clone 0 Private 2905. Modified 10047. Locked 0.
    DeviceMap fffffa8000004950
    Token                             fffffa800122a060
    ElapsedTime                       77 Days 02:14:26.109
    UserTime                          00:00:04.156
    KernelTime                        00:00:02.359
    QuotaPoolUsage[PagedPool]         143128
    QuotaPoolUsage[NonPagedPool]      191072
    Working Set Sizes (now,min,max)  (541, 50, 345) (2164KB, 200KB, 1380KB)
    PeakWorkingSetSize                6323
    VirtualSize                       108 Mb
    PeakVirtualSize                   118 Mb
    PageFaultCount                    212547
    MemoryPriority                    BACKGROUND
    BasePriority                      13
    CommitCharge                      3733

[...]
```

```
THREAD fffffadfe68f2040  Cid 017c.0198  Teb: 000007fffffd7000 Win32Thread: fffff97ff4a09010 WAIT:
(Unknown) UserMode Non-Alertable
    fffffadfe7133160  Semaphore Limit 0x7fffffff
    fffffadfe68f20f8  NotificationTimer
sNot impersonating
DeviceMap                 fffffa8000004950
Owning Process            fffffadfe718c040        Image:        winlogon.exe
Attached Process          N/A            Image:        N/A
Wait Start TickCount      426298731      Ticks: 51 (0:00:00:00.796)
Context Switch Count      2215076                   LargeStack
UserTime                  00:00:00.187
KernelTime                00:00:00.468
Start Address 0x0000000077d6b6e0
Stack Init fffffadfe4481e00 Current fffffadfe4481860
Base fffffadfe4482000 Limit fffffadfe447a000 Call 0
Priority 14 BasePriority 13 PriorityDecrement 0
Child-SP          RetAddr           Call Site
fffffadf`e44818a0 fffff800`0103b093 nt!KiSwapContext+0x85
fffffadf`e4481a20 fffff800`0103c433 nt!KiSwapThread+0xc3
fffffadf`e4481a60 fffff800`012d25ae nt!KeWaitForSingleObject+0x528
fffffadf`e4481af0 fffff800`0104113d nt!NtReplyWaitReceivePortEx+0x8c8
fffffadf`e4481c00 00000000`77ef0caa nt!KiSystemServiceCopyEnd+0x3 (TrapFrame @ fffffadf`e4481c70)
00000000`00bcfb98 000007ff`7fd6ff61 ntdll!NtReplyWaitReceivePortEx+0xa
00000000`00bcfba0 00000000`000d2340 0x7ff`7fd6ff61
00000000`00bcfba8 00000000`00bcfde0 0xd2340
00000000`00bcfbb0 00000000`014cd220 0xbcfde0
00000000`00bcfbb8 00000000`000c1d30 0x14cd220
00000000`00bcfbc0 00000000`00bcfe18 0xc1d30
00000000`00bcfbc8 0000ffff`00001f80 0xbcfe18
00000000`00bcfbd0 *00000000`006c0044* 0xffff`00001f80
00000000`00bcfbd8 00000000`000006ec firefox+0x2c0044
00000000`00bcfbe0 00000000`000007b0 0x6ec
00000000`00bcfbe8 00000000`419b8385 0x7b0
00000000`00bcfbf0 00000000`00000000 0x419b8385


kd> lmu m firefox
start             end               module name
00000000`00400000 00000000`00b67000   firefox   T (no symbols)
```

We have the return address 00000000`006c0044 that is just *firefox+0x2c0044 (*00000000`00400000 + 2c0044). We correct it by reloading user space symbols.

```
kd> .reload /user
```

```
kd> !process fffffadfe718c040
[...]
THREAD fffffadfe68f2040  Cid 017c.0198  Teb: 000007fffffd7000 Win32Thread: fffff97ff4a09010 WAIT:
(Unknown) UserMode Non-Alertable
    fffffadfe7133160  Semaphore Limit 0x7fffffff
    fffffadfe68f20f8  NotificationTimer
Not impersonating
DeviceMap                 fffffa8000004950
Owning Process            fffffadfe718c040      Image:      winlogon.exe
Attached Process          N/A         Image:        N/A
Wait Start TickCount      426298731   Ticks: 51 (0:00:00.796)
Context Switch Count      2215076                LargeStack
UserTime                  00:00:00.187
KernelTime                00:00:00.468
Start Address kernel32!BaseThreadStart (0x0000000077d6b6e0)
Stack Init fffffadfe4481e00 Current fffffadfe4481860
Base fffffadfe4482000 Limit fffffadfe447a000 Call 0
Priority 14 BasePriority 13 PriorityDecrement 0
Child-SP          RetAddr           Call Site
fffffadf`e44818a0 fffff800`0103b093 nt!KiSwapContext+0x85
fffffadf`e4481a20 fffff800`0103c433 nt!KiSwapThread+0xc3
fffffadf`e4481a60 fffff800`012d25ae nt!KeWaitForSingleObject+0x528
fffffadf`e4481af0 fffff800`0104113d nt!NtReplyWaitReceivePortEx+0x8c8
fffffadf`e4481c00 00000000`77ef0caa nt!KiSystemServiceCopyEnd+0x3 (TrapFrame @ fffffadf`e4481c70)
00000000`00bcfb98 000007ff`7fd6ff61 ntdll!NtReplyWaitReceivePortEx+0xa
00000000`00bcfba0 000007ff`7fd45369 RPCRT4!LRPC_ADDRESS::ReceiveLotsaCalls+0x2a5
00000000`00bcfeb0 000007ff`7fd65996 RPCRT4!RecvLotsaCallsWrapper+0x9
00000000`00bcfee0 000007ff`7fd65d51 RPCRT4!BaseCachedThreadRoutine+0xde
00000000`00bcff50 00000000`77d6b71a RPCRT4!ThreadStartRoutine+0x21
00000000`00bcff80 00000000`00000000 kernel32!BaseThreadStart+0x3a
```

Commands like **.process /r /p** fffffadfe718c040 or **!process** fffffadfe718c040 **3f** do that automatically.

Another case for incorrect module names is malformed unloaded modules information:

```
0:000> lmt
start      end        module name
[...]
7c800000 7c907000   kernel32  Mon Apr 16 16:53:05 2007 (46239BE1)
7c910000 7c9c7000   ntdll     Wed Aug 04 08:57:08 2004 (411096D4)
7c9d0000 7d1ef000   shell32   Tue Dec 19 21:49:37 2006 (45885E71)
7df20000 7dfc0000   urlmon    Wed Aug 22 14:13:03 2007 (46CC365F)
7e360000 7e3f0000   user32    Thu Mar 08 15:36:30 2007 (45F02D7E)
Missing image name, possible paged-out or corrupt data.
```

```
Unloaded modules:
00410053 008a00a3   Unknown_Module_00410053
    Timestamp: Tue Mar 17 20:27:26 1970 (0064002E)
    Checksum:  006C006C
00010755 007407c5   l
    Timestamp: Wed Feb 04 21:26:01 1970 (002E0069)
    Checksum:  006C0064
00000011 411096d2   eme.dll
    Timestamp: Thu Apr 02 01:33:25 1970 (00780055)
    Checksum:  00680054
Missing image name, possible paged-out or corrupt data.
0064002e 00d0009a   Unknown_Module_0064002e
    Timestamp: unavailable (00000000)
    Checksum:  00000000
```

Here parts of UNICODE module names appear in checksums and timestamps as well. Such partial module names can appear on thread stacks and raw stack data, for example:

```
0:000> kL
ChildEBP RetAddr
[...]
0015ef3c 0366afc2 ModuleA!Validation+0x5b
WARNING: Frame IP not in any known module. Following frames may be wrong.
0015efcc 79e7c7a6 <Unloaded_ure.dll>+0x366afc1
03dc9b70 00000000 mscorwks!MethodDesc::CallDescr+0x1f
```

Default analysis falls victim too and suggests *ure.dll* that you would try hard to find on your system:

```
MODULE_NAME: ure

IMAGE_NAME:   ure.dll

DEBUG_FLR_IMAGE_TIMESTAMP:   750063

FAILURE_BUCKET_ID:   ure.dll!Unloaded_c0000005_APPLICATION_FAULT
```

The timestamp is suspiciously UNICODE-like. In such cases, we can even reconstruct the module name:

```
00000011 411096d2   eme.dll
    Timestamp: Thu Apr 02 01:33:25 1970 (00780055)
    Checksum:  00680054


0:000> .formats 00780055
Evaluate expression:
  Hex:      00000000`00780055
  Decimal: 7864405
  Octal:    0000000000000036000125
  Binary:   00000000 00000000 00000000 00000000 00000000 01111000 00000000 01010101
  Chars:    .....x.U
  Time:     Thu Apr 02 01:33:25 1970
  Float:    low 1.10204e-038 high 0
  Double:   3.88553e-317
```

```
0:000> .formats 00680054
Evaluate expression:
  Hex:      00680054
  Decimal:  6815828
  Octal:    00032000124
  Binary:   00000000 01101000 00000000 01010100
  Chars:    .h.T
  Time:     Fri Mar 20 21:17:08 1970
  Float:    low 9.55101e-039 high 0
  Double:   3.36747e-317
```

We concatenate UNICODE *Ux* and *Th* with *eme.dll* to get *UxTheme.dll* which is a real DLL name we can find on a system.

Injected Symbols

This pattern can be used to add missing symbols when we have **Reduced Symbolic Information** (page 921) like it was done previously in this old case study[105]. For example, TestWER[106] module was compiled with static MFC and CRT libraries and its private PDB file contains all necessary symbols including MSG structure. We can load that module into notepad.exe process space and apply symbols:

```
0:000:x86> lm
start            end              module name
00fc0000 00ff0000   notepad    (pdb
symbols)         c:\mss\notepad.pdb\E325F5195AE94FAEB58D25C9DF8C0CFD2\notepad.pdb
10000000 10039000   WinCRT     (deferred)
727f0000 7298e000   comctl32   (deferred)
72aa0000 72af1000   winspool   (deferred)
72b10000 72b19000   version    (deferred)
72e40000 72e48000   wow64cpu   (deferred)
72e50000 72eac000   wow64win   (pdb
symbols)         c:\mss\wow64win.pdb\B2D08CC152D64E71B79167DC0A0A53E91\wow64win.pdb
72eb0000 72eef000   wow64      (deferred)
733d0000 733e3000   dwmapi     (deferred)
735b0000 73606000   uxtheme    (deferred)
746f0000 746fc000   CRYPTBASE  (deferred)
74700000 74760000   sspicli    (deferred)
747c0000 74817000   shlwapi    (deferred)
74830000 7547a000   shell32    (deferred)
755d0000 7564b000   comdlg32   (deferred)
75650000 7567e000   imm32      (deferred)
75770000 75810000   advapi32   (deferred)
75810000 75920000   kernel32   (pdb
symbols)         c:\mss\wkernel32.pdb\1C690A8592304467BB15A09CEA7180FA2\wkernel32.pdb
75920000 759b0000   gdi32      (deferred)
759b0000 759f7000   KERNELBASE (deferred)
75a00000 75b00000   user32     (pdb
symbols)         c:\mss\wuser32.pdb\0FCE9CC301ED4567A819705B2718E1D62\wuser32.pdb
75b00000 75b8f000   oleaut32   (deferred)
[...]
76e40000 76fe9000   ntdll      (deferred)
77020000 771a0000   ntdll_77020000  (pdb
symbols)         c:\mss\wntdll.pdb\D74F79EB1F8D4A45ABCD2F476CCABACC2\wntdll.pdb


0:000:x86> .sympath+ C:\DebuggingTV\TestWER\x86
Symbol search path is: srv*;C:\DebuggingTV\TestWER\x86
Expanded Symbol search path is:
SRV*c:\mss*http://msdl.microsoft.com/download/symbols;c:\debuggingtv\testwer\x86


0:000:x86> .reload /f /i C:\DebuggingTV\TestWER\x86\TestWER.exe=10000000
```

[105] Coping with Missing Symbolic Information, Memory Dump Analysis Anthology, Volume 1, page 199
[106] http://support.citrix.com/article/CTX111901

```
0:000:x86> lm
start             end             module name
00fc0000 00ff0000  notepad    (pdb symbols)         c:\mss\notepad.pdb\E325F5195AE94FAEB58D25C9DF8C0CFD2\notepad.pdb
10000000 10039000  TestWER    (private pdb symbols) c:\debuggingtv\testwer\x86\TestWER.pdb
727f0000 7298e000  comct132   (deferred)
72aa0000 72af1000  winspool   (deferred)
72b10000 72b19000  version    (deferred)
72e40000 72e48000  wow64cpu   (deferred)
72e50000 72eac000  wow64win   (pdb symbols)         c:\mss\wow64win.pdb\B2D08CC152D64E71B79167DC0A0A53E91\wow64win.pdb
72eb0000 72eef000  wow64      (deferred)
733d0000 733e3000  dwmapi     (deferred)
735b0000 73606000  uxtheme    (deferred)
746f0000 746fc000  CRYPTBASE  (deferred)
74700000 74760000  sspicli    (deferred)
747c0000 74817000  shlwapi    (deferred)
74830000 7547a000  shell32    (deferred)
755d0000 7564b000  comdlg32   (deferred)
75650000 7567e000  imm32      (deferred)
75770000 75810000  advapi32   (deferred)
75810000 75920000  kernel32   (pdb symbols)         c:\mss\wkernel32.pdb\1C690A8592304467BB15A09CEA7180FA2\wkernel32.pdb
75920000 759b0000  gdi32      (deferred)
759b0000 759f7000  KERNELBASE (deferred)
75a00000 75b00000  user32     (pdb symbols)         c:\mss\wuser32.pdb\0FCE9CC301ED4567A819705B2718E1D62\wuser32.pdb
75b00000 75b8f000  oleaut32   (deferred)
[...]
76e40000 76fe9000  ntdll      (deferred)
77020000 771a0000  ntdll_77020000 (pdb symbols)     c:\mss\wntdll.pdb\D74F79EB1F8D4A45ABCD2F476CCABACC2\wntdll.pdb


0:000:x86> kv
ChildEBP RetAddr  Args to Child
0013fe34 75a1790d 0013fe74 00000000 00000000 user32!NtUserGetMessage+0x15
0013fe50 00fc148a 0013fe74 00000000 00000000 user32!GetMessageW+0x33
0013fe90 00fc16ec 00fc0000 00000000 00354082 notepad!WinMain+0xe6
0013ff20 758233aa 7efde000 0013ff6c 77059ef2 notepad!_initterm_e+0x1a1
0013ff2c 77059ef2 7efde000 57785ae5 00000000 kernel32!BaseThreadInitThunk+0xe
0013ff6c 77059ec5 00fc3689 7efde000 00000000 ntdll_77020000!__RtlUserThreadStart+0x70
0013ff84 00000000 00fc3689 7efde000 00000000 ntdll_77020000!_RtlUserThreadStart+0x1b


0:000:x86> dt -r MSG 0013fe74
TestWER!MSG
   +0x000 hwnd          : 0x0007149c HWND__
      +0x000 unused      : ??
   +0x004 message       : 0x113
   +0x008 wParam        : 0x38a508
   +0x00c lParam        : 0n1921500630
   +0x010 time          : 0x2079a177
   +0x014 pt            : tagPOINT
      +0x000 x           : 0n1337
      +0x004 y           : 0n448
```

Inline Function Optimization

Managed Code

In addition to **Inline Function Optimization** (page 578) of unmanaged and native code we can see similar approach to JIT-compiled code:

```
public class ClassMain
{
    public bool time2stop = false;

    public static void Main(string[] args)
    {
        new ClassMain().Main();
    }

    public void Main()
    {
        while (!time2stop)
        {
            DoWork();
        }
    }

    volatile int inSensor, outSensor;

    void DoWork()
    {
        outSensor ^= inSensor;
    }
}
```

```
0:000> kL
ChildEBP RetAddr
WARNING: Frame IP not in any known module. Following frames may be wrong.
001fefa0 79e7c6cc 0x3200a4
001ff020 79e7c8e1 mscorwks!CallDescrWorkerWithHandler+0xa3
001ff160 79e7c783 mscorwks!MethodDesc::CallDescr+0x19c
001ff17c 79e7c90d mscorwks!MethodDesc::CallTargetWorker+0x1f
001ff190 79eefb9e mscorwks!MethodDescCallSite::Call_RetArgSlot+0x18
001ff2f4 79eef830 mscorwks!ClassLoader::RunMain+0x263
001ff55c 79ef01da mscorwks!Assembly::ExecuteMainMethod+0xa6
001ffa2c 79fb9793 mscorwks!SystemDomain::ExecuteMainMethod+0x43f
001ffa7c 79fb96df mscorwks!ExecuteEXE+0x59
001ffac4 736455ab mscorwks!_CorExeMain+0x15c
001ffad0 73747f16 mscoreei!_CorExeMain+0x38
001ffae0 73744de3 mscoree!ShellShim__CorExeMain+0x99
001ffae8 76573833 mscoree!_CorExeMain_Exported+0x8
001ffaf4 77c1a9bd kernel32!BaseThreadInitThunk+0xe
001ffb34 00000000 ntdll!_RtlUserThreadStart+0x23
```

```
0:000> r
eax=00000000 ebx=001fefbc ecx=015316e0 edx=0037a238 esi=0037a238 edi=00000000
eip=003200a4 esp=001fef90 ebp=001fefa0 iopl=0 nv up ei pl zr na pe nc
cs=001b ss=0023 ds=0023 es=0023 fs=003b gs=0000 efl=00000246
003200a4 80790c00 cmp byte ptr [ecx+0Ch],0 ds:0023:015316ec=00


0:000> !IP2MD 003200a4
MethodDesc:      000d3048
Method Name:     ClassMain.Main()
Class:           000d1180
MethodTable:     000d3060
mdToken:         06000002
Module:          000d2c3c
IsJitted:        yes
m_CodeOrIL:      00320098


0:000> .asm no_code_bytes
Assembly options: no_code_bytes


0:000> !U 003200a4
Normal JIT generated code
ClassMain.Main()
Begin 00320098, size 13
00320098 cmp byte ptr [ecx+0Ch],0
0032009c jne 003200aa
0032009e mov eax,dword ptr [ecx+4]
003200a1 xor dword ptr [ecx+8],eax
>>> 003200a4 cmp byte ptr [ecx+0Ch],0
003200a8 je 0032009e
003200aa ret
```

We see that *DoWork* code was inlined into *Main* function code.

Unmanaged Code

Sometimes compilers optimize code by replacing function calls with their bodies. This procedure is called function inlining and functions themselves are called inline. On one platform, we can see the real function call on the stack trace but on another platform or product version we only see the same problem instruction. Fortunately, the rest of stack trace should be the same. Therefore when comparing **Stack Traces** (page 1033), we should not pay attention only to the top function call.

This pattern is frequently seen when threads crash while copying or moving memory. Consider this stack trace:

```
0: kd> kL
ChildEBP RetAddr
f22efaf4 f279ec3d driver!QueueValue+0x26b
f22efb30 8081dcdf driver!BufferAppendData+0x35f
f22efc7c 808f47b7 nt!IofCallDriver+0x45
f22efc90 808f24ee nt!IopSynchronousServiceTail+0x10b
f22efd38 80888c7c nt!NtWriteFile+0x65a
f22efd38 7c82ed54 nt!KiFastCallEntry+0xfc
```

When looking at *rep movs* instruction we might suspect that *QueueValue* was copying memory:

```
0: kd> r
eax=00000640 ebx=89b23000 ecx=00000190 edx=89b3c828 esi=02124220 edi=e2108f58
eip=f279c797 esp=f22efadc ebp=f22efaf4 iopl=0 nv up ei pl nz na pe nc
cs=0008 ss=0010 ds=0023 es=0023 fs=0030 gs=0000 efl=00010206
driver!QueueValue+0x26b:
f279c797 f3a5 rep movs dword ptr es:[edi],dword ptr [esi] es:0023:e2108f58=dfefbecf
ds:0023:02124220=????????
```

On x64 platform, the same driver had the similar stack trace but with *memcpy* at its top:

```
fffffadf`8955f4a8 fffffadf`8d1bef46 driver!memcpy+0x1c0
fffffadf`8955f4b0 fffffadf`8d1c15c9 driver!QueueValue+0x2fe
fffffadf`8955f550 fffff800`01273ed9 driver!BufferAppendData+0x481
...
```

We also see how *QueueValue+0x2fe* and *QueueValue+0x26b* are close. In fact, the source code for the driver calls *RtlCopyMemory* function only once, and it is defined as *memcpy* in *wdm.h*. The latter function is also exported from *nt* module:

```
0: kd> x nt!
...
80881780 nt!memcpy = <no type information>
...
```

but usually can be found in any driver that links with C runtime library, for example, on x64 Windows:

```
1: kd> x nt!memcpy
fffff800`01c464e0 nt!memcpy = <no type information>
```

```
1: kd> x srv!memcpy
fffff980`0eafdf20 srv!memcpy = <no type information>

1: kd> x win32k!memcpy
fffff960`000c1b40 win32k!memcpy = <no type information>
```

Therefore, we see that when compiling for x86 platform Visual C++ compiler decided to inline *memcpy* code but AMD compiler on the x64 platform did not inline it. The overall stack trace without offsets is very similar, and we can suppose that the problem was identical.

Instrumentation Information

Application and Driver Verifiers (including *gflags.exe* tool from Debugging Tools for Windows) set flags that modify the behavior of the system that is reflected in additional information being collected such as memory allocation history and in WinDbg output changes such as stack traces. These tools belong to a broad class of instrumentation tools. To check in a minidump, kernel, and complete memory dumps whether Driver Verifier was enabled we use **!verifier** WinDbg command:

```
1: kd> !verifier

Verify Level 0 ... enabled options are:

Summary of All Verifier Statistics

RaiseIrqls                          0x0
AcquireSpinLocks                    0x0
Synch Executions                    0x0
Trims                               0x0


Pool Allocations Attempted          0x0
Pool Allocations Succeeded          0x0
Pool Allocations Succeeded SpecialPool 0x0
Pool Allocations With NO TAG        0x0
Pool Allocations Failed             0x0
Resource Allocations Failed Deliberately   0x0


Current paged pool allocations      0x0 for 00000000 bytes
Peak paged pool allocations         0x0 for 00000000 bytes
Current nonpaged pool allocations   0x0 for 00000000 bytes
Peak nonpaged pool allocations      0x0 for 00000000 bytes


0: kd> !verifier

Verify Level 3 ... enabled options are:
      Special pool
      Special irql


Summary of All Verifier Statistics

RaiseIrqls                          0xdea5
AcquireSpinLocks                    0x87b5c
Synch Executions                    0x17b5
Trims                               0xab36


Pool Allocations Attempted          0x8990e
Pool Allocations Succeeded          0x8990e
Pool Allocations Succeeded SpecialPool 0x29c0
Pool Allocations With NO TAG        0x1
Pool Allocations Failed             0x0
Resource Allocations Failed Deliberately   0x0
```

```
Current paged pool allocations          0x0 for 00000000 bytes
Peak paged pool allocations             0x0 for 00000000 bytes
Current nonpaged pool allocations       0x0 for 00000000 bytes
Peak nonpaged pool allocations          0x0 for 00000000 bytes
```

To check in a process user dump that Application Verifier (and gflags) was enabled we use **!avrf** and **!gflags** WinDbg extension commands:

```
0:001> !avrf
Application verifier is not enabled for this process.
Page heap has been enabled separately.


0:001> !gflag
Current NtGlobalFlag contents: 0x02000000
    hpa - Place heap allocations at ends of pages
```

Here is an example of an instrumented stack trace:

```
68546e88 verifier!AVrfpDphFindBusyMemoryNoCheck+0xb8
68546f95 verifier!AVrfpDphFindBusyMemory+0x15
68547240 verifier!AVrfpDphFindBusyMemoryAndRemoveFromBusyList+0x20
68549080 verifier!AVrfDebugPageHeapFree+0x90
77190aac ntdll!RtlDebugFreeHeap+0x2f
7714a8ff ntdll!RtlpFreeHeap+0x5d
770f2a32 ntdll!RtlFreeHeap+0x142
75fb14d1 kernel32!HeapFree+0x14
748d4c39 msvcr80!free+0xcd
[...]
00a02bb2 ServiceA!ServiceMain+0x302
767175a8 sechost!ScSvcctrlThreadA+0x21
75fb3677 kernel32!BaseThreadInitThunk+0xe
770f9d42 ntdll!__RtlUserThreadStart+0x70
770f9d15 ntdll!_RtlUserThreadStart+0x1b
```

Here is another example that shows instrumentation difference. We run **Double Free** (page 289) fault modeling application and see its stack trace from a crash dump:

```
0:000> !gflag
Current NtGlobalFlag contents: 0x00000000
```

```
0:000> kL 100
Child-SP          RetAddr           Call Site
00000000`002dec38 00000000`77735ce2 ntdll!NtWaitForSingleObject+0xa
00000000`002dec40 00000000`77735e85 ntdll!RtlReportExceptionEx+0x1d2
00000000`002ded30 00000000`77735eea ntdll!RtlReportException+0xb5
00000000`002dedb0 00000000`77736d25 ntdll!RtlpTerminateFailureFilter+0x1a
00000000`002dede0 00000000`77685148 ntdll!RtlReportCriticalFailure+0x96
00000000`002dee10 00000000`776a554d ntdll!_C_specific_handler+0x8c
00000000`002dee80 00000000`77685d1c ntdll!RtlpExecuteHandlerForException+0xd
00000000`002deeb0 00000000`776862ee ntdll!RtlDispatchException+0x3cb
00000000`002df590 00000000`77736cd2 ntdll!RtlRaiseException+0x221
00000000`002dfbd0 00000000`77737396 ntdll!RtlReportCriticalFailure+0x62
00000000`002dfca0 00000000`777386c2 ntdll!RtlpReportHeapFailure+0x26
00000000`002dfcd0 00000000`7773a0c4 ntdll!RtlpHeapHandleError+0x12
00000000`002dfd00 00000000`776dd1cd ntdll!RtlpLogHeapFailure+0xa4
00000000`002dfd30 00000000`77472c7a ntdll! ?? ::FNODOBFM::`string'+0x123b4
00000000`002dfdb0 00000000`6243c7bc kernel32!HeapFree+0xa
00000000`002dfde0 00000001`3f8f1033 msvcr90!free+0x1c
00000000`002dfe10 00000001`3f8f11f2 InstrumentedApp!wmain+0x33
00000000`002dfe50 00000000`7746f56d InstrumentedApp!__tmainCRTStartup+0x11a
00000000`002dfe80 00000000`776a3281 kernel32!BaseThreadInitThunk+0xd
00000000`002dfeb0 00000000`00000000 ntdll!RtlUserThreadStart+0x1d
```

Then we enable Application Verifier and full page heap in *gflags.exe* GUI. Actually two crash dumps are saved at the same time (we had set up *LocalDumps* registry key[107] on x64 W2K8 R2) with slightly different stack traces:

```
0:000> !gflag
Current NtGlobalFlag contents: 0x02000100
    vrf - Enable application verifier
    hpa - Place heap allocations at ends of pages


0:000> kL 100
Child-SP          RetAddr           Call Site
00000000`0022e438 00000000`77735ce2 ntdll!NtWaitForSingleObject+0xa
00000000`0022e440 00000000`77735e85 ntdll!RtlReportExceptionEx+0x1d2
00000000`0022e530 000007fe`f3ed26fb ntdll!RtlReportException+0xb5
00000000`0022e5b0 00000000`77688a8f verifier!AVrfpVectoredExceptionHandler+0x26b
00000000`0022e640 00000000`776859b2 ntdll!RtlpCallVectoredHandlers+0xa8
00000000`0022e6b0 00000000`776bfe48 ntdll!RtlDispatchException+0x22
00000000`0022ed90 000007fe`f3eca668 ntdll!KiUserExceptionDispatcher+0x2e
00000000`0022f350 000007fe`f3ec931d verifier!VerifierStopMessage+0x1f0
00000000`0022f400 000007fe`f3ec9736 verifier!AVrfpDphReportCorruptedBlock+0x155
00000000`0022f4c0 000007fe`f3ec99cd verifier!AVrfpDphCheckNormalHeapBlock+0xce
00000000`0022f530 000007fe`f3ec873a verifier!AVrfpDphNormalHeapFree+0x29
00000000`0022f560 00000000`7773c415 verifier!AVrfDebugPageHeapFree+0xb6
00000000`0022f5c0 00000000`776dd0fe ntdll!Rtl*Debug*FreeHeap+0x35
00000000`0022f620 00000000`776c2075 ntdll! ?? ::FNODOBFM::`string'+0x122e2
00000000`0022f960 000007fe`f3edf4e1 ntdll!RtlFreeHeap+0x1a2
```

---

[107] Local Crash Dumps in Vista, Memory Dump Analysis Anthology, Volume 1, page 606

```
00000000`0022f9e0 00000000`77472c7a verifier!AVrfpRtlFreeHeap+0xa5
00000000`0022fa80 000007fe`f3ee09ae kernel32!HeapFree+0xa
00000000`0022fab0 00000000`642bc7bc verifier!AVrfpHeapFree+0xc6
00000000`0022fb40 00000001`3fac1033 msvcr90!free+0x1c
00000000`0022fb70 00000001`3fac11f2 InstrumentedApp!wmain+0x33
00000000`0022fbb0 00000000`7746f56d InstrumentedApp!__tmainCRTStartup+0x11a
00000000`0022fbe0 00000000`776a3281 kernel32!BaseThreadInitThunk+0xd
00000000`0022fc10 00000000`00000000 ntdll!RtlUserThreadStart+0x1d


0:000> kL 100
Child-SP          RetAddr           Call Site
00000000`0022e198 000007fe`f3ee0f82 ntdll!NtWaitForMultipleObjects+0xa
00000000`0022e1a0 000007fe`fd8513a6 verifier!AVrfpNtWaitForMultipleObjects+0x4e
00000000`0022e1e0 000007fe`f3ee0e2d KERNELBASE!WaitForMultipleObjectsEx+0xe8
00000000`0022e2e0 000007fe`f3ee0edd verifier!AVrfpWaitForMultipleObjectsExCommon+0xad
00000000`0022e320 00000000`77473143 verifier!AVrfpKernelbaseWaitForMultipleObjectsEx+0x2d
00000000`0022e370 00000000`774e9025 kernel32!WaitForMultipleObjectsExImplementation+0xb3
00000000`0022e400 00000000`774e91a7 kernel32!WerpReportFaultInternal+0x215
00000000`0022e4a0 00000000`774e91ff kernel32!WerpReportFault+0x77
00000000`0022e4d0 00000000`774e941c kernel32!BasepReportFault+0x1f
00000000`0022e500 00000000`7770573c kernel32!UnhandledExceptionFilter+0x1fc
00000000`0022e5e0 00000000`77685148 ntdll! ?? ::FNODOBFM::`string'+0x2365
00000000`0022e610 00000000`776a554d ntdll!_C_specific_handler+0x8c
00000000`0022e680 00000000`77685d1c ntdll!RtlpExecuteHandlerForException+0xd
00000000`0022e6b0 00000000`776bfe48 ntdll!RtlDispatchException+0x3cb
00000000`0022ed90 000007fe`f3eca668 ntdll!KiUserExceptionDispatcher+0x2e
00000000`0022f350 000007fe`f3ec931d verifier!VerifierStopMessage+0x1f0
00000000`0022f400 000007fe`f3ec9736 verifier!AVrfpDphReportCorruptedBlock+0x155
00000000`0022f4c0 000007fe`f3ec99cd verifier!AVrfpDphCheckNormalHeapBlock+0xce
00000000`0022f530 000007fe`f3ec873a verifier!AVrfpDphNormalHeapFree+0x29
00000000`0022f560 00000000`7773c415 verifier!AVrfDebugPageHeapFree+0xb6
00000000`0022f5c0 00000000`776dd0fe ntdll!Rtl*Debug*FreeHeap+0x35
00000000`0022f620 00000000`776c2075 ntdll! ?? ::FNODOBFM::`string'+0x122e2
00000000`0022f960 000007fe`f3edf4e1 ntdll!RtlFreeHeap+0x1a2
00000000`0022f9e0 00000000`77472c7a verifier!AVrfpRtlFreeHeap+0xa5
00000000`0022fa80 000007fe`f3ee09ae kernel32!HeapFree+0xa
00000000`0022fab0 00000000`642bc7bc verifier!AVrfpHeapFree+0xc6
00000000`0022fb40 00000001`3fac1033 msvcr90!free+0x1c
00000000`0022fb70 00000001`3fac11f2 InstrumentedApp!wmain+0x33
00000000`0022fbb0 00000000`7746f56d InstrumentedApp!__tmainCRTStartup+0x11a
00000000`0022fbe0 00000000`776a3281 kernel32!BaseThreadInitThunk+0xd
00000000`0022fc10 00000000`00000000 ntdll!RtlUserThreadStart+0x1d
```

We also see above that enabling instrumentation triggers debug functions of runtime heap (*RtlDebugFreeHeap*).

Instrumentation Side Effect

Sometimes added instrumentation via gflags, Application and Driver Verifier options affect system, service or application performance and resources. For example, after enabling full page heap, one process on an x64 machine was growing up to 24GB, and its user memory dump shows that every heap allocation was recorded in a stack trace database:

```
0:055> !gflag
Current NtGlobalFlag contents: 0x02000000
hpa - Place heap allocations at ends of pages


0:055> ~*kc

[...]


48 Id: 117fc.c164 Suspend: 1 Teb: 000007ff`fff52000 Unfrozen
Call Site
ntdll!ZwWaitForSingleObject
ntdll!RtlpWaitOnCriticalSection
ntdll!RtlEnterCriticalSection
verifier!AVrfpDphEnterCriticalSection
verifier!AVrfpDphPreProcessing
verifier!AVrfDebugPageHeapAllocate
ntdll!RtlDebugAllocateHeap
ntdll! ?? ::FNODOBFM::`string'
ntdll!RtlAllocateHeap
msvcrt!malloc
ModuleA!foo1
[...]


49 Id: 117fc.de80 Suspend: 1 Teb: 000007ff`fff54000 Unfrozen
Call Site
ntdll!RtlCompareMemory
ntdll!RtlpLogCapturedStackTrace
ntdll!RtlLogStackTrace
verifier!AVrfpDphPlaceOnFreeList
verifier!AVrfDebugPageHeapFree
ntdll!RtlDebugFreeHeap
ntdll! ?? ::FNODOBFM::`string'
ntdll!RtlFreeHeap
kernel32!HeapFree
msvcrt!free
ModuleB!foo2
[...]
```

```
50 Id: 117fc.3700 Suspend: 1 Teb: 000007ff`fff4e000 Unfrozen
Call Site
ntdll!ZwWaitForSingleObject
ntdll!RtlpWaitOnCriticalSection
ntdll!RtlEnterCriticalSection
verifier!AVrfpDphEnterCriticalSection
verifier!AVrfpDphPreProcessing
verifier!AVrfDebugPageHeapFree
ntdll!RtlDebugFreeHeap
ntdll! ?? ::FNODOBFM::`string'
ntdll!RtlFreeHeap
kernel32!HeapFree
msvcrt!free
ModuleC!foo3
[...]


0:055> !runaway
User Mode Time
Thread Time
38:d090          0 days 0:02:28.793
44:ca48          0 days 0:01:04.459
48:c164          0 days 0:00:56.909
43:4458          0 days 0:00:54.475
50:3700          0 days 0:00:43.992
45:6f98          0 days 0:00:38.953
49:de80          0 days 0:00:24.211
1:391c           0 days 0:00:00.639
0:7e90           0 days 0:00:00.109
55:a300          0 days 0:00:00.046
34:10c9c         0 days 0:00:00.015
21:d054          0 days 0:00:00.015
56:b0a0          0 days 0:00:00.000
54:8b78          0 days 0:00:00.000
53:155b8         0 days 0:00:00.000
52:b444          0 days 0:00:00.000
```

Top Modules (page 1127) ModuleA(B, C) from **Spiking** (page 992) and heap intensive threads are from **Same Vendor** (page 943).

We were able to get a 200x27349 slice from that dump using ImageMagick[108], and it shows almost all virtual memory space filled with traces of this pictorial form (magnified by x8):

---

[108] http://www.imagemagick.org/

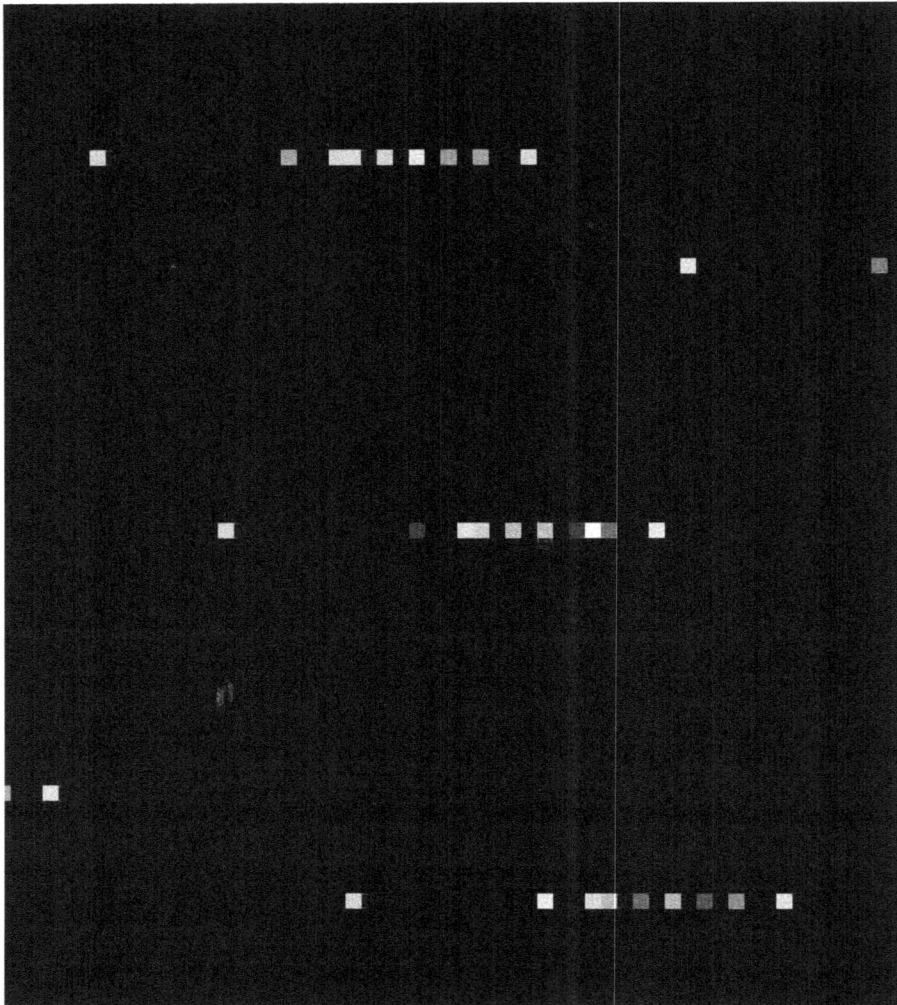

Comments

Another side-effect from object tracking:

```
kd> !poolused 3
Sorting by NonPaged Pool Consumed

Pool Used:
NonPaged Paged
Tag Allocs  Frees   Diff Used     Allocs Frees Diff Used
ObRt 4384299 4383686 615  54256308 0      0     0    0     object reference stack tracing , Binary: nt!ob
```

Insufficient Memory

Committed Memory

Insufficient Memory pattern can be seen in many complete and kernel memory dumps. This condition can cause a system to crash, become slow, hang or refuse to provide the expected functionality, for example, refuse new terminal server connections. There are many types of memory resources, and we can classify them initially into the following categories:

- Committed memory
- Virtual memory
  - Kernel space
    - Paged pool
    - Non-paged pool
    - Session pool
    - PTE limits
    - Desktop heap
    - GDI limits
  - User space
    - Virtual regions
    - Process heap

What we outline here is committed memory exhaustion. Committed memory is an allocated memory backed up by some physical memory or by a reserved space in the page file(s). Reserving the space needs to be done in case OS wants to swap out that memory data to disk when it is not used, and there is no physical memory available for other processes. If that data is needed again, OS brings it back to physical memory. If there is no space in the page file(s), then physical memory is filled up. If committed memory is exhausted, most likely, the system will hang or result in a bugcheck soon so checking memory statistics shall always be done when we get a kernel or a complete memory dump. Even access violation bugchecks could result from insufficient memory when some memory allocation operation failed, but a kernel mode component didn't check the return value for NULL. Here is an example:

```
BugCheck 8E, {c0000005, 809203af, aa647c0c, 0}

0: kd> !analyze -v
...
...
...
TRAP_FRAME: aa647c0c -- (.trap ffffffffaa647c0c)
...
...
...

0: kd> .trap ffffffffaa647c0c
ErrCode = 00000000
```

```
eax=00000000 ebx=bc1f3cfc ecx=89589250 edx=000018c1 esi=bc1f3ce0 edi=aa647d14
eip=809203af esp=aa647c80 ebp=aa647c80 iopl=0 nv up ei pl zr na pe nc
cs=0008 ss=0010 ds=0023 es=0023 fs=0030 gs=0000 efl=00010246
nt!SeTokenType+0x8:
809203af 8b8080000000 mov eax,dword ptr [eax+80h] ds:0023:00000080=????????


0: kd> k
ChildEBP RetAddr
aa647c80 bf8173c5 nt!SeTokenType+0x8
aa647cdc bf81713b win32k!GreGetSpoolMessage+0xb0
aa647d4c 80834d3f win32k!NtGdiGetSpoolMessage+0x96
aa647d4c 7c82ed54 nt!KiFastCallEntry+0xfc
```

If we enter **!vm** command to display memory statistics we would see that all committed memory is filled up:

```
0: kd> !vm
*** Virtual Memory Usage ***
 Physical Memory:       999294 (   3997176 Kb)
 Page File: \??\C:\pagefile.sys
   Current:   4193280 Kb  Free Space:      533744 Kb
   Minimum:   4193280 Kb  Maximum:       4193280 Kb
 Available Pages:        18698 (     74792 Kb)
 ResAvail Pages:        865019 (   3460076 Kb)
 Locked IO Pages:          290 (      1160 Kb)
 Free System PTEs:      155265 (    621060 Kb)
 Free NP PTEs:           32766 (    131064 Kb)
 Free Special NP:            0 (         0 Kb)
 Modified Pages:           113 (       452 Kb)
 Modified PF Pages:         61 (       244 Kb)
 NonPagedPool Usage:     12380 (     49520 Kb)
 NonPagedPool Max:       64799 (    259196 Kb)
 PagedPool 0 Usage:      40291 (    161164 Kb)
 PagedPool 1 Usage:       2463 (      9852 Kb)
 PagedPool 2 Usage:       2455 (      9820 Kb)
 PagedPool 3 Usage:       2453 (      9812 Kb)
 PagedPool 4 Usage:       2488 (      9952 Kb)
 PagedPool Usage:        50150 (    200600 Kb)
 PagedPool Maximum:      67584 (    270336 Kb)


********** 18 pool allocations have failed **********


 Shared Commit:         87304 (    349216 Kb)
 Special Pool:              0 (         0 Kb)
 Shared Process:        56241 (    224964 Kb)
 PagedPool Commit:      50198 (    200792 Kb)
 Driver Commit:          1892 (      7568 Kb)
 Committed pages:     2006945 (   8027780 Kb)
 Commit limit:        2008205 (   8032820 Kb)


********** 1216024 commit requests have failed **********
```

There might have been a memory leak or too many terminal sessions with fat applications to fit in physical memory and the page file.

Control Blocks

Certain system and subsystem architectures and designs may put a hard limit on the amount of data structures created to manage resources. If there is a dependency on such resources from other subsystems, there could be starvation and blockage conditions resulting in sluggish system behavior, the absence of functional response and even in some cases perceived system, service or application freeze. For example, **!filecache** WinDbg command diagnoses low VACB (Virtual [or View] Address Control Block) conditions.

```
7: kd> !filecache
***** Dump file cache******
  Reading and sorting VACBs ...
  Removed 0 nonactive VACBs, processing 1907 active VACBs …
File Cache Information
  Current size 408276 kb
  Peak size    468992 kb
  1907 Control Areas
[...]
```

Handle Leak

Sometimes **Handle Leaks** (page 464) also result in insufficient memory especially if handles point to structures allocated by OS. Here is the typical example of the handle leak resulted in freezing several servers. The complete memory dump shows exhausted non-paged pool:

```
0: kd> !vm

*** Virtual Memory Usage ***
 Physical Memory:      1048352 (    4193408 Kb)
 Page File: \??\C:\pagefile.sys
   Current:   4190208 Kb  Free Space:    3749732 Kb
   Minimum:   4190208 Kb  Maximum:       4190208 Kb
 Available Pages:       697734 (    2790936 Kb)
 ResAvail Pages:        958085 (    3832340 Kb)
 Locked IO Pages:           95 (        380 Kb)
 Free System PTEs:      199971 (     799884 Kb)
 Free NP PTEs:             105 (        420 Kb)
 Free Special NP:            0 (          0 Kb)
 Modified Pages:           195 (        780 Kb)
 Modified PF Pages:        195 (        780 Kb)
 NonPagedPool Usage:     65244 (     260976 Kb)
 NonPagedPool Max:       65503 (     262012 Kb)
 ********** Excessive NonPaged Pool Usage *****
 PagedPool 0 Usage:       6576 (      26304 Kb)
 PagedPool 1 Usage:        629 (       2516 Kb)
 PagedPool 2 Usage:        624 (       2496 Kb)
 PagedPool 3 Usage:        608 (       2432 Kb)
 PagedPool 4 Usage:        625 (       2500 Kb)
 PagedPool Usage:         9062 (      36248 Kb)
 PagedPool Maximum:      66560 (     266240 Kb)


 ********** 184 pool allocations have failed **********


 Shared Commit:           7711 (      30844 Kb)
 Special Pool:               0 (          0 Kb)
 Shared Process:         10625 (      42500 Kb)
 PagedPool Commit:        9102 (      36408 Kb)
 Driver Commit:           1759 (       7036 Kb)
 Committed pages:       425816 (    1703264 Kb)
 Commit limit:         2052560 (    8210240 Kb)
```

Looking at non-paged pool consumption reveals an excessive number of thread objects:

```
0: kd> !poolused 3
   Sorting by  NonPaged Pool Consumed

  Pool Used:
            NonPaged
 Tag    Allocs    Frees     Diff      Used
 Thre   772672   463590   309082 192867168  Thread objects , Binary: nt!ps
 MmCm       42        9       33  12153104  Calls made to MmAllocateContiguousMemory , Binary: nt!mm
 ...
 ...
 ...
```

The next logical step would be to list processes and find their handle usage. Indeed, there is such a process:

```
0: kd> !process 0 0
...
...
...
PROCESS 88b75020  SessionId: 7  Cid: 172e4    Peb: 7ffdf000  ParentCid: 17238
    DirBase: c7fb6bc0  ObjectTable: e17f50a0  HandleCount: 143428.
    Image: iexplore.exe
...
...
...
```

Making the process current and listing its handles shows contiguously allocated handles to thread objects:

```
0: kd> .process 88b75020
Implicit process is now 88b75020

0: kd> .reload /user

0: kd> !handle
...
...
...
0d94: Object: 88a6b020  GrantedAccess: 001f03ff Entry: e35e1b28
Object: 88a6b020  Type: (8b780c68) Thread
    ObjectHeader: 88a6b008
        HandleCount: 1  PointerCount: 1

0d98: Object: 88a97320  GrantedAccess: 001f03ff Entry: e35e1b30
Object: 88a97320  Type: (8b780c68) Thread
    ObjectHeader: 88a97308
        HandleCount: 1  PointerCount: 1

0d9c: Object: 88b2b020  GrantedAccess: 001f03ff Entry: e35e1b38
Object: 88b2b020  Type: (8b780c68) Thread
    ObjectHeader: 88b2b008
        HandleCount: 1  PointerCount: 1
```

```
0da0: Object: 88b2a730  GrantedAccess: 001f03ff Entry: e35e1b40
Object: 88b2a730  Type: (8b780c68) Thread
    ObjectHeader: 88b2a718
        HandleCount: 1  PointerCount: 1


0da4: Object: 88b929a0  GrantedAccess: 001f03ff Entry: e35e1b48
Object: 88b929a0  Type: (8b780c68) Thread
    ObjectHeader: 88b92988
        HandleCount: 1  PointerCount: 1


0da8: Object: 88a57db0  GrantedAccess: 001f03ff Entry: e35e1b50
Object: 88a57db0  Type: (8b780c68) Thread
    ObjectHeader: 88a57d98
        HandleCount: 1  PointerCount: 1


0dac: Object: 88b92db0  GrantedAccess: 001f03ff Entry: e35e1b58
Object: 88b92db0  Type: (8b780c68) Thread
    ObjectHeader: 88b92d98
        HandleCount: 1  PointerCount: 1


0db0: Object: 88b4a730  GrantedAccess: 001f03ff Entry: e35e1b60
Object: 88b4a730  Type: (8b780c68) Thread
    ObjectHeader: 88b4a718
        HandleCount: 1  PointerCount: 1


0db4: Object: 88a7e730  GrantedAccess: 001f03ff Entry: e35e1b68
Object: 88a7e730  Type: (8b780c68) Thread
    ObjectHeader: 88a7e718
        HandleCount: 1  PointerCount: 1


0db8: Object: 88a349a0  GrantedAccess: 001f03ff Entry: e35e1b70
Object: 88a349a0  Type: (8b780c68) Thread
    ObjectHeader: 88a34988
        HandleCount: 1  PointerCount: 1


0dbc: Object: 88a554c0  GrantedAccess: 001f03ff Entry: e35e1b78
Object: 88a554c0  Type: (8b780c68) Thread
    ObjectHeader: 88a554a8
        HandleCount: 1  PointerCount: 1
...
```

Examination of these threads shows their stack traces and start addresses:

```
0: kd> !thread 88b4a730
THREAD 88b4a730  Cid 0004.1885c  Teb: 00000000 Win32Thread: 00000000 TERMINATED
Not impersonating
DeviceMap                 e1000930
Owning Process            8b7807a8       Image:         System
Wait Start TickCount      975361         Ticks: 980987 (0:04:15:27.921)
Context Switch Count      1
UserTime                  00:00:00.0000
KernelTime                00:00:00.0000
Start Address mydriver!StatusWaitThread (0xf5c5d128)
Stack Init 0 Current f3c4cc98 Base f3c4d000 Limit f3c4a000 Call 0
Priority 8 BasePriority 8 PriorityDecrement 0
ChildEBP RetAddr  Args to Child
f3c4ccac 8083129e ffdff5f0 8697ba00 a674c913 hal!KfLowerIrql+0x62
f3c4ccc8 00000000 808ae498 8697ba00 00000000 nt!KiExitDispatcher+0x130

0: kd> !thread 88a554c0
THREAD 88a554c0  Cid 0004.1888c  Teb: 00000000 Win32Thread: 00000000 TERMINATED
Not impersonating
DeviceMap                 e1000930
Owning Process            8b7807a8       Image:         System
Wait Start TickCount      975380         Ticks: 980968 (0:04:15:27.625)
Context Switch Count      1
UserTime                  00:00:00.0000
KernelTime                00:00:00.0000
Start Address mydriver!StatusWaitThread (0xf5c5d128)
Stack Init 0 Current f3c4cc98 Base f3c4d000 Limit f3c4a000 Call 0
Priority 8 BasePriority 8 PriorityDecrement 0
ChildEBP RetAddr  Args to Child
f3c4ccac 8083129e ffdff5f0 8697ba00 a674c913 hal!KfLowerIrql+0x62
f3c4ccc8 00000000 808ae498 8697ba00 00000000 nt!KiExitDispatcher+0x130
```

We can see that these threads have been terminated, and their start address belongs to *mydriver.sys*. Therefore, we can say that mydriver code has to be examined to find the source of our handle leak.

Comments

Enabling Application Verifier using *gflags.exe* before running the leaking application and then using **!htrace** WinDbg command can show stack traces for handle usage. For example, quick test for *notepad.exe*:

```
0:001> !htrace 0x00000100
---------------------------
Handle = 0x00000100 - CLOSE
Thread ID = 0x00002d7c, Process ID = 0x0000237c

00x7c836b0c: ntdll!LdrGetDllHandleEx+0x000002b8
0x7c836cf9: ntdll!LdrGetDllHandle+0x00000018
0x77e645c2: kernel32!GetModuleHandleForUnicodeString+0x00000049
0x77e66516: kernel32!BasepGetModuleHandleExW+0x0000017f
0x77e663f4: kernel32!GetModuleHandleW+0x00000029
0x773a2eb3: USER32!_InitializeImmEntryTable+0x00000047
0x773c5369: USER32!_UserClientDllInitialize+0x00000163
0x5a61897f: verifier!AVrfpStandardDllEntryPointRoutine+0x0000014f
0x7c82257a: ntdll!LdrpCallInitRoutine+0x00000014
0x7c8358fb: ntdll!LdrpRunInitializeRoutines+0x00000367
---------------------------
Handle = 0x00000100 - OPEN
Thread ID = 0x00002d7c, Process ID = 0x0000237c

00x7c836b0c: ntdll!LdrGetDllHandleEx+0x000002b8
0x7c836cf9: ntdll!LdrGetDllHandle+0x00000018
0x77e645c2: kernel32!GetModuleHandleForUnicodeString+0x00000049
0x77e66516: kernel32!BasepGetModuleHandleExW+0x0000017f
0x77e663f4: kernel32!GetModuleHandleW+0x00000029
0x773a2eb3: USER32!_InitializeImmEntryTable+0x00000047
0x773c5369: USER32!_UserClientDllInitialize+0x00000163
0x5a61897f: verifier!AVrfpStandardDllEntryPointRoutine+0x0000014f


---------------------------
Parsed 0x2EC stack traces.
Dumped 0x2 stack traces.
```

Another example from the complete memory dump where Application Verifier was enabled for *MyApp.exe*:

```
03: kd> .process /p /r 0x8896e670
Implicit process is now 8896e670
Loading User Symbols

03: kd> dt _PEB 7ffdd000
ntdll!_PEB
+0x000 InheritedAddressSpace : 0 ''
+0x001 ReadImageFileExecOptions : 0x1 ''
+0x002 BeingDebugged : 0 ''
+0x003 BitField : 0 ''
+0x003 ImageUsesLargePages : 0y0
+0x003 SpareBits : 0y0000000 (0)
+0x004 Mutant : 0xffffffff
+0x008 ImageBaseAddress : 0x00400000
```

```
+0x00c Ldr : 0x7c889e00 _PEB_LDR_DATA
+0x010 ProcessParameters : 0x00020000 _RTL_USER_PROCESS_PARAMETERS
+0x014 SubSystemData : (null)
+0x018 ProcessHeap : 0x00140000
+0x01c FastPebLock : 0x7c889d40 _RTL_CRITICAL_SECTION
+0x020 AtlThunkSListPtr : (null)
+0x024 SparePtr2 : (null)
+0x028 EnvironmentUpdateCount : 1
+0x02c KernelCallbackTable : 0x77382970
+0x030 SystemReserved : [1] 0
+0x034 SpareUlong : 0
+0x038 FreeList : (null)
+0x03c TlsExpansionCounter : 0
+0x040 TlsBitmap : 0x7c888910
+0x044 TlsBitmapBits : [2] 0xffff
+0x04c ReadOnlySharedMemoryBase : 0x7f6f0000
+0x050 ReadOnlySharedMemoryHeap : 0x7f6f0000
+0x054 ReadOnlyStaticServerData : 0x7f6f0688 -> (null)
+0x058 AnsiCodePageData : 0x7ffb0000
+0x05c OemCodePageData : 0x7ffc1000
+0x060 UnicodeCaseTableData : 0x7ffd2000
+0x064 NumberOfProcessors : 4
+0x068 NtGlobalFlag : 0x100
+0x070 CriticalSectionTimeout : _LARGE_INTEGER 0xffffe86d`079b8000
+0x078 HeapSegmentReserve : 0x100000
+0x07c HeapSegmentCommit : 0x2000
+0x080 HeapDeCommitTotalFreeThreshold : 0x10000
+0x084 HeapDeCommitFreeBlockThreshold : 0x1000
+0x088 NumberOfHeaps : 0xb
+0x08c MaximumNumberOfHeaps : 0x10
+0x090 ProcessHeaps : 0x7c888340 -> 0x00140000
+0x094 GdiSharedHandleTable : 0x015f0000
+0x098 ProcessStarterHelper : (null)
+0x09c GdiDCAttributeList : 0x14
+0x0a0 LoaderLock : 0x7c889d94 _RTL_CRITICAL_SECTION
+0x0a4 OSMajorVersion : 5
+0x0a8 OSMinorVersion : 2
+0x0ac OSBuildNumber : 0xece
+0x0ae OSCSDVersion : 0x100
+0x0b0 OSPlatformId : 2
+0x0b4 ImageSubsystem : 2
+0x0b8 ImageSubsystemMajorVersion : 4
+0x0bc ImageSubsystemMinorVersion : 0
+0x0c0 ImageProcessAffinityMask : 0
+0x0c4 GdiHandleBuffer : [34] 0
+0x14c PostProcessInitRoutine : (null)
+0x150 TlsExpansionBitmap : 0x7c888908
+0x154 TlsExpansionBitmapBits : [32] 1
+0x1d4 SessionId : 1
+0x1d8 AppCompatFlags : _ULARGE_INTEGER 0x0
+0x1e0 AppCompatFlagsUser : _ULARGE_INTEGER 0x0
+0x1e8 pShimData : (null)
+0x1ec AppCompatInfo : (null)
+0x1f0 CSDVersion : _UNICODE_STRING "Service Pack 1"
+0x1f8 ActivationContextData : (null)
+0x1fc ProcessAssemblyStorageMap : (null)
```

```
+0x200 SystemDefaultActivationContextData : 0x00130000 _ACTIVATION_CONTEXT_DATA
+0x204 SystemAssemblyStorageMap : (null)
+0x208 MinimumStackCommit : 0
+0x20c FlsCallback : 0x001454a8 -> (null)
+0x210 FlsListHead : _LIST_ENTRY [ 0x141f60 - 0x169018 ]
+0x218 FlsBitmap : 0x7c888388
+0x21c FlsBitmapBits : [4] 7
+0x22c FlsHighIndex : 2


03: kd> !process 0 0
**** NT ACTIVE PROCESS DUMP ****
PROCESS 8896e670 SessionId: 1 Cid: 24b4 Peb: 7ffdd000 ParentCid: 1270
DirBase: 48e9f000 ObjectTable: e11109d0 HandleCount: 8717.
Image: MyApp.exe


03: kd> !handle
processor number 3, process 8896e670
PROCESS 8896e670 SessionId: 1 Cid: 24b4 Peb: 7ffdd000 ParentCid: 1270
DirBase: 48e9f000 ObjectTable: e11109d0 HandleCount: 8717.
Image: MyApp.exe


...


Handle table at e50ed000 with 8717 Entries in use
0004: Object: 88f39978 GrantedAccess: 00000410 Entry: e102a008
Object: 88f39978 Type: (8a392ca0) Process
ObjectHeader: 88f39960 (old version)
HandleCount: 8459 PointerCount: 8507


00008: Object: 88f39978 GrantedAccess: 00000410 Entry: e102a010
Object: 88f39978 Type: (8a392ca0) Process
ObjectHeader: 88f39960 (old version)
HandleCount: 8459 PointerCount: 8507


0000c: Object: 88f39978 GrantedAccess: 00000410 Entry: e102a018
Object: 88f39978 Type: (8a392ca0) Process
ObjectHeader: 88f39960 (old version)
HandleCount: 8459 PointerCount: 8507


...


03: kd> !htrace 0 8896e670
Process 0x8896e670
ObjectTable 0xe11109d0


--------------------
Handle 0x8878 - OPEN
Thread ID = 0x00000ca4, Process ID = 0x000024b4

00x809b94d8: nt!ExpUpdateDebugInfo+0x16D
0x8097232e: nt!ExCreateHandle+0x4A
0x8092b6ba: nt!ObpCreateHandle+0x3DE
0x80927674: nt!ObOpenObjectByPointer+0xA8
```

```
0x8093c2a5: nt!NtOpenProcess+0x22C
0x80834d3f: nt!KiFastCallEntry+0xFC
0x66861404: MyDLL!GetProcHandle+0x20
0x66862966: MyDLL!MainWndProc+0x1CC
0x7739c3b7: USER32!InternalCallWinProc+0x28
0x7739c484: USER32!UserCallWinProcCheckWow+0x151
0x7739ca68: USER32!DispatchClientMessage+0xD9
0x7739ce7a: USER32!__fnDWORD+0x24
0x7c82ec9e: ntdll!KiUserCallbackDispatcher+0x2E
0x66863244: MyDLL!Load+0x377
0x5a614cb0: verifier!AVrfpStandardThreadFunction+0x60
```

Example of handle leak in System process:

```
kd> !process 0 0
**** NT ACTIVE PROCESS DUMP ****
PROCESS 8d1615d8 SessionId: none Cid: 0004 Peb: 00000000 ParentCid: 0000
DirBase: bffba020 ObjectTable: e1002e08 HandleCount: 10879.
Image: System

3: kd> !handle 0 12

Kernel Handle table at e1765000 with 10879 Entries in use

1c20: Object: e4fca908 GrantedAccess: 00000004 Entry: e4b18840
Object: e4fca908 Type: (8d18a110) Directory
ObjectHeader: e4fca8f0 (old version)

1c24: Object: e5bf14c8 GrantedAccess: 00000004 Entry: e4b18848
Object: e5bf14c8 Type: (8d18a110) Directory
ObjectHeader: e5bf14b0 (old version)

1c28: Object: e496d490 GrantedAccess: 00000004 Entry: e4b18850
Object: e496d490 Type: (8d18a110) Directory
ObjectHeader: e496d478 (old version)

1c2c: Object: ea4a1370 GrantedAccess: 00000004 Entry: e4b18858
Object: ea4a1370 Type: (8d18a110) Directory
ObjectHeader: ea4a1358 (old version)

1c30: Object: e68558d0 GrantedAccess: 00000004 Entry: e4b18860
Object: e68558d0 Type: (8d18a110) Directory
ObjectHeader: e68558b8 (old version)

1c34: Object: e49f7d88 GrantedAccess: 00000004 Entry: e4b18868
Object: e49f7d88 Type: (8d18a110) Directory
ObjectHeader: e49f7d70 (old version)

1c38: Object: e3d8c6e8 GrantedAccess: 00000004 Entry: e4b18870
Object: e3d8c6e8 Type: (8d18a110) Directory
ObjectHeader: e3d8c6d0 (old version)
```

```
1c3c: Object: eb435bb8 GrantedAccess: 00000004 Entry: e4b18878
Object: eb435bb8 Type: (8d18a110) Directory
ObjectHeader: eb435ba0 (old version)


1c40: Object: ebd53f30 GrantedAccess: 00000004 Entry: e4b18880
Object: ebd53f30 Type: (8d18a110) Directory
ObjectHeader: ebd53f18 (old version)


1c44: Object: e7314698 GrantedAccess: 00000004 Entry: e4b18888
Object: e7314698 Type: (8d18a110) Directory
ObjectHeader: e7314680 (old version)


1c48: Object: eb32c378 GrantedAccess: 00000004 Entry: e4b18890
Object: eb32c378 Type: (8d18a110) Directory
ObjectHeader: eb32c360 (old version)


1c4c: Object: ece075c0 GrantedAccess: 00000004 Entry: e4b18898
Object: ece075c0 Type: (8d18a110) Directory
ObjectHeader: ece075a8 (old version)


3: kd> !object ebd53f30
Object: ebd53f30 Type: (8d18a110) Directory
ObjectHeader: ebd53f18 (old version)
HandleCount: 1 PointerCount: 2
Directory Object: e62c4ab8 Name: WindowStations


Hash Address Type Name
---- ------- ---- ----


3: kd> !object ece075c0
Object: ece075c0 Type: (8d18a110) Directory
ObjectHeader: ece075a8 (old version)
HandleCount: 1 PointerCount: 2
Directory Object: ec331ae0 Name: WindowStations


Hash Address Type Name
---- ------- ---- ----


3: kd> !object eb92af60
Object: eb92af60 Type: (8d18a110) Directory
ObjectHeader: eb92af48 (old version)
HandleCount: 1 PointerCount: 2
Directory Object: e67cfbc8 Name: WindowStations
```

We can also use "Miscellaneous Checks" option in Driver Verifier to enable handle traces in the System process[109].

---

[109] https://docs.microsoft.com/en-gb/windows-hardware/drivers/devtest/miscellaneous-checks

Kernel Pool

Although **Handle Leaks** (page 464) may result in insufficient pool memory, many drivers allocate their own private memory and specify a 4-letter ASCII tag, for example, here is the non-paged pool from my x64 Vista workstation:

```
1kd> !poolused 3
   Sorting by  NonPaged Pool Consumed


  Pool Used:
            NonPaged
  Tag    Allocs     Frees    Diff      Used
  EtwB      304       134     170   6550080   Etw Buffer , Binary: nt!etw
  File 32630649 32618671   11978   3752928   File objects
  Pool       16        11       5   3363472   Pool tables, etc.
  Ntfr   204791    187152   17639   2258704   ERESOURCE , Binary: ntfs.sys
  FMsl   199039    187685   11354   2179968   STREAM_LIST_CTRL structure , Binary: fltmgr.sys
  MmCa   250092    240351    9741   2134368   Mm control areas for mapped files , Binary: nt!mm
  ViMm   135503    134021    1482   1783824   Video memory manager , Binary: dxgkrnl.sys
  Cont       53        12      41   1567664   Contiguous physical memory allocations for device drivers
  Thre    72558     71527    1031   1234064   Thread objects , Binary: nt!ps
  VoSm      872       851      21   1220544   Bitmap allocations , Binary: volsnap.sys
  NtFs  8122505   8110933   11572   1190960   StrucSup.c , Binary: ntfs.sys
  AmlH        1         0       1   1048576   ACPI AMLI Pooltags
  SaSc    20281     14820    5461   1048512   UNKNOWN pooltag 'SaSc', please update pooltag.txt
  RaRS     1000         0    1000    960000   UNKNOWN pooltag 'RaRS', please update pooltag.txt
...
...
...
```

If the pool tag is unknown, we can use recommendations from Microsoft article KB298102 that explains how to locate the corresponding driver[110]. We can also use memory search in WinDbg to locate kernel space addresses and see what modules they correspond to (**Value References** pattern, page 1172).

WinDbg shows the number of failed pool allocations and also shows a message when pool usage is nearly its maximum. Below I put some examples with possible troubleshooting hints.

Session pool

```
3: kd> !vm

*** Virtual Memory Usage ***
        Physical Memory:     1572637 (    6290548 Kb)
        Page File: \??\C:\pagefile.sys
        Current:   3145728 Kb  Free Space:    3001132 Kb
        Minimum:   3145728 Kb  Maximum:       3145728 Kb
        Available Pages:     1317401 (    5269604 Kb)
```

---

[110] https://support.microsoft.com/en-gb/help/298102/how-to-find-pool-tags-that-are-used-by-third-party-drivers

```
        ResAvail Pages:      1478498 (    5913992 Kb)
        Locked IO Pages:         114 (        456 Kb)
        Free System PTEs:     194059 (     776236 Kb)
        Free NP PTEs:          32766 (     131064 Kb)
        Free Special NP:           0 (          0 Kb)
        Modified Pages:          443 (       1772 Kb)
        Modified PF Pages:       442 (       1768 Kb)
        NonPagedPool Usage:    13183 (      52732 Kb)
        NonPagedPool Max:      65215 (     260860 Kb)
        PagedPool 0 Usage:     11328 (      45312 Kb)
        PagedPool 1 Usage:      1473 (       5892 Kb)
        PagedPool 2 Usage:      1486 (       5944 Kb)
        PagedPool 3 Usage:      1458 (       5832 Kb)
        PagedPool 4 Usage:      1505 (       6020 Kb)
        PagedPool Usage:       17250 (      69000 Kb)
        PagedPool Maximum:     65536 (     262144 Kb)


        ********** 3441 pool allocations have failed **********


        Shared Commit:          8137 (      32548 Kb)
        Special Pool:              0 (          0 Kb)
        Shared Process:         8954 (      35816 Kb)
        PagedPool Commit:      17312 (      69248 Kb)
        Driver Commit:          2095 (       8380 Kb)
        Committed pages:      212476 (     849904 Kb)
        Commit limit:        2312654 (    9250616 Kb)
```

Paged and non-paged pool usage is far from maximum, therefore, we check session pool:

```
3: kd> !vm 4


        Terminal Server Memory Usage By Session:


        Session Paged Pool Maximum is 32768K
        Session View Space Maximum is 20480K


        Session ID 0 @ f79a1000:
        Paged Pool Usage:       9824K
        Commit Usage:          10148K


        Session ID 2 @ f7989000:
        Paged Pool Usage:       1212K
        Commit Usage:           2180K
  [...]


        Session ID 9 @ f79b5000:
        Paged Pool Usage:      32552K


        *** 7837 Pool Allocation Failures ***


        Commit Usage:          33652K
```

Paged pool

We might have a direct warning here:

```
1: kd> !vm

*** Virtual Memory Usage ***
 Physical Memory:    511881    ( 2047524 Kb)
 Page File: \??\S:\pagefile.sys
    Current:    2098176Kb Free Space:    1837740Kb
    Minimum:    2098176Kb Maximum:       2098176Kb
 Page File: \??\R:\pagefile.sys
    Current:    1048576Kb Free Space:     792360Kb
    Minimum:    1048576Kb Maximum:       1048576Kb
 Available Pages:    201353    (  805412 Kb)
 ResAvail Pages:     426839    ( 1707356 Kb)
 Modified Pages:      45405    (  181620 Kb)
 NonPagedPool Usage: 10042     (   40168 Kb)
 NonPagedPool Max:   68537     (  274148 Kb)
 PagedPool 0 Usage:  26820     (  107280 Kb)
 PagedPool 1 Usage:   1491     (    5964 Kb)
 PagedPool 2 Usage:   1521     (    6084 Kb)
 PagedPool 3 Usage:   1502     (    6008 Kb)
 PagedPool 4 Usage:   1516     (    6064 Kb)
 ********** Excessive Paged Pool Usage *****
 PagedPool Usage:    32850     (  131400 Kb)
 PagedPool Maximum:  40960     (  163840 Kb)
 Shared Commit:      14479     (   57916 Kb)
 Special Pool:           0     (       0 Kb)
 Free System PTEs:  135832     (  543328 Kb)
 Shared Process:     15186     (   60744 Kb)
 PagedPool Commit:   32850     (  131400 Kb)
 Driver Commit:       1322     (    5288 Kb)
 Committed pages:   426786     ( 1707144 Kb)
 Commit limit:     1259456     ( 5037824 Kb)
```

If there is no warning we can check the size manually, and if paged pool usage is close to its maximum, but for the non-paged pool it is not, then, most likely, failed allocations were from the paged pool:

```
0: kd> !vm

*** Virtual Memory Usage ***
      Physical Memory:      4193696 (  16774784 Kb)
      Page File: \??\C:\pagefile.sys
        Current:    4193280 Kb  Free Space:    3313120 Kb
        Minimum:    4193280 Kb  Maximum:       4193280 Kb
      Available Pages:      3210617 (  12842468 Kb)
      ResAvail Pages:       4031978 (  16127912 Kb)
      Locked IO Pages:          120 (        480 Kb)
      Free System PTEs:       99633 (     398532 Kb)
      Free NP PTEs:           26875 (     107500 Kb)
      Free Special NP:            0 (          0 Kb)
      Modified Pages:           611 (       2444 Kb)
```

```
        Modified PF Pages:       590 (      2360 Kb)
        NonPagedPool 0 Used:    8271 (     33084 Kb)
        NonPagedPool 1 Used:   13828 (     55312 Kb)
        NonPagedPool Usage:    37846 (    151384 Kb)
        NonPagedPool Max:      65215 (    260860 Kb)
        PagedPool 0 Usage:     82308 (    329232 Kb)
        PagedPool 1 Usage:     12700 (     50800 Kb)
        PagedPool 2 Usage:     25702 (    102808 Kb)
        PagedPool Usage:      120710 (    482840 Kb)
        PagedPool Maximum:    134144 (    536576 Kb)


    ********** 818 pool allocations have failed **********


        Shared Commit:        80168 (    320672 Kb)
        Special Pool:             0 (         0 Kb)
        Shared Process:       55654 (    222616 Kb)
        PagedPool Commit:    120772 (    483088 Kb)
        Driver Commit:         1890 (      7560 Kb)
        Committed pages:    1344388 (   5377552 Kb)
        Commit limit:       5177766 (  20711064 Kb)
```

!poolused 4 WinDbg command will sort paged pool consumption by pool tag:

```
0: kd> !poolused 4
   Sorting by  Paged Pool Consumed


  Pool Used:
           NonPaged              Paged
 Tag    Allocs     Used     Allocs     Used
 MmSt        0        0      85622 140642616    Mm section object prototype ptes , Binary: nt!mm
 Ntff        5     1040      63715 51991440     FCB_DATA , Binary: ntfs.sys
```

Here Microsoft article KB312362 may help[111].

Non-paged pool

```
0: kd> !vm


 *** Virtual Memory Usage ***
        Physical Memory:      851775 (   3407100 Kb)
        Page File: \??\C:\pagefile.sys
          Current:   4190208 Kb  Free Space:   4175708 Kb
          Minimum:   4190208 Kb  Maximum:      4190208 Kb
        Available Pages:      147274 (    589096 Kb)
        ResAvail Pages:       769287 (   3077148 Kb)
        Locked IO Pages:         118 (       472 Kb)
```

---

[111] https://support.microsoft.com/en-gb/help/312362/server-is-unable-to-allocate-memory-from-the-system-paged-pool

```
Free System PTEs:       184910 (     739640 Kb)
Free NP PTEs:              110 (        440 Kb)
Free Special NP:             0 (          0 Kb)
Modified Pages:            168 (        672 Kb)
Modified PF Pages:         168 (        672 Kb)
NonPagedPool Usage:      64445 (     257780 Kb)
NonPagedPool Max:        64640 (     258560 Kb)
********** Excessive NonPaged Pool Usage *****
PagedPool 0 Usage:       21912 (      87648 Kb)
PagedPool 1 Usage:         691 (       2764 Kb)
PagedPool 2 Usage:         706 (       2824 Kb)
PagedPool 3 Usage:         704 (       2816 Kb)
PagedPool 4 Usage:         708 (       2832 Kb)
PagedPool Usage:         24721 (      98884 Kb)

PagedPool Maximum:      134144 (     536576 Kb)


********** 429 pool allocations have failed **********


Shared Commit:            5274 (      21096 Kb)
Special Pool:                0 (          0 Kb)
Shared Process:           3958 (      15832 Kb)
PagedPool Commit:        24785 (      99140 Kb)
Driver Commit:           19289 (      77156 Kb)
Committed pages:        646282 (    2585128 Kb)
Commit limit:          1860990 (    7443960 Kb)
```

!poolused 3 WinDbg command will sort non-paged pool consumption by pool tag:

```
0: kd> !poolused 3
   Sorting by  NonPaged Pool Consumed


 Pool Used:
           NonPaged
Tag    Allocs    Frees    Diff
Ddk   9074558  3859522  5215036  Default for driver allocated memory (user's of ntddk.h)
MmCm    43787    42677     1110  Calls made to MmAllocateContiguousMemory , Binary: nt!mm
LSwi        1        0        1  initial work context
TCPt  3281838  3281808       30  TCP/IP network protocol , Binary: TCP
```

Regarding Ddk tag, please see "The Search for Tags" case study[112].

We can use **xpool** command from old *kdex2×86.dll* extension which even works for Windows 2003 dumps:

```
0: kd> !w2kfre\kdex2x86.xpool -map
unable to get NT!MmSizeOfNonPagedMustSucceed location
unable to get NT!MmSubsectionTopPage location
unable to get NT!MmKseg2Frame location
unable to get NT!MmNonPagedMustSucceed location


Status Map of Pool Area Pages
==============================
  'O': one page in use                            ('P': paged out)
  '<': start page of contiguous pages in use      ('{': paged out)
  '>': last page of contiguous pages in use       ('}': paged out)
  '=': intermediate page of contiguous pages in use ('-': paged out)
  '.': one page not used


Non-Paged Pool Area Summary
---------------------------
Maximum Number of Pages  = 64640 pages
Number of Pages In Use   = 36721 pages (56.8%)


          +00000  +08000   +10000   +18000    +20000  +28000    +30000  +38000
82780000: ..00.00.00..0.00 .0..00.00.00..0. 00.0..00.0..00.. ..00.0..00.00.00
827c0000: .0..00....00..0. 00.00.00....00.. 0....0..00....00 .0..00.0..00..0.
82800000: ..0............. ................ ................ ................
82840000: ................ ................ ................ ................
82880000: ......0.....0... ..0.0.....0..... 0.....0.....0... ..0.....0.......
828c0000: ..0.........0... ......000.....0. ....0.....0..... 0.....0.........
82900000: .0.........00... 0....0.........0. ......00....... 00.0..0.......
82940000: ...............0 ..0.00.......00 ................ ...0.....0.....
82980000: 0.........0..0.. ....0.........0. .........0.....0. ..0.........0...
829c0000: ........0....... ..0.........0. .0..0...0..0.... ..0........0...
82a00000: ......0..0...... 0.........0..... ....0.........0. ................
82a40000: ...........0... 0..0.0......00.. ......0.....0... ..0.....0...0.00
...
...
...
893c0000: ................ ................ ................ ................
89400000: ..........=..=.. ....=.....=..... =..=......=..=.. ....=..=......=.
89440000: ..=............. ..........=... =..=....=..=... =..=.=.....==..
89480000: ....==......=.=. ..........=.... ====.=.=........ ...............
894c0000: ................ ................ .........=.=.... ...==.........
89500000: ..=............. ....=.......... ..=............. ..=.........
89540000: ..=............. ..........=.... ..=........... ..=...=.....=..=
89580000: ......=..=..... =..=......=.==== ==.,==.=....=... .=....=....=.==.
895c0000: =.....==...... ..=........... =..=......=...=. ...............
89600000: ........=...=..= .....=......=..= ==....=......... ..........=....=.
```

```
89640000:  ..=...===...=... ==.......=..=..=. ..=..=.......=... .......=.=.....=.
...
...
...
```

Here is another example:

```
0: kd> !vm

*** Virtual Memory Usage ***
  Physical Memory:     786299   ( 3145196 Kb)
  Page File: \??\C:\pagefile.sys
     Current:    4193280Kb Free Space:    3407908Kb
     Minimum:    4193280Kb Maximum:       4193280Kb
  Available Pages:     200189   (  800756 Kb)
  ResAvail Pages:      657130   ( 2628520 Kb)
  Modified Pages:         762   (    3048 Kb)
  NonPagedPool Usage:   22948   (   91792 Kb)
  NonPagedPool Max:     70145   (  280580 Kb)
  PagedPool 0 Usage:    19666   (   78664 Kb)
  PagedPool 1 Usage:     3358   (   13432 Kb)
  PagedPool 2 Usage:     3306   (   13224 Kb)
  PagedPool 3 Usage:     3312   (   13248 Kb)
  PagedPool 4 Usage:     3309   (   13236 Kb)
********** Excessive Paged Pool Usage *****
  PagedPool Usage:      32951   (  131804 Kb)
  PagedPool Maximum:    40960   (  163840 Kb)
  Shared Commit:         9664   (   38656 Kb)
  Special Pool:             0   (       0 Kb)
  Free System PTEs:    103335   (  413340 Kb)
  Shared Process:       45024   (  180096 Kb)
  PagedPool Commit:     32951   (  131804 Kb)
  Driver Commit:         1398   (    5592 Kb)
  Committed pages:     864175   ( 3456700 Kb)
  Commit limit:       1793827   ( 7175308 Kb)


0: kd> !poolused 4
   Sorting by Paged Pool Consumed


 Pool Used:
          NonPaged              Paged
 Tag    Allocs     Used     Allocs     Used
 CM         85     5440      11045 47915424
 MyAV        0        0        186 14391520
 MmSt        0        0      11795 13235744
 Obtb      709    90752       2712 11108352
 Ntff        5     1120       9886  8541504
 ...
 ...
 ...
```

MyAV tag seems to be the prefix for *MyAVDrv* module, and this is hardly a coincidence. Looking at the list of drivers we see that *MyAVDrv.sys* was loaded and unloaded several times. Could it be that it did not free its non-paged pool allocations?

```
0: kd> lmv m MyAVDrv.sys
start     end         module name

Unloaded modules:
a5069000 a5084000    MyAVDrv.sys
    Timestamp: unavailable (00000000)
    Checksum:  00000000
a5069000 a5084000    MyAVDrv.sys
    Timestamp: unavailable (00000000)
    Checksum:  00000000
a5069000 a5084000    MyAVDrv.sys
    Timestamp: unavailable (00000000)
    Checksum:  00000000
b93e1000 b93fc000    MyAVDrv.sys
    Timestamp: unavailable (00000000)
    Checksum:  00000000
b9ae5000 b9b00000    MyAVDrv.sys
    Timestamp: unavailable (00000000)
    Checksum:  00000000
be775000 be790000    MyAVDrv.sys
    Timestamp: unavailable (00000000)
    Checksum:  00000000
```

Also, we see that CM tag has the most allocations and **!locks** command shows hundreds of threads waiting for the registry, one example of **High Contention** pattern (page 537):

```
0: kd> !locks

Resource @ nt!CmpRegistryLock (0x80478b00)    Shared 10 owning threads
    Contention Count = 9149810
    NumberOfSharedWaiters = 718
    NumberOfExclusiveWaiters = 21
```

Therefore, we see at least two problems in this memory dump: excessive paged pool usage and high thread contention around registry resource slowing down if not halting the system.

Comments

Another example from ntdebugging blog[113]:

To see session pool usage we need to switch to a session process first:

```
1: kd> !sprocess 3
[...]
PROCESS 88b0dd88 SessionId: 3 Cid: 1b90 Peb: 7ffde000 ParentCid: 1b84
DirBase: 4072d000 ObjectTable: d8651450 HandleCount: 414.
Image: ApplicationA.exe
[...]

1: kd> .process /r /p 88b0dd88
Implicit process is now 88b0dd88
Loading User Symbols

1: kd> !poolused 8
Sorting by Session Tag
[...]
```

Excessive nonpaged pool memory usage messages may be false positive for some WinDbg versions.

!poolused 5 produces the same level of detail for paged pool as **!poolused 3** for nonpaged pool.

---

[113] https://docs.microsoft.com/en-us/archive/blogs/ntdebugging/nonpagedpool-depletion

Module Fragmentation

Here we discuss the user space case when we do not have enough virtual memory available for reservation due to memory fragmentation. For example, a java virtual machine is pre-allocating memory for its garbage-collected heap. However, after installing some 3rd-party software, the amount of pre-allocated memory is less than expected. In such cases, it is possible to do comparative memory dump analysis to see the difference in virtual address spaces. Original memory dump has this module distribution in memory:

```
0:000> lm
start    end           module name
00400000 0040b000  javaw      (deferred)
009e0000 009e7000  hpi        (deferred)
00a30000 00a3e000  verify     (deferred)
00a40000 00a59000  java       (deferred)
00a60000 00a6d000  zip        (deferred)
03ff0000 03fff000  net        (deferred)
040a0000 040a8000  nio        (deferred)
040b0000 0410a000  hnetcfg    (deferred)
041d0000 042e2000  awt        (deferred)
04540000 04591000  fontmanager    (deferred)
04620000 04670000  msctf      (deferred)
047c0000 047de000  jpeg       (deferred)
05820000 05842000  dcpr       (deferred)
05920000 05932000  pkcs11wrapper    (deferred)
08000000 08139000  jvm        (deferred)
10000000 100e0000  moduleA    (deferred)
68000000 68035000  rsaenh     (deferred)
6e220000 6e226000  RMProcessLink    (deferred)
71ae0000 71ae8000  wshtcpip   (deferred)
71b20000 71b61000  mswsock    (deferred)
71bf0000 71bf8000  ws2help    (deferred)
71c00000 71c17000  ws2_32     (deferred)
71c20000 71c32000  tsappcmp   (deferred)
71c40000 71c97000  netapi32   (deferred)
73070000 73097000  winspool   (deferred)
76290000 762ad000  imm32      (deferred)
76920000 769e2000  userenv    (deferred)
76aa0000 76acd000  winmm      (deferred)
76b70000 76b7b000  psapi      (deferred)
76ed0000 76efa000  dnsapi     (deferred)
76f10000 76f3e000  wldap32    (deferred)
76f50000 76f63000  secur32    (deferred)
76f70000 76f77000  winrnr     (deferred)
76f80000 76f85000  rasadhlp   (deferred)
77380000 77411000  user32     (deferred)
77670000 777a9000  ole32      (deferred)
77ba0000 77bfa000  msvcrt     (deferred)
77c00000 77c48000  gdi32      (deferred)
77c50000 77cef000  rpcrt4     (deferred)
77e40000 77f42000  kernel32   (deferred)
77f50000 77feb000  advapi32   (deferred)
78130000 781cb000  msvcr80    (deferred)
7c800000 7c8c0000  ntdll      (pdb symbols)
```

We see the big gap between 100e0000 and 68000000 addresses. This means that it is theoretically possible to reserve and/or commit up to 57F20000 bytes (about 1.4Gb). **!address** WinDbg command shows that at least 1.1Gb region (shown in bold below) was reserved indeed:

```
0:000> !address
00000000 : 00000000 - 00010000
                Type       00000000
                Protect    00000001 PAGE_NOACCESS
                State      00010000 MEM_FREE
                Usage      RegionUsageFree
00010000 : 00010000 - 00001000
                Type       00020000 MEM_PRIVATE
                Protect    00000004 PAGE_READWRITE
                State      00001000 MEM_COMMIT
                Usage      RegionUsageEnvironmentBlock
00011000 : 00011000 - 0000f000
                Type       00000000
                Protect    00000001 PAGE_NOACCESS
                State      00010000 MEM_FREE
                Usage      RegionUsageFree
00020000 : 00020000 - 00001000
                Type       00020000 MEM_PRIVATE
                Protect    00000004 PAGE_READWRITE
                State      00001000 MEM_COMMIT
                Usage      RegionUsageProcessParametrs
00021000 : 00021000 - 0000f000
                Type       00000000
                Protect    00000001 PAGE_NOACCESS
                State      00010000 MEM_FREE
                Usage      RegionUsageFree
00030000 : 00030000 - 00003000
                Type       00020000 MEM_PRIVATE
                Protect    00000140 <unk>
                State      00001000 MEM_COMMIT
                Usage      RegionUsageStack
                Pid.Tid    97c.1b3c
...
...
...
100e0000 : 100e0000 - 000a0000
                Type       00020000 MEM_PRIVATE
                Protect    00000040 PAGE_EXECUTE_READWRITE
                State      00001000 MEM_COMMIT
                Usage      RegionUsageIsVAD
           10180000 - 05cc0000
                Type       00020000 MEM_PRIVATE
                State      00002000 MEM_RESERVE
                Usage      RegionUsageIsVAD
           15e40000 - 004f3000
                Type       00020000 MEM_PRIVATE
                Protect    00000040 PAGE_EXECUTE_READWRITE
                State      00001000 MEM_COMMIT
                Usage      RegionUsageIsVAD
           16333000 - 45bad000
                Type       00020000 MEM_PRIVATE
                State      00002000 MEM_RESERVE
```

```
        Usage       RegionUsageIsVAD
      5bee0000 - 00ac0000
          Type      00020000 MEM_PRIVATE
          Protect   00000040 PAGE_EXECUTE_READWRITE
          State     00001000 MEM_COMMIT
          Usage     RegionUsageIsVAD
      5c9a0000 - 03540000
          Type      00020000 MEM_PRIVATE
          State     00002000 MEM_RESERVE
          Usage     RegionUsageIsVAD
5fee0000 : 5fee0000 - 00120000
          Type      00000000
          Protect   00000001 PAGE_NOACCESS
          State     00010000 MEM_FREE
          Usage     RegionUsageFree
...
...
...
```

Looking at the problem memory dump, we see that the gap is smaller (less than 1.1Gb):

```
0:000> lm
start    end      module name
00400000 0040b000 javaw      (deferred)
08000000 08139000 jvm        (deferred)
10000000 10007000 hpi        (deferred)
51120000 511bb000 msvcr80  # (private pdb symbols)
520f0000 520fe000 verify     (deferred)
52100000 52119000 java       (deferred)
52120000 5212d000 zip        (deferred)
52130000 5213f000 net        (deferred)
52140000 52148000 nio        (deferred)
52150000 52262000 awt        (deferred)
52270000 522c1000 fontmanager    (deferred)
522d0000 52320000 MSCTF      (deferred)
52330000 5234e000 jpeg       (deferred)
52350000 52372000 dcpr       (deferred)
52510000 52522000 pkcs11wrapper   (deferred)
5f270000 5f2ca000 hnetcfg    (deferred)
60000000 60029000 3rdPartyHook   (deferred)
61e80000 61e86000 detoured   (export symbols)
68000000 68035000 rsaenh     (deferred)
71ae0000 71ae8000 wshtcpip   (deferred)
71b20000 71b61000 mswsock    (deferred)
71bf0000 71bf8000 ws2help    (deferred)
71c00000 71c17000 ws2_32     (deferred)
71c20000 71c32000 tsappcmp   (deferred)
71c40000 71c97000 netapi32   (deferred)
73070000 73097000 winspool   (deferred)
76290000 762ad000 imm32      (deferred)
76920000 769e2000 userenv    (deferred)
76aa0000 76acd000 winmm      (deferred)
76b70000 76b7b000 psapi      (deferred)
76ed0000 76efa000 dnsapi     (deferred)
76f10000 76f3e000 wldap32    (deferred)
76f50000 76f63000 secur32    (deferred)
```

```
76f70000 76f77000    winrnr      (deferred)
76f80000 76f85000    rasadhlp    (deferred)
77380000 77411000    user32      (pdb symbols)
77670000 777a9000    ole32       (deferred)
77ba0000 77bfa000    msvcrt      (deferred)
77c00000 77c48000    gdi32       (deferred)
77c50000 77cef000    rpcrt4      (deferred)
77e40000 77f42000    kernel32    (pdb symbols)
77f50000 77feb000    advapi32    (pdb symbols)
7c340000 7c396000    msvcr71     (deferred)
7c800000 7c8c0000    ntdll       (pdb symbols)
```

!address command shows that less memory was reserved in the latter case (about 896Mb):

```
0:000> !address
...
...
...
10010000 : 10010000 - 000a0000
            Type      00020000 MEM_PRIVATE
            Protect   00000040 PAGE_EXECUTE_READWRITE
            State     00001000 MEM_COMMIT
            Usage     RegionUsageIsVAD
          100b0000 - 04a70000
            Type      00020000 MEM_PRIVATE
            State     00002000 MEM_RESERVE
            Usage     RegionUsageIsVAD
          14b20000 - 004a6000
            Type      00020000 MEM_PRIVATE
            Protect   00000040 PAGE_EXECUTE_READWRITE
            State     00001000 MEM_COMMIT
            Usage     RegionUsageIsVAD
          14fc6000 - 3804a000
            Type      00020000 MEM_PRIVATE
            State     00002000 MEM_RESERVE
            Usage     RegionUsageIsVAD
          4d010000 - 00ac0000
            Type      00020000 MEM_PRIVATE
            Protect   00000040 PAGE_EXECUTE_READWRITE
            State     00001000 MEM_COMMIT
            Usage     RegionUsageIsVAD
          4dad0000 - 03540000
            Type      00020000 MEM_PRIVATE
            State     00002000 MEM_RESERVE
            Usage     RegionUsageIsVAD
51010000 : 51010000 - 00110000
            Type      00000000
            Protect   00000001 PAGE_NOACCESS
            State     00010000 MEM_FREE
            Usage     RegionUsageFree
...
...
...
```

Looking at module list again we notice that most java runtime modules were shifted to 50000000 address range. We also notice that new the *3rdPartyHook* and detoured modules appear in our problem memory dump.

Module information is missing for detoured module:

```
0:000> lmv m detoured
start    end         module name
61e80000 61e86000   detoured   (deferred)
    Image path: C:\WINDOWS\system32\detoured.dll
    Image name: detoured.dll
    Timestamp:        Thu Feb 07 04:14:16 2008 (47AA8598)
    CheckSum:         0000EF91
    ImageSize:        00006000
    File version:     0.0.0.0
    Product version:  0.0.0.0
    File flags:       0 (Mask 0)
    File OS:          0 Unknown Base
    File type:        0.0 Unknown
    File date:        00000000.00000000
    Translations:     0000.04b0 0000.04e0 0409.04b0 0409.04e0
```

Applying **Unknown Component** pattern (page 1150) we see that is Microsoft Research Detours Package:

```
0:000> db 61e80000 61e86000
61e80000  MZ.............
61e80010  ........@.......
61e80020  ...............
61e80030  ...............
61e80040  ........!..L.!Th
61e80050  is program canno
61e80060  t be run in DOS
61e80070  mode....$.......
61e80080  5...q...q...q...
61e80090  ....r...q...p...
61e800a0  V%..p...V%..p...
61e800b0  V%..p...V%..p...
61e800c0  Richq...........
61e800d0  ...............
61e800e0  PE..L......G....
61e800f0  .......!........
61e80100  ...............
...
...
...
...
61e84390  ..P.r.o.d.u.c.t.
61e843a0  N.a.m.e....M.i.
61e843b0  c.r.o.s.o.f.t. .
61e843c0  R.e.s.e.a.r.c.h.
61e843d0  .D.e.t.o.u.r.s.
61e843e0  .P.a.c.k.a.g.e.
61e843f0  ....j.#...P.r.o.
61e84400  d.u.c.t.V.e.r.s.
```

```
61e84410  i.o.n…P.r.o.f.
61e84420  e.s.s.i.o.n.a.l.
61e84430  .V.e.r.s.i.o.n.
61e84440  .2…1.  .B.u.i.
61e84450  l.d._.2.1.0…..
61e84460  D…..V.a.r.F.i.
...
...
...

0:000> du 61e843a0+C
61e843ac  "Microsoft Research Detours Packa"
61e843ec  "ge"
```

We can also see that *3rdPartyHook* module imports this library and lots of *kernel32* API related to memory allocation, file mapping and loading DLLs (see **No Component Symbols** pattern, page 819):

```
0:000> !dh 60000000
...
...
...
OPTIONAL HEADER VALUES
     10B magic #
    8.00 linker version
   18000 size of code
    F000 size of initialized data
       0 size of uninitialized data
   13336 address of entry point
    1000 base of code
         ----- new -----
60000000 image base
    1000 section alignment
    1000 file alignment
       2 subsystem (Windows GUI)
    4.00 operating system version
    0.00 image version
    4.00 subsystem version
   29000 size of image
    1000 size of headers
   3376F checksum
00100000 size of stack reserve
00001000 size of stack commit
00100000 size of heap reserve
00001000 size of heap commit
       0 [       0] address [size] of Export Directory
   218CC [      8C] address [size] of Import Directory
   25000 [     5F4] address [size] of Resource Directory
       0 [       0] address [size] of Exception Directory
   28000 [    19E0] address [size] of Security Directory
   26000 [    2670] address [size] of Base Relocation Directory
   19320 [      1C] address [size] of Debug Directory
       0 [       0] address [size] of Description Directory
       0 [       0] address [size] of Special Directory
       0 [       0] address [size] of Thread Storage Directory
   1F3C0 [      40] address [size] of Load Configuration Directory
       0 [       0] address [size] of Bound Import Directory
```

```
   19000 [      2B0] address [size] of Import Address Table Directory
       0 [        0] address [size] of Delay Import Directory
       0 [        0] address [size] of COR20 Header Directory
       0 [        0] address [size] of Reserved Directory
...
...
...

0:000> dds 60000000+19000 60000000+19000+2B0
60019064  7c82b0dc ntdll!RtlReAllocateHeap
60019068  77e4ec39 kernel32!HeapDestroy
6001906c  77e41fba kernel32!GetSystemTimeAsFileTime
60019070  77e619d1 kernel32!GetTickCount
60019074  77e69577 kernel32!QueryPerformanceCounter
60019078  7c82a9be ntdll!RtlSizeHeap
6001907c  77e82060 kernel32!SetUnhandledExceptionFilter
60019080  77e7690d kernel32!UnhandledExceptionFilter
60019084  77e42004 kernel32!TerminateProcess
60019088  7c82a136 ntdll!RtlRestoreLastWin32Error
6001908c  77e77a5f kernel32!SuspendThread
60019090  77e76a26 kernel32!SetThreadContext
60019094  77e77ae3 kernel32!GetThreadContext
60019098  77e73347 kernel32!FlushInstructionCache
6001909c  77e5f38b kernel32!ResumeThread
600190a0  77e616a8 kernel32!InterlockedCompareExchange
600190a4  77e645a9 kernel32!VirtualAlloc
600190a8  77e41fe3 kernel32!VirtualProtect
600190ac  77e66ed1 kernel32!VirtualQuery
600190b0  77e44960 kernel32!GetLogicalDriveStringsA
600190b4  77eab401 kernel32!GetVolumeNameForVolumeMountPointA
600190b8  77e6794d kernel32!GetACP
600190bc  77e6f3cf kernel32!GetLocaleInfoA
600190c0  77e622b7 kernel32!GetThreadLocale
600190c4  77e69d74 kernel32!GetVersionExA
600190c8  77e4beab kernel32!RaiseException
600190cc  77e60037 kernel32!GetSystemDirectoryA
600190d0  77e52bf4 kernel32!GetWindowsDirectoryA
600190d4  77e5c7a8 kernel32!lstrcmpA
600190d8  77e46c99 kernel32!OutputDebugStringA
600190dc  77e5bd7d kernel32!CreateEventA
600190e0  77e62311 kernel32!SetEvent
600190e4  77e51281 kernel32!ExpandEnvironmentStringsA
600190e8  77e9f365 kernel32!MoveFileA
600190ec  77e5da00 kernel32!IsDebuggerPresent
600190f0  77e9e4b1 kernel32!QueryDosDeviceA
600190f4  7c829e08 ntdll!RtlGetLastWin32Error
600190f8  77e63d7a kernel32!GetProcAddress
600190fc  77e41dc6 kernel32!LoadLibraryA
60019100  7c829e17 ntdll!RtlFreeHeap
60019104  77e62419 kernel32!LocalFree
60019108  7c829fd6 ntdll!RtlAllocateHeap
6001910c  77e63ec7 kernel32!GetProcessHeap
60019110  77ea2186 kernel32!VerifyVersionInfoA
60019114  7c81379f ntdll!VerSetConditionMask
60019118  77e63143 kernel32!WideCharToMultiByte
6001911c  77e70550 kernel32!SizeofResource
```

```
60019120  77e6b11b kernel32!SetHandleCount
60019124  77e69bf9 kernel32!LoadResource
60019128  77e511e1 kernel32!FindResourceA
6001912c  77e7388c kernel32!FindResourceExA
60019130  77e5be30 kernel32!lstrlenA
60019134  77e424de kernel32!Sleep
60019138  77ea2cb1 kernel32!WaitNamedPipeA
6001913c  77e63e6f kernel32!CloseHandle
60019140  77e5e123 kernel32!OpenEventA
60019144  77e622c9 kernel32!lstrlenW
60019148  77e62fc7 kernel32!GetCurrentThreadId
6001914c  77e5fdd4 kernel32!OpenProcess
60019150  77e63c78 kernel32!GetCurrentProcessId
60019154  7c81a3ab ntdll!RtlLeaveCriticalSection
60019158  7c81a360 ntdll!RtlEnterCriticalSection
6001915c  77e4cabf kernel32!GetComputerNameA
60019160  77e6f032 kernel32!ProcessIdToSessionId
60019164  77e645ff kernel32!GetModuleFileNameA
60019168  77e6474a kernel32!GetModuleHandleA
6001916c  77e62f9d kernel32!GetCurrentProcess
60019170  77e49968 kernel32!GetCurrentDirectoryA
60019174  77e61c7b kernel32!WaitForSingleObject
60019178  77e63868 kernel32!GetCurrentThread
6001917c  7c82c988 ntdll!RtlDeleteCriticalSection
60019180  77e67861 kernel32!InitializeCriticalSection
60019184  77e6b1a1 kernel32!FreeLibrary
60019188  77e63f41 kernel32!UnmapViewOfFile
6001918c  77e643f1 kernel32!MapViewOfFile
60019190  77e6b65f kernel32!OpenFileMappingA
60019194  77e61694 kernel32!InterlockedExchange
60019198  77e4d2fb kernel32!DeleteFileA
...
...
...
60019294  00000000
60019298  61e81000 detoured!Detoured
6001929c  00000000
...
...
...
```

This warrants the suspicion that *3rdPartyHook* somehow optimized the virtual address space for its own purposes, and this resulted in more fragmented virtual address space.

Comments

!address -summary WinDbg command also gives various output about region type usage and the largest available blocks per region type.

Physical Memory

Sometimes there is not enough physical memory, and a system experiences the so-called **disk** or **page file** *thrashing* trying to resolve page faults. This can be seen in some memory dumps coming from frozen environments showing signs of double traps in running threads, the first trap is a normal memory access fault (shown in bold) and the second is forced NMI bugcheck[114] to save a memory dump (shown in bold italics):

```
1: kd> .bugcheck
Bugcheck code 00000080
Arguments 004f4454 00000000 00000000 00000000


1: kd> !thread
THREAD 88939b20  Cid 360.378  Teb: 7ffdb000  Win32Thread: a20a7ac8 RUNNING
IRP List:
    86be9e68: (0006,0100) Flags: 00000070  Mdl: 00000000
    88939e68: (0006,0100) Flags: 00000070  Mdl: 00000000
    88939128: (0006,0100) Flags: 00000070  Mdl: 00000000
Not impersonating
Owning Process 889456e0
Wait Start TickCount    2357431        Elapsed Ticks: 9
Context Switch Count    18267                    LargeStack
UserTime                   0:00:08.0218
KernelTime                 0:12:28.0109
Start Address KERNEL32!BaseThreadStartThunk (0x7c57b740)
Win32 Start Address msafd!SockAsyncThread (0x74fd3113)
Stack Init bef9e000 Current bef9db60 Base bef9e000 Limit bef9b000 Call 0
Priority 11 BasePriority 11 PriorityDecrement 0 DecrementCount 0


ChildEBP RetAddr
8904aff0 80469211 hal!HalHandleNMI+0x193
8904aff0 80438621 nt!KiTrap02+0x41
bef9dc10 8043799a nt!MiTrimWorkingSet+0xa7
bef9dc38 804378ec nt!MiDoReplacement+0x2e
bef9dc50 804453cf nt!MiLocateAndReserveWsle+0x1e
bef9dc68 804444e0 nt!MiAddValidPageToWorkingSet+0x89
bef9dc8c 804443a2 nt!MiCompleteProtoPteFault+0xf6
bef9dcb8 804436e8 nt!MiResolveProtoPteFault+0x160
bef9dcfc 8044ccd0 nt!MiDispatchFault+0xfc
bef9dd4c 8046b063 nt!MmAccessFault+0xd1c
bef9dd4c 74fd31e0 nt!KiTrap0E+0xc7
016effb4 7c57b3bc msafd!SockAsyncThread+0xcd
016effec 00000000 KERNEL32!BaseThreadStart+0x52
```

---

[114] Bugchecks Depicted, NMI_HARDWARE_FAILURE, Memory Dump Analysis Anthology, Volume 1, page 135

If we check virtual memory stats we see the low number of available pages:

```
1: kd> !vm

*** Virtual Memory Usage ***
 Physical Memory:     524165    ( 2096660 Kb)
 Page File: \??\C:\pagefile.sys
    Current:    4190208Kb Free Space:    3298704Kb
    Minimum:    4190208Kb Maximum:       4190208Kb
 Page File: \??\E:\pagefile.sys
    Current:    4190208Kb Free Space:    3339860Kb
    Minimum:    4190208Kb Maximum:       4190208Kb
 Available Pages:       1098    (    4392 Kb)
 ResAvail Pages:      410646    ( 1642584 Kb)
 Modified Pages:      282384    ( 1129536 Kb)
 NonPagedPool Usage: 10046    (   40184 Kb)
 NonPagedPool Max:    68609    (  274436 Kb)
 PagedPool 0 Usage:   15391    (   61564 Kb)
 PagedPool 1 Usage:    1906    (    7624 Kb)
 PagedPool 2 Usage:    1925    (    7700 Kb)
 PagedPool 3 Usage:    1937    (    7748 Kb)
 PagedPool 4 Usage:    1892    (    7568 Kb)
 PagedPool Usage:     23051    (   92204 Kb)
 PagedPool Maximum:   87040    (  348160 Kb)
 Shared Commit:       16867    (   67468 Kb)
 Special Pool:            0    (       0 Kb)
 Free System PTEs:    65288    (  261152 Kb)
 Shared Process:      38655    (  154620 Kb)
 PagedPool Commit:    23051    (   92204 Kb)
 Driver Commit:        1060    (    4240 Kb)
 Committed pages:   1049592    ( 4198368 Kb)
 Commit limit:      2580155    (10320620 Kb)
[...]
```

In W2K dumps we can also see locking on a working set resource (the name is guessed from **Ws** shortcut here):

```
1: kd> !locks
**** DUMP OF ALL RESOURCE OBJECTS ****

Resource @ nt!MmSystemWsLock (0x804869c0)    Exclusively owned
    Contention Count = 33083
    NumberOfExclusiveWaiters = 237
[...]
```

and the huge number of threads in the Ready state for every thread priority.

Looking at the current process owning the running thread shows the large number of page faults and increased kernel CPU time compared to time spent in user mode:

```
1: kd> !process 889456e0
PROCESS 889456e0  SessionId: 0  Cid: 0360    Peb: 7ffdf000  ParentCid: 01a8
    DirBase: 102af000  ObjectTable: 88945c08  TableSize: 622.
    Image: Application.EXE
    VadRoot 88944468 Clone 0 Private 838. Modified 30691412. Locked 188.
    DeviceMap 89049288
    Token                             e28db550
    ElapsedTime                       10:13:30.0684
    UserTime                          0:00:12.0578
    KernelTime                        0:12:38.0625
    QuotaPoolUsage[PagedPool]         31568
    QuotaPoolUsage[NonPagedPool]      68266
    Working Set Sizes (now,min,max)   (49, 50, 345) (196KB, 200KB, 1380KB)
    PeakWorkingSetSize                1956
    VirtualSize                       131 Mb
    PeakVirtualSize                   131 Mb
    PageFaultCount                    46180598
    MemoryPriority                    BACKGROUND
    BasePriority                      10
    CommitCharge                      1247
```

PTE

In order to maintain virtual to physical address translation, OS needs page tables. These tables occupy memory too. If memory is not enough for new tables the system will fail to create processes, allocate I/O buffers and memory from pools. We might see the following diagnostic message from WinDbg:

```
4: kd> !vm

*** Virtual Memory Usage ***
  Physical Memory:        851422 (    3405688 Kb)
  Page File: \??\C:\pagefile.sys
    Current:    2095104 Kb  Free Space:    2081452 Kb
    Minimum:    2095104 Kb  Maximum:        4190208 Kb
  Available Pages:        683464 (    2733856 Kb)
  ResAvail Pages:         800927 (    3203708 Kb)
  Locked IO Pages:           145 (        580 Kb)
  Free System PTEs:        23980 (      95920 Kb)

******* 356363 system PTE allocations have failed ******

  Free NP PTEs:             6238 (      24952 Kb)
  Free Special NP:             0 (          0 Kb)
  Modified Pages:            482 (       1928 Kb)
  Modified PF Pages:         482 (       1928 Kb)
  NonPagedPool Usage:      18509 (      74036 Kb)
  NonPagedPool Max:        31970 (     127880 Kb)
  PagedPool 0 Usage:        8091 (      32364 Kb)
  PagedPool 1 Usage:        2495 (       9980 Kb)
  PagedPool 2 Usage:        2580 (      10320 Kb)
  PagedPool 3 Usage:        2552 (      10208 Kb)
  PagedPool 4 Usage:        2584 (      10336 Kb)
  PagedPool Usage:         18302 (      73208 Kb)
  PagedPool Maximum:       39936 (     159744 Kb)

********** 48530 pool allocations have failed **********

  Shared Commit:            5422 (      21688 Kb)
  Special Pool:                0 (          0 Kb)
  Shared Process:           5762 (      23048 Kb)
  PagedPool Commit:        18365 (      73460 Kb)
  Driver Commit:            2347 (       9388 Kb)
  Committed pages:        129014 (     516056 Kb)
  Commit limit:          1342979 (    5371916 Kb)
```

We can also see another diagnostic message about pool allocation failures which may be the consequence of PTE allocation failures.

The cause of system PTE allocation failures might be the incorrect value of SystemPages registry key that needs to be adjusted as explained in the following TechNet article: The number of free page table entries is low, which can cause system instability[115].

Another cause would be /3GB boot option on x86 systems especially used for hosting terminal sessions.

In our case, the system was booted with /3GB:

```
4: kd> vertarget
Windows Server 2003 Kernel Version 3790 (Service Pack 2) MP (8 procs) Free x86 compatible
Product: Server, suite: Enterprise TerminalServer
Built by: 3790.srv03_sp2_gdr.070304-2240
Kernel base = 0xe0800000 PsLoadedModuleList = 0xe08af9c8
Debug session time: Fri Feb  1 09:10:17.703 2008 (GMT+0)
System Uptime: 6 days 17:14:45.528
```

Normal Windows 2003 systems have different kernel base address which can be checked from Reference Stack Traces for Windows Server 2003 (Appendix A):

```
kd> vertarget
Windows Server 2003 Kernel Version 3790 (Service Pack 2) UP Free x86 compatible
Product: Server, suite: Enterprise TerminalServer SingleUserTS
Built by: 3790.srv03_sp2_rtm.070216-1710
Kernel base = 0x80800000 PsLoadedModuleList = 0x8089ffa8
Debug session time: Wed Jan 30 17:54:13.390 2008 (GMT+0)
System Uptime: 0 days 0:30:12.000
```

Comments

According to Windows Internals 6th Edition Part 2, page 236, we can create DWORD TrackPtes value in the HKLM\SYSTEM\CurrentControlSet\Control\Session Manager\Memory Management key and set it to 1, and then see allocation history by using **!sysptes 4** WinDbg command.

---

[115] https://docs.microsoft.com/en-us/previous-versions/office/exchange-server-analyzer/aa995783(v=exchg.80)

Region

While working on **Insufficient Memory** pattern for stack trace database (page 627) we noticed the expansion of certain memory regions. Of course, after some time expanding region consumes remaining free or reserved space available before some other region. Generalizing from this, we may say there can be **Insufficient Memory** pattern variant for any expanding region. Region expansion may also be implemented via its move into some other position in memory virtual address space. This movement also has its limits. For example, we created this modeling application and found out it stops reallocating memory long before it reaches 2,000,000,000 byte size:

```
int _tmain(int argc, _TCHAR* argv[])
{
        int i = 100000000;
        void *p = malloc(i);
        for (i = 200000000; i < 2000000000; i+=100000000)
        {
                p = realloc(p, i);
                getc(stdin);
        }
        return 0;
}
```

We took memory dumps after each loop iteration and after 6 or 8 iterations the memory size was constant, and there were no further reallocations:

```
0:000> !heap -s
[...]
Virtual block: 0000000006370000 - 0000000006370000 (size 0000000000000000)
[...]

0:000> !address
[...]
; Start       End         Size
+ 0`00550000 0`06370000 0`05e20000 MEM_FREE    PAGE_NOACCESS  Free
+ 0`06370000 0`1222d000 0`0bebd000 MEM_PRIVATE MEM_COMMIT PAGE_READWRITE Heap [ID: 0; Handle: 0000000000310000; Type: Large block]
+ 0`1222d000 0`77710000 0`654e3000 MEM_FREE    PAGE_NOACCESS  Free
+ 0`77710000 0`77711000 0`00001000 MEM_IMAGE MEM_COMMIT PAGE_READONLY Image [kernel32; "C:\windows\system32\kernel32.dll"]
[...]

0:000> !heap -s
[...]
Virtual block: 0000000012230000 - 0000000012230000 (size 0000000000000000)
[...]

0:000> !address
[...]
+ 0`005d0000 0`12230000 0`11c60000 MEM_FREE    PAGE_NOACCESS  Free
+ 0`12230000 0`2404b000 0`11e1b000 MEM_PRIVATE MEM_COMMIT PAGE_READWRITE Heap [ID: 0; Handle: 0000000000310000; Type: Large block]
+ 0`2404b000 0`77710000 0`536c5000 MEM_FREE    PAGE_NOACCESS  Free
+ 0`77710000 0`77711000 0`00001000 MEM_IMAGE MEM_COMMIT PAGE_READONLY Image [kernel32; "C:\windows\system32\kernel32.dll"]
[...]

0:000> !heap -s
[...]
Virtual block: 0000000024050000 - 0000000024050000 (size 0000000000000000)
[...]
```

```
0:000> !address
[...]
+ 0`00590000 0`24050000 0`23ac0000 MEM_FREE PAGE_NOACCESS Free
+ 0`24050000 0`3bdc9000 0`17d79000 MEM_PRIVATE MEM_COMMIT PAGE_READWRITE Heap [ID: 0; Handle: 0000000000310000; Type: Large block]
+ 0`3bdc9000 0`77710000 0`3b947000 MEM_FREE PAGE_NOACCESS Free
+ 0`77710000 0`77711000 0`00001000 MEM_IMAGE MEM_COMMIT PAGE_READONLY Image [kernel32; "C:\windows\system32\kernel32.dll"]
[...]
```

We skip a few iterations and finally come to a region that does not move and not increase:

```
0:000> !heap -s
[...]
Virtual block: 0000000041d30000 - 0000000041d30000 (size 0000000000000000)
[...]
```

```
0:000> !address
[...]
+ 0`006c0000 0`41d30000 0`41670000 MEM_FREE PAGE_NOACCESS Free
+ 0`41d30000 0`6b8c3000 0`29b93000 MEM_PRIVATE MEM_COMMIT PAGE_READWRITE Heap [ID: 0; Handle: 0000000000310000; Type: Large block]
+ 0`6b8c3000 0`77710000 0`0be4d000 MEM_FREE PAGE_NOACCESS Free
+ 0`77710000 0`77711000 0`00001000 MEM_IMAGE MEM_COMMIT PAGE_READONLY Image [kernel32; "C:\windows\system32\kernel32.dll"]
[...]
```

Reserved Virtual Memory

Allocated dynamic memory such as process heap can remain reserved after deallocation, and its virtual memory region might become unavailable for usage. One example of this we encountered while debugging a .NET service. During peak usage, it reported various out-of-memory events, but its managed heap was healthy and didn't consume much. However, its process heap statistics showed a large reserved heap segment missing in a similar memory dump from a development environment. Remaining allocated entries in that heap segment contained a specific **Module Hint** (page 781) that allowed us to suggest removing a 3rd-party product from a production environment.

In order to provide a proof of that possible scenario of reserved heap regions we created a special modeling application:

```
int _tmain(int argc, _TCHAR* argv[])
{
    static char *pAlloc[1000000];
    for (int i = 0; i < 1000000; i++)
    {
        pAlloc[i] = (char *)malloc (1000);
    }
    getc(stdin);
    for (int i = 0; i < 1000000; i++)
    {
        free(pAlloc[i]);
    }
    getc(stdin);
    return 0;
}
```

Here is the debugging log:

```
0:001> .symfix c:\mss

0:001> .reload
Reloading current modules
.....
```

After allocation:

```
0:001> !heap -s
LFH Key : 0x156356e0
Termination on corruption : ENABLED
Heap      Flags    Reserv  Commit  Virt     Free   List UCR Virt Lock Fast
(k)       (k)      (k)     (k)      length  blocks cont. heap
-------------------------------------------------------------------------
00520000 00000002 1024     112     1024     8      1    1   0    0    LFH
007e0000 00001002 1019328 1012444 1019328 131     68   67  0    0    LFH
-------------------------------------------------------------------------
```

```
0:001> g
(1588.14b0): Break instruction exception - code 80000003 (first chance)
eax=7efda000 ebx=00000000 ecx=00000000 edx=770ff85a esi=00000000 edi=00000000
eip=7707000c esp=00f0f7e4 ebp=00f0f810 iopl=0 nv up ei pl zr na pe nc
cs=0023 ss=002b ds=002b es=002b fs=0053 gs=002b efl=00000246
ntdll!DbgBreakPoint:
7707000c cc  int 3
```

After deallocation:

```
0:001> !heap -s
LFH Key : 0x156356e0
Termination on corruption : ENABLED
Heap     Flags    Reserv  Commit Virt    Free   List UCR  Virt Lock Fast
(k)      (k)      (k)     (k)     length  blocks cont. heap
-------------------------------------------------------------------------
00520000 00000002 1024    112    1024    8      1    1    0 0 LFH
007e0000 00001002 1019328 73040  1019328 71365  419  165  0 0 LFH
External fragmentation 97 % (419 free blocks)
Virtual address fragmentation 92 % (165 uncommited ranges)
-------------------------------------------------------------------------
```

```
0:001> !address -summary
--- Usage Summary --------------- RgnCount ----------- Total Size -------- %ofBusy %ofTotal
Free                             26                  3fbe7000 (1019.902 Mb)         49.80%
<unclassified>                   752                 3f8ec000 (1016.922 Mb)  98.92% 49.66%
Image                            41                  76b000 ( 7.418 Mb)      0.72%  0.36%
Stack                            6                   200000 ( 2.000 Mb)      0.19%  0.10%
MemoryMappedFile                 8                   1af000 ( 1.684 Mb)      0.16%  0.08%
TEB                              2                   2000 ( 8.000 kb)        0.00%  0.00%
PEB                              1                   1000 ( 4.000 kb)        0.00%  0.00%


--- Type Summary (for busy) ------ RgnCount ----------- Total Size -------- %ofBusy %ofTotal
MEM_PRIVATE                      734                 3f8a2000 (1016.633 Mb)  98.89% 49.64%
MEM_IMAGE                        68                  9b8000 ( 9.719 Mb)      0.95%  0.47%
MEM_MAPPED                       8                   1af000 ( 1.684 Mb)      0.16%  0.08%


--- State Summary --------------- RgnCount ----------- Total Size -------- %ofBusy %ofTotal
MEM_FREE                         26                  3fbe7000 (1019.902 Mb)         49.80%
MEM_RESERVE                      374                 3f6e8000 (1014.906 Mb)  98.72% 49.56%
MEM_COMMIT                       436                 d21000 ( 13.129 Mb)     1.28%  0.64%


--- Protect Summary (for commit) - RgnCount ----------- Total Size -------- %ofBusy %ofTotal
PAGE_READWRITE                   383                 725000 ( 7.145 Mb)      0.69%  0.35%
PAGE_EXECUTE_READ                10                  414000 ( 4.078 Mb)      0.40%  0.20%
PAGE_READONLY                    29                  1cd000 ( 1.801 Mb)      0.18%  0.09%
PAGE_WRITECOPY                   10                  12000 ( 72.000 kb)      0.01%  0.00%
PAGE_READWRITE|PAGE_GUARD        4                   9000 ( 36.000 kb)       0.00%  0.00%
```

```
--- Largest Region by Usage ----------- Base Address -------- Region Size ----------
Free                                    3f0c0000              33050000 ( 816.313 Mb)
<unclassified>                          158a1000              fcf000 ( 15.809 Mb)
Image                                   1083000               3d1000 ( 3.816 Mb)
Stack                                   200000                fd000 (1012.000 kb)
MemoryMappedFile                        7efe5000              fb000 (1004.000 kb)
TEB                                     7efda000              1000 ( 4.000 kb)
PEB                                     7efde000              1000 ( 4.000 kb)
```

We see that free memory available for allocation was only 816 Mb.

Session Pool

Although we briefly mentioned session pool in **Insufficient Memory** (kernel pool) pattern (page 599) we factored it into a separate (sub)pattern to provide WinDbg commands for analysis of possible leaks. The following output shows the sequence of commands that gives an idea although the example itself was taken from a healthy dump so no highlights in bold font (we had seen leaks in session pool happening mostly in 32-bit cases):

```
1: kd> !vm 4

Terminal Server Memory Usage By Session:

Session ID 0 @ fffff8800324d000:
Paged Pool Usage:        4128K
Commit Usage:            7488K


Session ID 1 @ fffff88002f65000:
Paged Pool Usage:        32852K
Commit Usage:            36488K


1: kd> !session
Sessions on machine: 2
Valid Sessions: 0 1
Error in reading current session


1: kd> !session -s 1
Sessions on machine: 2
Implicit process is now fffffa80`07d79730
Using session 1


1: kd> !poolused 8
Sorting by Session Tag


Pool Used:
NonPaged             Paged
Tag     Allocs     Used     Allocs     Used
TOTAL            4     4208       9500 33475120
[...]
```

Stack

Insufficient stack memory may not result in **Stack Overflow** (page 1019) if there are internal thread checks or external watchdog threads. In some way, this is a specialization of a more general **Insufficient Memory** (region, page 621) analysis pattern.

Consider this thread stack trace we see when we open a crash dump in WinDbg:

```
0:003> kc
# Call Site
00 EdgeContent!wil::details::ReportFailure
01 EdgeContent!wil::details::ReportFailure_Hr
02 EdgeContent!wil::details::in1diag3::FailFast_Hr
03 EdgeContent!`anonymous namespace'::MemoryLimitWatchdogThreadProc
04 kernel32!BaseThreadInitThunk
05 ntdll!RtlUserThreadStart
```

The reported error is related to general security checks and does not reveal much:

```
0:003> .lastevent
Last event: 10e0.25fc: Security check failure or stack buffer overrun - code c0000409 (first/second
chance not available)
debugger time: Sat Sep 29 21:30:31.531 2018 (UTC + 1:00)
```

However, from **Stack Trace Motif** (page 1061) we may infer that the failure was related to some memory limit.

When looking at **Stack Trace Collection** (page 1053) we notice the thread #11 which has the long sequence of frames:

```
11 Id: 10e0.d68 Suspend: 2 Teb: 000000ca`e96e3000 Unfrozen
# Call Site
00 ntdll!NtWaitForSingleObject
01 KERNELBASE!WaitForSingleObjectEx
02 Chakra!Memory::Recycler::WaitForConcurrentThread
03 Chakra!Memory::Recycler::FinishConcurrentCollect
04 Chakra!ThreadContext::ExecuteRecyclerCollectionFunction
05 Chakra!Memory::Recycler::FinishConcurrentCollectWrapped
06 Chakra!Memory::Recycler::LargeAlloc<0>
07 Chakra!Memory::Recycler::AllocLeaf
08 Chakra!Js::CompoundString::GetSz
09 Chakra!Js::JSONStringifier::ReadProperty
0a Chakra!Js::JSONStringifier::ReadObject
0b Chakra!Js::JSONStringifier::ReadProperty
0c Chakra!Js::JSONStringifier::Stringify
0d Chakra!JSON::Stringify
0e Chakra!amd64_CallFunction
0f Chakra!Js::InterpreterStackFrame::OP_CallCommon<Js::OpLayoutDynamicProfile<
Js::OpLayoutT_CallIWithICIndex<Js::LayoutSizePolicy<0> > > >
10 Chakra!Js::InterpreterStackFrame::ProcessUnprofiled
11 Chakra!Js::InterpreterStackFrame::Process
12 Chakra!Js::InterpreterStackFrame::InterpreterHelper
```

```
13 Chakra!Js::InterpreterStackFrame::InterpreterThunk
[...]
fa Chakra!ThreadContext::ExecuteImplicitCall<<
lambda_5a46706206cf607f01fe0fb33b6e8acf> >
fb Chakra!Js::DynamicObject::CallToPrimitiveFunction
fc Chakra!Js::DynamicObject::ToPrimitiveImpl<409>
fd Chakra!Js::DynamicObject::ToPrimitive
fe Chakra!Js::JavascriptConversion::OrdinaryToPrimitive
ff Chakra!Js::JavascriptConversion::MethodCallToPrimitive
```

It looks like the thread stack is really long that we suspect the possibility of overflow:

```
0:003> ~11kc 0xffff
[...]
c473 Chakra!amd64_CallFunction
c474 Chakra!Js::JavascriptFunction::CallFunction<1>
c475 Chakra!Js::JavascriptFunction::CallRootFunctionInternal
c476 Chakra!Js::JavascriptFunction::CallRootFunction
c477 Chakra!ScriptSite::CallRootFunction
c478 Chakra!ScriptSite::Execute
c479 Chakra!ScriptEngineBase::Execute
c47a edgehtml!CMutationObserver::PerformMicrotaskCheckpoint
c47b edgehtml!CObserverManager::InvokeObserversForCheckpoint
c47c edgehtml!CObserverManager::MicroTaskExecutionCallback
c47d edgehtml!HTML5TaskScheduler::RunReadiedTask
c47e edgehtml!HTML5TaskScheduler::PerformMicrotaskCheckpoint
c47f edgehtml!CJScript9Holder::ExecuteCallback
c480 edgehtml!CScriptTimer::ExecuteTimer
c481 edgehtml!CScriptTimerManager::OnTick
c482 edgehtml!CPaintAlignedTimerManager<CPaintBeat>::ProcessTimers
c483 edgehtml!CPaintBeat::OnProcessTimersTask
c484 edgehtml!GWndAsyncTask::Run
c485 edgehtml!HTML5TaskScheduler::RunReadiedTask
c486 edgehtml!TaskSchedulerBase::RunReadiedTasksInTaskQueueWithCallback
c487 edgehtml!HTML5TaskScheduler::RunReadiedTasks
c488 edgehtml!HTML5EventLoopDriver::DriveLowPriorityTaskExecution
c489 edgehtml!GlobalWndOnPaintPriorityMethodCall
c48a edgehtml!GlobalWndProc
c48b user32!FilteredProcessRedirectingWndProcW
c48c user32!UserCallWinProcCheckWow
c48d user32!DispatchClientMessage
c48e user32!_fnDWORD
c48f ntdll!KiUserCallbackDispatcherContinue
c490 win32u!NtUserDispatchMessage
c491 user32!DispatchMessageWorker
c492 EdgeContent!CBrowserTab::_TabWindowThreadProc
c493 EdgeContent!LCIETab_ThreadProc
c494 edgeIso!_IsoThreadProc_WrapperToReleaseScope
c495 kernel32!BaseThreadInitThunk
c496 ntdll!RtlUserThreadStart
```

However, the current stack pointer is the way above the stack region limit:

```
0:003> ~11s
ntdll!NtWaitForSingleObject+0x14:
00007ffa`b0d99f74 c3              ret

0:011> r rsp
rsp=000000caeb033348

0:011> !teb
TEB at 000000cae96e3000
ExceptionList:        0000000000000000
StackBase:            000000caeba00000
StackLimit:           000000caeb00b000
SubSystemTib:         0000000000000000
FiberData:            0000000000001e00
ArbitraryUserPointer: 0000000000000000
Self:                 000000cae96e3000
EnvironmentPointer:   0000000000000000
ClientId:             00000000000010e0 . 0000000000000d68
RpcHandle:            0000000000000000
Tls Storage:          000001e915185590
PEB Address:          000000cae96a8000
LastErrorValue:       1455
LastStatusValue:      c000012d
Count Owned Locks:    0
HardErrorMode:        0
```

The last error code shows possible **Insufficient Memory** (committed memory, page 587) pattern but there was enough space in the page file and the same crashes were observed in a much more spacious memory environment:

```
0:011> !error c000012d
Error code: (NTSTATUS) 0xc000012d (3221225773) - {Out of Virtual Memory}  Your system is low on virtual
memory. To ensure that Windows runs properly, increase the size of your virtual memory paging file. For
more information, see Help.

0:011> !error 0n1455
Error code: (Win32) 0x5af (1455) - The paging file is too small for this operation to complete.
```

When we look at a raw stack trace region though, we see it was used to the fullest:

```
0:011> dps 000000caeb00b000 L30
000000ca`eb00b000 00000000`00000000
000000ca`eb00b008 00000000`00000000
000000ca`eb00b010 00000000`00000000
000000ca`eb00b018 00000000`00000000
000000ca`eb00b020 00000000`00000000
000000ca`eb00b028 00000000`00000000
000000ca`eb00b030 00000000`00000000
000000ca`eb00b038 00000000`00000000
000000ca`eb00b040 00000000`00000000
```

```
000000ca`eb00b048  00000000`00000000
000000ca`eb00b050  00000000`00000000
000000ca`eb00b058  00000000`00000000
000000ca`eb00b060  00000000`00000000
000000ca`eb00b068  00000000`00000000
000000ca`eb00b070  00000000`00000000
000000ca`eb00b078  00000000`00000000
000000ca`eb00b080  00000000`00000000
000000ca`eb00b088  00000000`00000000
000000ca`eb00b090  00000000`00000000
000000ca`eb00b098  000001e9`258805c0
000000ca`eb00b0a0  00000000`00000000
000000ca`eb00b0a8  00000000`00000000
000000ca`eb00b0b0  00000000`00000131
000000ca`eb00b0b8  00007ffa`8de137a9 Chakra!Js::DictionaryTypeHandlerBase<unsigned>::GetProperty+0x119
000000ca`eb00b0c0  00000000`00000006
000000ca`eb00b0c8  000001e9`258805c0
000000ca`eb00b0d0  000001e9`258805c0
000000ca`eb00b0d8  000001e9`283d4e70
000000ca`eb00b0e0  000000ca`eb00b210
000000ca`eb00b0e8  00000000`00000000
000000ca`eb00b0f0  00000000`00000131
000000ca`eb00b0f8  000001f1`71863c70
000000ca`eb00b100  00007ffa`8e3cd468 Chakra!Js::BuiltInPropertyRecords::number
000000ca`eb00b108  00000000`00000000
000000ca`eb00b110  000001f1`71863c70
000000ca`eb00b118  000000ca`eb00b210
000000ca`eb00b120  000001e9`258805c0
000000ca`eb00b128  00007ffa`8de103d3 Chakra!Js::DynamicObject::GetPropertyQuery+0x53
000000ca`eb00b130  000001e9`24cc65b0
000000ca`eb00b138  000001e9`258805c0
000000ca`eb00b140  000001e9`258805c0
000000ca`eb00b148  00000000`00000131
000000ca`eb00b150  000000ca`eb00b210
000000ca`eb00b158  00000000`00000000
000000ca`eb00b160  000001f1`71863c70
000000ca`eb00b168  00000000`00000000
000000ca`eb00b170  00000000`00000000
000000ca`eb00b178  00007ffa`8df79864 Chakra!Js::JavascriptOperators::GetProperty_InternalSimple+0x64
```

We also see **Execution Residue** (page 395) possibly indicating catch exception processing:

```
0:011> dpS 000000caeb00b000 L100
00007ffa`8de137a9 Chakra!Js::DictionaryTypeHandlerBase<unsigned short>::GetProperty+0x119
00007ffa`8e3cd468 Chakra!Js::BuiltInPropertyRecords::number
00007ffa`8de103d3 Chakra!Js::DynamicObject::GetPropertyQuery+0x53
00007ffa`8df79864 Chakra!Js::JavascriptOperators::GetProperty_InternalSimple+0x64
00007ffa`b0d470d0 ntdll!RtlSetLastWin32Error+0x40
00007ffa`b0d470d0 ntdll!RtlSetLastWin32Error+0x40
00007ffa`b048a5da msvcrt!getptd_noexit+0x6e
00007ffa`8dfb36d6 Chakra!`Js::JavascriptExceptionOperators::StackTraceAccessor'::`1'::catch$8
+0x50
00007ffa`b048a553 msvcrt!getptd+0xb
00007ffa`b045aad6 msvcrt!_DestructExceptionObject+0x46
00007ffa`b0463798 *msvcrt!_CxxCallCatchBlock+0x1e8*                  ,
00007ffa`8ddb6d54 Chakra!Js::JavascriptExceptionOperators::StackTraceAccessor+0x2a4
```

```
00007ffa`8e324798 Chakra!ValueType::PrimitiveOrObject+0xa80
00007ffa`8dfb3686 Chakra!`Js::JavascriptExceptionOperators::StackTraceAccessor'::`1'::catch$8
00007ffa`8dd20000 Chakra!_jscriptinfo_IID_Lookup <PERF> (Chakra+0x0)
00007ffa`b04635b0 msvcrt!_CxxCallCatchBlock
00007ffa`b0d9e2b3 ntdll!RcConsolidateFrames+0x3
00007ffa`8ddb6d54 Chakra!Js::JavascriptExceptionOperators::StackTraceAccessor+0x2a4
00007ffa`8de137a9 Chakra!Js::DictionaryTypeHandlerBase<unsigned short>::GetProperty+0x119
00007ffa`8e3cd468 Chakra!Js::BuiltInPropertyRecords::number
00007ffa`8de103d3 Chakra!Js::DynamicObject::GetPropertyQuery+0x53
00007ffa`8df79864 Chakra!Js::JavascriptOperators::GetProperty_InternalSimple+0x64
00007ffa`b0d470d0 ntdll!RtlSetLastWin32Error+0x40
00007ffa`b0d470d0 ntdll!RtlSetLastWin32Error+0x40
00007ffa`b048a5da msvcrt!getptd_noexit+0x6e
00007ffa`8dfb36d6 Chakra!`Js::JavascriptExceptionOperators::StackTraceAccessor'::`1'::catch$8
+0x50
00007ffa`b048a553 msvcrt!getptd+0xb
00007ffa`b045aad6 msvcrt!_DestructExceptionObject+0x46
00007ffa`b0463798 msvcrt!_CxxCallCatchBlock+0x1e8
00007ffa`8ddb6d54 Chakra!Js::JavascriptExceptionOperators::StackTraceAccessor+0x2a4
```

Another similar crash on a different machine with much more memory available had **Active Thread** (page 74) **Exception Stack Trace** (page 386):

```
0:013> kc
# Call Site
00 ntdll!NtQueryWnfStateNameInformation
01 ntdll!SignalStartWerSvc
02 ntdll!SendMessageToWERService
03 ntdll!ReportExceptionInternal
04 kernel32!WerpReportFaultInternal
05 kernel32!WerpReportFault
06 KERNELBASE!UnhandledExceptionFilter
07 Chakra!FatalExceptionFilter
08 Chakra!ReportFatalException$filt$0
09 msvcrt!_C_specific_handler
0a ntdll!RtlpExecuteHandlerForException
0b ntdll!RtlDispatchException
0c ntdll!RtlRaiseException
0d KERNELBASE!RaiseException
0e Chakra!ReportFatalException
0f Chakra!OutOfMemory_fatal_error
10 Chakra!Js::Exception::RaiseIfScriptActive
11 Chakra!Js::Throw::OutOfMemory
12 Chakra!Memory::Recycler::LargeAlloc<0>
13 Chakra!Memory::Recycler::AllocLeaf
14 Chakra!Js::LazyJSONString::GetSz
15 Chakra!Js::CompoundString::AppendGeneric<Js::CompoundString>
16 Chakra!Js::JavascriptExceptionOperators::StackTraceAccessor
17 Chakra!Js::InlineCache::TryGetProperty<1,1,1,1,0>
18 Chakra!Js::CacheOperators::TryGetProperty<1,1,1,1,1,1,1,0,0>
19 Chakra!Js::JavascriptOperators::PatchGetValue<1,Js::InlineCache>
1a js!d.toString
[...]
```

which showed the Javascript URL:

```
0:013> .frame 1a
1a 00000037`4671e5e0 00007ffe`1753f1a1 js!d.toString [https://yastatic.net/awaps-ad-sdk-js-bundles/1.0-
889/bundles/inpage.bundle.js @ 8,36454]
```

The stack region was also almost full of execution residue including exception catch processing. But this time it shows "stack space" hint:

```
0:013> !teb
TEB at 00000037456dc000
ExceptionList:          0000000000000000
StackBase:              0000003747100000
StackLimit:             000000374670a000
SubSystemTib:           0000000000000000
FiberData:              0000000000001e00
ArbitraryUserPointer:   0000000000000000
Self:                   00000037456dc000
EnvironmentPointer:     0000000000000000
ClientId:               0000000000005914 . 0000000000001150
RpcHandle:              0000000000000000
Tls Storage:            000001a5bcfd88d0
PEB Address:            00000037456bd000
LastErrorValue:         0
LastStatusValue:        c000012d
Count Owned Locks:      0
HardErrorMode:          0

0:013> s-su 000000374670a000 00000037`46720000
[...]
00000037`4670d210 "tack space"
[...]
```

Note: Regardless of the actual root cause and mechanism for these crash dumps, such stack region monitoring can also be used for software prognostics purposes.

The example dump is available for download[116].

---

[116] http://www.patterndiagnostics.com/SoftwareDiagnosticsCorpus/SDC3.zip

Stack Trace Database

Once we have seen a sequence of process memory dumps with the largest one almost 4GB. They were all saved from the process with growing memory consumption from 200MB initially. Initially, we suspected process heap **Memory Leak** (page 732). However, heap statistics (**!heap -s**) was normal. There were not even large block allocations[117]. The dumps were also supplied with UMDH logs, but their difference only showed **Memory Fluctuation** (page 714) and not increase. **Stack Trace Collection** (page 1042) revealed one **Spiking Thread** (page 989) was logging a heap allocation into user mode stack trace database. We could also see that it was **Distributed Spike** (page 265). Inspection of address space showed a large number of sequential regions of the same size with **Stack Trace Database** (page 1026) entries inside. So we concluded that it was stack trace logging **Instrumentation Side Effect** (page 584) and advised to limit stack backtrace size in *gflags.exe*.

To make sure we understood that problem correctly, we decided to model it. We did not come to the same results probably due to different logging implementation, but the memory dumps clearly show the possibility of **Insufficient Memory** pattern variant. Here's the source code:

```
void foo20 (int size)
{
    free(malloc(size));
}

#define FOO(x,y) void foo##x (int size) { foo##y(size); }

FOO(19,20)
FOO(18,19)
FOO(17,18)
FOO(16,17)
FOO(15,16)
FOO(14,15)
FOO(13,14)
FOO(12,13)
FOO(11,12)
FOO(10,11)
FOO(9,10)
FOO(8,9)
FOO(7,8)
FOO(6,7)
FOO(5,6)
FOO(4,5)
FOO(3,4)
FOO(2,3)
FOO(1,2)

typedef void (*PFN) (int);

#define ARRSZ 20
```

---

[117] Models of Software Behaviour, Memory Leak (Process Heap) Pattern, Memory Dump Analysis Anthology, Volume 5, page 315

```
PFN pfnArr[ARRSZ]  = {foo1, foo2, foo3, foo4, foo5, foo6, foo7,
    foo8, foo9, foo10, foo11, foo12, foo13, foo14,
    foo15, foo16, foo17, foo18, foo19, foo20};

int _tmain(int argc, _TCHAR* argv[])
{
    int i;
    for (i = 1; i < 1000000000; ++i)
    {
        pfnArr[i%ARRSZ](i);
    }
    Sleep(-1);
    return 0;
}
```

It allocates and then frees heap entries of different size from 1 byte to 1,000,000,000 bytes all with different 20 possible stack traces. We choose different stack traces to increase the number of different *{size, stack backtrace}* pairs as several allocations of similar size having the same stack trace may be recorded only once in the database. We emulate different stack traces by calling different entries in *pfnArr*. Each call then leads to *foo20,* but the resulting stack trace depth is different. We also enabled *"Create user mode stack trace database"* checkbox in *gflags.exe* for our application called *AllocFree.exe*.

Then we see the expansion of **Stack Trace Database** regions (addresses are different because memory dumps were taken from different application runs):

```
0:000> !address
[...]
; Start        End         Size
+ 0`00240000 0`00312000 0`000d2000 MEM_PRIVATE MEM_COMMIT PAGE_READWRITE Other [Stack Trace Database]
0`00312000 0`01a37000 0`01725000 MEM_PRIVATE MEM_RESERVE Other [Stack Trace Database]
0`01a37000 0`01a40000 0`00009000 MEM_PRIVATE MEM_COMMIT PAGE_READWRITE Other [Stack Trace Database]

0:000> !address
[...]
+ 0`001b0000 0`0188c000 0`016dc000 MEM_PRIVATE MEM_COMMIT PAGE_READWRITE Other [Stack Trace Database]
0`0188c000 0`0188d000 0`00001000 MEM_PRIVATE MEM_RESERVE Other [Stack Trace Database]
0`0188d000 0`019b0000 0`00123000 MEM_PRIVATE MEM_COMMIT PAGE_READWRITE Other [Stack Trace Database]
```

Heap stays the same:

```
0:000> !heap -s
NtGlobalFlag enables following debugging aids for new heaps:
stack back traces
LFH Key                  : 0x000000f841c4f9c0
Termination on corruption : ENABLED
          Heap      Flags    Reserv  Commit  Virt  Free  List  UCR  Virt  Lock  Fast
                             (k)     (k)     (k)   (k)  length    blocks cont. heap
-----------------------------------------------------------------------------------
0000000001a40000 08000002   4096    1444    4096  1164   4      3    0      0   LFH
External fragmentation  80 % (4 free blocks)
0000000000010000 08008000    64      4       64    1     1      1    0      0
0000000000020000 08008000    64      64      64    61    1      1    0      0
-----------------------------------------------------------------------------------

0:000> !heap -s
NtGlobalFlag enables following debugging aids for new heaps:
stack back traces
LFH Key                  : 0x000000473a639107
Termination on corruption : ENABLED
          Heap      Flags    Reserv  Commit  Virt  Free  List  UCR  Virt  Lock  Fast
                             (k)     (k)     (k)   (k)  length    blocks cont. heap
-----------------------------------------------------------------------------------
00000000019c0000 08000002   4096    1444    4096  1164   4      3    0      0
    LFH
External fragmentation  80 % (4 free blocks)
0000000000010000 08008000    64      4       64    1     1      1    0      0
0000000000020000 08008000    64      64      64    61    1      1    0      0
-----------------------------------------------------------------------------------
```

However, we see the thread consuming much CPU (**Spiking Thread**, page 992) and that it was caught while logging stack backtrace:

```
0:000> kc
Call Site
ntdll!RtlpStdLogCapturedStackTrace
ntdll!RtlStdLogStackTrace
ntdll!RtlLogStackBackTraceEx
ntdll!RtlpAllocateHeap
ntdll!RtlAllocateHeap
AllocFree!_heap_alloc
AllocFree!malloc
AllocFree!foo20
AllocFree!foo19
AllocFree!foo18
AllocFree!foo17
AllocFree!foo16
AllocFree!foo15
AllocFree!foo14
AllocFree!foo13
AllocFree!foo12
AllocFree!foo11
AllocFree!foo10
AllocFree!foo9
```

```
AllocFree!foo8
AllocFree!foo7
AllocFree!foo6
AllocFree!foo5
AllocFree!foo4
AllocFree!foo3
AllocFree!foo2
AllocFree!foo1
AllocFree!wmain
AllocFree!__tmainCRTStartup
kernel32!BaseThreadInitThunk
ntdll!RtlUserThreadStart

0:000> !runaway f
 User Mode Time
   Thread       Time
    0:53b8      0 days 3:22:02.354
 Kernel Mode Time
   Thread       Time
    0:53b8      0 days 0:20:39.022
 Elapsed Time
   Thread       Time
    0:53b8      0 days 10:11:23.596
```

If we dump some portion of the region we see recorded stack backtraces:

```
0:000> dps 0`0188c000-200 L200/8
00000000`0188be00 00000000`77891142 ntdll!RtlpAllocateHeap+0x33bd
00000000`0188be08 00000000`778834d8 ntdll!RtlAllocateHeap+0x16c
00000000`0188be10 00000001`3fcc13cb AllocFree!malloc+0x5b
00000000`0188be18 00000001`3fcc1015 AllocFree!foo20+0x15
00000000`0188be20 00000001`3fcc1041 AllocFree!foo19+0x11
00000000`0188be28 00000001`3fcc1061 AllocFree!foo18+0x11
00000000`0188be30 00000001`3fcc12e3 AllocFree!wmain+0x53
00000000`0188be38 00000001`3fcc156c AllocFree!__tmainCRTStartup+0x144
00000000`0188be40 00000000`777259ed kernel32!BaseThreadInitThunk+0xd
00000000`0188be48 00000000`7785c541 ntdll!RtlUserThreadStart+0x1d
00000000`0188be50 00000000`0188b1d0
00000000`0188be58 0009457d`00024fff
00000000`0188be60 00000000`77891142 ntdll!RtlpAllocateHeap+0x33bd
00000000`0188be68 00000000`778834d8 ntdll!RtlAllocateHeap+0x16c
00000000`0188be70 00000001`3fcc13cb AllocFree!malloc+0x5b
00000000`0188be78 00000001`3fcc1015 AllocFree!foo20+0x15
00000000`0188be80 00000001`3fcc1041 AllocFree!foo19+0x11
00000000`0188be88 00000001`3fcc12e3 AllocFree!wmain+0x53
00000000`0188be90 00000001`3fcc156c AllocFree!__tmainCRTStartup+0x144
00000000`0188be98 00000000`777259ed kernel32!BaseThreadInitThunk+0xd
00000000`0188bea0 00000000`7785c541 ntdll!RtlUserThreadStart+0x1d
00000000`0188bea8 00000000`00000000
00000000`0188beb0 00000000`0188b230
00000000`0188beb8 0008457e`00023fff
00000000`0188bec0 00000000`77891142 ntdll!RtlpAllocateHeap+0x33bd
00000000`0188bec8 00000000`778834d8 ntdll!RtlAllocateHeap+0x16c
00000000`0188bed0 00000001`3fcc13cb AllocFree!malloc+0x5b
00000000`0188bed8 00000001`3fcc1015 AllocFree!foo20+0x15
00000000`0188bee0 00000001`3fcc12e3 AllocFree!wmain+0x53
```

```
00000000`0188bee8 00000001`3fcc156c AllocFree!__tmainCRTStartup+0x144
00000000`0188bef0 00000000`777259ed kernel32!BaseThreadInitThunk+0xd
00000000`0188bef8 00000000`7785c541 ntdll!RtlUserThreadStart+0x1d
00000000`0188bf00 00000000`0188b280
00000000`0188bf08 001b457f`0002dfff
00000000`0188bf10 00000000`77891142 ntdll!RtlpAllocateHeap+0x33bd
00000000`0188bf18 00000000`778834d8 ntdll!RtlAllocateHeap+0x16c
00000000`0188bf20 00000001`3fcc13cb AllocFree!malloc+0x5b
00000000`0188bf28 00000001`3fcc1015 AllocFree!foo20+0x15
00000000`0188bf30 00000001`3fcc1041 AllocFree!foo19+0x11
00000000`0188bf38 00000001`3fcc1061 AllocFree!foo18+0x11
00000000`0188bf40 00000001`3fcc1081 AllocFree!foo17+0x11
00000000`0188bf48 00000001`3fcc10a1 AllocFree!foo16+0x11
00000000`0188bf50 00000001`3fcc10c1 AllocFree!foo15+0x11
00000000`0188bf58 00000001`3fcc10e1 AllocFree!foo14+0x11
00000000`0188bf60 00000001`3fcc1101 AllocFree!foo13+0x11
00000000`0188bf68 00000001`3fcc1121 AllocFree!foo12+0x11
00000000`0188bf70 00000001`3fcc1141 AllocFree!foo11+0x11
00000000`0188bf78 00000001`3fcc1161 AllocFree!foo10+0x11
00000000`0188bf80 00000001`3fcc1181 AllocFree!foo9+0x11
00000000`0188bf88 00000001`3fcc11a1 AllocFree!foo8+0x11
00000000`0188bf90 00000001`3fcc11c1 AllocFree!foo7+0x11
00000000`0188bf98 00000001`3fcc11e1 AllocFree!foo6+0x11
00000000`0188bfa0 00000001`3fcc1201 AllocFree!foo5+0x11
00000000`0188bfa8 00000001`3fcc1221 AllocFree!foo4+0x11
00000000`0188bfb0 00000001`3fcc1241 AllocFree!foo3+0x11
00000000`0188bfb8 00000001`3fcc1261 AllocFree!foo2+0x11
00000000`0188bfc0 00000001`3fcc1281 AllocFree!foo1+0x11
00000000`0188bfc8 00000001`3fcc12e3 AllocFree!wmain+0x53
00000000`0188bfd0 00000001`3fcc156c AllocFree!__tmainCRTStartup+0x144
00000000`0188bfd8 00000000`777259ed kernel32!BaseThreadInitThunk+0xd
00000000`0188bfe0 00000000`7785c541 ntdll!RtlUserThreadStart+0x1d
00000000`0188bfe8 00000000`00000000
00000000`0188bff0 00000000`00000000
00000000`0188bff8 00000000`00000000
```

Internal Stack Trace

Occasionally, we look at **Stack Trace Collection** (page 1052) and notice **Internal Stack Trace**. This is a stack trace that is shouldn't be seen in a normal crash dump because statistically, it is rare (we planned to name this pattern **Rare Stack Trace** initially). This stack trace is also not **Special Stack Trace** (page 986) because it is not associated with the special system events or problems. It is also not a stack trace that belongs to various **Wait Chains** (page 1199) or **Spiking Threads** (page 989). This is also a real stack trace and not a reconstructed or hypothetical stack trace such as **Rough Stack Trace** (page 940) or **Past Stack Trace** (page 886). This is simply a thread stack trace that shows some internal operation, for example, where it suggests that message hooking was involved:

```
THREAD fffffa8123702b00 Cid 11cc.0448 Teb: 000007fffffda000 Win32Thread: fffff900c1e6ec20 WAIT:
(WrUserRequest) UserMode Non-Alertable
fffffa81230cf4e0 SynchronizationEvent
Not impersonating
DeviceMap fffff8a0058745e0
Owning Process fffffa81237a8b30 Image: ProcessA.exe
Attached Process N/A Image: N/A
Wait Start TickCount 1258266 Ticks: 18 (0:00:00:00.280)
Context Switch Count 13752 IdealProcessor: 1 NoStackSwap LargeStack
UserTime 00:00:00.468
KernelTime 00:00:00.187
Win32 Start Address ProcessA!ThreadProc (0x000007feff17c608)
Stack Init fffff8800878c700 Current fffff8800878ba10
Base fffff8800878d000 Limit fffff88008781000 Call fffff8800878c750
Priority 12 BasePriority 8 UnusualBoost 0 ForegroundBoost 2 IoPriority 2 PagePriority 5
Child-SP RetAddr Call Site
fffff880`0878ba50 fffff800`01a6c8f2 nt!KiSwapContext+0x7a
fffff880`0878bb90 fffff800`01a7dc9f nt!KiCommitThreadWait+0x1d2
fffff880`0878bc20 fffff960`0010dbd7 nt!KeWaitForSingleObject+0x19f
fffff880`0878bcc0 fffff960`0010dc71 win32k!xxxRealSleepThread+0x257
fffff880`0878bd60 fffff960`000c4bf7 win32k!xxxSleepThread+0x59
fffff880`0878bd90 fffff960`000d07a5 win32k!xxxInterSendMsgEx+0x112a
fffff880`0878bea0 fffff960`00151bf8 win32k!xxxCallHook2+0x62d
fffff880`0878c010 fffff960`000d2454 win32k!xxxCallMouseHook+0x40
fffff880`0878c050 fffff960`0010bf23 win32k!xxxScanSysQueue+0x1828
fffff880`0878c390 fffff960`00118fae win32k!xxxRealInternalGetMessage+0x453
fffff880`0878c470 fffff800`01a76113 win32k!NtUserRealInternalGetMessage+0x7e
fffff880`0878c500 00000000`771b913a nt!KiSystemServiceCopyEnd+0x13 (TrapFrame @ fffff880`0878c570)
00000000`053ff258 000007fe`fac910f4 USER32!NtUserRealInternalGetMessage+0xa
00000000`053ff260 000007fe`fac911fa DUser!CoreSC::xwProcessNL+0x173
00000000`053ff2d0 00000000`771b9181 DUser!MphProcessMessage+0xbd
00000000`053ff330 00000000`774111f5 USER32!_ClientGetMessageMPH+0x3d
00000000`053ff3c0 00000000`771b908a ntdll!KiUserCallbackDispatcherContinue (TrapFrame @
00000000`053ff288)
00000000`053ff438 00000000`771b9055 USER32!NtUserPeekMessage+0xa
00000000`053ff440 000007fe`ebae03fa USER32!PeekMessageW+0x105
00000000`053ff490 000007fe`ebae4925 ProcessA+0x5a
[...]
00000000`053ff820 00000000`773ec541 kernel32!BaseThreadInitThunk+0xd
00000000`053ff850 00000000`00000000 ntdll!RtlUserThreadStart+0x1d
```

We see that this thread was neither waiting for significant time nor consuming CPU. It was reported that *ProcessA.exe* was very slow responding. So perhaps this was slowly punctuated thread execution with periodic small waits. In fact, **Execution Residue** (page 395) analysis revealed Non-**Coincidental Symbolic Information** (page 148) of the 3rd-party **Message Hook** (page 748) and its **Module Product Process** (page 783) was identified. Its removal resolved the problem.

Interrupt Stack

Interrupts can happen in either kernel or user mode. In the latter case, upon transition to kernel mode, a special memory region is used for interrupt processing in kernel space, distinct from the thread's kernel stack, that we call **Interrupt Stack**. It can also be used for mining **Execution Residue** (page 395).

```
2: kd> !thread -1 1f
THREAD fffffa801a9fa3e0  Cid 0f74.0804  Teb: 000007ffffdf8000 Win32Thread: 0000000000000000 RUNNING on
processor 2
Not impersonating
DeviceMap                 fffff88000007400
Owning Process            fffffa801a949c10     Image:          App.exe
Attached Process          N/A              Image:      N/A
Wait Start TickCount      81642662         Ticks: 0
Context Switch Count      58671950         IdealProcessor: 4
UserTime                  01:33:39.702
KernelTime                00:01:11.401
Win32 Start Address 0x000007fef9b1050c
Stack Init fffffa6005af4db0 Current fffffa6005af4950
Base fffffa6005af5000 Limit fffffa6005aef000 Call 0
Priority 8 BasePriority 8 PriorityDecrement 0 IoPriority 2 PagePriority 5
Child-SP          RetAddr           Call Site
fffffa60`01793b98 fffff800`01a58eee nt!KeBugCheckEx
fffffa60`01793ba0 fffff800`01a57dcb nt!KiBugCheckDispatch+0x6e
fffffa60`01793ce0 fffffa60`00eb279b nt!KiPageFault+0x20b (TrapFrame @ fffffa60`01793ce0)
fffffa60`01793e70 fffffa60`00e62739 tcpip! ?? ::FNODOBFM::`string'+0x3883b
fffffa60`01794020 fffffa60`00e62194 tcpip!TcpMatchReceive+0x1b9
fffffa60`01794120 fffffa60`00e52ddd tcpip!TcpPreValidatedReceive+0x2e4
fffffa60`017941c0 fffffa60`00e52e89 tcpip!IppDeliverListToProtocol+0x4d
fffffa60`01794280 fffffa60`00e52463 tcpip!IppProcessDeliverList+0x59
fffffa60`017942f0 fffffa60`00e5176c tcpip!IppReceiveHeaderBatch+0x223
fffffa60`017943d0 fffffa60`00e50d54 tcpip!IpFlcReceivePackets+0x8dc
fffffa60`017945d0 fffffa60`00e61133 tcpip!FlpReceiveNonPreValidatedNetBufferListChain+0x264
fffffa60`017946b0 fffffa60`009a40bc tcpip!FlReceiveNetBufferListChain+0xd3
fffffa60`01794700 fffffa60`0096c8c9 NDIS!ndisMIndicateNetBufferListsToOpen+0xac
fffffa60`01794750 fffffa60`008016f7 NDIS!ndisMDispatchReceiveNetBufferLists+0x1d9
fffffa60`01794bd0 fffffa60`02b4e2d3 NDIS!NdisMIndicateReceiveNetBufferLists+0x67
fffffa60`01794c10 fffffa60`02b3de0c Driver+0x152d3
fffffa60`01794de0 fffffa60`02b3df6b Driver+0x4e0c
fffffa60`01794e20 fffffa60`02b3e0b3 Driver+0x4f6b
fffffa60`01794e60 fffffa60`00801670 Driver+0x50b3
fffffa60`01794ec0 fffff800`01a5d367 NDIS!ndisInterruptDpc+0xc0
fffffa60`01794f40 fffff800`01a5bc35 nt!KiRetireDpcList+0x117
fffffa60`01794fb0 fffff800`01a5ba47 nt!KyRetireDpcList+0x5 (TrapFrame @ fffffa60`01794e70)
fffffa60`05af4bf0 fffff800`01aa1b28 nt!KiDispatchInterruptContinue
fffffa60`05af4c20 000007fe`f7e5c55a nt!KiDpcInterrupt+0xf8 (TrapFrame @ fffffa60`05af4c20)
00000000`4deae430 00000000`00000000 0x000007fe`f7e5c55a
```

```
2: kd> !address fffffa60`01794e60
Usage:
Base Address:        fffffa60`011ff000
End Address:         fffffa60`019dc000
Region Size:         00000000`007dd000
VA Type:             SystemDynamicSpace
VAD Address:         0x27676e69727473
Commit Charge:       0x244a0f51940
Protection:          0x244a0f51940 []
Memory Usage:        Private
No Change:           yes
More info:           !vad 0xfffffa60011ff000

2: kd> !address fffffa60`05af4c20
Usage:               Stack
Base Address:        fffffa60`05aef000
End Address:         fffffa60`05af5000
Region Size:         00000000`00006000
VA Type:             SystemDynamicSpace

2: kd> dpS fffffa60`01793b98 fffffa60`01794fb0
[...]
fffffa60`05657c3f Driver2+0x4c3f
fffffa60`05656369 Driver2+0x3369
[...]
fffffa60`00801670 NDIS!ndisInterruptDpc+0xc0
fffff800`01a5d367 nt!KiRetireDpcList+0x117
fffff800`01a5bc35 nt!KyRetireDpcList+0x5
fffffa60`008015b0 NDIS!ndisInterruptDpc

2: kd> ub fffffa60`05657c3f
Driver2+0x4c25:
fffffa60`05657c25 8bf2        mov     esi,edx
fffffa60`05657c27 33d2        xor     edx,edx
fffffa60`05657c29 418be8      mov     ebp,r8d
fffffa60`05657c2c 488bd9      mov     rbx,rcx
fffffa60`05657c2f 448d4240    lea     r8d,[rdx+40h]
fffffa60`05657c33 488d48b8    lea     rcx,[rax-48h]
fffffa60`05657c37 418bf9      mov     edi,r9d
fffffa60`05657c3a e8010e0000  call    Driver2+0x5a40 (fffffa60`05658a40)

2: kd> ub fffffa60`05656369
Driver2+0x334d:
fffffa60`0565634d cc          int     3
fffffa60`0565634e cc          int     3
fffffa60`0565634f cc          int     3
fffffa60`05656350 4889542410  mov     qword ptr [rsp+10h],rdx
fffffa60`05656355 48894c2408  mov     qword ptr [rsp+8],rcx
fffffa60`0565635a 4883ec58    sub     rsp,58h
fffffa60`0565635e 488d4c2428  lea     rcx,[rsp+28h]
fffffa60`05656363 ff15972c0000 call   qword ptr [Driver2+0x6000 (fffffa60`05659000)]
```

Invalid Exception Information

Here we show how to recognize this pattern and get a stack trace right when a debugger is not able to locate a crash point. For example, WinDbg default analysis command is not able to locate the exception context for a crash and provides a heuristic stack trace:

```
0:000> !analyze -v

[...]

EXCEPTION_RECORD:  001150fc -- (.exr 0x1150fc)
ExceptionAddress: 7c7e2afb (kernel32!RaiseException+0x00000053)
   ExceptionCode: 0eedfade
  ExceptionFlags: 00000001
NumberParameters: 7
   Parameter[0]: 0098fa49
   Parameter[1]: 0374c200
   Parameter[2]: 00000000
   Parameter[3]: 005919b4
   Parameter[4]: 01d80010
   Parameter[5]: 00115704
   Parameter[6]: 001154a4

[...]

CONTEXT:  0012ffb4 — (.cxr 0x12ffb4)
eax=00000000 ebx=00000000 ecx=0000019c edx=00000214 esi=00000000 edi=00000000
eip=000003b0 esp=000002d8 ebp=2d59495b iopl=0 nv up ei ng zr na pe nc
cs=0032 ss=0010 ds=0002 es=0000 fs=0000 gs=0000 efl=000003e4
0032:000003b0 ??              ???

[...]

STACK_TEXT:
7c910328 ntdll!`string'+0x4
7c7db7d0 kernel32!ConsoleApp+0xe
7c7db7a4 kernel32!ConDllInitialize+0x20f
7c7db7b9 kernel32!ConDllInitialize+0x224
7c915239 ntdll!bsearch+0x42
7c91542b ntdll!RtlpLocateActivationContextSection+0x15a
7c915474 ntdll!RtlpCompareActivationContextDataTOCEntryById+0x0
7c916104 ntdll!RtlpFindUnicodeStringInSection+0x23d
7c91534a ntdll!RtlpFindNextActivationContextSection+0x61
7c915742 ntdll!RtlFindNextActivationContextSection+0x46
7c9155ed ntdll!RtlFindActivationContextSectionString+0xde
7c915ce9 ntdll!RtlDecodeSystemPointer+0x9e7
7c915d47 ntdll!RtlDecodeSystemPointer+0xb0b
7c9158ff ntdll!RtlDecodeSystemPointer+0x45b
7c915bf8 ntdll!RtlDosApplyFileIsolationRedirection_Ustr+0x346
7c915c5d ntdll!RtlDosApplyFileIsolationRedirection_Ustr+0x3de
7c97e214 ntdll!DllExtension+0xc
00800000 ApplicationA+0x400000
```

```
7c910000 ntdll!RtlFreeHeap+0x1a4
7c914a53 ntdll!LdrLockLoaderLock+0x146
7c912d04 ntdll!LdrLockLoaderLock+0x1d2
7c912d71 ntdll!LdrUnlockLoaderLock+0x88
7c916768 ntdll!LdrGetDllHandleEx+0xc9
7c912d80 ntdll!`string'+0x84
7c91690e ntdll!LdrGetDllHandleEx+0x2f1
7c912d78 ntdll!LdrUnlockLoaderLock+0xb1
7c97ecc0 ntdll!LdrpHotpatchCount+0x8
7c9167e8 ntdll!`string'+0xc4
7c9168d6 ntdll!LdrGetDllHandleEx+0x2de
7c9166b8 ntdll!LdrGetDllHandle+0x18
7c7de534 kernel32!GetModuleHandleForUnicodeString+0x1d
7c7de544 kernel32!GetModuleHandleForUnicodeString+0xa0
7c7de64b kernel32!BasepGetModuleHandleExW+0x18e
7c7de6cb kernel32!BasepGetModuleHandleExW+0x250
79000000 mscoree!_imp__EnterCriticalSection <PERF> +0x0
7c809ad8 kernel32!_except_handler3+0x0
7c7de548 kernel32!`string'+0x28
79002280 mscoree!`string'+0x0
02080000 xpsp2res+0xc0000
7c7db6d4 kernel32!_BaseDllInitialize+0x7a
7c7db6e9 kernel32!_BaseDllInitialize+0x488
7c917ef3 ntdll!LdrpSnapThunk+0xbd
7c9048b8 ntdll!$$VProc_ImageExportDirectory+0x14b8
7c9000d0 ntdll!RtlDosPathSeperatorsString <PERF> +0x0
7c905d48 ntdll!$$VProc_ImageExportDirectory+0x2948
7c910228 ntdll!RtlpRunTable+0x448
7c910222 ntdll!RtlpAllocateFromHeapLookaside+0x42
7c911086 ntdll!RtlAllocateHeap+0x43d
7c903400 ntdll!$$VProc_ImageExportDirectory+0x0
7c7d9036 kernel32!$$VProc_ImageExportDirectory+0x6a0a
791c6f2d mscorwks!DllMain+0x117
7c917e10 ntdll!`string'+0xc
7c918047 ntdll!LdrpSnapThunk+0x317
7c7d00f0 kernel32!_imp___wcsnicmp <PERF> +0x0
7c7d903c kernel32!$$VProc_ImageExportDirectory+0x6a10
7c917dba ntdll!LdrpGetProcedureAddress+0x186
7c900000 ntdll!RtlDosPathSeperatorsString <PERF> +0x0
7c917e5f ntdll!LdrpGetProcedureAddress+0x29b
7c7d262c kernel32!$$VProc_ImageExportDirectory+0x0
7c7d0000 kernel32!_imp___wcsnicmp <PERF> +0x0
79513870 mscorsn!DllMain+0x119
7c913425 ntdll!RtlDecodePointer+0x0
00726574 ApplicationA+0x326574
7c917e09 ntdll!LdrpGetProcedureAddress+0xa6
7c917ec0 ntdll!LdrGetProcedureAddress+0x18
7c9101e0 ntdll!CheckHeapFillPattern+0x54
7c9101db ntdll!RtlAllocateHeap+0xeac
40ae17ea msxml6!calloc+0xa9
40ae181f msxml6!calloc+0xde
40a30000 msxml6!_imp__OpenThreadToken <PERF> +0x0
7c910323 ntdll!RtlpImageNtHeader+0x56
7c910385 ntdll!RtlImageDirectoryEntryToData+0x57
00400100 ApplicationA+0x100
7c928595 ntdll!LdrpCallTlsInitializers+0x1d
```

```
00400000 ApplicationA+0x0
7c9285c7 ntdll!LdrpCallTlsInitializers+0xd8
7c90118a ntdll!LdrpCallInitRoutine+0x14
00a23010 ApplicationA+0x623010
7c9285d0 ntdll!`string'+0x18
7c935e24 ntdll!LdrpInitializeThread+0x147
7c91b1b7 ntdll!LdrpInitializeThread+0x13b
778e159a SETUPAPI!_DllMainCRTStartup+0x0
7c91b100 ntdll!`string'+0x88
7c91b0a4 ntdll!_LdrpInitialize+0x25b
7c90de9a ntdll!NtTestAlert+0xc
7c91b030 ntdll!`string'+0xc8
7c91b02a ntdll!_LdrpInitialize+0x246
7c90d06a ntdll!NtContinue+0xc
7c90e45f ntdll!KiUserApcDispatcher+0xf
00780010 ApplicationA+0x380010
7c951e13 ntdll!DbgUiRemoteBreakin+0x0
7c97e178 ntdll!LdrpLoaderLock+0x0
00d10000 ApplicationA+0x910000
7c951e40 ntdll!DbgUiRemoteBreakin+0x2d
7c90e920 ntdll!_except_handler3+0x0
7c951e60 ntdll!`string'+0x7c
```

Compare our invalid context data with the normal one having good efl and segment register values:

```
cs=0023 ss=002b ds=002b es=002b fs=0053 gs=002b efl=00010206
```

We look at our stack trace after resetting the context and using **kv** command. We see that *KiUserExceptionDispatcher* has the valid exception context, but exception pointers for *UnhandledExceptionFilter* are not valid:

```
0:000> .ecxr

0:000> kv
ChildEBP RetAddr  Args to Child
001132d0 7c90df4a 7c7d9590 00000002 001132fc ntdll!KiFastSystemCallRet
001132d4 7c7d9590 00000002 001132fc 00000001 ntdll!ZwWaitForMultipleObjects+0xc
00113370 7c7da115 00000002 001134a0 00000000 kernel32!WaitForMultipleObjectsEx+0x12c
0011338c 6993763c 00000002 001134a0 00000000 kernel32!WaitForMultipleObjects+0x18
00113d20 699382b1 00115018 00000001 00198312 faultrep!StartDWException+0x5df
00114d94 7c834526 00115018 00000001 00000000 faultrep!ReportFault+0x533
00115008 0040550c 00115018 7c9032a8 001150fc kernel32!UnhandledExceptionFilter+0x55b
WARNING: Stack unwind information not available. Following frames may be wrong.
00115034 7c90327a 001150fc 0012ffb4 0011512c ApplicationA+0x550c
001150e4 7c90e48a 00000000 0011512c 001150fc ntdll!ExecuteHandler+0x24
001150e4 7c7e2afb 00000000 0011512c 001150fc ntdll!KiUserExceptionDispatcher+0xe (CONTEXT @ 0011512c)
0011544c 0057ac37 0eedfade 00000001 00000007 kernel32!RaiseException+0x53
00115470 0098fa49 0eedfade 00000001 00000007 ApplicationA+0x17ac37
[...]
0012268c 7e398816 017d0f87 000607e8 0000001a USER32!InternalCallWinProc+0x28
001226f4 7e3a8ea0 00000000 017d0f87 000607e8 USER32!UserCallWinProcCheckWow+0x150
```

```
0:000> dd 00115018 L4
00115018  001150fc 0012ffb4 0011512c 001150d0
```

So we use the valid context pointer now:

```
0:000> .cxr 0011512c
eax=001153fc ebx=0eedfade ecx=00000000 edx=001537a8 esi=001154a4 edi=00000007
eip=7c7e2afb esp=001153f8 ebp=0011544c iopl=0         nv up ei pl nz na po nc
cs=001b  ss=0023  ds=0023  es=0023  fs=003b  gs=0000         efl=00200202
kernel32!RaiseException+0x53:
7c7e2afb 5e              pop     esi
```

```
0:000> kv
  *** Stack trace for last set context - .thread/.cxr resets it
ChildEBP RetAddr  Args to Child
0011544c 0057ac37 0eedfade 00000001 00000007 kernel32!RaiseException+0x53
WARNING: Stack unwind information not available. Following frames may be wrong.
00115470 0098fa49 0eedfade 00000001 00000007 ApplicationA+0x17ac37
[...]
0012268c 7e398816 017d0f87 000607e8 0000001a USER32!InternalCallWinProc+0x28
001226f4 7e3a8ea0 00000000 017d0f87 000607e8 USER32!UserCallWinProcCheckWow+0x150
00122748 7e3aacd1 00fd2ad0 0000001a 00000000 USER32!DispatchClientMessage+0xa3
00122778 7c90e473 00122788 00000030 00000030 USER32!__fnINSTRING+0x37
001227b4 7e3993e9 7e3993a8 00122840 00000000 ntdll!KiUserCallbackDispatcher+0x13
001227e0 7e3aa43b 00122840 00000000 00000000 USER32!NtUserPeekMessage+0xc
0012280c 004794d9 00122840 00000000 00000000 USER32!PeekMessageA+0xeb
001228bc 00461667 0012ff7c 00461680 001228e0 ApplicationA+0x794d9
[...]
```

Invalid Handle

General

Invalid handle exception (0xC0000008) is frequently seen in crash dumps. It results from an invalid handle value passed to *CloseHandle* function and other Win32 API or when a handle or a return status is checked manually for validity and the same exception is raised via *RaiseException* or internally via *RtlRaiseStatus* (**Software Exception**, page 977).

For example, critical sections are implemented using events and invalid event handle can result in this exception:

```
STACK_TEXT:
025bff00 7c94243c c0000008 7c9010ed 00231af0 ntdll!RtlRaiseStatus+0x26
025bff80 7c90104b 0015b4ac 77e76a6f 0015b4ac ntdll!RtlpWaitForCriticalSection+0x204
025bff88 77e76a6f 0015b4ac 010d2040 00000000 ntdll!RtlEnterCriticalSection+0x46
025bffa8 77e76c0a 0015b420 025bffec 7c80b683 rpcrt4!BaseCachedThreadRoutine+0xad
025bffb4 7c80b683 001feae8 010d2040 00000000 rpcrt4!ThreadStartRoutine+0x1a
025bffec 00000000 77e76bf0 001feae8 00000000 kernel32!BaseThreadStart+0x37
```

By default, unless raised manually, this exception does not result in a default postmortem debugger launched to save a crash dump. In order to do this we need to run the application under a debugger and save a crash dump upon this exception or use exception monitoring tools that save first-chance exceptions like Debug Diagnostics, ADPlus or Exception Monitor (see **Early Crash Dump** pattern, page 335):

```
0:002> g
(7b0.d1c): Invalid handle - code c0000008 (first chance)
First chance exceptions are reported before any exception handling.
This exception may be expected and handled.
eax=00000001 ebx=00000000 ecx=00000000 edx=00000000 esi=7d999906 edi=00403378
eip=7d61c92d esp=0012ff68 ebp=0012ff70 iopl=0 nv up ei pl nz na po nc
cs=0023 ss=002b ds=002b es=002b fs=0053 gs=002b efl=00000202
ntdll!NtClose+0x12:
7d61c92d c20400          ret     4


0:000> g
(7b0.d1c): Invalid handle - code c0000008 (!!! second chance !!!)
eax=00000001 ebx=00000000 ecx=00000000 edx=00000000 esi=7d999906 edi=00403378
eip=7d61c92d esp=0012ff68 ebp=0012ff70 iopl=0 nv up ei pl nz na po nc
cs=0023 ss=002b ds=002b es=002b fs=0053 gs=002b efl=00000202
ntdll!NtClose+0x12:
7d61c92d c20400          ret     4
```

In order to catch it using postmortem debuggers, we can use Application Verifier and configure its basic checks to include invalid handles. Then we will have crash dumps if a postmortem debugger or WER is properly configured. The typical stack might look like below and point straight to the problem component:

```
EXCEPTION_RECORD:  ffffffff -- (.exr 0xffffffffffffffff)
ExceptionAddress: 6b006369
   ExceptionCode: 80000003 (Break instruction exception)
  ExceptionFlags: 00000000
NumberParameters: 1
   Parameter[0]: 00000000

DEFAULT_BUCKET_ID:  STATUS_BREAKPOINT

0:000> kL
ChildEBP RetAddr
0301ff44 0489a480 ntdll!NtClose+0x12
WARNING: Stack unwind information not available. Following frames may be wrong.
0301ff54 7d4d8e4f vfbasics+0xa480
0301ff60 04894df9 kernel32!CloseHandle+0x59
0301ff70 00401022 vfbasics+0x4df9
0301ffc0 7d4e7d2a BadHandle+0x1022
0301fff0 00000000 kernel32!BaseProcessStart+0x28
```

or it might look like this:

```
0:000> kL
Child-SP          RetAddr           Call Site
00000000`0012ed58 00000000`01f9395a ntdll!DbgBreakPoint
00000000`0012ed60 00000000`023e29a7 vrfcore!VerifierStopMessageEx+0x846
00000000`0012f090 00000000`023d9384 vfbasics+0x129a7
00000000`0012f0f0 00000000`77f251ec vfbasics+0x9384
00000000`0012f180 00000000`77ee5f36 ntdll!RtlpCallVectoredHandlers+0x26f
00000000`0012f210 00000000`77ee6812 ntdll!RtlDispatchException+0x46
00000000`0012f8c0 00000000`77ef325a ntdll!RtlRaiseException+0xae
00000000`0012fe00 00000000`77d6e314 ntdll!KiRaiseUserExceptionDispatcher+0x3a
00000000`0012fed0 00000001`40001028 kernel32!CloseHandle+0x5f
00000000`0012ff00 00000001`40001294 BadHandle+0x1028
00000000`0012ff30 00000000`77d5964c BadHandle+0x1294
00000000`0012ff80 00000000`00000000 kernel32!BaseProcessStart+0x29
```

vfbasics and *vrfcore* modules are Application Verifier DLLs that possibly translate an invalid handle exception to a breakpoint exception and, therefore, trigger the launch of a postmortem debugger from an unhandled exception filter. Application Verifier version (x64 or x86) must match the application platform (64-bit or 32-bit)[118].

If invalid handle exception is raised manually we get the status code and possibly problem component immediately from **!analyze** command:

```
FAULTING_IP:
kernel32!RaiseException+53
7d4e2366 5e              pop     esi
```

---

[118] Memory Dump Analysis Anthology, Volume 2, page 413

```
EXCEPTION_RECORD:  ffffffff -- (.exr 0xffffffffffffffff)
ExceptionAddress: 7d4e2366 (kernel32!RaiseException+0x00000053)
   ExceptionCode: c0000008 (Invalid handle)
  ExceptionFlags: 00000000
NumberParameters: 0
Thread tried to close a handle that was invalid or illegal to close

DEFAULT_BUCKET_ID:  STATUS_INVALID_HANDLE

PROCESS_NAME:  BadHandle.exe

ERROR_CODE: (NTSTATUS) 0xc0000008 - An invalid HANDLE was specified.

STACK_TEXT:
0012ff64 00401043 c0000008 00000000 00000000 kernel32!RaiseException+0x53
WARNING: Stack unwind information not available. Following frames may be wrong.
0012ffc0 7d4e7d2a 00000000 00000000 7efde000 BadHandle+0x1043
0012fff0 00000000 004012f9 00000000 00000000 kernel32!BaseProcessStart+0x28

FAULTING_THREAD:  00000b64

PRIMARY_PROBLEM_CLASS:  STATUS_INVALID_HANDLE

BUGCHECK_STR:  APPLICATION_FAULT_STATUS_INVALID_HANDLE
```

Because we have WinDbg warning about stack unwind we can double check the disassembly of *RaiseException* return address:

```
0:000> ub 00401043
BadHandle+0x1029:
00401029 push    offset BadHandle+0x212c (0040212c)
0040102e push    0
00401030 call    esi
00401032 push    0
00401034 push    0
00401036 push    0
00401038 push    0C0000008h
0040103d call    dword ptr [BadHandle+0x2004 (00402004)]

0:000> dps 00402004 l1
00402004  7d4e2318 kernel32!RaiseException
```

In such cases, the real problem could be memory corruption overwriting stored valid handle values.

Comments

We can also check if the handle value is valid or not:

```
STACK_TEXT:
0fbef7f8 7581c455 00000aa4 00000aa4 0fbef818 ntdll!ZwClose+0x12
0fbef808 76051438 00000aa4 0000000d 00000000 KERNELBASE!CloseHandle+0x2d
0fbef818 5fa2632a 00000aa4 5fa24b9c 00000000 kernel32!CloseHandleImplementation+0x3f
[...]

0:017> !handle 0000aa4
Handle 00000aa4
Type

0:017> !handle 0000aa0
Handle 00000aa0
Type Thread

0:017> !handle 0000aa8
Handle 00000aa8
Type Event
```

Enabling application verifier in *gflags.exe* to catch handle close stack traces may also reveal who closed the handle originally before we got the second invalid handle close. Use **!htrace** command there.

Managed Space

We recently encountered **Invalid Handle** pattern in the context of .NET program execution. We decided to model it and wrote a small C# program:

```
namespace SafeHandle
{
    class Program
    {
        static void Main(string[] args)
        {
            SafeFileHandle hFile =
                new SafeFileHandle(new IntPtr(0xDEAD), true);
            Console.WriteLine("About to close");
            Console.ReadKey();
        }
    }
}
```

Of course, when we execute it nothing happens. Invalid handles are ignored by default. However, to change the behavior we enabled "*Enable close exception*" in *gflags.exe*:

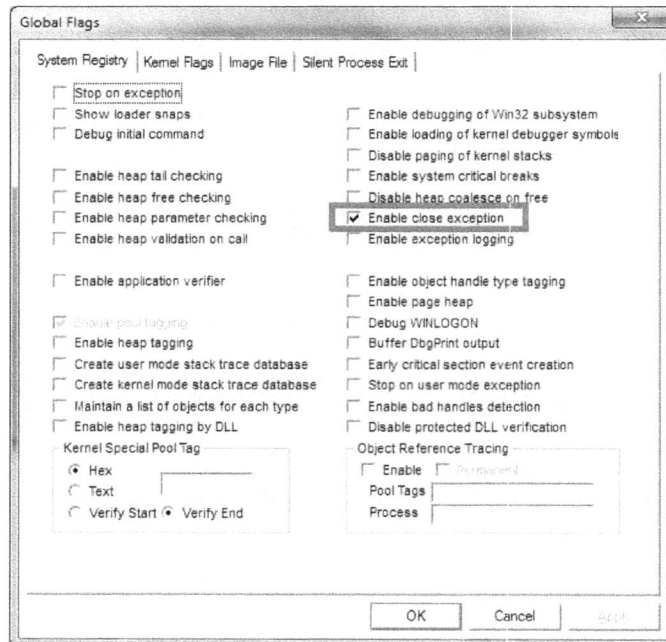

Moreover, if we run it we get this **Managed Stack Trace** (page 704):

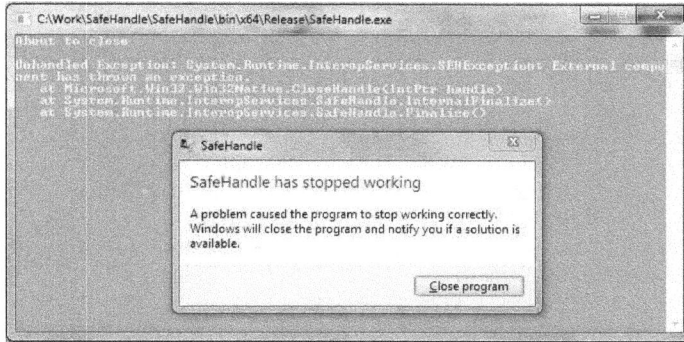

We could have detected invalid handle if we enabled *Application Verifier,* but then we would not have **Managed Code Exception** (page 697).

So we load a crash dump (saved because we enabled LocalDumps[119]) and load SOS extension:

```
0:002> lmv m clr
start end module name
000007fe`ed880000 000007fe`ee1eb000 clr (pdb symbols)
Loaded symbol image file: clr.dll
Image path: C:\Windows\Microsoft.NET\Framework64\v4.0.30319\clr.dll
[...]


0:002> .load C:\Windows\Microsoft.NET\Framework64\v4.0.30319\sos


0:002> !pe
Exception object: 0000000002ab5fe8
Exception type: System.Runtime.InteropServices.SEHException
Message: External component has thrown an exception.
InnerException:
StackTrace (generated):
SP IP Function
000000001B40EDD0 0000000000000000 mscorlib_ni!Microsoft.Win32.Win32Native.CloseHandle(IntPtr)+0x1
000000001B40F2F0 0000000000000000
mscorlib_ni!System.Runtime.InteropServices.SafeHandle.InternalFinalize()+0x1
000000001B40F2F0 000007FEEC62F7A6 mscorlib_ni!System.Runtime.InteropServices.SafeHandle.Finalize()+0x26


StackTraceString:
HResult: 80004005
```

Our unmanaged **CLR Thread** (page 135) **Exception Stack Trace** (page 386) is quite simple:

```
0:002> k
Child-SP RetAddr Call Site
00000000`1b40d6e8 000007fe`fd651430 ntdll!NtWaitForMultipleObjects+0xa
00000000`1b40d6f0 00000000`77621723 KERNELBASE!WaitForMultipleObjectsEx+0xe8
00000000`1b40d7f0 00000000`7769b5e5 kernel32!WaitForMultipleObjectsExImplementation+0xb3
00000000`1b40d880 00000000`7769b767 kernel32!WerpReportFaultInternal+0x215
00000000`1b40d920 00000000`7769b7bf kernel32!WerpReportFault+0x77
00000000`1b40d950 00000000`7769b9dc kernel32!BasepReportFault+0x1f
00000000`1b40d980 00000000`778b3398 kernel32!UnhandledExceptionFilter+0x1fc
00000000`1b40da60 00000000`778385c8 ntdll! ?? ::FNODOBFM::`string'+0x2365
00000000`1b40da90 00000000`77849d2d ntdll!_C_specific_handler+0x8c
00000000`1b40db00 00000000`778391cf ntdll!RtlpExecuteHandlerForException+0xd
00000000`1b40db30 00000000`778397c8 ntdll!RtlDispatchException+0x45a
00000000`1b40e210 00000000`778712c7 ntdll!RtlRaiseException+0x22f
00000000`1b40ebc0 000007fe`fd651873 ntdll!KiRaiseUserExceptionDispatcher+0x3a
00000000`1b40ec90 00000000`77621991 KERNELBASE!CloseHandle+0x13
00000000`1b40ecc0 000007fe`ec720418 kernel32!CloseHandleImplementation+0x3d
00000000`1b40edd0 000007fe`ed8e9e03 mscorlib_ni+0x580418
00000000`1b40eea0 000007fe`ed8e9e7e clr!CallDescrWorkerInternal+0x83
00000000`1b40eee0 000007fe`ed8ec860 clr!CallDescrWorkerWithHandler+0x4a
00000000`1b40ef20 000007fe`ed8f1a1d clr!DispatchCallSimple+0x85
00000000`1b40efb0 000007fe`ed8f19ac clr!SafeHandle::RunReleaseMethod+0x69
00000000`1b40f050 000007fe`ed8f180a clr!SafeHandle::Release+0x122
00000000`1b40f120 000007fe`eda4863e clr!SafeHandle::Dispose+0x36
00000000`1b40f190 000007fe`ec62f7a6 clr!SafeHandle::Finalize+0xa2
00000000`1b40f2f0 000007fe`ed8e9d56 mscorlib_ni+0x48f7a6
00000000`1b40f330 000007fe`eda83c4e clr!FastCallFinalizeWorker+0x6
00000000`1b40f360 000007fe`eda83bc3 clr!MethodDesc::RequiresFullSlotNumber+0x72
00000000`1b40f3a0 000007fe`eda83b0f clr!MethodTable::CallFinalizer+0xa3
00000000`1b40f3e0 000007fe`ed9fee46 clr!SVR::CallFinalizer+0x5f
00000000`1b40f420 000007fe`ed9aac5b clr!SVR::CallFinalizer+0x102
00000000`1b40f4e0 000007fe`ed8f458c clr!WKS::GCHeap::IsPromoted+0xee
00000000`1b40f520 000007fe`ed8f451a clr!Frame::Pop+0x50
00000000`1b40f560 000007fe`ed8f4491 clr!COMCustomAttribute::PopSecurityContextFrame+0x192
00000000`1b40f660 000007fe`ed9d1bfe clr!COMCustomAttribute::PopSecurityContextFrame+0xbd
00000000`1b40f6f0 000007fe`ed9d1e59 clr!ManagedThreadBase_NoADTransition+0x3f
00000000`1b40f750 000007fe`ed9533de clr!WKS::GCHeap::FinalizerThreadStart+0x193
00000000`1b40f790 00000000`776159ed clr!Thread::intermediateThreadProc+0x7d
00000000`1b40f850 00000000`7784c541 kernel32!BaseThreadInitThunk+0xd
00000000`1b40f880 00000000`00000000 ntdll!RtlUserThreadStart+0x1d
```

We see that exception processing happened during object finalization. We can infer the value of the handle (maybe **Small Value**, page 975) via disassembly if this is possible:

```
0:002> kn
# Child-SP RetAddr Call Site
00 00000000`1b40d6e8 000007fe`fd651430 ntdll!NtWaitForMultipleObjects+0xa
01 00000000`1b40d6f0 00000000`77621723 KERNELBASE!WaitForMultipleObjectsEx+0xe8
02 00000000`1b40d7f0 00000000`7769b5e5 kernel32!WaitForMultipleObjectsExImplementation+0xb3
03 00000000`1b40d880 00000000`7769b767 kernel32!WerpReportFaultInternal+0x215
04 00000000`1b40d920 00000000`7769b7bf kernel32!WerpReportFault+0x77
05 00000000`1b40d950 00000000`7769b9dc kernel32!BasepReportFault+0x1f
06 00000000`1b40d980 00000000`778b3398 kernel32!UnhandledExceptionFilter+0x1fc
07 00000000`1b40da60 00000000`778385c8 ntdll! ?? ::FNODOBFM::`string'+0x2365
08 00000000`1b40da90 00000000`77849d2d ntdll!_C_specific_handler+0x8c
09 00000000`1b40db00 00000000`778391cf ntdll!RtlpExecuteHandlerForException+0xd
0a 00000000`1b40db30 00000000`778397c8 ntdll!RtlDispatchException+0x45a
0b 00000000`1b40e210 00000000`778712c7 ntdll!RtlRaiseException+0x22f
0c 00000000`1b40ebc0 000007fe`fd651873 ntdll!KiRaiseUserExceptionDispatcher+0x3a
0d 00000000`1b40ec90 00000000`77621991 KERNELBASE!CloseHandle+0x13
0e 00000000`1b40ecc0 000007fe`ec720418 kernel32!CloseHandleImplementation+0x3d
0f 00000000`1b40edd0 000007fe`ed8e9e03 mscorlib_ni+0x580418
10 00000000`1b40eea0 000007fe`ed8e9e7e clr!CallDescrWorkerInternal+0x83
11 00000000`1b40eee0 000007fe`ed8ec860 clr!CallDescrWorkerWithHandler+0x4a
12 00000000`1b40ef20 000007fe`ed8f1a1d clr!DispatchCallSimple+0x85
13 00000000`1b40efb0 000007fe`ed8f19ac clr!SafeHandle::RunReleaseMethod+0x69
14 00000000`1b40f050 000007fe`ed8f180a clr!SafeHandle::Release+0x122
15 00000000`1b40f120 000007fe`eda4863e clr!SafeHandle::Dispose+0x36
16 00000000`1b40f190 000007fe`ec62f7a6 clr!SafeHandle::Finalize+0xa2
17 00000000`1b40f2f0 000007fe`ed8e9d56 mscorlib_ni+0x48f7a6
18 00000000`1b40f330 000007fe`eda83c4e clr!FastCallFinalizeWorker+0x6
19 00000000`1b40f360 000007fe`eda83bc3 clr!MethodDesc::RequiresFullSlotNumber+0x72
1a 00000000`1b40f3a0 000007fe`eda83b0f clr!MethodTable::CallFinalizer+0xa3
1b 00000000`1b40f3e0 000007fe`ed9fee46 clr!SVR::CallFinalizer+0x5f
1c 00000000`1b40f420 000007fe`ed9aac5b clr!SVR::CallFinalizer+0x102
1d 00000000`1b40f4e0 000007fe`ed8f458c clr!WKS::GCHeap::IsPromoted+0xee
1e 00000000`1b40f520 000007fe`ed8f451a clr!Frame::Pop+0x50
1f 00000000`1b40f560 000007fe`ed8f4491 clr!COMCustomAttribute::PopSecurityContextFrame+0x192
20 00000000`1b40f660 000007fe`ed9d1bfe clr!COMCustomAttribute::PopSecurityContextFrame+0xbd
21 00000000`1b40f6f0 000007fe`ed9d1e59 clr!ManagedThreadBase_NoADTransition+0x3f
22 00000000`1b40f750 000007fe`ed9533de clr!WKS::GCHeap::FinalizerThreadStart+0x193
23 00000000`1b40f790 00000000`776159ed clr!Thread::intermediateThreadProc+0x7d
24 00000000`1b40f850 00000000`7784c541 kernel32!BaseThreadInitThunk+0xd
25 00000000`1b40f880 00000000`00000000 ntdll!RtlUserThreadStart+0x1d


0:002> .frame /c d
0d 00000000`1b40ec90 00000000`77621991 KERNELBASE!CloseHandle+0x13
rax=00000000c0000001 rbx=000000000000dead rcx=00000000009a0000
rdx=0000000000000001 rsi=000000001b40efd0 rdi=000000001b40eff8
rip=000007fefd651873 rsp=000000001b40ec90 rbp=000000001b40edf0
r8=000000001b40ce08 r9=000000001b40cf70 r10=0000000000000000
r11=0000000000000246 r12=0000000000000001 r13=0000000040000000
r14=000000001b40ef40 r15=0000000000000000
iopl=0         nv up ei pl zr na po nc
cs=0033 ss=002b ds=002b es=002b fs=0053 gs=002b efl=00000246
KERNELBASE!CloseHandle+0x13:
000007fe`fd651873 85c0            test eax,eax
```

```
0:002> ub 00000000`77621991
kernel32!CloseHandleImplementation+0x1e:
00000000`7762196e 83f9f4          cmp   ecx,0FFFFFFF4h
00000000`77621971 0f83952e0100    jae   kernel32!TlsGetValue+0x3ef0 (00000000`7763480c)
00000000`77621977 488bc3          mov   rax,rbx
00000000`7762197a 2503000010      and   eax,10000003h
00000000`7762197f 4883f803        cmp   rax,3
00000000`77621983 0f847f8dfeff    je    kernel32!CloseHandleImplementation+0x56 (00000000`7760a708)
00000000`77621989 488bcb          mov   rcx,rbx
00000000`7762198c e81f000000      call  kernel32!CloseHandle (00000000`776219b0)
```

Here we also check the value from the managed stack trace or **Execution Residue** (page 393):

```
0:002> !CLRStack -a
OS Thread Id: 0x1390 (2)
Child SP IP Call Site
000000001b40edf8 000000007787186a [InlinedCallFrame: 000000001b40edf8]
Microsoft.Win32.Win32Native.CloseHandle(IntPtr)
000000001b40edf8 000007feec720418 [InlinedCallFrame: 000000001b40edf8]
Microsoft.Win32.Win32Native.CloseHandle(IntPtr)
000000001b40edd0 000007feec720418 DomainNeutralILStubClass.IL_STUB_PInvoke(IntPtr)
PARAMETERS:
    <no data>


000000001b40eff8 000007feed8e9e03 [GCFrame: 000000001b40eff8]
000000001b40f148 000007feed8e9e03 [GCFrame: 000000001b40f148]
000000001b40f1f8 000007feed8e9e03 [HelperMethodFrame_1OBJ: 000000001b40f1f8]
System.Runtime.InteropServices.SafeHandle.InternalFinalize()
000000001b40f2f0 000007feec62f7a6 System.Runtime.InteropServices.SafeHandle.Finalize()
PARAMETERS:
    this (0x000000001b40f330) = 0x0000000002ab2d78


000000001b40f6a8 000007feed8e9d56 [DebuggerU2MCatchHandlerFrame: 000000001b40f6a8]


0:002> !dso
OS Thread Id: 0x1390 (2)
RSP/REG Object Name
000000001B40EEA0 0000000002ab2d78 Microsoft.Win32.SafeHandles.SafeFileHandle
000000001B40EFD0 0000000002ab2d78 Microsoft.Win32.SafeHandles.SafeFileHandle
000000001B40F038 0000000002ab2d78 Microsoft.Win32.SafeHandles.SafeFileHandle
000000001B40F050 0000000002ab2d78 Microsoft.Win32.SafeHandles.SafeFileHandle
000000001B40F090 0000000002ab2d78 Microsoft.Win32.SafeHandles.SafeFileHandle
000000001B40F120 0000000002ab2d78 Microsoft.Win32.SafeHandles.SafeFileHandle
000000001B40F190 0000000002ab2d78 Microsoft.Win32.SafeHandles.SafeFileHandle
000000001B40F1B8 0000000002ab2d78 Microsoft.Win32.SafeHandles.SafeFileHandle
000000001B40F240 0000000002ab2d78 Microsoft.Win32.SafeHandles.SafeFileHandle
000000001B40F2F8 0000000002ab2d78 Microsoft.Win32.SafeHandles.SafeFileHandle
000000001B40F330 0000000002ab2d78 Microsoft.Win32.SafeHandles.SafeFileHandle
000000001B40F360 0000000002ab5e10 System.Threading.Thread
000000001B40F390 0000000002ab2d78 Microsoft.Win32.SafeHandles.SafeFileHandle
000000001B40F3E0 0000000002ab2d78 Microsoft.Win32.SafeHandles.SafeFileHandle
000000001B40F3F0 0000000002ab2d78 Microsoft.Win32.SafeHandles.SafeFileHandle
000000001B40F430 0000000002ab58a8 Microsoft.Win32.SafeHandles.SafeViewOfFileHandle
000000001B40F4E0 0000000002ab2d78 Microsoft.Win32.SafeHandles.SafeFileHandle
```

```
0:002> !do 0000000002ab2d78
Name:              Microsoft.Win32.SafeHandles.SafeFileHandle
MethodTable:       000007feec88a260
EEClass:           000007feec34d340
Size:              32(0x20) bytes
File: C:\windows\Microsoft.Net\assembly\GAC_64\mscorlib\v4.0_4.0.0.0__b77a5c561934e089\mscorlib.dll
Fields:
MT                 Field     Offset  Type              VT  Attr      Value  Name
000007feec88a338  400060d  8         System.IntPtr    1   instance   dead   handle
000007feec8892b8  400060e  10        System.Int32     1   instance   3      _state
000007feec887de0  400060f  14        System.Boolean   1   instance   1      _ownsHandle
000007feec887de0  4000610  15        System.Boolean   1   instance   1      _fullyInitialized
```

Please note that we do not have global application flags:

```
0:002> !gflag
Current NtGlobalFlag contents: 0x00000000
```

Here is the exception stack trace from a different crash dump when we enable *Application Verifier*:

```
0:002> !gflag
Current NtGlobalFlag contents: 0x02000100
vrf - Enable application verifier
hpa - Place heap allocations at ends of pages
```

```
0:002> k
Child-SP RetAddr Call Site
00000000`24bac4a8 00000000`77cd3072 ntdll!NtWaitForSingleObject+0xa
00000000`24bac4b0 00000000`77cd32b5 ntdll!RtlReportExceptionEx+0x1d2
00000000`24bac5a0 000007fe`fa2c26fb ntdll!RtlReportException+0xb5
00000000`24bac620 00000000`77c2a5db verifier!AVrfpVectoredExceptionHandler+0x26b
00000000`24bac6b0 00000000`77c28e62 ntdll!RtlpCallVectoredHandlers+0xa8
00000000`24bac720 00000000`77c61248 ntdll!RtlDispatchException+0x22
00000000`24bace00 000007fe`fa2bae03 ntdll!KiUserExceptionDispatch+0x2e
00000000`24bad500 000007fe`fa2c268a verifier!VerifierStopMessageEx+0x6fb
00000000`24bad850 00000000`77c2a5db verifier!AVrfpVectoredExceptionHandler+0x1fa
00000000`24bad8e0 00000000`77c28e62 ntdll!RtlpCallVectoredHandlers+0xa8
00000000`24bad950 00000000`77c297c8 ntdll!RtlDispatchException+0x22
00000000`24bae030 00000000`77c612c7 ntdll!RtlRaiseException+0x22f
00000000`24bae9e0 000007fe`fa2d2386 ntdll!KiRaiseUserExceptionDispatcher+0x3a
00000000`24baeab0 000007fe`fdbd1873 verifier!AVrfpNtClose+0xbe
00000000`24baeae0 000007fe`fa2d4031 KERNELBASE!CloseHandle+0x13
00000000`24baeb10 000007fe`fa2d40cb verifier!AVrfpCloseHandleCommon+0x95
00000000`24baeb40 00000000`77a11991 verifier!AVrfpKernelbaseCloseHandle+0x23
00000000`24baeb80 000007fe`fa2d4031 kernel32!CloseHandleImplementation+0x3d
00000000`24baec90 000007fe`fa2d409c verifier!AVrfpCloseHandleCommon+0x95
*** WARNING: Unable to verify checksum for mscorlib.ni.dll
00000000`24baecc0 000007fe`e6a40418 verifier!AVrfpKernel32CloseHandle+0x2c
00000000`24baed00 000007fe`ec0e9e03 mscorlib_ni+0x580418
00000000`24baedd0 000007fe`ec0e9e7e clr!CallDescrWorkerInternal+0x83
00000000`24baee10 000007fe`ec0ec860 clr!CallDescrWorkerWithHandler+0x4a
00000000`24baee50 000007fe`ec0f1a1d clr!DispatchCallSimple+0x85
00000000`24baee90 000007fe`ec0f19ac clr!SafeHandle::RunReleaseMethod+0x69
00000000`24baef80 000007fe`ec0f180a clr!SafeHandle::Release+0x122
```

```
00000000`24baf050 000007fe`ec24863e clr!SafeHandle::Dispose+0x36
00000000`24baf0c0 000007fe`e694f7a6 clr!SafeHandle::Finalize+0xa2
00000000`24baf220 000007fe`ec0e9d56 mscorlib_ni+0x48f7a6
00000000`24baf260 000007fe`ec283c4e clr!FastCallFinalizeWorker+0x6
00000000`24baf290 000007fe`ec283bc3 clr!MethodDesc::RequiresFullSlotNumber+0x72
00000000`24baf2d0 000007fe`ec283b0f clr!MethodTable::CallFinalizer+0xa3
00000000`24baf310 000007fe`ec1fee46 clr!SVR::CallFinalizer+0x5f
00000000`24baf350 000007fe`ec1aac5b clr!SVR::CallFinalizer+0x102
00000000`24baf410 000007fe`ec0f458c clr!WKS::GCHeap::IsPromoted+0xee
00000000`24baf450 000007fe`ec0f451a clr!Frame::Pop+0x50
00000000`24baf490 000007fe`ec0f4491 clr!COMCustomAttribute::PopSecurityContextFrame+0x192
00000000`24baf590 000007fe`ec1d1bfe clr!COMCustomAttribute::PopSecurityContextFrame+0xbd
00000000`24baf620 000007fe`ec1d1e59 clr!ManagedThreadBase_NoADTransition+0x3f
00000000`24baf680 000007fe`ec1533de clr!WKS::GCHeap::FinalizerThreadStart+0x193
00000000`24baf6c0 000007fe`fa2d4b87 clr!Thread::intermediateThreadProc+0x7d
00000000`24baf780 00000000`77a059ed verifier!AVrfpStandardThreadFunction+0x2b
00000000`24baf7c0 00000000`77c3c541 kernel32!BaseThreadInitThunk+0xd
00000000`24baf7f0 00000000`00000000 ntdll!RtlUserThreadStart+0x1d


0:002> !pe
There is no current managed exception on this thread


0:002> !CLRStack
OS Thread Id: 0x51e4 (2)
Child SP IP Call Site
0000000024baed28 0000000077c612fa [InlinedCallFrame: 0000000024baed28]
Microsoft.Win32.Win32Native.CloseHandle(IntPtr)
0000000024baed28 000007fee6a40418 [InlinedCallFrame: 0000000024baed28]
Microsoft.Win32.Win32Native.CloseHandle(IntPtr)
0000000024baed00 000007fee6a40418 DomainNeutralILStubClass.IL_STUB_PInvoke(IntPtr)
0000000024baef28 000007feec0e9e03 [GCFrame: 0000000024baef28]
0000000024baf078 000007feec0e9e03 [GCFrame: 0000000024baf078]
0000000024baf128 000007feec0e9e03 [HelperMethodFrame_1OBJ: 0000000024baf128]
System.Runtime.InteropServices.SafeHandle.InternalFinalize()
0000000024baf220 000007fee694f7a6 System.Runtime.InteropServices.SafeHandle.Finalize()
0000000024baf5d8 000007feec0e9d56 [DebuggerU2MCatchHandlerFrame: 0000000024baf5d8]


0:002> !dso
OS Thread Id: 0x51e4 (2)
RSP/REG Object Name
0000000024BAEDD0 000000000c282d78 Microsoft.Win32.SafeHandles.SafeFileHandle
0000000024BAEF00 000000000c282d78 Microsoft.Win32.SafeHandles.SafeFileHandle
0000000024BAEF68 000000000c282d78 Microsoft.Win32.SafeHandles.SafeFileHandle
0000000024BAEF80 000000000c282d78 Microsoft.Win32.SafeHandles.SafeFileHandle
0000000024BAEFC0 000000000c282d78 Microsoft.Win32.SafeHandles.SafeFileHandle
0000000024BAF050 000000000c282d78 Microsoft.Win32.SafeHandles.SafeFileHandle
0000000024BAF0C0 000000000c282d78 Microsoft.Win32.SafeHandles.SafeFileHandle
0000000024BAF0E8 000000000c282d78 Microsoft.Win32.SafeHandles.SafeFileHandle
0000000024BAF170 000000000c282d78 Microsoft.Win32.SafeHandles.SafeFileHandle
0000000024BAF228 000000000c282d78 Microsoft.Win32.SafeHandles.SafeFileHandle
0000000024BAF260 000000000c282d78 Microsoft.Win32.SafeHandles.SafeFileHandle
0000000024BAF290 000000000c285e10 System.Threading.Thread
0000000024BAF2C0 000000000c282d78 Microsoft.Win32.SafeHandles.SafeFileHandle
0000000024BAF310 000000000c282d78 Microsoft.Win32.SafeHandles.SafeFileHandle
0000000024BAF320 000000000c282d78 Microsoft.Win32.SafeHandles.SafeFileHandle
```

```
0000000024BAF360 000000000c2858a8 Microsoft.Win32.SafeHandles.SafeViewOfFileHandle
0000000024BAF410 000000000c282d78 Microsoft.Win32.SafeHandles.SafeFileHandle


0:002> !CLRStack -a
OS Thread Id: 0x51e4 (2)
Child SP               IP Call Site
0000000024baed28 0000000077c612fa [InlinedCallFrame: 0000000024baed28]
Microsoft.Win32.Win32Native.CloseHandle(IntPtr)
0000000024baed28 000007fee6a40418 [InlinedCallFrame: 0000000024baed28]
Microsoft.Win32.Win32Native.CloseHandle(IntPtr)
0000000024baed00 000007fee6a40418 DomainNeutralILStubClass.IL_STUB_PInvoke(IntPtr)
PARAMETERS:
    <no data>


0000000024baef28 000007feec0e9e03 [GCFrame: 0000000024baef28]
0000000024baf078 000007feec0e9e03 [GCFrame: 0000000024baf078]
0000000024baf128 000007feec0e9e03 [HelperMethodFrame_1OBJ: 0000000024baf128]
System.Runtime.InteropServices.SafeHandle.InternalFinalize()
0000000024baf220 000007fee694f7a6 System.Runtime.InteropServices.SafeHandle.Finalize()
PARAMETERS:
    this (0x0000000024baf260) = 0x000000000c282d78


0000000024baf5d8 000007feec0e9d56 [DebuggerU2MCatchHandlerFrame: 0000000024baf5d8]


0:002> !do 0x000000000c282d78
Name: Microsoft.Win32.SafeHandles.SafeFileHandle
MethodTable:    000007fee6baa260
EEClass:        000007fee666d340
Size:           32(0x20) bytes
File: C:\windows\Microsoft.Net\assembly\GAC_64\mscorlib\v4.0_4.0.0.0__b77a5c561934e089\mscorlib.dll
Fields:
MT               Field     Offset Type            VT Attr      Value Name
000007fee6baa338 400060d 8       System.IntPtr   1  instance   dead  handle
000007fee6ba92b8 400060e 10      System.Int32    1  instance   3     _state
000007fee6ba7de0 400060f 14      System.Boolean  1  instance   1     _ownsHandle
000007fee6ba7de0 4000610 15      System.Boolean  1  instance   1     _fullyInitialized
```

Comments

Enabling application verifier in *gflags.exe* to catch handle close stack traces may also reveal who closed the handle originally before we got the second invalid handle close. Use **!htrace** command there.

Invalid Parameter

Process Heap

This is a general pattern of passing unexpected values to functions. Here we look at invalid heap block parameter pattern specialization. It is different from **Dynamic Memory Corruption** (page 330) or **Double Free** (page 289) pattern because no corruption happens in heap structures before detection and the parameter value has never been correct before its use. For example, we have this stack trace:

```
0:003> kL 100
ChildEBP RetAddr
01b2e6f0 77f27d0c ntdll!ZwWaitForSingleObject+0x15
01b2e774 77f27e3a ntdll!RtlReportExceptionEx+0x14b
01b2e7cc 77f4dc2e ntdll!RtlReportException+0x86
01b2e7e0 77f4dcab ntdll!RtlpTerminateFailureFilter+0x14
01b2e7ec 77ef05c4 ntdll!RtlReportCriticalFailure+0x67
01b2e800 77ef0469 ntdll!_EH4_CallFilterFunc+0x12
01b2e828 77ed8799 ntdll!_except_handler4+0x8e
01b2e84c 77ed876b ntdll!ExecuteHandler2+0x26
01b2e8fc 77e9010f ntdll!ExecuteHandler+0x24
01b2e8fc 77f4dc9b ntdll!KiUserExceptionDispatcher+0xf
01b2ecc4 77f4eba1 ntdll!RtlReportCriticalFailure+0x57
01b2ecd4 77f4ec81 ntdll!RtlpReportHeapFailure+0x21
01b2ed08 77efdda0 ntdll!RtlpLogHeapFailure+0xa1
01b2ed38 76bc14d1 ntdll!RtlFreeHeap+0x64
01b2ed4c 75694c39 kernel32!HeapFree+0x14
01b2ed98 726f167d msvcr80!free+0xcd
01b2eda4 7270613d DllA!FreeData+0xd
[...]
01b2fe38 77eb9d42 kernel32!BaseThreadInitThunk+0xe
01b2fe78 77eb9d15 ntdll!__RtlUserThreadStart+0x70
01b2fe90 00000000 ntdll!_RtlUserThreadStart+0x1b
```

We see that the failure was detected and logged immediately without any **Instrumentation Information** (page 580):

```
0:003> !gflag
Current NtGlobalFlag contents: 0x00000000
```

If we enable full page heap we get this default analysis output and the following stack trace:

```
0:003> !gflag
Current NtGlobalFlag contents: 0x02000000
hpa - Place heap allocations at ends of pages
```

```
0:003> !analyze -v

[...]

APPLICATION_VERIFIER_HEAPS_CORRUPTED_HEAP_BLOCK_EXCEPTION_RAISED_FOR_PROBING (c)
Exception raised while verifying the heap block.
This situation happens if we really cannot determine any particular type of corruption for the block. For
instance you will get this if during a heap free operation you pass an address that points to a non-
accessible memory area.
This can also happen for double free situations if we do not find the block among full page heap blocks
and we probe it as a light page heap block.
Arguments:
Arg1: 05eb1000, Heap handle used in the call.
Arg2: 00720071, Heap block involved in the operation.
Arg3: 00000000, Size of the heap block.
Arg4: c0000005, Reserved.

[...]

0:003> kL 100
ChildEBP RetAddr
0818dca4 75fa0962 ntdll!ZwWaitForMultipleObjects+0x15
0818dd40 76bc162d KERNELBASE!WaitForMultipleObjectsEx+0x100
0818dd88 76bc1921 kernel32!WaitForMultipleObjectsExImplementation+0xe0
0818dda4 76be9b0d kernel32!WaitForMultipleObjects+0x18
0818de10 76be9baa kernel32!WerpReportFaultInternal+0x186
0818de24 76be98d8 kernel32!WerpReportFault+0x70
0818de34 76be9855 kernel32!BasepReportFault+0x20
0818dec0 77ef06e7 kernel32!UnhandledExceptionFilter+0x1af
0818dec8 77ef05c4 ntdll!__RtlUserThreadStart+0x62
0818dedc 77ef0469 ntdll!_EH4_CallFilterFunc+0x12
0818df04 77ed8799 ntdll!_except_handler4+0x8e
0818df28 77ed876b ntdll!ExecuteHandler2+0x26
0818dfd8 77e9010f ntdll!ExecuteHandler+0x24
0818dfd8 71a6ba58 ntdll!KiUserExceptionDispatcher+0xf
0818e344 71a69ee0 verifier!VerifierStopMessage+0x1f8
0818e3a8 71a66f11 verifier!AVrfpDphReportCorruptedBlock+0x2b0
0818e3bc 71a819ec verifier!AVrfpDphFindBusyMemoryNoCheck+0x141
0818e3d0 71a8174e verifier!_EH4_CallFilterFunc+0x12
0818e3f8 77ed8799 verifier!_except_handler4+0x8e
0818e41c 77ed876b ntdll!ExecuteHandler2+0x26
0818e4cc 77e9010f ntdll!ExecuteHandler+0x24
0818e4cc 71a66e88 ntdll!KiUserExceptionDispatcher+0xf
0818e868 71a66f95 verifier!AVrfpDphFindBusyMemoryNoCheck+0xb8
0818e88c 71a67240 verifier!AVrfpDphFindBusyMemory+0x15
0818e8a8 71a69080 verifier!AVrfpDphFindBusyMemoryAndRemoveFromBusyList+0x20
0818e8c4 77f50aac verifier!AVrfDebugPageHeapFree+0x90
0818e90c 77f0a8ff ntdll!RtlDebugFreeHeap+0x2f
0818ea00 77eb2a32 ntdll!RtlpFreeHeap+0x5d
0818ea20 76bc14d1 ntdll!RtlFreeHeap+0x142
0818ea34 75694c39 kernel32!HeapFree+0x14
0818ea80 726f167d msvcr80!free+0xcd
0818ea8c 7270613d DllA!FreeData+0xd
[...]
0818fb20 77eb9d42 kernel32!BaseThreadInitThunk+0xe
```

```
0818fb60 77eb9d15 ntdll!__RtlUserThreadStart+0x70
0818fb78 00000000 ntdll!_RtlUserThreadStart+0x1b
```

In both examples above we see that 00720071 value was passed to *free* function (we also verify from the code using **ub** command that there was no parameter optimization, **Optimized Code** pattern, page 853):

```
0:003> kv
ChildEBP RetAddr Args to Child
[...]
01b2ed98 726f167d *00720071* 01b2edb0 7270613d msvcr80!free+0xcd
[...]
```

We recognize that value as Unicode as an example of **Wild Pointer** (page 1271), but parameters need not be pointers in a general case. We can also consider **Invalid Handle** (page 646) pattern as another specialization of **Invalid Parameter** pattern.

Runtime Function

This is another variant of **Invalid Parameter** pattern where an invalid parameter is passed to either statically or dynamically linked C runtime function. Exception codes may vary, for example, 0xc000000d and c0000417 as the following examples illustrate:

```
0:000> k
Child-SP          RetAddr           Call Site
00000000`0289e858 00007ff8`cf4f13ed ntdll!NtWaitForMultipleObjects+0xa
00000000`0289e860 00007ff8`d1157d51 KERNELBASE!WaitForMultipleObjectsEx+0xe1
00000000`0289eb40 00007ff8`d1157773 kernel32!WerpReportFaultInternal+0x581
00000000`0289f0b0 00007ff8`cf5d1cdf kernel32!WerpReportFault+0x83
00000000`0289f0e0 00007ff6`f0225095 KERNELBASE!UnhandledExceptionFilter+0x23f
00000000`0289f1d0 00007ff6`f021ec89 ModuleA!_invalid_parameter+0xc5
00000000`0289f790 00007ff6`f01a2636 ModuleA!vswprintf_s+0x79
[...]
00000000`0289fdc0 00007ff8`d20b5454 kernel32!BaseThreadInitThunk+0x22
00000000`0289fdf0 00000000`00000000 ntdll!RtlUserThreadStart+0x34

0:000> !analyze -v
[...]
EXCEPTION_RECORD:  ffffffffffffffff -- (.exr 0xffffffffffffffff)
ExceptionAddress: 00007ff6f021ec89 (ModuleA!vswprintf_s+0x0000000000000079)
  ExceptionCode: c000000d
  ExceptionFlags: 00000000
NumberParameters: 0
[...]
EXCEPTION_CODE: (NTSTATUS) 0xc000000d - An invalid parameter was passed to a service or function.

0:000> k
 # ChildEBP RetAddr
00 002e6de8 74a01606 ntdll!NtWaitForMultipleObjects+0xc
01 002e6f7c 74a014b8 KERNELBASE!WaitForMultipleObjectsEx+0x136
02 002e6f98 7431a02a KERNELBASE!WaitForMultipleObjects+0x18
03 002e73d4 74319ac6 kernel32!WerpReportFaultInternal+0x545
04 002e73e4 742fcf09 kernel32!WerpReportFault+0x7a
05 002e73ec 74a1a013 kernel32!BasepReportFault+0x19
06 002e7480 73edcc2c KERNELBASE!UnhandledExceptionFilter+0x1b3
07 002e77b8 73ea75b4 msvcr90!_invoke_watson+0xf9
08 002e77e0 5f29a294 msvcr90!wcsncpy_s+0x41
09 002e77fc 5f434563 ModuleB+0x6a294
[...]
44 002efda8 76f19e54 kernel32!BaseThreadInitThunk+0x24
45 002efdf0 76f19e1f ntdll!__RtlUserThreadStart+0x2f
46 002efe00 00000000 ntdll!_RtlUserThreadStart+0x1b
```

```
0:000> !analyze -v
[...]
EXCEPTION_RECORD:  (.exr -1)
ExceptionAddress: 73ea75b4 (msvcr90!wcsncpy_s+0x00000041)
   ExceptionCode: c0000417
   ExceptionFlags: 00000001
NumberParameters: 0
[...]
EXCEPTION_CODE: (NTSTATUS) 0xc0000417 - An invalid parameter was passed to a C runtime function.
```

We can inspect parameters passed to the function where it is possible. In 32-bit memory dumps, we may see the first 3 parameters in the output of **kv** WinDbg command. More than 3 function parameters require the analysis of the raw stack region. 64-bit memory dumps may require disassembled code analysis of the caller (via **ub** WinDbg command).

Invalid Pointer

General

Invalid Pointer pattern is just a number saved in a register or in a memory location, and when we try to interpret it as a memory address itself and follow it (dereference) to fetch memory contents (value) it points to, OS with the help of hardware tells us that the address does not exist or inaccessible due to security restrictions.

In Windows, we have our process memory partitioned into two big regions: kernel space and process space. Space partition is a different concept than execution mode (kernel or user, ring 0 or ring 3) which is a processor state. Code executing in kernel mode (a driver or OS, for example) can access memory that belongs to user space.

Based on this, we can make the distinction between invalid pointers containing kernel space addresses (starting from 0x80000000 on x86, no /3Gb switch) and invalid pointers containing user space addresses (below 0x7FFFFFFF).

On Windows x64 user space addresses are below 0x000007ffffffffff, and kernel space addresses start from 0xFFFFF80000000000.

When we dereference invalid kernel space address we get a bugcheck immediately:

```
UNEXPECTED_KERNEL_MODE_TRAP (7F)
```

```
PAGE_FAULT_IN_NONPAGED_AREA (50)
```

There is no way we can catch it in our code (by using SEH).

However, when we dereference user space address the course of action depends on whether our processor is in kernel mode (ring 0) or in user mode (ring 3). In any mode, we can catch the exception (by using appropriate SEH handler) or leave this to the operating system or a debugger. If there was no component willing to process the exception when it happened in user mode we get our process crash and in kernel mode, we get the following bugchecks:

```
SYSTEM_THREAD_EXCEPTION_NOT_HANDLED (7E)
```

```
KERNEL_MODE_EXCEPTION_NOT_HANDLED (8E)
```

We summarized all of this on the following UML class diagram:

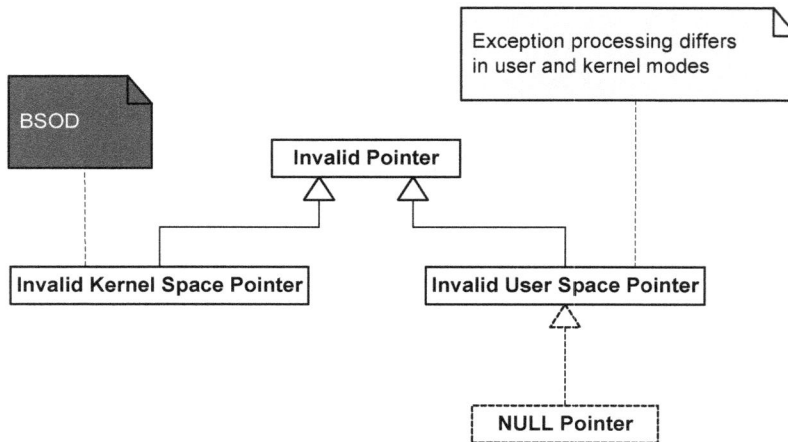

NULL pointer is a special class of user space pointers. Usually, its value is in the range of 0x00000000 - 0x0000FFFF. We can see them used in instructions like

```
mov   esi, dword ptr [ecx+0x10]
```

where ecx value is 0x00000000, and we try to access the value located at 0x00000010 memory address.

When we get a crash dump, and we see an invalid pointer pattern the next step is to interpret the pointer value which should help in understanding possible steps that led to the crash.

Objects

In addition to generic **Invalid Pointer** pattern (page 663) that maps to visible pointer dereference in C and C++ code, plain **NULL Code Pointers** (page 836) and **NULL Data Pointers** (page 838) that are visible **Small Values** (page 975), and **Wild Pointers** (page 1271) showing ASCII or **Regular Data** (such as UNICODE fragments, page 934), we also have implicit dereference (from C++ source code perspective) crash dump analysis patterns that we call **Invalid Pointer (Objects)**. When seeing them in a high-level debugger (could be just an exception during debugging) developers are confused since they do not see the usual pointer dereference:

```
struct Resource
{
    void DoSomething()
    {
        ++m_usageCounter;
    }
    std::size_t m_usageCounter{};
};
```

However, the function call was ordinary (not virtual, otherwise we would have **NULL Code Pointer**), and the object address to access its members was passed via RCX register, but the memory of the object was invalid; hence we have an exception inside the method call when trying to access object members:

```
0:000> .ecxr
*** WARNING: Unable to verify checksum for InvalidPointerObject.exe
rax=0000022c837e0000 rbx=0000022c83905ca0 rcx=0000022c837e0000
rdx=0000000000000000 rsi=0000000000000000 rdi=0000022c83907540
rip=00007ff6d65630ba rsp=00000098812ffc18 rbp=0000000000000000
r8=00000098812ffbe8 r9=0000000000000000 r10=0000000000000000
r11=0000000000000246 r12=0000000000000000 r13=0000000000000000
r14=0000000000000000 r15=0000000000000000
iopl=0         nv up ei pl nz na pe nc
cs=0033 ss=002b ds=002b es=002b fs=0053 gs=002b efl=00010202
InvalidPointerObject!Resource::DoSomething+0xa:
00007ff6`d65630ba 488b00 mov rax, qword ptr [rax] ds:0000022c`837e0000=????????????????


0:000> !address @rax

Usage:
Base Address:          0000022c`837e0000
End Address:           0000022c`837e1000
Region Size:           00000000`00001000 ( 4.000 kB)
State:                 00002000 MEM_RESERVE
Protect:
Type:                  00020000 MEM_PRIVATE
Allocation Base:       0000022c`837e0000
Allocation Protect:    00000004 PAGE_READWRITE
```

```
0:000> kL
# Child-SP          RetAddr           Call Site
00 00000098`812fe748 00007ffd`62278027 ntdll!NtWaitForMultipleObjects+0x14
01 00000098`812fe750 00007ffd`62277f0e KERNELBASE!WaitForMultipleObjectsEx+0x107
02 00000098`812fea50 00007ffd`63d871fb KERNELBASE!WaitForMultipleObjects+0xe
03 00000098`812fea90 00007ffd`63d86ca8 kernel32!WerpReportFaultInternal+0x51b
04 00000098`812febb0 00007ffd`6231f868 kernel32!WerpReportFault+0xac
05 00000098`812febf0 00007ffd`64ee4b32 KERNELBASE!UnhandledExceptionFilter+0x3b8
06 00000098`812fed10 00007ffd`64ecc6d6 ntdll!RtlUserThreadStart$filt$0+0xa2
07 00000098`812fed50 00007ffd`64ee121f ntdll!_C_specific_handler+0x96
08 00000098`812fedc0 00007ffd`64eaa289 ntdll!RtlpExecuteHandlerForException+0xf
09 00000098`812fedf0 00007ffd`64edfe8e ntdll!RtlDispatchException+0x219
0a 00000098`812ff500 00007ff6`d65630ba ntdll!KiUserExceptionDispatch+0x2e
0b 00000098`812ffc18 00007ff6`d656313c InvalidPointerObject!Resource::DoSomething+0xa
0c 00000098`812ffc20 00007ff6`d6568454 InvalidPointerObject!wmain+0x6c
0d (Inline Function) ---`--- InvalidPointerObject!invoke_main+0x22
0e 00000098`812ffc70 00007ffd`63d37bd4 InvalidPointerObject!__scrt_common_main_seh+0x10c
0f 00000098`812ffcb0 00007ffd`64eaced1 kernel32!BaseThreadInitThunk+0x14
10 00000098`812ffce0 00000000`00000000 ntdll!RtlUserThreadStart+0x21

0:000> ub 00007ff6`d656313c
InvalidPointerObject!wmain+0x45:
00007ff6`d6563115 488b4c2428     mov rcx,qword ptr [rsp+28h]
00007ff6`d656311a e891ffffff     call InvalidPointerObject!Resource::DoSomething (00007ff6`d65630b0)
00007ff6`d656311f 41b800400000   mov r8d,4000h
00007ff6`d6563125 33d2           xor edx,edx
00007ff6`d6563127 488b4c2420     mov rcx,qword ptr [rsp+20h]
00007ff6`d656312c ff15ce0e0200   call qword ptr [InvalidPointerObject!_imp_VirtualFree
(00007ff6`d6584000)]
00007ff6`d6563132 488b4c2428     mov rcx,qword ptr [rsp+28h]
00007ff6`d6563137 e874ffffff     call InvalidPointerObject!Resource::DoSomething (00007ff6`d65630b0)

0:000> u InvalidPointerObject!Resource::DoSomething
InvalidPointerObject!Resource::DoSomething:
00007ff6`d65630b0 48894c2408     mov qword ptr [rsp+8],rcx
00007ff6`d65630b5 488b442408     mov rax,qword ptr [rsp+8]
00007ff6`d65630ba 488b00         mov rax,qword ptr [rax]
00007ff6`d65630bd 48ffc0         inc rax
00007ff6`d65630c0 488b4c2408     mov rcx,qword ptr [rsp+8]
00007ff6`d65630c5 488901         mov qword ptr [rcx],rax
00007ff6`d65630c8 c3             ret
00007ff6`d65630c9 cc             int 3
```

The example memory dump, the application PDB file, and source code are available for download[120].

---

[120] http://www.patterndiagnostics.com/SoftwareDiagnosticsCorpus/SDC6.zip

J

JIT Code

.NET

Sometimes the assembly code looks almost wild (not like generated by a favorite compiler, **Wild Code**, page 1268). Here is an example that also shows .NET runtime native unhandled exception processing:

```
0:000> kL 100
ChildEBP RetAddr
0014dbb4 77189254 ntdll!KiFastSystemCallRet
0014dbb8 75fec244 ntdll!ZwWaitForSingleObject+0xc
0014dc28 75fec1b2 kernel32!WaitForSingleObjectEx+0xbe
0014dc3c 72605389 kernel32!WaitForSingleObject+0x12
0014dc6c 726058e7 mscorwks!ClrWaitForSingleObject+0x24
0014e128 72608084 mscorwks!RunWatson+0x1df
0014e86c 7260874a mscorwks!DoFaultReportWorker+0xb59
0014e8a8 72657452 mscorwks!DoFaultReport+0xc3
0014e8cc 7265c0c7 mscorwks!WatsonLastChance+0x3f
0014e924 7265c173 mscorwks!CLRAddVectoredHandlers+0x209
0014e92c 7603f4be mscorwks!InternalUnhandledExceptionFilter+0x22
0014e9e8 771a85b7 kernel32!UnhandledExceptionFilter+0x127
0014e9f0 77139a14 ntdll!__RtlUserThreadStart+0x6f
0014ea04 771340f4 ntdll!_EH4_CallFilterFunc+0x12
0014ea2c 77189b99 ntdll!_except_handler4+0x8e
0014ea50 77189b6b ntdll!ExecuteHandler2+0x26
0014eb00 771899f7 ntdll!ExecuteHandler+0x24
0014eb00 03ca0141 ntdll!KiUserExceptionDispatcher+0xf
WARNING: Frame IP not in any known module. Following frames may be wrong.
0014ee28 634c2f42 0x3ca0141
0014ee34 67715e44 System_ni+0x132f42
0014ee70 72431b4c System_ServiceProcess_ni+0x25e44
0014ee80 724421f9 mscorwks!CallDescrWorker+0x33
0014ef00 72456571 mscorwks!CallDescrWorkerWithHandler+0xa3
0014f03c 724565a4 mscorwks!MethodDesc::CallDescr+0x19c
0014f058 724565c2 mscorwks!MethodDesc::CallTargetWorker+0x1f
0014f070 724afac5 mscorwks!MethodDescCallSite::CallWithValueTypes+0x1a
0014f1d4 724af9e5 mscorwks!ClassLoader::RunMain+0x223
0014f43c 724aff35 mscorwks!Assembly::ExecuteMainMethod+0xa6
0014f90c 724b011f mscorwks!SystemDomain::ExecuteMainMethod+0x456
0014f95c 724b004f mscorwks!ExecuteEXE+0x59
0014f9a4 72f57c24 mscorwks!_CorExeMain+0x15c
0014f9b4 75fe4911 mscoree!_CorExeMain+0x2c
0014f9c0 7716e4b6 kernel32!BaseThreadInitThunk+0xe
0014fa00 7716e489 ntdll!__RtlUserThreadStart+0x23
0014fa18 00000000 ntdll!_RtlUserThreadStart+0x1b
```

We set exception context:

```
0:000> kv 100
ChildEBP RetAddr  Args to Child
[...]
0014e9e8 771a85b7 0014ea18 77139a14 00000000 kernel32!UnhandledExceptionFilter+0x127 (FPO: [SEH])
[...]


0:000> .exptr 0014ea18


----- Exception record at 0014eb18:
ExceptionAddress: 03ca0141
   ExceptionCode: c0000005 (Access violation)
  ExceptionFlags: 00000000
NumberParameters: 2
   Parameter[0]: 00000000
   Parameter[1]: 00000000
Attempt to read from address 00000000


----- Context record at 0014eb34:
eax=00000001 ebx=08394ff8 ecx=00000000 edx=00000001 esi=056a2a94 edi=00000000
eip=03ca0141 esp=0014ee00 ebp=0014ee28 iopl=0         nv up ei pl zr na pe nc
cs=001b  ss=0023  ds=0023  es=0023  fs=003b  gs=0000              efl=00010246
03ca0141 3909        cmp       dword ptr [ecx],ecx  ds:0023:00000000=????????
```

Then we disassemble the code at the crash point, and it looks strange because it includes calls through DS data segment:

```
0:000> .asm no_code_bytes
Assembly options: no_code_bytes


0:000> u 03ca0141
03ca0141 cmp        dword ptr [ecx],ecx
03ca0143 call       dword ptr ds:[36067C0h]
03ca0149 mov        ecx,dword ptr [esi+5Ch]
03ca014c cmp        dword ptr [ecx],ecx
03ca014e call       dword ptr ds:[3606D10h]
03ca0154 mov        dword ptr [ebp-1Ch],0
03ca015b mov        dword ptr [ebp-18h],0FCh
03ca0162 push       3CA0180h
```

However further disassembly finally reaches RET instruction:

```
0:000> u
03ca0167 jmp        03ca0169
03ca0169 movzx      edx,byte ptr [ebp-24h]
03ca016d mov        ecx,dword ptr [ebp-28h]
03ca0170 call       System_ServiceProcess_ni+0x25140 (67715140)
03ca0175 pop        eax
03ca0176 jmp        eax
03ca0178 lea        esp,[ebp-0Ch]
03ca017b pop        ebx
```

```
0:000> u
03ca017c pop        esi
03ca017d pop        edi
03ca017e pop        ebp
03ca017f ret
[...]
```

Backward disassembling shows the matching function prolog code:

```
0:000> ub 03ca0141
03ca0127 movzx      eax,byte ptr [ebp-24h]
03ca012b test       eax,eax
03ca012d je         03ca0154
03ca012f cmp        dword ptr [esi+60h],0
[...]
```

```
0:000> ub 03ca0127
03ca0114 push       esi
03ca0115 push       ebx
03ca0116 sub        esp,1Ch
03ca0119 xor        eax,eax
03ca011b mov        dword ptr [ebp-18h],eax
03ca011e mov        dword ptr [ebp-28h],ecx
03ca0121 mov        dword ptr [ebp-24h],edx
03ca0124 mov        esi,dword ptr [ebp-28h]
```

```
0:000> ub 03ca0114
03ca0102 retf
03ca0103 add        eax,dword ptr [eax+36h]
03ca0106 retf
03ca0107 add        ebx,dword ptr [esi+esi-35h]
03ca010b add        esi,esp
03ca010d cmp        eax,8B550360h
03ca0112 in         al,dx
03ca0113 push       edi
```

From the stack trace, we suspect this code as JIT-compiled .NET code of the main assembly method. And indeed, we can find the similar call signatures in the following MSDN article "Drill Into .NET Framework Internals to See How the CLR Creates Runtime Objects"[121]:

```
03ca0141 cmp        dword ptr [ecx],ecx
03ca0143 call       dword ptr ds:[36067C0h]
```

Comments

!IP2MD extension command from SOS will give us method name, class and module addresses for 0x3ca0141.

---

[121] https://docs.microsoft.com/en-us/archive/msdn-magazine/2005/may/net-framework-internals-how-the-clr-creates-runtime-objects

Java

JIT compiling is not restricted to .NET in Windows and we decided to add Java variant of **JIT Code (.NET)** analysis pattern (page 667). Here is one thread example from *java.exe* process memory dump:

```
0:071> k
#  ChildEBP RetAddr
00 536cf424 770c15ce ntdll!NtWaitForSingleObject+0x15
01 536cf490 76f31194 KERNELBASE!WaitForSingleObjectEx+0x98
02 536cf4a8 76f31148 kernel32!WaitForSingleObjectExImplementation+0x75
03 536cf4bc 59207cb3 kernel32!WaitForSingleObject+0x12
WARNING: Stack unwind information not available. Following frames may be wrong.
04 536cf4e4 5918dbb1 jvm!JVM_FindSignal+0x5833
05 536cf558 03b6db25 jvm!JVM_Clone+0x30161
06 536cf588 03c4b0f4 0x3b6db25
07 536cf690 0348339a 0x3c4b0f4
08 536cf7d8 034803d7 0x348339a
09 536cf7e4 591a0732 0x34803d7
0a 536cf870 75bb9cde jvm!JVM_Clone+0x42ce2
0b 536cf87c 5926529e msvcrt!_VEC_memzero+0x82
0c 536cf8c4 591a1035 jvm!JVM_FindSignal+0x62e1e
0d 536cf908 591a1097 jvm!JVM_Clone+0x435e5
0e 536cf978 5914c49f jvm!JVM_Clone+0x43647
0f 536cf9d4 591c22dc jvm!jio_printf+0xaf
10 536cfa20 591c2d37 jvm!JVM_Clone+0x6488c
11 536cfa58 592071e9 jvm!JVM_Clone+0x652e7
12 536cfc98 5d34c556 jvm!JVM_FindSignal+0x4d69
13 536cfcd0 5d34c600 msvcr100!_endthreadex+0x3f
14 536cfcdc 76f3338a msvcr100!_endthreadex+0xce
15 536cfce8 77829902 kernel32!BaseThreadInitThunk+0xe
16 536cfd28 778298d5 ntdll!__RtlUserThreadStart+0x70
17 536cfd40 00000000 ntdll!_RtlUserThreadStart+0x1b
```

We see that the return addresses are indeed return addresses saved on the stack with the preceding call instruction:

```
0:071> ub 03b6db25
03b6db03 50                       push    eax
03b6db04 57                       push    edi
03b6db05 e876586455               call    jvm!JVM_Clone+0x55930 (591b3380)
03b6db0a 83c408                   add     esp,8
03b6db0d 8d9730010000             lea     edx,[edi+130h]
03b6db13 891424                   mov     dword ptr [esp],edx
03b6db16 c7876c01000004000000 mov dword ptr [edi+16Ch],4
03b6db20 e8dbff6155               call    jvm!JVM_Clone+0x300b0 (5918db00)
```

```
0:071> ub 03c4b0f4
03c4b0cd 891c24           mov     dword ptr [esp],ebx
03c4b0d0 894c2404         mov     dword ptr [esp+4],ecx
03c4b0d4 899c2480000000   mov     dword ptr [esp+80h],ebx
03c4b0db 898c2484000000   mov     dword ptr [esp+84h],ecx
03c4b0e2 b928b0b91a       mov     ecx,1AB9B028h
03c4b0e7 89bc248c000000   mov     dword ptr [esp+8Ch],edi
03c4b0ee 90               nop
03c4b0ef e8ac29f2ff       call    03b6daa0


0:071> ub 034803d7
034803c6 89049c           mov     dword ptr [esp+ebx*4],eax
034803c9 43               inc     ebx
034803ca 49               dec     ecx
034803cb 75f5             jne     034803c2
034803cd 8b5d14           mov     ebx,dword ptr [ebp+14h]
034803d0 8b4518           mov     eax,dword ptr [ebp+18h]
034803d3 8bf4             mov     esi,esp
034803d5 ffd0             call    eax


0:071> ub 591a0732
jvm!JVM_Clone+0x42ccc:
591a071c 57               push    edi
591a071d 89461c           mov     dword ptr [esi+1Ch],eax
591a0720 e8ab110000       call    jvm!JVM_Clone+0x43e80 (591a18d0)
591a0725 6a08             push    8
591a0727 6a06             push    6
591a0729 57               push    edi
591a072a 894514           mov     dword ptr [ebp+14h],eax
591a072d e86e9af2ff       call    jvm+0x6a1a0 (590ca1a0)
```

www.ingramcontent.com/pod-product-compliance
Lightning Source LLC
Chambersburg PA
CBHW081210220326
41598CB00037B/6739

9 781912 636280